Strategic Management for Tourism, Hospitality and Events

Strategic Management for Tourism, Hospitality and Events is the must-have text for students approaching this subject. It introduces students to fundamental strategic management principles in a tourism, hospitality and events context and brings theory to life by integrating a host of industry-based case studies and examples throughout.

Among the new features and topics included in this edition are:

- Extended coverage to hospitality and events to reflect the increasing need and importance of a combined sector approach to strategy.
- New international tourism, hospitality and events case studies from both SMEs and large-scale businesses are integrated throughout to show applications of strategic management theory, such as objectives, products and markets and strategic implementation. Longer combined sector case studies are also included at the end of the book for seminar work.
- New content on emerging strategic issues affecting the tourism, hospitality and events industries, such as innovation, employment, culture and sustainability.
- Web support for tutors and students providing explanation and guidelines for instructors on how to use the textbook and case studies, and additional exercises, questions and resources for students.

This book is written in an accessible and engaging style and structured logically with useful features throughout to aid students' learning and understanding. This book is an essential resource to tourism, hospitality and events students.

Nigel Evans is Assistant Dean of the School of Social Sciences, Business and Law at Teesside University. He has published widely in tourism and management and taught strategy for many years on varied programmes including MBA and BA (Hons) Travel and Tourism programmes at Teesside and Northumbria Universities.

'Nigel Evans' textbook has long been essential reading for students on Strategic Management in Tourism courses. This new edition is very welcome and extending the coverage to hospitality and events and the inclusion of diverse international case studies and an extensive glossary is timely and will be well received by students and course tutors. The book should also be of interest to practitioners in tourism, hospitality and events.'

Dr Philip Long, *Associate Dean, Head of Tourism Academic Group,*
School of Tourism, Bournemouth University, UK

'Nigel Evans has provided great cases and updated perspectives on the nature of the closely entwined tourism, hospitality and events sectors and their internationalized dimension. The style of the book is attractive and interesting, using lots of graphics and illustrations as well as many examples and cases to keep students not only engaged but also firmly in touch with the realities and implications of strategic management.'

Professor Ray Pine, *Dean, Faculty of Management and Hospitality,*
Technological & Higher Education Institute of Hong Kong

 A range of further resources for this book are available on the Companion Website: www.routledge.com/cw/evans

Strategic Management for Tourism, Hospitality and Events

Second edition

Nigel Evans

Routledge
Taylor & Francis Group

LONDON AND NEW YORK

First edition published 2003
Second edition 2015
by Routledge
2 Park Square, Milton Park, Abingdon, Oxon OX14 4RN

and by Routledge
711 Third Avenue, New York, NY 10017

Routledge is an imprint of the Taylor & Francis Group, an informa business

British Library Cataloguing in Publication Data
A catalogue record for this book is available from the British Library

Library of Congress Cataloging in Publication Data
Library of Congress Cataloging-in-Publication Data
Evans, Nigel, 1955-
    Strategic management for tourism, hospitality and events /
    Nigel Evans. — Second edition.
        pages cm
    Includes bibliographical references and index.
    1. Tourism—Management. 2. Hospitality industry—Management.
    3. Strategic planning. I. Title.
    G155.A1E927 2014
    910.68'4—dc23   2014020183

ISBN: 978-0-415-83727-9 (hbk)
ISBN: 978-0-415-83724-8 (pbk)
ISBN: 978-0-203-77149-5 (ebk)

Typeset in Iowan Old Style
by Keystroke, Station Road, Codsall, Wolverhampton

Printed and bound by CPI Group (UK) Ltd, Croydon, CR0 4YY

To my wife Michelle and daughters Lydia, Megan and Laura
without whose love and support the book would not have been possible.

Contents

Figures

Tables

Preface

This international text is aimed at being the textbook of choice for three important sets of readers:

- Students studying strategy and/or marketing (probably in their final undergraduate year or postgraduate) as part of their studies in tourism, hospitality and events management.
- Students and researchers who have chosen to study tourism, hospitality or events management organizations for their dissertation, projects or assignments, who want to understand the unique characteristics of the industry and to gain knowledge of the relevant literature.
- Managers and practitioners working in tourism, hospitality and events (or seeking a career in these sectors), who want to gain an understanding of the challenges faced by managers and some of the managerial responses which can be considered.

Putting aside definitional debates, fundamentally:

- *strategy* is about making you think ahead regarding key issues affecting organizations; and
- *strategic management* is about giving you concepts, frameworks, tools and techniques to help you do so.

Consequently this book aims to make readers think ahead about the key issues facing tourism, hospitality and events management organizations and provides concepts, frameworks, tools and techniques to help you do so.

The first edition of this book was published as *Strategic Management for Travel and Tourism* in 2003 (for which I thank my two co-authors Professors David Campbell and George Stonehouse). This text builds on the first edition, but much has changed in the intervening years and consequently this edition is completely modified and its scope extended. The text is global in its orientation and explicitly encompasses hospitality and events along with tourism recognizing the inextricably linked nature of these sectors. The text is contemporary in that the broad range of academic literature which has emerged in recent years is incorporated as are recent industry developments.

The book contextualizes and applies relevant material from the strategic management and tourism, hospitality and events management literature and takes an international approach to what are inherently internationally oriented industry sectors. This approach is reflected in:

- the application of concepts and principles;
- links to a wide range of relevant literature enabling further study;
- a particular focus on smaller organizations (SMEs) recognizing that they form an important part of these sectors;
- taking an explicitly international approach for what are inherently internationally oriented sectors;
- emphasis of key points affecting this industry in particular; and
- use of short illustrative examples and a series of longer cases drawn from across the industry and focusing on different parts of the world.

There are of course many existing strategic management titles. There are, however comparatively few textbooks which apply strategy to 'services' contexts and in particular to the service sectors of tourism, hospitality and events. These service sectors are inextricably linked and have grown to represent one of the world's most important industries.

The strategic management challenges facing managers in service contexts are often different in a number of ways from the challenges facing managers in manufacturing industries. These different challenges reflect the characteristics of services. Furthermore, tourism, hospitality and events represent a distinctive set of services which entail an understanding of their own specific characteristics. Hence it is appropriate that a dedicated text should consider the strategic implications of managing in this important and rapidly developing industry (which is one of the world's largest), in particular.

Clearly there are many examples to illustrate a text such as this, and I have chosen those which: I consider to be relevant, can gain access to information, can link with the academic material or have personal experience. However, I recognize that other illustrations could have been chosen. I would like to encourage readers to submit further contributions and illustrations, which would be fully attributed if they were to appear on the companion website which supports this book and contains further material. Any feedback on this edition would also be gratefully received.

Finally, I would like to thank colleagues at Teesside University and elsewhere who have commented on parts of this book and the publishers for all their help and support throughout the book's production.

Nigel G. Evans
n.evans@tees.ac.uk
October 2014

Study guide

How to use this book

In this book strategic management is studied in a structured way following a logical sequence.

The principles and concepts developed in studying strategic management are applied to the tourism, hospitality and events sectors.

Additionally, the book is enhanced with learning features to:

- reinforce your learning;
- provide opportunities to explore topics further; and
- test your knowledge as you study.

Each chapter contains:

- Introduction and chapter overview;
- Learning objectives;
- Small business focus;
- Chapter summary; and
- References and further reading.

In order to bring the subject alive, aid understanding and make it memorable, throughout the book you will find sections which highlight and illustrate the material:

> **DEFINITION/QUOTATION**
>
> Encourages you to engage with primary sources.

KEY CONCEPT

Highlights important principles that underpin your understanding.

STRATEGY IN PRACTICE

Illustrates how as a manager you might implement elements of strategy.

SHORT CASE ILLUSTRATION

Provides an example of how strategy is actually working in a real situation taken from tourism, hospitality or events contexts.

THINK POINTS

Provide review and discussion questions to enable you to test your knowledge and understanding as you progress through the book.

SMALL BUSINESS FOCUS

Focuses on how strategic management principles can be applied to the many smaller businesses operating in *THE*.

CASE LINKAGES

Enable you to link the material in each chapter to illustrations contained in the case studies contained at the end of the book.

Part

Strategy and the tourism, hospitality and events contexts

Introduction

This introduction to Part 1 of the book has two purposes in that it provides readers with:

1. An introduction to the approach that this book takes to the study of strategy – *The strategy process.*
2. A rationale for the approach taken by this book in applying strategic management tools, techniques and concepts in the context of the tourism, hospitality and events sectors – *Strategy in a tourism, hospitality and events (THE) context.*

The strategy process

Why do we often refer to strategy as a *process*? The answer is that it is never a once-and-for-all event – it goes on and on.

There is a need to continually review *strategic objectives* because the environment within which organizations operate is continually changing. The purpose of strategy is to make an organization fit into its environment. By achieving this, the probabilities that it will survive and prosper are enhanced.

Part 1 of this book is concerned with introducing the subject matter of strategy in a specific context, namely that of tourism, hospitality and events.

Thus in Part 1:

1. Chapter 1 discusses concepts, definitions and the nature of objectives.
2. Chapter 2 highlights the particular characteristics of tourism, hospitality and events which are relevant to understanding how organizations within the industry are managed in a strategic way.

The subsequent parts of this book are concerned with examining the distinct 'stages' in the strategic process. It can be argued that strategy is a process because it contains distinct 'stages' and that there are three main interrelated stages to the process.

In practice, the strategic management process has three main components or stages as shown in Figure P1.1 below:

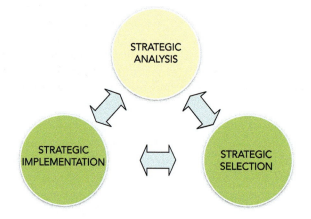

Figure P1.1 A schematic of the strategic process

Strategic analysis

The purpose of strategic analysis is to gather information and to analyse it systematically and thoroughly. None of us would be wise to make an important decision about anything in life without adequate and relevant information, and nor would tourism, hospitality and events organizations.

There are two main stages in strategic analysis:

- Strategic analysis involves an examination of an organization's internal environment (*internal analysis*). This takes the form of a thorough analysis of the internal processes and structures of a business in much the same way as a doctor might carry out a thorough medical examination on a person. The purpose of internal analysis is to establish what the organization is good at (its *strengths*) and what it is not so good at (its *weaknesses*). We discuss the internal environment in Part 2 of this book.
- The second stage in strategic analysis involves an examination of the organization's external environment (*external analysis*). This takes the form of a thorough analysis of two 'layers' of external environment – the *micro* or *near* environment, and the *macro* or *far* environment. The external environment will be encountered in Part 3 of the book.

The macro environment contains a range of influences that have an impact not only on an organization in an industry, but also on the whole industry itself. It follows that a single organization is usually unable to affect the factors in the macro environment but successful strategy usually involves learning to cope and adapt to changes. This book explains the macro environment in terms of five main areas of influence – socio-demographic, political, economic, environmental and technological – which are discussed in Chapter 7.

The micro environment comprises the industry in which the organization competes. The organization is usually affected by the factors in this environment and it may be able to have an influence upon it. However unlike the internal environment the organization does not have control over its micro environment. The micro environment, which is discussed in Chapter 8, is sometimes referred to as the *competitive environment* because it is within this sphere that an organization competes, both for its resource inputs and to sell its product outputs.

From the information gathered from the external analysis, we seek to establish which influences represent *opportunities* and which are, or might develop into, *threats*.

Once we have established the organization's internal strengths and weaknesses, and its external opportunities and threats, the challenge becomes the selection of an appropriate strategy. Such a strategy is required to address the weaknesses and threats whilst at the same time, building upon the identified strengths and exploiting opportunities. It is important to understand that a detailed internal and external analysis is a necessary prerequisite for producing a summary of the strengths, weaknesses, opportunities and threats – the *SWOT*. In other words the SWOT emerges from the internal and external analyses and is a summary of the main results.

The process sometimes involves an additional stage of condensing the strengths, weaknesses, opportunities and threats into a survey of the *key issues*. These are the most pressing or important elements of the SWOT statement – those which require the most urgent action or which the strategy should be particularly designed to address. The SWOT is discussed in Chapter 9.

Strategic selection

The second stage in the strategic process involves taking the important information gathered from the strategic analysis stage and using it to make an intelligent and informed strategic *selection* or *choice* of the most appropriate courses of action for the future. These strategic choices are covered in Part 4 of the book.

Specifically strategic choices are required for tourism, hospitality and events organizations (or their constituent parts) in relation to three key aspects:

- How will the organization compete?
- What is the strategic direction that the organization will take?
- What methods will be utilised by the organization?

These aspects of strategic selection are discussed in Chapters 10 and 11.

It is at this stage that the importance of the strategic analysis can be appreciated. If insufficient or flawed information from the analysis has been gathered, then the strategy selection process will not be built on solid foundations. In other words, inappropriate strategic options could be selected.

Strategic selection therefore begins with an examination of the strategic analysis. Once we are acquainted with it, we normally formulate a list of the options open to the organization, paying particular attention to how each option will address the key issues. After this, we evaluate each option using a number of criteria. Finally, the most appropriate strategic option is selected. Strategic evaluation and selection is covered in Chapter 12.

Strategic implementation and management

The third stage in the strategic process involves taking the selected strategic options and actually putting them into practice. The implementation and management of chosen strategies are discussed in Part 5 of the book.

This is a complex stage of the process as it concerns putting detailed aspects of the strategy into practice. It involves actually carrying out the strategy and this brings into focus a number of other managerial issues. There are a number of areas which we need to be aware in order to effectively implement a strategy within tourism, hospitality and events organizations. Implementation typically involves taking into account the following:

- the adequacy of the organization's resource base (Chapter 13);
- the readiness of the organization's culture and structure to undertake the proposed strategy (Chapter 13);
- the management of any changes that are needed to implement the strategy (Chapter 13);
- the extent to which the organization positions itself in respect to its geographic coverage and international presence (Chapter 14).

In implementing the strategic process it is necessary to be aware not only of changes occurring to the internal and external environment, but also of changes to the subject matter itself. Strategic Management is a complex area of study. Whilst in this book we study a particular view of the subject matter there are alternative views which could be taken and the subject matter is continually evolving. Thus Chapter 15 considers the present and future trends occurring in the study of strategic management to give students some understanding of the complexity and evolving themes of the subject. The chapter also considers how strategy might be presented in a practical sense, so that it is easily and convincingly presented to internal and external stakeholders.

The feedback link

Finally, the progress of strategy is monitored continually through feedback from the implementation stage back to the analysis stage. As a strategy proceeds, it may have an effect on the organization's internal environment and it may also have an effect on the external environment. In addition, independent influences may have brought internal or external changes about since the strategic analysis was first carried out.

In order to ensure that the selected strategy is still appropriate, therefore, a review of the strategic analysis is necessary. If nothing has changed, then the company may decide that no amendment to the strategy is necessary. If the environment (internal or external) has changed, however, some modification to the strategy may become necessary. Increasingly environments are changing ever more quickly and thus there is a need for organizations to maintain flexibility so that they can respond quickly to any changes.

Study progress

Thus the book is divided into five parts that follow the *strategic process* in a logical sequence.

The diagram below is replicated (in modified form) at the start of each part. The chapters being studied in the part are highlighted so as to indicate the progress you are making in studying the book's contents and to indicate where the chapters are placed within the overall strategic process, which follows a logical sequence.

Part 1 Strategy and the tourism, hospitality and events contexts		Part 2 Analysing the internal environment	Part 3 Analysing the external environment and SWOT	Part 4 Strategic selection	Part 5 Strategic implementation and strategy in theory and practice
Chapter 1 Strategy and strategic objectives for tourism, hospitality and event organizations	Chapter 2 Introduction to strategy for tourism, hospitality and events	Chapters 3, 4, 5 and 6	Chapters 7, 8 and 9	Chapters 10, 11 and 12	Chapters 13, 14, and 15

Strategy in tourism, hospitality and events (*THE*) contexts

This text utilizes strategic management concepts and principles in a *THE* context through its:

- application of concepts and principles;
- emphasis on key points affecting these sectors in particular; and
- use of short illustrative examples and longer case studies.

Each chapter contains specific references to *THE*, but it should be stressed that this book is *Strategic Management* for *Tourism, Hospitality and Events*, thereby implying that the theory is largely generic (though services rather than manufacturing oriented) and it is adapted and applied to the needs of these particular commercial sectors.

The book explicitly recognises that these sectors (which are closely aligned) are service-based rather than manufacturing and therefore that certain aspects of strategic management are particularly emphasised and the language used is modified accordingly. *For example* – the word 'operations' is used in place of 'production' and the intangibility, perishability, cash flow implications, difficulty of maintaining quality standards, etc. of service-based products will be specifically emphasized.

It is recognized that there are some difficulties with this approach. Tourism, hospitality and events sectors, although similar and linked, are distinctive to some degree. It can be argued that tourism, hospitality and events represent separate sectors with their own literature and constructs.

In this book the view is taken that

- the distinctions are outweighed by the similarities between them;
- any difficulties can be successfully overcome; and consequently
- the sectors can be studied at the *strategic* level together.

It is important to stress the final point. Whilst at the strategic (high-level decision making) it is sensible to study the three closely linked sectors together, it may be far less sensible to do so at the more detailed operational level.

For example – the operational detail of managing a tour operator will be very different from managing a hotel, since they operate in very different ways requiring different skills. However, at the strategic level – in terms of decisions like how resources are allocated or how they compete – they may have very similar sets of issues and indeed may in many cases be parts of the same organization.

In fact, it can be further argued that not only is it possible to cover the three sectors together at a strategic level, but it is desirable to do so. This is because tourism, hospitality and events management are highly interrelated and there are many examples of cross-ownership. The demand and supply in one sector has direct effects on other parts of THE and in many cases there are shared ownership structures across the three sectors.

We now turn to a brief discussion of the individual sectors we are considering in this book.

Tourism management

Tourism and the international travel industry that has grown up to support it

- is a vast and complex industry;
- is highly fragmented in its ownership and control;
- has a wide diversity of products and destinations; and
- is often divided between public and private sectors.

The United Nations World Tourism Organization (UNWTO) defines tourism as:

> *Activities of persons traveling to and staying in places outside their usual environment for more than one day but not more than one consecutive year for leisure, business or other purposes.*
> *(Chadwick, 1994:65)*

Tourism such as pilgrimages or visiting other cities and states to trade has taken place throughout history. The origins of what is often termed *mass international tourism* are more recent and can be traced back to Thomas Cook in 1850s Britain (Withey, 1998; Hamilton, 2006; Holloway and Humphreys, 2012). As a highly structured sector of many economies, it can primarily be viewed as a creation of more recent times. Its rise has been traced by a number of authors including Gee *et al.* (1997), Page (2011) and Holloway and Humphreys (2012). Since the early 1950s the growth of tourism both domestically in the developed countries and internationally has been phenomenal in its scale and remarkably resilient to periodic economic and political adversity (Evans, 2012:215).

The growth has been spatially uneven and has taken place against the backdrop of dramatic changes in the business environment. This dynamic environment creates both managerial opportunities and dilemmas both for private sector leaders and public sector policy makers. Given the dominance and drive of the private sector in the development of tourism and the growth in the services which support this, a business management approach to tourism studies has evolved over the past 25 years or so (Evans, 2012:217), which this book addresses at a strategic level.

Tourism products have a number of characteristics which are of relevance to the way in which they are managed and are thus relevant to any business-oriented study of tourism. Some of these characteristics are shared with other service products, whilst others are, if not unique, certainly of particular relevance to travel and tourism products in particular. The characteristics are thus highly distinctive and warrant specific study as in this book.

The operational management issues can be viewed as being highly context-specific, varying greatly according to the type, location and scope of the business and thus beyond the scope of this book. They are, however, discussed in, for example: Sharpley (2002); Cooper *et al.* (2008); Goeldner and Brent Ritchie (2011); and Holloway and Humphreys (2012). The operational issues also vary greatly between tourism, hospitality and events management, so while it is possible to take a combined approach to the study of the three sectors at a strategic level, such an approach is not possible at an operational level.

Hospitality management

Although hospitality is recognized as one of the largest industries, it still remains as a composite of diverse sub-sectors. In a wide-ranging review of the problems of delineating hospitality, Ottenbacher *et al.* (2009) point out that there is still no consensus on the scope and exposure of this field as a whole among academics and hospitality professionals. However, in common usage the hospitality industry is often associated with the tourism industry but most people relate it to hotels and restaurants (Powers and Barrows, 2012).

Widening the definition of hospitality slightly, Harrison *et al.* (2005:23) argue that the hospitality industry:

> *primarily consists of businesses that provide accommodation, food and beverage or some combination of these activities.*

This provides a working definition of hospitality that provides an understanding of the subject matter which is followed in this book.

Notwithstanding the problems associated with the term, many hospitality and hotel management courses have grown up around the world and in many cases tourism and/or events also appear in the title of such courses, thus giving a practical illustration of the close linkages which exist.

The definitional difficulties described serve in many ways to demonstrate the close interaction between tourism and hospitality and the fuzziness and flexibility of the boundaries between the two. Indeed, several definitions combine the hospitality and tourism fields (Ottenbacher *et al.*, 2009) under the umbrella of 'travel and tourism' (e.g. Walker, 2010). Certainly tourism and hospitality are closely related and are not mutually exclusive – since hospitality is at least partly concerned with providing for the needs of tourists.

Although the approach taken here is to consider strategic management for hospitality not in isolation, but together with tourism and events management, Harrington and Ottenbacher (2011) adopted a different approach. They summarised research relating strategic management specifically to the context of hospitality, albeit recognizing the definitional difficulties involved.

Events management

The conceptual problems in defining the hospitality management field are to a large extent replicated in events management.

Indeed it can be argued that the definitional problems are even more acute since, unlike hospitality,

- the subject area has been studied for a shorter period of time;
- the industry has few recognizable brand names (a measure of its fragmentation); and
- the literature in the field is both more sparse and of more recent origin.

It is generally accepted (and it is the approach adopted in this book) that events management is concerned with managing the following contexts:

- event management companies;
- sports events;
- concerts and performances;
- festivals;
- exhibitions;
- meetings and conferences.

The subject area is emerging and Getz (2007) defines event studies as 'the study of all planned events, with particular reference to the nature of the event experience and meanings attached to events and event experiences'. In a further discussion of the events field of study Getz (2012) recognizes the interactions with other related applied fields such as tourism, leisure and sports studies. Events interact (with the other related fields) in that they are used for various purposes, and they vary in the nature of the experience. However, within the related fields though planned events are highly important they represent only one phenomenon of many that are relevant.

In identifying the often crucial role of events in destination development and marketing Getz (2012) identifies five core roles in that events:

1. Attract tourists whose spending generate economic benefits.
2. Create positive images for the destination and help brand it.
3. Contribute to place marketing by making cities more liveable and attractive to investors.
4. Animate cities, resorts, parks, urban spaces and venues making them more attractive.
5. Act as catalysts for urban renewal, infrastructure development, voluntarism and improved marketing capability.

A number of textbooks cover the operational aspects of the subject matter and support the growth of events and events management as a field of study including: Raj *et al.* (2008); Allen *et al.* (2010); Bowdin *et al.* (2011); and Goldblatt (2011). In addition there are many more practical books from the event practitioner's point of view, such as the series written by Judy Allen including Allen (2009). However, there are currently no texts (to the author's knowledge) which consider events in a purely strategic way and which integrate events with the study of tourism and hospitality.

Tourism, hospitality and events management – an integrated approach

The previous sections illustrate the complexity of studying tourism, hospitality and events as industrial sectors, since there is debate as to sector boundaries and clearly there is a large degree of interrelation between them.

In each of the fields of study, many courses have emerged in recent years around the world – some of which consider the fields separately, whilst others combine the fields under a plethora of titles. In addition a large body of both academic and commercial literature has emerged in each of these fields and quite a large number of peer reviewed international journals have become established. Some of these journals are dedicated to one of the fields: (e.g. *Tourism Management*, *Event Management* and the *International Journal of Hospitality Management*), whereas others combine the fields (e.g. the *Journal of Hospitality and Tourism Research* and the *Journal of Convention and Event Tourism*). Even though the titles might appear to make the sector boundaries clear, the content within the journal is frequently not as clear as it often crosses over. For example, many articles in *Tourism Management* cover hospitality issues or particular events arranged for tourists.

Much of the relevant literature concentrates on detailed operational or context-specific aspects of tourism, hospitality and events. At this detailed operational level it is unarguable that tourism, hospitality and events are (although still linked) usually highly distinctive. The operational issues raised in managing an airline, a resort destination or a music concert, for example, are highly context-specific and thus require individual treatment.

At the strategic level, however, a more integrative approach is possible and helpful, given the obvious commonalities. Thus in this book the view is taken that at the 'strategic' as opposed to the 'operational' level the distinctions between tourism, hospitality and events are far less important. Operationally they may be very different but at the strategic level (that we are concerned with) they are not. Each of the three sectors are *service* sectors sharing similar characteristics and in many cases they overlap. Consequently tourism, hospitality and events can successfully be included in the remit of this book.

For example – tour operators engaged with organizing tourism may also own or manage accommodation and manage events of various kinds.

The approach here will be to include the three sectors together since many of the companies involved are integrated examples from a range of different organizations of differing sizes, spread throughout the sectors (and their sub-sectors) and the illustrations are taken from around the world.

Tourism, hospitality and events share many of the same characteristics and issues for management which are considered in various parts of this book. These shared features include the following, as they are all sectors with:

- products which are service-based;
- a scope that is international;
- a heavy reliance on human resources for successful delivery;
- perishable and intangible products;
- a wide use of *price discrimination* and *yield management* techniques; and
- rapidly changing means of distribution.

SMALL BUSINESS FOCUS

A further relevant issue relates to scale. Whilst the tourism and hospitality industries can be identified broadly as a certain subset of mostly larger companies (such as airlines, hotel groups and tour operators) providing services to customers and tourists, they also encompass a diverse, highly fragmented network of small-to-medium-sized companies and other organizations. This is particularly relevant in these industries. The events sector is also highly fragmented with low barriers to entry, and represents a wide-ranging and diverse set of organizations with few large companies or generally recognizable brands.

Much of the strategic management literature relates primarily to larger businesses, and is sometimes viewed as being irrelevant for smaller organizations, such as those in the sectors we are concerned with. However, many of the principles embodied in the literature are applicable to smaller businesses and 'not-for-profit organizations', but they need to be applied in a rather different way. Therefore the approach adopted here is to focus primarily on larger-scale businesses, but each chapter also contains a specific section illustrating the relevance of strategic management to small-to-medium-sized enterprises (SMEs).

SUMMARY

This chapter discussed the approach that this book will take to the study of strategic management in a *THE* context. The chapter introduced the three parts of the strategic process – strategic analysis, strategic selection and strategic implementation – and the importance of recognizing strategy as a continuous process requiring a feedback loop.

The chapter went on to introduce the individual sectors – tourism, hospitality and events – and describe the definitional debates surrounding these sectors. An argument was proposed as to why these three sectors could be studied together at the strategic but not the operational level and that the approach adopted by the book would be to integrate the three strands of *THE*.

Finally the aspect of scale was discussed in that many strategy books focus on larger-scale organizations, but the approach of this book would be to also contain discussions of particular relevance to smaller organizations.

REFERENCES

Allen, J. (2009) *Event Planning: The Ultimate Guide To Successful Meetings, Corporate Events, Fundraising Galas, Conferences, Conventions, Incentives and Other Special Events*, 2nd edn, New York: John Wiley.

Allen, J., W. O'Toole, R. Harris and I. McDonnell (2010) *Festival and Special Event Management*, 5th edn, Milton: John Wiley & Sons Australia.

Bowdin, G., J. Allen, W. O'Toole, R. Harris and I. McDonnell (2011) *Events Management*, 3rd edn, Oxford: Butterworth-Heinemann.

Chadwick, R. (1994) 'Concepts, Definitions and Measures Used in Travel and Tourism Research', in J. R. Brent Ritchie and C. Goeldner (eds.) *Travel, Tourism and Hospitality Research*, 2nd edn, New York: John Wiley, pp. 65–80 .

Cooper, C., J. Fletcher, A. Fyall, D. Gilbert and S. Wanhill (2008) *Tourism Principles and Practice*, 4th edn, Harlow: Pearson Education.

Evans, N. (2012) 'Tourism: A Strategic Business Perspective', in T. Jamal and M. Robinson (eds.) *The Sage Handbook of Tourism Studies*, Thousand Oaks, Calif.: Sage, pp. 215–34.

Gee, C. Y., J. C. Makens and D. J. L. Choy (1997) *The Travel Industry*, 3rd edn, New York: John Wiley.

Getz, D. (2007) *Event Studies: Theory, Research and Policy for Planned Events*, Oxford: Elsevier.

—— (2012) 'Event Studies: Discourses and Future Directions', *Event Management*, 16 (2): 171–87.

Goeldner, C. R. and C. R. Brent Ritchie (2011) *Tourism: Principles, Practices, Philosophies*, 12th edn, New York: John Wiley.

Goldblatt, J. (2011) *Special Events: A New Generation and the Next Frontier*, 6th edn, New York: Wiley.

Hamilton, J. (2006) *Thomas Cook: The Holiday Maker*, Stroud: Sutton Publishing Ltd.

Harrington, R. J. and M. C. Ottenbacher (2011) 'Strategic Management: An Analysis of Its Representation and Focus in Recent Hospitality Research', *International Journal of Contemporary Hospitality Management*, 23 (4): 439–62.

Harrison, J. S., C. A. Enz and R. Leyh (2005) *Hospitality Strategic Management: Concepts and Cases*, Hoboken, NJ: John Wiley & Sons.

Holloway, C. and C. Humphreys (2012) *The Business of Tourism*, 9th edn, Harlow: Pearson.

Ottenbacher, M., R. Harrington and H. G. Parsa (2009) 'Defining the Hospitality Discipline: A Discussion of Pedagogical and Research Implications', *Journal of Hospitality and Tourism Research*, 33 (3): 263–83.

Page, S. (2011) *Tourism Management*, 4th edn, London and New York: Routledge.

Powers, T. and C. Barrows (2012) *Introduction to Management in the Hospitality Industry*, 5th edn, Hoboken, NJ: John Wiley.

Raj, R., P. Walters and T. Rashid (2008) *Event Management: An Integrated and Practical Approach*, London: Sage.

Sharpley, R. (ed.) (2002) *The Tourism Business: An Introduction*, Sunderland: Business Education Publishers.

Walker, J. R. (2010) *Introduction to Hospitality Management*, 3rd edn, Upper Saddle River, NJ: Pearson Education.

Withey, L. (1998) *Grand Tours and Cook's Tours: A History of Leisure Travel, 1750 to 1915*, London: Aurum Press.

Strategy and strategic objectives for tourism, hospitality and event organizations

Introduction and chapter overview

Strategic thinking and strategic management can be viewed as the most important activities undertaken by any business or public sector organization. Strategic decisions are the key decisions which have to be taken by any organization; and from the strategic decisions which establish the framework, a series of more detailed operational decisions can be made. How skilfully these activities are carried out will determine the eventual long-term success or failure of the organization.

In this chapter, the basic concepts of strategy are introduced.

Definitions of the word *strategy* are discussed and we then explore the levels of decision making in successful strategic management (at the strategic and operational levels). These are defined and the links between the levels are discussed. Finally, we discuss the nature of strategic objectives – who is responsible for setting them and what they are essentially about.

LEARNING OBJECTIVES

After studying this chapter, you should be able to:

- define *strategy* and *strategic management*;
- explain Mintzberg's Five Ps framework of strategy;
- appreciate the importance and organizational context of strategic decision making;
- distinguish between deliberate (prescriptive) and emergent strategy;

- explain what strategy often contains in practice;
- distinguish between *strategic, tactical* and *operational* decisions;
- explain the meaning of mission, vision and values and describe the typical contents of these statements;
- analyse examples of mission and vision statements from relevant tourism, hospitality and events (*THE*) contexts;
- explain what is meant by *hierarchical congruence* and why is it important;
- employ the stakeholder model to explain how strategic decisions are arrived at;
- explain the most typical types of objective that are sought through strategic management and how they might be written; and
- understand how the strategy concepts introduced in the chapter can be applied to relevant tourism, hospitality and events (*THE*) contexts.

What is strategy?

Strategy is a complex study area in that it involves:

- few (if any) facts that can be learned;
- many views put forward by academics, practitioners and consultants, which can sometimes appear contradictory;
- a lot of jargon – where different words are used to describe essentially the same aspect *or* conversely the same words are used to describe aspects of strategy which are essentially different;
- a vast academic and commercial body of literature;
- different schools of thought and approaches adopted by various academics and consultants involved in this field;
- dealing with a dynamic set of circumstances;
- integrating subject matter from other fields.

In this book we attempt to find a way through this complexity by presenting the material in a logical order and by trying to present views on the subject matter which are widely accepted, taught and practised.

This book is entitled *Strategic Management for Tourism, Hospitality and Events*, and for the sake of brevity we will use *THE* throughout this book.

The implication of this title is that whist there are aspects of strategic management that need to be particularly stressed in the context of these three sectors, the conceptual material is largely generic. That is, most of the conceptual material is relevant for many industrial sectors (including tourism, hospitality and events), but the way in which it is applied will vary because of the particular nature of the sectors in question. As we will see in Chapter 2 there are some aspects of *THE* that are distinguishing features and that consequently we need to pay particular attention to.

Definition

The obvious starting point at the beginning of a book on strategy is the question 'what is strategy?'. However, the answer to the question, as implied above, is rather more complicated than it might at first appear. The growth of the subject of study has led to the use of the term strategy (and strategic management) in various ways and numerous definitions have emerged.

Fundamentally though, putting aside the definitional debates, we can distinguish between strategy and strategic management:

- *strategy* is about making you think ahead regarding key issues affecting organizations;
- *strategic management* is about giving you concepts, frameworks, tools and techniques to help you do so.

Many organizations operating in *THE* (as in other sectors) are hindered by short-termism, concentrating on the most pressing immediate tasks at hand, rather than looking ahead and taking a longer-term view. This is, perhaps, understandable given the pressures of modern business, but is not the most sensible way to manage.

It is extremely difficult for organizations to plan ahead, in the same way as it is difficult to forecast the weather or foresee future interest rate movements, because there are so many aspects of uncertainty and change. In order to facilitate the process of strategic management, concepts, frameworks, tools and techniques have been developed. The overall aim of strategic management is thus to develop a framework for thinking ahead – for planning strategically.

Historically the term strategy has military roots with commanders employing strategy in dealing with their opponents (see, for example, John Keegan's *The Mask of Command: A Study of Generalship*, 2004). Indeed dictionaries often continue the military theme defining strategy as 'the art of war'. In viewing strategy in such a way the fundamental underlying premise of strategy becomes the notion that an adversary can defeat a rival (even a larger more powerful one) if it can out manoeuvre the rival.

As in the military arena, so in business: organizations attempt to outmanoeuvre rivals. In so doing strategies have to be developed that rely on various disciplines such as marketing, finance and human resource management.

Since the beginning of commercial transactions businesses have had strategies determining their future courses of action. It is only since the 1960s, however, that the subject area has been widely considered as a topic of academic interest and hence widely taught in business schools and on business-based courses.

The subject is also widely taught as part of *THE*-related courses. As we progress through the book the *THE* literature relevant to each part of strategic management will be introduced. In some areas of strategy (for example, strategic alliances, which are covered in Chapter 12, and market entry strategy and globalization, which are covered in Chapter 14) the range of *THE* literature is quite extensive whereas in many others it is far less so.

The range of literature also varies considerably in terms of its coverage of the three sectors we are considering, with the literature applying business concepts to events being generally more recent and less extensive than is the case in relation to tourism and hospitality. There are though some general texts which consider strategy and planning in *THE* contexts including: Holloway (1998a and b); Olsen *et al.* (2007); Phillips and Moutinho (1998); and Moutinho (2000).

Chandler's definition

A number of writers have tried to sum up the meaning of strategy succinctly to make it easier for students to understand. One such definition, which despite its age is still widely quoted and adapted, was offered by Professor Chandler of Harvard Business School in 1962.

> **DEFINITION/QUOTATION**
>
> Strategy is *the determination of the basic long-term goals and objectives* of an enterprise, and *the adoption of courses of action* and *the allocation of resources* necessary for carrying out these goals.
>
> (Chandler, 1962; emphasis added)

The elements of strategy

This definition clearly shows the three elements (or components) of strategy. The italics in the definition above emphasize long-term goals; actions to achieve the goals and allocation of resources:

- The *determination of the basic long-term goals and objectives* concerns the conceptualization of coherent and attainable strategic objectives. Without objectives, nothing else can happen. If you do not know where you want to go, how can you act in such a way as to get there?

- The *adoption of courses of action* refers to the actions taken to arrive at the objectives that have been previously set.

- The *allocation of resources* refers to the fact that there is likely to be a cost associated with the actions required in order to achieve the objectives. If the course of action is not supported with adequate levels of resource, then the objective will not be accomplished.

The short case illustration below uses the analogy of a journey to illustrate the three elements of Chandler's definition of strategy.

SHORT CASE ILLUSTRATION

A journey from Berlin to Paris

By way of analogy we can consider a journey, say from Berlin to Paris.

Your objective is clear: to arrive in Paris, travelling from Berlin.

However, in making this journey there are various courses of action available to you. You might travel by train, by car, by coach or by plane. You might travel on certain days or at certain times of day. You might take advantage of certain concessionary fares and you might make a booking through an intermediary such as a travel agent, internet search site such as Expedia or book directly with the principal company (the airline or train company).

Thus as a result of wanting to travel to Paris from Berlin, a whole range of options need to be considered and detailed decisions have to be taken as to which options to select. Hence strategy contains three elements:

1. Your objective is clearly stated as arriving in Paris at a certain date and time.

2. In order to achieve this objective certain actions are necessary which are chosen from a range of alternative options available. If might be decided that flying is the best option. Thus a specified flight is booked through a travel agent and a plane is boarded at the airport.

3. However, the actions could not be achieved if they could not be resourced. You need the resources of a plane with a suitably qualified pilot, an airport, money to pay for your flight and other such 'inputs'. If any one of these is missing, you will be unable to meet your objective.

When we consider organizations we often talk about resources, which are divided up into various types. The Key Concept overleaf considers what we mean by resources.

KEY CONCEPT

Resources

Resource inputs (sometimes called factors of production) are those inputs that are essential to the normal functioning of the organizational process.

These are the inputs without which an organization simply could not continue to exist or meet its objectives. We can readily appreciate that human beings rely upon certain vital inputs such as air, water, nutrition, warmth, shelter, etc., but organizations have similar needs.

An organization's resource inputs fall into four key categories:

1. *Financial resources* – Money for capital investment and working capital. Sources include shareholders, banks, bondholders, etc.

2. *Human resources* – Appropriately skilled employees to add value in operations and to support those that add value (e.g. supporting employees in marketing, accounting, personnel, etc.). Sources include the labour markets for the appropriate skill levels required by the organization.

3. *Physical (tangible) resources* – Land, buildings (offices, accommodation, warehouses, etc.), plant, equipment, stock for production, transport equipment, etc.

4. *Intellectual (intangible) resources* – Inputs that cannot be seen or felt but which are essential for continuing business success, for example 'know-how', legally defensible patents and licences, brand names, registered designs, logos, 'secret' formulations and recipes, business contact networks, databases, etc.

The practice of strategy

The number and range of academics, consultants, authors and practitioners claiming to be involved in strategy in some way is vast. Given this diversity, it is unsurprising that, notwithstanding how we might formally define the term strategy, in practice the term has been used in numerous ways.

It was this multiplicity of uses of the term that led Professor Henry Mintzberg of McGill University in Montreal, Canada, originally writing in the late 1980s (Mintzberg, 2002: 3–9), to propose his 'five Ps' of strategy.

Mintzberg's five Ps

Mintzberg suggested that nobody can claim to own the word 'strategy' and that the term can legitimately be used in several ways.

A strategy can be:

- a plan;
- a ploy;
- a pattern of behaviour;
- a position in respect to others;
- perspective.

Note: It is important not to see each of these five Ps in isolation from each other. One of the problems of dividing ideas into frameworks, like the five Ps, is that they are necessarily simplified. The five Ps are not mutually exclusive, i.e. it is possible for an organization to show evidence of more than one interpretation of strategy.

PLAN STRATEGIES

A plan is probably the way in which most people use the word strategy. It tends to imply something that is intentionally put in place and its progress is monitored from the start to a predetermined finish. Some business strategies follow this model. 'Planners' tend to produce internal documents that detail what the company will do for a period of time in the future (say five years). It might include a statement on the overall direction that the organization will take in seeking new business opportunities as well as a schedule for new product launches, acquisitions, financing (i.e. raising money), human resource changes, marketing, etc.

PLOY STRATEGIES

A ploy is generally taken to mean a short-term strategy, and is concerned with the detailed tactical actions that will be taken. It tends to have very limited objectives and it may be subject to change at very short notice. Mintzberg describes a ploy as 'a manoeuvre intended to outwit an opponent or competitor' (Mintzberg *et al.*, 2002: 3). He points out that some companies may use ploy strategies as threats. They may threaten to, say, decrease the price of their products simply to destabilize competitors.

PATTERN STRATEGIES

A 'pattern of behaviour' strategy is one in which progress is made by adopting a consistent form of behaviour. Unlike plans and ploys, patterns 'just happen' as a result of the consistent behaviour.

SHORT CASE ILLUSTRATION

Plan, ploy and pattern strategies: a Northern European tour operator

A large tour operator which operates to various Mediterranean destinations offering holidays mainly to Northern Europeans might operate plan, ploy and pattern strategies in various parts of its business.

- *Plan* – A large tour operator, for instance, might decide that it plans to implement a strategy concerned with expanding its share of the market and that this will be achieved by setting prices at lower levels than competitors and by acquiring smaller firms.

- *Ploy* – Whilst the tour operator concerned has an overall strategy which it has planned that includes offering lower price levels than competitors, it might also develop a short-term ploy. The company might suddenly discount its prices within six weeks of customers' departure in order to destabilize its competitors and to sell excess capacity

- *Pattern* – In keeping with the consolidation that has taken place in the industry the tour operator concerned in this illustration might have acquired a small specialist operation offering summer villa and apartment holidays to a particular Greek island to a small but loyal group of customers. This might be viewed as following a pattern strategy. The company is unlikely to produce elaborate plans, simply renewing contracts with property owners and transport providers annually. If offered a new villa on favourable terms, then the operator would probably contract the property and feature it on its website without thinking about it. It is an opportunity that is taken, as it appears too good to miss. However, the tour operator would probably not feature a hotel in Majorca, although it may be available to the company, because that would be outside their pattern of business behaviour.

Questions

Consider other *THE* situations you are familiar with and provide an example of

1. a plan strategy;
2. a ploy strategy;
3. a pattern strategy.

Such patterns of behaviour are sometimes unconscious, meaning that they do not even realize that they are following a consistent pattern. Nevertheless, if it proves successful, it is said that the consistent behaviour has *emerged* into a success. This is in direct contrast to planning behaviour.

KEY CONCEPT

Deliberate and emergent strategy

There is a key difference between two of Mintzberg's Ps of strategy – plan and pattern. The difference is to do with the source of the strategy. He drew attention to the fact that some strategies are deliberate whilst others are emergent.

Deliberate strategy (sometimes called planned or prescriptive strategy) is meant to happen. It is preconceived, premeditated and usually monitored and controlled from start to finish. It has a specific objective.

Emergent strategy has no specific objective. It does not have a preconceived route to success *but* it may be just as effective as a deliberate strategy. By following a consistent pattern of behaviour an organization may arrive at the same position as if it had planned everything in detail.

The difference between these is fundamental in studying strategy. In practice few companies have a totally deliberate or totally emergent strategy, but have a combination of the two to some degree. To have a totally deliberate strategy would imply a lack of flexibility which would be dangerous for any organization when the environment can change quickly and fundamentally. To have a totally emergent strategy could also be dangerous in that it possibly implies a lack of forward thinking.

These concepts are discussed in greater detail in Chapter 15.

POSITION STRATEGIES

A position strategy is appropriate when the most important issue to an organization is perceived to be how it relates or is positioned in respect to its competitors or its markets (i.e. its customers). In other words, the organization wishes to achieve or defend a certain position.

In business, companies tend to seek objectives such as market share, profitability, superior research, reputation, etc. It is plainly obvious that not all companies are equal when such criteria are considered.

> **THINK POINTS**
>
> - What are Mintzberg's five Ps of strategy?
> - Define and distinguish between deliberate and emergent strategy.
> - What are the three components of strategy as described by Chandler?

PERSPECTIVE STRATEGIES

Perspective strategies are about changing the culture (the beliefs and the 'feel'; the way of looking at the world) of a certain group of people – usually the members of the organization itself. Some companies want to make their employees think in a certain way, believing this to be an important way of achieving success. They may, for example, try to get all employees to think and act courteously, professionally or helpfully.

> **SHORT CASE ILLUSTRATION**
>
> **Position and perspective strategies: hotels and airlines**
>
> Many *THE* companies such as international airlines or hotel operators have enviable reputations for reliability and quality whilst others are not so fortunate.
>
> - *Position* – The competitors with a reputation to defend will use a position strategy to ensure that the reputation they enjoy is maintained and strengthened. This may include advertising and public relations activities, but it may also include a focus on other activities such as improving or adding product features, or pricing incentives. Marketing messages may even extend to pointing out the deficiencies in competitors' products whilst pointing out the positive features of their own international hotel groups and some airlines have also developed a number of sub-brands in order to ensure that they are able to have a position they can defend in every segment of the market.
> - *Perspective* – This view of strategy is often of central importance to many *THE* companies since they rely on delivering services of consistent quality. In *THE* the quality of service delivery is often judged by the quality and attitude of those members of staff that are involved with delivering services. Consequently many *THE* companies invest heavily in developing a strong organizational culture which focuses greatly on the attitude of employees and their quality. Many large hotel groups and airlines, for example, go further and feature such a culture as a core strength. Employees (usually smiling!) are frequently featured in their advertising and other promotional activities since it is the quality of their encounter with customers which is seen as being the key factor in achieving high degrees of customer satisfaction.

Levels of strategic decisions

Different 'levels'

It is useful at this stage to gain an understanding of what characterizes strategic decisions. Management decisions in an organization can be classified in three broad and sometimes overlapping categories: strategic, tactical and operational. These can be illustrated as a hierarchy (See Figure 1.1) in which higher level decisions tend to shape those at lower levels of the organization.

Figure 1.1 Levels of strategic decision-making

Strategic, tactical and operational decisions within an organization differ from each other in terms of their:

- focus;
- level in the organization at which they are made;
- scope;
- time horizon;
- degree of certainty or uncertainty;
- complexity.

The differences between the three levels of decision making are summarized in Table 1.1.

Table 1.1 Comparison of strategic operational and tactical decisions

	Strategic	Tactical	Operational
Focus of decision	Achieving competitive advantage	Implementation of strategy	Day-to-day operations
Level of decision making	Senior management/ board of directors	Head of business unit or functional area	Supervisory
Scope	Corporate/whole organization	Business unit or functional area e.g. marketing	Department
Time horizon	Medium to long term (years)	Medium term (months to years)	Short to medium term (weeks to months)
Certainty/ uncertainty	High uncertainty	Some uncertainty	High certainty
Complexity	Highly complex	Moderately complex	Comparatively simple
Examples	Decisions to launch new products, enter new markets, takeover competitors, investment decisions	Decision to advertise adjust prices, alter product features etc.	Scheduling of work rotas, re-ordering supplies etc.

Strategic level decisions

Strategic decisions (which are our primary focus) are concerned with:

- the acquisition of *sustainable competitive advantage* (in a commercial organization);
- the setting of long-term objectives;
- the formulation, evaluation, selection and monitoring of strategies to achieve these objectives.

Strategic decisions normally have a number of characteristic features in that they:

- are made by senior managers (usually directors);
- affect the whole organization (or a substantial discrete part of the whole organization);
- are medium to long-term in nature;
- are complex and often based upon uncertain or incomplete information.

Managers at the strategic level require multi-conceptual skills – the ability to consider the effects of multiple internal and external influences on the business and the possible ways in which strategy can be adjusted to account for such influences.

Tactical level decisions

Tactical decisions are concerned with how strategic level objectives are to be met and how strategies are implemented. They are dependent upon overall strategy and involve fine tuning and adjustment. They are usually made at the head of business unit, department or functional area level and they have an effect only in parts of the organization. They are normally medium-term in timescale, semi-complex and usually involve some uncertainty but not as much as at the strategic level.

Operational level decisions

Operational decisions are concerned with the shorter-term objectives of the business and with its day-to-day management. They are dependent upon strategy and tactics. These decisions are made at junior managerial or supervisory level, are based on a high degree of certainty, and are not complex.

The different levels of decision making are illustrtated in the case of a hypothetical Australian events management company shown below.

SHORT CASE ILLUSTRATION

Levels of decision making: an Australian events management company

Total Event Solutions (TES) is a hypothetical events management company based in Sydney, Australia. The company has successfully operated in that market for many years organizing conferences, meetings, exhibitions and other events for both large and small clients in the local region and throughout the state of New South Wales. The market is extremely competitive and many of the larger companies TES works with have stated that they have difficulties in extending their working relationship with TES, though they are very satisfied with the service they have received. This is because the larger companies they represent have a nationwide presence and they need a partner to manage events that can also work on a nationwide basis.

TES's Board of Directors met and decided that in order to prosper in the future and compete effectively with national and international rivals in the market, TES had to expand to cover the entire Australian market. It was determined that it would do so by opening branch offices in each of the country's other five state capitals. However, to expand too rapidly can be an extremely risky aspect of business and lead to so-called *overtrading*. In such a situation, though the underlying business may be sound, investment may mean that cash-flow is negative for a period of time and has to be financed in some way. This occurs because financial and other resources need to be deployed before sales are achieved and revenue flows in. If there are unexpected adverse changes to the business environment, or levels of expected sales are not achieved, those providing finance (generally shareholders or banks) might withdraw the finance thereby leading to potential business failure.

Consequently, the Board of Directors laid down the condition that national coverage should be achieved, not immediately, but within five years through a phased opening of state offices in the key cities of Melbourne, Perth, Adelaide, Brisbane and Hobart. The CEO and his senior team subsequently met to consider the growth plan and determined a schedule for opening the offices, which involved a phased opening over five years starting with Melbourne and Brisbane in the subsequent year. As usual, annual sales targets were set for the Sydney office and new annual targets were set for TES's first new offices which would be opened in the coming year in Melbourne and Brisbane.

Questions

1. Distinguish between strategic, tactical and operational level decisions in the TES example.
2. Explain what is meant by the term *overtrading*.

Congruency and 'fit'

The success of strategy rests upon a very important, but rather obvious principle. Once the strategic level objectives have been set, the tactical and operational objectives must be set in such a way that they contribute to the achievement of the strategic objectives. In other words, the tactical and operational decisions must 'fit' the strategic objectives. This introduces the concept of *hierarchical congruence*, i.e. that objectives set at various levels must be aligned with each other in such a way that each level of organizational decision making contributes to the organization's overall strategic objectives.

The decision-making framework can be visualized as a pyramid-shaped hierarchy (see Figure 1.1). The top, where the strategic decisions are made, is thin whilst the bottom (operational decisions) is fatter. This representation is meant to show that strategic decisions are taken infrequently, whilst tactical and operational decisions are taken more often. Strategic decisions are few and far between, tactical decisions are taken with increasing frequency, whilst operational decisions are taken weekly, daily or even hourly. For every one strategic decision, there may be hundreds of individual operational decisions.

> **THINK POINTS**
>
> • Explain the meaning and significance of the term 'hierarchical congruence' for an organization.
> • Why is hierarchical congruence important in successful strategy?

Time and planning horizons

One of the key differences between the levels of decision making in organizations is the timescale with which they are concerned. It is usually considered that the higher up the organization, the longer the timescale with which management is concerned. Certainly this is true in most manufacturing companies. However, in service organizations, such as those we are concerned with *THE* organizations, the situation is often somewhat different.

Service delivery is of prime importance to service-based companies, and consequently relatively senior staff can often be involved to some degree in operational decision making. In the delivery of services it is vital that managers ensure that the service provided is:

- delivered to specified quality standards;
- capable of being replicated;
- resilient (i.e. service standards can resist unexpected changes).

The differing time horizons for decision making are illustrated below in the case of a group of hotels.

Strategic management involves taking account of a large number of environmental variables. The longer ahead that a manager seeks to plan for, the more uncertainty is introduced into the analysis.

SHORT CASE ILLUSTRATION

Decision-making time horizons: a hotel group

A group of hotels demonstrates the different levels of decision-making and the differeing time horizons that are usually involved with each level.

In a group of hotels most of the staff will be concerned with ensuring that the daily schedule of bookings run to plan and are delivered satisfactorily. The manager and senior hotel staff will, however, have wider concerns. They will probably have weekly, monthly and annual budgets and sales targets to hit. These requirements of their roles means that they will need to consider the hotel's position up to a year ahead. The chief executive of the whole group of hotels may have a longer time-frame as this person and their senior team may be considering what the potential threats and opportunities in the marketplace might be and how this particular hotel group might respond.

Questions

1. Explain why the hierarchy of decision making might be differnt in some service based companies such as those in *THE*.
2. Why is service delivery likely to be so important to all managers at every level in this case?

Objectives

Types of objectives

The different levels of decision making are reflected in the way in which organizations set objectives. Objectives can be written in two forms:

- *Closed* – stated in quantitative terms, specific in form and timescale.
- *Open* – stated in qualitative terms, general in form and timescale.

It is important at the outset to understand two important points about the way in which objectives are used in practice in organizations:

- Objectives take different forms (open or closed) at the various levels of the organization.
- Objectives can be described in different ways. That is, organizations will use varying terminology to describe their objectives.

Objectives in an organization are often portrayed as a hierarchy in which the organization sets out:

- an overall enduring purpose by way of – its *mission;*
- a desired future position it is trying to reach – its *vision;*
- how the mission and vision will be translated into specific targets – *corporate objectives, business objectives, unit and personal objectives.*

Hierarchy of objectives

The hierarchy of decision making in organizations is reflected in a hierarchy of objectives as shown in Table 1.2. The mission, vision and corporate objectives can be cascaded down the hierarchy of the organization. In this way the overall mission and vision of the organization are translated to give meaning for each constituent part and in some cases each individual employee.

Mission, vision and values: overview

An organization's mission, vision and values can be viewed as manifestations of an organization's identity; its 'personality', which is visible to both internal groups within the organization and, often, external groups (stakeholders) as well.

A great deal of management literature has been devoted to the successful adoption of statements relating to missions, vision and values (see for example Kantabutra and Avery, 2010; and Powers, 2012), and in essence the intention is that the statements should be clear and inspiring so that employees have a common

Table 1.2 A hierarchy of objectives

Level of hierarchy	Focus	Type	Timescale
Mission	Strategic – Overall organization	Open	Long term
Values	Strategic – Overall organization	Open	Long term
Vision	Strategic – Overall organization	Open	Medium to long term
Corporate objectives	Strategic – Overall organization	Primary – Closed Secondary – Open and Closed	Medium to long term
Business objectives	Strategic/tactical – *Strategic Business Unit*	Closed	Medium term
Unit/team objectives	Operational	Closed	Short term
Personal	Operational	Closed	Short term

framework of objectives which they can understand and aspire to while external stakeholders have a clear view of what the organization is striving to achieve.

Here we encounter some of the confusion that is often evident in dealing with strategy since different terminology can be encountered to describe essentially the same aspect, and the position of different aspects of strategy can be altered.

For example – terminology such as 'strategic intent', 'company philosophy' and 'corporate goals', can sometimes be encountered to describe the mission and vision. In some cases the mission might be subordinated to vision (rather than the other way round) which is more usual.

In some organizations the mission, vision and values are not labelled at all, or the values are incorporated into the mission statement. Thus, organizations create different presentational norms (the presentation of strategy is discussed further in Chapter 15) and use varying terminology, or no terminology at all, but the intent is clear:

> *The statements are intended to create a clear framework for decision making within the organization and are disseminated through the organizational hierarchy as shown in Table 1.2.*

KEY CONCEPT

Mission, vision and values

The mission, vision and values of organizations can take many forms in different organizations, and different words can often be substituted for these terms. Much discussion has also taken place in the academic literature about what is entailed in each of these concepts; the usefulness of these statements and how they should be presented. One view (Hill and Jones, 2009) of what each of the statements is trying to achieve is presented below:

- *Mission* – an organization's mission describes what the organization does.
- *Vision* – an organization's vision sets out some desired future state; it articulates, often in bold terms, what the company would like to achieve.
- *Values* – an organization's values state how managers and employees should conduct themselves, how they should do business, and what kind of organization they should build to help the organization achieve its mission.

Mission and mission statements

Powers (2012) argues that management professionals generally agree that the critical first step in planning is the definition of an organizational mission. A mission statement articulates the fundamental purpose of the organization and often contains several components (Hitt *et al.*, 2012), among them:

- company philosophy;
- company identity or self-concept;
- principal products or services;
- customers and markets;
- geographic focus;
- obligations to shareholders;
- commitment to employees.

The mission is the objective that subsumes all others beneath it and for some organizations the mission is very easy to articulate; but for large commercial businesses it tends to be more complex. Differing views for writing mission statements have emerged, and while there does not appear to be universal acceptance of any one particular format or set of attributes Powers (2012) usefully summarizes the different approaches. Williams (2008) assesses the mission statements in relation to the performance of larger American companies in the Fortune 1000 list. Similarly, in a study of Dutch mission statement Sidhu (2003) concludes that mission statements can lead to superior performance.

Some organizations attempt to frame their mission in a formal statement, which is often to be seen adorning office walls, printed on employee identity cards and published in annual reports. Mission statements are commonly found both in the commercial sector and in the non-commercial (*not-for-profit*) sector. Since the mission statement represents a long-term perspective, it often is retained by organizations for many years despite the many changes that may occur within the organization and in the external environment.

The American low-cost airline Southwest, for example, retains a mission statement originally conceived in January 1988 as illustrated below.

SHORT CASE ILLUSTRATION

Mission statement: Southwest Airlines

The mission statement of Southwest Airlines (which has been unchanged from January 1988 to the present) is testimony to what for many organizations is the enduring nature of such statements. Since the statement is about the purpose for which the organization exists, it can remain unchanged for long periods. This mission statement places particular emphasis on customer service and on its employees in the knowledge that it is the employees that can deliver the excellent customer service that is required. The full mission statement can be found on the company's website www.southwest.com, but the following extract provides a flavour of the style adopted:

> The mission of Southwest Airlines articulates a dedication to the highest quality of customer service which is . . . delivered with a sense of warmth, friendliness, individual pride, and Company Spirit. . . . Employees will be provided the same concern, respect, and caring attitude within the organization that they are expected to share externally.
>
> *www.southwest.com, accessed May 2014*

Questions

1. Why do you think the Southwest Aitrlines mision statement has remain unchanged for so long?
2. What sort of behaviour do you think Southwest Airlines is trying to encourage by employees?

A mission statement has a number of possible purposes. It can be used to clearly communicate the objectives and values of the organization to the various *stakeholder* groups and it can be argued that it assists in achieving *strategic congruence*.

In other words it sets a framework for the setting of other objectives, so that they are developed in a consistent manner at different levels of the organization. It may also have an effect in influencing the behaviour and attitudes of employees, although this is somewhat debatable as anecdotal evidence suggests that many employees have not in fact read their organization's mission statement.

A mission statement can be seen as the starting point for an organization's entire planning process since it requires senior management to seriously consider where the firm is now and where it should be in the future. This point is emphasized by two leading management writers, in the quotation below.

DEFINITION/QUOTATION

In business like in art, what distinguishes leaders from laggards, and greatness from mediocrity, is the ability to uniquely imagine what could be.

(Hamel and Prahalad, 1994:25)

However, establishing an organization's mission is not easy or without controversy and as a result styles and content vary enormously. As Peter Drucker (1974:94) points out in the quotation below.

DEFINITION/QUOTATION

Defining the purpose and mission of the business is difficult, painful and risky. But it alone enables a business to set objectives, to develop strategies, to concentrate its resources and to go to work. It alone enables a business to be managed for performance.

(Peter Drucker, 1974:94)

Campbell and Yeung (1998) emphasize that whilst the mission statement itself is clearly important, it is also important for managers to instil a 'sense of mission' in employees. The success of the mission requires the behaviour of employees to match the values of the company, but such harmony is difficult to achieve and requires the mission as it is implemented to become embedded as part of the organizational culture.

One view of what effective mission statements should contain is provided below.

STRATEGY IN PRACTICE

Effective mission statements

The mission statement should be:

- *Clearly articulated* – simple to comprehend so that employees and other stakeholders can clearly understand the principles and values that will guide them in their dealings with the organization. The statement must be specific enough to have an impact upon the behaviour of individuals.

- *Relevant* – appropriate to the organization in terms of its history, culture and shared values. The mission should not be too broad or too narrow. Too broad may result in lack of focus. Too narrow may mean factors that are potentially important to the organization are overlooked.

- *Current* – an unchanged mission statement may no longer be able to act as a driving force guiding the organization into the future.

- *Positive in tone* – written in such a way that encourages commitment and energizes or inspires employees.

- *Individual* – sets the organization apart from other organizations establishing its individuality if not its uniqueness through an emphasis on the advantages of the organization based on an objective assessment of organizational strengths and weaknesses.
- *Enduring* – cannot be continually altered, as this would be confusing, so they are likely to remain in place for a number of years. Consequently they must be written to allow for some flexibility.
- *Adapted* – written with various target audiences in mind, some for employees only, some for shareholders and other external groups, and others for all audiences. The information and style should reflect the relevant target audience.

Source: Stone (1996)

What does a mission statement contain?

The style, content and terminology of mission statements vary enormously. Some are long and detailed whereas others are short and to the point. Some are focused on a particular audience (such as employees or customers) others are written with multiple target audiences in mind. There are probably no 'rights' or 'wrongs' of how it should be presented or what it should contain; it all depends upon the organization and its culture.

In assessing mission statements the reader will find many examples of the use of language that is ambiguous in its meaning or is questionable in its use of 'hype' to inflate the image of the organization. In practice many mission statements contain a statement on the aspects listed below.

STRATEGY IN PRACTICE

Mission statement content

In practice, mission statements usually contain one or more of the following:

- Some indication of the industry or business the organization is mainly concerned with.
- An indication of the realistic market share or market position the organization should aim towards.
- A brief summary of the values and beliefs of the organization in relating to key stakeholder groups such as customers and employees.
- An indication of the ownership or control of the organization.
- A summary of the geographical location or scope of organizational activities.
- Specific and highly context-dependent objectives are sometimes expressed in the mission statement.

A selection of mission statements taken from a range of *THE* organizations in various sectors of the industry is presented in the following short case illustrations.

SHORT CASE ILLUSTRATION

Values, vision and purpose: Rezidor Hotel Group

The Rezidor Hotel Group is a fast growing international hotel company headquartered in Brussels, Belgium but its origins lie in Scandinavia and it has a primary stock market listing in Sweden.

The company focuses on an 'asset-light' business model by which it manages and franchises properties operating brands (including, Radisson Blu, Park Inn by Radisson, Hotel Missoni and Regent) at different price levels targeting various market segments. The company operates more than 440 hotels in city centres and key suburban locations, at gateway airports and exclusive resorts. It has over 96,000 rooms and more than 35,000 employees in more than 72 countries across Europe, the Middle East and Africa.

Rezidor's full mission, values and vision can be found on the company's website www.rezidor.com.

Rezidor defines its mission simply (as indeed many companies do), by means of a simple easily recalled statement. In Rezidor's case this is providing unique 'yes I can' service.

The simple Mission is aligned with several supporting statements (which is also a common approach). In this case the supporting statements are its Vision and Values.

Rezidor's Vision (what it wants to be known for) stresses the passion of its hoteliers; that it is responsive and innovative; that it wants to be viewed as the most dynamic hotel company in its territory of Europe, Middle East and Africa; and that it wants to be the preferred hotel group to do business with.

In its values the hotel group mentions that its values are: "Being Host' which is concerned with being professionl, responsible and being focused on service levels; and delivering what the brand pronioses. Its values continue through 'Fighting the "Z" spirit', which it defines in terms of speedy decision making and being innovative and 'Living Trust', which is concerned with empowering employees to deliver results.

www.rezidor.com, accessed May 2014

SHORT CASE ILLUSTRATION

Vision, mission and objectives: Kerala Tourism Organisation

The beautiful southern Indian state of Kerala has encountered a rapid increase in overseas tourist arrivals rising from 50,000 in 1986 to 0.6 million in 2010. The Kerala Tourism Policy which was published in 2012 and which is available at the Kerala Tourism Organisation's website (www.keralatourism.org) is that:

> Tourism becomes a vibrant and significant contributor to the sustainable development of the state of Kerala.

The Vision is supported by a Mission which mentions several aspects of tourism development such as Kerala providing a world-class visitor experience and positioning itself as a visible brand in global tourism achieving an enhanced market share outside India.

In turn the Mission is supported by a number of more detailed statements which are termed the 'Objectives' of the policy.

(www.keralatourism.org, accessed May 2014)

SHORT CASE ILLUSTRATION

Vision, mission and value: VISIT FLORIDA

VISIT FLORIDA, the state's official tourism marketing corporation, serves as Florida's official source for travel planning to visitors across the globe. VISIT FLORIDA is not a government agency, but rather a not-for-profit corporation created as a public/private partnership.

As the state's number one industry, Florida received 87.3 million visitors in 2011 who spent more than $67.2 billion, and over 1 million were employed in the industry.

Mission

To promote travel and drive visitation to and within Florida.

Vision

Establishes Florida as the No. 1 travel destination in the world.

Values

- Integrity
- Excellence
- Innovation
- Inclusiveness
- Welcoming
- Fun
- Teamwork.

www.visitflorida.org

SHORT CASE ILLUSTRATION

Mission statement: South by Southwest Festival, Austin Texas

Austin the state capital of Texas is a fast growing city with major technology industries and is also home to the University of Texas. The city labels itself as The Live Music Capital of the World, partly because of the numerous music venues operating in the city, but also because of South by Southwest (SXSW).

Though best known for its music festival, SXSW also hosts, interactive and film festivals and conferences in spring every year since its inception in 1987. It has grown to become one of the world's largest festivals.

The Mission statement of SXSW Interactive Festival is as follows:

The values of innovation, inspiration and creativity shape everything that we do at the SXSW Interactive Festival. Innovation means that we try to showcase up-and-coming technologies and industry leaders at SXSW. Inspiration means that we always aim for programming that will leave registrants enlivened and energized and excited. Creativity means that the process of generating new ideas is often more important than the process of generating new technologies.

As organizers, we understand the importance of the community in growing the quantity of registrants and the quality of programming at the SXSW Interactive Festival. The PanelPicker is a manifestation of this commitment to the community. The innovative interface allows anyone from the community to suggest programming ideas. The PanelPicker also empowers anyone in the community to vote on which suggested ideas should be part of the event (and to explain their vote via comments). Our commitment to community values also shines through with the Dewey Winburne Awards as well as the various social good sessions that we program during the event.

Finally, we acknowledge that SXSW Interactive is always a work-in-progress. Every year, we tinker with the formula and the event continues to improve. But every year we also discover more elements that need re-thinking and re-working. Many of the best improvements at SXSW Interactive come as a result of community input from engaged people such as yourself. If you have ideas on changes that we can implement to make the event better, then please contact us.

www.sxsw.com

Questions

Compare and contrast the Rezidor, Kerala, Florida and SXSW statements above.

1. Assess who you think the primary audiences for the statements might be in each case?
2. How effective is each statement in your judgement and why?

Vision and values

As with the mission, there is no firm, generally accepted definition of vision or values, and different styles with various features can be encountered.

Although strategy and leadership writers have proposed different characteristics that a vision should have, some commonly shared characteristics can be identified. Kantabutra and Avery (2010) for instance identified seven characteristics that might be found in vision statements that are perceived as making a difference to organizational performance.

STRATEGY IN PRACTICE

What do 'powerful' visions look like?

- *Conciseness* – visions should be easy to communicate and remember.
- *Clarity* – visions directly point at a prime goal. They can be understood without extended presentation and discussion.
- *Future orientation* – visions that are powerful do not consist of a one-time, specific goal or productivity target (e.g. sales or profit), that can be met and then discarded.
- *Stability* – visions do not shift in response to short-term trends, technology or market changes. They must be flexible enough to weather fluctuations.
- *Challenge* – visions that are effective are challenging since it motivates staff members to try their best to achieve desired outcomes.

- *Abstractness* – visions that are abstract suggest a longer-term goal that also allows for individual interpretations.
- *Desirability or ability to inspire* – powerful visions must be highly desirable and inspiring. They state a goal that directly inspires staff.

Source: Kantabutra and Avery, 2010

Just as with individuals we have a set of values which govern the way in which we conduct our behaviour, so it is with organizations. Organizations will have a set of guiding principles, i.e. values, though they may not be explicitly expressed in a statement or they be subsumed within the mission statement.

The organizations' values can be viewed as the philosophical principles that the great majority of its members hold in common (Haberberg and Rieple, 2001:48). The values are normally enduring and often closely associated with the organizational leadership since they set the parameters within which the organization operates.

The content of corporate objectives

In strict terms, the most important of all objectives is to simply survive as a going concern. Other objectives depend upon the type of organization and the nature of its environment. The objectives are not necessarily mutually exclusive in that an organization can usually pursue more than one type of objective at the same time. Two leading writers refer to them as 'the end the firm seeks and the criteria the firm uses to determine its effectiveness' (Glueck and Jauch, 1988:12).

The objectives can be written in a *closed* manner in that they are stated in quantitative terms and are specific in relation to form and timescale or an *open* manner in that they are stated in qualitative terms and are general in form and timescale.

Objectives are essential to the successful accomplishment of the managerial function in any formal organization in that they:

- provide a sense of direction;
- provide a standard of measurement and a means of controlling performance; and
- project an image of the organization's style.

Corporate objectives translate the mission and vision into specific long-term targets that can usually be quantified and measured. Corporate objectives are strategic-level objectives that can be used as a starting point in the setting *business* and tactical or *operational objectives*, which are more detailed objectives set lower down the organizational hierarchy. Business objectives will usually relate to important constituent parts of the overall organization – often termed *Strategic Business Units* (SBUs) – whilst the operational objectives will usually relate to smaller units or teams within each SBU.

Corporate objectives normally:

- relate to the whole organization;
- apply to the medium-to-long-term (see note overleaf);
- are set by senior management;
- relate to a number of key areas of concern; and
- can be pursued simultaneously.

Note – time horizons vary considerably and will depend largely upon the nature of the business, especially the lead time taken to launch new products and services. In some sectors where heavy capital expenditure is required development is time-consuming and lead times may be long. As a working rule, the long term is often considered to be over five years, the medium term one to five years, and the short term under one year.

For example – in many cases in service industries such as *THE*, lead times can be comparatively short, since launching a new destination, a new route or planning and staging most events can be achieved relatively quickly. However, where large capital investment is required as with hotel construction or new aircraft or cruise ship purchases, lead times are likely to be quite long.

Care must be taken in writing corporate objectives so that they are clear and easily understood.

STRATEGY IN PRACTICE

Objective writing is a *CRIME*

A common view is that objective writing is a *CRIME* in that corporate objectives should be:

- *C – Communicable* – capable of being easily communicated down the line to the workforce and other internal and external stakeholder groups;
- *R – Realistic* – capable of being achieved within the timescale;
- *I – Internally consistent* – consistent with the overall organizational mission, the operational objectives and the strategy for achieving the objectives set;
- *M – Measurable* – capable of being quantified so that they can be measured and it is possible to assess whether the objectives have been achieved;
- *E – Explicit* – written in clear and unambiguous language, precise in relation to both targets set and to timescale.

Corporate objectives often relate to economic and social concerns, and to matters of growth and competitive advantage. The main issues addressed by corporate objectives will now be considered.

Economic objectives

Economic objectives are those that can be measured in financial ways. For commercial organizations, objectives will usually include measures such as *return*. Return is an accounting term to describe the proportion of either sales or investment capital that is left over as profit. In commercial organizations the economic objective is often referred to as the *primary objective*, with other objectives being *secondary* to the achievement of the financial objective.

Return on sales, sometimes referred to as profit margin, is an indication of how well the company has controlled its costs, whilst *return on assets* (or *return on capital employed*) is an indication of how efficiently the company has used its investors' money. Both of these are important business objectives: to provide sufficient return to retain some profits for future investment and to provide investors with a dividend on their shareholding.

Not-for-profit organizations also have economic objectives, but they are measured in different ways. Organizations like destination marketing offices, charities and government departments tend to measure economic performance by using *cost-benefit* or *value-for-money* objectives. These organizations usually rely in large part on income over which they have little control – it may, for example, be fixed by central or local government. The objectives set will typically involve extracting the maximum benefit in terms of outputs from the income they have.

Social objectives

It should not be assumed that all organizational objectives are financial in nature. Many exist, either in part or totally, to deliver social benefits. Many publicly funded organizations such as museums, art galleries, heritage attractions and so on exist to deliver services to society in general. Charities exist primarily to provide social benefit to one or more allegedly worthwhile constituencies. For organizations of this type, economic objectives may be secondary to their desire to deliver socially desirable ends.

Commercial organizations are also gradually adopting social objectives in their strategic planning as part of what they view as their corporate social responsibilities. Although they are usually subordinate to their economic objectives, commercial organizations may espouse social or environmental causes that they purport to believe in. They may, for example, recognize the social value of supporting local community projects or seconding (at their own expense) some of their people to serve with charities.

Growth or market share objectives

At some stages in the life of an organization, objectives concerning growth and expansion become among the most important. This is especially true of businesses who must grow and maintain market position in order to 'keep up with' or 'keep ahead of' competitors.

Size and market position offer a number of advantages and it is these that an organization seeks when growth is a key objective. Size gives an organization economy of scale advantages in both product and resource markets. It means that a larger organization attracts resource inputs at preferential unit costs compared to smaller concerns and its larger presence in its product markets increases its pricing power and its ability to subjugate competitors. We will consider the basis for this type of objective in more depth in Chapter 11.

Competitive advantage objectives

Finally, and importantly, many strategic objectives concern the company's position in respect to its competitors. Competitive advantage objectives concern how the company's position compares to others – especially to competitors. The objectives are limited to ensuring simply that 'we beat you' or 'we are better than you'. Superior performance is the only objective and if a company can achieve ascendancy over its nearest competitors, then the objective will have been accomplished.

How do businesses set objectives?

Earlier in this chapter, we introduced the idea that strategic objectives, since they represent the most important level of decision making, are set by an organization's senior management, usually the board of directors. In setting objectives, however, senior managers are likely to be influenced by a range of different groups, which have an interest in the organization.

Who or what influences the senior management in their objective setting? Two broad schools of thought have emerged: the stockholder approach and the stakeholder approach.

The stockholder approach

The stockholder approach argues that businesses exist primarily for their owners (usually shareholders). Accordingly, any business behaviour that renders profit performance sub-optimal is not only theft from shareholders but will also, eventually, lead to a level of business performance that will harm all other groups such as employees, customers and suppliers.

Nobel Laureate, Professor Milton Friedman (1984), contended that the moral obligation of business is to increase its profits. Friedman argues that the one and only obligation of company directors (who are the legal agents of shareholders' financial interests) is to act in such a way as to maximize the financial rate of return on the owners' shares.

The stakeholder approach

There are many examples of different stakeholders, and the term is defined below.

> **DEFINITION/QUOTATION**
>
> A stakeholder can be defined as:
>
> > Any group or individual who can affect or is affected by the achievement of an organization's objectives.
> >
> > (Freeman, 1984:46)

This definition draws in almost everybody that is in, or may be potentially involved in, the life of an organization. It consequently goes without saying that not all stakeholders are equal in their influence on an organization's objectives.

The stakeholder approach – as advocated for example by Donaldson and Preston, 1995 and Campbell, 1997 – argues that organizations, like individual people, are characterized by their relationships with various groups and individuals such as employees and customers. A group or individual qualifies as a stakeholder if it has a legitimate interest in the organization's activities and thus has the power to affect the firm's performance and/or has a stake in the firm's performance.

The implications of this proposition are far-reaching. In essence, *stakeholder theory* argues that shareholders are neither the sole owners of a business nor the sole beneficiaries of its activities. Whilst shareholders are undeniably one stakeholder group (in a commercial business), they are far from being the only group who expect to benefit from business activity and, accordingly, are just one of those groups who have a legitimate right to influence a company's strategic objectives. Some of these groups are internal to the organization whilst others are external.

Stakeholder groups, which might be able to exert an influence over the setting of objectives, are shown in Table 1.3.

Stakeholders and objectives

One widely used and useful model for understanding how stakeholders exert influence on an organization's objectives was proposed by Mendelow (1991). According to this model, stakeholders can be 'ranked' depending upon two variables: the stakeholders' *interest* and *power*.

- Stakeholder *power* refers to the *ability* to influence the organization.
- Stakeholder *interest* refers to the *willingness* to influence the organization. In other words, interest concerns the extent to which the stakeholder cares about what the organization does.

It then follows that:

> *Stakeholder influence = power × interest*

Table 1.3 A summary of stakeholder groups

Internal stakeholders	External stakeholders
Board of directors	Shareholders
Employees collectively	Creditors (existing & potential)
Individual employees (e.g. founding entrepreneur)	Suppliers (existing & potential)
Employees' representatives (trade unions, trade associations etc)	Customers (existing & potential)
Functional business areas (marketing, finance etc)	Trade bodies (e.g. ABTA, the UK's Association of British Travel Agents)
Geographical areas of the organization (e.g. Europe, Asia etc.)	Pressure groups (e.g. environmental)
	Competitors (current and future, national and international)
	Government (legal, fiscal, and regulatory impacts)
	Private individuals
	International regulatory bodies (e.g. IATA, the International Air Transport Association)
	The local community

The actual influence that a stakeholder is able to exert will depend upon where the stakeholder is positioned with respect to their ability and willingness to influence. A stakeholder with both high power and high interest will be more influential than one with low power and low interest. We can map stakeholders by showing the two variables on a grid comprising two intersecting continua as shown in Figure 1.2).

Once constructed, the map can be used to assess two aspects:

1. Which stakeholder is likely to exert the most influence upon the organization's objectives.
2. The stakeholders that are most likely to be in potential conflict over strategic objectives (where two or more stakeholders are in close proximity in the high power–high interest part of the map).

The managing director and the board of directors are examples of stakeholders with both high power and high interest. This is because they lead and manage the business, depend upon it for their jobs and their

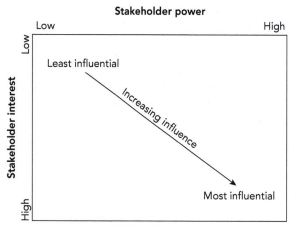

Figure 1.2 The stakeholder map

positions within the organization give them power with which to implement their decisions. The local community (in most cases) will not concern itself with the setting of organizational objectives and have limited power to impose their views. Organizations will have a range of stakeholders, some of whom might have opposing views.

In applying stakeholder theory in a tourism planning context, Sautter and Leissen (1999) produce a conceptualization of how it might be used as a tourism planning tool. They argue that it can be used to promote collaboration among key players in the planning process and that planners must proactively seek to include certain stakeholders in the planning process.

THINK POINTS

- What is a mission statement?
- In what ways might a mission statement help in achieving strategic objectives?
- What is a stakeholder and in what ways might stakeholders affect objective setting?
- Explain how the power–interest map helps to identify the most influential stakeholders.

The Australian Council of National Trusts (see below), for example, will have a wide range of stakeholder views which need to be considered.

SHORT CASE ILLUSTRATION

Stakeholders: The Australian Council of National Trusts

The National Trust of Australia is a community-based, non-government organization, committed to promoting and conserving Australia's indigenous, natural and historic heritage through its advocacy work and its custodianship of heritage places and objects.

The Australian National Trust movement was established in New South Wales in 1945 by Annie Wyatt who, along with a group of other citizens, raised community consciousness of widespread destruction of the built and natural heritage in Sydney.

The National Trust movement quickly spread across Australia with the other States establishing National Trust offices throughout the 1950s and 1960s. The Northern and Australian Capital Territories were the last to establish a National Trust in 1976. Each State and Territory National Trust is a fully autonomous entity in its own right responsible for managing its own affairs.

Collectively the organization owns or manages over 300 heritage places (the majority held in perpetuity) and manages a volunteer workforce of 7,000. The National Trust of Australia relies heavily on community support generated through membership subscriptions, sponsorship, donations and bequests, property admissions and retail sales. Of the collective total operational revenue generated by the organization less than 10% is sourced from government.

www.nationaltrust.org.au

Questions

1. Identify the principal stakeholder groups in this case.
2. Which stakeholder groups are likely to be the most influential and why?

SMALL BUSINESS FOCUS

SMEs are often sadly neglected in the strategic management literature, with a concentration on large internationally diversified corporations instead. Many of the tools and techniques that have been developed are certainly primarily explained in the context of such enterprises, but in many cases they can be applied appropriately to smaller enterprises.

One of the key facets about the *THE* sectors is that in most cases they are highly fragmented. While vehicle or aircraft manufacture are examples of highly *concentrated* industries with production dominated by a few large corporations, this is not the case in *THE* sectors. Some large international diversified companies have developed in *THE* sectors (and continue to do so); nevertheless it is true to say that these sectors remain highly fragmented, particularly in developing countries.

The larger companies (such as Tui, Marriott, Air France/KLM) will certainly be used as examples in this book, but it is important to remember that even in highly developed economies there is often a much larger number of SMEs that have less well-known brand names.

Indeed, in one of the sectors we are considering, (events management), arguably no strong internationally recognized brand exists, but rather a plethora of SMEs. Many smaller businesses exist and many family enterprises continue to thrive, as entry costs are often low and individuality and service flexibility are often valued.

Small businesses are certainly different from larger businesses in several respects. They are likely to be competing in a limited number of markets with a limited range of products and they are often 'private' companies as opposed to 'public' companies making access to finance more difficult. However, many of the strategic concepts, tools and techniques discussed in this book are applicable to SMEs (or can be adapted to them). For example as Johnson *et al.* (2011) point out, unless the company is specializing in a particular market segment (and has established a specific niche) it is likely to face significant competitive pressures. Thus, those areas we will consider in this text when dealing with competitive strategy are particularly relevant in this context.

In this chapter we introduced the notion that strategy is essentially about 'thinking ahead' in considering the most important issues an organization faces. Furthermore we considered the mission, vision, values and setting objectives. These aspects of strategic management, it can be argued, are valid regardless of organizational size. Competitive pressures, the dynamic nature of the environment and the expectations of stakeholder groups (such as banks and other investors) means that thinking ahead is of vital importance to SMEs just as it is to their larger competitors.

CHAPTER SUMMARY

This chapter discussed the meanings of the terms *strategy* and *strategic management* and introduced the concepts of *deliberate* and *emergent* strategies. It went on to explain the components of strategy before discussing the levels of strategic decision making in organizations and the important concept of strategic congruence. The concepts of mission, vision and values were introduced and the role of stakeholders in objective setting was discussed. The main 'types' of objective were explained and their content was discussed.

REFERENCES

Campbell, A. (1997) 'Stakeholders: The Case in Favour', *Long Range Planning*, 30 (3): 446–9.

Campbell, A. and S. Yeung (1998) 'Creating a Sense of Mission', in S. Segal-Horn (ed.) *The Strategy Reader*, Oxford: Blackwell, pp. 284–95.

Chandler, A. D. (1962) *Strategy and Structure*, Boston, Mass.: MIT Press.

Donaldson, T. and L. E. Preston (1995) 'The Stakeholder Theory of the Corporation: Concepts, Evidence and Implications', *Academy of Management Review*, 20 (1): 65–91.

Drucker, P. F. (1974) *Management: Tasks, Responsibilities, Practices*, New York: Harper & Row.

Freeman, R. E. (1984) *Strategic Management: A Stakeholder Approach*, Boston, Mass.: Pitman.

Friedman, M. (1970) 'A Theoretical Framework for Monetary Analysis', *The Journal of Political Economy*, 78 (2): 193–238.

Glueck, F. and L. R. Jauch (1988) *Strategic Management and Business Policy*, 3rd edn, New York: McGraw-Hill.

Haberberg, A. and A. Rieple (2001) *The Strategic Management of Organisations*, Harlow: FT Prentice Hall.

Hamel, G. and C. K. Prahalad (1994) *Competing for the Future*, Boston, Mass.: Harvard Business School Press.

Hill, C. W. and G. R. Jones (2009) *Strategic Management: An Integrated Approach*, 3rd edn, Mason, OH: Cengage Learning.

Hitt, M., R. D. Ireland and R. Hoskisson (2012) *Strategic Management Cases: Competitiveness and Globalization*, 10th edn, Mason, Ohio: South-Western Cengage Learning.

Holloway, S. (1998a) *Changing Planes: A Strategic Management Perspective on an Industry in Transition*, vol. I: *Situation Analysis*, Farnham: Ashgate.

—— (1998b) *Changing Planes: A Strategic Management Perspective on an Industry in Transition*, vol. II: *Strategic Choice, Implementation and Outcome*, Farnham: Ashgate.

Johnson, G., R. Whittington, K. Scholes and S. Pyle (2011) *Exploring Strategy: Text and Cases*, 9th edn, Harlow: Financial Times Prentice Hall.

Kantabutra, S. and G. C. Avery (2010) 'The Power of Vision: Statements that Resonate', *Journal of Business Strategy*, 31 (1): 37–45.

Keegan, J. (1988) *The Mask of Command: A Study of Generalship*, New York: Viking Penguin.

Mendelow, A. (1991) *Proceedings of 2nd International Conference on Information Systems*, New York: Society for Management Information Systems.

Mintzberg, H., J. Lampel, J.B. Quinn and S. Ghoshal (2002) *The Strategy Process: Global*, 4th edn, Hemel Hempstead: Prentice Hall.

Moutinho, L. (2000) 'Strategic Planning', in L. Moutinho (ed.) *Strategic Management in Tourism*, Wallingford: CABI, pp. 259–82.

Olsen, M. D., J. West and E. C. Tse (2007) *Strategic Management in the Hospitality Industry*, 3rd edn, New York: John Wiley.

Phillips, P. A. and L. Moutinho (1998) *Strategic Planning Systems in Hospitality and Tourism*, Wallingford: CABI.

Powers, E. L. (2012) 'Organizational Mission Statement Guidelines Revisited', *International Journal of Management and Information Systems (IJMIS)* 16 (4): 281–90.

Sautter, E. T. and B. Leisen (1999) 'Managing Stakeholders: A Tourism Planning Model', *Annals of Tourism Research*, 26 (2): 312–28.

Sidhu, J. (2003) 'Mission Statements: Is It Time to Shelve Them?' *European Management Journal*, 21 (4): 439–46.

Stone, R. A. (1996) 'Mission Statements Revisited', *SAM Advanced Management Journal*, 61: 31–43.

Williams, L. S. (2008) 'The Mission Statement: A Corporate Reporting Tool with a Past, Present and Future', *Journal of Business Communication*, 45 (2): 94–119.

WEBSITES

www.keralatourism.org
www.nationaltrust.org.au
www.rezidor.com
www.southwest.com
www.sxsw.com
www.visitflorida.org

Reference	Focus
Argenti, J. (1997) 'Stakeholders: The Case Against', *Long Range Planning*, 30 (3): 442–5.	Stakeholders Objective setting
Athiyaman, A. (1995) 'The Interface of Tourism and Strategy Research: An Analysis', *Tourism Management*, 16 (6): 447–53.	Strategy Tourism Research
Athiyaman, A. and R. W. Robertson (1995) 'Strategic Planning in Large Tourism Firms: An Empirical Analysis', *Tourism Management*, 16 (3): 199–205.	Strategy Tourism Research
Baetz, M. C. and C. K. Bart (1996) 'Developing Mission Statements Which Work', *Long Range Planning*, 29 (4): 526–33.	Mission statement Objective setting
Bart, C. K. (1997) 'Sex, Lies and Mission Statements', *Business Horizons*, 40 (6): 9–18.	Mission statement Objective setting
Campbell, A. (1997) 'Mission Statements', *Long Range Planning*, 30 (6): 931–2.	Mission statement Objective setting
Dev, C. S. (1989) 'Operating Environment and Strategy: The Profitable Connection', *Cornell Hotel and Restaurant Administration Quarterly*, 30 (2): 9–14.	Strategy Hotels Environmental analysis
McKiernan, P. (1997) 'Strategy Past; Strategy Futures', *Long Range Planning*, 30 (5): 790–8.	Strategy Approaches to strategy History of strategic thought
Mitchell, R. K., B. R. Agle and D. J. Wood (1997) 'Toward a Theory of Stakeholder Identification and Salience: Defining the Principle of Who and What Really Counts', *Academy of Management Review*, 22 (4): 853–88.	Stakeholders Objective setting
Olsen, M. D. (1991) 'Strategic Management in the Hospitality Industry: A Literature Review', in C. P. Cooper and A. Lockwood (eds.) *Progress in Tourism, Recreation and Hospitality Management, Volume 3*: 215–31.	Strategy Hospitality Literature review
Phillips, P. A. (1996) 'Strategic Planning and Business Performance in the UK Hotel Sector: Results of an Exploratory Study', *International Journal of Contemporary Hospitality Management*, 15 (4): 347–62.	Strategy Hotels Performance
Soteriou, E. C. and C. Toberts (1998) 'The Strategic Planning Process in National Tourism Organizations', *Journal of Travel Research*, 37 (August): 21–9.	Strategy Tourism planning
Teare, R. and R. Boer (1991) *Strategic Hospitality Management*, London: Cassell.	Strategy Hospitality
Tribe, J. (1997) *Corporate Strategy for Tourism*, London: International Thomson Business Press.	Strategy Objective Setting Mission statements

Case 2	Tourism Queensland
Case 6	Reed Exhibitions

Chapter **2**

Introduction to strategy for tourism, hospitality and events

Introduction and chapter overview

Formulating tourism, hospitality and events strategy represents a complex set of challenges for managers operating in these sectors because of the nature of the products being sold and because of the distinctiveness of the environment in which these sectors exist.

In particular, strategy is informed by the fact that *THE* products are 'services' rather than goods (physical products) which has certain implications for managers in these sectors. Furthermore *THE* products have certain specific features, which, if not unique, are certainly highly distinctive characteristics in comparison with other service sectors.

In this chapter we consider the nature of service products and the particular distinctive characteristics of *THE* products. An understanding of these features and the managerial implications that flow from them is necessary, as it informs and underpins the strategy formulation process.

> **LEARNING OBJECTIVES**

After studying this chapter, you should be able to:

- define goods and services;
- describe the key characteristics of service products and how they are relevant to *THE* organizations;
- explain the defining characteristics of *THE* products in particular;
- assess the impacts of the key features of *THE* products on managers working in these sectors;
- explore some of the ways in which managers respond to the key features of *THE* products.

Tourism, hospitality and events as service industry sectors

Goods and services

In a book on strategy for tourism, hospitality and events, it is appropriate to consider the nature of the products that comprise the central themes that we will be studying. If you have studied business or economics before, you will recall that there are two basic types of product: goods and services:

- goods are *tangible* – things you can own;
- services are *intangible* – things done on your behalf or for your benefit. You do not own service products, but instead you have use of them.

For example – as a customer you do not own an aircraft seat on a flight, a hotel room, or an event that you attend, but instead you make use of the services offered.

The reason that we make this distinction (and we will go on to consider the issues raised by this distinction in greater detail) is that it has a fundamental effect on managing in these sectors.

Products in *THE* have a number of key or defining characteristics which are important because they are of relevance to the way in which managers have to make decisions in these sectors. Some of these characteristics they share with other service products, which are discussed in the following section. Some other characteristics can be viewed as characteristics of *THE* products in particular. These defining characteristics are also relevant to *THE* managers and they are discussed later in the chapter.

Service product characteristics

There are a number of factors which make services different from physical goods.

These distinguishing factors are:

- intangibility
- inseparability
- perishability
- heterogeneity
- ownership.

We will consider each characteristic in turn.

Intangibility

Services cannot normally be seen, touched, smelt, tasted, tried on for size or stored on a shelf prior to purchase. Their intangibility makes them harder to buy, since you cannot test them, but easier to distribute, since there is no physical product to distribute.

The fact that *THE* products are not normally physical objects but amalgams of 'invisible' services does create certain problems for organizations operating in these sectors. To overcome this intangibility, organizations operating in these sectors sometimes attempt to create some form of tangible offering that potential customers can relate to, such as a free gift, t-shirts sold at a concert or a free DVD which shows product features. It also means that managers have to ensure that promotional activities are effective and that distribution of the product enables potential customers to gain access to the product so that purchases can be made. In some cases it might also be possible to try out the product prior to acquiring it.

For example – a buyer working for a tour operator, event manager or travel intermediary might be able to sample the food and accommodation prior to contracting the supplier. However, the exact quality of the accommodation and meals that the customer will receive is still intangible. This is because the quality of the accommodation or the meals that the customer receives (or their perception of them) may be different from those sampled prior to contracting.

With the growth in the home ownership of DVD players, personal and tablet computers, and smart phones, tour operators, destinations, hotels and event organizers are now able to record or stream the features of their products for viewing by potential customers. This takes away some of the uncertainty the customer may have when buying these services before they are actually provided. Similarly, brochures, 'flyers' and pamphlets promoting *THE* products help to overcome the intangibility problem, and this is why so much effort, expense and creativity are devoted to their design.

KEY CONCEPT

Packages and tour operators

A 'package' can be defined as a pre-arranged combination, sold or offered for sale at an inclusive price of not less than two of the following three elements:

- transport;
- accommodation; and
- other tourist services not ancillary to transport or accommodation and accounting for a significant part of the package.

The growth of the package has been a major cause of the increase in the holiday market in Europe and elsewhere since the 1950s. The role of the package company goes beyond that of the wholesaler, in that they not only purchase or reserve the separate components in bulk but, in combining these components into an 'inclusive tour', they also become producers in the holiday market. The traditional appeal of the tour operators' product has been to offer a complete holiday package at the lowest price to a population often lacking the linguistic or general knowledge and confidence to organize independent travel.

In recent years, tour operators have come under increasing pressure as the internet and the growth of low-cost airlines have enabled consumers to construct their own packages, and have taken away the advantages offered by charter airlines operated by the major tour operators. Notwithstanding these changes, tour operators, and the packages they provide, remain major features of the holiday market in many tourist-generating countries.

Inseparability

The production and consumption of services, including those in *THE* sectors, are inseparable.

For example – to take advantage of a festival music event you have to be at the event at the time it is taking place. In other words, the event is being delivered (produced) at the same time as you are listening to it (consuming). Similarly, for you to make use of an air flight or a bus service, both you and the means of transport must make the journey at the same time, i.e. the service is provided and consumed simultaneously.

The implication of this inseparability is important for managers in service sectors such as *THE* in that the consumers of the service have direct experience of the production of that service. They are, in effect, in the 'service factory' at the time of production. This has profound implications for the staff and managers in service industries.

When a physical product is purchased, it usually comes packaged and the customer is likely to assess the product purely upon its product features (such as taste, size, specification, reliability, durability, quality, etc.). Managers have time to plan these aspects of product management to ensure that customers' satisfaction is achieved. The circumstances under which the product is produced and how it is delivered are usually of little relevance to the customer.

In the case of a service product, however, the position is often different. Customers are likely to be very concerned about the way in which the product is delivered, i.e. the level of customer service.

For example – at a hotel reception desk or the welcome desk for an exhibition or convention, the customer is likely to notice if the reception staff are rude or unwelcoming. Conversely, the customer will also appreciate the production of the product if the reception staff are efficient, courteous and helpful.

The task of satisfying customers for the provider of a service is in many ways much more difficult than it is for the manufacturer of a product. With the provision of a manufactured product there is a time delay between the production of the product and its distribution and consumption. This delay allows for mistakes to be rectified. In service industries such as *THE* sectors the position is somewhat different.

Since production and consumption are inseparable (as they occur simultaneously), there is no chance to correct errors. Everything should be 'right first time, all the time' and any mistake can prove very costly in terms of lost future custom. How service personnel conduct themselves in the customer's presence – what they say; what they don't say; how competent they are; how personable they are; how presentable they are – can determine whether the customer buys from the business again. If mistakes are made, as inevitably they will be, how these are followed up and dealt with are crucial in determining customer loyalty.

The implications of inseparability for managers in *THE* sectors are that it places a great emphasis on the importance of front-line staff, in that they need to be carefully selected, well trained and have the appropriate skills and aptitude for customer service roles.

Perishability

Since production and consumption are simultaneous, *THE* services are instantly perishable; if the services are not sold at the time they are offered, then they perish and no income is received.

For example – an event which takes place and is not full to capacity; an empty train seat; an unoccupied hotel bedroom; or, an unsold holiday, all represent lost opportunities. They are sales that have not taken place and that can never be recovered because they are services offered on a certain date and cannot be 'stored' for when demand increases. The income foregone cannot be recovered.

Unlike manufacturers of goods, service providers cannot just keep on producing services and store them for future sales. Striking the correct balance of capacity and sales (supply and demand) is extremely difficult and represents a key managerial challenge for those operating in *THE* sectors.

KEY CONCEPT

Capacity, occupancy rate, load factors and attendance rate

In *THE*, capacity refers to the number of people that can be accommodated at an event, in a hotel, on an aircraft or bus, at a resort, at a destination, etc. It may be, for example, that a hotel has a capacity of 300 and an aircraft might be able to seat 130.

The important figure, however is how much of the capacity is actually used at any time and it is often referred to in different ways. This is normally:

- the occupancy rate for accommodation;
- the load factor for transportation;
- the attendance numbers (or attendance rate) for events and venues;
- the carrying capacity for destinations and resorts.

For example – if a hotel is only full on a quarter of the nights in a year, then it is paying the 'fixed costs' (building costs, mortgage payments, taxes, etc.) on the empty rooms without any income from them. The management of capacity is particularly important when considering seasonality and also explains why prices fall in the low season – to maintain as high an occupancy rate as possible to help to cover the hotel's total costs.

The problems of perishability can be made even more acute in *THE* by fluctuating demand for services, but a relatively fixed supply. Demand can vary during the day, week or from season to season of the year.

For example – many resort hotels, for instance, are full for only a few months of the year. Capacity may therefore be insufficient to meet demand at peak times, but in excess of what is required at slack times. Similarly, the demand for visiting an art exhibition may be greatest during holiday periods and when people are not generally working, i.e. weekends and evenings. Consequently, during these busy periods numbers attending may have to be restricted (because the exhibition has a given capacity level), whereas at other times there is excess capacity.

Demand can fluctuate for all sorts of reasons, such as: seasonal changes; changes due to the level of economic activity; changes due to climatic conditions; changes due to publicity or advertising; and changes in trends and fashions. Changes in demand can also occur very suddenly and can have a dramatic impact on service suppliers.

For example – a single reported terrorist attack in a destination area, or more widespread instability, such as the instability that has been caused in Egypt following political changes in 2012, could severely limit demand for visits and accommodation. Following the terrorist attack on the twin towers in New York in September 2011, the airline industry world-wide faced a major and immediate downturn in demand which could not have been foreseen and which continued to be felt for a number of years.

Supply, however, is often much more difficult to alter, at least in the short term.

For example – a hotel has a fixed bed-stock (number of beds) that it has to try and fill. A scheduled airline has an obligation to fly between advertised points regardless of the number of empty seats on the aircraft and the aircraft capacity cannot be altered. A tour operator or an event organizer enters a contractual obligation, often months in advance. In the case of a tour operator there may be an agreement to fill a certain specified number of rooms or in the case of an event organizer agreements may be put in place with event locations and event participants. All of the supply arrangements listed here can be very difficult to alter, at least in the short term.

The management challenge, therefore, is to ensure that the organization is operating at full capacity for as much of the time as possible. To be successful, the organization will need carefully designed actions for instance: to stimulate demand, lengthen seasons or offer appropriate pricing levels to manage and 'smooth out' occupancy levels, load factors and attendance figures.

Break-even point

In *THE*, the break-even point is often referred to as a crucial stage to reach in operating the particular service that the organization is involved in delivering.

The break-even point is the point at which costs or expenses and revenue are equal, i.e. there is no net loss or gain, and the activity has 'broken even'. Beyond that point all costs have been met by revenues so the revenues received are profits or surplus. This can often be more easily understood in relation to what is being delivered.

Thus, a coach operator with a 54-seat coach may have a break-even point of 30 seats; a concert venue might have a capacity of 1,200 seats at which a break-even point is reached when 1,000 tickets have been sold.

In reality the situation is not always quite so clear, since seats on the coach or concert tickets might be sold at different price levels, but clearly it is helpful if managers have some knowledge of when the break-even point is likely to be reached.

Heterogeneity

Services, unlike mass-produced manufactured goods, are never identical. One hotel in a chain of hotels, one person's holiday or one person's experience of an event will never be identical to another. The human element and other factors in delivering services, ensures that services will be heterogeneous, i.e. varied.

THE products are human resource intensive i.e. 'people oriented', and the human factor plays a key role.

For example – the enjoyment gained from a foreign holiday cannot be separated from the personalities who go to make up that holiday: the personnel employed in the travel agency; the airline crew; the hotel staff; the tour operator's representative; employees at destination attractions; and, of course, the other holiday-makers. All of these have a role to play in ensuring that the holiday lives up to the customer's expectations. Similarly, the experiences in all hotels and hospitality outlets and events are closely linked to the attitude, competence and personality of those charged with delivering the particular service.

The importance of human resources is illustrated by the London Olympic Games in the short case illustration below.

The importance of human resources in delivering services: London 2012 Olympic 'Games Makers'

The London 2012 Olympic and Paralympic Games required a vast army of volunteers – the 'Games Makers', and their role in making the games such a success, has been widely acclaimed. However, with such a vast army of heterogeneous volunteers there was a significant managerial challenge to ensure that a good customer experience was achieved.

Almost a quarter of a million people applied to be Games Makers, from which the final 70,000 were selected to carry out countless crucial tasks. Significantly, nearly half of those appointed had never volunteered before. All Games Makers were offered the chance to complete a customer service qualification as part of their job.

According to Ian Hembrow, a senior consultant writing in the *Guardian* newspaper, three factors really stand out about the Games Makers' achievement in that volunteers:

- *had a specific, time-limited challenge:* Signed up only to help make the event run smoothly;
- *played to strengths:* Carefully screened and matched to roles, making the most of skills and personalities; and
- *gained something in return:* Properly briefed, trained and provided with quality accessories, and made to feel a vital part.

Questions

1. Does this case illustrate whether heterogeneity is; 'good' or 'bad' when delivering services in *THE* contexts?
2. What key lessons about motivating staff might be drawn from the experience of Games Makers?

Listening to and understanding the customer, anticipating customer needs and giving a high priority to customer satisfaction are key attributes to encourage in staff, particularly those in front-line positions. To many customers, the contact person *is* the organization in their eyes. The organization is only as competent, knowledgeable, courteous and reliable as the person who represents it. In most cases the person in the front line representing the company is not a member of the senior management team, but a relatively junior member of staff: a waiter, receptionist, air steward, etc.

For example – the importance of front-line staff in terms of customer service is illustrated by the case of an airline and its staff. The ability of an airline pilot to successfully fly the plane you are travelling on is of prime importance for safety and it is assumed the pilot is suitably qualified. However, passengers rarely meet the pilot and it is the check-in staff, air stewards, ground handling staff, etc. that are more likely to frame attitudes towards customer service.

Human behaviour, however, is highly variable and it is difficult for a company to ensure that its employees display good customer relation skills all of the time. Similarly, the company has no influence over the behaviour of the customer. The customer's attitudes and behaviour will also contribute to the pleasure gained from hospitality received, an event attended or a holiday. This means that there is an uncontrollable element inherent in the operation of a *THE* product which can lead to the customer being dissatisfied or disappointed with the service delivery.

To take account of this problem, it is important that accurate and timely information is provided in advance to the potential customer in order to manage their expectations. This will reduce the risk of the customer purchasing an unsuitable *THE* product at the outset. Special attention has also to be paid to the personnel who will deal with the client on a face-to-face basis. It is necessary to make certain that they have suitable personalities and attributes for dealing with customers and that they receive appropriate and regular training and development so that they are aware of expectations and how to deal with customers.

Heterogeneity should not, however, be viewed necessarily as a negative factor, though clearly it presents managerial challenges. In many cases with regard to *THE* products, the customer is actually attracted by heterogeneity. Tourists would become bored if every tourist destination was identical; hotel chains strive to maintain a consistent brand image, whilst at the same time trying to differentiate each hotel location through varying design features. Customers would be less likely to pay high prices for concert tickets if each performance were to be absolutely identical.

The attraction of heterogeneity for customers is understandable, but it does make it very difficult for potential purchasers to evaluate services and for managers to deliver products of a consistent quality, as illustrated by the case of Radisson Hotels below.

SHORT CASE ILLUSTRATION

Managing heterogeneity: Radisson Hotels

Radisson Hotels are part of the privately owned Carlson group of companies based in Minneapolis, USA. Other companies in the group include leading restaurant chain TGI Friday's and the international Carlson Wagonlit travel business.

Radisson has grown rapidly in recent years, despite problems elsewhere in the hotel sector, because it focused on management contracts and franchising in its hotels rather than on real estate investment, i.e. another company owns the physical structure of the hotels. The company has concentrated on its strengths in management, marketing and sales. Radisson is a two-tiered brand offering a choice of an 'upper upscale' hospitality experience at Radisson Blu hotels or an 'upscale' experience at Radisson hotels. As of March 2012, Radisson had 419 hotels operating throughout the world with 94,372 rooms and 108 hotels in the development pipeline with an additional 23,733 rooms.

Carlson's 'Ambition 2015' growth strategy includes the development of flagship properties in the top five U.S. cities and a global focus on adding key hotels in major cities, airport gateways, leisure destinations and other important locations with plans to grow the portfolio to at least 600 hotels by 2015.

Radisson owns very few of these hotels and manages about 50, while the rest are franchised – managed by franchisees operating in partnership with Radisson. In 2011 it entered into a strategic partnership with the Rezidor group (based in Brussels) in which Radisson has become the major shareholder with just over 50 per cent of the company.

The challenge for a company such as Radisson is to ensure that the same levels of quality are provided around the world, when:

- staff come from many cultural and linguistic backgrounds;
- locations vary greatly in their geographical, climatic and cultural characteristics; and
- the company does not actually own the buildings in which it operates.

The strength of a brand such as Radisson relies upon such standards being ensured, but in practice it is a very difficult management task, since even communicating effectively with world-wide locations in different time zones can be problematic.

Radisson relies heavily on alliances with local 'quality' hoteliers, places a great emphasis on training, has a consistent statement of vision and values, standardizes procedures where possible, carefully words all its management and franchising agreements, and has sophisticated international communications.

www.carlson.com/hotels/radisson

Questions

1. Explain the challenges Radisson faces in managing heterogeneity.
2. Explain how Radisson has responded to these challenges.

Ownership

When a customer buys a manufactured product there will usually be a document, such as a receipt, which transfers ownership from seller to buyer. When a consumer buys a service he or she does not usually receive ownership of anything tangible.

For example – a car is hired, but ownership is not transferred; a hotel room is reserved for a period of time but nothing in it is ever owned by the customer; a concert ticket provides access to the concert venue only for the time that the concert is taking place. Even a credit card actually remains the property of the issuing company.

Service buyers are therefore buying only access to or use of something, which has important management implications. Since transfer of ownership is not involved, the task of building a relationship with customers, of retaining their custom, and building brand loyalty becomes more difficult.

THINK POINTS

- Explain the meaning of the terms intangibility, inseparability, perishability and heterogeneity in *THE* contexts.

- Why might heterogeneity be valued by many *THE* customers and what challenges might this present for *THE* managers?

- Explain why perishability is affected by the difficulties of changing supply in the short-to-medium term in many *THE* settings.

Loyalty schemes such as the frequent flyer programmes operated by many airlines and frequent guest programmes operated by hotel groups are examples (as illustrated in the short case below) of managerial responses to the problems of building brand loyalty in *THE* organizations.

Quite a large academic literature has emerged which explores the building of relationships with customers and loyalty programmes in a *THE* context. (See for example: McKercher *et al.* (2012) for a critique and literature review in a tourism context; Gartner and Ruzzier (2011) in relation to tourist destinations; Gallarza *et al.* (2012) in relation to tourism services; Kayaman and Arasli (2007); Hsu *et al.* (2012) in relation to Hospitality; and Lu and Cai (2011) in relation to exhibition events.

SHORT CASE ILLUSTRATION

Airline and hotel loyalty programmes

When American Airlines launched the first frequent flyer programme in 1981, few imagined how successful airline loyalty (frequent flyer) programmes would become (DeKay *et al.*, 2009) and the reasons for the success among consumers is investigated by Dolnicar *et al.* (2011). The American Airlines' *Advantage Programme* (the largest) now has 57 million members. Following American's example, InterContinental Hotels two years later developed the first hotel frequent guest programme, *Priority Club Rewards* which now numbers 37 million members. Loyal customers are highly attractive to businesses because they are less price sensitive and require a lower effort to communicate with (Gomez *et al.* 2006).

Numerous loyalty schemes have subsequently developed. DeKay *et al.* (2009) in comparing hotel loyalty programmes and Airline Frequent Flyer programmes point out that some observers have considered the hotel programmes as costly, financially unprofitable, and poor investments (see, for example, Mattila, 2006 and Skogland and Siguaw, 2004), while on the other hand, several major airlines have been kept flying by creditors mainly in order to retain their highly profitable frequent flyer programmes.

In response, hotel loyalty programmes are increasingly offering more attractive rewards that are starting to be interchangeable and less restricted (Toh *et al.* 2008) and with fewer rules and restrictions. The entire Marriott family of hotels, for example – which includes Residence Inn, Fairfield, and Renaissance as well as Marriott – shares the same loyalty programme.

Questions

1. Explain the characteristic of *THE* contexts to which loyalty programmes represent one response.
2. Consider what problems might arise for managers in a *THE* company because of the spread of loyalty programmes throughout the industry?

Tourism, hospitality and events – specific service characteristics

Six tourism, hospitality and events characteristics

The five characteristics of services cited in the preceding sections change the emphasis of a manager's task when compared to dealing with physical products. The characteristics apply to all service products to some degree – which includes banking, insurance and professional services (legal accounting, etc.). Thus the characteristics considered previously, whilst certainly applicable to *THE* sectors are not unique to these sectors, but applicable across all service sectors.

Six further characteristics can be identified, which are particularly applicable to these sectors (though to varying degrees in the three sectors). Consequently these characteristics have a particular influence on decision making for managers operating in these three sectors.

The six further factors, which are relevant in *THE* contexts, are:

- high cost
- seasonality
- ease of entry/exit
- interdependence
- impact on society
- the effect of external shocks.

Whilst most of these factors are not unique to *THE* sectors, they are certainly very important to any consideration of strategic management in such contexts. The fifth of these factors, however, the impact on society, is (arguably) unique to tourism, in that no other service sector can claim to have such a visible and profound impact on society. This is highly significant in the way in which organizations and destinations are managed. Each of the six characteristics will be considered in turn.

High cost

THE products often represent a relatively high-cost purchase for the consumer. Taking a holiday, buying an airline ticket or staying at a hotel are expensive and attending events and festivals can also be very expensive when all costs are considered. Indeed, in some cases such purchases will represent the largest single item of expenditure for a consumer in a given year, and in all the *THE* sectors there is often a great deal of choice, so that potential customers are very discerning.

Consequently, making such a purchase decision does not usually occur without a great deal of thought and a comparison of alternative offerings. It is not like buying a *fast moving consumer good*, a bar of chocolate for example, which may be done on impulse. There may of course be some exceptions in *THE* where supply is limited.

For example – with regard to some events, demand far exceeds supply. In such cases there is little chance for reflection and comparison and a speedy impulse decision is necessary. Where a popular band announces they are to give a series of concerts or a popular sporting event is scheduled, often potential buyers have to react quickly to ensure success in purchasing tickets. There is thus little chance for reflection, comparison or negotiation in such cases.

The high cost of many *THE* products has important managerial implications when formulating strategy, especially with regard to marketing aspects. Potential customers will want reassurance about the reliability of the product, the value for money the purchase represents, and the quality and value provided. With myriad internet search sites and apps freely available consumers have ever more accurate pricing information at their disposal, which in most cases enables price comparisons to be easily made. This places an emphasis on the organization to provide product features of a consistent quality and build brand values that consumers trust. It also suggests that *relationship marketing* is important, since products are less likely to be bought on impulse. Consequently companies have to build up a relationship with customers over a period of time to provide reassurance before the purchase decision is made.

Seasonality

THE products often have some of the most seasonal patterns of demand for any category of product or service and a number of writers have covered the implications.

For example – Baum and Lundtorp (2001) bring together a collection of studies that draw lessons from various parts of the world that experience the effects of seasonality in tourism; Parrilla *et al.* (2007) consider the implications for accommodation; and Tum and Norton (2006) discuss the effects of seasonality on the implementation and delivery of events.

Writing in a tourism context (though it also often equally applies to hospitality and events), Bull (1995:44), argues that tourism has:

> *. . . less variation than the demand for Christmas cards or air conditioners, but more than nearly all high-value individual purchases.*

This seasonality of demand for the product is largely related to climate, but is also related to factors such as school holidays, religious festivals and historic travel patterns (Baron, 1999; Allcock, 1995; Evans, 2002:358).

Skiing holidays, outdoor festivals, and childrens' summer camps which are particularly popular in North America are three examples of *THE* provision which, for obvious reasons, have highly seasonal demand patterns. This seasonality has important managerial implications in terms of aspects of management such as: managing cash flow; product pricing; managing the quantity of products supplied; and dealing with labour (and wider societal) issues relating to the need to employ, motivate and retain seasonal employees.

For example – the seasonality of demand often leads to a highly seasonal pattern of cash flows (which is discussed in greater detail in Chapter 6) for organizations in these sectors which has to be carefully managed if staff and suppliers are to be paid promptly at low points in the cycle. Consequently, at some times of the year, companies in these sectors may have relatively large surplus cash balances to invest whilst, at

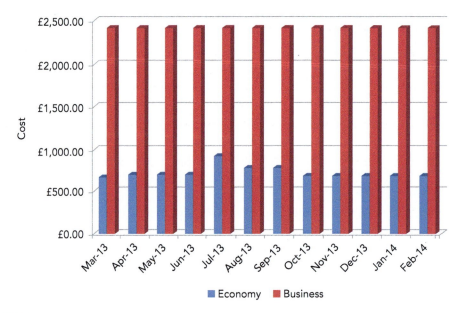

Figure 2.1 Seasonality of fares at British Airways

other times, only small amounts of cash may be available or it may even be necessary to borrow to meet cash requirements (Evans, 2002:358).

One way in which management can respond to these problems of seasonality is to develop or acquire counter-seasonal businesses, i.e. to develop from their own resources or to purchase businesses that operate primarily at other times of the year.

For example – many tour operators selling mainly to Northern European markets have attempted over the years to reduce the effects of seasonality by introducing 'winter sun' and skiing products to provide cash flows for these companies when cash flow from the sales of their summer products is weak.

Figure 2.1 shows the seasonal patterns for air travel on one of the world's busiest routes between London's Heathrow Airport and New York during 2013/14.

Figure 2.1 shows the seasonal fluctuation of economy fares in particular. Economy fares, purchased by a high proportion of leisure travellers, show a peak season in July (when school holidays start) and what is often termed the 'shoulder' season, in this case during August and September, with a low season for the remaining months. Leisure travellers tend to travel during school holidays and when weather conditions are favourable, whereas business travellers (although sometimes showing some seasonal variations) often have to travel throughout the year as implied by the consistency of the fares in the graph.

SHORT CASE ILLUSTRATION

Managing variations in seasonal demand: Kuoni

Kuoni is a leading global travel and destination management services company. Kuoni, which has more than 12,000 employees in over 80 countries, is based in Zurich, Switzerland, where it is quoted on the Swiss Stock Market.

The Kuoni Group of companies' business activities are divided in five distinct main areas: the traditional tour operating business, destination management travel services, specialist travel business, operations in Emerging Markets and visa services. These areas are structured into three divisions in the group's organizational structure: Outbound Europe (where it has particularly strong sales in Scandinavia, the UK, Belgium, the Netherlands and its home Swiss market); Global Travel Services and Emerging Markets; and Specialists. Kuoni, unlike some other European-based tour operators, owns very few of its own aircraft or hotels pursuing what the company describes as its 'asset light' strategy.

Kuoni, as with many European travel companies (depending heavily on Northern European markets), experiences a high degree of seasonality of demand. Such seasonality of demand causes some managerial problems for European-based tour operators:

Profits are concentrated in the second half of the financial year, and losses or small profits are often incurred for the first six months. During 2011, Kuoni, for example, made a loss (earnings before interest and taxes) of 32.5m Swiss Francs on a turnover of 2,084m Swiss Francs in the first six months to the end of June. In contrast, for the whole year earnings were 398m Swiss Francs on a turnover of 5,111m Swiss Francs. Such uneven performances experienced by many travel companies can make the financial markets uneasy and this, in turn, can lead to share price volatility and make it more difficult to raise new finance.

Large fluctuations in cash flow often occur. Typically cash flows in during the early part of the calendar year as bookings are made and paid for, but then cash is drained over the course of the summer months as the companies have to pay accommodation, airline and other expenses. Net cash levels are usually at their lowest levels during the autumn and early winter months. Many companies have to rely on bank borrowing facilities to support them during this period and some companies have failed due to banks' refusal to support them through their cash deficit months.

'Integrated' travel companies such as Tui and Thomas Cook own charter airlines. Whilst it is usually possible to keep the airlines flying with very high load factors over the summer season, capacity has to be carefully managed so that aircraft capacity is not underutilized during the winter. European-based companies may respond by having aircraft leased on flexible contracts, developing counter-cyclical business opportunities, such as skiing and winter sun holidays or sending the aircraft to other markets, such as Canada, where there is strong winter demand.

www.kuoni.com

Questions

1. Explain the nature of the seasonality issues faced by Kuoni.
2. Explain the actions managers in a company like Kuoni might take to deal with the seasonality issues.

Ease of entry/exit

Barriers to entry have been a popular field of research since the seminal work of Bain (1956) and a large literature on this particular aspect of economics has developed (see for example Pehrsson, 2009). Barriers which are obstacles preventing entrant firms from being established in a particular market (Porter, 1980) vary from industry to industry and from one country or trading block (such as the European Union) to another. Pehrsson (2009), categorizes and summarizes a number of such barriers to entry, including:

- capital required for establishing a business;
- cost incurred by customers in switching between suppliers; and
- access to distribution channels.

KEY CONCEPT

Barriers to entry and contestability

Barriers to entry describe the barriers preventing potential suppliers coming into the market to compete for sales. Economists talk about the relative size of the barriers and the *contestability* of markets. In recent years the theory of *contestable markets* has become prominent, associated primarily with its proponent William J. Baumol (1982).

The theory is that what is crucial in determining prices and setting levels of supply is not whether an industry is actually a monopoly or in contrast highly competitive, but whether there is a real threat of competition. A contestable market is characterized by insignificant entry and exit barriers, so there are negligible entry and exit costs (Sinclair and Stabler, 1997:61). The deregulation of the United States airline market from the late 1970s, for example, was very much influenced by this theory in removing barriers to entry to make the airline market contestable.

In some cases the barriers are virtually impossible to overcome, for example where the government grants one company a monopoly to provide flights or rail services on certain routes, but in most cases barriers to entry are not insurmountable though they vary considerably in different parts of *THE* and between different national markets.

Significant barriers to entry include:

- government requirements for companies to hold financial bonds or licences to operate;
- significant start-up capital requirements;
- planning restrictions;
- the pricing actions and tactics of established companies.

In many areas of *THE* it is relatively easy to set up in business or indeed to exit from the industry, i.e. entry and exit costs are relatively low (compared to some other industries). To establish an oil refinery or a vehicle manufacturing plant would require a large initial capital outlay (i.e. they are *capital intensive* industries), but this is not the case in many parts of *THE*.

For example – the capital outlay to set up a tour operator, or an event organizer, is generally quite low (when compared to other industrial sectors). Many of the services included in the product are leased, or are purchased as and when required. The greatest (up-front) cost involved is often in producing brochures and other promotional materials and marketing the products to agents and the public. Similarly, travel agents do not generally purchase products from tour operators until the customer pays for them, and so do not incur the risk of unsold stock or stock-holding costs.

Mainly as a result of the relatively low barriers to entry in most areas of the world, *THE* is dominated by small-to-medium-sized enterprises (SMEs). The sectors of *THE* are generally highly fragmented and this is documented by a number of authors. (See for example: Pechlaner *et al.*, 2004; and Thomas *et al.*, 1999.) *THE* sectors with relatively low market entry barriers are comparatively attractive for SMEs, since various types of firms require only minor capital investments, few staff and low operating costs (Stickdorn and Zehrer, 2009).

Therefore, in many parts of *THE* entry to the industry might be considered to be relatively straightforward and this means that if one company is seen to be successful in a particular segment of the market then it is not difficult for a competitor to offer a similar product. In other parts of *THE* however, barriers to entry may be greater.

For example – setting up an airline, a cruise line or building a hotel normally require quite hefty capital outlays and in the case of an airline has traditionally been subject to quite stringent regulatory pressures. Even in these parts of *THE*, entry barriers are becoming lower as initial capital costs are avoided by such means as leasing equipment in cruising and airline operations and through franchising and management contracts in hotel developments. Furthermore the gradual removal of international regulatory barriers in the international airline industry, has further lowered barriers in that sector.

For managers the implications of relatively low barriers to entry (or barriers which are lower than they were previously) include the need to:

- find ways of differentiating the product, possibly on the basis of price or by adding additional features to the product which are valued by customers;
- establish and build a brand that is recognized and reassures customers;
- consider working cooperatively with other organizations through alliances and other arrangements.

Interdependence

In the introduction to part one, the difficulties of defining and delineating the component parts of tourism, hospitality and events were considered. It was concluded that there is a great deal of overlap between the constituent parts and that at the strategic level they could usefully be considered together. Exactly where the boundaries lie is not material, but clearly there are linkages between the component parts.

Hence, the industry we are considering, *THE*, can be viewed as comprising six component sectors:

- hospitality
- events management
- attractions
- transport
- travel organizers
- destination organizations.

Each of these sectors can be further broken down into several sub-sectors (as shown in Figure 2.2). Some of the sub-sectors, such as tour operators, are operated for profit (on a commercial basis), while others such as museums and national parks are often operated on a non-commercial basis.

The important point to note in this context, however, is that the sectors are all linked and depend upon one another; there is interdependence between them.

For example – the hospitality sector relies upon the transport sector to transport guests to and from the accommodation. Similarly, the transport and hospitality sectors both rely upon the travel organizers and event managers to provide them with customers.

If one sub-sector fails to deliver a service, it has an impact on other sub-sectors.

For example – the success of a music festival organized by an event management company may be judged on the arrangements for catering and accommodation provided by hospitality suppliers. Similarly, if a tour operator organizes a holiday including seats on an aircraft, the quality of the holiday will be judged partly upon the quality of the airline regardless of whether the tour operator has any direct control over that airline's activities.

THINK POINTS

- Explain the effects of seasonality on the way in which management is carried out in *THE* organizations.

- Explain the interdependence of *THE* organizations.

- Provide a brief explanation of the structure of the tourism, hospitality and events sectors and explain the linkages between them.

Figure 2.2 The sectors and sub-sectors of tourism, hospitality and events

Thus the success of a product often depends on a *supply chain* in which there are many interdependent links. Managers need to be aware of the linkages which exist and where particular problems might occur if, for instance, demand increased suddenly. In response to the interdependence that exists, managers might try to gain greater control of the supply chain by:

- buying suppliers, distributors or competitors;
- encouraging greater co-operation between suppliers, distributors or competitors;
- establishing rigorous quality standards for suppliers and distributors.

Figure 2.2 illustrates how the various sectors of the industry 'fit' together and interact with the transport sector at the centre, implying that all the sectors of *THE* rely on transport to some extent in moving customers to the place where the service is delivered. In reality, the world is not as simple as the diagram implies. Individual companies will often straddle two or more of the sectors.

DEFINITION/QUOTATION

Tourism supply chain

A tourism supply chain is defined as:

> A network of tourism organizations engaged in different activities ranging from the supply of different components of tourism products/services such as flights and accommodation to the distribution and marketing of the final tourism product at a specific tourism destination, and involves a wide range of participants in both the private and public sectors.
>
> (Zhang et al., 2009)

The tourism supply chain clearly illustrates the interdependence of the component parts of *THE* (and indeed other suppliers), since as Tapper and Font (2004) point out, tourism supply chains involve many components – not just accommodation, transport and excursions, but also bars and restaurants, handicrafts, food production, waste disposal, and the infrastructure that supports tourism in destinations. This infrastructure can include the various events, festivals, exhibitions and conferences which both create a demand for tourism in the first place and support tourists when they arrive at a destination.

For example – some hotel companies organise inclusive tour packages and organize and manage events thereby also operating in the travel organizers and events sectors. Similarly, the 1990s consolidation of European-based travel companies led to a small number of large pan-European travel groups being formed, operating worldwide from their European head offices under a number of different brand names (see for example Evans, 2001 and Holloway and Humphreys, 2012). Thus, Tui plc, based in the UK but with a majority German-owned parent company (Tui AG, based in Hanover); Thomas Cook plc, group of companies based in the UK; and the Swiss-based Kuoni and Cosmos group of companies all became large internationally diversified travel companies during the 1990s.

These companies (to varying degrees) undertook strategies of 'vertical integration' whereby a single group of companies formed to:

- sell travel arrangements to customers through shops and online (retail distribution);
- provide travel and accommodation arrangements (tour operations);
- transport customers (airline operations); and, in some cases
- own or manage accommodation.

Table 2.1 Vertically and horizontally integrated structure of Thomas Cook plc (adapted from: www.thomascookgroup.com)

	Thomas Cook group plc Group Structure					
	UK, Ireland & Middle East	Central Europe	West Europe	Northern Europe	Airlines Germany	North America
	Turnover: £3,109m Operating profit: £13m	Turnover: £2,587m Operating profit: £50m	Turnover: £1,467m Operating profit: £2m	Turnover: £1,167m Operating profit: £101m	Turnover: £1,165m Operating profit: £36m	Turnover: £296m Operating profit: £22m
Retail Distribution	6.6m passengers 1,089 retail outlets 86.3% Controlled distribution 34.7% Internet distribution	4.7m passengers 1,625 retail outlets 23.4% Controlled distribution 6.8% Internet distribution	2.7m passengers 793 retail outlets 60.2% Controlled distribution 27.1% Internet distribution	1.5m passengers 11 retail outlets 87.1% Controlled distribution 69.4% Internet distribution		1.0m passengers 119 retail outlets 14.1% Controlled distribution 35.7% Internet distribution
Tour Operations (Main Brands)	Thomas Cook Club 1830 Direct Holidays Neilson Airtours	Thomas Cook Neckermann Öger Tours	Thomas Cook Aquatour Jet tours	Spies Ving Tjäreborg	Condor	Alba Tours Intair FunSun Vacations
Aircraft	35	0	6	12	38	0
Hotels and resorts		Sentido				

Horizontal integration also took place whereby acquisitions, mergers and internal development took place so that the group of companies was able to sell its products in different markets around the world.

This vertically and horizontally integrated structure can be illustrated by looking at the structure of the Thomas Cook group of companies shown in Table 2.1. Thomas Cook plc is a British global online/offline travel company created in June 2007 by the merger of Thomas Cook AG and MyTravel Group plc when the business was floated on the UK stock market. Thomas Cook is one of the most recognized brands in the international travel industry, with a protracted history (documented by Hamilton, 2006; and Withey, 1998). Dating back to 1841, Thomas Cook, a cabinet-maker, formed a company to carry temperance supporters by railway between the cities of Leicester, Nottingham, Derby and Birmingham. However, recent years have proved financially challenging for the group of companies with a *turnaround* plan being put in place during 2013.

Impact of tourism

Perhaps the one area where tourism (and importantly the hospitality and event management sectors which support it) is unique is in its impact on society. It is probably fair to say that no other industrial service sector comes close, since tourism by definition involves the transportation of people (often in large numbers) to a destination area away from home. But the impacts that tourism has are both wide-ranging and controversial.

The focus of attention is usually upon the impact tourism has upon host destinations. Figure 2.3 summarizes some of these impacts. The impacts can be classified as economic, social and environmental and classified into positive and negative impacts. However, it is important to point out that the issues involved are often complex, interrelated and involve tourism together with other industrial sectors including hospitality and events.

Many destination areas have been profoundly changed by the influx of tourists. The Spanish Balearic Islands (Majorca, Ibiza, Menorca); Australia's Gold Coast; the Thai Island of Phuket; and Dubai are examples of the way in which tourism has profoundly and visibly affected the host destinations in recent years, economically, socially and environmentally.

The impacts may rather simplistically be labelled as 'positive' or 'negative', but often whether the impacts can be viewed as positive or negative depends on whose view you take, or on achieving an appropriate balance between the differing types of impact.

For example – if a piece of land is cleared to make way for a new hotel development next to a beach, the overall economic effect may be highly positive for the region in which it is built. However, those residents who have been displaced may not feel so positively disposed towards the development.

Tourism can also have an impact on tourist-generating areas and on the territories affected by the travel between destinations and tourist-generating areas (Mason, 2008). The changed perceptions towards food and culture in Northern Europe and the impact of returning international students to China are evidence of this. Tourists (albeit long-term tourists in the case of returning students) have gained an insight into other cultures as a result of the increase in travel and brought back their changed perceptions, needs and wants to the tourist-generating areas.

A large tourism literature has emerged which explores the range of issues relating to the impacts resulting from development of tourism and the related terms of sustainable development and responsible tourism which are often used. See for example: Buckley, 2012; Wall and Mathieson, 2006; Farrell and Twining-Ward, 2005; and the various international case studies presented in Laws *et al.*, 1998. Mbaiwa and Stronza (2010) trace the effects of tourism in the environmentally sensitive Okavango Delta of Botswana and report that tourism development is achieving its goal of improved livelihoods for rural communities.

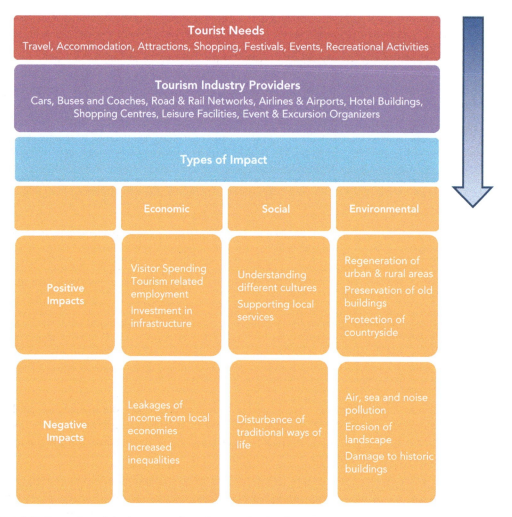

Figure 2.3 Examples of the impacts of tourism on destination areas

Understanding tourism impacts

It can be argued that tourism is different from other services in at least one important respect – its impact on society. Evans (2012:221) argues that:

> tourism is highly visible as well as invisible in its impact and is capable of making profound societal and cultural changes, not only to host destinations, but also to tourist 'exporting' areas. Though it is clear that the impacts are wide-ranging, and that some of the impacts are both easy to identify and measure while others are not, the topic is often controversial in practice and subject to much debate in the academic literature.

This controversy has been illustrated by Krippendorf (and many others subsequently).

The Swiss academic, Jost Krippendorf was one of the founding fathers of the concept of 'sustainable tourism' (Müller and Lane, 2003). In his influential work *The Holiday Makers – Understanding the Impacts of Leisure and Travel* (1999), he discussed aspects of the impact tourists have on their destination.

Krippendorf cites a leading Swiss researcher writing in the early 1960s who argued that since its focal point is people, tourism can be one of the most important means, especially in developing countries, of bringing nations closer together and of maintaining good international relations (Evans, 2012:221)

Krippendorf takes a contrary view when he argues that this was the theory twenty years ago. Today, when travelling has become a mass phenomenon, the tale of understanding among peoples is nothing more than wishful thinking.

> I do not share this faith nor do I know many positive experiences and examples. On the contrary, I believe that the chances for real human contact between holidaymakers and locals could hardly be less hopeful. The contact is usually only skin deep, the relationship a mere illusion. Where the main reason for travelling is to get away from things, where the tourist ignores the existence of other people; where assembly line techniques are the only way of dealing with huge numbers, where profit making rules supreme, where there are feelings of superiority and inferiority, no communication can develop.
>
> Adapted from Krippendorf (1999)

A full exploration of these topics (related to the impacts *of* tourism) is beyond the scope of this book. However, for managers operating in *THE*, an understanding of the impacts of tourism (and hospitality and events) is important in considering ways in which those impacts can be managed satisfactorily. The needs of the various *stakeholders* require consideration and to be dealt with in an appropriately balanced way as part of any strategic plan.

Any discussion of the impacts of tourism usually centres on the effects of so-called 'mass tourism'. However, in recent years far more is being done to address the issues associated with such mass tourism through smaller-scale alternatives such as ecotourism and other forms of low-impact and responsible travel (Getz and Page, 1997).

DEFINITION/QUOTATION

Mass tourism

Mass tourism has been defined as:

> a phenomenon of large-scale packaging of standardised leisure services at fixed prices for sale to a mass clientele.
>
> Poon (1993:32)

Poon (1993) identifies five key forces as having been responsible for the spread of this mass, standardized and rigidly packaged tourism:

- *consumers*: Sun-lust, and inexperienced mass consumers;
- *technology*: Jet aircraft, automobile, computer reservations and accounting systems, credit cards;

- *production*: Cheap oil, charter flights, packaged tours, hotel over-building, mass production;
- *management*: Economies of scale, hotel and holiday branding, promotional airfares, mass marketing;
- *frame conditions*: Post-war peace and prosperity, paid holidays, regulation of air transportation, incentives to attract hotel chains to establish operations.

In North America and Europe, different drivers facilitated the development and spread of mass tourism. In the USA, multinational hotel chains, airlines and the growth in car usage were prevalent. In Europe by comparison, powerful tour operators, charter flights and packaged tours to Mediterranean 'sun' destinations were the key agents in the rapid growth of mass tourism.

One of the key questions facing managers in *THE* contexts today is to what extent mass tourism will continue with what some regard as its socially, culturally and environmentally harmful patterns of growth?

Poon (1993), in her book *Tourism, Technology and Competitive Strategies*, claims that what she terms as a 'new tourism' is increasingly emerging. The signs of the emerging new tourism include:

- The growing demand for 'independent', non-packaged holidays.
- The growing demand for choice and flexibility.
- Information technologies, such as Computer Reservations Systems (CRS) and the Internet, rapidly diffusing and allowing customers to deal directly with companies and organizations as a means to flexibly make travel arrangements as an alternative to package holidays.
- The slowing rate of growth of the traditional sun package tour business.
- The increasing environmental planning and control of tourism in host countries such as Belize and Bermuda.
- The increasing 'segmentation' of travel markets to cater for differing lifestyle characteristics.
- The travel behaviour and motivation of tourists changing toward shorter breaks and activity-orientated travel.

In addition to the factors identified, a further important factor could be added, namely the rapid growth of domestic, inbound and outbound tourism in many emerging markets such as China, India and Brazil.

The case below illustrates some of the challenges raised by tourism and responses to these challenges at a local level.

SHORT CASE ILLUSTRATION

Grootbos, South Africa

Tourist destinations and companies are increasingly coming to realize that limits have to be placed on growth if the impacts of tourist developments are not to destroy the attractions that tourists sought in the first place. In the tourism literature the terms 'tourist carrying capacity' and 'sustainable tourism' have been used to describe the maximum desirable level of tourism development that could be sustained over a medium-to-long-term period.

There are many examples from around the world of destinations, hospitality providers and event managers who are adapting their business models so that they recognize the importance of operating according to principles of sustainability. One such example is Grootbos Private Nature Reserve and Lodge in South Africa. Grootbos is a luxury camp two hours north of Cape Town.

Grootbos, which is operated as a charitable foundation, provides five-star accommodation for guests providing a crucial revenue stream. It is also an important nature reserve set in the Fynbos area. Fynbos is an area of natural heathland vegetation occurring in a small belt of the Western Cape with a Mediterranean climate and is known for its exceptional degree of biodiversity. The Grootbos nature reserve was instrumental in setting up the Walker Bay Fynbos Conservancy in 1999 and currently consists of 21 landowners, who manage approximately 12,000 hectares of Fynbos.

The Grootbos private foundation also offers a number of different sustainability initiatives:

- 'Growing the Future' – trains a number of people each year in the growing of vegetables and fruit, beekeeping and the principles of successful animal husbandry.
- 'Green Future' – provides annual, practical-based training programmes for unemployed local people in the fields of landscaping, horticulture and ecotourism.
- 'Spaces for Sport' – offers a multipurpose facility which is considered a community development project.

The site was chosen due to its unique position in the centre of three racially diverse communities. Guests are given the opportunity to plant a tree in a patch which was damaged by a fire in February of 2006. Approximately 1,000 trees have been planted to date. Each guest receives a tree planting certificate with the co-ordinates of where the trees have been planted.

www.grootbos.com

Questions

1. Explain the issues raised by Grootbos in relation to the impacts of tourism.
2. Explain the business model Grootbos has developed and assess its effectiveness.

The relevance of the preceding discussion on the impacts of tourism raises a number of issues for managers in the tourism, hospitality and events sectors:

Modern consumers are becoming ever more sensitive to the impacts of what they consume; whether it is the effect that the detergents they use might have on the environment, the amount of water used in irrigating a golf course in hot climates or the impacts that tourism has on the culture of the host community.

In successfully managing their tourism, hospitality and event products, managers and marketers must be sensitive to this issue in a way in which they often failed to be in the past.

Whilst mass tourism is obviously here to stay, nevertheless changes are taking place in the marketplace. Consumers are becoming more knowledgeable, experienced and sophisticated in their tastes and rather more complicated to understand. Furthermore, additional consumers are being added as emerging markets such as Brazil, Russia, India and China (the so called 'BRIC' countries) develop.

Managers have to research and attempt to understand these changes that are undoubtedly taking place. Furthermore, in the highly competitive sectors of the industry we are concerned with, they have to design their products to appeal to these changing tastes and then to promote, distribute and price the products appropriately.

Many new forms of tourism, and associated events and hospitality products, have emerged to suit the needs of this vastly more discriminating travel market including: wine tourism; culinary tourism; 'dark' tourism; extreme adventures; sport, festival and event tourism; and various specialized forms of learning-based travel.

These new forms of tourism are creating additional opportunities and challenges which managers need to research, understand and design and deliver targeted products.

The effect of external shocks

Tourism, hospitality and events are particularly prone to external shocks beyond the control of its managers.

Internal corporate shocks such as financial irregularities by contrast are also important to the industry, but these are not distinguishing characteristics, for as the events in other industries have demonstrated they are prevalent in many industries where management have proved to be too ambitious, fraudulent or incompetent (Evans and Elphick, 2005).

THE as a service sector is unique (among service industries) in its vulnerability, since the sector is highly exposed to risks and prone to crises as the result of external events. Unlike internal events, which can be assessed and controlled by managers, external events are beyond their control and therefore inherently provide a greater degree of risk and uncertainty.

Furthermore, the inherent characteristics of these service sectors (such as the perishability of the product and the interdependence of elements of the product) make the risks potentially very difficult to manage, since supply often cannot quickly be matched to rapid declines in demand (Evans and Elphick, 2005).

The external shocks such as wars, hurricanes, terrorist attacks, pollution, adverse publicity or accidents can have a dramatic and speedy effect upon levels of business and disruption to planned activities and events. The external shocks can quickly develop into crises and indeed can, and should be, viewed as a central concern of competent managers in the industry.

Quite a large and varied academic literature covers 'crisis management' in this sector. (See for example Glaesser, 2012; Pforr and Hosie, 2009; Hall, 2010; Wang and Ritchie, 2011).

For example – in a study of Indian upscale hotels, Israeli *et al.* (2011) found that Indian Hotels were not prepared to handle a crisis such as the terror attacks in Mumbai involving two luxury hotels in November 2008. The attacks reduced hotel occupancy levels to 30 per cent for several weeks and charter tours were cancelled in South India, some 2000 km away. The result was the loss of millions of dollars of revenue for tourism, hotel and related industries.

By their nature these events are unpredictable in relation to their geographical location, their timing and their scale, and hence provide difficulties for industry managers in a number of ways in that:

- it is difficult to forecast such events in the first place and to foresee the full implications;
- the management steps that need to be taken can be complex at a strategic level;
- the effective implementation of management actions at an operational level is also complex and needs careful coordination of resources and communications;
- a brand which may have been assiduously developed over many years can be severely damaged or even destroyed by sudden events;
- recovery from crises has to be planned and stresses the importance of a strategy that is flexible so that rapid unforeseen changes can be incorporated.

The terrorist attacks in New York and Washington on September 11 2001 had an immediate effect upon the industry as illustrated by the case of Accor Hotels.

Other examples include the following:

- The Gulf War led to a severe downturn in travel and tourism in the early 1990s (which extended far beyond the Middle East location of the conflict).
- The devastating Indian Ocean tsunami, which occurred on 26th December 2004, was among the deadliest natural disasters in human history with over 230,000 people killed in 14 countries bordering the Indian Ocean. As well as the devastation in terms of the tragic loss of life, long-term effects included long-lasting impacts on tourism in Indonesia, Thailand and Sri Lanka.

SHORT CASE ILLUSTRATION

The effects of September 11 2001: Accor hotel group

Accor is a Paris-based multi-brand network, which in 2001 had 3,600 hotels in 90 countries that were fully integrated in terms of sales and technology. Hotel development is based on well-known international brands (such as Sofitel, Novotel, Mercure, Ibis, Formule 1, as well as Motel 6 and Red Roof Inns in the United States) which cover the full range of hotel segments, from budget to luxury class. Accor properties are now well represented around the globe, particularly in America, Europe and Asia.

The travel industry, faced with a slowdown that was already perceptible in spring 2001, had to cope with one of the worst crises in its history: the events of September 11th, 2001 in America. The tragic events had two consequences. The first was immediate and of an unprecedented magnitude – a psychological shock. The second was the aggravation of the global economic slowdown affecting America, Europe and Asia simultaneously.

As a result of the events, some hotel investments were postponed but very few were cancelled and the group still planned 250 new hotel openings over the subsequent few years. The group was protected to some extent from the worst effects of the downturn by the diversity of its hotel portfolio both geographically and in terms of quality. However, some effects on hotel bookings were inevitable. For example, the luxury hotel industry in Paris was severely affected, whereas the economy hotel segment in Europe held up well. Thus Sofitel's bookings dropped by 33% in October and 18% in November 2001, while Formule 1 and Ibis budget brands in Europe recorded an increase of 3.5% in their October bookings and 4.6% in November. In the US, Sofitel's bookings declined by 25%–30%, whereas Red Roof Inns and Motel 6 (budget brands) registered a limited drop of 8.2% in October and then 6% in November 2001.

www.accor.com

Questions

1. Explain how Accor was affected by the 9/11 terrorist attacks.
2. Explain the managerial responses of Accor after the attacks.

- SARS (Severe Acute Respiratory Syndrome), a kind of pneumonia, was a recent occurrence that first appeared in November 2002 in southern China. It spread quickly until on March 15th 2003 the World Health Organization (WHO) issued a warning suggesting that tourists should not travel to countries or regions that were affected by it. In China and Hong Kong the number of inbound tourists and international tourism receipts decreased sharply after March 2003. However, within a period of a few months from the onset of the disease, the crisis had passed, markets had recovered and a "normal" situation prevailed (Gu and Wall, 2006).

Managers, whilst not able to plan directly for such events, need to be able to:

- identify the risks to which the organization (destination or event) may be susceptible;
- assess the possible impact of those risks;
- have contingency plans in place so that the organization is able to react quickly and effectively.

The contingency plans that a *THE* organization puts in place need to include detailed operating procedures for which key staff might be involved; how communications with customers, relatives and the media might be organized; and how operations can be reorganized to minimize the disruption.

One approach is to spread the risks so that one crisis does not destroy the business entirely.

For example – a tour operator or event manager specializing in tours or events in only one country would be at risk if a war or environmental catastrophe were to occur, but by operating in several countries the risks are spread and the overall risk is reduced.

SHORT CASE ILLUSTRATION

Crisis management: Ryanair and Icelandic volcanic ash

In 2010 a volcano on Iceland's Eyjafjallajökull glacier caused travel chaos for Europe's airlines during April and May as vast swathes of European airspace were closed. The ash cloud moved unpredictably across much of Northern Europe, potentially threatening air safety.

The budget airline Ryanair, for example, despite protests from the airline itself that it was unnecessary, was forced to cancel 9,400 flights and disrupted the travel plans of 1.5 million passengers. It was reported that the incident cost the Irish airline £42m (€65m).

In such unpredictable circumstances it is important that a company:

- communicates accurately and at an early stage with customers with regular updated information;
- provides as much operational flexibility as possible; and
- is sufficiently diversified so that one serious and unpredictable incident does not lead to the organization's demise.

In the case of Ryanair its full year profits increased despite the severe impacts of the ash clouds.

www.ryanair.com

Questions

1. Explain what the lessons of this case might be for dealing with crisis situations for *THE* companies.
2. Consider other examples of crisis situations that have occurred for *THE* organizations.

SMALL BUSINESS FOCUS

THE sectors can often be regarded as highly fragmented. A fragmented industry is normally characterized by a large numbers of small and medium-sized businesses and a lack of market leaders with a significant share of the market. The sectors do have some strong, international companies and undoubtedly both the power and the market share of these players are increasing year by year. The context varies across the sectors in that large international brands are established with regard to hotel chains, cruise lines, tour operators and airlines whereas there are few such large internationally diversified companies currently operating in the events management sector.

However, alongside these large organizations there is a proliferation of smaller businesses, such as owner-operated guest houses and restaurants, transport operators, visitor attractions, travel agents, tour guides and resorts.

A number of the aspects discussed in this chapter are relevant to smaller businesses operating in *THE* sectors. In some cases the characteristics that have been outlined can work against smaller businesses.

For example – in some sub-sectors there are high barriers to entry such as capital requirements, regulatory restrictions or well established brand names. These barriers vary considerably between different markets, but where they exist in airlines, cruising and in some hotel markets it is difficult for smaller companies to compete.

In other sub-sectors such as tour operating and acting as a travel agent or event organiser, barriers to entry are usually quite low thereby allowing smaller companies to often compete successfully.

Some of the other characteristics can at times work in favour of smaller companies.

For example:

- *Heterogeneity* – the desire many customers have for something that is different often means that smaller companies can provide *niche* products which are attractive to customers.

- *Inseparability* – the simultaneous consumption and production of *THE* products implies that a great emphasis is on customer service. Whilst larger companies make great efforts to achieve high levels of service, it is difficult given their diversity and size to ensure it is always delivered successfully. Smaller organizations with fewer staff and less complexity may be more agile and be able to more easily ensure standards are maintained.

- *Ownership* – since customers have use of *THE* products rather than own them, the need to successfully build up a relationship with potential customers is implied. Many smaller companies successfully target particular types of customer or a particular market niche, and build up loyalty and repeat customers through effective more personal communications and promotional activities.

- *Impacts of THE* – many smaller *THE* companies are able to present themselves successfully as being more sustainable in the way that they operate. In this way they are stressing that they are minimizing the negative impacts of tourism that have been identified.

The short case illustration overleaf shows how smaller tour operators have acted collaboratively to form a trade association which stresses the particular benefits (based on the underlying characteristics we have discussed) that these SMEs are able to offer.

A summary of the key characteristics and their implications for *THE* managers

This chapter has considered a total of 11 characteristics of *THE*. Some of these are common in many service sectors, but some are particularly important to *THE* settings.

Whichever might be the case, it is important that managers working in *THE* are aware of these factors and consider the managerial implications that are associated with each. The strategy which organizations put in place should reflect an understanding of these characteristics and the impacts they might have on the organizations concerned.

Table 2.2 summarizes the key characteristics of *THE* we have explored in this chapter and provides examples of their implications for managers.

Table 2.2 A summary of key *THE* characteristics and their implications for managers

Characteristic	Summary (examples)	Managerial implications (examples)
Intangibility	Products cannot be tested or sampled	Effective promotion & distribution are essential
Inseparability	Production and consumption take place at the same time	'Front-line' staff must deliver good service
Perishability	Products cannot be stored	Stimulate demand so all products are sold at required time
Heterogeneity	Products are not identical	Good, well trained staff are essential
Ownership	Customers use services rather than own them	Loyalty programmes are important
High cost product	Often a relatively expensive purchase	Customers need reassurance about reliability
Seasonality	Products often have very seasonal demand patterns	Different seasonal prices charged
Ease of entry/exit	Often relatively low barriers to entry	Product differentiation
Interdependence	The sub-sectors of *THE* are closely linked	Coordination or control of the supply chain
Impact on society	Tourism has a high impact on society	Produce 'sustainable' products
External shocks	Prone to external shocks, beyond managers' control	Have contingency plans in place

SHORT CASE ILLUSTRATION

Association of Independent Tour Operators

In the UK, the Association of Independent Tour Operators (AITO) represents over 150 smaller tour operators which are able to successfully challenge larger tour operators through offering niche products.

The products may relate to types of tourism such as adventure; battlefield; wine and gastronomy; cycling, or to particular parts of the world. The products offered are highly diverse, as are the companies that provide them. In some case the particular niche segments identified are too small or new for the larger operators to have targeted them. In other cases the companies involved are competing directly with the larger operators and to do so they concentrate on higher and consistent levels of customer service, building up a relationship with clients and offering products which are differentiated from 'mainstream' products.

AITO stresses its sustainable tourism credentials and potential members are examined before they join, to ensure that sustainable principles are adhered to. Sustainable travel guidelines for its members are based upon five key objectives:

- to protect the environment – its flora, fauna and landscapes;
- to respect local cultures – traditions, religions and built heritage;
- to benefit local communities – both economically and socially;
- to conserve natural resources – from office to destination; and
- to minimise pollution – through noise, waste disposal and congestion.

www.aito.co.uk

Questions

1. Explain which characteristics of *THE* does AITO help SMEs with in competing with larger competitors.
2. Explain how belonging to AITO helps SMEs compete effectively.

CHAPTER SUMMARY

In this chapter, we have introduced some of the key themes in tourism, hospitality and events that are relevant to strategy. These include understanding the nature of *THE* products and in this context we looked at some of the properties of service products. These properties apply to tourism, hospitality and events products as they also apply to other service sectors.

We also identified six further factors that apply particularly to this sector (high cost, seasonality, ease of entry/exit, interdependence, impact on society, and the effect of external shocks). Understanding these characteristics and their implications for managers is a key issue in determining the success of strategy in *THE*. We will return to them, and re-emphasize their importance, at several points in this book.

REFERENCES

Allcock, J. B. (1995) 'Seasonality', in S. F. Witt and L. Moutinho (eds.) *Tourism Marketing and Management Handbook*, London: Prentice Hall, pp. 92–104.

Bain, J. (1956) *Barriers to New Competition*, Cambridge, Mass.: Harvard University Press.

Baron, R. R. V. (1999) 'The Measurement of Seasonality and Its Economic Impacts', *Tourism Economics*, 5 (4): 437–58.

Baum, T. and S. Lundtorp (2001) *Seasonality in Tourism*, Oxford: Pergamon.

Baumol, W. J. (1982) 'Contestable Markets: An Uprising in the Theory of Industrial Structure', *American Economic Review*, 72 (1): 1–15.

Buckley, R. (2012) 'Sustainable Tourism: Research and Reality', *Annals of Tourism Research*, 39 (2): 528–46.

Bull, A. (1995) *The Economics of Travel and Tourism*, 2nd edn, Melbourne: Longman Australia.

Dekay, F., R. S. Toh and P. Raven (2009) 'Loyalty Programmes: Airlines Outdo Hotels', *Cornell Hospitality Quarterly*, 50 (3): 371–82.

Dolnicar, S., K. Grabler, B. Grun and A. Kulnig (2011) 'Key Drivers of Airline Loyalty', *Tourism Management*, 32 (5): 1020–6.

Evans, N. (2001) 'The UK Air Inclusive-Tour Industry: A Reassessment of the Competitive Positioning of the "Independent" Sector', *International Journal of Tourism Research*, 3 (6): 477–91.

—— (2002) 'Financial Management for Travel and Tourism', in R. Sharpley (ed.) *The Tourism Business: An Introduction*, Sunderland: Business Education Publishers, pp. 345–66.

—— (2012) 'Tourism: A Strategic Business Perspective', in T. Jamal and M. Robinson (eds.) *The Sage Handbook of Tourism Studies*, Thousand Oaks, Calif.: Sage, pp. 215–34.

Evans, N. and S. Elphick (2005) 'Models of Crisis Management: An Evaluation of Their Value for Strategic Planning in the International Travel Industry', *International Journal of Tourism Research*, 7 (3): 135–50.

Farrell, B. and L. Twining-Ward (2005) 'Seven Steps towards Sustainability: Tourism in the Context of New Knowledge', *Journal of Sustainable Tourism*, 13 (2): 109–22.

Gallarza, M. G., S. Gil-Saura and M. B. Holbrook (2012) 'Customer Value in Tourism Services: Meaning and Role for a Relationship Marketing Approach', in R. H. Tsiotsou and R. E. Goldsmith (eds.) *Strategic Marketing in Tourism Services*, Bingley: Emerald, pp. 147–62.

Gartner, W. C. and M. K. Ruzzier (2011) 'Tourism Destination Brand Equity Dimensions Renewal Versus Repeat Market', *Journal of Travel Research*, 50 (5): 471–81.

Getz, D. and S. J. Page (1997) 'Conclusions and Implications for Rural Business Development', in S. J. Page and D. Getz (eds.) *The Business of Rural Tourism: International Perspectives*, London: International Thomson Business Press, pp. 191–205.

Glaesser, D. (2012) *Crisis Management in the Tourism Industry*, London and New York: Routledge.

Gomez, B. G., A. G. Arranz and J. G. Cillan (2006) 'The Role of Loyalty Programmes in Behavioural and Affective Loyalty', *Journal of Consumer Marketing*, 23 (7): 387–96.

Gu, H. and G. Wall (2006) 'The Effects of SARS on China's Tourism Enterprises', *Tourism*, 54 (3): 225–33.

Hall, C. M. (2010) 'Crisis Events in Tourism: Subjects of Crisis in Tourism', *Current Issues in Tourism*, 13 (5): 401–17.

Hamilton, J. (2006) *Thomas Cook: The Holiday Maker*, Stroud: Sutton Publishing Ltd.

Hembrow, I. (2012) 'Lessons for Local Government from the 2012 Games Makers', *The Guardian*, 5 September.

Holloway, C. and C. Humphreys (2012) *The Business of Tourism*, 9th edn, Harlow: Pearson.

Hsu, C. H., H. Oh and A. G. Assaf (2012) 'A Customer-Based Brand Equity Model for Upscale Hotels', *Journal of Travel Research*, 51 (1): 81–93.

Israeli, A. A., A. Mohsin and B. Kumar (2011) 'Hospitality Crisis Management Practices: The Case of Indian Luxury Hotels', *International Journal of Hospitality Management*, 30 (2): 367–74.

Kayaman, R. and H. Arasli (2007) 'Customer Based Brand Equity: Evidence from the Hotel Industry', *Managing Service Quality*, 17 (1): 92–109.

Krippendorf, J. (1999) *Holiday Makers*, Oxford: Butterworth-Heinemann.

Laws, E., B. Faulkner and G. Moscardo (eds.) (1998) 'Embracing and Managing Change in Tourism: International Case Studies', London and New York: Routledge.

Lu, T. Y. and L. A. Cai (2011) 'An Analysis of Image and Loyalty in Convention and Exhibition Tourism in China', *Event Management*, 15 (1): 37–48.

Mason, P. (2008) *Tourism Impacts, Planning and Management*, 2nd edn, Oxford: Butterworth-Heinemann.

Mattila, A. S. (2006) 'How Affective Commitment Boosts Guest Loyalty (and Promotes Frequent Guest Programs)', *Cornell Hotel and Restaurant Administration Quarterly*, 47 (2): 147–81.

Mbaiwa, J. E. and A. L. Stronza (2010) 'The Effects of Tourism Development on Rural Livelihoods in the Okavango Delta, Botswana', *Journal of Sustainable Tourism*, 18 (5): 635–56.

McKercher, M., B. Denisxci-Guillet and E. Ng (2012) 'Rethinking Loyalty', *Annals of Tourism Research*, 39 (2): 708–73.

Müller, H. and B. Lane (2003) 'Jost Krippendorf: Obituary', *Journal of Sustainable Tourism*, 11 (1): 3.

Parrilla, J. C., A. R. Font and J. R. Nadal (2007) 'Accommodation Determinants of Seasonal Patterns', *Annals of Tourism Research*, (34): 2: 422–36.

Pechlaner, H., F. Raich, A. Zehrer and M. Peters (2004) 'Growth Perceptions of Small and Medium-Sized Enterprises (SMEs): The Case of South Tirol', *Tourism Review*, 59 (4): 7–13.

Pehrsson, A. (2009) 'Barriers to Entry and Market Strategy: A Literature Review and a Proposed Model', *European Business Review*, 21 (1): 64–77.

Pforr, C. and P. Hosie (2009) *Crisis Management in the Tourism Industry: Beating the Odds?* Farnham: Ashgate.

Poon, A. (1993) *Tourism, Technology and Competitive Strategy*, Wallingford: CAB International.

Porter, M. E. (1980) *Competitive Strategy*, New York: Free Press.

Sinclair, M. T. and M. Stabler (1997) *The Economics of Tourism*, London and New York: Routledge.

Skogland, I. and J. A. Siguaw (2004) 'Are Your Satisfied Customers Loyal?', *Cornell Hotel and Restaurant Administration Quarterly*, 45 (3): 221–34.

Stickdorn, M. and A. Zehrer (2009) 'Service Design in Tourism: Customer Experience Driven Destination Management', First Nordic Conference on Service Design and Service Innovation, Oslo, Norway, November.

Tapper, R. and X. Font (2004) 'Tourism Supply Chains: Report of a Desk Research Project for the Travel Foundation', Leeds Metropolitan University, Environment Business and Development Group. Available online at http://www.lmu.ac.uk/lsif/the/tourism-supply-chains.pdf (accessed 28 February 2013).

Thomas, R., M. Friel and S. Jameson (1999) 'Small Business Management', in R. Thomas (ed.) *The Management of Small Tourism and Hospitality Firms*, London: Cassell, pp. 10–25.

Toh, R. S., F. Dekay and P. Raven (2008) 'Characteristics of Members of Hotel Frequent-Guest Programmes: Implications for the Hospitality Industry', *Tourism Analysis*, 13 (3): 271–80.

Tum, J. and P. Norton (2006) *Management of Event Operations*, London and New York: Routledge, pp. 187–238.

Wall, G. and A. Mathieson (2006) *Tourism: Change, Impacts and Opportunities*, Harlow: Pearson Education.

Wang, J. and B. W. Ritchie (2011) 'Understanding Accommodation Managers' Crisis Planning Intention: An Application of the Theory of Planned Behaviour', *Tourism Management*, 33 (5): 1057–67.

Zhang, X., H. Song and G. Q. Huang (2009) 'Tourism Supply Chain Management: A New Research Agenda', *Tourism Management*, 30 (3): 345–58.

WEBSITES

www.aito.co.uk
www.accor.com
www.britishairways.com/
www.carlson.com/hotels/radisson
www.grootbos.com
www.kuoni.com
www.ryanair.com

FURTHER READING

Reference	Focus
Abukhalifeh, A. N., A. P. M. Som and A. R. Albattat (2013) 'Strategic Human Resource Development in Hospitality Crisis Management: A Conceptual Framework for Food and Beverage Departments', *International Journal of Business Administration*, 4 (1): 39–45.	Managing crises Hospitality
Albayrak, T., M. Caber and Ş. Aksoy (2010) 'Relationships of the Tangible and Intangible Elements of Tourism Products with Overall Customer Satisfaction', *International Journal of Trade, Economics and Finance*, 1 (2): 140–3.	Intangibility Tourism Customer satisfaction
Blake, A. and M. T. Sinclair (2003) 'Tourism Crisis Management: US Response to September 11', *Annals of Tourism Research*, 30 (4): 813–32.	Crisis management Tourism
Boo, S., J. Busser and S. Baloglu (2009) 'A Model of Customer-Based Brand Equity and Its Application to Multiple Destinations', *Tourism Management*, 30 (2): 219–31.	Brand equity Loyalty schemes Tourist destinations
Bowen, D. and J. Clarke (2002) 'Reflections on Tourist Satisfaction Research: Past, Present and Future', *Journal of Vacation Marketing*, 8 (4): 297–308.	Heterogeneity Tourism

Castro, C. B., E. Martín Armario and D. Martín Ruiz (2007) 'The Influence of Market Heterogeneity on the Relationship between a Destination's Image and Tourists' Future Behaviour', *Tourism Management*, 28 (1): 175–87.	Heterogeneity Tourism
Dwyer, L., R. Mellor, N. Mistilis and T. Mules (2000) 'A Framework for Assessing "Tangible" and "Intangible" Impacts of Events and Conventions', *Event Management*, 6 (3): 175–89.	Intangibility Tourism impacts
Hall, C. M. (2010) 'Crisis Events in Tourism: Subjects of Crisis in Tourism', *Current Issues in Tourism*, 13 (5): 401–17.	Crisis management Tourism
Hyun, S. and W. Kim (2011) 'Dimensions of Brand Equity in the Chain Restaurant Industry', *Cornell Hospitality Quarterly*, 52 (4): 429–37.	Brand equity Loyalty schemes Hospitality
Israeli, A. A. and A. Reichel (2003) 'Hospitality Crisis Management Practices: The Israeli Case', *International Journal of Hospitality Management*, 22 (4): 353–72.	Crisis management Hospitality Israel
Reisinger, Y. B. (2001) 'Unique Characteristics of Tourism, Hospitality and Leisure Services', in J. Kandampully, C. Mok and B. Sparks (eds.) *Service Quality Management in Hospitality, Tourism and Leisure*, New York: Routledge, pp. 15–47.	Characteristics Tourism
Ritchie, B. W. (2004) 'Chaos, Crises and Disasters: A Strategic Approach to Crisis Management in the Tourism Industry', *Tourism Management*, 25 (6): 669–83.	Crisis management Tourism
Stafford, G., L. Yu and A. Kobina Armoo (2002) 'Crisis Management and Recovery: How Washington, DC, Hotels Responded to Terrorism', *The Cornell Hotel and Restaurant Administration Quarterly*, 43 (5): 27–40.	Crisis management Hospitality Hotels
Vidal González, M. (2008) 'Intangible Heritage: Tourism and Identity', *Tourism Management*, 29 (4): 807–10.	Intangibility Tourism
Xu, J. B. and A. Chan (2010) 'A Conceptual Framework of Hotel Experience and Customer-Based Brand Equity: Some Research Questions and Implications', *International Journal of Contemporary Hospitality Management*, 22 (2): 174–93.	Brand equity Loyalty schemes Hotels

CASE LINKAGES

Case 1	Strategic alliances in the airline industry
Case 4	Hyatt Hotels
Case 5	Days Inn
Case 7	Thomas Cook

Part **2**

Analysing the internal environment

Introduction

Internal analysis

The previous part of this book was concerned with considering the context of *THE* organizations which make managing in *THE* distinctive. Strategic management as a subject of study was also introduced and specifically objectives, mission, vision and values were considered.

In Part 2 we turn towards the internal analysis of organizations and to consider in turn the operational context, including the competencies, resources and competitive advantage; followed by the human, financial and product/market aspects of internal strategic analysis. Part 3 goes on to consider the external aspects of strategic analysis.

Study progress:

Part 1	Part 2				Part 3	Part 4	Part 5
Strategy and the tourism, hospitality and events contexts	Analysing the internal environment				Analysing the external environment and SWOT	Strategic selection	Strategic implementation and strategy in theory and practice
Chapters 1 and 2	Chapter 3 Competencies resources and competitive advantage	Chapter 4 The human resources context	Chapter 5 The financial context	Chapter 6 Products and markets	Chapters 7,8 and 9	Chapters 10, 11 and 12	Chapters 13, 14 and 15

Purposes of internal analysis

Internal analysis is concerned with providing the management of *THE* organizations with a detailed understanding of their organizations with respect to:

- how effective current strategies are;
- how effectively resources have been deployed in support of chosen strategies.

In carrying out internal analysis managers may gain insights and understanding of how *competitive advantage* might be achieved and also an appreciation of where remedial action must be taken in order to ensure survival.

This Section of the book introduces and evaluates the main techniques and frameworks which can be employed to enable *THE* managers to produce a comprehensive internal analysis of their organization.

THE organizations should carry out an internal analysis for a number of reasons including to:

- identify resources, competencies and core competencies to be developed and exploited;
- evaluate how effectively value added activities are organized;
- identify areas of weaknesses to be addressed by the formulation of future strategies and their successful implementation;
- evaluate the performance of products;
- evaluate financial performance;

- evaluate investment potential if finance is being sought from external sources;
- assess the performance and future requirements for human resources; and
- provide the analytical underpinning for the 'strengths' and 'weaknesses' section of the SWOT.

The components of internal analysis

An internal analysis will usually cover some or all of the following aspects:

- resource analysis;
- competence identification and analysis;
- internal activities analysis using Porter's value chain analysis;
- financial resources and financial performance;
- products and their position in the market.

These aspects of internal analysis are covered in Chapters 3 to 6 which form Part 2 of this book. A number of 'techniques' and frameworks are introduced to help *THE* managers in carrying out the analysis and in organizing the information.

Part 1 of the book introduced strategy as being a three part process involving: strategic analysis; strategic selection; and, strategic implementation. Figure P2.1 develops this model further and indicates the way in which internal analysis provides a firm evidence base which enables the Strengths and Weaknesses of the organisation to be identified as part of the so-called SWOT analysis.

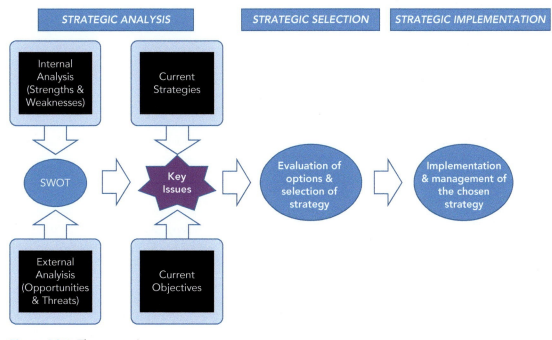

Figure P2.1 The strategic process

Chapter **3**

Tourism, hospitality and event organizations

The operational context: competencies, resources and competitive advantage

Introduction and chapter overview

In Chapter 1 we encountered the concept of competitive advantage as one of the key objectives of business strategy. There has been considerable debate in the academic literature as to the causes of competitive advantage. Essentially the debate asks the question, 'how do organizations achieve superior performance?' Two positions have emerged as the most prominent.

The *competitive positioning* school of thought, based primarily on the work of Professor Michael Porter of Harvard Business School (1985), stresses the importance of how the organization is positioned in respect to its competitive environment or industry (which we discuss in Chapter 7). The *resource* or *competence* school (Prahalad and Hamel, 1990; Heene and Sanchez, 1997) on the other hand, argues that it is the competencies (abilities) of the business and the distinctive way that it organizes its activities which determines its ability to outperform competitors. As with most controversies, we suggest that both schools of thought have their merits – both are partial explanations of the source of competitive advantage.

This is the first of four chapters which cover the internal analysis of THE organizations. This is a crucial building block in the strategy process – how can you move the organization forward successfully into the future (with which strategic management is concerned) unless you have a good understanding of its current position?

Subsequent chapters consider what are sometimes termed the functional areas of organizations, namely: the human resources; financial; and product and market contexts. The other key area of all organizations relates to their operations.

The nature of operations is such, though, that they are very specific to each organization; no two organizations are identical. However, they are similar in that they are trying to configure and coordinate their operational resources and processes in such a way that they add value and in so doing achieve an advantage over competitors – *competitive advantage*.

This chapter concentrates on developing an understanding of the major factors governing the level of performance of the business, namely its resources, competencies (particularly its core competencies), and its 'value-adding' activities.

Much of the writing and many case study examples found in strategy texts and academic papers relate mainly to manufacturing and the production of physical goods. Some writers have argued that different factors have to be considered in the context of services, such as those considered in *THE* sectors. This has led to the development of specific conceptual models such as the 'Service Profit Chain' and the academic framework, so-called 'Service Dominant Logic'. These services-oriented topics are covered towards the end of the chapter.

LEARNING OBJECTIVES

After studying this chapter you should be able to:

- explain the concepts of *core competencies*, *competencies*, *resources* and the relationships between them;
- apply core competencies, competencies and resources to relevant *THE* contexts;
- explain the concept of the *value chain* and the value chain framework;
- explain the relationships between core competencies and core activities;
- apply the value chain framework to relevant *THE* settings;
- explain how the configuration of value adding activities can improve business performance;
- explain the potential benefits of collaboration with suppliers, distributors and customers for *THE* organizations;
- explain why established frameworks and analytical tools may be less relevant in a service industry context;
- explain the concept of the Service Profit Chain and how it relates to *THE* organizations;
- explain the developing academic debate relating to Service Dominant Logic.

Resources, competencies, core competencies and competitive advantage

The sources of competitive advantage

In all industries, including *THE*, some organizations are more successful than others regardless of whether the average profitability for the sector is relatively high or low. The superior performers conceivably possess something special that competitors do not have access to that allows them to outperform their rivals.

The sources of *competitive advantage* lie in combining:

- the superior application of competencies (skills);
- the deployment of superior resources (assets);
- in creating value for consumers.

Strategy and *THE* texts often use the term *sustainable* (or sustainability) in connection with the notion of advantage. However, it is also acknowledged that in *THE* texts in particular, the term is also often used in different contexts to denote sustainability in relation to the physical environment.

Sustainability is achieved when the advantage resists erosion by competitive behaviour (Porter, 1985: 20), in that it cannot be copied, substituted or eroded by the actions of rivals, and it is not made redundant by developments in the environment. In other words, in order to achieve the goal of reaching a position of sustainable competitive advantage, a business's competitive advantage must be capable of resisting duplication by other companies (Barney, 2002).

Competence and capability

The terms *competence* and *capability*, *core competence* and *distinctive capability* are often used interchangeably in textbooks on strategy. Although some writers (e.g. Stalk *et al.*, 1992) argue that there are significant differences between the terms *competence* and *capability*, here the terms will be taken to mean broadly the same things based upon the following definitions.

DEFINITION/QUOTATION

Competence, core competence and resources

A competence is:

> An attribute or collection of attributes possessed by all or most of the organizations in a sector of industry.

A core competence is:

> An attribute or collection of attributes specific to a particular organization which enables it to produce above industry average performance.

A resource is:

> An input employed in the activities of the business.

Competencies

Without competencies a business cannot enter or survive in the industry. Competencies develop from resources and embody skills, technology or 'know-how'.

For example – in order to operate as an outbound tour operator involved in air-inclusive 'package' tours, a company must possess a range of competencies in arranging:

- a means of distributing, marketing and selling their product;
- licences to operate the required capacity to the specified destinations;
- air transportation to and from the destination;
- suitable accommodation at the destination;
- ground-handling activities to ensure customers are checked onto their flights and that they are transported to and from their accommodation.

Every successful survivor in the industry must possess these areas of competence.

Core competencies

Core competencies arise from the way in which the organization has employed its competencies and resources *more effectively* than its competitors. The result of a distinctive capability is an output which customers value higher than those of competitors. The basis upon which their core competencies are achieved is considered later in the chapter.

Resources

In employing resources, success rests in large part upon the efficiency by which the business converts its resources (inputs) into outputs. Resources fall into five broad categories (although sometimes the physical and operational categories are combined):

- human;
- financial;
- physical (e.g. buildings, equipment, stock, etc.);
- operational (e.g. aeroplanes, ships, coaches, computers, etc.);
- intangible (e.g. 'knowhow', patents, legal rights, brand names, registered designs, licences, etc.).

KEY CONCEPT

Competitive advantage

Competitive advantage is often seen as the overall purpose of strategy. Some texts use the phrase 'superior performance' to mean the same thing.

Essentially, a business can be said to possess competitive advantage if it is able to return higher profits than its competitors. The higher profits mean that it will be able to commit more retained profit to reinvestment in its strategy, thus maintaining its lead over its competitors in an industry. When this superiority is maintained successfully over time, a sustainable competitive advantage has been achieved. Competitive advantage can be lost when management fail to reinvest the superior profits in such a way that the advantage is not maintained.

How core competencies 'work'

Core competencies tend to be both complex and intangible, so it is necessary to explore the nature of resources and competencies which underpin them before exploring the concept further. The purpose of such analysis is to allow managers to identify which resources and competencies act as the foundation of existing or potential core competencies. It is important to note that not all the competitors in an industry will possess core competencies or distinctive capabilities (Kay, 1995). It is only those organizations, which are producing above average performance, that can be considered to possess core competencies.

THINK POINTS

- What are the major purposes of internal analysis?
- Define and explain the relationships between resources, competencies and core competencies.
- Provide an example of a core competence in a *THE* organization you are familiar with.
- Describe and distinguish between the two conceptual approaches to strategic management which have been introduced in this chapter.

Figure 3.1 The links between resources, competencies and core competencies

Those with only average or below average performance possess competencies and resources (without which they could not compete in the industry at all), but not core competencies. For further discussion of these concepts, see Prahalad and Hamel, 1990; Kay, 1995; Heene and Sanchez, 1997; Petts, 1997; and Javidan, 1998. The links between competencies, resources and core competencies are summarized in Figure 3.1.

Core competence (distinctive capability) when applied in a market creates value for customers – this represents *competitive advantage.*

These terms will now be considered in greater detail.

Resource analysis

Tangible and intangible resources

Resources can be either *tangible* or *intangible*. They are the inputs or assets that enable an organization to carry out its activities. Tangible assets include: stocks, materials, machinery, buildings, human resources and finance. Intangible resources include: skills, knowledge, brand names, goodwill and patent rights. A number of writers have studied the nature and significance of intangible resources (see for example Hall, 1992; Fernandez *et al.*, 2000; Galbreath, 2005; and Hall, 2006), while Choi and Parsa (2012) and FitzPatrick *et al.* (2013) consider such resources applied in relation to hotels specifically.

Tangible resources are obtained from outside organizations. Such resources are obtained in *resource markets* in competition with organizations from within and outside the industry. Intangible resources can often be developed within an organization, but as with tangible resources they have a value attached to them which, although sometimes difficult to quantify (or even identify), can be bought and sold in markets. Relationships with the suppliers of resources can form an important part of the organization's core competence as, for example, with its ability to attract the most appropriately skilled human resources in the job market.

Tourism though, it can be argued (and by extension, owing to the close linkages and overlaps, also in relation to hospitality and events), is different from most other industries in that what economists typically refer to as *free resources* are a vital part of the product. Free resources are those resources available freely which do not require a market mechanism to allocate them.

KEY CONCEPT

Free resources

'Free' resources are those available in such abundance naturally, such as air, the sea, climate, culture, etc., that there is no need for an allocative mechanism (a market), in order to allocate them to users or consumers. However, it can be argued that free resources are also limited in supply and subject to degradation and therefore they have to be utilised carefully in 'sustainable' ways.

Scarce resources on the other hand are the tangible and intangible resources which are limited in their supply, relative to the demand of consumers, and are therefore allocated in a market.

Bull (1995) argues that the basis for tourism lies in building upon free resources (or 'renewable resources' as they are sometimes termed) with a mixture of public sector and private sector resources. Free resources together with scarce resources are combined to form what most tourists perceive as the 'product' they consume and which suppliers produce. It may be argued, as Bull (1995) points out, that in today's world there are few truly free resources since any human activity makes demands on the world's resources and, as a consequence, ultimately someone will have to pay a price. Indeed the concept of *sustainable tourism* largely rests upon the recognition of such a line of argument.

All resources have competing demands made upon them so that if they are used for one form of activity they cannot be used in other ways.

For example, a large flat land coastal area might be suitable for the development of a resort area for tourism including hotels and event venues or alternatively as a site for heavy industry such as steel and chemicals production. If tourism is chosen ahead of heavy industry, an opportunity to develop heavy industry on this site has been lost. The cost of this choice is known as the *opportunity cost*, which represents the potential economic returns that are being given up in favour of developing tourism.

A number of points are pertinent to a consideration of the use of resources and to their management in *THE* sectors. Particular challenges presented to *THE* managers in the use of resources include:

Resource immobility

Many resources that are used cannot be moved either in terms of place or time.

For example – a particular beach or mountain, the Empire State Building or the culture of Spain are geographically fixed. The Alpine snows of February cannot be replicated in May and the 'midnight sun', a tourist attraction in far northern latitudes, can be observed only during mid-summer. The Vienna Philharmonic Orchestra and the New York Marathon have their homes in those cities and represent important and prestigious parts of their cultural and sporting offerings which cannot be moved.

Resource substitution

It is often difficult to substitute one resource category with those of another.

For example – in a car factory efficiency gains may be possible, and indeed have been achieved, through replacing employees by machines i.e. the substitution of human resources with operational resources. In the cases of a luxury hotel, a concert or conference venue, an airline or a cruise ship, for instance, the quality of service is often perceived as being fundamentally linked with the quality and number of staff. Consequently it is often difficult to replace human resources with operational resources such as computers. As a result *THE* sectors are usually viewed as being 'labour intensive', i.e. relying heavily on human resouces in delivering products.

Resource conflict and competition

THE frequently makes extensive demands on the use of certain resources which can be in serious conflict or competition with other uses. Such resource conflict or competition may be partially resolved through pricing mechanisms by which the activity that is able to pay the most is able to use the resources. Similarly regulatory restrictions such as the geographical zoning of areas to permit specified activities only within a particular zone may resolve some conflicts. Some degree of conflict frequently remains.

For example – in the UK, the competing demands of the British army in using gunnery ranges in the Isle of Purbeck, Dorset (an area of outstanding natural beauty) and in the Northumberland National Park at Otterburn, Northumberland, are in conflict with tourist demands for unspoilt environments. Cultural and sporting events and tourism are often important contributors to local economies but have to compete for funding with other activities.

In a local setting tourism and events often have to compete for public funding with other activities such as education, social services and health. These activities normally have far larger budgets than tourism and events and it is difficult to argue that tourism and events should be favoured in budget allocations over these activities. Recognizing this reality, government authorities throughout the world have attempted to form various types of public–private partnerships in order to place promotional and organizational aspects in the private (commercial) sector. In doing so tourism and events can form the central focus of a particular dedicated organization rather than remain as a fringe activity in a larger body always competing for scarce resources.

SHORT CASE ILLUSTRATION

Resource competition: Sunderland Live

Sunderland, a coastal city in north east England, has a heritage in ship building and is home to Britain's largest car plant operated by Nissan. In common with all cities in the UK, local government has been forced to operate with reduced budgets and has experienced competition for the scarce resources available.

Sunderland, although often viewed as an industrial city, has an excellent beach and has a good and growing reputation for events, which include an International Air Show and a series of summer outdoor rock concerts staged at the city's Premier League football ground.

Sunderland City Council launched an independent events company in April 2013 to provide an increased ability to bring commercial funding into the city through sponsorship and partnership arrangements. The events team, which previously was part of the city council, transferred to the new company, 'Sunderland Live'. The launch of Sunderland Live represents an innovative attempt to protect and grow the city's event programme at a time when public finances are increasingly under pressure and provides an organization that is solely focused on providing successful events for the city and its region.

www.sunderlandlive.co.uk

Questions

1. What are the reasons for public sector bodies forming separate companies for developing and managing events?
2. Consider the issues that might arise from public and private sectors working together in the way described.

Resource ownership and control

THE managers, frequently have to utilize resources that are neither owned nor controlled by the companies operating within the sectors. The lack of ownership and control of resources that is evident is a demonstration of the interdependence that exists between organizations operating in these sectors.

For example:

- Airlines depend upon the physical resources provided by airports and the operating resources provided by air traffic control services. Although the airlines may have some influence over the way in which these resources are managed, they are rarely directly owned and managed.

- Projects aimed at regenerating decaying urban environments often have tourism, event venues, hotels and hospitality outlets at their heart. Such projects are often developed as *public–private partnerships*. With such arrangements the public sector (local and national government) manage and control the overall redevelopment and provide limited funding, sometimes termed 'pump priming'. Private sector companies in such cases provide the major part of the financial resources. Examples of such public–private partnerships include the redevelopment of Cardiff Bay in the UK and of the Baltimore waterfront in Maryland, USA.

Seasonality

Demand for most *THE* resources and hence the products that they contribute to, whether business- or leisure-based, is highly seasonal. This in turn is the result of factors such as climate, the distribution of holiday entitlements, the timing of events and festivals and historic travel patterns.

Consequently, the price that organizations have to pay for their resource inputs, and the prices that consumers have to pay those organizations, vary according to the season.

For example – many resort hotels situated in coastal areas close during the winter period and have lower rates in early Spring and Autumn to reflect differences in seasonal demand patterns.

Low rewards

THE sectors are often viewed as relatively low-margin sectors of business. Whilst this is not necessarily the case, it is certainly true to say that the rewards from *THE* are often slow to materialize and susceptible to wide swings in cash flow and profitability.

As Bull (1995) points out, rewards in tourism (though it also applies in hospitality and events) may be low for several reasons. The industry is often perceived as being relatively clean and pleasant both to invest in and to work in. Consequently, employees may be prepared to work for lower wages than in other industries, as they would rather work in such an attractive industry than elsewhere. Some destination areas have few alternative land uses and employment opportunities, thus little competition is provided for the use of resources thereby keeping rewards in terms of prices paid for land and development, and wages paid to employees, low.

For example – the development of tourism in the Yucatán Peninsula on the Caribbean coast of Mexico has taken place over recent years in an area that is economically poorly developed and which is remote from major markets for goods and services. Hence the development of hospitality and tourism in this beautiful region does not face strong competition from other industries for the use of resources and the costs of rewarding resources (in terms of land costs and wages) are relatively low.

Capacity constraints

The capacity of *THE* resources is frequently constrained in some way as we noted in the previous chapter.

Thus in tourism the *carrying capacity* for a destination is often referred to. This refers to the ability of a site, resort or region to absorb tourism use without deteriorating. The notion of carrying capacity is central to the concept of sustainability.

For example – the rapid development of Spain's Costa del Sol from the 1950s onwards demonstrates the need to constrain development. Extensive linear development along the coast to the west of Malaga led to over-building with poor planning controls. The relative popularity of the resort areas subsequently diminished as consumers opted for more recent and better-planned resorts elsewhere. Thus the over use of resources led to the carrying capacity being exceeded and deterioration in the environment that had attracted tourists in the first place.

Similarly the capacity of physical and operational resources in *THE* is often constrained, at least in the short- to medium period.

For example – if a hotel (physical resource) is full, or an airline flight or a theatre (operational resources) are fully booked, it is difficult to add capacity quickly. By contrast, if additional demand is apparent for a manufactured product, capacity can often be increased by overtime working, by putting on an extra shift of work or by running production lines at a faster rate.

Thus in *THE* supply is often relatively fixed (at least in the short- to medium term) whereas demand fluctuates.

The managerial implication of this is that managers will often (in the short- to medium term) try to influence demand rather than supply. Thus pricing levels and promotional activities will be altered in order to increase or reduce demand so that it matches the supply that is available.

For example – it has become common for UK outbound tour operators to alter prices in a very active manner in the weeks immediately prior to the date of departure and hotels often make late alterations to their accommodation rates. This active management of prices, which can be moved upwards or downwards to inhibit or encourage demand respectively, is a way of managing the demand so that it matches the supply which has been previously fixed.

Time

Unlike the purchase of household goods or many services, *THE* consumers must also give up a scarce resource in addition to money, namely time. In a similar way to money, time has an *opportunity cost* attached to it, i.e. other ways in which it might be spent to which a value can be attached. Whilst much time is spent on *THE* activities willingly, other time spent travelling to destinations or queuing at an event venue may be viewed, by some consumers, as a burden that if at all possible should be avoided or curtailed.

The managerial implication of this is that consumers may choose different products or may be willing to pay a premium for certain services. Alternatively they may take advantage of discounted prices for travel or last-minute theatre tickets, for instance, in return for some extra inconvenience.

For example – flights between Australia and Europe have become increasingly popular for leisure travellers in recent years as newer aircraft types have needed only one intermediate refuelling stop thereby reducing journey times to about 21 hours. The more efficient use of time also explains why overnight long haul flights and early morning trains are usually more expensive. The recent rapid growth in the popularity of low-cost airlines is explained partly by the fact that passengers are willing to trade some degree of inconvenience for lower fares. The airlines often utilise 'secondary airports' (such as London Luton Airport in the UK or Dallas Love Field in the USA) which are further away from the main urban centres that they serve or have fewer facilities and onward transit opportunities.

Analysing resources

When we analyse a company's resources as part of an internal analysis, several frameworks can be employed to provide a comprehensive review.

Analysis by category

First we might, for example, consider them by *category* – physical, operational, human, financial and intangible resources. These resources are then evaluated quantitatively (how much or how many) and qualitatively (how effectively they are being employed). Much of this analysis is covered in Chapters 4, 5 and 6.

- *Physical resources* (buildings, land, materials) and *operational resources* (computers, machines, aircraft, systems, etc.) are typically audited for capacity, utilization, age, condition, contribution to output and value.

- *Financial resources* (the amount and type of finance available to the organization) are considered in terms of the balance between different types of finance and the relative cost and risks of each of these types of finance.

- *Human resources* (employees, junior, middle and senior management, board directors) are considered in terms of numbers, education, skills, training, experience, age, motivation, wage costs and productivity in relation to the needs of the organization.

- *Intangible resources* (brand, reputation, goodwill, skills, licences and 'free' resources) are assessed in terms of their overall value to the organization.

SHORT CASE ILLUSTRATION

Resource analysis: Marriott International

Marriott International is a leading worldwide hospitality company with its headquarters near Washington DC in Bethesda, Maryland, USA. It manages and franchises hotels under a number of recognized international brand names including Marriott, Renaissance and Courtyard.

Table 3.1 Resource analysis: Marriott International

Resource Category	Analysis of Marriott resources
Physical resources	Almost 3,700 operating units and 17 brands in the United States and 72 other countries.
	Properties range from luxurious (Ritz-Carlton) to budget (Courtyard and Fairfield Inn).
Operational resources	Each brand has a detailed set of operating procedures which is constantly updated and refined.
	Worldwide reservations system with industry leading costs per reservation.
	Common reservations system for all brands allowing for cross-selling opportunities.
	Large web sales volume.
	Marriott Rewards is one of the largest frequent guest programmes in the hospitality sector and is linked to over 30 international airlines.
Financial resources	Most hotels are financed by third parties with less than 1% of properties being company-owned.
	As a hotel manager and franchisor significant and more stable cash flows are generated than through real estate ownership.
	Strong balance sheet and profitability record.
Human resources	Over 150,000 employees worldwide.
	Extensive staff training and advancement opportunities.
	Consistently listed in *Fortune* magazine annual list of 100 best companies to work for in United States.

Table 3.1 continued

Resource Category	Analysis of Marriott resources
Intangible resources	Strong range of brand names many of which are clear leaders within their market tiers.
	Customer and owner loyalty achieved through a strong rewards programme.
	Distinct market positioning of each brand.
	Many hotels situated at scenic locations.

Source: www.marriott.com

Questions

1. Summarize the purpose of carrying out a resource analysis for a *THE* company such as Marriott.

2. What conclusions would you draw from the resource analysis of Marriott?

Analysis by specificity

Second, we can analyse resources according to their *specificity*. Resources can be specific or non-specific.

For example – skilled workers tend to have specialized and industry-specific knowledge and skills. Some technology, such as computer software, is for general (non industry-specific) business use, like word-processing, database and spreadsheet software. Other computer software applications, like airline or hotel computer reservation systems or yield management programmes, are written for highly specialized uses.

Whereas non-specific resources tend to be more flexible and form the basis of competencies, industry-specific resources are more likely to act as the foundations of core competencies.

For example – the specialized knowledge of procurement managers responsible for contracting accommodation in the tour operating sector, or the front of house staff of a hotel chain, may have knowledge, expertise or training which can be viewed as industry-leading by their companies and thereby constitute a source of core competence.

Analysis by performance

Third, resources can be evaluated on the basis of how they contribute to internal and external measures of performance.

Internal measures include their contribution to:

- business objectives and targets – financial, performance and output measures;
- historical comparisons – measures of performance over time (e.g. against previous years);
- business unit or divisional comparisons – comparisons with other parts of the same organization.

External measures can include:

- comparisons with industry norms – standards of performance accepted as exemplary across the sector;
- comparisons with competitors – particularly those who are industry leaders and those who are the closest competitors in its *strategic grouping* (see Chapter 6);
- comparisons with companies – in other service-based industries such as banking or insurance.

By employing these techniques of analysis, an organization is able to internally and externally *benchmark* its performance as a stimulus to improving performance in the future. Performance, however, is based on more than resources, and competencies must be similarly analysed and evaluated.

Competencies

Competencies are attributes like skills, knowledge, technology and relationships that are common among the competitors in an industry.

For example – all companies in the airline industry possess similar competencies (basic abilities) in operations, marketing and distribution.

They are less tangible than resources and are consequently more difficult to evaluate. Competencies are more often developed internally, but may also be acquired externally or by collaboration with suppliers, distributors or customers.

Competencies are distinguished from core competencies by the fact that they do not produce superior performance and are not distinctive when compared to the competencies possessed by other companies in the industry. On the other hand, competencies are essential for survival in a particular line of business. Competencies also have the potential to be developed into core competencies.

THINK POINTS

- Explain what is meant by *free resources* in *THE* contexts.
- Explain what is meant by *resource immobility* and *resource substitution* and explain their relevance in *THE* contexts.
- Explain the different ways in which resources might be analysed.

Core competencies

Core competencies are distinguished from competencies in several ways in that they are:

- only possessed by those companies whose performance is superior to the industry average;
- unique to the company;
- more complex;
- difficult to emulate (copy);
- related to fulfilling customer needs;
- adding greater value than competencies;
- often based on distinctive relationships with customers, distributors and suppliers;
- based upon superior organizational skills and knowledge.

Core competence arises from the unique and distinctive way that the organization builds, develops, integrates and deploys its resources and competencies. An existing core competence can be evaluated for:

- *Customer focus* – does it adequately focus on customer needs by contributing to something that is valued by them, i.e. is there an economic value?
- *Uniqueness* – can it be imitated by competitors and if so, how easily?

- *Flexibility* – can it be easily adapted if market or industry conditions change?
- *Contribution to value* – to what extent does it add value to the product or service? Are there close substitute products available?
- *Sustainability* – how long can its superiority be sustained over time? Is it relatively difficult to imitate?

Harrison (2003), writing in the context of hospitality, provides a model demonstrating the linkages between resources, competencies and competitive advantages shown in Figure 3.2. The model demonstrates at practical level some of the questions managers have to ask themselves about how resources are deployed and which competencies should be sought.

Competencies, as opposed to core competencies, can also be judged against these criteria in order to evaluate their potential to form the basis upon which new core competencies can be built.

Core competencies can never be regarded as being permanent. The pace of changing technology and society are such that core competencies must be constantly adapted and new ones cultivated. *THE* organizations normally operate in highly competitive environments and have to be responsive to changes and challenge competitors by utilizing their core competencies to the full.

In a *THE* context the core competencies are sometimes the result of holding a particular market position, but they can also result from aspects of regulation or geography which are difficult for others to replicate.

For example – transport operators are often subject to regulatory restrictions which prevent new companies from entering the market to compete while the beaches of Florida or the South by Southwest set of film, interactive, and music festivals and conferences (which have taken place every spring since 1987 in Austin, Texas) cannot be moved to a different location. For a discussion of core competencies in *THE* contexts see for example Denicolai *et al.* (2010); Peters *et al.* (2011); Harrison (2003); and Dwyer *et al.* (2013).

However, in some albeit limited cases core competencies can be maintained over a prolonged period of time.

For example – Kay (1995) identified British Airways' core competencies as: its dominance at London's key hub (Heathrow Airport); licences to fly on certain routes; and its strong brand attributes. Arguably, 20 years on, British Airways' core competencies remain intact.

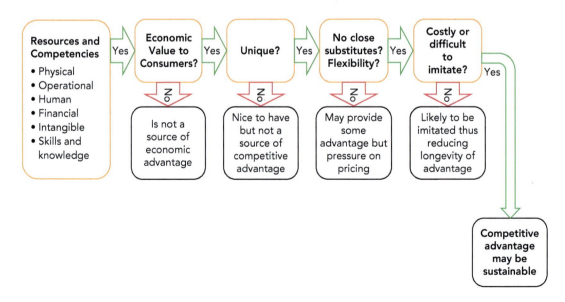

Figure 3.2 The links between resources, competencies and competitive advantage

Core competencies and distinctive capabilities

Kay (1995) presents a slightly different explanation, arguing that competitive advantage is based upon what he terms *distinctive capability*. According to Kay, distinctive capability can develop from four sources.

Architecture

A network of relationships within or around the organization. The relationships may be among employees (internal architecture), with their suppliers and customers (external architecture) or among a group of organizations engaged in related activities (networks).

For example – the strategic alliances that have been built up by the major international airlines in recent years are examples of using networks to strengthen the competitive position of individual airlines through shared activities and extended geographical scope. Similarly the various marketing alliances of hotel consortia such as Best Western are examples of how independent owners of hotels can reap the marketing, branding, technology and training benefits of being part of a network of hotels.

Reputation

In service markets reputation is an extremely important contributor to consumer choice of product, but given the intangibility of the product, reputation is usually built up slowly and at some cost as consumers gain experience. Given the high value and public profile of travel products reputations can easily be damaged, for example through disaster. A coach or aeroplane crash, a ferry sinking or a hotel fire quickly erodes the reputation of the organization responsible. Though the reputation may have been built up carefully over several years it can take only a short time for the reputation to be severely damaged.

Strategic assets

The strength of market position or dominance of a market is often based upon the possession of strategic assets. They can be of three types. First, an organization may benefit from a monopoly position in a market; second, an organization may have already incurred the costs of supplying a market which inhibits the ability of new entrants to compete effectively; and third, some companies may benefit from the possession of licences or regulation that prevent competition.

For example – the dominant position of major international airlines at their 'hub' airports (such as Lufthansa at Frankfurt, United at Chicago and American Airlines at Dallas/Fort Worth) is often the result of costs expended and local regulatory regimes that have allocated take-off and landing slots to these airlines over the years.

Innovation

Through innovation, companies are often capable of providing a distinctive product and/or reducing costs. However, innovations can often be copied (particularly in service industries) and the additional returns are often not forthcoming for the innovative company.

For example – British Airways was the world's first airline to introduce flat beds for some of its business class passengers, but other airlines quickly followed its lead.

SHORT CASE ILLUSTRATION

Core competencies: British Airways

In the airline sector all airlines have the competencies and resources required to operate flights between certain destinations. A company like British Airways (Kay, 1995) possesses core competencies relating to its:

- dominance of take-off and landing slots at London's Heathrow Airport;
- licences it holds to operate certain routes to which access is denied for other airlines; and
- brand attributes which act as the basis of its reputation for high quality service.

These core competencies, although initially identified by the author in the early 1990s, are still valid in the contemporary market. However, it could be argued that the web of cooperative partnerships with other airlines through the 'One World' strategic alliance in allowing for greater destination choice and flexibility of arrangements provides a further area of core competence for the airline. Thus British Airways has core competencies (or distinctive capabilities in Kay's terminology) in terms of strategic assets (Heathrow slots and licences), its reputation (brand attributes) and architecture (strategic alliance).

The possession of these core competencies enable the airline to charge premium prices for its products by targeting business travellers in particular and by altering aircraft seat configurations to accommodate a greater proportion of business and first class passengers. The airline has maintained a strong competitive position on the key Trans-Atlantic routes (partly built on its dominance at its London hub), which enjoy a strong level of premium traffic.

In this way, core competencies are applied to the marketplace and in so doing form the basis of an organization's competitive advantage.

Questions

1. What threats might emerge to challenge British Airways' core competencies?

2. What steps might British Airways take to defend its core competencies?

Outcomes of the analyses

The aim of an analysis of resources, competencies and core competencies (distinctive capabilities) is, therefore, to:

- understand the nature and sources of particular core competencies;
- identify the need for and methods of adaptation of existing core competencies;
- identify the need for new core competence building;
- identify potential sources of core competence based on resources and competencies;
- ensure that core competencies remain focused on customer needs.

Resources, competencies and core competencies are obviously closely related to the ways that a business organizes and performs its value-adding activities. It is therefore also necessary to analyse the way in which value-adding activities are configured and co-ordinated.

Competence leveraging and competence building

Competence leveraging

Refers to the ability of a business to exploit its core competencies in new markets, thus meeting new customer needs. It can also refer to the ability of the business to modify and improve existing core competencies.

Competence building

Takes place when the business builds new core competencies, based upon its resources and competencies. It is often necessary to build new competencies alongside existing ones when entering new markets as it is unlikely that existing competencies will fully meet new customer needs.

From distinctive capability to competitive advantage

According to Kay (1995), distinctive capability (core competence) becomes a competitive advantage when it is applied in a relevant market.

Each distinctive capability will have a market (or group of markets) in which the organization can achieve a competitive advantage. Competitive advantage is a relative rather than absolute notion and can be viewed in several ways.

Organizations can enjoy a competitive advantage relative to:

- other suppliers in the same market;
- other firms in the same industry; or
- other competitors in the same strategic grouping.

In establishing competitive advantage therefore, it is imperative that activities are correctly matched up to the organization's capabilities. It is also important that organizations are able to fully understand the inherent differences between 'the market', 'the industry' and 'the strategic group':

- the *market* refers to the needs of customers and potential customers;
- the *industry* an organization is in refers to a group of products linked by common technology, supply or distribution channels;
- the *strategic group* refers to those organizations that are identified as primary competitors.

In a *THE* context, Kandampully and Duddy (2001) produce a conceptual model: the 'service system.' The model stresses the role of superior service levels in delivering competitive advantage. In particular the service strategies of employee empowerment, service guarantees and service recovery are emphasized in assisting hospitality and tourism firms in delivering superior service while, simultaneously, gaining a competitive advantage.

> ### KEY CONCEPT
>
> **Markets, industries and strategic groups**
>
> The market
>
> - defined by demand conditions
> - based on consumer needs
> - characterized by 'the law of one price'.
>
> The industry
>
> - determined by supply conditions
> - based on production or operations technology
> - defined by the markets chosen by organizations.
>
> The strategic group
>
> - defined by the strategic choices of firms
> - based on distinctive capabilities and market positioning
> - subjective in determination.
>
> During the 1980s Britain's largest brewer, Bass, viewed the market for beer as having unexciting growth prospects and redefined its core business as 'leisure'. Consequently the company bought Horizon Travel, a leading UK tour operator of the time. Bass was correct in its observation that pubs and holidays were alternative ways of spending leisure time and that they competed for the same share of consumer expenditure. However, the skills involved in brewing beer and managing an estate of public houses were quite different from those required to run a tour operator. As a result the tour operator was subsequently sold through a sale to the market leader, Thomson. Bass perhaps failed to fully appreciate that there is a leisure market but that there is not a leisure industry. They did not possess the necessary operating skills to supply the market effectively.
>
> *(Kay 1995)*

Analysis of value-adding activities

What is value adding?

Value chain analysis (Porter, 1985) seeks to provide an understanding of how much value an organization's activities add to its products and services compared to the costs of the resources used in their production. Although it has been applied widely in the manufacturing sector, several writers have applied the model successfully to a service setting. Poon (1993), for example, adapts the model to the travel and tourism industry. Fleisher and Bensoussan (2003) offer a useful resource in devoting a whole chapter of their book to an application and critique of value chain analysis.

A given product can be produced by organizing activities in a number of different ways. Value chain analysis helps managers to understand how effectively and efficiently the activities of their organization are configured and co-ordinated. The 'acid test' is how much value is added in the process of turning inputs into outputs, which are products in the form of goods and services. Value is measured in terms of the price that customers are willing to pay for the product.

Value added can be increased in two ways. It can be increased by:

1. changing customer perceptions of the product so that they are willing to pay a higher price than for similar products produced by other businesses; or

2. reducing operating costs below those of competitors.

KEY CONCEPT

Value added

In simple terms, the value added to a good or service is the difference in the financial value of the finished product compared to the financial value of the inputs. As a sheet of metal passes through the various stages in car production, value is added so that a tonne of metal worth a few hundred dollars becomes a motor car worth several thousand. The rate at which value is added is dependent upon how well the operations process is managed. If the car manufacturer suffers a cost disadvantage by, say, holding a high level of stock or working with out-of-date machinery, then the value added over the process will be lower.

Similarly a tour operator gathers together various inputs in terms of transportation, accommodation, on-site services and ground handling arrangements and 'packages' them together and in so doing adds value to the customer. Efficiencies in procurement, for instance, achieved through the use of buying in bulk can be passed on to the customer.

There are clear linkages between value-adding activities, core competencies, competencies and resources:

- resources form the inputs to the organization's value-adding activities;
- competencies and core competencies provide the skills and knowledge required to carry out the value-adding activities; and
- the more that core competencies can be integrated into value-adding activities, the greater the value added.

The value-adding process

Businesses can be regarded as systems which transform inputs (resources, materials, etc.) into outputs (goods and services). This is illustrated in Figure 3.3.

The activities inside the organization *add value* to the inputs. The value of the products or services is equivalent to the price that a customer is willing to pay for them. The difference between the end value (payable by the customer) and the total costs is the *margin* (the quantity that accountants would refer to as the *profit margin* – before interest, taxation and extraordinary items).

The rate at which value is added varies. If value is not being added as fast as it could be then *waste* is occurring and the organization in not operating as efficiently as it could be.

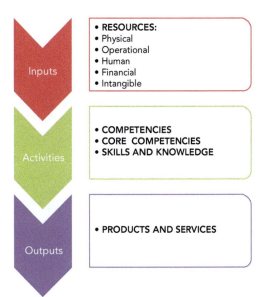

Figure 3.3 A simplified schematic of the value adding process.

For example – poor quality, low utilization, under occupancy and an under-skilled workforce are all examples of waste.

Increased added value can be achieved through reduction in costs or increasing the price that the customer is willing to pay for the output.

The value chain

Frameworks have increasingly been developed which purport to represent not merely a way of measuring the success of an organization but go further in that they offer managers a 'road map' by which they can manage (Evans, 2012:223). One of the most widely used approaches – 'value chain analysis' (Porter, 1985) – seeks to provide an understanding of how much value an organization's activities add to its products and services compared to the costs of the resources used in their production. In doing so it seeks to help managers to understand how effectively and efficiently the activities of their organization are configured and coordinated.

The activities of the organization can be broken down into a sequence of activities known as the value chain.

Although it has been applied widely in the manufacturing sector (and not so widely in a services context), several writers have discussed the model in *THE* settings, including Soteriades and Dimou (2011) in relation to the management of events and Poon (1993) who applied and adapted Porter's value chain to the tourism industry (see Figure 3.4).

The activities within the chain may be classified into *primary* activities and *support* activities.

- *Primary activities* are those which *directly add value* to the final product.
- *Support activities* do not directly add value themselves, but *indirectly add value* by supporting the effective execution of primary activities.

The nature of the primary activities and the way in which they can add value vary greatly between differing types of *THE* organization according to the organizational context. By contrast, the secondary activities are common in most organizational contexts.

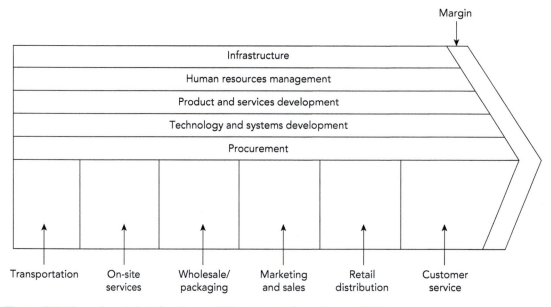

Figure 3.4 The value chain (after Poon, 1993, adapted from Porter, 1985)

Tables 3.2 and 3.3 describe the primary and secondary activities respectively relating to *THE* and how they might add value.

Table 3.2 Primary activities (adapted from Poon, 1993)

Activity	Description	Examples of how value might be added
Transportation services	Transportation to and from the destination or event, and at the destination or event	Information provision Scheduling Gate operations Ticketing Baggage handling Passenger management In-flight/on-board services Reservations Route and yield management Equipment age and specification Timekeeping
Services on site	Services delivered to visitors at their destination or event	Repair and maintenance of accommodation and facilities Age and specification of accommodation and facilities Quality of entertainment Added services provided e.g. valet parking, excursions Accommodation and venue locations Quality of company representatives
Wholesaling and packaging	Assembling or 'packaging' the product or service	Commission and fee negotiations Product development Pricing Assembling, integrating and coordinating ('packaging') aspects of the product
Retail distribution	Distributing the product to the market	Retail locations Choice of distribution channels Internet search optimization Commission levels Cost of sales Client database management Customer retention levels
Marketing and sales	Making the product available to the market and persuading people to buy.	Brochure production and distribution Advertising Public relations Sales-force management Managing customer loyalty programmes Point of sales materials Developing the value of the brand
Customer service	Installation and after sales support.	Customer complaint management Management and monitoring customer satisfaction Speed of responsiveness Client advice

Table 3.3 Secondary activities (adapted from Poon, 1993)

Activity	Description	Examples of how value might be added
Procurement	Purchasing, leasing or renting of services and equipment	Obtaining inputs at lower prices Better contract terms Obtaining bulk purchase discounts Working collaboratively with suppliers
Technology and systems development	Developing and implementing technology and systems in support of primary activities	Computer reservation systems Internet applications 'Real-time' sales reports Yield management applications Price discrimination between different customer segments
Products and services development	Developing new products, services and market opportunities	Developing new market segments Developing new products or enhancing existing products Developing new destinations, new venues, new accommodation etc. Developing partnerships and alliances with suppliers and/or distributors
Human resource management	Recruitment, selection, training, reward and motivation	Quality of employees and managers Employee *empowerment* Team working Level of training Outsourcing selected activities Replacing human resources with technology
Infrastructure	General management, financial control and accounting, planning, legal affairs, quality control	Speed and quality of decision making Costs of providing infrastructure Coherent and consistent standards Efficient organizational structure Communicating effectively with workforce

Analysis of the value chain

An organization's value chain links into the value chains of other organizations, particularly those of suppliers and distributors. This 'chain' of value chains is sometimes called the *value system* or *total supply chain*. Linkages with suppliers are known as *upstream* linkages while those with distributors and customers are *downstream* linkages.

Different types of organization will have very different value chains.

For example – the value chain of Thomas Cook plc (a vertically integrated UK-based tour operator), includes transportation of clients, and retail and internet distribution. In a smaller tour operator such as the independent UK tour operator Sunvil, however, the position is somewhat different. In the case of this company, which operates air holidays to Greece, Cyprus and other destinations, retail distribution and transportation are undertaken by other companies on a commercially agreed basis. Consequently these aspects do not form a part of the company's value chain but are important elements of the value system described above. Significantly though, internet distribution allows both the large and smaller companies described above to distribute directly to customers thereby forming part of both companies' value chain.

Similarly, not all of an organization's activities are of equal importance in adding value to its products. Those which are of greatest importance can be considered as *core activities* and are often closely associated with core competencies.

For example – in an upscale hotel, clients are willing to pay premium prices because the level, type and consistency of customer service are of a high standard. Thus this aspect may be of greatest importance in adding value and the organization's core competencies could be concentrated in this area. Conversely, in a budget chain of hotels (such as the Premier Inn chain in the UK or the Holiday Inn Express chain operating in many countries), offering value-for-money, consistent standards and many convenient locations are of greatest importance in delivering value.

A further point to stress is the importance of linkages between the component parts of the model. In some cases a key source of value-added activity might lay in the way in which organizations link different aspects, as opposed to the aspects on their own.

For example – for a tour operator, event manager or a hotel operator, it is important that demand and supply are closely co-ordinated so that excess capacity which cannot be sold is avoided and so that there is enough supply to meet customer demand. This involves close linkages and coordination between the transportation; wholesaling and packaging; retail distribution; and marketing and sales aspects.

Analysis of value-adding activities helps to identify where the most value is added and where there is potential to add greater value by changing the way in which activities are configured and by improving the way in which they are co-ordinated. It is important to note that an organization's value chain is not analysed in isolation but that it is considered in conjunction with its external linkages to suppliers, distributors and customers. Table 3.4 provides a classification of various internal and external linkages encountered.

A value chain analysis would be expected to include:

- a breakdown of all the activities of the organization;
- identification of core activities and their relationships to core competencies and current organizational strategies;
- identification of the effectiveness and efficiency of the individual activities;

Table 3.4 Classification of internal and external linkages

Internal linkages		External linkages	
Type of activity	Example	Type of activity	Example
Primary–primary	Interdepartmental co-ordination	Links with suppliers – backward linkages (upstream)	Tour operator linking with a hotel group
			Festival organizer linking with transport & accommodation providers
Primary–support	Computer-based sales management systems	Links with distributors – forward linkages (downstream)	Tour operator securing 'racking agreement' with a travel agency group for its brochures
			Hotel group working with destination management organizations
Support–support	Training for new technologies	Links with other companies at same stage of operations	Airlines collaborating in some of their activities through the formation of strategic alliances

- examination of *linkages* between activities for additional added value;
- identification of *blockages* which reduce the organization's competitive advantage.

A useful technique in value chain analysis involves comparison with the value chains of competitors to identify the benefits and drawbacks of alternative configurations.

The aim of value chain analysis is to identify ways in which the performance of the individual activities and the linkages between them can be improved. This may involve identification of improved configurations for activities or improved co-ordination of them. It is particularly important to consider the extent to which value chain activities support the current strategy of the organization.

For example – if the current strategy is based upon high quality then the activities must be configured so as to ensure high-quality products. On the other hand, if the organization competes largely on the basis of price, then activities must be organized so as to minimize costs.

Core activities, non-core activities and outsourcing

An increasing trend in recent years has been for organizations to concentrate on core activities associated with core competencies and to *outsource* activities which are not regarded as core to other organizations for which they are. Outsourcing (which is also discussed in Chapter 14 in the context of internationalization) refers to the practice of a firm entrusting to an external entity the performance of an activity that was performed erstwhile in-house (Varadarajan, 2009).

In recent years outsourcing has become a popular strategic option in parts of *THE*. It has become particularly prevalent amongst airline and hotel operators (see for example Espino-Rodríguez and Padrón-Robaina, 2005; Rieple and Helm, 2008; Gonzalez *et al.*, 2011) and in relation to outsourcing festivals and event management from the public to private or public–private partnerships, as discussed (see Getz, 2009).

For example – British Airways has outsourced some of its accounting and information technology functions to external suppliers and several airlines, such as American Airlines, United Airlines and Cathay Pacific, have sold what they regarded as non-core divisions such as their repair shops and now subcontract maintenance, in some cases to a joint venture. By contrast some airlines such as Delta and Lufthansa are increasingly building on their existing capabilities in the maintenance function and offering this facility to other carriers (Rieple and Helm, 2008).

It is also why local and central government agencies around the world are devolving responsibility. The responsibility for tourism; organizing festivals and events; and destination management and promotion are being devolved to private sector providers or to private/public partnerships run at 'arms-length' from their parent bodies.

SHORT CASE ILLUSTRATION

Outsourcing: The airline industry

Over the last 20–25 years, this sector has been characterized by poor financial performance and returns that would be, according to the UK's Civil Aviation Authority (2006), 'unsustainable' in most industries. Consequently airlines have been under enormous pressure to find ways of cutting costs and maximizing revenues to ensure survival.

One study of outsourcing in the industry, focused on major international, full-service, legacy (i.e. formed prior to the industry's deregulation that occurred throughout the 1980s) airlines that are broadly comparable in the customer segments they serve, as well as in their operational requirements.

The study focused on five aspects of activity (termed functions by the authors) that are commonly considered for outsourcing in the industry. The study found that, though examples of outsourcing activities in their entirety are rare (and there is differential practice between the airlines), examples of partial outsourcing were common in the sample investigated. The results are shown in the table below:

Table 3.5 Outsourcing: the airline industry

Airline function	Air France	British Airways	American Airlines	United Airlines	Cathay Pacific	Qantas	SAS
Plane acquisition and ownership	B	B	B	B	B	B	B
Engineering and aircraft maintenance	A	A	B	B	B	A	B
Customer sales and ticketing	B	B	B	B	B	B	B
In-flight catering	C	B	D	A	A	A	D
Corporate identity and brand management	B	B	B	B	B	B	B

A – Undertaken wholly in house or by wholly owned division or subsidiary

B – Partly undertaken in house or by wholly owned subsidiary, partly outsourced

C – Wholly outsourced to partly owned subsidiary or joint venture

D – Wholly outsourced to an external supplier.

Adapted from Rieple and Helm (2008)

Questions

1. What do you consider the motivations for outsourcing to be in the airline industry?
2. What factors might prevent outsourcing being developed more widely in *THE* contexts?

The combination of complementary core competencies adds to the competitive advantage of all the collaborating companies and organizations. Value chain analysis should therefore also seek to identify where outsourcing might potentially add greater value than performing the activity in-house.

THINK POINTS

- Explain the idea of the business as a value chain.
- Explain the relationships between primary and secondary activities.
- What is meant by blockages and linkages in the value chain?

- Explain with an example from *THE* what is meant by the value system.

- Provide an example of a core competence in a *THE* organization you are familiar with.

- Describe and distinguish between the two conceptual approaches to strategic management which have been introduced in this text.

The Service Profit Chain

During the 1990s an alternative framework was introduced by a team of researchers at Harvard University: *The Service Profit Chain* (Heskett *et al.*, 1994). Heskett and Sasser (2010) also assess the sources of profitability and growth in labour-dominated service firms. Such companies are defined as those service companies where labour is both an important component of total cost and capable of differentiating the firm's service from that of its competitors.

DEFINITION/QUOTATION

The Service Profit Chain

The Service Profit Chain hypothesize that:

> Profit (in a for-profit organization) or other measures of success (in a not-for-profit organization) results from customer loyalty generated by customer satisfaction, which is a function of value delivered to customers. Value for customers in turn results from employee loyalty and satisfaction, which is directly related to the internal quality (or value) created for employees.
>
> Heskett *et al.* (1994)

The purpose of the Service Profit Chain is to provide managers with a framework to help them manage such companies by enabling them to focus on (predominantly) quantifiable measures that lead to financial performance measures (Hallowell and Schlesinger, 2000) and as such is similar in its approach to the 'Balanced Scorecard' approach to strategy developed by Kaplan and Norton (1996). However, focusing as it does on the service delivery aspects of performance, the model is useful but does not represent a holistic approach to managing service-based organizations (Evans, 2012:224).

The Service Profit Chain (shown in Figure 3.5) emphasizes the following three factors as key drivers of profitability and revenue growth:

- the roles of employees internally to the organization;
- the way in which services are delivered; and
- the targeting of marketing to customers' needs.

Thus the ways in which the organization effectively utilizes its human resources and the ways in which it positions its products so that they appeal to particular target markets are two of the most important aspects of an organization's competitive strategy. A number of authors discuss the application of the Service Profit Chain in a *THE* context such as Bouranta *et al.* (2009) in relation to hotels and Abdullah *et al.* (2011) in relation to the Malaysian hospitality sector, while Dodds (2007), adopting a case study approach, relates how the concept has been applied to US low-cost airline Jet Blue.

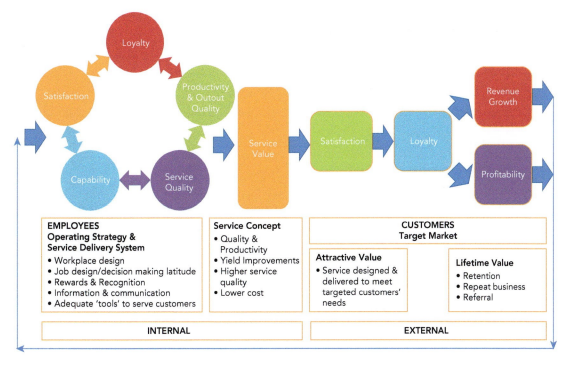

Figure 3.5 The service profit chain

The Profit Impact of Market Strategy (PIMS) study

The Profit Impact of Market Strategy (PIMS) study is a major, long-running study which was initiated in the 1970s by senior managers working at the American General Electric Company who wanted to know why some of their business units were more profitable than the others. The study which has been administered by the American Strategic Planning Institute since 1975 has developed into a major database which is founded upon examining thousands of companies in many industries.

One of the key findings in examining the data is that a primary determinant of profitability is market share (Moore, 1992) and the relationship is summarized and examined in detail by Uslay *et al.* (2010). The link which data appears to establish is certainly important in that several strategic management techniques which have been developed subsequently (such as the Boston Consultancy Group Matrix; see Chapter 6) apply the logic in their analyses.

However, other researchers have maintained that the relationship between profitability and market share has been exaggerated (Szymanski *et al.*, 1993) and have also questioned the findings in relation to service companies in particular, concluding that customer loyalty is a more important determinant of profit in these companies (Reicheld and Sasser, 1990). The Service Profit Chain builds on this doubt in service settings in that it establishes links between profitability, customer loyalty; and employees' satisfaction, loyalty and productivity. The links in the chain (Heskett *et al.*, 1994) are as follows:

- profit and growth are stimulated primarily by customer loyalty;
- customer loyalty is a direct result of customer satisfaction;
- customer satisfaction is largely influenced by the value of services provided to customers;
- value is created by satisfied, loyal and productive employees;

- employee satisfaction results primarily from high-quality support services and policies that enable employees to deliver results to customers.

Over the past two decades the theory and practice of service quality and value has received considerable attention from academics and practitioners alike (Hu *et al.*, 2009). Value has been defined according to the SERVQUAL framework developed by Zeithaml *et al.* (1990). Value is viewed as:

> *The perceived service quality received relative to the service quality delivered, all of which is relative to price.*

Service Dominant Logic

The implication of the work of Heskett *et al.* (1997), and the issues discussed in the previous chapters, is that that organizations providing services are 'different' from other organizations and that lessons derived mainly from studying manufacturing companies might have to be modified in a services setting.

The provision of services after all represent the dominant portion of most developed economies, but traditionally have received less academic attention than manufacturing. Perhaps this is partly due to the difficulties involved in identifying, measuring and assessing the provision of intangible products. The differences inherent in services apply to *THE* organizations as with others working in a services setting, and indeed as has been argued (in the previous chapter) that there are some characteristics which, if not unique, are certainly of particular relevance to *THE* organizations.

This perceived need to study services in a different way has found a strong voice since the early years of this century through the development of a strong strand of academic thought termed *Service Dominant Logic* and the developing field of *services science*.

The first article on what has become known as service dominant (S-D) logic appeared in 2004 (Vargo and Lusch, 2004) and has since been cited over 3,000 times. Many subsequent articles (by these authors and others) and conferences have followed, though few writers (with the exception of Li and Petrick, 2008; Shaw *et al.*, 2011; and FitzPatrick *et al.*, 2013) have hitherto applied the concept in a *THE* setting.

At the centre of Vargo and Lusch's proposition is a change of the dominant logic of marketing from exchanges of goods to service provision. Specifically, as Li and Petrick (2007) point out in relation to tourism, this new logic focuses on:

- intangible rather than tangible resources;
- co-creation of value rather than embedded value;
- relationships rather than transactions.

THINK POINTS

- Explain the concept of the *Service Profit Chain* and its relevance to *THE* organizations.
- Explain what is meant by *Service Dominant Logic*.
- Explain how *Service Dominant Logic* might be applied to *THE* contexts.

Vargo and Lusch argue that service marketing had been built on the same goods- and manufacturing-based model as the marketing of goods, and called this perspective 'goods dominant' (G-D) logic (Vargo and Lusch 2004). G-D logic suggests that the firm 'produces' value and that customers are exogenous to value creation (outside the process) and, as such, constitute *operand* resources i.e. resources on which an operation or act is performed to produce benefit for the producing firm. Operand resources can be contrasted with *operant* resources i.e. resources capable of causing benefit by directly acting on other resources, either operand or operant, to create benefit.

KEY CONCEPT

Service dominant logic

S-D logic is captured in ten foundational premises (Vargo and Lusch, 2008). The central tenet of S-D logic is that service is the fundamental basis of exchange. That is, service is exchanged for service. The essential elements of S-D logic thus begin with the definition of service: the process of using one's competencies (knowledge and skills) for the benefit of another party.

Perhaps the second most important tenet of S-D logic is found in its conceptualizations of value and value creation. In G-D logic, value is a property of goods, which are created by the firm and distributed to 'consumers' who destroy (consume) it. In S-D logic, the firm cannot create value but can only offer value propositions and then collaboratively create value with the beneficiary. Thus, the service provided (directly or through a good) is only input into the value-creating activities of the customer. Thus, value creation is always a collaborative and interactive process that takes place in the context of a unique set of multiple exchange relationships, somewhat tacitly and indirectly.

Vargo (2009)

SMALL BUSINESS FOCUS

Although large, powerful, diversified international organizations are emerging, in many countries *THE* is characterized by a large proportion of SMEs. In these organizations family and private ownership are common and market entry is encouraged by relatively low barriers to entry (Getz and Carlsen, 2000). However, SME providers have to cope with competitive disadvantages, which according to Zehrer (2009) include:

- poor economies of scale and scope;
- minimal potential for diversification and innovation;
- inadequate information about the market;
- limited access to capital markets;
- high debt to capital ratios.

Adding to this list in a *THE* context, Abou-Shouk *et al.* (2012) point out that SMEs, particularly in developing countries, are regarded as slow adopters of technology.

Notwithstanding the disadvantages identified, however, SMEs also possess certain potential advantages which can in certain circumstances be developed into core competencies and provide sources of competitive advantage. Clearly smaller organizations are likely to be able to react more quickly to market changes and offer services more flexibly than larger organizations which have to consider wider implications and for whom decision making is often more centralized and consequently slower.

SMEs can also compete on more favourable terms by collaborating with each other or with suppliers and distributors, through networking and formation of marketing alliances and joint ventures.

For example – in the UK over 150 smaller tour operators collaborate in joint marketing and distribution through the Association of Independent Tour Operators (AITO) in order to compete effectively with the large, internationally diversified tour operator companies such as Tui and Thomas Cook.

Independent hotel owners have also long worked collaboratively in consortia in order to compete effectively. A hotel consortium can be defined as 'a grouping of predominantly single, indepentently owned hotels that share corporate costs, such as marketing while retaining independence of ownership and operation' (Morrison and Harrison, 1998:351). Fyall and Garrod (2005), building on the work of Slattery *et al.* (1985), categorize five types of consortia ranging from involvement as part of a reservations system to full involvement with all marketing and purchasing aspects of the business.

Examples of hotel consortia include:

- *Best Western* – founded in 1946 in the USA and has over 4,000 member hotels in 80 countries, each one independently owned and managed.
- *Classic British Hotels* – represents over 80 Britsish independent hotels, largely in rural locations.
- *Irish Country Hotels* – was founded in 1984 and represents over 26 family-run hotels throughout Ireland.
- *Relais et Chateaux* – established in France in 1954, the consortium represents over 500 individually owned and operated luxury hotels and restaurants in about 60 countries.
- *Small Luxury Hotels of the World* – created in 1991 as the result of a merger between Prestige Hotels Europe and Small Luxury Hotels and Resorts of North America, the two groups combined in order to represent the collective interests of luxurious, independent hotels and resorts around the world. Currently the consortium has over 520 members in over 70 countries.
- *Your Hotel Worldwide* – established in Sweden in 1999 represents some 90 independently owned hotels around Europe.
- *HotelREZ* – established in 2004, is a global representation company providing hotel and internet distribution, revenue and marketing support to over 1,000 independent hotels and small groups of hotels.

The adoption of a so-called 'service orientation' by service businesses has become of increasing interest in recent years as a crucial factor in the enhancement of profit, growth, customer satisfaction, customer loyalty and employee satisfaction. In general terms, a 'service orientation' is an organizational predisposition that encourages a distinctive approach to all aspects of the consumer market (Zehrer, 2009). More specifically, Grönroos (1990:9) suggested six principles of services management, which can be said to represent an organizational commitment to what would now be called a 'service orientation'.

These principles include the notion that 'decision making has to be decentralized as close as possible to the interface between organization and customer'. Given their scale, SMEs should be in a more favoured position to expeditie decision making in a more customer-focused, responsive and flexible manner in comparison with larger competitors.

Internal analysis centres on the identification of the organization's potential for generating competitive advantage.

This chapter is concerned with the way in which *THE* organizations try to configure and coordinate their operational resources and processes in such a way that they add value and in so doing achieve an advantage over competitors – competitive advantage. It is very important in the strategy process for organizations to have a good understanding of the resources they have available to them and how these are used to create value. Some *THE* organizations are better at doing this than others by utilizing resources efficiently, achieving core competencies and applying them in markets to gain a competitive advantage.

This chapter has focused on the analysis of resources, competencies, core competencies the value chain and the Service Profit Chain. Core competencies and the configuration and co-ordination of value-adding activities have been identified as primary sources of competitive advantage. It is important to examine the links between current strategies, core competencies and core activities in the value chain as these are where the major potential for competitive advantage lies. Similarly it is important to examine other resources, competencies and activities to identify the potential for building new core competencies and core activities. The analysis also helps to identify opportunities for efficiency gains by re-configuring activities and by improving their integration so as to remove blockages from the system. This analysis allows a business to consider the potential of collaboration with suppliers, distributors and customers for improving performance.

The service profit chain provides a focus for analysis specifically for service-based organizations. This technique focuses particularly on the human aspects of service delivery and can be used together with value chain analysis or as an alternative. It is from all of this analysis that many of the elements of future strategy can be identified. In recent years the academic literature has focused on a new strand of thought – Service Dominant Logic – that attempts to distinguish between marketing and strategy in services as opposed to manufacturing.

REFERENCES

Abdullah, R. B., M. Musa, H. Zahari, R. Rahman and K. Khalid (2011) 'The Study of Employee Satisfaction and Its Effects towards Loyalty in Hotel Industry in Klang Valley, Malaysia', *International Journal of Business and Social Science*, 2 (3): 147–55.

Abou-Shouk, M., P. Megicks and W. M. Lim (2012) 'Perceived Benefits and e-Commerce Adoption by SME Travel Agents in Developing Countries: Evidence from Egypt', *Journal of Hospitality and Tourism Research*, 37 (4): 490–515.

Barney, J. B. (2002) *Gaining and Sustaining Competitive Advantage*, 2nd edn, Upper Saddle River, NJ: Prentice-Hall.

Bouranta, N., L. Chitiris and J. Paravantis (2009) 'The Relationship between Internal and External Service Quality', *International Journal of Contemporary Hospitality Management*, 21 (3): 275–93.

Bull, A. (1995) *Economics of Travel and Tourism*, 2nd edn, Melbourne: Longman Australia.

Buzzell, R. D. and T. G. Bradley (1992) 'Robert D. Buzzell and Bradley T. Gale' in J. I. Moore (ed.) *Writers on Strategy and Strategic Management*, London: Penguin, pp. 59–71.

Choi, G. and H. G. Parsa (2012) 'Role of Intangible Assets in Foreign-Market Entry-Mode Decisions: A Longitudinal Study of American Lodging Firms', *International Journal of Hospitality and Tourism Administration*, 13 (4): 281–312.

Denicolai, S., G. Cioccarelli and A. Zucchella (2010) 'Resource-Based Local Development and Networked Core-Competencies for Tourism Excellence', *Tourism Management*, 31 (2): 260–6.

Dodds, B. (2007) 'Jetblue Airways: Service Quality as a Competitive Advantage', *Journal of Business Case Studies (JBCS)* 3 (4): 33–44.

Dwyer, L. M., L. K. Cvelbar, D. J. Edwards and T. A. Mihali (2013) 'Tourism Firms' Strategic Flexibility: The Case of Slovenia', *International Journal of Tourism Research*, 16 (4): 377–87.

Espino-Rodríguez, T. F. and V. Padrón-Robaina (2005) 'A Resource-Based View of Outsourcing and Its Implications for Organizational Performance in the Hotel Sector', *Tourism Management*, 26 (5): 707–21.

Evans, N. (2012) 'Tourism: A Strategic Business Perspective', in T. Jamal and M. Robinson (eds.) *The Sage Handbook of Tourism Studies*, Thousand Oaks, Calif.: Sage, pp. 215–34.

Fernandez, E., J. M. Montes and C. J. Vasquez (2000) 'Typology and Strategic Analysis of Intangible Resources: A Resource Based Approach', *Technovation*, 20 (2): 81–92.

Fitzpatrick, M., J. Davey, L. Muller and H. Davey (2013) 'Value-Creating Assets in Tourism Management: Applying Marketing's Service-Dominant Logic in the Hotel Industry', *Tourism Management*, 36 (1): 86–98.

Fleisher, C. S. and B. E. Bensoussan (2003) *Strategic and Competitive Analysis: Methods and Techniques for Analyzing Business Competition*, Upper Saddle River, NJ: FT Press.

Fyall, A. and B. Garrod (2005) *Tourism Marketing: A Collaborative Approach*, Clevedon: Channel View Publications.

Galbreath, J. (2005) 'Which Resources Matter the Most to Firm Success? An Exploratory Study of Resource-Based Theory', *Technovation*, 25 (9): 979–87.

Getz, D. (2009) 'Policy for Sustainable and Responsible Festivals and Events: Institutionalization of a New Paradigm', *Journal of Policy Research in Tourism, Leisure and Events*, 1 (1): 61–78.

Getz, D. and J. Carlsen (2000) 'Characteristics and Goals of Family and Owner-Operated Businesses in the Rural Tourism and Hospitality Sectors', *Tourism Management*, 21 (6): 547–60.

Gonzalez, R., J. Llopis and J. Gasco (2011) 'What Do We Know about Outsourcing in Hotels?' *The Service Industries Journal*, 31 (10): 1669–82.

Grönroos, C. (1990) *Service Management and Marketing*, Lexington, Mass.: Lexington Books.

Hall, R. (1992) 'The Strategic Analysis of Intangible Resources', *Strategic Management Journal*, 13 (2): 135–44.

—— (2006) 'A Framework Linking Intangible Resources and Capabilities to Sustainable Competitive Advantage', *Strategic Management Journal*, 14 (8): 607–18.

Hallowell, R. and L. A. Schlesinger (2000) 'The Service Profit Chain, Intellectual Roots, Current Realities and Future Prospects', in T. A. Swartz and D. Iacobucci (eds.) *Handbook of Services Marketing and Management*, Thousand Oaks, Calif.: Sage, pp. 203–21.

Harrison, J. S. (2003) 'Strategic Analysis for the Hospitality Industry', *Cornell Hotel and Restaurant Administration Quarterly*, 44 (2): 139–52.

Heene, A. and R. Sanchez (1997) *Competence-Based Strategic Management*, London: John Wiley.

Heskett, J. L., T. O. Jones, G. W. Loveman, W. E. Sasser and L. A. Schlesinger (1994) 'Putting the Service Profit Chain to Work', *Harvard Business Review*, 72 (2): 164–70.

Heskett, J. L., W. E. Sasser and L. A. Schlesinger (1997) *The Service Profit Chain*, New York: Simon & Schuster.

Heskett, J. L. and W. E. Sasser (2010) 'The service profit chain: from satisfaction to ownership' in P. P. Maglio, C. A. Kieliszewski and J. C. Spohrer (eds.) *Handbook of Service Science: Research and Innovations in the Service Economy*, New York: Springer, pp. 19–29.

Hu, H. H., Kandampully, J. and Juwaheer, T. D. (2009) 'Relationships and Impacts of Service Quality, Perceived Value, Customer Satisfaction and Image: An Empirical Study', *The Service Industries Journal*, 29 (2): 111–25.

Javidan, M. (1998) 'Core Competence: What Does It Mean in Practice?' *Long Range Planning*, 31 (1): 60–71.

Kandampully, J. and R. Duddy (2001) 'Service System: A Strategic Approach to Gain a Competitive Advantage in the Hospitality and Tourism Industry', *International Journal of Hospitality and Tourism Administration*, 2 (1): 27–47.

Kaplan R. S. and D. P. Norton (2001) *The Strategy Focused Organization*, Boston, Mass.: Harvard Business School Press.

Kay, J. (1995) *Foundations of Corporate Success*, Oxford: Oxford University Press.

Li, X. R. and J. F. Petrick (2008) 'Tourism Marketing in an Era of Paradigm Shift', *Journal of Travel Research*, 46 (3): 235–44.

Morrison, A. J. and A. Harrison (1998) 'From Corner Shop to Electronic Shopping Mall?' *Progress in Tourism and Hospitality Research*, 4 (4): 349–56.

Peters, M., L. Siller and K. Matzler (2011) 'The Resource-Based and the Market-Based Approaches to Cultural Tourism in Alpine Destinations', *Journal of Sustainable Tourism*, 19 (7): 877–93.

Petts, N. (1997) 'Building Growth on Core Competencies: A Practical Approach', *Long Range Planning*, 30 (4): 551–61.

Poon, A. (1993) *Tourism, Technology and Competitive Strategy*, Wallingford: CAB International.

Porter, M. E. (1985) *Competitive Advantage*, New York: Free Press.

Prahalad, C. K. and G. Hamel (1990) 'The Core Competence of the Corporation', *Harvard Business Review*, 68 (3): 79–91.

Reichheld, F. E. and W. E. Sasser (1990) 'Zero Defections: Quality Comes to Services', *Harvard Business Review*, 68 (5): 105–11.

Rieple, A. and C. Helm (2008) 'Outsourcing for Competitive Advantage: An Examination of Seven Legacy Airlines', *Journal of Air Transport Management*, 14 (5): 280–5.

Shaw, G., A. Bailey and A. Williams (2011) 'Aspects of Service-Dominant Logic and Its Implications for Tourism Management: Examples from the Hotel Industry', *Tourism Management*, 32 (2): 207–14.

Slattery, P., A. Roper and A. Boer (1985) 'Hotel Consortia: Their Activities, Structure and Growth', *Service Industries Journal*, 5 (2): 192–9.

Soteriades, M. D. and I. Dimou (2011) 'Special Events: A Framework for Efficient Management', *Journal of Hospitality Marketing and Management*, 20 (3/4): 329–46.

Stalk, G., P. Evans and L. E. Shulmann (1992) 'Competing on Capabilities: The New Rules of Corporate Strategy', *Harvard Business Review*, 63 (March–April): 57–69.

Szymanski, D. M., S. G. Bharadwaj and P. Rajan Varadarajan (1993) 'An Analysis of the Market Share–Profitability Relationship', *Journal of Marketing*, 57 (July): 1–18.

UK Civil Aviation Authority (2006) *Ownership and Control Liberalization*, London: Civil Aviation Authority.

Uslay, C., Z. A. Altintig and R. D. Winsor (2010) 'An Empirical Examination of the "Rule of Three": Strategy Implications for Top Management, Marketers and Investors', *Journal of Marketing*, 74 (2): 20–39.

Varadarajan, R. (2009) 'Outsourcing: Think More Expansively', *Journal of Business Research*, 62 (11): 1165–72.

Vargo, S. L. (2009) 'Toward a Transcending Conceptualization of Relationship: A Service-Dominant Logic Perspective', *Journal of Business and Industrial Marketing*, 24 (5/6): 373–9.

Vargo, S. L. and R. F. Lusch (2004) 'Evolving to a New Dominant Logic for Marketing', *Journal of Marketing*, 68 (1): 1–17.

—— (2008) 'Service-Dominant Logic: Continuing the Evolution', *Journal of the Academy of Marketing Science*, 36 (1): 1–10.

Zehrer, A. (2009) 'Service Experience and Service Design: Concepts and Application in Tourism SMEs', *Managing Service Quality*, 19 (3): 332–49.

Zeithaml, V. A., A. Parasuraman and L. L. Berry (1990) *Delivering Quality Service: Balancing Customer Perceptions and Expectations*, New York: The Free Press.

WEBSITES

www.bestwestern.com
www.classicbritishhotels.com
www.hotelrez.net
www.irishcountryhotels.com
www.relaischateaux.com
www.slh.com
www.yourhotelsworldwide.net
www.sunderlandlive.co.uk
www.marriott.com

FURTHER READING

Reference	Focus
Aung, M. (2000) 'The Accor Multinational Hotel Chain in an Emerging Market: Through the Lens of the Core Competency Concept', *Service Industries Journal*, 20 (3): 43–60.	Core competency Hotels Accor Group
Connolly, P. and G. McGing (2007) 'High Performance Work Practices and Competitive Advantage in the Irish Hospitality Sector', *International Journal of Contemporary Hospitality Management*, 19 (3): 201–10.	Competitive advantage Hospitality Ireland
Dwyer, L. and C. Kim (2003) 'Destination Competitiveness: Determinants and Indicators', *Current Issues in Tourism*, 6 (5): 369–414.	Competitive advantage Tourism Destinations

Henderson, S. (2011) 'The Development of Competitive Advantage through Sustainable Event Management', *Worldwide Hospitality and Tourism Themes*, 3 (3): 245–57.	Competitive advantage Event management Sustainability
Kim, B. Y. and H. Oh (2004) 'How Do Hotel Firms Obtain a Competitive Advantage?' *International Journal of Contemporary Hospitality Management*, 16 (1): 65–71.	Competitive advantage Hotels
Kozak, M. and M. Rimmington (1999) 'Measuring Tourist Destination Competitiveness: Conceptual Considerations and Empirical Findings', *International Journal of Hospitality Management*, 18 (3): 273–83.	Competitive advantage Tourism Destinations
Lemmetyinen, A. and F. M. Go (2009) 'The Key Capabilities Required for Managing Tourism Business Networks', *Tourism Management*, 30 (1): 31–40.	Key apabilities Tourism Networks
Morrison, A. and R. Teixeira (2004) 'Small Business Performance: A Tourism Sector Focus', *Journal of Small Business and Enterprise Development*, 11 (2): 166–73.	Competitive advantage Tourism SMEs
Phillips, P. A. (1999) 'Hotel Performance and Competitive Advantage: A Contingency Approach', *International Journal of Contemporary Hospitality Management*, 11 (7): 359–65.	Competitive advantage Hotels Performance measurement
Weeden, C. (2002) 'Ethical Tourism: An Opportunity for Competitive Advantage?' *Journal of Vacation Marketing*, 8 (2): 141–53.	Competitive advantage Tourism Ethical tourism

CASE LINKAGES

Case 1	Strategic alliances in the airline industry
Case 2	Tourism Queensland
Case 3	Ryanair
Case 4	Hyatt Hotels
Case 5	Days Inn
Case 6	Reed Exhibitions

Chapter **4**

Tourism, hospitality and event organizations

The human resources context

Introduction and chapter overview

This chapter continues the internal analysis of organizations in examining one of the functional areas that organizations are often divided into – the human context. The subsequent chapters will examine the other functional areas, namely finance (Chapter 5) and marketing (Chapter 6)

Human resources are one of the key resource inputs to any organizational process. *THE* sectors are often said to be labour intensive (as opposed to capital intensive) in their orientation which places an even greater reliance on the management of human resources. A thorough analysis of this resource is an important part of strategic analysis and this chapter explains the resource audit – one of the most widely used tools for this purpose.

Closely linked to human resources is the issue of an organization's personality or culture. We define culture and then go on to explain its importance to an organization. The cultural web is discussed – a model used to explain the way that the features of culture determine the organization's paradigm. Finally, we discuss three cultural typologies which provide frameworks for analysing culture in organizations.

LEARNING OBJECTIVES

After studying this chapter, you should be able to:

- define and explain the importance of human resources to *THE* organizations;
- explain the employment and working conditions in *THE* organizations;
- explain the importance of the guest-employers encounter to *THE* organizations;

- explain the linkages between service quality and human resources;
- explain the purpose of a human resource audit;
- describe what a human resource gap is;
- explain what a human resource audit contains and what it can be used for;
- describe human resource benchmarking;
- explain what a critical success factor (CSF) is and how human resources can be CSFs;
- define culture, explain its determinants and why it is important;
- explain the components of the cultural web and the nature of paradigms; and
- describe and apply three typologies of cultural types.

Human resources

The importance of human resources in tourism, hospitality and events

The sectors of *THE* are labour-intensive service sectors in which the human factor is often the key differentiator between different competing organizations (Evans, 2012:224). Employees (or groups of employees) are often critical to an organization's strategic success and thus represent what is often referred to in the literature as a 'critical success factor' (CSF).

People are an important resource to most organizations, but in service-based organizations in particular it is often the human resources, i.e. people, that represent the key factor in delivering successful performance. As Richard Lynch puts it, 'There are some industries where people are not just important but they are the *key factor* for successful performance as, for example, in leisure and tourism, where a company has a direct, intangible interface that relies on individual employees to give interest and enjoyment to customers' (Lynch, 2003:254). Few people would reject the proposition that the human element in *THE* organizations is critical for service quality, customer satisfaction and loyalty, competitive advantage and organizational performance (Kusluvan *et al.*, 2010).

Similarly, Baum (1997) considers the experience of the guest or consumer within the tourism industry to be both highly intense and intimate in a way rarely replicated in other service industries. Furthermore, their interactive experience is commonly with front-line staff who generally are those who have the lowest status, are the least highly trained and are the poorest paid employees.

Thus the consideration of human resource issues is vital to the successful implementation of strategy in most organizations operating in *THE* contexts. As with the other functional areas of organizations we consider in subsequent chapters (finance and marketing), we are most interested in the *key* areas of human resource management in that they have an impact on the successful formulation and implementation of strategy. In studying strategy we are less interested in all the myriad detailed human resource issues that may occur in any organization. These issues are covered in detail elsewhere, see, for example, Mullins and Dossor (2013).

Strategy has to take a holistic view of an organization covering key aspects of activity. Sometimes modules covering strategic management in universities are referred to as 'capstone' modules recognizing that the modules draw together detailed study of individual functional areas in a holistic manner. In studying strategy we are not only concerned with studying the key issues of the functional areas themselves, but also the interaction between them. In some situations it is the interaction between the functions which gives the organization a core competence or conversely makes the organization less competitive rather than the way in which the functional area itself is managed.

Given the labour intensity of most *THE* organizations and the centrality of human resources to commercial success it is unsurprising that issues related to this field have received a considerable degree of academic attention in *THE* literature in recent years. In the context of tourism and hospitality the extensive literature (see, for example, Kusluvan *et al.*, 2010) relating to the management of human resource issues is very much interwoven with hospitality, often viewed as a constituent component of tourism (or vice versa). Both sectors often share similar characteristics when employing staff and many of these characteristics are shared by the events sector. These issues are considered in the next section.

The events sector, though sharing many characteristics with tourism and hospitality, is also often distinctive in certain ways:

- *Work is usually geared towards a particular point in time* when the events are taking place (or the event may be repeated at regular or irregular intervals). This facet of events often gives rise to job insecurity, high recruitment costs and relatively poor working conditions as pressure builds before and during the event. However, as Bowdin *et al.* (2012: Ch. 10) point out, if an event seeks to grow in size and attendance each time it is repeated, a human resource strategy (as part of an overall strategy) becomes essential in order to support increased staff recruitment and to support additional and probably more sophisticated training.

- *Volunteers often form an important part of the workforce* and indeed many events, such as the 2012 London Olympic Games, would not be feasible without the involvement of a large-scale volunteer workforce. Recruiting, managing, motivating and controlling such a workforce presents certain challenges when the normal authority engendered by the employee–employer relationship underpinned by payments and contracts does not exist (see for example Smith and Holmes, 2012).

- *Staff numbers have often had to quickly expand and then contract*. Hanlon and Jago (2004) developed the concept of the 'pulsating' organization to describe many organizations in the events sector. Many such organizations have to grow quickly as the event approaches, take on additional staff for the event itself and then quickly contract when the event finishes.

The factors outlined above give rise to specific challenges for managers in the events sector (Bowdin *et al.*, 2012:324). These challenges might include:

- obtaining paid staff of the right calibre given the short-term nature of the employment offered;
- working to short timescales to hire and select staff, and to implement effective staff training;
- shedding staff after the event quickly.

If volunteers are part of the workforce, specific challenges include sourcing sufficient volunteers; quality control; asserting management control; integration and cooperation with paid employees; motivation and training.

The Australian Open Championships provide an illustration of some of the human resource challenges encountered in managing an annual sporting event.

SHORT CASE ILLUSTRATION

A 'pulsating' organization: the Australian Open Tennis Championships

The Australian Open Tennis Championships, together with the French and US Open and Wimbledon (UK), represents one of the four major titles on the world professional tennis circuit – the so-called 'grand slams'. The event held in Melbourne in January each year provides an illustration of a 'pulsating' organization, a concept developed by Hanlon and Jago (2004) and subsequently adopted by other authors in the field.

Deery (2009) described the 2008 event which employed some 4,500 staff including: 319 ball kids; 365 umpires; 195 courtesy car drivers; and 45 statisticians. Most of these staff are, however only needed during the two week event itself. Many of the staff work at the championships year after year, but others have to be recruited annually with the recruiting process for the next event commencing shortly after the conclusion of the current year's. Many volunteers as well as paid staff are employed and rewards include access to available seats, free meals, uniforms and some free transport.

www.ausopen.com

Questions

1. Why might The Australian Open be described as a 'pulsating' organization?

2. What would you consider the human resource challenges for managers might be in this case?

The general literature relating to human resources in *THE* contexts is supplemented by numerous studies considering *THE* human resource issues, in particular geographical settings. According to Zhang and Wu (2004), for example, there are many human resource challenges facing China's hotel and tourism industry. They argue that the key issues in this context are: the lack of qualified staff at both operational and managerial levels; high staff turnover rates; the unwillingness of university graduates to enter the industry; and the gap between what is taught in schools and colleges and the realities of the industry itself.

Employment and working conditions in tourism, hospitality and events

THE represents a sizable proportion of worldwide employment and though comparisons are difficult, it is likely that these sectors employ more than the automotive industry but slightly less than education, and employment opportunities are continuing to increase.

The World Travel and Tourism Council (WTTC, 2012) estimates that when the wider impacts of the industry are taken into account, in terms of the supply chain, investment and consumer spending, travel and tourism is estimated to support almost 255 million jobs – about one in every 12. Remarkably, 48 per cent of worldwide travel and tourism jobs during 2011 were directly supported in India and China. The much higher share of global travel and tourism employment relative to GDP, for the two countries, is explained by their size and their lower-than-global-average industry productivity.

It is not only the size of the workforce that is distinctive but also its composition. The human resources which make up the workforce in *THE* sectors are often characterized by:

- a large proportion of female employees;
- a large proportion of young employees;
- a large number of part-time and seasonal workers;
- high staff turnover rates;
- recruitment difficulties;
- poor levels of training;
- relatively low pay;
- mobility of labour between different employers and geographically;
- working patterns involving work at nights and weekends;
- importance of volunteer workforce, particularly for large events.

By way of illustration, Figure 4.1 provides a comparison of the factors affecting the supply and demand for labour in ten countries of the Asia-Pacific region from data derived from a United Nations World Tourism Organization (UNWTO) conference. The countries concerned are at various stages in their economic development, are subject to different political systems and have differences in their tourism and hospitality infrastructures. Nevertheless, some of the characteristics (such as high turnover and poor training) of the workforce in *THE* identified in Table 4.1 clearly emerge as common themes in this sample of countries.

Table 4.1 Factors affecting demand and supply of labour in tourism and hospitality in ten Asia/Pacific countries (adapted from Ruhanen and Cooper, 2009)

Country	Factors affecting labour supply and demand
Australia	Lower salary levels than other industries Quality education and training in place Negative perceptions of working conditions and career progression Low unemployment rate leads to competition for labour Strict immigrant rules restricting inflow of labour High degree of labour mobility Tensions between expectations of older and younger workers A lack of planned management of human resources in SMEs
China	Lower salary levels than other industries Negative perceptions of working in tourism and hospitality Need further development of skills and capabilities to meet demand for managers Improved opportunities needed for students to gain skills Need improved human resource strategies in the industry
India	Demand for skilled labour cannot be met through current supply Additional training and education institutes are necessary Insufficient educators available with necessary skills and experience Low inter-regional mobility among the population limiting supply in some regions Proficient in English but lack language skills for emerging Chinese market
Indonesia	Fluctuating tourism demand impacting stability of labour market Low wages and unfavourable working conditions in some parts of the industry Need standardization and more training capacity to meet demand for skilled workers
Iran	Improvements needed to training and education especially at management levels Image of service based positions not favourable High rate of female participation requiring a focus on HR policies and practices Require focus on developing career opportunities to reduce high labour turnover
Japan	Actual and perceived reputation of industry providing low wages High labour turnover and increased temporary positions particularly amongst women Shortages of skilled labour particularly those with appropriate language skills Further development of training and educations system required to meet skill shortages
Malaysia	Low and un-standardized wage rates Tendency to recruit migrant labour to fill senior positions High mobility of skilled labour with English proficiency Difficult to recruit and retain employees in accommodation and food and beverage
Republic of Korea	Lower salary levels than other industries Perceived lack of career paths particularly for those at lower levels Increased tendency to employ temporary employees Cannot meet demand for staff with English, Japanese and Chinese language proficiency Lack of continual training and education for employees Significant proportion of relevant graduates not entering the industry Strict national regulations restricting inflow of migrant labour

Table 4.1 continued

Country	Factors affecting labour supply and demand
Sri Lanka	Exodus of skilled labour (to Middle East and Maldives) leading to high turnover rates Lack of higher education and training institutes to meet demand for skilled labour Perceived lack of career opportunities and reluctance by young people to enter the industry Low wages and unfavourable working conditions Reluctance of SMEs to invest in education and training for employees
Thailand	Negative perceptions of industry in terms of low wages and career paths Lack of standardized curriculum in education and training institutes Business owners and managers need to acquire more skills in human resource management

Each of the human resource characteristics identified can raise challenges for managers working in *THE*. The relatively high levels of staff turnover in many cases can be particularly problematic because it can lead to higher costs relating to additional recruitment activities, wasted training and development and difficulties in maintaining quality standards.

A number of studies have reported on the high employee turnover rates in parts of the industry and discuss strategies for retaining and motivating employees.

For example – Chalkiti and Sigala (2010) report on employee turnover rates and suggest strategies such as *job rotation* for retaining staff in Greece. One study in the United States (Woods *et al*., 1998) found that annual staff turnover in the hotel sector was running at 51.7 per cent for 'front-line' employees (although the figures were somewhat lower for supervisory and managerial staff).

As a result of the high staff turnover rates encountered many *THE* employers go to great lengths to recruit the right calibre of staff and to retain and motivate them once they have been recruited.

The case of Starwood Hotels provides an illustration of the importance one major *THE* employer attaches to selection, recruitment and retention of staff.

SHORT CASE ILLUSTRATION

Employee recruitment: Starwood Hotels

America-based Starwood Hotels brings together some well-known international hospitality brands such as Sheraton, Le Meridien, Westin and Four Points.

Notwithstanding the sales oriented language, designed to attract potential recruits, the following statements adapted from Starwood clearly illustrates the importance this hotel and resorts group attaches to selecting, recruiting and motivating its associates (employees). Similar statements are to be found on many of the websites of leading international hospitality brands.

- *Core Belief:* people want a better way to experience the world extends not only to Starwood's guests and customers, but to also to the global team of associates.
- *Unparalleled Experience:* The exceptional service and personal touches that they give Starwood's guests demonstrate commitment to turning everyday moments into memorable branded experiences.

For Starwood to deliver to this high standard of excellence, it must provide an unparalleled experience for its associates. These are the people who live the brands every day and devote their energy to bringing them to life for guests.

Starwood goes on to state that it is committed to building a workforce that is the envy of the industry, a trusted resource to its guests and a driver of exceptional business results. Starwood states that it focuses its leading edge recruiting efforts on the best and the brightest. It is not only working to win the war for talent in a new age of guest expectation – it is defining it.

- *World-Class Training and Development Starwood* states that it strives to challenge itsr associates to grow through world-class training and development programmes, which support their differences across generations, cultures and geographies. As a truly global enterprise, operating more than 1,134 hotels and resorts in 100 countries, Starwood claims to embrace the fact that it is a diverse business and uses that energy and creativity to power the business, care for communities and work toward environmental sustainability. Strawood focuses on the environment and its communities and leverages its people, brands, relationships and global reach; because it argues that it is uniquely equipped to help associates and guests create a better world to experience.

- *Reach Your True Potential:* Starwood claims to understand that great ideas can come from anywhere at any time. Therefore, it insists on open dialogue and sharing as it continues to build for the future of the industry. From leadership discussions to engagement surveys to all manner of live events, it claims to be a company that goes beyond the expected to make certain that its associates reach their true potential.

Adapted from www.starwoodhotels.com

Questions

1. Why does Starwood give so much attention to employee recruitment?
2. Consider the difficulties involved in managing staff at chains of hotels such as those managed by Starwood brands.

As a counter-balance to some of the perceived negative aspects of the industry sectors, it can be argued that it is often viewed as an attractive industry in which to work. Indeed, travelling and working in tourism, hospitality and events are often linked. Staff often have access to concessionary travel and accommodation rates, opportunities are presented to attend events, for meeting people and seeing something of the world, and many employees are situated in attractive surroundings.

For many young people in particular, in various places globally, being able to travel and undertake tourism and hospitality work become intertwined (Duncan *et al.*, 2013). In some cases the attraction of the work is such that parts of the workforce can be volunteers accepting no payment for their work (Smith and Holmes, 2012).

In such circumstances the challenge for managers is to recruit and retain talented staff, take actions to motivate employees and try to ensure an appropriate work–life balance is maintained (Deery, 2008). In order to be successful in these actions, employers may offer more training opportunities, career progression opportunities, travel incentives, and higher levels of pay and bonuses. Critically though, employers need to pay attention to the design of jobs and roles through measures such as:

- *Job enlargement* – by which employees' jobs are made more worthwhile and interesting in that they are given a wider variety of tasks to carry out.

- *Job rotation* – by which employees rotate jobs between them so that teamwork is encouraged, knowledge and skills are gained, and everyone has to take a share of less popular tasks.
- *Job enrichment* – by which employees are given a greater deal of discretion or *empowerment* to make decisions.
- *Job sharing* – by which employees' jobs are shared between two or more employees thereby sharing burdens and responsibilities and providing cover for staff leave or sickness absences.

In service industries such as *THE*, managers are often working in relative isolation and many organizations or business units are relatively small. Thus managers often have to work in diverse locations which are away from the central organizational support services such as sales and marketing, customer services, etc. (or organizations are too small to have such support services). It may also be the case that managers have to work shift patterns which means organizational support is unavailable when called upon. However, managers can be called upon to take decisions as a result of operational difficulties or customer pressure.

THINK POINTS

- Explain why human resources are so important to operating successful *THE* organizations.
- Identify the key differentiating characteristics of working in many *THE* organizations.
- Assess how managers in *THE* might address problems of high staff turnover rates.

Thus empowerment of managers (and indeed all employees) to take decisions is often a vital issue for many *THE* organizations and it has consequently received quite a lot of attention in the academic literature, particularly in relation to hospitality employers. Though they stress the importance of empowerment, Ro and Chen (2011) argue that it needs to be supported by hiring customer-oriented people, guiding them with service training, providing a valid reward system and facilitating communication of service standards in order to increase perceived empowerment.

Managers and employers in many *THE* settings have to work remotely or at hours when support is unavailable. In such circumstances many *THE* employers stress the importance of empowering their employees so that they can take decisions and resolve issues as they occur. Such empowerment is illustrated by the case of Ritz Carlton hotels.

SHORT CASE ILLUSTRATION

Empowerment: Ritz-Carlton Hotels

Employee empowerment can be described as enabling or authorizing employees to make decisions to solve customer issues by themselves.

It is particularly advocated in services because of their heterogeneity. Employees in their contact with customers need to adapt their behaviours to the demands of each and every service encounter (Ueno, 2008) in order to ensure consistent levels of service delivery are maintained. Ro and Chen (2011) emphasize the importance of careful recruitment to successful empowerment of employees in that efforts must be made to select 'empowerable' employees who can be inculcated with the skills and attitudes conducive to exercising an acceptable and responsible decision making.

A few companies have embraced the concept of employee empowerment in their service delivery. The Ritz-Carlton hotel chain (a subsidiary of Marriott) is an upscale international chain with 82 hotels in 27 countries. The company's 'Gold Standards' of service encapsulate the values and philosophy of the company. Among the 12 service values for staff are the statements 'I am empowered to create unique, memorable and personal experiences for our guests' and 'I own and immediately resolve guest problems'. In making these bold statements meaningful, employees are empowered to spend up to $2,000 a day per guest not just in resolving guest problems but to 'wow' them with 'legendary service'.

Adapted from www.corporate.ritzcarlton.com

Questions

1. What managerial difficulties is the Ritz-Carlton chain attempting to overcome through employee empowerment?
2. Consider the benefits and potential drawbacks of empowerment in this case.

The management of the guest–employee encounter

The management of the guest/customer–employee encounter remains one of the most difficult but ultimately most important tasks for *THE* managers (Baum, 1997). In fast-moving markets, especially in service industries which are relatively 'labour intensive', it may be

- the ability and knowledge of people;
- the ability of people to learn;
- the ability of people to adapt to change.

in delivering the services that are the true source of sustainable competitive advantage (discussed in the previous chapter).

Writers on service quality have suggested that the proof of service quality is in its flawless performance (Berry and Parasuraman, 1991; Augustyn and Ho, 1998), a concept similar to the notion of 'zero defects' which is often discussed in a manufacturing context. From the customer's point of view, the most immediate evidence of service quality occurs in the service encounter or 'the moment of truth' when the customer interacts with the organization (Bitner *et al.*, 1994).

The derivation of the term 'moment of truth' is often attributed to Jan Carlzon (1987), a past President of Scandinavian Airline Systems (SAS), when he used the terminology to describe every point of contact that a customer, or potential customer, has with the organization in question.

As Baum (1995) and Ryan (1996) have argued, the tourism industry (though it also applies in many cases to hospitality and events) presents particular challenges in the management of 'moments of truth' because of the fragmentation of the experience for many customers. For example, the purchase of a typical 'package' holiday or a concert ticket may involve contact with a wide range of intermediaries, as indicated in Table 4.2.

The concept of the 'moment of truth' as a manifestation of the guest/customer–employee encounter clearly has applicability throughout the three parts (traveller generator region, transit route region and tourist destination region) of what Leiper (1990) has called 'the tourism system'.

Baum (1997) building on Leiper's representation (Leiper, 1990) has produced a model of 'moments of truth' in relation to the wide range of organizations that go to make up the tourism system. The model presented as Figure 4.1 recognises that 'moments of truth' need not carry equal weighting i.e. that some will be more important to customers than others: 'so that as far as the guest is concerned . . . a positive

Table 4.2 Comparison of possible intermediaries encountered in purchasing a typical package holiday or a concert ticket

Package tour purchase: possible intermediaries	Concert ticket purchase: possible intermediaries
Retail travel agent or internet intermediary	Ticket agent, concert promoter or internet intermediary
Insurance companies	Transport to and from the venue
Ground transport to and from the airport	Catering staff at the venue or providers in the locality
Airport handling agents (at outbound and inbound airports);	Sellers of merchandise associated with the concert
Immigration and customs services	Promoters of other concerts and events which may be of interest
Local ground transportation	The hotel or other overnight accommodation (if required).
Hotel or other accommodation	Artists and performers at the concert
Tour services at the destination	Emergency and first-aid services at the venue
Companies selling goods and services at the destination	
Emergency services at the destination	
Service providers such as restaurants, entertainment venues, attractions, festival and event organisers	

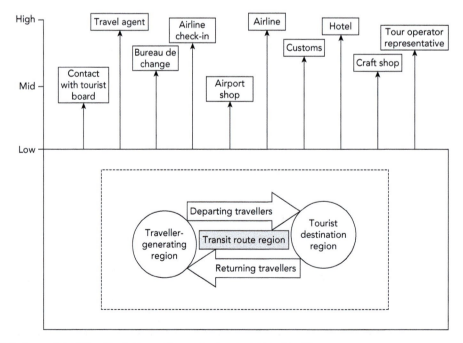

Figure 4.1 A model of the tourist experience and moments of truth

or negative experience in one area may elicit a very different response to a similar experience elsewhere in the guest cycle' (Baum, 1997).

The model provides through its vertical axis a measure (albeit rather crude and subjective) of the intensity and therefore the importance of the interaction to customers. In so doing the model allows tourism managers who are responsible for the tourists' experience to attempt to predict those areas of greatest potential impact and consequently to recognize those areas on which resources might be focused.

Human resources and service quality

Service quality can be viewed as an important strategy for gaining a competitive advantage in firms as many authors including Baum (1997) and Crick and Spencer (2011) have argued. Service quality in *THE* is to a large degree determined by the quality and attitude of owners, managers and employees – the human resources – as a service industry quality in *THE* sectors depends on a range of human skills adopted during the service encounter. As we have seen, the recognition of the centrality of human resources to the successful delivery of service quality has led to the adoption of concepts such as managing 'moments of truth' (Carlzon, 1987) and also to what Albrecht (1992) has described as a 'spirit of service'.

In essence, human resources 'contribute to sustained competitive advantage through facilitating the development of competencies that are firm specific' (Lado and Wilson, 1994). This link between the development of sustained competitive advantage and the quality of an organization's human resources is illustrated by Kusluvan *et al.* (2010):

- services are intangible;
- they are produced and consumed simultaneously, usually at the service providers' location;
- customers are present or participating in the service, usually with interpersonal interaction between customers and service providers.

Owing to these features, services are made tangible in the personality, appearance, attitudes and behaviour of the service provider; thus, employees become part of the product, represent the organization, and help to form the image of the organization (Kandampully, 1997; Swanson and Hsu, 2009). In providing service quality there are important cross-cultural dimensions in achieving customer satisfaction that need to be considered (Weiermair, 2000).

It should be recognised that in many *THE* settings delivering the service involves customers and employees who are diverse in their backgrounds, expectations, religion and cultural norms in different parts of the world. Consequently the way in which services are delivered has to reflect and respect these differences and be adjusted accordingly.

Figure 4.2 illustrates the way in which a 'virtuous circle' may be formed in service organizations such as those operating in *THE*:

1. People who are carefully selected, well trained and highly motivated are more likely to deliver services of high quality.
2. Since the quality of services offered is high they are likely to be valued by customers leading to customer satisfaction and loyalty.
3. This leads to the creation of a competitive advantage since a competence (delivery of high quality services) has been successfully delivered to customers (in a market).
4. Gaining advantage over competitors leads to high level of organizational performance and business success.
5. The success of the business allows for additional resources to be deployed in rewarding existing people and recruiting additional people of a high calibre who are attracted by the success of the organization.

Figure 4.2 'The virtuous circle' linking human resources with business success

The most widely used model to translate theories of customer satisfaction into management practice is that of SERVQUAL (Soutar, 2001:103), The SERVQUAL model of service quality was developed in the mid-1980s by Zeithaml, Parasuraman and Berry defines service quality in terms of the difference (the 'gap') between customer expectations and customer perception of service received.

Although it has been challenged on a number of grounds (see for example Bennington and Cumane, 1998) and other models have been developed (such as those associated with Grönroos (1984) and the FESTPERF model developed by Tkaczynski and Stokes (2010) in relation to festivals and events), the SERVQUAL model remains important, and indeed, one leading writer (Mill, 2011) maintains that 'the SERVQUAL model presents *the best* mechanism to explain customer satisfaction in hospitality and tourism'.

The 'gap' in service quality occurs when the perception of service received is less than what is expected (Zeithaml *et al.*, 1990).

According to Zeithaml *et al.* (1990) there are five dimensions of service which can usefully be remembered through the acronym '*RATER*':

- Responsiveness: Willingness to help customers and provide prompt service, e.g. problem solving by hotel reception staff, advice offered by call centres.
- Assurance: Knowledge and courtesy of employees and their ability to convey trust and confidence, e.g. level of training for flight attendants, providing itemized bills for services delivered.
- Tangibles: Appearance of physical facilities, equipment, personnel, and communication materials, e.g. comfort of the hotel room, facilities at the concert venue, aeroplane passenger features.
- Empathy: Caring, individualized attention the company provides its customers, e.g. treating each customer at a restaurant individually according to their needs.
- Reliability: Ability to perform the promised service dependably and accurately e.g. trains' arrival times, accuracy of bills, conference running according to schedule.

The gap between what customers expect and what they perceive they get is for one or more of the following reasons (Zeithaml *et al.* 1990):

- Gap 1: Management does not know what guests expect.
- Gap 2: Management is not willing or able to put the systems in place to match or exceed customer expectations – service–quality standards are not developed.
- Gap 3: The service–performance gap – when employees are unable and/or unwilling to perform the service at the desired level.
- Gap 4: When promises do not match delivery.

The management task in responding to these perceived gaps is to identify effective strategic options for closing the gaps. Mill (2011) suggests that a sequential five-step approach should be adopted which address the four gaps:

1. Identify whether or not a problem exists.
2. Manage customer expectations so they are realistic with the service offering. (Gap 4)
3. Identify customer needs and expectations of quality service. (Gap 1)
4. Develop service quality standards based on customer expectations. (Gap 2)
5. Re-evaluate the human resource system to hire, train and motivate employees who are willing and able to deliver quality service. (Gap 3)

THINK POINTS

- Explain the link between human rersources and the quality of service delivery in *THE* contexts.
- According to Zeithaml *et al.* what are the five dimensions of service quality and how might they be applied to *THE* organizations?
- Explain what is meant by 'moments of truth' and why are they crucially important in *THE* contexts.

A key tool in identifying where gaps exist is the human resource audit which is discussed in the following section.

The human resource audit

The purpose of HR audit

Decisions about the future strategy of the organization are made by people and strategies are implemented by people. The success or failure of a current strategy will depend not only on decisions made in the past but also on how those decisions are being implemented now by people employed by the organization. It is therefore important to ask questions about who, how and why people are doing what they are doing and what they should do in strategic implementation. In short, human resources add value, manage the business and, conversely, can make spectacular errors that can be very costly to the organization.

An understanding of the capabilities of individuals and groups in terms of attitudes, abilities and skills, as well as an understanding of how individuals relate one to another, is an important part in the preparation and development of strategy. A key 'tool' in gaining an understanding of an organization's human resources is the human resource audit.

The human resource audit is an investigation into the size, skills, structure and all other issues surrounding those currently employed by the organization. The audit reviews the ability of the human resources to implement a chosen strategy or a range of strategic options.

Most organizations employ accountants to maintain a constant review of financial resources and each year limited companies subject themselves (by law) to a formal external financial audit. Human resources are another resource input and are equally important, and although they are not subject to legal verification, an organization would be foolish to pursue a strategy without a thorough review of its human resources: its people.

Once the audit has been completed, management should be able to answer the key question: Are the human resources in the organization capable of implementing the proposed strategy? If any gaps are identified, then a human resource strategy may be put in place to close the gap.

Human resource gaps

A 'gap' can occur in any area of human resource management. It rests upon a simple calculation.

Human resource characteristic necessary for the proposed strategy

Minus

Current state of the human resource characteristic

Equals

The human resource gap.

Gaps can occur in particular skills. In sectors like tourism, for example, skills gaps may be identified in particular areas such as those with knowledge and experience of computer reservation systems. It may be that the audit reveals a deficit of 30 people who can operate such systems – a negative gap. The task of the human resource department thus becomes to successfully appoint or retrain to gain the requisite number of skilled operators.

Positive gaps may also be identified – surpluses of a particular type of employee. The human resource strategy thus has to put measures in place to 'dispose' of the excess labour.

Gaps may be closed by using the 'five Rs' individually or in combination. The five Rs are:

- retirement;
- retraining;
- redeployment;
- redundancy; or
- recruitment.

The contents of a human resource audit

The contents of a human resource audit may vary from organization to organization depending on its size, geographic coverage, and type of activity. However, a typical audit checklist is as follows.

- The number of employees by a number of counting methods – the total number, by division, by location, by skill type, by grade or place in hierarchy, by age or length of service, by gender and by ethnic group.
- Employee costs – usually measured by salary costs and 'add-ons' like benefits and taxes payable by the organization.
- The organizational structure and the position of employees within the structure.
- Recruitment and selection procedures and their effectiveness.
- The quality and effectiveness of training and development programmes used.
- The level of employee motivation and morale.
- The quality of employee or industrial relations between management and employees.
- The internal and external networks that employees in the organization have developed (and their effectiveness for various purposes).
- The monitoring of the effectiveness of existing human resource policies and control procedures.

Formal and informal human resource audits

The information provided by the audit can provide management with important information about the state of the organization's human resources. In most types of organization, regular audits are essential to success. However, for some organizations connected with events such as a professional football club or an orchestra, the state of the human resources is completely transparent and the audit occurs continually – although it may never be formally conducted. A football team that loses every match or an orchestra that sounds terrible will have obvious human resource skill deficits. A formal audit is hardly necessary in such circumstances.

Formal audits may be carried out by personnel specialists on a regular basis (say annually), or whenever management need the information for the purposes of a strategic analysis. Practitioners in this area make the point that the simple following of 'lists', like that outlined above, is only a starting point. As points of interest are raised, such as key skill deficiencies, then it is imperative that the reasons for the shortage (or surplus) are also examined as an integral part of the audit.

The outcomes of a human resource audit

The problem of measurement

The various components of a human resource audit present differing problems of quantification. We can intuitively understand that entries like employee costs, numbers, skills shortages or surpluses can be measured in numerical terms. Industrial relations measures can usually be measured by such things as days lost through strikes. Other parts of the audit present more difficulty in respect of measurement.

For example – how might we measure staff morale or motivation? We might be able to say that staff morale is high or low, but any 'in-betweens' might be difficult to assign a value to in the same way as for, say, employee costs. The same problems arise with the levels of staff motivation and job satisfaction. It is also probably true to say that in most organizations large disparities exist between employees in respect of these intangibles. Some employees will be highly motivated and will enjoy good morale whilst others will not. It is for these reasons that a 'checklist' approach to human resource audit is rarely possible – it usually contains some subjective assessments of some parts of the audit.

Human resource benchmarking

The concept of *benchmarking* is one that we will encounter several times in this book. Essentially, benchmarking is a tool for comparing a feature of one organization with the same feature of another. It is particularly useful for comparison against the best in an industry for the feature in question. Followers of the best in the industry might then ask why the leader company has achieved the superior performance (see discussion of benchmarking in finance, Chapter 5). Increasingly, however, companies in the service industries are also benchmarking themselves against companies in different sectors.

For example – it may be that in the area of offering customer service, hotel companies are able to learn from practices in banking, insurance companies, airlines or car dealers.

The feature examined in a benchmarking analysis will depend upon what the organization needs to know.

For example – if a company identifies a negative gap in a key skill area which it has found difficult to close (say of good quality graduates), a benchmark study will enable the company to find out about its competitors. If Company A is known to be able to attract the best graduates, then an examination of its human resource policies will enable other companies (competitors) to benchmark their own practices against it. It may be that Company A is identified as offering the best career-progression planning, the highest salaries or the best development opportunities. If this is found to be the case, then competitors will want to examine their own provision in these areas to see where they can be improved.

Lead companies may also be analysed for the ways in which they not only manage their internal human resources, but also the ways in which they interact with external sources of labour.

For example – many airlines close skills gaps by making extensive use of contract workers, 'outsource' some of their work to outside suppliers or use consultants. The ability to attract these 'mobile' workers can be just as important as attracting permanent employees.

Identifying human resources as critical success factors

As well as using a human resource audit to identify gaps, it can also be used to establish which, if any, employees or groups of employees are critical to strategic success. These are the people that the organization's success may have been built upon in the past and it is likely that the existing structures are centred on them.

THINK POINTS

- What is the purpose of a human resource audit applied to *THE* organizations?
- What is a human resource gap and how might the gaps be addressed by *THE* organizations?
- Explain what a human resource audit analyses.
- Consider what the potential difficulties of human resource audit are, in relation to *THE* organizations.
- What is human resource benchmarking and when might *THE* organizations use the technique?
- What are critical success factors?

In some organizations, critical success human resources may be found on the board of directors, giving strategic direction to the company as a whole. In others, they might be found in research and development, developing the new products upon which the future success will be built. Certain marketing personnel or operations managers might also be critical in some businesses.

For example, in some tour operators the management of the operational aspects of tours may involve local knowledge and experience of destination areas and individual suppliers. Similarly the organization of events such as concerts or festivals might involve the use of highly specialist staff with a range of skills such as lighting and sound engineers, stage managers, etc.

This knowledge and experience may be held by key individuals whose sudden loss to a company could cause operational problems. Well-managed companies try to reduce this risk through measures such as documented procedures, rotating staff to widen the experience base, and training procedures.

KEY CONCEPT

Critical success factors

It is usually the case that there are one or more reasons why superior performers in an industry are in the positions that they are. These key reasons for success are called critical success factors (CSFs). Some companies have uniquely skilled employees, such as particularly skilled financiers, product development specialists or staff selected and trained to give exceptional levels of customer service. In these cases, the CSF is a human resource. In other businesses, the CSF might be a unique location, a brand image, an enviable reputation, a legally protected patent or licence, or a unique production process or technology. This is not to say that other parts of the organization are unimportant, merely that the CSF is the key cause of the success.

In terms of competitive strategy, the approach to a CSF is to defend it – in some cases at whatever cost it might take. This usually takes a form of 'locking it in' to ensure that the advantage is maintained or that competitors are prevented from gaining the same advantage. If the CSF is in the form of a human resource this might involve contractual arrangements providing financial incentives, long periods of notice to leave the company or providing the right working environment to motivate employees.

The importance of the human resources as critical success factors in a business and the steps that may be taken to motivate, train and retain key staff is illustrated by the case of China's fast growing Home Inns chain.

SHORT CASE ILLUSTRATION

HR management and culture: China's Home Inns

International hotel groups from North America and Europe announce new hotel projects in China nearly on a daily basis and they occupy prominent sites in leading Chinese cities. However, Chinese-controlled hotel brands continue to dominate this massive, fast-developing market. The market is becoming highly competitive particularly in the 'budget' segment (which is considered by Chan and Ni, 2011), though hotel groups such as Jinjiang hotels are also providing strong competition for foreign competitors in star-rated properties.

The leading chains are opening new properties at an astonishing rate but in 2013 the largest hotel chain (according to www.tophotelchains.com), with about 850 properties, is the Shanghai-based company Home Inns, followed by:

- Jinjiang Inns (400) and Jinjiang Hotels (346)
- 7 Days Inn (658)
- Green Tree Hotels (600)
- The Lodging Group and their brand Hanting Inns & Hotels (580).

Home Inns, for example, has tapped into the biggest potential market in China: domestic tourism. The style of the typical Home Inn is simple yet unique and certainly eye-catching. 'Its multi-story buildings have bright yellow exteriors, which are highly visible in crowded cities. Bright colours are also on display in the interiors: pink bedspreads and orange walls provide a pleasant and cosy feeling' (Zhang et al., 2013).

In their paper, Zhang et al. (2013) discuss the academic literature concerning CSFs and through their research attempt to identify the relevant CSFs in the case of Home Inns (while by way of contrast, in a recent study Avcikurt et al., 2011 examine CSFs in a Turkish hotel context).

Although other CSFs were identified, two of the key success factors identified related to people and culture. The Chief Executive David Sun in stressing that people are central to business success said that, 'the design, concept, and even strategies and techniques can be easily copied by others, while the core of the organization – people – cannot be duplicated in the same manner' (Zhang et al. 2013).

The provision of training and development opportunities for employees together with a supportive corporate culture appear to have aided retention and resulted in a comparatively low staff turnover rate of under 25 per cent. Early in its development, Home Inns established training and development programmes hosted at The Educational Institute of Home Inns situated in Shanghai. It is reported that new employees can be developed into unit managers within 3–6 years.

Culture, as the term suggests, is not something that can be directly seen or touched, but is a strong invisible force for both customers and employees. Home Inns provides a written promise to create a home-like environment for customers and employees and seems to produce strong loyalty from employees. From all levels of management, to the front-line workers, people in Home Inns appear to be approachable and easy to communicate with and many employees report on the caring attitude of the company. David Sun said, 'It is a very simple idea – if you want to keep these people, you treat them nicely by providing a nice living environment, and draw them a clear career path . . . We create a sense of belonging, we respect our employees, and we get along harmoniously . . . When the staff is happy, they stay'. One example is that free meals and accommodation are often provided for staff which is perceived as a popular benefit in cities like Shanghai, where accommodation is expensive, and many employees are from other areas of the country.

Zhang et al., 2013; www.tophotelchains.com; and www.phx.corporate-ir.net

Questions

1. Explain what is meant by *critical success factors* and identify what you think they are in this case.
2. What issues in relation to human resources might China's Home Inns faces when expanding in China?

Organizational culture

What is culture?

Culture is the organizational equivalent of a human's personality. As with human personality, organizational culture can be somewhat difficult to explain and define, and consequently many different definitions exist. Ralph Stacey (2010) provides one definition.

DEFINITION/QUOTATION

Organizational culture

The culture of any group of people is that set of beliefs, customs, practices and ways of thinking that they have come to share with each other through being and working together. It is a set of assumptions people simply accept without question as they interact with each other. At the visible level the culture of a group of people takes the form of ritual behaviour, symbols, myths, stories, sounds and artefacts.

Stacey (2010)

According to Charles Handy, a leading writer on management, the difficulties encountered with defining culture mean that it cannot be precisely defined, for in essence it is 'something that is perceived, something felt' (Handy, 1996).

Organizational culture can vary enormously from one organization to another, as Handy points out. Organizations are as different and varied as the nations and societies of the world. They have differing cultures – sets of values and norms and beliefs – reflected in different structures and systems. And the cultures are affected by the events of the past and by the climate of the present, by the technology of the type of work, by their aims and the kind of people that work in them (Handy, 1996).

Culture can thus be explained in terms of the 'feel' of an organization or its 'character' or as it has sometimes been described as 'the way we do things round here'. Definitions can be a bit inaccessible, but the importance of an organization's culture lies in the fact that it can be 'felt' whenever it is encountered.

From a strategic point of view, the important point is that all organizations have some sort of culture and that the culture can have a significant effect upon organizational performance. Consequently THE managers must attempt to understand the culture of their organization and the effect it is having (positive or negative) upon organizational performance. Managers may subsequently find it necessary to take steps to implement a programme that attempts to change the prevailing culture in order to improve performance.

The principles relating to organizational culture have been applied, research carried out and the strategic implications considered in various parts of THE. See, for example, Getz et al. (2010); Tsang (2011); and Chen et al. (2012).

Organizations are as individual as people and in many ways, there are as many cultures as there are organizations – each one is unique. This is not to say, however, that we cannot identify common features between organizational cultures.

The determinants of culture

The reason why an organization has a particular type of culture is as complicated a question as asking why a human has a particular personality. It has many possible influences, the net effects of which forge culture over a period of time. Any list would be necessarily incomplete, but the following are some of the most important reasons.

- The philosophy of the organization's founders, especially if it is relatively young.
- The nature of the activities in the business and the character of the industry it competes in.
- The nature of the interpersonal relationships and the nature of industrial or employee relationships.
- The management style adopted and the types of control mechanism, for example, the extent to which management style is autocratic or democratic.
- The national or regional character of the areas in which the organization's activities are located. This, in turn, can affect the *power distance*, which also influences culture.
- The structure of the organization, particularly its 'height' and 'width' (see Chapter 13).
- The dependency the organization has on technology and the type of technology employed (the growth of email, for example, has had an influence of the culture of some organizations).

Why is culture important?

Culture is important because it can and does affect all aspects of an organization's activities. The metaphor of human personality may help us to understand this. Some people's personality means they are motivated, sharp, exciting to be with, etc. Others are dull, tedious, apathetic and conservative. These personality features will affect all aspects of their lives.

The same is true of an organization's 'personality'. Culture is important because of the following (non-exhaustive) reasons. Culture can have an influence on:

- employee motivation;
- the attractiveness of the organization as an employer and hence the rate of staff turnover;
- employee morale and 'goodwill';
- productivity and efficiency;
- the quality of work;
- the nature of the employee and industrial relations;
- the attitude of employees in the workplace; and
- innovation and creativity.

The point to make after such a list is simply that culture is *very* important. It is essential that management understand the culture of the organization both in analysing the organizations's strategic positioning and then in the implementation of strategy.

Many *THE* organizations have recognized the central importance of developing a strong and consistently applied organizational culture. The development of a strong culture enables the organization concerned to strive to deliver consistent standards of service but can also be used as a promotional tool not only externally to customers but also internally to employees, giving them a sense of pride and motivation. The culture is often summed up in a short advertising slogan, many of which have become synonymous with the *THE* organization in question, such as: 'Now everyone can fly' (Air Asia); 'We try harder' (Avis); and 'Incredible India' (India Ministry of Tourism).

Building a strong sense of organizational culture is difficult in organizations such as those in *THE* which are often geographically dispersed and operating internationally. Furthermore, developing a strong sustainable culture that can help drive an organization forward successfully often takes a long period of time.

THINK POINTS

- Providing relevant examples from *THE*, explain what is meant by organizational culture.
- Explain why organizational culture is so important to the success of organizations.
- Assess what factors determine the culture of an organization.

Most of the organizations operating in the tourism and hospitality sectors operate in a continuing fashion aiming to trade successfully year after year and being able to develop a successful culture on that basis. In the events sector, however, this is often not the case, as events such as major sporting events – for example, the 2016 Rio de Janeiro Olympic Games – may be organized only on one occasion by the host city or festivals may be organized on a recurring basis once a year.

Nevertheless, the successful delivery of these events may rely heavily on instilling a strong organizational culture in the workforce and volunteers enabling the festival or event to be delivered successfully. The case of Edmonton, Canada, illustrates the importance of recruiting a strong volunteer workforce to deliver events and festivals successfully.

SHORT CASE ILLUSTRATION

Eventful cities: Edmonton, Canada

Many so-called 'eventful cities' are placing festivals and events at the heart of their development and promotional strategies, recognizing the key role that they can have in developing positive images of a location and enhancing economic activity. By way of example, Richards and Palmer (2012) cite, amongst others, the cases of Melbourne, Australia, which has labelled itself as 'the world's event city'; Seoul, South Korea which has claimed to be 'one of the most eventful cities in the world'; and, on a less global scale, Reno-Tahoe territory in Nevada, USA, which has promoted itself as 'the most eventful city in America'.

Among these cities promoting themselves in this way is Edmonton in Alberta Canada, which refers to itself as 'Canada's Festivals City', setting itself in competition with other Canadian cities, Montreal and Quebec City, which define themselves in similar terms (Richards and Palmer, 2012:3). Although Edmonton, a city of about a million people, is somewhat isolated from other large urban centres, research in 2008 indicated that it hosts an array of colourful, entertaining festivals every year including Canada's largest folk music festival and North America's largest and longest-running International Fringe Theatre Festival.

Like other cities which have limited promotional budgets, Edmonton has had to rely heavily on a volunteer workforce. Since adopting this strategy of promoting itself through its festivals provision in 2008, the city has promoted a strong culture of volunteering among the population. In particular it promotes a culture of involvement through its Edmonton Magical Volunteer Army and has a dedicated website (edmontonstories.com) which encourages visitors and residents to share their stories about their experiences.

Richards and Palmer (2012); www.edmonton.com, www.edmontonstories.ca

Questions

1. Consider the benefits and potential difficulties volunteers bring to events such as those in Edmonton.
2. Consider how efficiently cities such as Edmonton are able to utilize resources in providing and managing events.

The centrality of a successful organizational culture is illustrated by the cases of two airlines: Southwest Airlines in USA, and a later follower of the airline's cultural attributes in Canada, WestJet. Southwest Airlines explicitly (and famously) place employees at the heart of what they do. To Southwest it is a simple equation: happy employees = happy customers.

SHORT CASE ILLUSTRATION

Organizational culture: Southwest Airlines

The culture of Southwest Airlines which emphasizes employees as the airline's 'first customers' and passengers as the second has been integral to Southwest Airlines' success. Dallas-based Southwest has grown significantly and profitably since its first services in 1971 and continues to do so, drawing in thousands of new employees to the airline's ways and raising questions about whether it can keep its culture intact.

In 1990, the airline had 8,600 on its payroll, which has now risen to about 46,000 employees. The airline has also flown beyond its Texas roots into other regions of the USA and today it serves almost 100 destinations. In an attempt to address this, a committee focusing on new employees was created. As turnover edges up, an internal branding campaign reminds employees of the 'freedoms' that working at Southwest brings. The airline is also in the relatively new position of having to search for applicants rather than wait for candidates to come to it.

It takes a lot of hard work to maintain the culture, but the airline regularly finds a place towards the top lists of Best Companies to Work for in America. Southwest's charismatic founder and leader, 82-year-old Herb Kelleher, has devoted much time and energy to creating and maintaining the company's distinctive corporate culture.

Southwest, which began operating in 1971, now challenges the major North American 'legacy' airlines such as American, United and Delta. Originally offering flights in a triangle between Dallas, San Antonio and Houston, the idea of offering fares so cheap that people would abandon their cars for jets has proved very attractive to consumers and has been widely copied. Its low-cost operating model has been copied and adapted by numerous airlines across the world such as easyJet and Ryanair in Europe; Air Asia, Tiger Airways and Lion Airways in Asia; and FastJet and Gol in Africa and South America respectively. The airline's core offering is to offer lots of short flights between pairs of cities, though in recent years it has been offering more long flights. Reinforcing the low fares is a culture of relaxed professionalism which includes flight attendants who might crack jokes or burst into song.

Southwest's employees appear to understand what's made the airline succeed which provides clarity of purpose at Southwest that makes it easy to retain the culture while growing.

Throughout the company, employees are encouraged to hold 'celebrations' to mark birthdays, engagements and other milestones. Creativity also is emphasized, especially when it comes to finding relief in high-stress jobs. Customer relations workers may come to work in pyjamas for a day. Profit sharing ties employees' directly to company performance. Southwest built an infrastructure that ensures that when an employee does something good, many of the organization's other employees know about it. The lives of Southwest employees, along with the company's history, are highlighted on the headquarters' walls, and 'special' days are held such as a Halloween celebration on 31st October.

To help facilitate communications, a 'culture committee' was established in 1990 aiming to do what was necessary to create, enhance and enrich the Southwest spirit and the committee has now been replicated across the company with local culture committees having also been established in cities across Southwest's network. In one way or another, the committee tries to ensure that fellow workers are appreciated and that people appreciate other difficulties involved with other people's positions. A committee focusing on new employees has also been added in order to make sure that new employees are inducted appropriately and receive proper guidance and mentoring during their early careers.

The company is also paying more attention to employee retention as turnover creeps up and an internal branding campaign established eight 'basic freedoms' of working at Southwest. Employees, the company says, get the freedom to: pursue good health; travel; learn and grow; stay connected; have financial security; work and have fun; make a positive difference; and be creative and innovative.

Various newspaper articles and www.southwestairlines.com

Questions

1. Explain the main features of Southwest's corporate culture.
2. Consider the difficulties that Southwest might have in maintaining its corporate culture as it grows and develops.

The cultural web

Since culture is so important to successful adoption of strategy and yet it is difficult to define, understand and measure, it is important to have a model that enables us to provide some understanding. One of the most commonly used ways of making sense of an organization's culture is to use the cultural web (Johnson, 1992). It is a schematic representation of the elements of an organization's culture in such a way that we can see how each element influences the paradigm (See Figure 4.3). Each component is interrelated and has an impact on the overall cultural paradigm of the organization.

KEY CONCEPT

Paradigm

A paradigm is a worldview – a way of looking at the world. It is expressed in the assumptions that people make and in their deep-rooted beliefs. The paradigm of an organization or a national culture is important because it determines how it will behave in a given circumstance. Given a certain moral dilemma or similar choice, we might expect the paradigms of a person living in one country or culture will lead them to arrive at different conclusions from those living in another country or culture. The things that cause one culture to adopt one paradigm and another culture to espouse a different one are set out in the cultural web.

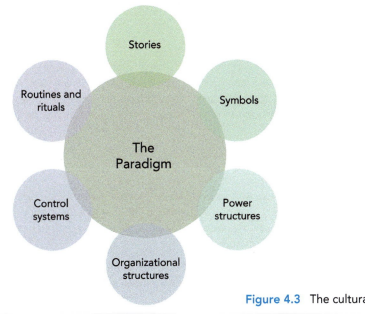

Figure 4.3   The cultural web (adapted from Johnson, 1992)

The main elements of the web are described below.

Stories

Stories are those narratives that people within the organization talk to each other about; what they tell new recruits and outsiders about the organization. The stories typically recount events and people from the past and present – stories of famous victories and defeats. They tend to highlight what is considered important to the members of the organization.

Routines and rituals

Routines are the procedures for doing things within the organization. They are repeated on a regular basis to the extent they are taken as 'the way things are done'. Rituals have a longer time-frame and can be either formal or informal. Formal routines and rituals are a part of the organization's practice, such as the 'long service award' or the company annual sporting event, that work teams might go on from time to time. Informal routines and rituals might include the way that people behave at the annual Christmas party or the extent to which colleagues do or do not go for a drink together after work.

Symbols

Symbolic aspects of organizational life concern those things that symbolize something to some people – a certain level of promotion, the company car they drive, the position of their office, their job title. In some companies, these symbols have no apparent importance at all. In others, they matter a great deal. The way that employees respond to these symbols can tell us a great deal about the culture.

Structure

The structure of an organization can mean more than just those formal relationships that are shown on an organization diagram. Informal structures can also exist through interpersonal relationships that transcend the formal structures. Some organizations have highly developed informal structures whilst others do not.

Control systems

The ways in which activities are controlled, whether 'tight' or 'loose', is closely aligned to culture. This has a strong link to power distance and the nature of the activities that the organization is engaged in. Control systems, by definition, concern activity in which performance is gauged against a predetermined standard and the methods of both standard-setting and monitoring performance vary significantly according to culture.

Power structures

The core assumptions that contribute to the paradigm are likely to be made by the most powerful management groupings in the organization. In some companies, this power resides in the research department; in others it will be the production people or those from another department. In some organizations, there may be arguments about what is important between one or more groupings.

Each component of the cultural web exerts its own influence upon the organization's paradigm. The paradigm describes the aggregate effects of the cultural influences on the way the members of the organization look at the world. This can apply to regions of the world just as it applies to organizations. People indigenous to the Middle East are often thought to have a different view of the world than citizens of countries in North Western Europe. This difference is because of the influence that each component of the cultural web exerts on the national or regional paradigm.

SHORT CASE ILLUSTRATION

Application of the cultural web at WestJet

WestJet was founded in 1996 by a team of Calgary entrepreneurs, headed by Clive Beddoe (who remains as Chairman), as a western Canadian regional carrier with three aircraft flying to five cities. Today, the airline (Canada's second largest) offers scheduled service to over 70 destinations in Canada, the United States, Mexico and the Caribbean, with a modern fleet of over 100 Boeing 'Next Generation' 737-series aircraft. The airline's headquarters are in Calgary which remains a major hub, though Toronto (where the airline is also quoted on the stock exchange) is the airline's largest hub.

WestJet is based on the low-cost carrier business model pioneered by Southwest Airlines and Morris Air in the United States. Its original routes were all located in Western Canada, which gave the airline its name. In 2012, WestJet carried over 17 million passengers.

Stories

- Three used Boeing 737's at the start up in 1996.
- Early changes in senior management.
- Taking on a well-established 'legacy' airline Air Canada which subsequently strengthened its dominant position with the purchase of Canadian Airlines (Canada's No. 2 airline at the time) in 2001.
- Learning from other low-cost airlines and taking advantage of opportunities arising from North American airline deregulation.

Symbols

- Aircraft are painted distinctively in white except for some lettering on parts of the aircraft.
- Calgary headquarters attained gold certification under the Leadership in Energy and Environmental Design (LEED) program.
- Winner of numerous awards: claiming top spot in Waterstones' study of Canada's 10 Most Admired Corporate Cultures for four years and inducted into its Hall of Fame in 2010; in 2011 designated as a J.D. Power 'Customer Service Champion' – one of two companies in Canada and the only airline to make the list.

Power structure

- Non-unionized flexible workforce.
- Some codeshare agreements with other airlines but not a member of any airline alliance.
- 85 per cent of employees are shareholders giving rise to the advertising slogan 'Owners Care'.
- Head office in Canadian regional centre giving rise to strong loyalty.

Organizational structure

- Outsourcing some key business functions e.g. aircraft catering provided by local suppliers in major cities.

- Strong emphasis on teamwork and 'WestJetters' (employees) contribution to business success: 'Owners Care – sure, it's our aircraft that fly you places, but it's really our people who get you there' (www.westjet.com).
- Employee representative sits on the company's Board of Directors.
- Strong leadership from Chairman and experienced Board of Directors including a majority of non-executive directors.

Control system

- Economies of scale through operating variants of the same aircraft type.
- Extensive connectivity between the networks of WestJet and about 30 global partner airlines.
- Strict adherence to budgeting, target setting and operating a 'low-cost' model.
- Motivating WestJetters through share ownership scheme, competitive pay levels and other benefits.

Rituals and routines

- Light-hearted attitude. Issued 'joke' press releases as part of 1st April Fool's Day – the introduction of 'sleeper cabins' in overhead bins.
- Strong ethos of community investment, environmental initiatives and sponsorship by the company and its 9,000 WestJetters.
- Employees as 'owners': 'We're looking to fill a number of positions, starting with Owner'.

Paradigm

- Value for money.
- WestJetter's interests aligned with those of the company.
- Growth with responsibility – to environment, communities and stakeholders.

www.westjet.com and various press sources

Questions

1. Consider what purpose is served by producing a *cultural web* for a company such as Westjet and how might it be utilized by managers.
2. Consider a *THE* organization you are familiar with and apply the *cultural web* analysis to it.

Cultural typologies

A number of writers in organizational theory have attempted to group culture types together. The thinking behind such attempts at *typology* is that if organizations can describe their cultures by type, then this would help in strategic analysis. We will briefly consider three of these attempts which might be useful in analysing *THE* organizations in various contexts.

Handy's culture types

An influential writer, Charles Handy (1996) suggested that organizational cultures could be divided into four broad types: power cultures, role cultures, task cultures and person cultures.

Power cultures

This type of organization is dominated by either a very powerful individual or a dominant small group. It is typified by an organization that has grown as a result of entrepreneurial flair. Strategic decisions and many operational ones are made by the centre and few decisions are devolved to other managers. As the organization is dependent on the abilities and personality of the powerful individual, the ability of the organization to change in response to changes in the environment are sometimes limited by the centre.

Power cultures are common in small entrepreneurial (owner-managed) companies and in some notable larger organizations with a charismatic leader.

Role cultures

This type of culture is found in many long-established organizations that have traditionally operated in stable environments. They tend to be very hierarchical and rely on established procedures, systems and precedent. They often respond slowly to change as it takes time for change to be recognized through the reporting mechanisms. Delays are also encountered in the slow-thought and considered decision-making process.

Role cultures are common in traditional bureaucracies such as the civil service. The task of management in a role culture is to manage procedure. There is usually a high degree of decentralization and the organization is run by rules and laid-down procedures.

Task cultures

Task cultures are found in organizations engaged in activities of a non-repetitive nature, often high-value, one-off tasks. Activities are normally based around flexible multi-disciplinary teams containing expertise in the major disciplines required to complete the project. Teams tend to be small but flexible and find change easy to identify and adjust to. Strategic planning tends to concentrate on the task in hand.

As their name suggests, task cultures can be found in organizations that are dedicated to a particular task. Consortia that work on large civil engineering projects may demonstrate task culture, as might missionary teams that work together on a medical project in the developing world.

Person cultures

Person cultures are those that exist primarily for the benefit of the members of the organization itself and hence they tend to be rare in commercial businesses. They can have a very different 'feel' to the other cultures as all members of the organizations work for the benefits of themselves and the other members.

They can be found in learned professional societies, in trade unions, in co-operatives, in some charities and in some religious organizations.

In reality, few organizations fit perfectly into just one classification and they may demonstrate elements of two or more. Some diversified organizations may have divisions that fall into all the categories and the cultures may change over time. Many start as power cultures and then tend towards a role culture as size increases.

> ### KEY CONCEPT
>
> **Power distance**
>
> The term is used to describe how removed subordinates feel from their superiors in a social meaning of the word 'distance'. In a high power distance culture, inequality is accepted. In a low power distance culture, inequalities and overt status symbols are minimized and subordinates expect to be consulted and to share decisions with approachable managers.

In assessing the appropriateness of the four cultural types, three criteria might be used. Does the dominant culture identified:

- fit with prescriptive or emergent forms of strategy formulation;
- deliver competitive advantage for the organization;
- have the ability to cope with strategic change.

In assessing the four main cultural types however, three important qualifications should be made:

1. organizations change over time;
2. several types or variations of culture often exist in the same organization;
3. different cultures may predominate depending on the headquarters and ownership of the company.

Miles and Snow's culture types

Since its emergence, the typology of cultural types produced by Miles and Snow (1978) has been widely used and cited in the academic literature (see for example, Desarbo *et al.*, 2005). Miles and Snow categorized cultures into four types, based on how they tend to react in strategic terms.

Defenders

These organizations tend to seek a competitive advantage in terms of targeting niche markets through cost reduction and specialization. They tend to operate in stable, mature markets and, as the name suggests, they favour defending their current market share by service improvements or further cost savings. Defenders therefore tend to be centralized, have rigid control systems and a hierarchical management structure that does not enjoy sudden change.

Prospectors

These organizations enjoy the challenge of developing and introducing new products to the market place. They actively seek out new markets for their products. These favoured strategies require organizations to constantly monitor the environment and be willing and able to respond quickly to changes that may occur. To that end, they are decentralized and flexible.

Analysers

These organizations are 'followers' and are conservative in nature. Steady growth through market penetration is the favoured option as this can be achieved without radical changes to structure. Moves into new markets and products only occur after extensive evaluation and market research. They learn from the mistakes of others and tend to balance power between the centre and divisions with complex control systems.

Reactors

Reactors are a bit like analysers in that they tend to follow rather than innovate. They differ from analysers in that they are less conservative and sometimes behave impulsively, having failed to fully consider the implications of their actions. These organizations may lack proper control systems and typically have a weak but dominant leader.

The four cultural types of Miles and Snow and their strategic implications are summarised in Table 4.3.

Cross-cultural differences based on the work of Hofstede

Professor Geert Hofstede is an influential Dutch researcher in the field of organizational culture. His cross-cultural studies demonstrated that there are important national and regional cultural groups. The importance of these groups is that they exert a significant influence on the behaviour of organizations (and societies more generally). *THE*, by its nature, is international in orientation, with organizations frequently operating across borders and working in various cultural contexts.

Consequently, it is important that managers in these sectors have an understanding of the influence of national culture and the effects the differences might have upon the successful implementation of strategy.

DEFINITION/QUOTATION

National culture

There is no single agreed definition of national culture, but to Hofstede (1980) it is:

> The collective programming of the mind which distinguishes the members of one human group from another . . . Culture, in this sense, includes systems of values; and values are among the building blocks of culture.

Table 4.3 Summary of the strategic implications of Miles and Snow's typology

Cultural type	Strategic implications	Environmental conditions	Organizational characteristics
Defenders	Hold on to current market position Retrench	Stable	Tight control Centralized Operational efficiency Low overheads
Prospectors	Innovate Find new market opportunities Grow Take Risks	Dynamic and growing	Creative Innovative Flexible Decentralized
Analyser	Maintain current market with moderate innovation	Moderate change	Tight control and flexibility Efficient operations Creativity
Reactors	No clear strategy React to specific conditions Drift	Any condition	No clear organizational approach Depends on current needs

Some have criticised Hofstede's work on methodological grounds, since his work was based largely on samples of employees from the company he worked for – IBM. See for example the critique by McSweeney (2002) and the overview by Williamson (2002). Furthermore, clearly national cultures are also subject to change over time; important regional and ethnic variations within countries and describing such cultures leads to potential national stereotyping.

Nevertheless, his work has been widely cited, adapted by others, and applied to particular circumstances. The concepts of Hofstede and others have been widely applied to cross-cultural studies in an attempt to understand why managers and employees in different parts of the world think and act in different ways.

Hickson and Pugh (2003), for example, building on the work of Hofstede and others, usefully provide an analytical journey around the world when they consider managerial and organizational differences in different parts of the world. In doing so they distinguish between managerial differences of: the 'Anglos'; the 'Latins'; the 'Northern Europeans'; the 'East Central Europeans'; the 'Asians'; the 'Arabs of the Middle East'; and the 'Developing Countries'.

THINK POINTS

- Explain the concept of the cultural web and describe its components as applied in a *THE* context.
- Explain what is meant by the terms power distance and paradigm.
- Describe Handy's and Miles and Snow's cultural typologies and assess the usefulness of the concepts to *THE* organizations.
- Explain why an understanding of Hofstede's work is important to international managers operating in *THE* organizations.

Reisinger and Crotts (2010) apply Hofstede's analysis specifically to tourism, drawing from a sample of tourists from eight countries (Australia, Greece, United Kingdom, United States, China, Indonesia, Malaysia and Singapore) which completed Hofstede's original survey instruments. The results show strong support for Hofstede's national cultural measures in that only minor differences are revealed between their study and Hofstede's work. This finding provides strong support for Hofstede's dimensions as a measure of central tendencies of visitors from different nations.

Reisinger and Crotts (2010) also identify graphically contrasting respondents' values along the five cultural dimensions revealing that the between-nation differences are relatively small when compared to the within-nation variability, thus indicating that subcultures do exist within countries. The analysis also identifies international regions that cluster closely together, demonstrating that national cultural differences do not end at national borders.

Hofstede is best known for his work in developing his 'cultural dimensions theory' which encapsulates five dimensions, considered in Table 4.4.

There are a number of strategic considerations that are raised by the outcomes of Hofstede's work that managers operating in *THE* might need to be aware of when formulating and implementing their strategic plans. These considerations might include:

FOR ORGANIZATIONS OPERATING IN ONE NATIONAL MARKET:

Employees may come from a range of countries and different cultural backgrounds.

Table 4.4 Summary of Hofstede's cultural dimensions

Cultural dimension	Description	Findings
Power Distance	Extent to which the poorest in society are willing to accept their position or countries in which inequalities are less acceptable	Countries such as Panama, Malaysia and Venezuela were found to accept such inequalities, whereas countries such as Ireland, Israel, Denmark and Sweden found inequalities less acceptable.
Individualism/ collectivism	Extent to which countries are collections of individuals or are bound together as a cohesive whole	The more individual countries included USA, UK, Australia and Netherlands whereas South American countries tended more towards collectivism.
Masculinity versus femininity	Extent to which countries are placed on a spectrum from masculinity to femininity	In male cultures there is a sharp distinction between genders with males expected to emphasize work, power and wealth. In female cultures there is more equality. Japan, Austria and Italy tended towards greater masculinity whereas countries such as Sweden, Netherlands and Finland are more feminine.
Uncertainty avoidance	Extent to which members of a culture feel threatened by the unknown	In countries where uncertainty avoidance is weak people are willing to embrace uncertainty and ambiguous situations: precision and punctuality for meetings for instance were useful but not essential. These countries included Singapore, Denmark, Jamaica and Hong Kong. On the other hand, in strong uncertainty avoidance countries people appear to need certainty, planning and order. These cultures included those in Japan, Portugal, Greece and Belgium.
Long-termism versus short-termism	Hofstede later added this category. It relates to the extent to which different cultures have different time horizons – long-termism versus short-termism	Long-termism stresses the importance of taking a long view and adapting traditions to a modern context while stressing perseverance. China, Hong Kong and South Korea are examples of long termism. Short-termism stresses the importance of quick results as well as social obligations and status. Short-termism is typified by USA, Nigeria, UK and Canada.

For example – it is quite common for many employees at UK hotels to come from elsewhere, particularly from Eastern Europe and Mediterranean countries.

FOR ORGANIZATIONS WITH A RANGE OF OPERATIONS IN DIFFERENT COUNTRIES:

There might be a need to devise a strategy taking into account not only central HQ issues but also local cultural styles, values and expectations. For example, mission statements might have to be adapted and the rate of strategic change adjusted to local circumstances.

There might also be a need in such companies (or those with global operations) to find ways of bringing together and integrating the many cultures which exist. This might involve special integration programmes to break down barriers.

SMALL BUSINESS FOCUS

Human resource management frequently raises particular strategic challenges for managers in smaller *THE* organizations. 'The very size of small businesses creates a special condition – which can be referred to as resource poverty – that distinguishes them from their larger counterparts and requires some very different management approaches' (Welsh and White, 1981:18). In relation to human resources, Urbano and Yordanova (2008), writing in a Spanish tourism context, argue that there are several difficulties smaller companies may face relative to larger competitors. SMEs may:

- Have less access to formal training opportunities.
- Be unlikely to have HRM departments dedicated to resolving HR issues.
- Have owners and managers who are likely to combine HR responsibility with other responsibilities.
- Have more limited financial resources, limiting the adoption of costly HRM practices.
- Encounter difficulties in pursuing new approaches to people management due to lack of information about the developments in HRM in other companies.
- Encounter problems in competing for labour with larger organizations and recruiting and training employees.

While the factors outlined above are no doubt important (and there may be others), small businesses need to design strategies to overcome the difficulties encountered and to build on other factors which might be advantageous for SMEs.

For example, smaller businesses might seek to overcome their size disadvantages by:

- Working cooperatively in alliances to share resources.
- Forming trade associations to share knowledge and best practices.
- 'Clustering' together to achieve economies of scale in relation to aspects such as marketing and purchasing.
- Using technology (such as internet applications) effectively, e.g. in communicating with customers directly and providing training for employees.

Notwithstanding some of the potential disadvantages smaller organizations might have relative to larger competitors, they may also have potential advantages in relation to their human resources. The task for *THE* managers in smaller organizations is then to identify these advantages and maximize their potential in the strategies they adopt. Despite extensive training and development, active policies, extensive marketing, public relations and brand building, and managerial actions, larger companies frequently find it difficult to be viewed as responsive, friendly, customer-focused and having consistent service standards.

THE owners, managers and employees working in smaller organizations may be able to differentiate themselves by exhibiting superior:

- customer knowledge;
- responsiveness to enquiries and complaints;

- development of long-lasting relationships encouraging repeat business;
- attention to detail;
- consistent and reliable standards across the organization;
- friendliness, leaving the customer feeling important and reassured.

In addition, SMEs may be able to foster high standards of service delivery and the fostering of a service-oriented culture by the direct day-to-day involvement of owners and managers. Rather than being remote (as in some larger organizations) managers and owners who are directly involved can seek to foster high standards.

In particular, owners and managers are on hand to:

- monitor and experience the standards directly;
- make changes quickly when required;
- impose a sense of urgency and importance when customer problems arise;
- make decisions directly and deploy necessary resources when required;
- ensure that employees are appropriately rewarded and motivated.

CHAPTER SUMMARY

Both human resources and organizational culture are important parts of strategic analysis. An understanding of both of these areas is a vital part of internal analysis. The state of an organization's human resources can be assessed using a human resource audit – a tool that has its limitations, particularly in respect of measuring intangible aspects like job satisfaction, employee morale and motivation.

Since THE sectors are usually highly labour intensive, it is the human resources of an organization that can frequently represent the key differentiator between organizations. In particular, the quality of the service provided in customer/guest–employee encounters is often critical.

The configuration of human resources in an organization is a major determinant of its culture. We can think of an organization's culture as its personality and we can use the cultural web to analyse it. Finally, we encountered two ways of sub-dividing culture types. These can also be useful tools in strategic analysis.

REFERENCES

Albrecht, K. (1992) *The Only Thing That Matters: Bringing the Customer to the Center of Your Business.* New York: Harper Business.

Augustyn, M. and S. K. Ho (1998) 'Service Quality and Tourism', *Journal of Travel Research*, 37 (1): 71–5.

Avcikurt, C., H. Altay and O. Ilban (2011) 'Critical Success Factors for Small Hotel Businesses in Turkey: An Exploratory Study', *Cornell Hospitality Quarterly*, 52 (2): 153–64.

Baum, T. (1995) *Managing Human Resources in the European Hospitality and Tourism Industry: A Strategic Approach*, London: Chapman Hall.

— (1997) 'Making or Breaking the Tourist Experience: The Role of Human Resource Management', in C. Ryan (ed.) *The Tourist Experience: A New Introduction*, London: Cassell, pp. 92–111.

Bennington, L. and J. Cummane (1998) 'Measuring Service Quality: A Hybrid Methodology', *Total Quality Management*, 9 (6): 395–406.

Berry, L. L. and A. Parasuraman (1991) *Marketing Services*, New York: The Free Press.

Bitner, M. J., B. H. Booms and L. A. Mohr (1994) 'Critical Service Encounters: The Employee's Viewpoint', *Journal of Marketing*, 58 (October): 95–106.

Bowdin, G., J. Allen, R. Harris, I. McDonnell and W. O'Toole (2012) *Events Management*, London and New York: Routledge.

Carlzon, J. (1987) *Moments of Truth*, Cambridge, Mass.: Ballinger.

Chalkiti, K. and M. Sigala (2010) 'Staff Turnover in the Greek Tourism Industry: A Comparison between Insular and Peninsular Regions', *International Journal of Contemporary Hospitality Management*, 22 (3): 335–59.

Chan, W. W. and S. Ni (2011) 'Growth of Budget Hotels in China: Antecedents and Future', *Asia Pacific Journal of Tourism Research*, 16 (3): 249–62.

Chen, R. X., C. Cheung and R. Law (2012) 'A Review of the Literature on Culture in Hotel Management Research: What Is the Future?' *International Journal of Hospitality Management*, 31 (1): 52–65.

Crick, A. P. and A. Spencer (2011) 'Hospitality Quality: New Directions and New Challenges', *International Journal of Contemporary Hospitality Management*, 23 (4): 463–78.

Deery, M. (2008) 'Talent Management, Work-Life Balance and Retention Strategies', *International Journal of Contemporary Hospitality Management*, 20 (7): 792–806.

— (2009) 'Employee Retention Strategies for Events Management', in T. Baum, M. Deery, C. Hanlon, L. Lockstone and K. Smith (eds.) *People and Work in Events and Conventions*, Oxford: CABI, pp. 127–37.

Desarbo, W. S., C. Anthony Di Benedetto, M. Song and I. Sinha (2005) 'Revisiting the Miles and Snow Strategic Framework: Uncovering Interrelationships between Strategic Types, Capabilities, Environmental Uncertainty and Firm Performance', *Strategic Management Journal*, 26 (1): 47–74.

Duncan, T., D. G. Scott and T. Baum (2013) 'The Mobilities of Hospitality Work: An Exploration of Issues and Debates', *Annals of Tourism Research*, 41 (1): 1–19.

Evans, N. (2012) 'Tourism: A Strategic Business Perspective', in T. Jamal and M. Robinson (eds.) *The Sage Handbook of Tourism Studies*, Thousand Oaks, Calif.: Sage, pp. 215–34.

Getz, D., T. Andersson and J. Carlsen (2010) 'Festival Management Studies: Developing a Framework and Priorities for Comparative and Cross-Cultural Research', *International Journal of Event and Festival Management*, 1 (1): 29–59.

Grönroos, C. (1984) 'A Service Quality Model and Its Marketing Implications', *European Journal of Marketing*, 18 (4): 36–44.

Handy, C. B. (1996) *Understanding Organizations*, 4th edn, London: Penguin.

Hanlon, C. and L. Jago (2004) 'The Challenge of Retaining Personnel in Major Sport Event Organizations', *Event Management*, 9 (1–2): 1–2.

Hickson, D. J. and D. S. Pugh (2003) *Management Worldwide*, 2nd edn, London: Penguin.

Hofstede, G. (1980). *Culture's Consequences: International Differences in Work-related Values*. Beverly Hills, CA: Sage.

Holmes, K. and K. Smith (2012) *Managing Volunteers in Tourism*, Abingdon, UK: Routledge.

Johnson, G. (1992) 'Managing Strategic Change: Strategy, Culture and Action', *Long Range Planning*, 25 (1): 28–36.

Kandampully, J. (1997) 'Quality Service in Tourism', in M. Foley, J. Lennon and G. Maxwell (eds.) *Hospitality, Tourism and Leisure Management*, London: Cassell, pp. 3–20.

Kusluvan, S., Z. Kusluvan, I. Ilhan and L. Buyruk (2010) 'The Human Dimension: A Review of Human Resources Management Issues in the Tourism and Hospitality Industry', *Cornell Hospitality Quarterly*, 51 (2): 171–214.

Lado, A. A. and M. C. Wilson (1994) 'Human Resource Systems and Sustained Competitive Advantage: A Competency-Based Perspective', *Academy of Management Journal*, 19 (4): 699–727.

Leiper, N. (1990) 'Tourist Attraction Systems', *Annals of Tourism Research*, 17, 367–84.

Lynch, R. (2003) *Strategic Management*, 3rd edn, Harlow: Pearson Education.

McSweeney, B. (2002) 'Hofstede's Model of National Cultural Differences and the Consequences: A Triumph of Faith—A Failure of Analysis', *Human Relations*, 55 (1): 89–118.

Miles, R. E. and C. C. Snow (1978) *Organizational Strategy, Structure and Process*, New York: McGraw-Hill.

Mill, R. C. (2011) 'A Comprehensive Model of Customer Satisfaction in Hospitality and Tourism: Strategic Implications for Management', *International Business and Economics Research Journal*, 1 (6): 7–18.

Mullins, L. J. and P. Dossor (2013) *Hospitality Management and Organizational Behaviour*, 5th edn, Harlow: Pearson Education.

Reisinger, Y. and J. C. Crotts (2010) 'Applying Hofstede's National Culture Measures in Tourism Research: Illuminating Issues of Divergence and Convergence', *Journal of Travel Research*, 49 (2): 153–64.

Richards, G. and R. Palmer (2012) *Eventful Cities*, London and New York: Routledge.

Ro, H. and P. J. Chen (2011) 'Empowerment in Hospitality Organizations: Customer Orientation and Organizational Support', *International Journal of Hospitality Management*, 30 (2): 422–8.

Ruhanen, L. and C. Cooper (2009) 'The Tourism Labour Market in the Asia Pacific Region', in Tourism: An Engine for Employment Creation Conference, Bali, Indonesia, March, Madrid: UN World Tourism Organization.

Ryan, C. (1996) 'Market Research in Tourism: Shifting Paradigms for New Concerns', in L. Moutinho (ed.) *Marketing Research in Tourism*, London: Prentice Hall.

Smith, K. and K. Holmes (2009) 'Researching Volunteers in Tourism: Going Beyond', *Annals of Leisure Research*, 12 (3–4): 403–420.

Soutar, G.N. (2001). 'Service Quality, Customer Satisfaction and Value: An Examination of their Relationships', in Kandampully, J., C. Mok and B. Sparks (eds.) *Service Quality Management in Hospitality, Tourism, and Leisure*, New York: The Haworth Hospitality Press, pp. 97–110.

Stacey, R. (2010) *Strategic Management and Organizational Dynamics*, 6th edn, London: Pitman.

Swanson, S. R. and M. K. Hsu (2009) 'Critical Incidents in Tourism: Failure, Recovery, Customer Switching and Word-of-Mouth Behaviors', *Journal of Travel and Tourism Marketing*, 26 (2): 180–94.

Tkaczynski, A. and R. Stokes (2010) 'Festperf: A Service Quality Measurement Scale for Festivals', *Event Management*, 14 (1): 69–82.

Tsang, N. K. (2011) 'Dimensions of Chinese Culture Values in Relation to Service Provision in Hospitality and Tourism Industry', *International Journal of Hospitality Management*, 30 (3): 670–9.

Ueno, A. (2008) 'Is Empowerment Really a Contributory Factor to Service Quality?' *The Service Industries Journal*, 28 (9): 1321–35.

Urbano, D. and D. Yordanova (2008) 'Determinants of the Adoption of HRM Practices in Tourism SMEs in Spain: An Exploratory Study', *Service Business*, 2 (3): 167–85.

Weiermair, K. (2000) Tourists' Perceptions towards and Satisfaction with Service Quality in the Cross-Cultural Service Encounter: Implications for Hospitality and Tourism Management', *Managing Service Quality*, 10 (6): 397–409.

Welsh, J. and J. White (1981) 'A Small Business Is Not a Little Big Business', *Harvard Business Review*, 59 (4): 18–32.

Williamson, D. (2002) 'Forward from a Critique of Hofstede's Model of National Culture', *Human Relations*, 55 (11): 1373–95.

Woods, R. H., W. Heck and M. Sciarini (1998) *Turnover and Diversity in the Lodging Industry*, Washington DC: American Hotel Foundation.

World Travel and Tourism Council (2012) *Global Travel and Tourism in 2011: A Year of Challenge*, London: World Travel and Tourism Council.

Zeithaml, V., A. Parasuraman and L. L. Berry (1990) *Delivering Quality Service: Balancing Customer Perceptions and Expectations*, New York: The Free Press.

Zhang, H. Q., L. Ren, H. Shen and Q. Xiao (2013) 'What Contributes to the Success of Home Inns in China?' *International Journal of Hospitality Management*, 33 (June): 425–34.

Zhang, H. Q. and E. Wu (2004) 'Human Resources Issues Facing the Hotel and Travel Industry in China', *International Journal of Contemporary Hospitality Management*, 16 (7): 424–8.

WEBSITES

www.corporate.ritzcarlton.com
www.phx.corporate-ir.net/
www.southwestairlines.com
www.starwoodhotels.com
www.tophotelchains.com
www.westjet.com
www.ausopen.com
www.edmonton.com
www.edmontonstores.com

FURTHER READING

Reference	Focus
Albattat, A. R. S. and A. P. M. Som (2013) 'Employee Dissatisfaction and Turnover Crises in the Malaysian Hospitality Industry', *International Journal of Business and Management*, 8 (5): 62–71.	Hospitality Staff turnover Malaysia

Alleyne, P., L. Doherty and D. Greenidge (2006) 'Human Resource Management and Performance in the Barbados Hotel Industry', *International Journal of Hospitality Management*, 18 (2): 94–109.	Hospitality Human resource management Barbados
Boella, M. and S. Goss-Turner (2013) *Human Resource Management in the Hospitality Industry: A Guide to Best Practice*, London and New York: Routledge.	Hospitality Human resource management Best practice
Bresciani, S., A. Thrassou and D. Vrontis (2012) 'Human Resource Management-Practices, Performance and Strategy in the Italian Hotel Industry', *World Review of Entrepreneurship, Management and Sustainable Development*, 8 (4): 405–23.	Hospitality Human resource management Hotels Italy
Chan, S. H. and O. M. Kuok (2011) 'A Study of Human Resources Recruitment, Selection and Retention Issues in the Hospitality and Tourism Industry in Macau', *Journal of Human Resources in Hospitality and Tourism*, 10 (4): 421–41.	Hospitality Human resource management Macau
Chand, M. (2010a) 'Human Resource Management Practices in Indian Hospitality Enterprises: An Empirical Analysis', *Managing Leisure*, 15 (1–2): 4–16.	Hospitality Human resource management India
Chand, M. (2010b) 'The Impact of HRM Practices on Service Quality, Customer Satisfaction and Performance in the Indian Hotel Industry', *The International Journal of Human Resource Management*, 21 (4): 551–66.	Hospitality Human resource management Hotels India
Chand, M. (2010c) 'Measuring the Service Quality of Indian Tourism Destinations: An Application of SERVQUAL Model', *International Journal of Services Technology and Management*, 13 (3): 218–33.	Tourism Service quality Servqual India
Chang, S., Y. Gong and C. Shum (2011) 'Promoting Innovation in Hospitality Companies through Human Resource Management Practices', *International Journal of Hospitality Management*, 30 (4): 812–18.	Hospitality Human resource management Innovation
Chen, C. F. and F. S. Chen (2010) 'Experience Quality, Perceived Value, Satisfaction and Behavioral Intentions for Heritage Tourists', *Tourism Management*, 31 (1): 29–35.	Tourism Service quality Heritage
Chen, R. X., C. Cheung and R. Law (2012) 'A Review of the Literature on Culture in Hotel Management Research: What Is the Future?' *International Journal of Hospitality Management*, 31 (1): 52–65.	Hospitality Hotels Organizational culture
Cho, S., R. H. Woods, S. Jang and M. Erdem (2006) 'Measuring the Impact of Human Resource Management Practices on Hospitality Firms' Performances', *International Journal of Hospitality Management*, 25 (2): 262–77.	Hospitality Human resource management
Choy, D. (1995) 'The Quality of Tourism Employment', *Tourism Management*, 16 (2): 129–37.	Tourism Human resource management Employment
Coyne, B. S. and E. J. Coyne Snr. (2001) 'Getting, Keeping and Caring for Unpaid Volunteers for Professional Golf Tournament Events', *Human Resource Development International*, 4 (2): 199–216.	Events Sport Volunteering
Cronin, J. J. Jr and A. Taylor (1994) 'SERVPERF versus SERVQUAL: reconciling performance-based and perception-minus-expectations measurement of service quality', *Journal of Marketing*, 58 (1): 125–31.	Customer satisfaction Service quality Servqual

Cuskelly, G., R. Hoye, and C. Auld (2006), *Working with Volunteers in Sport: Theory and Practice*, Abingdon UK: Routledge.	Events Sport Volunteering
Davidson, M. C., R. McPhail and S. Barry (2011) 'Hospitality HRM: Past, Present and the Future', *International Journal of Contemporary Hospitality Management*, 23 (4): 498–516.	Hospitality Human resource management
Davidson, M. C., N. Timo and Y. Wang (2010) 'How Much Does Labour Turnover Cost?: A Case Study of Australian Four- and Five-Star Hotels', *International Journal of Contemporary Hospitality Management*, 22 (4): 451–66.	Hospitality Staff turnover Hotels Australia
Dawson, M., J. Abbott and S. Shoemaker (2011) 'The Hospitality Culture Scale: A Measure Organizational Culture and Personal Attributes', *International Journal of Hospitality Management*, 30 (2): 290–300.	Hospitality Organizational culture
Devine, F., T. Baum, N. Hearns and A. Devine (2007) 'Cultural Diversity in Hospitality Work: The Northern Ireland Experience', *International Journal of Human Resource Management*, 18 (2), 333–49.	Hospitality Organizational culture Northern Ireland
Elstad, B. (1996) 'Volunteer Perception of Learning and Satisfaction in a Mega-event: The Case of the XVII Olympic Winter Games in Lillehammer', *Festival Management and Event Tourism*, 4 (3–4), 75–83.	Events Sport Volunteering
Elstad, B. (2003) 'Continuance Commitment and Reasons to Quit: A Study of Volunteers at a Jazz Festival', *Event Management*, 8 (2), 99–108.	Events Festivals Volunteering
Fâilte Ireland (2005) *A Human Resource Development Strategy for Irish Tourism: Competing Through People, 2005–2012*. Dublin: Fâilte Ireland.	Tourism Human resource management Ireland
Fick, G. R. and J. R. B. Ritchie (1991) 'Measuring service quality in the travel and tourism industry' *Journal of Travel Research*, 30 (2), 2–9.	Tourism Travel industry Service quality
Getz, D., M. O'Neill and J. Carlsen (2001) 'Service Quality Evaluation at Events Through Service Mapping', *Journal of Travel Research*, 39 (4), 380–90.	Events Service quality Service evaluation
Hanlon, C., and G. Cuskelly (2002) 'Pulsating Major Sport Event Organizations: A Framework for Inducting Managerial Personnel', *Event Management*, 7 (4), 231–43.	Events Human resource management Sport
Hogg, G. (ed.) (1997) *Contemporary Services Marketing Management: A Reader*, London: The Dryden Press, 149–70.	Services Marketing management
Goodale, P. A. and R. C. Wood (1997) 'Organizational Culture in Luxury Hotels', in Foley, M., J. Lennon and G. Maxwell (eds.) *Hospitality, Tourism and Leisure Management*, London: Cassell, pp. 37–50.	Hospitality Hotels Organizational culture
Hartline, M. D. and O. C. Ferrell (1996) 'The Management of Customer-Contact Service Employees: An Empirical Investigation', *Journal of Marketing*, 60 (4): 52–70.	Services Human resource management Customer service
Hon, A. H. and A. S. Leung (2011). 'Employee Creativity and Motivation in the Chinese Context: The Moderating Role of Organizational Culture', *Cornell Hospitality Quarterly*, 52 (2): 125–34.	Hospitality Organizational culture China

Hoque, K. (1999) 'New Approaches to HRM in the UK Hotel Industry', *Human Resource Management Journal*, 9 (2): 64–76.	Hospitality Hotels Human resource management United Kingdom
Jones, P. and A. Davies (1991) 'Empowerment: A Study of General Managers at Four-Star Hotel Properties in the UK', *International Journal of Hospitality Management*, 10 (3): 211–17.	Hospitality Hotels Empowerment
Knutson, B. J., P. Stevens, M. Patton and F. Yokoyama (1990) 'The Service Scoreboard: A Service Quality Measurement Tool for the Hospitality Industry', *Hospitality Education and Research Journal*, 14 (2): 413–20.	Hospitality Service quality Service Measurement
Ladkin, A., and V. McCabe (2010) 'Human Resource Issues and Industry Trends in the UK Conventions and Exhibitions Industry', *CAUTHE Conference 2010: Tourism and Hospitality: Challenge the Limits*, 825-837.	Events Conventions and exhibitions Human resource management
Lashley, C. (1995) 'Towards an Understanding of Employee Empowerment in Hospitality Service', *International Journal of Contemporary Hospitality Management*, 7 (1): 27–32.	Hospitality Human resource management Empowerment
Liu, A., and G. Wall (2006) 'Planning Tourism Employment: A Developing Country Perspective', *Tourism Management*, 27 (1): 159–170.	Tourism Employment Developing countries
Lucas, R. and M. Deery (2004) 'Significant Developments and Emerging Issues in Human Resource Management', *International Journal of Hospitality Management*, 23 (5): 459–72.	Hospitality Human resource management
MacLaurin, D. J. (2002) 'Human Resource Issues for the Convention Industry', in Weber, K. and K. S. Chon *Convention Tourism: International Research and Industry Perspectives*, Binghampton NY: Haworth Hospitality Press, 79–100.	Events Conventions and exhibitions Human resource management
Mahesh, V. S. (1993) 'Human Resource Planning and Development a Focus on Service Excellence', in Baum, T (ed.) *Human Resource Issues in International Tourism*, Oxford: Butterworth-Heinemann, 22–9.	Tourism Human resource management Service quality
Marco-Lajara, B. and M. Úbeda-García (2013) 'Human Resource Management Approaches in Spanish Hotels: An Introductory Analysis', *International Journal of Hospitality Management*, 35: 339–47.	Hospitality Human resource management Hotels Spain
Maxwell, G. A. (1997) 'Empowerment in the UK Hospitality Industry', in Foley, M., J. Lennon and G. Maxwell (eds.) *Hospitality, Tourism and Leisure Management*, London: Cassell, 53–68.	Hospitality Empowerment United Kingdom
Mok, C., B. Sparks and J. Kadampully (2013) *Service Quality Management in Hospitality Tourism and Leisure*, Routledge.	Tourism Hospitality Service quality
Mullins, L. J. and P. Dossor (2013) *Hospitality Management and Organizational Behaviour*, 5th edn, Harlow UK: Pearson Education.	Hospitality Human resource management Organizational behaviour
Muskat, B., M. Muskat and D. Blackman (2013) 'Understanding the Cultural Antecedents of Quality Management in Tourism', *Managing Service Quality*, 23 (2): 131–48.	Tourism Service quality Organizational culture

Narayan, B., C. Rajendran, L. P. Sai and R. Gopalan (2009) 'Dimensions of Service Quality in Tourism: An Indian Perspective', *Total Quality Management*, 20 (1): 61–89.	Tourism Service quality India
Nickson, D. (2000) 'Human Resource Issues in Travel and Tourism', in Moutinho, L. (ed.) *Strategic Management in Tourism*, Wallingford Oxford UK: CABI Publishing, pp. 169–86.	Tourism Travel industry Human resource management
Nickson, D. (2007) *Human Resource Management for the Hospitality and Tourism Industries*, Abingdon UK: Routledge.	Tourism Hospitality Human resource management
Riley, M., A. Ladkin and E. Szivas (2002) *Tourism Employment: Analysis and Planning*, Clevedon UK: Channel View.	Tourism Employment Planning
Saad, S. K. (2013) 'Contemporary Challenges of Human Resource Planning in Tourism and Hospitality Organizations: A Conceptual Model', *Journal of Human Resources in Hospitality and Tourism*, 12 (4): 333–54.	Hospitality Tourism Human resource management
Safrit, R. D., and R. Schmiesing (2011) 'Volunteer Models and Management', in Connors, T. D. (ed.) *The Volunteer Management Handbook: Leadership Strategies for Success*, 2nd edn, Hoboken NJ: John Wiley, pp. 1–30.	Events Human resource management Volunteers
Tesone, D. (2008) *Handbook of Hospitality Human Resources Management (Handbooks of Hospitality Management)*, Oxford: Butterworth-Heinemann.	Hospitality Human resource management
Tsang, N. K. (2011). 'Dimensions of Chinese Culture Values in Relation to Service Provision in Hospitality and Tourism Industry', *International Journal of Hospitality Management*, 30 (3): 670–9.	Hospitlaity Tourism Organizational culture China
Van der Wagen, L. (2007) *Human Resource Management for Events: Managing the Event Workforce*, Burlington, MA: Butterworth-Heinemann.	Events Human resource management
Weber, K., and A. Ladkin (2004) 'Trends Affecting the Convention Industry in the 21st Century', *Journal of Convention and Event Tourism*, 6 (4): 47–63	Events Conventions & exhibitions Human resource management
Yang, J. T., C. S. Wan and Y.J. Fu (2012) 'Qualitative Examination of Employee Turnover and Retention Strategies in International Tourist Hotels in Taiwan', *International Journal of Hospitality Management*, 31 (3): 837–48.	Hospitality Staff turnover Taiwan

CASE LINKAGES

Case 3	Ryanair
Case 4	Hyatt Hotels

Chapter **5**

Tourism, hospitality and event organizations

The financial context

Introduction and chapter overview

This chapter continues the internal analysis of organizations in examining one of the functional areas that organizations are often divided into – the financial context. The previous chapter considered the human resource functional area and the following chapter will examine the other functional area, namely Marketing (Chapter 6).

The ability to make sense of an organization's financial situation is an important part of strategic analysis. In order to carry out a financial analysis of a company's situation or of an industry, it is necessary to understand some of the fundamentals of finance and its sources.

This chapter begins with a discussion of the sources of corporate finance and then goes on to discuss the costs of the various types of capital. This information helps students to make sense of a company's financial structure before the tools of conventional financial analysis are discussed. The concept of benchmarking is explained and its use in financial analysis is discussed.

Two topics of particular relevance in *THE* contexts are outlined towards the end of the chapter: exchange rate risk and cash flow risk analysis.

LEARNING OBJECTIVES

After studying this chapter, readers should be able to:

- identify the primary distinguishing aspects of financial management in parts of *THE*;
- understand what is meant by financial analysis in *THE* contexts;

- identify the sources of funds available to companies and the relative advantages and disadvantages of each;
- assess a company's potential for further funding based on the current position, future prospects and past performance;
- understand the cost and non-cost issues involved in raising and using various forms of capital;
- understand the importance of the cost of capital;
- understand the limitations of a company report and accounts as a source of data for financial analysis;
- utilise the major tools that can be used to analyse a company's financial position and to understand their limitations;
- analyse and understand the characteristics of foreign exchange risks in *THE* contexts;
- analyse and understand the characteristics of cash flow risks in *THE* contexts.

Financial resources in tourism, hospitality and events contexts

Introduction

Although *THE* sectors cover a wide diversity of different organizations including: tour operators; transport and accommodation providers; event organisers; destination organizations; internet intermediaries; and travel agencies, financial management is important to all of them.

When dealing with finance much of the material is quite generic in that the accounting conventions, ratio analysis techniques and the fundamentals of raising finance are similar for *THE* organizations as in other business fields. Nevertheless, in this chapter they will be applied to *THE* organizations to illustrate the relevant financial principles.

There are, however, also some highly significant and distinctive features of managing finance in many *THE* contexts that are characteristic of the sectors and that we consider briefly below.

Cash management

All companies have a need to hold cash or have the ability to borrow cash. Cash is used to pay creditors (suppliers). Cash management is concerned with the investing of cash surpluses and financing of cash shortages.

During the course of trading, companies often generate cash surpluses for which there is no current requirement and which can therefore be invested for a period of time. Sometimes companies that have such surpluses are referred to as 'cash rich' and many in *THE* are in this category, at least for part of each year, because of the seasonality of many businesses in these sectors.

THE organizations make profits predominantly from their operations such as selling holidays, accommodation, transportation or events. However, many organizations in *THE* also derive substantial revenues from investing the cash they receive from their customers at certain times of the year. Many parts of the industry are highly seasonal with large cash accumulations in some periods and an exodus of cash during other times of the year.

Such a situation is illustrated by the major events and entertainment group Live Nation below.

The importance of cash management: Live Nation

Live Nation, headquartered in Beverly Hills, California, is probably the largest entertainment company in the world. The company organizes and promotes concerts and festivals around the world, owns or leases concert and festival venues and sells tickets for events through its 'Ticketmaster' operations.

However, many of its operations are highly seasonal in nature with outdoor events such as concerts and festivals being concentrated during the spring and summer. Consequently the results of operations vary from quarter to quarter and year over year. Typically the company experiences its poorest financial performance in the first and fourth quarters of the calendar year as its outdoor venues are primarily used, and the festivals it organizes primarily occur, during May through to September. The seasonality of the underlying businesses creates volatile cash flows.

Live Nation Entertainment 2012 Annual Report available at http://phx.corporate-ir.net/

Questions

1. What is meant by cash management?

2. Why is cash management important to an organization such as Live Nation?

Managing foreign exchange risk

Many businesses in *THE* operate internationally (across national boundaries), producing costs and revenues in various currencies. Since the rate of exchange between one currency and another varies, this produces a risk (commonly called 'exposure') that needs to be managed.

Such risks are of course not unique to *THE* businesses. Given the underlying nature of the business, however, the size of the exposure to movements in foreign exchange rates is often large relative to the size of the organization; far larger than for most companies engaged in other areas of the economy. The very purpose of companies involved in tour operating, international air transportation or hotel groups operating internationally implies that they are operating across national boundaries and consequently they are exposed to foreign exchange risks

The cases of a German airline and a British tour operator illustrate the sort of foreign exchange risks that *THE* companies are often exposed to.

Exposure to foreign exchange risks

Many companies in *THE* operate internationally which produces costs and revenues denominated in foreign currencies. Since the rate of exchange between most currencies varies, as the rate is set by the vast international foreign exchange markets, a risk is created. The risk is basically that planned revenues are lower and costs are higher than expected when converted into the company's home currency.

For example a German airline may:

- sell its tickets in many currencies;
- buy its fuel and aircraft in US Dollars;
- pay most of its staff and report its profits in Euros.

Similarly a British-based outbound tour operator may:

- receive most of its income in £ Sterling;
- buy or lease aircraft and pay for fuel in US Dollars;
- pay most of its staff in £ Sterling;
- pay its accommodation and other suppliers in the various currencies of the destination country.

In the cases above, if the value of the US Dollar were to rise against the Euro and £ Sterling, costs would be higher, putting a strain on the profitability of the operations of the two companies.

Questions

1. Explain the nature of the foreign exchange exposure for the German Airline.
2. Explain the nature of the foreign exchange exposure for the British based outbound tour operator.

Capital intensity

Levels of capital intensity vary enormously in different parts of THE. Capital intensity refers to the amount of capital used in businesses relative to the other factors of production, particularly human resources. Capital-intensive industries use a large portion of capital to buy expensive equipment compared to their labour costs.

Thus, industries such as oil refining and iron and steel production are often thought of as 'capital intensive'. The capital intensity of THE businesses varies enormously. Accommodation including hotels and transport including airlines and cruising are often viewed as capital intensive parts of the industry.

Conversely, in other parts of THE capital requirements are usually relatively low. Thus the capital requirements in setting up a travel agent, an internet intermediary or an event management company, for example, are often relatively low.

The relative capital intensity of parts of the industry has three important implications for managers working in the industry.

- *Barrier to competition* – Capital intensity can often act as a barrier to new companies entering the market to compete. Often new companies or smaller companies have insufficient access to capital from the financial markets and banks which prevents them from entering the market to compete with more established companies.
- *Long lead times* – Projects which require large amounts of capital often have very long lead times between the decision to invest and the asset becoming available. This requires careful planning and scheduling. For example, if an airline decides to invest in new aircraft it may have to raise the capital it needs to invest (from banks or financial markets), place an order with the aircraft manufacturer, have a period of aircraft testing and staff training, and alter operational procedures and systems. In most cases this requires lead times of several years. The six launch customers for the Airbus 380 aircraft (currently the largest civil aircraft flying) were received in 2000, but did not enter service with Singapore Airlines until 2007.

- *Asset ownership or management* – The need for large quantities of capital can in some parts of *THE* be mitigated by the fact that many companies do not actually own the assets concerned (and therefore do not need to finance them), but instead they manage or lease the assets. Hotels, for example, are often under management contracts or franchising arrangements. Airlines often lease some or all their aircraft from leasing companies such as General Electric Commercial Aviation Services (GECAS) and International Lease Finance Corporation (ILFC).

The contrast between Carnival Cruises and Travel Counsellors below illustrates the differences in capital intensity for two parts of *THE*.

SHORT CASE ILLUSTRATION

Capital intensity: Carnival Cruises and Travel Counsellors

Carnival Corporation and plc is a company listed in New York and London with headquarters in Miami and London. It operates some of the world's leading cruise brands including: Carnival, Holland-America, Cunard, P&O and Princess.

In order to grow and compete with other cruise lines the company has to spend heavily on new cruise ships and refurbishments for its existing fleet. These investments have to be carefully planned since they have very long lead times and require substantial financial commitments over a number of years.

During 2012, for example, the company ordered two new cruise ships. One of the ships being built by Fincantieri of Italy will be the largest vessel in the Carnival Cruise Lines fleet. The ship, named Carnival Vista with a gross tonnage of 135,000, is scheduled to be delivered in the winter of 2016, some four years following the initial order, a demonstration of the long lead times involved. In total the company reported (in late 2012) that it had nine ships on order at a total cost of $5.9 billion.

By contrast, Travel Counsellors represents a labour-intensive (as opposed to capital-intensive) part of the industry. Travel Counsellors was launched in 1994 by David Speakman in Bolton, UK.

The travel intermediary has grown substantially to become a £0.5 billion business, but is based on a low capital outlay business model. The company has an international network of self-employed travel counsellors working from home who are paid on a commission basis based on the travel sales they achieve. Since they are self-employed, experienced and highly motivated, they are able to provide high customer service levels which are difficult to match on the internet or by traditional travel agents operating from shop premises.

www.travelcounsellors.co.uk and Carnival Corporation and plc Annual Report 2012, available at www.carnival.com

Questions

1. Explain what is meant by capital intensity.
2. Contrast the capital intensity of Carnival Corporation and Travel Counsellors and comment on the implications.

The importance of finance

Financial management is that part of the total management function concerned with the effective and efficient raising and use of funds.

Like physical, operational, marketing or human resources, finance:

- has a large number of competing uses;
- is scarce, but can be obtained at a price;
- is bought and sold in markets.

Financial management is concerned with managing this scarce resource so as to ensure that finance is:

- available in *sufficient quantities at the right time*;
- obtained at the *lowest possible cost*;
- used in the *most profitable* ways.

The importance of finance to hospitality managers is illustrated below.

SHORT CASE ILLUSTRATION

The importance of finance to hospitality managers

Tsai *et al.* (2011) stress the importance of good financial management for managers working in hospitality.

The authors argue that 'financial management is the backbone of any business, including firms involved in hospitality (including but not limited to hotels, restaurants, and casinos)'. However, although financial management is important at all levels of hospitality organizations, the focus of financial management alters. At the property level managers are 'charged with using owners' invested assets to enhance revenues and reduce expenses to achieve desired net profits. However, managers at the corporate level are more involved in issues related to investing excess cash and raising debt and equity capital. Dividend policy and decisions, which to some extent signal board-level views on the firm's future development opportunities, also play a significant role in hospitality finance' (Tsai *et al.*, 2011).

Since the hospitality industry is relatively *capital-intensive* (Karadeniz *et al.*, 2009; Lee, 2007), managers at all levels are required to have adequate financial management skills and access to strategies for achieving the goal of financial management, namely value enhancement or creation for owners.

Questions

1. Why is financial management important for hospitality managers?
2. Distinguish between the likely focus of financial management at the corporate and property level for hospitality managers.

Most university business courses have accounting and finance content. You may consequently be familiar with some of the content of this chapter and this will be to your advantage. This chapter takes the material from the other modules and develops the material specifically in the context of strategic analysis. There are certain elements of finance that we need to concentrate on when carrying out a strategic analysis.

THINK POINTS

- Explain in what respects there are aspects of financial management which are characteristic of many *THE* organizations.

- Explain why an American hotel group operating hotels in Asia may be susceptible to foreign exchange risk.
- Identify the managerial implications for managers operating in high- or low-capital intensity parts of *THE*.

Financial management is often complex and frequently laden with specific terminology. We are primarily concerned with the impact finance, its availability and price will have on the adoption of successful strategies. For a more detailed examination of financial management and accounting in a *THE* context a number of sources are available including: Evans (2002); Guilding (2009); Bowdin *et al.* (2012); and Harris (2012). A large number of generic texts also examine financial management in detail, see for example Marsh (2012) and Arnold (2012).

Finance, or the lack of it, is central to the strategic development of all organizations large or small. It is one of the key resource inputs and cannot be ignored. The most original strategies and the most complex plans for the future of a business are meaningless unless managers have considered the financial position of the organization at the outset and during the period covered by the strategy.

The ability of an organization to finance both current and future strategies is central to any analysis of the organization's position. A central theme to this chapter will be the ability of the company to finance current strategies – its ability to raise the funding required for future developments.

The success or failure of the organization is judged by its ability to meet its strategic objectives. The financial information (in the form of annual and sometimes quarterly financial 'corporate' reports) produced by organizations provides a quantifiable means of assessing success. It is important to recognize, however, that other quantifiable information, such as efficiency and productivity data, and non-quantifiable data such as the company's image, can also be used to make such judgements. In this chapter we will examine the value of information extracted from financial reports specifically as a source from which judgements can be made.

Corporate reports are, however, just one source of information about a company's financial state. Managers have a number of ways of gathering information about their own and competitors' finances and we will discuss these later in the chapter.

An introduction to financial analysis

Understanding financial structure and profitability

At the outset it is necessary to have an understanding of a business's financial structure. An organization's annual accounts will normally contain two key statements which we will examine briefly:

- The balance sheet; and
- The profit and loss statement.

Understanding the balance sheet

Assets, which may be *long-term* or *current* assets, are financed (and 'matched' in the balance sheet) by capital and liabilities. Liabilities may be *current* (less than one year) or *long term* (over one year).

> *Capital + Liabilities = Assets*

The principles underpinning a balance sheet are shown in Figure 5.1.

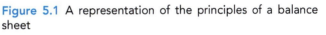

Figure 5.1 A representation of the principles of a balance sheet

Table 5.1 A simplified balance sheet for Air New Zealand

	Item	Value NZ$ (m)	Examples
A	Fixed assets	3,754	Semi-permanent assets – property, plant, vehicles, aircraft etc.
B	Current assets	1,858	Trading assets – stock, debtors, cash
C	Current liabilities	(1,710)	Trading liabilities – creditors, overdrafts
	Net current assets or *working capital* (B–C)	148	
	CAPITAL EMPLOYED (A + B + C)	3,902	
D	Shareholder finance	1,816	Share capital, retained profits
E	Long-term liabilities	2,086	Medium- and long-term loans
	SOURCES OF FINANCE (D + E)	3,902	

Source: Air New Zealand Financial Results 2013, available at www.airnewzealand.com.

A simplified example of a balance sheet for Air New Zealand is shown in Table 5.1 as an example.

Understanding the profit and loss account

The profit and loss statement matches the revenue earned in a period with the costs incurred in earning it.

A simplified profit and loss account for Air New Zealand is shown in Table 5.2 as an example.

Sources of corporate funding

Financial resources, as we have already learned, are an essential input to strategic development. Capital for development can be raised from several sources and these are summarised here.

Table 5.2 A simplified profit and loss account for Air New Zealand

	Item	Value NZ$ (m)	Examples
A	Sales or operating revenue	4,618	Passenger and freight revenue, contract services
B	Costs or operating expenditure	(3,720)	Labour, fuel, maintenance, aircraft operations, sales and marketing
C	OPERATING PROFIT (A + B)	898	
D	Depreciation, amortization, rental & lease costs	(588)	
E	EARNINGS BEFORE FINANCE COSTS AND TAXATION (C + D)	310	
F	Finance costs	(54)	
G	PROFIT BEFORE TAXATION (E + F)	256	
H	Taxation	(74)	
	NET PROFIT ATTRIBUTABLE TO SHAREHOLDERS (G – H)	182	

Source: Air New Zealand Financial Results 2013, available at www.airnewzealand.com

KEY CONCEPT

Capital

Accountants use the term capital to describe one particular type of 'money'. It is usually contrasted with revenue. Revenue is money that is earned through normal business transactions – through sales, rents or whatever the company 'does' through its normal activities. Capital is money that is used to invest in the business – to buy new equipment, new capacity, extra aircraft, etc. The investment of capital enables the business to expand and, through that expansion, to increase its revenue and profits in future years. Capital can be raised from shareholders, through retained profits, through loan capital or through the disposal of assets.

Share capital

For *limited liability* companies, a sizeable proportion of capital is raised from shareholders (the financial owners of the company) in the form of share capital.

Historically, share capital has comprised the majority of capital for a limited company's start-up and subsequent development. In return for their investment, shareholders receive a return in accordance with the company's performance in a given year in the form of a 'dividend'. The dividend per share is taken as an important measure, by shareholders, of the company's success in its chosen strategy. Shares also confer on their holders a right to vote on company matters through resolutions at annual or extraordinary company meetings pro rata with the size of their holding. It follows that a shareholding in excess of 50% confers total control over a company's strategy.

Under normal circumstances, share capital is considered to be permanent – it is not paid back by the company. It is thus unlike other forms of capital (e.g. loan capital). The shareholders' only 'payback' is in the form of dividends and through capital growth – an increase in the value of the shares. Shareholders who wish to divest their stock in a company must usually sell it via a stock exchange (in the case of shares in a *public* limited company) or through a private sale (in the case of a *private* company). In exceptional circumstances, some companies offer a 'buyback' of their own shares.

Shareholders can be individuals or 'institutional shareholders'. Some individuals hold their personal share portfolio, but the vast majority of shares are held by institutional shareholders (whose business it is to invest on behalf of others) such as pension funds, life assurance companies and investment trusts. The profile of shareholders varies from company to company and from country to country.

KEY CONCEPT

Share value and share volume

Share value is the price of a given company's shares at a given point in time. Like any other commodity, the forces of supply and demand determine its value. Given that in normal circumstances the supply is fixed over the short-to-medium term, its price is determined by how many people want to buy it. If the market has confidence in a company's prospects, its price will rise. If a company's prospects are considered poor, fewer people will want to buy its shares and the price will fall.

Share volume is the number of shares held by a shareholder. The larger the volume, the more influential the shareholder will be in the company's affairs.

Total share volume is the total number of shares that a company has issued for sale to the stock market or to employees of the organization. Broadly speaking, larger companies have greater share volumes than smaller concerns.

Rights issue capital

From time to time a company may seek to increase its capital for expansion by means of a *rights issue*. This is when a company issues new shares to the stock market, normally giving its own shareholders the first refusal *pro rata* with their current proportion of the company's share volume.

The decision to go for a rights issue may well be a strategic decision for management because it can impact on the ownership of the company. If existing shareholders do not exercise their right to buy, then it is likely that ownership will be diluted – i.e. shareholders will find that they own a lower percentage of share volume than they used to.

Those shares not taken up by shareholders, who may be unable or unwilling to buy them, are normally covered by *underwriters* (institutional investors) at a price agreed, in advance. Underwriting is an important 'technical' feature of new share issues and as such is a major cost in the process. A rights issue is sometimes seen as a reward to loyal shareholders

A variation on a rights issue is *placing*. A placing involves the selling of shares direct to a small number of investors, usually large financial institutions. This may be marginally cheaper than a rights issue, but its major advantage is its flexibility in enabling new shareholders significant, possibly strategic holdings. *Placings* take place, for example, as a part of a joint venture agreement whereby the two companies exchange placed shareholdings as a sign of their mutual commitment to the alliance.

SHORT CASE ILLUSTRATION

Refinancing: Thomas Cook

Thomas Cook launched a package of measures in mid-May 2013 to enable it to restructure its financing structure and reduce its burden of debt which stood at £1.5 billion at that time. The international travel group had endured a turbulent few years of trading prior to 2013 as tough trading brought on by the global economic downturn, high fuel costs and social unrest in popular destinations such as Egypt and Tunisia forced it to negotiate banking lifelines and make disposals to raise cash and reduce debt. Sales worth £9.5 billion were made in 2012 to 23 million customers, but the sales were made at an overall loss of £590 million.

A new Chief Executive (Harriet Green) was appointed in July 2012, and as in many cases when a new boss is appointed a new course of direction was plotted which appears to be generating positive results. She embarked on a revised strategy which included more asset sales and cost-cutting measures to restore the group to financial health. These measures included the closing of many high street outlets, 2,500 redundancies in the UK and the sale of its North American division.

The Thomas Cook share price rallied considerably from Autumn 2012 and this renewed confidence in the company enabled the refinancing to take place. The refinancing includes:

- A deeply discounted (relative to the current market price) rights issue at 76 pence per share aimed at raising around £305million.
- A 'share placing' raising £120million.
- The issue of new bonds maturing in 2020 and £691 million of new debt facilities with lenders.

Harriet Green said it would reduce the company's 'very significant debt', lengthen its repayment profile and help it deliver its recovery plan. The company also suggested it would pave the way for reinstating its dividend.

www.thomascook.com/ and various newspapers

Questions

1. What were the financial issues which Thomas Cook faced when the new CEO was appointed?
2. Explain the measures which the new CEO took in order to address the financial issues.

Retained profit as a source of capital

Shareholders provide other funds for development by agreeing *not* to receive all the company's profits in a given year. *Retained profit,* that element of operating profit not paid to shareholders in the form of dividend, is arguably the most common method of funding strategic developments, particularly if the company is quite old in terms of years of operation. By using this form of funding organizations save on the costs involved in using alternatives such as fees to investment banks, lawyers and accountants. It also means management do not have to reveal nor justify their strategies to others and risk their plans becoming known to competitors.

It should be recognized that retained profits do not constitute a loss to shareholders as such, because the value of the organization and consequently the share price is normally increased when these funds are used for reinvestment. It is, however, important that companies recognize the need to balance the proportion of profits distributed and retained in order to satisfy those shareholders who need regular funds themselves (such as insurance and pension companies).

Loan capital

An important consideration in the use of retained profits to fund corporate development is clearly the ability of the company to actually make a profit that can be, at least in part, distributed to shareholders as dividends. Whilst a company may make a profit from its normal activities after taxation, some profits will be required to meet the cost of other forms of *debt finance* or loans.

Debt finance is shown in the balance sheet under two headings:

- *Creditors* – amounts falling due within one year; and
- *Creditors* – amounts falling due after more than one year.

The form of borrowing with most impact on strategic development is that falling due after more than one year – long-term debt. This form of borrowing can take a number of forms. In addition to the use of long term bank loans, a company can use debentures, convertible loan stock or corporate bonds.

Debt finance is normally for a set period of time and at a fixed rate of interest. The interest must be paid every year, regardless of the level of profit (often referred to as *servicing the debt*). The interest rate for this source is normally less than the cost of share capital (when the dividend payable on the shares is taken into account).

Comparison of share capital and loan capital

Each of the types of capital described above has its pros and cons. Share capital has the advantage that the amount paid on the capital is dependent upon company results. A company can decide not to pay a dividend if profits are poor in any given year. Loan capital, by contrast, must normally be serviced regardless of results, in much the same way that a mortgage on a house must be repaid regardless of other commitments.

Offsetting this advantage is the fact that share capital is permanent. As long as the company exists, it has an obligation to pay a dividend to its shareholders. Loan capital has the advantage to the company that it is time limited. Servicing the capital is restricted to the term of the loan (like a mortgage on a house) and when it is finally repaid in full, the business has no further obligation to the lender.

The fact that the repayment of debt finance takes precedence over dividends on shares means that shareholders bear an increased risk. If the company performs badly, their return on investment will be small or non-existent in a given year. Against this possibility, they usually expect to receive higher returns compared to providers of loan capital in the years when profits are good.

> **KEY CONCEPT**
>
> **Rewarding providers of debt and shareholders**
>
> Interest on debt capital must be paid regardless of the level of profit;
>
> interest on debt capital takes priority over dividends to shareholders;
>
> thus shareholders take a greater risk and expect to be rewarded accordingly.

The major advantages and disadvantages of share and loan capital are summarised in Table 5.3:

Table 5.3 Summary of the major advantages and disadvantages of share and loan capital

	Advantages	Disadvantages
Share capital	No fixed charges or legal obligation to pay a dividend No maturity date Issue of equity increases credit worthiness Marketable, i.e. can be traded	Extension of voting rights High issue costs May increase average cost of capital Dividends not tax deductible
Loan capital	Known and often lower cost No dilution of equity Interest payable is tax deductible	Increase in risk which may cause value of equity to fall Need for repayment Limit to amount of available funding

The strategic significance of sources of finance

Company ownership varies greatly in different countries. In some countries such as the UK, Australia, New Zealand, USA and Canada there is a strong tradition of share ownership by private individuals and public share quotations on the stock exchange. Other countries such as Germany, France, Italy and Spain exhibit different patterns, with more companies owned at least in part by banks, private trusts, families and government institutions (Lynch, 2003). Regardless of these differences however, the main sources of finance can be analysed and their strategic significance assessed.

> **THINK POINTS**
>
> - Why is money important to a business?
> - Define and distinguish between revenue and capital.
> - Define and distinguish between share capital and loan capital

Strategic developments for an organization normally imply that they:

- are of major importance to a company's future development;
- require a substantial commitment of resources (financial and other) by an organization;
- involve choices that have to be made about the deployment of finite resources between competing strategic options;
- involve key changes which need to be carefully managed;
- have an impact over a medium-to-long-term (more than a year) rather than short-term (less than one year) period because of their scope.

Because of the scope and timescale of strategic developments, some forms of finance are more suited to funding them than others. Table 5.4 considers the main categories of finance and considers their significance in funding strategic developments.

In Figure 5.2 the sources of finance for four well-known *THE* companies are summarized. It is, however, often difficult to obtain such detailed information for companies whose shares are not traded on major stock markets since they are not legally required to make such information widely available. Since there are

Table 5.4 Summary of the strategic significance of different sources of finance

Sources of finance	Strategic significance
Reserves and retained profits	Represent an accumulation over time. If not utilised, shareholders may demand that they are distributed to them as owners.
	Cheap and non-controversial.
	Typically the largest sources of finance for many companies.
	Finances the majority of strategic developments.
Shareholders	Useful to call on when major new strategic initiatives are envisaged.
	Relying on shareholders for further funding changes ownership, so risky in terms of retaining control.
Provisions for tax and pensions	Funds are committed for other purposes so not really useful for strategic developments.
Debt: long-term	Can be cheap, quick to set up and retains the existing shareholder structure thereby retaining control.
	High levels of debt (relative to equity) can be dangerous when interest rates are rising or when the economy is weak.
	The requirement to pay interest to 'service' the debt can be major burden on companies when earnings are weak.
Debt: short-term	Short-term means repayable inside one year, so only a temporary solution for major strategic initiatives.
	Funding could be quickly withdrawn by provider leaving the organization with a funding difficulty.

Source: Adapted from Lynch, 2003: 287.

many such businesses in *THE*, which are 'owner-managed' or family owned and do not have a stock market quotation, obtaining details of their funding position can be somewhat difficult.

The events management sector, for example, is highly fragmented with few large players with stock market quotations. There are also many event management operations which operate as subsidiaries of larger entities (such as in the case of Cox and Kings in Figure 5.2). Many of the larger quoted hotel groups, such as Marriott and Hilton for example, have event management capabilities that rely on the parent company's balance sheet for funding so cannot be analysed independently in terms of their sources of finance.

The companies chosen for comparison operate in different parts of *THE* and in differing markets and have done so with differing levels of financial success in recent years. Hence it is unsurprising that their balance sheets demonstrate different patterns of funding. The following companies are analysed in Figure 5.2:

- *Carnival Corporation and plc* is a global cruise company with stock market listings in both New York and London and a turnover of about $11 billion per annum. The company is one of the largest vacation companies in the world operating a portfolio of leading cruise brands which includes Carnival Cruise Lines, Holland America Line, Princess Cruises and Seabourn in North America; P&O Cruises and Cunard in the United Kingdom; AIDA Cruises in Germany; Costa Cruises in Southern Europe; Iberocruceros in Spain; and P&O Cruises in Australia. These brands attract about ten million customers annually (www.carnival.com).

- *Qantas*, an acronym for 'Queensland and Northern Territory Aerial Services', is Australia's largest airline and is also one of the world's oldest airlines. The airline has an extensive domestic and international network serving Europe and North America and serves the Asian market through its low-cost Jetstar subsidiary. Due to high fuel prices, intense competition and industrial disputes, Qantas reported a net loss in 2012, which was its first loss since Qantas was fully privatized 17 years previously, in 1995 (www.qantas.com.au).

- *Accor* which is based in France, is one of the world's leading hotel operators, with a particularly strong presence in Europe. It has some 450,000 rooms in more than 3,500 hotels in 92 countries. Its extensive brand portfolio – encompassing Sofitel, Pullman, Novotel, Mercure, Adagio, Ibis, and HotelF1 – provides a comprehensive range of options across the luxury to economy spectrum (www.accor.com).

- *Cox and Kings*, based in Mumbai, India, claims to be the longest-established travel company in the world, tracing its origins to the middle of the eighteenth century. The modern company has operations in 26 countries with a particular emphasis in India, Europe, Australia, US, Dubai, Japan and Singapore, selling packaged holidays for leisure travel. With the acquisition of the British Company Holidaybreak in September 2011, the group expanded to include brands such as Eurocamp (Camping and static caravan holidays), Explore (small group overland tours) and the European market leader in outdoor pursuits aimed at school children – PGL. In its home market of India the business also includes the organization and management of meetings, conferences, incentives and exhibition (MICE) and trade fairs for corporate clients (www.coxandkings.com).

Some conclusions can be made through an examination of the sources of finance in Figure 5.2:

- Carnival – Has a very high level of reserves and retained profit and relatively low levels of debt.
- Qantas – Has very low levels of reserves and retained profit (a reflection of poor levels of profitability in the airline industry in recent years) and high levels of both short- and long-term debt.
- Accor – Has moderate levels of reserves and retained profit, high levels of short-term debt and moderate levels of long-term debt.
- Cox and Kings – Has a very high level of reserves and retained profit, very low shareholders' funds, high levels of long-term debt and low levels of short-term debt.

In practice, business profits can vary significantly over time. In some years, it is preferable to use loan capital, especially when interest rates are low and profits are high. In other years, when profits are lower and interest rates are higher, share capital works out cheaper. The fact that the benefits are so finely divided means that most companies opt to use an element of both.

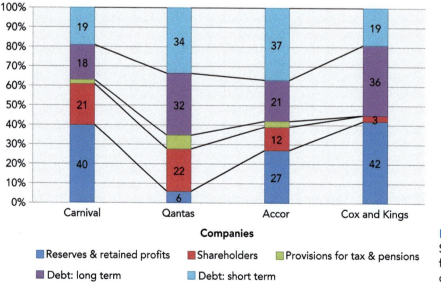

Figure 5.2
Sources of finance for four *THE* companies

Other sources of capital

Whilst the foregoing are the most common mechanisms of raising capital for development, others are available under some circumstances. One such method is to dispose of existing fixed assets. This can range from the selling of an aircraft, a hotel building or a performance venue to selling a subsidiary to a third party.

Marginal improvements in a company's capital situation can be achieved by improving the management of *working capital*, i.e. over the course of a financial year, small savings can accumulate to significant proportions, increasing both profitability and capital for reinvestment. This can be achieved by:

- extending the time taken to pay creditors;
- getting debtors to pay sooner; or
- spreading payments through leasing rather than purchasing assets.

KEY CONCEPT

Working capital

Working capital is the amount of money that a company has tied up in the normal operation of its business.

Working capital comprises money tied up in:

- stocks;
- debtors (money owed to the business);
- creditors (money the company owes);
- cash or current bank deposits.

A company's objective is usually to minimize this figure, or to manage the working capital in such a way that minimizes financing costs or maximizes earnings on cash balances. This is an important source of earnings for many companies in *THE* given the seasonality with which revenue is often received.

Working capital is needed to pay for goods, services and expenses before money can be recovered from creditors. The ability of a business to pay its cash commitments as they fall due shows that it has sufficient liquidity.

Inefficient management of working capital can lead to over-investment in working capital – over-capitalization. Conversely under-capitalization, also known as *overtrading*, often occurs when a company tries to do too much, too soon with too little long-term capital.

In this situation, a company can be trading profitably but runs out of cash to make payments, i.e. it becomes insolvent. Warning signs of overtrading include:

- a rapid increase in sales;
- a rapid increase in current assets;
- deterioration in liquidity ratios (such as the acid test ratio which measures the proportion of current assets less stocks to current liabilities).

Cost of capital

Availability of capital (where to get it from) is one issue when examining a company's capital funding, but another equally important consideration is its cost.

We learned above that providers of loans or share capital (equity) both require a return on their investments. Managers therefore need to know what return (profit) they need to make in order to meet the minimum requirements of capital providers. Failure to achieve this minimum will make the raising of future funds all the more difficult.

THINK POINTS

- Explain the advantages of employing share capital for development.
- Explain the advantages of employing loan capital for development.
- Explain what is meant by a 'rights issue'.
- Explain the importance of 'working capital' to successful business operation.

The *cost of capital* can be seen as the minimum return required on the company's assets, which in turn may influence the objectives of the company.

At its simplest, the cost of capital can be viewed as the annual amount payable (as a percentage) against the principal amount of money. Most of us will be aware that the return payable on loans varies between lenders and over time as interest rates rise or fall.

For example – the cost of loans on a credit card is much higher than a mortgage loan (where the security against the loan is mainly responsible for the difference).

Costs of debt capital

The costs of debt capital are relatively easy to calculate as they tend to correspond closely to the prevailing rate of interest.

Costs of share capital

Calculating the cost of share capital is slightly more complex as it contains more variables. Accounting academics spend a great deal of time discussing what should and should not be included in this calculation and how each component should be weighted. Reasons for this complexity include:

- the indefinite nature of the funding;
- the *opportunity cost* of undistributed profits;
- shareholders' expectations.

These factors mean that some models try to include components for inflation, industry averages and attitudes towards risk.

At its simplest, the cost of share capital can be calculated as follows:

> *Cost of share capital (equity) as a percentage = (Current net dividend per share/Current market price of share) × 100 + average percentage annual growth rate.*
>
> *Cost of share capital – example*

If the market price for shares is 400 cents per share, the annual dividend is 20 cents and the growth in profits average 10 per cent per annum, this gives:

Cost of share capital = (20/400) × 100 + 10%
= 15%

Models of capital costing

The CAPM model

The *Capital Asset Pricing Model* (CAPM) is a more complex but widely used model for calculating the cost of share capital.

Cost of share capital = Ri +β(Rm-Ri)

The model takes into account the competitor financial products available to potential investors. These range from the percentage return on virtually risk free government bonds (Ri) to a component covering the average interest for the share (equity) markets overall (Rm). The final element of the model represents the company itself, or more correctly its position relative to the market overall. The β coefficient is a measure of the volatility of the company's financial returns.

The CAPM model does have a number of drawbacks, which need to be recognized. First, the shares of the company need to be traded on a stock market. This means that the cost of equity in private companies cannot be calculated using this model. Second, the volatility of share prices in recent years causes problems in arriving at a date for 'acceptable' returns. The dynamic and complex nature of many industries and markets also suggest that historical data has limited value.

CAPM model – example

Assuming that risk-free government bonds are trading at 4 per cent and the average return on the market is 10 per cent. Also assuming that the volatility of the company has been calculated at 1.1, meaning the shares fluctuated slightly more than the market average.

Cost of share capital (equity) = 4% + 1.1 (10% – 4%)
= 10.6%

The WACC model

Whereas the CAPM model is used to calculate the cost of share capital, the *Weighted Average Cost of Capital* (WACC) can be used to determine the overall cost of funding to a company. The calculation of this information is relatively simple.

WACC = (proportion of loan finance × cost of loan finance) + (proportion of shareholders' funds × cost of shareholders' funds).

WACC model – example

Assuming that a company has $30 million of loan capital and $70 million equity funding, and the cost of each type has been calculated as 5 per cent and 15 per cent respectively, the calculation would be as follows:

Type of capital	Proportion	Cost (after tax)	Weighted cost
Loan finance	0.3	5%	1.5%
Shareholders funds	0.7	15%	10.5%
Total	1.0	12%	

Why calculate the cost of capital?

The cost of capital is usually an important figure to calculate because if it works out to be too high, the development that it is intended to fund may not be viable. Given that both debt and share capital attract servicing costs, the profit returns must exceed these servicing costs to the extent that the proposal is economically attractive.

If the projected returns on a strategic development (such as a new hotel or theatre) are not much more than the projected servicing costs, then management will have to make a judgement as to whether the investment is actually 'worth the risk'.

The whole situation is rendered more complex if debt capital is obtained at a variable rate of interest. Interest rates can vary substantially throughout an economic cycle and depend upon such things as government inflation targets, the currency exchange value and the amount of government funding taking place.

There are no guidelines as to the 'ideal' capital structure, regarding the balance between debt and equity finance.

The optimal structure will vary from company to company, from industry sector to industry sector and from year to year. Some companies will calculate their WACC and include factors which are difficult to quantify, such as the degree of risk faced by the industry, trends in interest rates and even the cost and availability of funds to competitors.

Generally, however, two guidelines might be that it is risky to:

- Rely heavily on short-term funding sources, since these can be quickly withdrawn. For that reason Figure 5.1 shows Current Assets being partly funded by long-term funding sources.
- Have a high level of debt relative to equity (the *gearing* ratio) since it risks increased costs if interest rates rise and interest payments to providers of debt have to be paid regardless of levels of profitability.

Financial analysis

Introduction

We would usually employ an analysis of a company's financial situation as part of an internal strategic analysis, in the same way as we consider other functional areas of an organization in relation to its operations; human resources and marketing. It is necessary to understand a company's finances in order to make an assessment of its 'health' or its readiness to undertake a phase of strategic development.

It is also necessary to have an understanding of the interaction between finance and the other functional areas.

For example, the strategic marketing plan that is developed may suggest that a major expansion into a foreign market requiring the takeover of a local supplier should take place and that heavy promotional activity should support the move. Such a strategic option however cannot be successful unless adequate financing is available at a price which allows profits to be made.

Three key areas of financial analysis are:

- *longitudinal* analysis (sometimes called trend or time-series analysis);
- *cross-sectional* analysis (or comparison analysis);
- *ratio* analysis.

To many *THE* organizations two further areas of finance are key to considering the overall financial situation, namely analyses of the organization's exposure to:

- foreign exchange risk;
- cash flow risk.

A comprehensive analysis of a company's financial situation would normally involve an element of all three of these analyses. One key aspect to bear in mind when looking at accounting statements is that they contain numbers in isolation. An accounting number on it own is just that – a number. In order to make any sense of it we must compare it with other accounting numbers.

In the next few sections Air New Zealand will be used to illustrate some of the 'tools' of financial analysis.

SHORT CASE ILLUSTRATION

Air New Zealand

Auckland-based Air New Zealand is the national airline and flag-carrier of New Zealand operating scheduled passenger flights to about 27 domestic and 29 international destinations in 15 countries across Asia, Europe, North America and Oceania. The airline is a member of the Star Alliance of global airline partners (which also includes Air China; Air Canada; Lufthansa; South African Airways; Singapore Airlines and United Airlines) and has an extensive domestic and international route network. The network focuses on providing services within Australasia and the South Pacific, with long-haul services to Asia, Europe and North America.

The airline traces its roots back to 1940 as Tasman Empire Airways Limited (TEAL), a flying boat company operating trans-Tasman flights between New Zealand and Australia. The New Zealand Government took full control of TEAL in 1965 and it was renamed Air New Zealand. The airline has a chequered recent financial history having been largely privatized in 1989, but subsequently returned to majority government ownership in 2001 after a failed merger with struggling Australian carrier Ansett Australia. Air New Zealand carries over 13 million passengers annually, utilizing a modern fleet of about 100 aircraft.

The difficult trading conditions in recent years during a downturn in the world economy can be illustrated from the following extract from the 2012 Air New Zealand Share holder review:

> Air New Zealand operates in a volatile industry. Ongoing challenges in the global economy have continued to suppress demand, escalate oil prices and destabilise financial markets, yet tough operating conditions do not justify poor financial results. We simply must adapt our business, improve our productivity and enhance our financial performance.

The airline reported that they had a range of initiatives, some of which had already been completed with further measures still in progress aimed at improving productivity and enhancing financial performance. The necessary changes are aided by Air New Zealand's strong financial position with more than $1 billion cash on hand. The airline's measures include: aggressively managing its costs and, growing revenue opportunities and strategic alliances to allow the company to expand its network without making significant capital commitments.

The airline's shareholder review went on to point out that Air New Zealand had undergone substantial changes that had enabled it to be well positioned to operate profitably into the future in the face of uncertain demand and high fuel costs. The challenge was how to commercialize this positioning and deliver levels of profitability in line with expectations.

Air New Zealand 2012 Shareholder review and Air New Zealand
Annual Report available at www.airnewzealand.com

Questions

1. What were the financial challenges that Air New Zealand faced in 2012?
2. What measures did Air New Zealand take to improve financial performance?

Longitudinal analysis

The simplest means of assessing any aspect of a company's finances is to compare the data for two or more years and see what has increased and decreased over that time period, and by how much. It goes without saying that the further back in time we look, the better idea we will get as to its current position in its historical context (see for example Figures 5.3 and 5.4). Many company corporate reports provide a five- or ten-year record and this can help us in constructing a longitudinal analysis.

The easiest way to perform this form of analysis is to conduct an initial scan of the figures to identify any major changes between the years. This involves simply looking along each line in turn and highlighting any larger-than-normal increases or decreases; for example, a scan along five years of fuel expenses shown in Figure 5.5 clearly indicates that fuel costs (a large component of total costs) were highly volatile over the period at a time when demand was weak.

Anomalies like these may need further investigation in order to find answers as to the reasons for such volatility. Further investigation of the balance sheet or profit and loss account, together with any notes to the accounts, may provide some clues. It may be important to discover how such an increase was financed, why there was a need to carry high levels of stock, and the impact on suppliers and customers.

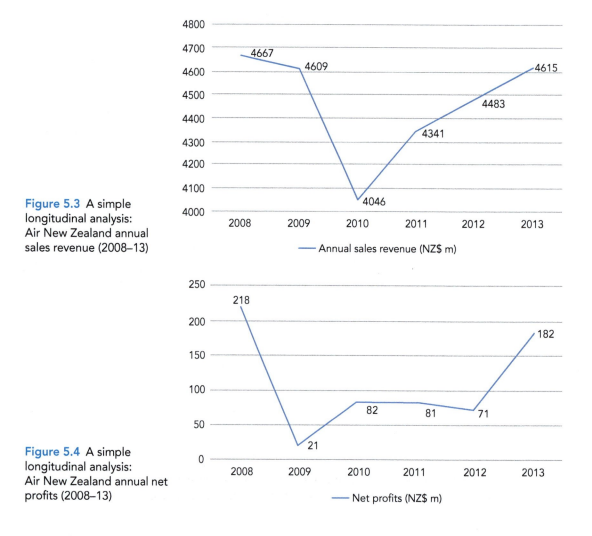

Figure 5.3 A simple longitudinal analysis: Air New Zealand annual sales revenue (2008–13)

Figure 5.4 A simple longitudinal analysis: Air New Zealand annual net profits (2008–13)

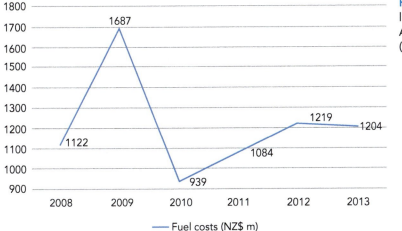

Figure 5.5 A simple longitudinal analysis: Air New Zealand fuel costs (2008–13)

The initial scan may need to be followed by a more detailed analysis which calculates the year-on-year increase/decrease in percentage terms. It is sometimes helpful to plot trends on a graph against time (such as in Figures 5.3, 5.4 and 5.5). This can help to highlight changes at particular points in time and to identify correlations between the various indicators.

The identification of trends in terms of, say, turnover, costs or of some items of a balance sheet (such as debtors), can therefore be valuable in our financial analysis.

Such trends should, however, be seen in their context.

For example, an organization operating in a static or slow-growth market may judge a 1 per cent year-on-year increase in turnover as a great success, whereas for a company in a buoyant market would judge a 1 per cent increase as a failure.

Cross-sectional analysis

Whilst longitudinal analysis helps us to assess performance within the context of historical trends, it tells us nothing of the company's performance against that of competitors or of similar companies in other industries.

For example, if we were to identify strong sales growth of 10 per cent a year in a longitudinal analysis of Company A's financial statements we might be tempted to think that the company was performing well. If we were then to compare this company with one of its competitors only to find that the industry average rate of growth was 15 per cent, then we would wish to modify our initial assessment of Company A's performance.

Inter-company comparison or financial *benchmarking* is a variation on cross-sectional analysis. It usually involves an analysis of 'like' companies, usually in the same industry but it can sometimes be an inter-industry analysis.

In order to make the benchmarking analysis meaningful, the company selection should usually be guided by similarity in terms of:

- company size (i.e. they should be comparable in terms of turnover, market value or similar);
- industry (in that the companies produce similar products); and
- market (i.e. the companies share a similar customer base).

In practice, sample selection for a benchmarking study always involves some compromise because no two companies are in all respects directly comparable. Many companies, for example, operate in more than one industry and this may render problematic any comparisons with another company that operates in only one industry.

Accountants and financial analysts have undertaken the practice of inter-company (cross-sectional) analysis using financial data for many years. Benchmarking, however, can be used to compare financial and, importantly, non-financial information between two or more companies, see for example Wöber (2002) for a discussion of benchmarking in a *THE* context.

Benchmarking is now used to compare the effectiveness of various processes, products and procedures against others. The objective is to identify where superior performance is found in whatever variable that is being used for comparison. Once the company with the highest performance is identified, the exercise becomes to explore the reasons behind the superior performance.

The benchmarking process therefore involves the following decisions:

- What are we going to benchmark? (Financial or non-financial data.)
- Who are we going to benchmark against? (Sample selection.)
- How will we get the information?
- How will we analyse the information?
- How will we use the results?

The value of benchmarking is in identifying not only which company has the superior performance in a sector, but also why this is the case. For example, if our analysis throws up the fact that Company X enjoys a return on sales significantly higher than the other companies in the sector, Company X thus occupies the profitability benchmark in the sector. The other companies may then wish to examine the practices within Company X that give rise to this level of performance.

For non-financial indicators, our analysis may highlight the fact that Company Y is able to attract the best-qualified people within a key category of human resources, such as the best sales and marketing professionals or computer programmers. In this case, Company Y demonstrates the benchmark in successful recruitment. Other companies who are unable to attract the best people would usually wish to examine Company Y to see why it is so successful in this regard.

THINK POINTS

- Distinguish between longitudinal and cross-sectional analyses.
- What are the main categories of accounting ratios?
- Explain what is meant by benchmarking.

Commonly sized accounts are particularly useful in cross-sectional analyses but it can also be used to analyse the same company's accounts from year to year. If we were, for example, to examine the profit and loss statements or balance sheets of two companies in the same industry, we may at first be unable to make sense of differences between the two. We can sometimes make sense of the two separate accounts by making the totals of both equal 100 and then dividing each entry by the resultant quotient accordingly.

A simplified example of commonly sized profit and loss is shown in Table 5.5 for our exemplar company, Air New Zealand and the Chinese airline and fellow Star Alliance member, Air China.

Although the companies operate in different currencies – New Zealand Dollars (NZ$) and Renminbi (RMB) respectively – and have different scales of operation, common sizing allows comparisons to be easily made.

Table 5.5 Simplified commonly sized P&L accounts for Air New Zealand and Air China (2011)

	Air New Zealand		Air China	
	NZ$ (m)	Common size	RMB (m)	Common size
Sales	4,341	100	98,409	100
Operating costs	3,678	84.7	92,150	93.6
Gross profits	663	15.3	6,259	6.4
Net Profits	81	1.9	7,062	7.2

Although such comparisons have to be interpreted with caution (because of detailed differences in accounting rules), Table 5.5 allows comparisons between the performances of the two companies to be made. The common sizing calculates operating costs, gross profits and net profits relative to sales which are set at 100. We can tell, for example, that overall Air New Zealand's operating costs are a lower proportion of sales than those of Air China. However, net profits are lower relative to sales at Air New Zealand indicating that it has higher depreciation, financing and tax costs than those of Air China since these costs are included in the net profits calculations.

We could draw comparable conclusions from other commonly sized components of the accounts.

KEY CONCEPT

Financial statements

One of the conditions usually placed upon limited companies is the requirement to file an audited annual report and accounts.

The details vary from country to country. There are usually elements such as:

- a chairman's statement;
- an auditor's report;
- a profit and loss statement;
- a balance sheet;
- a cash flow statement.

The accounting rules by which they are to be constructed are prescribed in financial reporting standards (which vary in different countries often making comparisons difficult) to ensure that all companies mean the same thing when they make an entry in one of the statements. When they are completed (following the company's financial year end), they become publicly available.

In the UK, for example, each shareholder receives a copy, and a copy is lodged at UK Companies House in Cardiff.

It is for the purposes of comparisons of this nature that cross-sectional analyses are important. As well as comparing accounting numbers like turnover, it is often helpful to compare two or more companies' ratios (see next section) such as return on sales or one of the working capital ratios.

Ratio analysis

The third important tool in the analysis of company performance is *ratio analysis*. A ratio is a comparison (by quotient) of two items from the same set of accounts. Given that there are a lot of numbers in a set of accounts, it will not come as a surprise to learn that a large number of ratios can be drawn – some of which are more useful than others.

Ratio analysis is an area of some academic debate and accordingly the way in which ratios are expressed may vary between accounting and strategy textbooks. What is important therefore is to employ a consistent approach to ratio analysis, especially in longitudinal and cross-sectional analyses.

For most purposes, we can divide ratios into five broad categories:

1. Performance ratios;
2. Efficiency ratios;
3. Liquidity ratios;
4. Investors' ratios;
5. Financial structure ratios.

Performance ratios

As their name suggests, performance ratios test to see how well a company has turned its inputs into profits. This usually involves comparing *return* (PBIT or profit before interest and tax) against either turnover or its capital. This is because the rates of tax and interest payable vary. Using profit after interest and tax would distort the performance figure.

Return on capital employed (ROCE) is perhaps the most important and widely used measure of performance. It indicates the return being made compared to the funds invested. At its simplest it is this figure that tests the gains of investing in a business as opposed to simply placing capital in a bank.

Where an organization can break down its figures by divisions or subsidiaries, individual performance can be measured and decisions relating to continued ownership made.

Return on equity or *return on ordinary shareholders' funds* gives an indication of how effectively the share capital has been turned into profit (i.e. it does not take account of loan capital). This ratio should be used carefully as the capital structure of the company can affect the ratio.

> *Performance ratios – examples*
>
> *Each expressed as a percentage by multiplying the ratio by 100.*
>
> *Return on capital employed = profit before interest and tax (PBIT from P&L account)/total capital employed (i.e. one side of the balance sheet) × 100*
>
> > AIR NZ, 2013 = (310/3902) × 100
> >   = 7.9%
>
> *Return on shareholders' funds = PBIT/shareholders' funds (from balance sheet) × 100*
>
> > AIR NZ, 2013 = (310/1816) × 100
> >   = 17.1%
>
> *Net return on sales = PBIT/total sales (also called turnover or revenue) × 100*
>
> > AIR NZ, 2013 = (310/4618) × 100
> >   = 6.7%

Gross return on sales = Gross profit/total sales × 100

$$AIR\ NZ,\ 2013 = (898/4618) \times 100$$
$$= 19.4\%$$

Note: Gross profit is the profit after direct (i.e. conversion) costs have been deducted from sales, but before indirect (i.e. administrative) costs. Gross margin is an indication of how effectively a company has managed its wages, energy and stocks.

Return on sales, or *profit margin*, either net or gross, is a popular guide to the profitability of a company. This ratio assesses the profit made per £ (or other currency) sold. Return on sales tends to vary from industry to industry and between companies within an industry. Airlines and tour operators, for example, typically make returns of less than 10 per cent whilst companies in the pharmaceuticals sector often make more than 20 per cent. Figure 5.6 shows a graphical representation of return on sales for Air New Zealand.

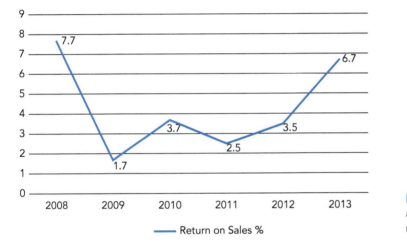

Figure 5.6 A longitudinal analysis of Air New Zealand return on sales (2008–13)

Efficiency ratios

These ratios show how efficiently a company has used its assets to generate sales. We can use any one of a number of a company's inputs to test against sales or profits. Common efficiency ratios include *sales per employee* and *profit per employee*, both of which test the efficiency with which a company uses its labour inputs.

KEY CONCEPT

Efficiency

The term efficiency is used in many ways – not just in accounting.

We may speak of an efficient engine on a cruise liner or an efficient ventilation system in a concert hall for instance. At its simplest, efficiency is a comparison of a system's output to its inputs with a view to testing how well the inputs have been turned into an output. It follows that a more efficient system will produce more output for a given input than a less efficient one.

It can be expressed mathematically as a quotient.

Efficiency = (work output/work input) × 100 (to arrive at a percentage)

Other commonly used efficiency ratios are *asset turnover* and a variant of this, *fixed asset turnover*. A high level of asset turnover indicates that the company is using its assets efficiently; conversely, a low level may indicate that the company is suffering from overcapacity. Stock turnover gives an indication of how well the company controls its stocks. A company that keeps stock moving will generally have a higher stock turnover than one that has lots of stock which cannot be sold or obsolete materials.

Efficiency ratios – examples

Sales per employee = total sales (from P&L)/number of employees (usually found in the notes to the accounts)

$$AIR\ NZ\ (2013) = NZ\$4,618\ million/10,336$$
$$= NZ\$0.446\ million\ (NZ\$\ 446,000)$$

Profit per employee = PBIT/number of employees

$$AIR\ NZ\ (2013) = NZ\$310\ million/10,336$$
$$= NZ\$0.0299\ million\ (NZ\$\ 29,900)$$

Liquidity ratios

These ratios test the company's ability to meet its short-term debts – an important thing to establish if there is reason to believe the company is in trouble. Essentially they ask the question, 'has the company enough funds to meet what it owes?'.

The *current ratio* is the best-known liquidity ratio. It is a measure of a company's total liabilities in comparison to its total assets and is thus calculated entirely from balance sheet figures. It is used to assess the company's ability to meet its liabilities by the use of its assets such as stock, debtors (receivables) and cash.

The *acid test ratio* is a variant of the current ratio and tests the company's ability to meet its short-term liabilities using its cash or 'near cash' assets. Many textbooks suggest a ratio of 2:1 should be a target for the current ratio and a target of 1:1 should be sought for the acid test ratio. These are simple guides and should not be taken as the norm for all industries.

Many companies in *THE* have low levels of stock (due to their services orientation) and as a result their current ratio may well be below 2:1, and consequently the acid test ratio provides a better guide in such cases.

Liquidity ratios – examples

Current Ratio = current assets/current liabilities

$$AIR\ NZ\ (2013) = NZ\$1,858/1,710$$
$$= 1.09$$

Acid test ratio = Current assets – stock/current liabilities

$$AIR\ NZ\ (2013) = NZ\$1,858 – 155/1,710$$
$$= 1.00$$

Investors' ratios

This family of ratios test for aspects of a company's performance that are important to a company's investors – usually its shareholders or potential shareholders. There are three that are widely used.

Earnings per share (EPS) are calculated by dividing profit after interest and tax (called earnings) by the number of shares. It shows how much profit is attributable to each share.

The *price earnings ratio* (P/E) gives an indication of the stock market's confidence in a company's shares. It is the current market price of the company's ordinary shares divided by its EPS at the last year-end and it follows therefore that the P/E varies with the share price. Broadly speaking it is a way of showing how highly investors value the earnings a company produces. A high P/E ratio (where the price is high compared to the last declared EPS) usually indicates growth potential whilst a low P/E suggests static profits. The P/E ratio for quoted companies is regularly published in the financial press.

Dividend yield is the third widely used investors' ratio. Potential shareholders often want to know what the most recent return on the share was in terms of percentage. Dividend yield is calculated by dividing the dividend per share at the last year-end by the current price (and then multiplying by 100 to arrive at a percentage).

> *Investors' ratios – examples*
>
> *EPS = profit after interest and tax/share volume.*
>
> > *AIR NZ (2013) = NZ$182 million/1,104 million*
> > *= NZ$0.16*
>
> *P/E = price of share (as of 'today' or in accounts)/EPS at most recent year-end.*
>
> > *AIR NZ (2013) = NZ$1.49/0.16*
> > *= 9.3*
>
> *Dividend yield = (gross dividend per share/current price of share) × 100*
>
> > *AIR NZ (2013) = 8.0 NZ cents/149 NZ cents*
> > *= 5.37%*

Financial structure ratios

We encountered financial structure above when we discussed the relative merits of loan and share capital earlier in the chapter. The way in which a company 'mixes' these forms of capital is referred to as its financial (or capital) structure.

The relationship of debt capital to shareholder capital is referred to as the company's gearing ratio. Gearing is an indication of how the company has arranged its capital structure.

The *gearing ratio* looks at the relationship between all the borrowings of the company (including short-term borrowings) and all the capital employed by the company. This provides a view of the extent to which borrowing forms part of the total capital base of the company and hence the risk associated with rising interest rates.

The *debt/equity ratio*, a variation on the gearing ratio, uses the shareholders' funds in the calculation rather than the total capital employed. This ratio provides a more direct comparison between the funds attributed to shareholders and liability of the company to loan providers.

> *Financial structure ratios – examples:*
>
> *Gearing ratio = Net debt (typically all borrowings less bank and other deposits)/Net debt + shareholders' funds × 100*
>
> > *AIR NZ = 1,168/1,168 + 1,816 × 100*
> > *= 39.1%*
>
> *Debt/equity ratio = debt capital (typically borrowings due after one year)/shareholders' funds × 100*

$$AIR\ NZ = 1,168/11,816 \times 100$$
$$= 64.3\%$$

Both are usually expressed as percentages by simply multiplying the quotient by 100.

It should be noted that (as with most ratios) there are several variants of the gearing ratio which use different measures of borrowing. It is important to be consistent in the ratio that is used when comparing the gearing of two or more companies or comparing the gearing of a single company over a period of time.

Using ratios in financial analysis

Compared to simply looking at accounting numbers, ratios provide a way of making some sense of published accounts. However, if a ratio is placed within its longitudinal or cross-sectional context, its usefulness is maximized.

If return on sales is taken as an example, we would usually want to know how Company A's figure this year compares not only with last year's (i.e. is it more or less), but also with Company A's competitors. This enables us to assess how Company A is performing over time and to make a judgement on its competitive position in its industry. This is because profitability is an important indicator of competitive success.

Limitations of financial information

For most purposes in strategic analysis, we can accept the proposition that the data we collect from a company's annual accounts is accurate and provides a truthful statement on its financial position. From time to time, however, we may need to qualify our analysis for of one or more reasons.

- *Accuracy* – Whilst the financial statements are audited for accuracy, other parts of the annual report are not. If our financial analysis consists of an examination of the entire document and not just the accounting sections, then we would need to be aware of this. Additional disclosures made in corporate reports may serve a number of purposes. Some commentators have suggested that such disclosures may be something of a public relations and marketing exercise.

- *Historic information* – It should be remembered that the financial information in a corporate report is historical, often published up to three months after the period they represent. Whilst historical information can be used to judge past performance, it may have limited use in predicting future performance. The balance sheet shows the financial position at 'a moment in time' (at the year-end). It does not (unlike the P&L) summarize a full year's trading and matters can sometimes change quickly after the year-end. In an attempt to avoid this potential problem, quoted companies in many parts of the world are required to produce interim reports, normally half-yearly and unaudited, which show their profit and turnover for that period. In the UK, quoted companies are also required to provide the UK Stock Exchange with information that may have a significant impact on its prospects such as changes on the Board or anything that gives rise to a 'profits warning'.

- *Presentation of accounts* – Those who prepare a company's financial statements (the financial accountants) sometimes have cause to 'hide' bad news so as to avoid alarming the company's investors. It is possible to employ legal financial restructuring so as to make some figures appear better than perhaps they are. Also although there are accounting conventions, which most organizations follow, they vary in detail in different countries. A year-on-year increase in the value of fixed assets, for example, may appear at first glance to be healthy, but it may be that the company has accumulated a high amount of debt to finance it. It is for this reason that we sometimes need to examine all parts of a company's financial statements to spot any countervailing bad news that has been obscured by the company in its reporting.

Foreign exchange risk and cash flow risk in *THE*

Two further financial topics are particularly pertinent to *THE* settings given the characteristics of the sectors being considered. These topics involve the recognition of risks relating to foreign exchange and cash flow risks. For a more detailed discussion of these topics see for example Evans (2002) and Buckley (2012).

Foreign exchange risk analysis

Given the nature of its products many *THE* companies operate internationally giving rise to international flows of funds in various currencies. Tour operators, airlines, hotel groups and cruise operators, and many event management companies, for example, typically have a very large exposure to movements in foreign exchange rates, almost certainly far larger than for most companies of a similar size engaged in other areas of the economy. The very purpose of these companies often implies that they are international in their activities, thereby leaving them exposed to international risks associated with foreign exchange transactions.

The profitability of any company that trades internationally is affected by changes in foreign exchange rates as Lockwood, in relation to travel and tourism, states below.

DEFINITION/QUOTATION

Foreign exchange risks for *THE* organizations

As a large part of the travel and tourist industry is concerned with persuading and assisting people to cross national boundaries and thus to buy goods and services priced in a foreign currency, the identification and management of exchange rate exposures is vital to the profitable operation of a travel and tourist business.

Lockwood (1989:175)

Thus foreign exchange management is very significant for many *THE* businesses. The lack of stability caused by the continual changes in exchange rates between currencies creates uncertainty.

Specifically uncertainty is created as to:

- what foreign income will be worth when it is received;
- what payments will cost when they have to be made; and
- what the value of foreign assets and liabilities might be in the future.

SHORT CASE ILLUSTRATION

Foreign exchange exposure: British Airways and Live Nation

The overall foreign exchange position of a company may be complicated and the measures taken to reduce the risks associated with foreign exchange rate movements can be illustrated by the position of one of the world's leading airlines, British Airways, and by a leading event management company Live Nation.

British Airways (BA)

Operating one of the most extensive international scheduled airline route networks, together with its joint business agreements, code share and franchise partners, BA flies to more than 400 destinations worldwide.

BA is exposed to currency risk on revenue, purchases and borrowings that are denominated in a currency other than sterling. The currencies in which these transactions are primarily denominated are US dollar, euro and Japanese yen. The group generates a surplus in most currencies in which it does business. The US dollar is an exception as capital expenditure, debt repayments and fuel payments denominated in US dollars normally create a deficit.

BA can experience adverse or beneficial effects arising from foreign exchange rate movements. BA seeks to reduce foreign exchange exposures arising from transactions in various currencies through a policy of matching, as far as possible, receipts and payments in each individual currency. Surpluses of convertible currencies are sold, either for US dollars or pounds sterling.

BA has substantial liabilities denominated in US dollar, euro and yen. BA utilises its US dollar, euro and yen debt repayments as a hedge of future US dollar, euro and yen revenues. Forward foreign exchange contracts and currency options are used to cover near-term future revenues and operating payments in a variety of currencies.

Live Nation

Live Nation is the largest producer of live music concerts in the world, connecting nearly 49 million fans to 22,000 events for over 2,300 artists in 2012. Live Nation operates in five main industries within the live entertainment business, including live music events, venue operations, ticketing services, sponsorship and advertising sales, and artist management and services with revenues of about $5.8 billion.

Live Nation has operations in countries throughout the world and the financial results of its foreign operations are measured in their local currencies. As a result, the financial results are affected by factors such as changes in foreign currency exchange rates.

As of December 31, 2012, the primary foreign exchange exposure included the euro, British Pound and Canadian Dollar. The company primarily uses forward currency contracts in addition to options to reduce its exposure to foreign currency risk associated with short-term artist fee commitments. Live Nation also enters into forward currency contracts to minimize the risks and/or costs associated with changes in foreign currency rates on forecasted operating income and short-term inter-company loans.

At the end of 2012, the company had forward currency contracts and options outstanding with a notional amount of $100 million.

British Airways (2012); Live Nation (2012).

Questions

1. Explain what the risks related to foreign exchange exposure are for British Airways and Live Nation.
2. Explain why managing foreign exchange exposure is often a particular difficulty for managers involved in *THE*.

It is imperative to the profitability of many companies operating in *THE* that this exposure to foreign exchange rate movements is recognized and managed appropriately. Though it is prudent to manage these risks it is common in reality for them to be ignored, especially by smaller companies.

In all cases, risk attributed to foreign exchange rate movements arises out of uncertainty about the future exchange rate between two currencies (Evans, 2002). This risk would be minimized if it were possible to predict future rate movements. Unfortunately, it is not possible to do so with any degree of accuracy, and for a company to try to do so can be financially dangerous.

If foreign exchange rates cannot be predicted, another option might be to pass on to the customer the effects of any adverse movements in exchange rates, and hence the company would incur no impact. In most cases, however, the highly competitive nature of most *THE* businesses prevents higher costs being passed on to the customer in this way.

We can identify three different types of foreign exchange risk or exposure a company may be faced with – transaction, translation and economic exposure – which are defined below.

DEFINITION/QUOTATION

Foreign exchange transaction, translation and economic risk

Transaction risk is the risk that transactions already entered into or for which the firm is likely to have a commitment in a foreign currency will have a variable value in the home currency because of exchange rate movements.

Translation risk arises because financial data denominated in one currency are then expressed in another currency. Between two accounting dates the figures can be affected by exchange rate movements.

Economic risk arises where a company's economic value may be affected by foreign exchange rate movements causing a loss in competitive strength.

Arnold (2012)

Transaction exposure

Transaction exposure relates to the foreign exchange exposure where contracts have already been entered into. When a company has contracted to receive or pay an amount of money in a foreign currency at some time in the future a risk is incurred.

The specific risk is that adverse exchange rate movements between now and the time of the eventual cash receipt/payment which will increase the amount to be paid out or decrease the amount to be received. The short case illustration below demonstrates the risks for a UK outbound tour operator.

SHORT CASE ILLUSTRATION

Transaction exposure: A UK outbound tour operator

A UK-based outbound tour operator selling holidays to America would receive its income in the local currency i.e. pounds sterling. Most of its payments to suppliers such as hoteliers, transportation companies, ground handling staff and other suppliers would be likely to be in US dollars. In order to make the payments, at some stage the company would have to convert the sterling the company receives in revenue into US dollars. This would entail a risk that the US dollar might rise in value (appreciate) against sterling, thereby making the payments more expensive in sterling terms:

Assume, for instance:

- the company had costed its hotel beds in its American programme at a rate of $1.50 to the pound (i.e. 1 pound buys 1.50 US dollars); and
- the total cost to purchase the required bed spaces was $1,500,000.

In the case outlined above, the planned cost in Sterling to the company would be $1,500,000/1.50 = £1,000,000.

Now if the rate subsequently fell to $1.40 the cost would increase to $1,500,000/1.40 = £1,071,429, an additional cost of over £71,000 to the company.

Questions

1. What would be the impact to the company if the exchange rate changed to $1.65 to the pound rather than $1.40 in the example?
2. Consider what steps managers in this company might take to deal with the issue in this example.

Translation exposure

Translation exposure arises on the consolidation of assets, liabilities and profits denominated in foreign currency in the process of preparing consolidated accounts. Values rise and fall in the accounts when revalued every year at the current prevailing exchange rate. However, unlike transaction exposure the real gain or loss is only realized when the asset is sold or the liability becomes payable.

Hence the concept is also known as *accounting exposure* and is illustrated by an American Hotel Company below.

SHORT CASE ILLUSTRATION

Translation exposure: An America-based hotel company

If an American hotel company which produces its annual results in its home currency US dollars purchases a hotel in Australia, it acquires an asset (the hotel) which is priced in the local currency, i.e. Australian dollars (AU$).

Each year when the balance sheet of the business is prepared, the value of the hotel would be translated into the company's 'home' currency, in this case US dollars, at the prevailing rate on the balance sheet date. The risk is that the hotel might therefore be worth less in US dollar terms as shown in the balance sheet of the company, than the cost of the asset when it was bought. This would be the case if the AU$ were to rise against the US$.

Assume, for instance:

- the company purchased the hotel when the US dollar/Australian dollar rate was 1.10, i.e. 1 US dollar buys 1.10 Australian dollars (AUS);
- the hotel cost AU$10 million.

In the case outlined above, the planned cost in US$ to the company would be AU$10,000,000/1.10 = US$9,090,909. This is the value of the property which will be recorded at the time of purchase.

If the rate of the AU$ subsequently strengthened and the exchange rate changed to $1.15, the value of the property recorded in the annual report (in US$) would fall to 10,000,000/1.15 = 8,695,652 – a drop in value of over US$395,000 which would be recorded in the annual accounts.

Questions

1. What would be the impact if the hotel company took out a loan of AU$10 million to pay for the hotel?
2. Explain why if a country's currency is historically very volatile it might deter investment in physical assets such as hotels in that country.

Economic exposure

Economic exposure (sometimes referred to as political exposure) arises from the effect of adverse exchange rate movements on future cash flows, where no contractual arrangement to receive or pay money has yet been made.

This kind of exposure which is longer term in nature and often difficult to quantify exactly and forecast accurately, and is illustrated by the case of a specialist tour operator shown below.

SHORT CASE ILLUSTRATION

Economic exposure: A European specialist tour operator

Suppose a specialist European tour operator operates most of its tour-operating programme to one country; say Egypt. The company will have an economic exposure to that country and its currency.

In some cases the political and economic circumstances are very uncertain and if, for example, the government should be replaced in a violent way, as occurred in recent years in Egypt, customers will be reluctant to book holidays to that country, thereby severely limiting the revenues of the specialist tour operator.

Questions

1. What steps might the company as described here take to protect itself against economic risks?
2. What other examples of economic risk affecting *THE* organizations you are familiar with could you cite?

Thus, movements in foreign exchange rates lead to a number of different problems or 'exposures' for *THE* companies. These exposures can be dealt with in a number of ways. The most obvious ways of dealing with such exposures are to avoid them altogether, either by trading in domestic markets only, or by passing the exposure over to suppliers or customers.

These alternatives are seldom possible in the competitive international sectors of *THE*, so other management methods such as the use of forward foreign exchange contracts or foreign exchange options have to be employed in order to reduce the risks. For a discussion of these methods see for example Arnold (2012: Ch. 22).

THINK POINTS

- What are the main limitations of financial information you need to be aware of?
- What are the three categories of foreign exchange risk? Provide an illustration of each of these risks from *THE*.
- Explain the possible impact of seasonality on cash flows in *THE*.

Cash flow risk analysis

As mentioned in Chapter 2, *THE* has one of the most highly seasonal patterns of demand for any group of products or services (Bull, 1995). This seasonality is largely due to climate, but is also related to factors such as school holidays, festivals and historic travel patterns.

For example – in temperate climates there is a strong tendency to travel, hold events and utilize hospitality services when the weather is more likely to be benign and daylight hours are longer, i.e. spring and summer.

Seasonality of demand for such products leads to a highly seasonal pattern of cash inflows and outflows.

Consequently at certain times of the year companies in these sectors may have large cash balances to invest and at other times of the year many companies need to borrow money in order to maintain payments to suppliers (creditors). The industry is also *cyclical* in nature, in that cash flows are very responsive to changes in the general level of economic activity.

In terms of cash management, tour operators, event managers, travel agents and airlines, for instance, are typically quite low-margin businesses. They often derive important parts of their income not from operating profits (through the selling of their services), but from interest income derived from investing cash surpluses they may be holding at certain times of the year. This source of income has, however, been rather less important in the low interest rate environment that has existed in recent years. Nevertheless, companies should take steps to maximize its effects.

An example of this seasonality of cash flow is provided by the international event organiser, Live Nation.

SHORT CASE ILLUSTRATION

Cash fluctuations: Event organizer Live Nation

Our intra-year cash fluctuations are impacted by the seasonality of our various businesses. Examples of seasonal effects include our concerts segment, which reports the majority of revenue in the second and third quarters. Cash inflows and outflows depend on the timing of event-related payments but the majority of the inflows generally occur prior to the event.

Live Nation (2012)

Questions

1. Consider what the implications of the seasonality of cash flow might be for a company such as Live Nation.
2. Can you cite other examples of companies involved in *THE* with such seasonal cash flows and what are the implications for managers in these companies?

The short case illustration below considers the seasonality of cash flow for a UK-based tour operator. The characteristics of the tour operating business outlined in the Illustrative example below have certain implications for cash flow analysis and cash management. Cash builds up and declines in a seasonal way.

During certain times of the year, particularly in the spring, large surplus cash balances are free to be invested until the cash is needed to pay bills during the summer season and for the remainder of the year. The size and timing of the cash balances, and the interest to be earned from the invested balances will vary from year to year, since the profile of bookings and level of interest rates also vary from year to year.

The period of greatest risk for many *THE* companies, however, usually comes in the autumn and winter, and historically this is when many such businesses have failed. Cash balances have been run down as seasonal payments have been made during the preceding summer season and the bulk of bookings for the subsequent season have yet to be made and cash will not be received until they have. Companies often have to rely on bank support to help them through this period.

In a case where a bank (or other party) fails to lend the necessary support, *insolvency* is the inevitable result. Insolvency (the inability to pay bills as they become due) has often befallen companies in these sectors when anticipated revenue from expected bookings have failed to materialize.

When a company reaches an insolvent position it normally leads to the company's failure and liquidation. A company can sometimes survive for many years without making profits or making very low levels of profit, but if they run out of cash it is difficult for them to survive, because employees and creditors must be paid.

Many *THE* companies routinely rely on banks to provide short-term finance for a part of the year, but it is when these negative cash balances are larger or more prolonged than usual and banks feel unable to provide finance that problems occur.

Analysing cash flow is an important strategic task which can provide a lot of information on how the company is trading at the time and to indicate likely future problems.

The case illustration below indicates the sort of seasonal cash flow issues associated with many *THE* companies, in this case a UK-based tour operator.

In Table 5.6 a specific (fictional) tour operator which exhibits the characteristics shown in the illustrative case below is used to show how a detailed cash flow analysis can be used to identify underlying financial

SHORT CASE ILLUSTRATION

Seasonality of cash flow: A UK outbound tour operator

Detailed patterns of seasonality will differ between sectors, companies and countries but most organizations in *THE* are prone to the effects of seasonality of cash flow to some degree.

If we take as an example a typical UK outbound tour operator selling 'package holidays' largely to southern Europe, it is greatly affected by the seasonality of the product and this directly affects its cash flow – and in turn its management.

Such an operator may have a number of operating characteristics:

The bulk of holidays sold would be 'summer sun' with the season lasting from April to September, but with the peak months being July and August during school holidays.

Summer sun holidays are typically booked in three distinct periods:

- Early booking period starting in August or September, when a significant number of people book. This applies especially to families and those who are tied to taking holidays between certain dates.

- Post-Christmas period from January to March which is usually the largest booking period.
- Late booking period, from April onwards, which has become increasingly significant in recent years, and may be a time of intense competition as operators try to sell remaining capacity and vary prices in order to do so.

Many tour operators have attempted to widen their range of activities and reduce the effects of seasonality by, for instance, introducing 'winter sun' and skiing programmes. The winter sun season normally lasts from October to April, whilst the skiing season normally lasts from December to April with peaks in February and at Easter. In most cases the combined size of these programmes, is far smaller than the summer programme in terms of receipts. Bookings for the winter sun and skiing programmes are taken throughout the summer and autumn, but the winter ski programme in particular is subject to a great deal of late booking in late autumn and early winter as customers wait to see what snow conditions are likely for the season.

The tour operator will have a number of seasonal costs such as airline fuel, staff working at resorts, and accommodation charges.

However, the tour operator will also have a high level of costs that have to be met throughout the year, such as the costs of head office staff, aircraft maintenance and computer facilities.

Questions

1. Explain the issues that the seasonality of cash flow might cause for managers in this case.
2. Explain the steps such a company might take to reduce the impact of this seasonality of cash flow.

issues. The effect of seasonality means that cash builds up and declines according to patterns linked to seasonal fluctuations.

Table 5.6 illustrates the cash flow problems described above for Interjet, a fictional outbound UK tour operator, which has a cash flow profile similar to the one described in the previous illustrative example.

Interjet is a small outbound tour operator with ambitious plans. The company plans to increase its sales turnover by around 25 per cent each year. However, like many tour operators, travel agents and other tourism businesses the company experiences annual seasonal cash flow difficulties.

A cash flow forecast has been prepared for the following financial years and this is shown below.

THINK POINTS

- Review the information on Interjet (Table 5.6).
- Identify foreseeable difficulties in the future cash flow position presented.

In analysing the cash flow it may be necessary to:

- insert all known income and payments for each period on to a cash flow schedule (as illustrated in the case of Interjet, Table 5.6);
- total income and payments to produce a balance carried forward to the next period;
- forecast future cash flow using available information;

Table 5.6 Interjet – cash flow forecast (in thousands GBP)

	1 Apr	2 May	3 Jun	4 Jul	5 Aug	6 Sep	7 Oct	8 Nov	9 Dec	10 Jan	11 Feb	12 Mar	TOT.
INFLOWS													
Receipts from debtors	230	250	120	50	60	75	80	90	110	150	220	320	1,755
Dividend on investment							45						45
TOTAL INFLOWS	230	250	120	50	60	75	125	90	110	150	220	320	1,800
OUTFLOWS													
Payments to creditors	102	80		80		88		88		88		92	516
Wages and other expenses		77	58	103	79	59	105	80	62	108	83	63	979
Payments for fixed assets				70	10	15					5		100
Dividend payable			80										80
Corporation tax									120				120
TOTAL OUTFLOWS	102	157	138	253	89	162	105	168	182	196	88	155	1,795
NET IN/OUT	128	93	–18	–203	–29	–87	20	–78	–72	–46	132	165	5
Bank balance													
Opening	30	158	251	233	30	1	–86	–66	–144	–216	–262	–130	
Closing	158	251	233	30	1	–86	–66	–144	–216	–262	–130	35	

Notes:
As a tour operator most funds are received by customers as a deposit and subsequent payment of balance. On average this results in three month's credit being granted to customers.

On average six weeks' credit is taken from customers.

Capital expenditure budget:

New computer facilities	Month 4	£40,000
Routine replacement of motor vehicles	Month 4	£30,000
Computer software and programming costs	Month 5	£10,000
Progress payment on building extensions	Month 6	£15,000
Office furniture and equipment	Month 11	£5,000

Negotiated overdraft facilities currently stand at £60,000

- produce 'senstivity' analyses. For example, what if sales were 10 per cent lower/higher than expected or jet fuel prices rose by 50 per cent; and
- produce a graph showing monthly or weekly balances to help indicate trends.

Analysis of the cash flow should prompt certain questions such as:

- How easily predictable are the cash flows?
- How seasonal or cyclical are the cash flows?
- Can the company keep within its borrowing limits?
- Is the company generating enough cash to ensure its survival?
- Does the company require further credit facilities?
- How long does it take customers to pay the company?
- How quickly does the company pay suppliers and others?

There are various actions managers may take in response to the identified issues as part of the implementation of strategy. These are outlined in Chapter 12.

SMALL BUSINESS FOCUS

Raising finance for smaller businesses in *THE* as in other industries is often problematic because:

- the asset backing (collateral for loans) is often lacking;
- they lack managerial expertise;
- some financing sources are unlikely to be available such as access to stock markets;
- providers of finance will demand higher returns because the risks and the set-up costs are greater;
- the company is less likely to have a long trading history to provide reassurance;
- with smaller resources or a more limited niche market, they may be less aware of the risks or have less ability to manage them or may be particularly dependent on one market segment rather than a balanced portfolio;
- with larger companies, banks and other providers of finance are likely to try harder to save failing companies because of the large losses they might incur.

Set against these difficulties for smaller companies in relation to raising finance there may be some advantages in that owner-managers are often very close to the business and can react quickly to adapt to market changes. Banks and other lenders prefer to lend to businesses in which the owners have their own money invested (as is likely to be the case in smaller businesses) because it might imply that the owner will work harder. It is also the case that if the business fails, it is the equity that is lost first, meaning that a cushion is provided for the bank and other lenders. Furthermore the owners of smaller businesses are often prepared to accept lower returns on their own investment in order to attract other investors and ensure long-term success.

Although in the modern world loan applications are often evaluated by computers according to centrally agreed lending criteria, building up a good relationship with banks and other investors often remains important. In the financing of smaller companies the credentials of the owners and key managers is often crucial in securing adequate financing, since if they leave the enterprise the impact is likely to be high.

It is important to realise that any time a small business seeks outside sources of finance its case almost certainly has to be presented in a formal way as part of a business plan or business case. This is because any investors will want to know what the investment is trying to achieve; is the amount of the investment sufficient to achieve the stated aims; and, crucially, how will the finance provider be rewarded and get their investment back.

In making a judgement on whether or not to invest, particularly in smaller companies, investors may need to be satisfied that the 'Five Cs of Credit' (Lasher, 1999) have been addressed:

- *Character* – The general character of the owner and/or key managers; specifically the probability that a person will attempt to pay off the debt and how serious is their intention.
- *Capacity* – A judgement on the borrower's ability to pay. Many small businesses attempt to grow too quickly and run out of the liquidity to service their loans which is often referred to as 'overtrading'.
- *Capital* – The general financial condition of the borrower as reflected in its financial statements.
- *Collateral* – The assets offered as security.
- *Conditions* – General economic conditions and the specific circumstances of the borrower's industry or geographic area. In periods of economic downturn even good well established businesses can fail and banks are reluctant to lend.

CHAPTER SUMMARY

An analysis of a company's financial position is an indispensable part of any strategic review. Decision makers need to know whether or not the company has the level of funding required to finance their strategies and, if not, financial resources will have to be raised.

It is usually important to know where a company has obtained its capital and the cost of this capital. Both share capital and loan capital have their advantages and disadvantages for use in strategic development. It is important to note whether current levels of profitability are sufficient to service the costs of capital. In *THE* settings it is also important to understand the relative capital intensity of the particular part of the industry being considered because it has important strategic consequences for managers.

There are a number of tools, which we can use to make sense of a company's financial statements. Longitudinal analysis examines trends over time while cross-sectional analysis compares a company's finances against its competitors. Ratio analysis enables us to make sense of accounts by dividing one accounting number by another. Benchmarking enables us to compare one company's performance on a number of fronts with similar companies.

Additionally foreign exchange risk and cash flow risk are important facets of strategic financial risk for many *THE* companies, so this chapter has provided tools for analysing such risks.

REFERENCES

Arnold, G. (2012) *Corporate Financial Management*, 5th edn, Harlow: Pearson.

Bowdin, G., J. Allen, R. Harris, I. McDonnell and W. O'Toole (2012) *Events Management*, London and New York: Routledge.

Buckley, A. (2012) *International Finance: A Practical Perspective*, Harlow: Pearson.

Bull, A. (1995) *The Economics of Travel and Tourism*, Melbourne: Longman Australia.

Evans, N. (2002) 'Financial Management for Travel and Tourism', in R. Sharpley (ed.) *Travel and Tourism*, Sunderland: Business Education Publishers, pp. 345–66.

Guilding, C. (2009) *Accounting Essentials for Hospitality Managers*, 2nd edn, Oxford: Butterworth Heinemann.

Harris, P. (ed.) (2012) *Accounting and Finance for the International Hospitality Industry*, London and New York: Routledge.

Karadeniz, E., S. Y. Kandir, M. Balcilar and Y. B. Onal (2009) 'Determinants of Capital Structure: Evidence from Turkish Lodging Companies', *International Journal of Contemporary Hospitality Management*, 21 (5): 594–609.

Lasher, W. R. (1999) *Strategic Thinking for Smaller Businesses and Divisions*, Oxford: Blackwell.

Lee, S. (2007) 'An Examination of Financial Leverage Trends in the Lodging Industry', *Journal of Hospitality Financial Management*, 15 (1): 35–45.

Lockwood, R. D. (1989) 'Foreign Exchange Management', in S. F. Witt and L. Moutinho (eds.) *Tourism Marketing and Management Handbook*, London: Prentice Hall, pp. 175–8.

Lynch, R. (2003) *Strategic Management*, 3rd edn, Harlow: Pearson Education.

Marsh, C. (2012) *Financial Management for Non-Financial Managers*, London: Kogan Page.

Tsai, H., S. Pan and J. Lee (2011) 'Recent Research in Hospitality Financial Management', *International Journal of Contemporary Hospitality Management*, 23 (7): 941–71.

Wöber, K. W. (2002) *Benchmarking in Tourism and Hospitality Industries: The Selection of Benchmarking Partners*, Wallingford: CABI.

WEBSITES

www.accor.com

www.britishairways.com

www.carnival.com

www.coxandkings.com

www.qantas.com.au

www.thomascook.com

www.travelcounsellors.co.uk

www//phx.corporate-ir.net

www.airnewzealand.com

www.livenation.com

www.airchina.com

FURTHER READING

Reference	Focus
Adams, D. (2006) *Management Accounting for Hospitality, Tourism and Leisure Industries: A Strategic Approach*, London UK: Thomson Learning.	Accounting Hospitality Tourism
Jones, T., H. Atkinson, A. Lorenz and P. Harris (2012), *Strategic Managerial Accounting: Hospitality, Tourism & Events Applications*, 6th edn, Oxford: Goodfellow.	Accounting Hospitality Tourism Events
Avci, U., M. Madanoglu and F. Okumus (2011) 'Strategic Orientation and Performance of Tourism Firms: Evidence from a Developing Country', *Tourism Management*, 32 (1): 147–57.	Performance management Tourism Turkey
Bridge, J. and L. Moutinho (2000) 'Financial Management in Tourism', in L. Moutinho (ed.) *Strategic Management in Tourism*, Wallingford: CABI.	Financial management Tourism
Burgess, C. (2007) 'Do Hotel Managers Have Sufficient Financial Skills to Help Them Manage Their Areas?' *International Journal of Contemporary Hospitality Management*, 19 (3): 188–200.	Financial management Hospitality Hotels

Burgess, C. (2010) *Essential Financial Techniques for Hospitality Managers: A Practical Manual*, Oxford: Goodfellow.	Financial management Hospitality
Collier, P. and A. Gregory (1995) 'Strategic Management Accounting: A UK Hotel Sector Case Study', *International Journal of Contemporary Hospitality Management*, 7 (1): 16–21.	Management accounting Hospitality Hotels
Damster, G. (2005) 'Events Accounting and Financial Management' in D. Tassiopoulos (ed.) *Events Management: A Professional and Developmental Approach*, Cape Town South Africa: Juta Academic, pp. 120–35.	Financial management Events
Della Lucia, M. (2013) 'Economic Performance Measurement Systems for Event Planning and Investment Decision Making', *Tourism Management*, 34: 91–100.	Performance management Events Investment decisions
Haktanir, M. and P. Harris (2005) 'Performance Measurement Practice in an Independent Hotel Context: A Case Study Approach', *International Journal of Contemporary Hospitality Management*, 17 (1): 39–50.	Performance management Hospitality Hotels
Harris, P. J. and J. Brander Brown (1998) 'Research and Development in Hospitality Accounting and Financial Management', *International Journal of Hospitality Management*, 17 (2): 161–82.	Accounting Financial management Hospitality
Hales, J. (2005) *Accounting and Financial Analysis in the Hospitality Industry*, London and New York: Routledge.	Accounting Financial management Hospitality
Hede, A. M. (2008) 'Managing Special Events in the New Era of the Triple Bottom Line', *Event Management*, 11 (1–2): 1–2.	Financial management Events
Lee, S. K. and S. S. Jang (2011) 'Foreign Exchange Exposure of US Tourism-Related Firms', *Tourism Management*, 32 (4): 934–48.	Foreign Exchange Exposure Tourism United States
Mia, L. and A. Patiar (2001) 'The Use of Management Accounting Systems in Hotels: An Exploratory Study', *International Journal of Hospitality Management*, 20 (2): 111–28.	Accounting Hospitality Hotels
Moncarz, E. S., N. D. J. Portocarrero and R. Davoodi (2004) *Accounting for the Hospitality Industry*, Upper Saddle River NJ: Prentice Hall.	Accounting Hospitality
Morrison, A. and R. Teixeira (2004) 'Small Business Performance: A Tourism Sector Focus', *Journal of Small Business and Enterprise Development*, 11 (2): 166–73.	Performance management Tourism Small Business
Owen, G. (1998) *Accounting for Hospitality, Tourism and Leisure*, 2nd edn, Harlow: Longman.	Accounting Hospitality Tourism
Pavlatos, O. and I. Paggios (2008) 'Management Accounting Practices in the Greek Hospitality Industry', *Managerial Auditing Journal*, 24 (1): 81–98.	Accounting Hospitality Greece

CASE LINKAGES

Case 4	Hyatt Hotels
Case 7	Thomas Cook

Chapter **6**

Tourism, hospitality and event organizations

The products and markets context

Introduction and chapter overview

So far in this part of the book in relation to *THE* organizations we have analysed the operational aspects, human aspects and financial aspects of organizations in Chapters 3, 4 and 5 respectively. This chapter examines the final part of the functional aspects of the organization – products and markets. The way in which an organization relates to its markets is one of the most important aspects of competitive strategy. The idea of a market as a place where buyers and sellers come together can apply to both inputs and outputs. Product markets are those in which an organization competes for sales whilst resource markets are those in which an organization competes for its resource inputs.

In this chapter, we discuss the key elements of this system – the nature of markets and the nature and importance of products in *THE* contexts. The way in which an organization configures itself in respect to these elements is crucial to the success of business strategy.

LEARNING OBJECTIVES

After studying this chapter, in relation to *THE* readers should be able to:

- explain the term *market* and describe the ways by which markets can be defined;
- understand the importance of markets and provide relevant examples from *THE*;
- explain the ways that markets can be segmented and be able to apply the principles to *THE* contexts;
- understand the concepts of targeting and positioning in relation to *THE* contexts;
- explain the term product, describe Kotler's five levels of product benefit and be able to illustrate the concepts with relevant *THE* examples;

- understand the stages in and uses of the product life cycle and its derivative application in tourism – the Tourist Area Life Cycle;
- explain the concept of a product portfolio and understand the underlying cash-flow implications; and
- understand the composition and limitations of selected strategic models such as PLC, the BCG Matrix and the GEC Matrix.

Strategic marketing for competitive advantage

The way in which an organization's products relate to its markets is one of the most important aspects of competitive strategy, the aim of which is to gain a competitive advantage over competitors. An organization may have great technical and operational capabilities but these capabilities only become a source of competitive advantage when such 'distinctive capabilities' are applied in the marketplace (Kay, 1995:127). Hence it is of critical importance that managers are able to define and understand the markets in which they are operating and the next section considers various ways in which markets can be defined.

Modern management writers view marketing less as one of the main constituent departments of an organization and more as a holistic, competitive orientation for a business (Evans, 2012:228). In such a way marketing takes on a strategic role for an organization and indeed the 'strategic' dimension to marketing reflects its growing impingement on traditional 'strategic management' territory (Fyall and Garrod, 2005). Thus the strategic management literature and the marketing academic literature are closely linked often covering similar concepts, tools and techniques.

The intention in this chapter is not to cover marketing in a *THE* context in great detail, since this is done elsewhere as indicated below, but instead to concentrate on those strategic aspects of marketing which are necessary to analyse as part of a holistic understanding of organizations' strategic position.

Marketing as applied to specific *THE* contexts has generated a large academic literature in recent years including a number of textbooks, with tourism and hospitality usually being considered jointly and separate texts available for events management. See, for example, Fyall and Garrod (2005); Hudson (2008); Middleton *et al.* (2009); Reid and Bojanic (2009) for further information with regard to tourism and hospitality marketing management. For a specific event marketing orientation see for example Kolb (2012); Preston, (2012); Yeoman *et al.* (2012).

Markets are rarely completely homogenous. Within markets there are groups of customers with requirements that are similar, and it is this similarity of needs and wants that distinguishes one market *segment* from another.

The most widely quoted authors on marketing (Kotler and Keller, 2012) uses these differences when he proposes that the heart of modern strategic marketing can be described as 'STP Marketing': Segmenting, Targeting and Positioning. In STP (or 'Target Marketing') the seller distinguishes the major *segments* (identifiable parts) of the market, *targets* one or more of these segments and *positions* products and marketing programmes so that they will appeal to the needs and wants of these chosen target segments. Kotler has also applied his approach specifically to tourism and hospitality (Kotler *et al.*, 2013) and to destinations (Kotler *et al.*, 1993).

Kotler's approach, which has been widely followed and adapted by other authors, will be followed in this chapter since it takes a strategic view of marketing within organizations, it is easy to understand and apply, and it is widely utilized in teaching and in practice.

Ways of defining and understanding markets

The importance of understanding markets

It is important before going on to consider how organizations approach their markets to consider exactly what we mean by the term markets.

Economists refer to a market as a system comprising two 'sides'. The demand side comprises buyers or consumers of a product or service. The supply side produces or operates products and services.

In strategy, we often use the term slightly differently. By market, we usually mean a group of actual or potential customers with similar needs or wants (the demand side). We usually refer to the supply side as an industry.

The definition and boundaries of an organization's markets represent a key starting point for the formulation of strategy and provide a basis for measuring competitive performance. The analysis and definition of markets will also provide key information concerning the threats and opportunities facing an organization.

A distinctive capability becomes a competitive advantage only when it is applied in a market or markets (Kay, 1995:127) so it is of critical importance that managers are able to define and understand the markets in which they are operating.

Specifically an understanding of markets is important for several reasons:

- it gives managers an indication of the demand and potential demand for an organization's products and services;
- it allows managers to assess the potential for market growth and gaining market share over competitors;
- it enables managers to recognize and evaluate the number, type and capabilities of competitors;
- it enables managers to position products and services in the market so that they are able to develop and sustain their competitive advantage.

Market attractiveness

Managers often consider the attractiveness of a market; they consider whether products offered in a particular market will deliver returns on investment that are attractive to the organization and its investors. A number of factors contribute to market attractiveness including market size, market growth and supplier concentration.

MARKET SIZE

In general terms the larger the size of a market the more attractive it will be in that it will offer wider opportunities for a larger number of organizations. Such a market, however, will also attract powerful suppliers who will attempt to dominate it by gaining a high market share.

For example – the market for mass holidays to Spain from Northern Europe, is large and consequently it is supplied by a large number of tour operators, whereas the market for activity holidays for European teenagers is far smaller and is consequently supplied by fewer companies.

MARKET GROWTH RATE

A growing market is normally more attractive than a static or declining market since growing markets allow opportunities for businesses to expand in line with the growth of the market. In static or declining markets, growth for individual organizations can only be achieved by taking market share away from competitors, which can be expensive and may lead to lower margins.

For example – the market for fast travel between China's major cities has been growing quickly in recent years and consequently state (or part state-owned) airlines, low-cost airlines, rail and road services have all considerably added to their capacity; whereas overall hotel capacity in English seaside resorts has been falling.

SUPPLIER CONCENTRATION

Concentration refers to the extent to which a market is dominated by its largest suppliers and is usually measured by the percentage market share of the top four or five. The short case illustration below outlines the relative lack of concentration in the case of international hotels.

Large organizations, which dominate the market, will tend to have advantages over smaller organizations in terms of costs, available promotional budgets and power over customers and suppliers in terms of setting prices and minimizing costs respectively. However, large organizations may find it difficult to increase their market share beyond a certain point due to regulatory restrictions and smaller organizations may compensate for their disadvantages.

In contrast, smaller organizations may be more flexible in their approach, know their customers' preferences more thoroughly, have access to a market niche (which is too small to attract larger organizations) and be less bureaucratic than larger competitors. In such circumstances it may be medium-sized organizations that find their competitive position is difficult to defend, since they possess neither the advantages of scale nor the benefits that small organizations may be able to exploit.

SHORT CASE ILLUSTRATION

Market concentration: Worldwide hotels

The hotel industry around the world has traditionally been highly fragmented. In many countries, small operators – often run by families with a single hotel – have dominated provision. However, this pattern is changing with large international groups becoming more active in many countries. As a result the market is becoming more concentrated in some countries, though the position varies considerably in different national markets.

Warwick Clifton, Research Director at a leading hotel consultancy organization 'Global Hotel Research Limited' (www.globalhoteldata.com), produced a report which analysed the extent to which the global hotel industry had been penetrated by the leading hotel groups in terms of the proportion of total room stock that was affiliated to the hotel groups. The proportion of total hotel room stock that was affiliated to one of the 2,100 groups of hotels was measured in percentage terms and the countries were categorized.

The data (for selected markets for which data was available), presented in the table below, indicates a marked difference in concentration between some national markets and others. According to this study, countries such as USA, UAE and New Zealand have particularly high levels of concentration whereas others such as Italy, Austria and Pakistan show evidence of a fragmented structure and low levels of concentration.

Table 6.1 Penetration by hotel groups in selected countries (2012)

>74%	50–74%	25–49%	10–24%	<10%
UAE	South Africa	Finland	Croatia	Austria
Djibouti	Singapore	Spain	Portugal	Pakistan
New Zealand	Dominican Republic	France	Germany	Italy
Cuba	India	Australia	Mexico	Argentina
Monaco	Norway	Netherlands	Morocco	Paraguay
Burundi	Canada	Denmark	Saudi Arabia	Ukraine
USA	UK	Sweden	Turkey	Peru
	China	Ireland	Switzerland	
		Swaziland	Japan	
		Egypt	Russia	

Source: Clifton (2013)

Questions

1. Why is worldwide hospitality relatively less concentrated than many other industry sectors?

2. Consider what the factors might be making worldwide hotels more concentrated.

Defining markets

We can also define the boundaries of markets in different ways. If different companies define a market in different ways, it is not surprising that the sum of their claimed market share may add to more or less than one hundred per cent. The problem is particularly difficult in many service industries because the boundaries between them often overlap and are sometimes difficult to define whereas the market for many manufactured products such as cars is obvious and relatively easy to define.

For example – the 'overseas holiday' market may mean different things to different companies. One company might include all holidays taken abroad whilst another company might only include such holidays taken by air or sold as part of a package.

The problem is perhaps even more difficult in a sector such as 'events' since its boundaries are difficult to define and recognize. The sector (as discussed in the Introduction to Part 1 of this book) has few recognizable brand names, a measure of its fragmentation, and there is some discussion as to the boundaries of the subject. It is, however, generally accepted that events management is concerned with managing in the contexts of:

- event management companies;
- sports events;
- concerts and performances;
- festivals;
- exhibitions; and
- meetings and conferences.

It is clearly important, therefore, that market share measures are stated explicitly with the market boundaries clearly defined.

Market share is a measure of an organization's performance with regard to its ability to win and retain customers relative to other organizations. It can be measured either by *volume* or by *value*.

- *Volume measures* concern the organization's share of units sold to the market.

  For example – the number of air-inclusive holidays sold by a tour operator in relation to the total number of air-inclusive holidays sold over a period; the number of beds sold by a hotelier relative to all bed sales; or the number of event tickets sold by an event manager relative to sales made by all event managers.

- *Value measures* concern the sales turnover of one company in proportion to the total value of the market.

  For example – the sales turnover of one air-inclusive tour operator relative to the turnover for all air-inclusive tour operators; the value of bed sales by one hotelier relative to the value of all bed sales; or the value of event tickets made by one manager relative to the value of all ticket sales.

There are three ways in which markets are commonly defined:

- based on *product*;
- based on *need satisfaction* or *function performed*; and
- based on *customer identity*.

We will briefly examine each of these in turn.

Market – definition based on product

If someone working for an organization is asked what market they are in, a common reply will be to describe the products sold, for example holidays or conferences and exhibitions. If the product definition is wide, this type of definition is close to describing an industry. Since government economic statistics are often produced on this basis, markets defined in this way often have the advantage of ease of measurement.

A drawback of this approach is that it sometimes fails to take into account that a product may provide a range of different benefits, and different products, often derived from completely different sources, might meet the same need.

The strategic implication of this is that it could lead to a failure to recognize threats that may come from a different industry altogether. Holidays, watching sport and attending arts festivals appear to be entirely different products with different markets, but they each compete for customers' discretionary income and time (the income and time left over when essentials have been dealt with). They can also both be considered as part of the wider 'leisure' market.

An advantage of a product-based definition of markets can be that economies of scale of operations may be gained by the sharing of particular processes. Taken to extreme, this can lead to a pragmatic view of the market. The market represents the sum total of the products that a company *happens* to produce even where they appear to have little in common.

For example – Saga Holidays is a UK-based tour operator selling holidays exclusively for the over-50 age group directly to the public. Using its database of clients it is also able to sell other products such as financial services to the same target market.

Market – definition based on need satisfaction or function performed

The reason why consumers purchase a good or service is to gain *utility*. The concept of utility infers that whenever a consumer makes a purchase, they make a cost–benefit calculation, making the judgement that the benefit they will get from the product is worth more than the price paid.

Table 6.2 Main benefits sought in types of events and attractions

Type of event/attraction	Main benefits sought
Theme park	Excitement, variety of on-site attractions, atmosphere
Beach	Sun tan, sea bathing, company of others *or* solitude, water-based activities
Cathedral	History, aesthetic pleasure derived from architecture, sense of peace or spirituality
Museum or gallery	Learning something new, nostalgia, purchasing replicas or souvenirs
Theatre	Entertainment, atmosphere, status – to be able to say 'you were there'
Leisure centre	Exercise, physical challenges, competing against others
Mountains	Solitude, beauty, activities, walking
Concert, event or festival	Entertainment, support, atmosphere, status – to be able to say 'you were there'

Source: Adapted from Swarbrooke (1995)

This understanding enables the organization to understand its markets according to customers' perceptions. Horner and Swarbrooke (1996) view success in the development of tourism, leisure and hospitality products depending upon 'the ability to match the product which is offered with the benefits sought by the customers'. The authors concede, however, that the matching of the two is a challenging process.

To illustrate this approach to defining markets, Table 6.2 considers the benefits being sought by visitors to various types of events and attractions

Whilst a definition based on satisfying needs can lead to a more open-minded approach to the formulation of strategy, its weakness can be that very broad definitions can lead to a view of markets that do not allow a practical approach to decision making.

For example – a restaurant chain, might define itself as being in the 'leisure' market, but it is probably wise for restaurant companies to also consider threats and opportunities that might arise from competing sources such as television, bars, computer games, holidays, etc. Opportunities only arise from leisure activities that the company's competencies would allow it to enter (see Chapter 2) and threats would come from activities that would be likely to provide adequate substitutes for customers' business.

KEY CONCEPT

Needs and wants

Whenever a customer makes a purchase decision, he or she expects to gain a benefit from the product purchased. This benefit satisfaction is usually expressed as a need or a want. The difference between the two is in the perception of the consumer – one customers' want is another's need.

The practical use of the distinction is in the price responsiveness of the product. Generally speaking, customers who need – or who believe they need – a product will be less price sensitive than those who merely want it. Hence, the greater the felt need, the more *price inelastic* the demand.

Market – definition based on customer identity

Groups of customers have requirements in common and differ from other groups of customers. In this way, the *identity* of customers can be used to define markets.

For example, we could consider the 'business travel market' as a quite distinct market. The market might be for products as diverse as airline flights, hotel rooms, meeting and exhibition spaces, event management services, car hire, etc. But the market could clearly be seen as the market for types of travel, hospitality and ancillary services needed by those travelling away from their offices for business purposes.

In terms of strategy formulation, the advantage of this approach is that it allows accurate targeting of the customer so that efficient use can be made of advertising, direct mail shots, personal selling, search engine optimization, etc. Its main disadvantage is that whilst marketing economies may be made, a number of different suppliers in the supply chain might need to be used to service the various requirements, so that the control of the quality of these suppliers becomes an issue of concern.

Market – combined definition

In practice, most businesses serve several markets with a range of products. They will define their markets with a combination of the ways listed here, and to the extent that one or another approach is uppermost, the advantages and disadvantages that we have already encountered will apply. A key task for management at a strategic level is to produce combinations that gain synergistic benefits and that enable the best opportunities to be chosen and exploited. In cases where change in aspects of the technology of supply or the characteristics of markets take place, so that synergies previously achievable are no longer available, a case exists for restructuring an organization to divest itself of some activities and/or to acquire new ones.

In terms of working out competitive success in markets, a key concept is that of the *served market* – that part of a market that the company is trading in. It is on that basis that the measure of market share is most meaningful.

THINK POINTS

- Explain how the term *market* can be defined and analysed.
- Explain why a detailed definition and understanding of the market is so important for *THE* managers.
- Explain the meanings of market *attractiveness* and supplier concentration and illustrate your answer by providing examples from *THE*.

STP marketing

Market segmentation has been considered one of the most fundamental aspects of marketing since William R. Smith (1956) published his influential article in the *Journal of Marketing*. Organizations cannot realistically engage and communicate with the entire population, so the overall population, or potential market, has to be broken down into manageable chunks. These chunks or 'segments' organizations can effectively engage with or, to use the terminology that is commonly used, 'reach'.

Thus market segmentation is concerned with the process of dividing a market into distinct groups of buyers with similar requirements.

To Kotler and Keller (2012:56), the essence of modern strategic marketing can be described as *STP* Marketing namely:

- segmenting;
- targeting; and
- positioning.

In STP or 'Target Marketing' (which Tsiotsou and Goldsmith, 2012 and Winston and Cahill, 2013 discuss in relation to tourism and hospitality respectively), the seller distinguishes the major *segments* (identifiable parts) of the market, *targets* one or more of these segments and *positions* products and marketing programmes so that they will appeal to the needs and wants of these chosen target segments. In this way organizations are able to define unique customer groups, select those they wish to serve, and then integrate the marketing mix to establish a unified image of the product relative to the competition (Jonk *et al.*, 2008).

Companies are increasingly adopting such an approach. Target marketing helps sellers to:

- identify marketing opportunities better;
- develop the right product features to attract each target market; and
- have the ability to adjust their prices, distribution channels and promotional activities to 'reach' the target market efficiently.

The approach can be seen as focusing marketing efforts on those customers that the organization has the greatest chance of satisfying. Underpinning this strategic process are two important information requirements:

- An organization needs to understand the process by which potential purchasers arrive at a decision to purchase a particular product i.e. *buyer behaviour*.
- In order to understand buyer behaviour and to gain an understanding of the structure of the market and competitive product offerings an organization requires attention to be given to the importance of detailed *marketing research*.

Market segmentation

Markets are rarely completely homogenous. Within markets there are groups of customers with requirements that are similar and it is this similarity of needs and wants that distinguishes one market segment from another. These 'sub markets' are known as *market segments*. By considering the extent to which the segments should be treated differently from others, and which ones will be chosen to serve, organizations can develop *target markets* and gain a focus for their commercial activity.

As Moutinho (2000:122) states: 'the concept of market segmentation arises from the recognition that consumers are different. Market segmentation is a strategy of allocation of marketing resources given a heterogeneous tourist population'.

KEY CONCEPT

Market segmentation

A market segment is a homogeneous group of customers with similar needs, wants, values and buying behaviour (Hollensen, 2010:284).

As such each market segment can be viewed as the sector of the overall market in which competition takes place. The marketer is concerned with identifying subsets of people with similar needs and characteristics that lead them to respond in similar ways to product offerings.

Hollensen (2010:283) identifies three reasons for the increasing importance of market segmentation in developing marketing strategies:

- Population growth has slowed and more product markets are maturing which in turn leads to more intense competition as companies seek growth through gains in market share.

- There is an important trend towards 'micro-segmentation' (one to one marketing). In manufacturing flexible production techniques allow cars for instance to be made to order to the customer's specifications. In *THE* technology has allowed, for example, customers to be offered individualized tour itineraries and potential events based on past purchasing histories.

- Expanding disposable incomes, higher educational attainment and more awareness of the world have produced customers with more varied and sophisticated needs, tastes and lifestyles.

Despite the advantages of segmenting a market there may also be potential difficulties as Gibson (2001) identifies.

The difficulties may include the following:

- Segmentation normally describes *current market segments* – the future position of segments may be different.

- Segmentation assumes *homogeneity within each identified segment* – this may not be the case.

- Segmentation implies competition-free segments – other competitors may identify the same segments.

- Segmentation may *identify the wrong segment* – other segments not identified may hold more opportunities.

This process of segmentation represents a powerful competitive tool. It is true to say that a business will prosper by giving the customer what the customer wants. Since not all customers are likely to want the same thing, identifying sub-groups and attending to their requirements more precisely is a way of gaining competitive advantage.

It could be argued that it is better to be hated by half of potential customers and loved by the other half than to be quite liked by them all. The latter is a recipe for being everyone's second choice and underlines the dangers of placing too much reliance on averages in market research.

By identifying a specific market segment and concentrating marketing efforts at it, many organizations can build a degree of *monopolistic power* (a mini-monopoly) in the segment and thereby achieve higher profit margins than would otherwise be achievable. Many organizations that have each identified a highly specific segment can each succeed and gain reasonable profits by configuring their internal activities to precisely meet the needs and wants of the customer group.

For the most part, we can assume that segments exist naturally in most markets and it is up to organizations as to how to exploit the differences that exist in the sub-markets. We do, however, have to recognize that activities of companies can also shape the segments to some extent. We could expect, for example, that men and women may buy differently. If, in those markets, suppliers offer and promote different products to men and women, then this tendency will be reinforced.

Before considering the ways in which market segments might be identified and specific segments targeted it is useful to consider the type of sub-groups, which exist within the different sectors of *THE* as shown in Table 6.3. Destination organizations are excluded since most are seen as having regard to all the segments identified.

Table 6.3 Consumer segments in the main constituent parts of tourism, hospitality and events

Tourism, hospitality and events	Principal consumer segments
Hotels	Corporate/business clients Visitors on group package tours Independent vacationers Visitors taking weekend/midweek package breaks Conference delegates
Tour operators	Young people, singles and couples, eighteen-to-thirty-year-olds Families with children Retired/senior citizens/empty nesters Activity/sports participants Culture seekers
Transport operators	First-class passengers Club-class passengers Standard-class passengers Charter groups Advance purchasers Purchasers close to departure 'last-minute'
Destination attractions, cultural, sporting and business events, restaurants	Local residents in the area Day visitors from outside local area – leisure and business Domestic tourists – leisure and business Foreign tourists – leisure and business School parties

Four approaches to segment marketing

Four broad approaches are recognized in respect to the ways that an organization can approach marketing to market segments (or sub-markets).

UNDIFFERENTIATED MARKETING

The first approach in relating to segmentation is called *undifferentiated* marketing. This means that the organization denies that its total markets are segmented at all and relates to the market assuming that demand is homogeneous in nature. The economies of a standardized approach to marketing outweigh any advantages of segmenting the market. Undifferentiated marketing is appropriate when the market the organization serves is genuinely homogeneous in nature.

DIFFERENTIATED MARKETING

Companies that adopt *differentiated* marketing recognize separate segments of the total market and treat each segment separately. Different segments need not always be different in every respect – it could be that some standard products can be promoted differently to different segments because of certain similarities or common characteristics. In other cases the product will be substantially or completely different and marketing to each segment will necessitate a distinctive approach to each one.

CONCENTRATED MARKETING

An extreme form of differentiated marketing is *concentrated* marketing, where an organization's effort is focused on a single market segment. In return for giving up substantial parts of the market, an effort is made to specialize in just one niche, and so we may see this referred to as *niche marketing*.

This approach offers the advantage that the organization can gain a detailed and in-depth knowledge of its segment, which, in turn, can enable an ever-improving match between the product and the customer requirement. The disadvantage relates to the extent to which the company may become dependent upon the one segment it serves. Any negative change in the demand pattern of the segment will leave the supplier vulnerable because of the narrowness of its market portfolio (see later in this chapter).

CUSTOMIZED MARKETING

Customized marketing occurs in cases where a market is viewed as being so diverse that an organization has to focus its marketing efforts on the needs of each individual customer. Such an approach enables the organization to modify its product or the way in which it is delivered, promoted or priced in order to satisfy individual requirements. However such an approach is costly since any potential economies of scale are lost but advances in technology make such approaches easier to implement than was previously the case.

A company operating with a large product range in many markets will typically use a multi-focus strategy – a combination of the above.

Criteria for segmentation

The reason why market segmentation occurs lies in the fact that organizations can no longer regard markets as being uniform, where all consumers wish to purchase the same product. Thus, each organization has to divide the market into clearly defined segments where each segment represents a discrete body of consumers, each of whom will have clearly defined needs, which warrant a separate marketing strategy.

However, the method by which the marketer or strategist divides the market into segments is extremely important.

For example – one method might be to divide the population into groups according to eye colour. We might end up with people with blue eyes, people with brown eyes, and people with mixed eye colours. This would be a perfectly valid method of classifying people into groups whose members were similar to each other and dissimilar from members of other groups. But what use would it be to the marketing of a tourist destination or a cultural event for instance? The answer, of course, is very little, since consumer needs and wants are unlikely to vary according to eye colour.

In *THE* sectors there are perhaps two major problems to consider when segmenting the market:

1. The product itself is, in many cases, highly inflexible. In other words, supply is usually fixed at least in the short-to-medium term. The basic attractions of the product are, to a great extent, given.

   For example – it is difficult to move a pre-planned festival at short notice to a different date, the attractions of a tourist destination (sun, sea, mountains, etc.) cannot be altered and cruise ship or hotel capacity cannot be changed quickly.

2. In many cases resources are extremely limited.

   For example – destinations, attractions, and national or regional tourism authorities often have very small promotional budgets; while the promoters of a festival or event will have a fixed promotional budget they are expected to adhere to.

The most important aspect of market segmentation is the choice of bases (criteria) used to divide customers into groups. The criteria selected must be relevant to the customers' needs and/or their behaviour in the market concerned.

Bases for segmentation

There is no single way of segmenting a market. Each organization has to choose *bases*, or variables, that it thinks are appropriate in respect of its consumers. It must never be forgotten that there is not only a great variety of *THE* products – countries, regions, cities, agencies, airlines, tour operators, festivals and events, etc. – but that the cost of promoting and distributing these products is extremely high. This forces each provider to critically consider all expenditure and to define clearly groups of customers that are most likely to purchase the products.

Furthermore, various writers differentiate between bases in various ways. Middleton *et al.* (2009), writing in a tourism context, refer to seven bases:

- purpose of travel;
- buyer needs, motivations and benefits sought;
- buyer behaviour/characteristics of product usage;
- demographic, economic and geographic characteristics;
- psychographic characteristics;
- geo-demographic profile; and
- price.

In the literature and in practice a distinction is often made between two groups of variables:

- socio-demographic variables
- geographic variables ⎱ *Consumer characteristics*
- psychographic variables ⎰
- behaviouristic variables } *Consumer responses*

Kotler and Keller (2012) point out that there is a basic distinction between geographic, demographic and psychographic variables on the one hand and behaviouristic on the other. Behaviouristic variables represent the responses that consumers exhibit to various marketing stimuli whereas the other categories of variable represent characteristics of the consumers themselves.

We will look briefly at each of these means of segmentation and add a fifth variable category; that of 'geo-demographic segmentation', which is really a combination of geographic and socio-demographic segmentation. For a detailed examination of the more common bases to segment markets in *THE* contexts, see for example: Middleton *et al.* (2009); Tkaczynski *et al.* (2009); Tkaczynski and Rundle-Thiele (2011); and Morritt and Weinstein (2012).

An important point to remember is that the various bases should generally be regarded not as alternative choices for segmentation, but as overlapping and complementary ways of sub-dividing the total market. In most cases the actual segments chosen by organizations represent a combination of bases sometimes referred to as *matrix segmentation*.

Socio-demographic segmentation

This form of segmentation addresses the question of *who* buys.

Perhaps the most common means of segmenting the market, particularly where the major travel companies are concerned, is by using demographic data.

For example – some tour operators specialize in providing packages for specific demographic groups. Contiki Tours (part of the Travel Corporation group of companies: www.thetravelcorporation.com) specialize in coach tours in Europe, Australia and New Zealand, Asia, Latin America and North America aimed at the 18–35 age groups located in many countries; whilst Saga Holidays specialise in tours for people over 50, predominantly located in the UK.

There are a number of demographic variables (characteristics), which may be of relevance to different markets and are summarised in Table 6.4. These variables usually refer to the age, gender, income, socio-economic group and stage in the family life cycle of the consumer.

Table 6.4 Socio-demographic segmentation variables

Socio-demographic variables	Comments
Age	Segmenting customers according to age bands is very common; children, for example, are clearly different to retired people in their needs.
Gender	Gender is a relevant segmentation criterion for many markets. Some THE products are, however, largely designed for either males or females while others appeal to both sexes. Spa days, for example, which have become increasingly popular at leading hotels, are primarily aimed at female customers.
Income	The personal disposable income of the consumer can be used as a segmentation variable. Some products are targeted at consumers with high disposable incomes – cruises, first-class travel, for example – while other products are aimed primarily at consumers with lower disposal incomes – camping holidays, for example.
Level of education	Sometimes the level of educational attainment is used as a segmentation variable. This criterion has obvious value with products requiring a certain level of intellectual application, such as books, but has also been found to influence other products as well. For example, people with lower levels of education often opt for the 'safety' of well-known destinations and established events whilst those with higher levels of education are more likely to have the confidence to try more diverse locations and events.
Family life cycle	The stage that consumers have reached in their family development can be an important variable. Two married couples with identical jobs and income levels, one with four children and the other childless will exhibit significant differences in their spending patterns.

Family life cycle segments might include:

• young single people;
• young couples with no children;
• families with young children;
• families with older children;
• middle aged couples with no children or whose children now live away from home;
• retired couples; and
• retired single people. |

Geographic segmentation

This form of segmentation addresses the question of *where* they buy.

An organization may segment its market according to the geographic location of its consumers. Similarly it is useful to be able to make distinctions between affluent and poor areas, and between various types of urban and rural areas.

For example – a visitor attraction or an event organizer will need to know where their customers are coming from in order to plan their strategy for attracting repeat custom and for targeting new geographical areas.

Psychographic segmentation

In psychographic segmentation, consumers are divided into different groups on the basis of social class, lifestyle and/or personality (see for example Gonzalez and Bello, 2002; Litvin, 2006; and Park and Jang, 2012).

The majority of people do not regard holidays, hospitality or attendance at events as status symbols. Rather, they are merely seeking to spend their time in the most effective ways, at the best possible price. When choosing a holiday destination, for example, some tourists might be motivated by the chance to learn about the local culture, but others might be seeking destinations that are less demanding and remind them of home.

In a frequently cited work, Plog (1974) identifies a continuum of tourist types, ranging from self-inhibited psychocentric tourists to extrovert allocentric tourists (Chang *et al.*, 2011). Thus Plog divided tourist consumers into five different psychographic traits; allocentrics, near allocentrics, midcentrics, near psychocentrics and psychocentrics. At the two extremes, allocentrics seek cultural and environmental differences from their norm, belong to higher income groups, are adventurous and require little in the way of tourism infrastructure. Psychocentrics seek familiar surroundings, belong to lower income groups, are unadventurous and require a high level of tourism infrastructure. A psychocentric New Yorker might favour Coney Island (a New York beach resort) whilst an allocentric New Yorker might favour an African Safari.

Attitudes and motivations, together with beliefs and perceptions, form the 'psychographic' profile of a consumer. Once the provider of *THE* products can understand this profile, they can infer a person's buying behaviour and devise the appropriate tourist products to cater for these segments of the market.

People's product interests are influenced by their lifestyle. It covers peoples' day-to-day habits, work patterns, leisure interests, attitudes and values. Lifestyle segments would be based on distinctive ways of living and social values portrayed by certain types of people.

This approach is sometimes felt to offer a more complete picture of the consumer than other approaches. Lifestyle market segmentation divides the market up according to the consumers way of life. It is this which has resulted in the marketing world labelling segments with acronyms such as:

- 'Yuppies' – young, upwardly mobile professionals;
- 'Dincs' – double-income, no children;
- 'Wooppies' – well-off old people; and
- 'Glammies' – the greying, leisured, affluent, middle-aged sector of the market.

A *THE* company which has taken a lifestyle approach can develop products that will appeal specifically to people with a particular way of life.

VALS (values, attitudes and lifestyles)

Many companies now utilize proprietary methodologies and software such as VALS (values, attitudes and lifestyles) for psychographic market segmentation. VALS was developed in 1978 by social scientist Arnold Mitchell and his colleagues at SRI International and is offered as a product of SRI's consulting services division. VALS draws heavily on the work of Harvard sociologist David Riesman and psychologist Abraham Maslow (see for example Novak and MacEvoy, 1990).

The main dimensions of the VALS framework are primary motivation (the horizontal dimension) and resources (the vertical dimension). The vertical dimension segments people based on the degree to which they are innovative and have resources such as income, education, self-confidence, intelligence, leadership skills and energy. The horizontal dimension represents primary motivations and includes three distinct types:

- Consumers driven by knowledge and principles are motivated primarily by ideals. These consumers include groups called Thinkers and Believers.
- Consumers driven by demonstrating success to their peers are motivated primarily by achievement. These consumers include groups referred to as Achievers and Strivers.
- Consumers driven by a desire for social or physical activity, variety and risk-taking are motivated primarily by self-expression. These consumers include the groups known as Experiencers and Makers.

At the top of the rectangle are the Innovators, who have such high resources that they could have any of the three primary motivations. At the bottom of the rectangle are the Survivors, who live complacently and within their means without a strong primary motivation of the types listed above.

PGL holidays in India

It is sometimes referred to as India's 'demographic dividend'; with more than half its 1.2 billion population under the age of 25, the country is expecting economic growth to be spurred on by a surge of new workers. The vast increase in the number of young people is in itself driving new business opportunities. Among these opportunities are American-style summer camps serving busy middle-class parents in India's burgeoning inner cities such as Mumbai and Delhi. With limited green spaces, traffic congestion, searing heat and pollution many families are choosing to send their children to the hills during the long school holidays. The camps offer everything from music tuition to back-packing and rafting. Many such camps are based close to the old colonial-era hill stations such as Shimla and Darjeeling in the Himalayan foothills, which have served as retreats for those seeking escape from oppressive summer heat for generations (Walsh, 2013).

PGL started life in the Wye Valley, straddling the English–Welsh border, in the late 1950s selling outdoor pursuits to young adults. In the seventies and eighties it expanded into permanent activity centres and started selling educational travel for schools. It is now one of the largest operators of residential adventure holidays for school groups and children. In February 2013 Holidaybreak (the owner of PGL) announced it was to export its outdoor activity holidays to India to tap into the growing demand from middle-class parents for safe and secure camps for their children. The impetus for the move has been provided by the £450 million takeover of Holidaybreak by the Indian travel group Cox and Kings in 2011. The group, which currently has twelve centres in Britain, three in France and one in Austria, has identified two sites in India near Mumbai and Delhi. A company spokesman was reported to have said that top private schools in India were interested in the PGL concept, particularly from a health and safety perspective (which had not always been emphasized in the past).

Questions

1. Explain the approach to product development taken by PGL.
2. Why might PGL's products be attractive to the Indian market?

Geo-demographic segmentation

Geo-demographic segmentation seeks to combine geographic and demographic principles of segmentation (see for example Middleton *et al.*, 2009).

Geo-demographic segmentation is based on two simple principles:

- People who live in the same neighbourhood are more likely to have similar characteristics than are two people chosen at random.
- Individual neighbourhoods can be categorized in terms of the characteristics of the population they contain. Any two neighbourhoods can be placed in the same category, i.e. they contain similar types of people, even though they are widely separated.

Geo-demographic segmentation is normally based on proprietary software systems offered by commercial suppliers such as Claritas Prizm and Tapestry in USA; CAMEO, ACORN and MOSAIC systems in the UK; with others having been developed elsewhere in the world.

For example – ACORN (A Classification of Residential Neighbourhoods) was developed in the UK in the late 1970s and classifies households according to the neighbourhood in which they are found. The underlying philosophy is that certain types of neighbourhood will not only display similar housing but also will have residents with similar demographic and social characteristics who will share common lifestyles and will tend to display similar purchasing behaviour.

For example, the developers of a new visitor attraction in a particular area of the UK aimed at families with young children in the local vicinity could use an ACORN map of the town. This would inform the managers of the attraction of the types of residential areas in the vicinity and hence those most likely to include the target customers.

Behaviour segmentation

In behavioural segmentation:

> *buyers are divided into groups on the basis of their knowledge, attitude, use, or response to a product.*

> *(Kotler and Keller, 2012:249)*

In the case of behavioural segmentation, unlike the use of other variables, we are concerned with consumer responses rather than consumer characteristics. Behaviour in the product field answers the question of *how* and *what* people buy. Consumers can be classified according to the brands they choose (or company loyalty), whether they are price-conscious and whether they are frequent or infrequent purchasers of *THE* products. Many markets can be segmented in terms of benefits sought by customers.

THE consumers are often attracted not by the product features but by the benefits they perceive they are likely to derive from their purchase. Consumers may be encouraged to buy a product if they recognize that they will benefit from it.

For example – customers who purchase an inclusive tour to the Australian Outback are not buying their package holiday simply for the flight on the aeroplane, the accommodation provided and the excursions that are arranged for them (which we could describe as the features of the holiday). Rather, the tourists are buying the complete package in order to enjoy the benefits of going away on a particular type of holiday. The holiday provides a chance to experience a different lifestyle, the opportunity to sample different forms of culture, a break from normal everyday routine and encounter wildlife not encountered in the home environment.

In order to take advantage of this knowledge, tour operators, for example, would have to identify the specific benefits that consumers in a particular market segment look for when going on holiday. When identified, the tour operator can devise holiday packages providing the specific benefits that are attractive to market segments.

Business-to-business (B2B) marketing

In this chapter up to this point we have primarily been concerned with businesses to consumers (B2C) marketing and segmentation. However, in many cases in *THE* as in other industries, organizations are concerned with marketing not directly to consumers but to other businesses – so-called B2B marketing.

The concept of B2B segmentation has demanded increasing academic attention in recent years (see for example Crittenden *et al.*, 2002; Powers and Sterling, 2008; and Hollensen, 2010:295–300).

B2B consumers differ in their needs, resources and buying habits. According to the widely cited model of Bonoma and Shapiro (1983), the B2B marketer typically segments organizations broadly classified into two major categories:

- *Macro segmentation* – Centres on the characteristics of the buying organization and situation, thus dividing the market by such organizational characteristics as size and geographical location.
- *Micro segmentation* – Requires a higher degree of market knowledge and focuses on the characteristics of decision making units within the macro-segment including buying decision criteria, perceived importance of the purchase and attitudes towards vendors.

The information required for the type of B2B segmentation outlined above is often difficult or costly to acquire. Consequently in practice many companies find it difficult to adequately segment their B2B marketing.

The notion of *reverse segmentation* or *supplier segmentation* as it is often referred to, has become common in recent years. Reverse segmentation highlights a process that parallels segmentation, by which customers select suppliers that meet particular specified criteria such as quality, financial stability, ethical stances, delivery reputation and collaborative development opportunities (Hollensen, 2010:299).

The implication is that a supplier that is able to exhibit appropriate reverse segmentation criteria to a customer can become significantly more attractive to buyers, not least because they demonstrate a greater degree of understanding of customer needs. Active seeking of a particular supplier segmentation variable could in itself become a significant segmentation variable, especially for those organizations seeking to benefit from long-term supplier–customer relationships such as in the car components industry or in corporate sponsorship markets (Mitchell and Wilson, 1998).

For example – hoteliers at a particular destination resort might target consistent and reliable deliverable quality standards in order to build up a long-term sustainable supplier–customer relationship with incoming tour operators. Similarly a conference venue might target well-trained staff delivering high levels of customer service and culinary excellence in order to attract repeat custom from corporate clients.

Targeting

When the possible range of segments has been identified and the characteristics of each of the segments has been analysed, the *THE* organization then has to decide which market segments to target.

When deciding which segments to target, a number of considerations should be borne in mind in relation to the segments. Each segment should reflect the following important characteristics:

- *Market size and market growth* – Each segment should be large enough, or demonstrating growth potential, to justify further investment of time and money by the company. As part of this evaluation an organization might consider the number and type of competitors in each segment.

  For example – it would probably be possible to construct and promote hotels solely for people in wheelchairs, but would this be a substantial enough segment of the population to ensure success?

- *Accessibility* – Each segment should be 'reachable', in the sense that it should be possible to give the consumers in that segment appropriate information about the organization's products.

  For example – a coach or bus operator finds that most customers are single and aged between 18 and 35, but unless they live in certain geographical areas they may be difficult to reach cost-effectively.

- *Measurability* – Each segment should be measurable, so that the likely demand for *THE* products in that segment can be identified. Research is very expensive and certain variables are very difficult to measure.

  For example – many people in deciding upon their holiday, do so in the expectation of receiving certain benefits such as peace and relaxation or a lively night life, but it is difficult to measure such 'motivations' especially when sometimes people are unwilling to answer personal questions in an honest manner. Some young people's true motivations for travel may be a desire to meet the opposite sex or to consume alcohol, but they may be reluctant to publicly acknowledge such motivations.

- *Actionability* – Each segment should be actionable, in that cost-effective programmes can be formulated for servicing the segments.

  For example – A small airline identifies seven market segments, but its staff and financial resources are too small to develop separate cost-effective marketing programmes for each segment identified.

However, some of the long-held assumptions that limit the smallest segments that can be economically reached are likely to change. Flexible technology is enabling products to be tailored to individual requirements more cheaply, thereby increasing choices available to consumers. In advertising, we are used to the concept of broadcasting. In the future we shall have to become used to the concept of *narrowcasting*, as a revolution in media takes place. If a company advertises on television and its product is only of interest to city dwellers, it is often also paying to reach all the rural viewers. Cable, satellite and mobile technology allows organizations to direct adverts much more accurately at prospective customers.

The same process is taking place with regard to direct marketing (mail shots) and web-based marketing, where data on buying habits and geo-demographic data allows accurately targeted marketing communications. The result of this process is that great rewards are available to organizations that can come up with sophisticated targeting strategies, as opposed to straightforward old-style mass marketing.

Product positioning

All organizations need to differentiate themselves and their products from competing organizations and products. Product positioning is the way in which a product or a brand is perceived in relation to preferences to segments of the market and in relation to competitive products.

The perceptual image that a consumer holds about an organization or product is important because a positive and favourable image can lead to the consumer purchasing products from the organization in question whereas a negative image inevitably results in consumers looking elsewhere for their product purchases. Thus *THE* strategists and marketers must seek to match the attributes of their product, and buyers' perceptions of those attributes, with the needs and priorities of customers in that segment. A number of authors have considered positioning in a *THE* context, see for example: Dev *et al.* (1999); Sahin and Baloglu (2011); Pike and Mason (2011); Morgan *et al.* (2012); Robertson and Wardrop (2011).

By way of example, assume that market research has been carried out which has identified that the two key attributes used by customers to rate specific airlines are:

- price
- quality.

This enables the market position of all the main competing products in that segment to be analysed by asking customers to rate each airline according to the two attributes of quality and price. The customer may be asked to rate each on a ten-point scale. The results can then be plotted on a scatter diagram where the position of each response can be accurately marked (see Figure 6.1 for an example).

The five competitors A, B, C, D and E, differ in sales volume as reflected by the sizes of the circles. The competitors' positions on the map are as follows:

- Competitor A occupies the high-quality/high-price position, sometimes termed a 'premium' position.
- Competitor B is perceived by the market as offering an average-quality product at an average price.
- Competitor C sells a low-quality product at a low price, sometimes termed a 'budget' position.
- Competitor D sells a high-quality product at a low price, sometimes termed a 'value-for-money' position.
- Competitor E sells a low-quality product at a high price, sometimes termed a 'cowboy' position.

The best position for a particular product can be determined. If they are very lucky the survey will have revealed an 'ideal' position not occupied by any existing product. If so, the objective of locating a group of customers with an unsatisfied need will have been achieved.

In Figure 6.1 a newcomer to the market might give consideration to locating at position F, where a high-quality product is provided at an average price. However, in reality, in today's very competitive markets the product-positioning map will probably not reveal such an obvious opportunity. The ideal

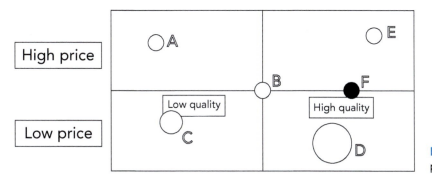

Figure 6.1 Product positioning

product may be close to or identical to an existing or several existing products. If so two basic positioning choices are possible:

- introduce a *me too* product, replicating the attributes of existing products occupying a similar position; or
- move into a gap on the product-positioning map, introducing a product bearing little similarity to any of the existing leading products.

If an organization finds a group of customers with a particular requirement for a combination not currently offered, it will literally have discovered a *gap* in the market (see the 'gap' on the bottom right of the chart). More likely, it will have to make the best of subtle differences in position, since all major combinations may be filled.

However, in the B2B market, it is company image considerations rather than the brand image (which we have considered here) which are more likely to be important in positioning. As Kalafatis *et al.* (2000) note, the brand-image-led positioning strategies that are prevalent in consumer goods marketing do not transfer well to business marketing.

SHORT CASE ILLUSTRATION

Product positioning: Marriott and IHG

Hotel brands are continually evolving and developing with new niche markets being served. The larger international hotel groups (such as IHG and Marriott) all have several sub-brands so that they can target differed segments successfully.

Richard Solomons, Chief Executive of UK based IHG plc (which runs brands such as Holiday Inn and Crowne Plaza), states 'customers are so much more discerning today, they are much clearer about what they want'. To illustrate the point Solomons draws an analogy with cars. 'When I grew up, it was a saloon, sports car or convertible. Now you've got SUVs and there are big SUVs and small SUVs and so on. Most consumer categories are becoming more segmented' (Goodman, 2013). Indeed, his own group, which already encompasses brands such as Holiday Inn, Crowne Plaza, Intercontinental and more recently Indigo, is planning the launch of two new brands. Hualuxe will be a brand aimed firmly at the Chinese market and catering for Chinese tastes as opposed to imposing Western tastes on the Chinese market while a further brand (as yet unnamed) will be aimed firmly at the growing perceived American market for a hotel brand focusing on wellbeing with healthy menus and workout options.

Marriott hotel group based in Washington DC currently has 15 brands (including Ritz-Carlton, Renaissance and luxury boutique brand Edition), but it is constantly searching for new niches to serve. The development of the Courtyard brand in the 1980s and 1990s and the current development of Moxy provide illustrations.

Courtyard, from its launch with three test hotels in 1983, has expanded rapidly in several countries and several hotel chains have attempted to duplicate the format. Research had identified a niche in the mid-level market, which was not being filled by any hotel concept at that time.

Marriott management identified three criteria, which had to be met in the design of the Courtyard concept:

- to assure that the new concept offered consumers good value for money;
- to minimize cannibalization (taking business away) from their other hotel offerings in the group;
- to establish a market position that offered management a substantial competitive advantage.

Marriott developed a product positioning statement for the hotel concept, which stated that the Courtyard product was to serve business travellers who wanted moderately priced hotels of consistent high quality, and pleasure travellers who wanted an affordable room that was a safe base of operations. A basic conceptual framework for the product was then developed. The product would have the following features (Crawford-Welch, 1994) in that it would:

- be tightly focused for the transient mid-priced market segment;
- be relatively small (150 rooms or fewer) to project a residential image;
- serve a limited menu and offer little public space and amenities;
- be a standardized product managed in clusters of hotels in one area;
- have the Marriott name attached for recognition and a 'halo' effect.

Moxy Hotels is Marriott's new entrant in the economy segment developed in partnership with the property division of Ikea Group, using modular construction techniques. Moxy will grow quickly to around 150 franchised locations in Europe during the next decade. The new three-star brand is designed specifically to target Generation Y and millennial travellers.

As the Moxy website says: 'Marriott International's newest player in the affordable three-star-tier segment for Millennial global nomads. It's got the power of Marriott behind it. The potency of style, innovation and tech-savvyness surrounding it. And a whole lot of wattage to light up its vibrant future' (www.moxyhotels.com).

Approximately two million of five million rooms in Europe are in economy hotels, but Arne Sorenson Marriott President and CEO argues that everywhere they turn customers are reminded that they are in an economy product. Thus the goal is to attract the emerging throngs of next-generation travellers who don't want to sacrifice comfort and design for an affordable price.

Technology and product design combined with Marriott's hospitality experience are aimed at attracting younger customers: Generation Y and Millenials. Moxy's 17-square-meter (183-square-foot) rooms will feature high-tech amenities, such as built-in universal-serial-bus ports and 42-inch flat-screen TVs with airplay connectivity. Each room will also feature a floor-to-ceiling signature art wall that is hand selected to reflect the local city or surroundings. Public spaces, meanwhile, will double as design-led hangouts with food and alcohol (Mayock, 2013).

Questions

1. Consider what advantages and possible disadvantages belonging to a powerful branded chain bring to Moxy.
2. Consider the reasons why Marriott is developing its Moxy brand.

Tourism destination positioning

The principles of positioning and repositioning can also be applied to destinations and a large literature has developed around the subject area. See for instance Scott *et al.* (2000); Gallarza *et al.* (2002); Pike and Ryan (2004); Usakli and Baloglu (2011); and Pike (2012).

However, destinations differ from organizations in that the assumptions of strong leadership and clear goal-driven decisions to which all participants adhere may be lacking. This is because destinations may be viewed as conglomerates of attractions, operators and agencies which each have individual objectives (Scott *et al.*, 2000:198–9).

SHORT CASE ILLUSTRATION

Tourism destination positioning in Queensland, Australia

Tourism is one of Queensland's key sectors, generating US$43 million per day – or US$16 billion per year in overnight visitor expenditure. Tourism also directly accounts for 124,000 (or 5.4 per cent) of Queensland's jobs and is the state's second largest export earner (behind coal). Tourism and Events Queensland (TEQ) is the Queensland Government's lead marketing, experience development and major events agency, representing the state's tourism and events industries.

In September 2010, after 18 months of extensive research and industry consultation, Tourism Queensland (now Tourism and Events Queensland) launched its first truly global tourism brand. 'Queensland, Where Australia Shines' introduces a new vision for Queensland as a tourism destination.

Though the new branding represents an umbrella brand to promote the whole of Queensland, the state has a unique position in Australia of having a number of strong destination brands, each having distinctive attributes, target markets and a sufficiently developed tourist industry to warrant a portfolio approach to their management as destinations. The approach reflects the diversity and scale of Queensland (and its tourism industry) and translates into different destination images, target markets, and positional and promotional programmes for each destination. These are summarised in Table 6.5 below:

Table 6.5 Queensland tourist destinations – positioning summary

Destinations	Positioning elements	Brand personality	% domestic visitors
Tropical North Queensland (TNQ)	Great Barrier Reef and tropical rainforest	Relaxed, friendly, natural, adventurous, active	57
Brisbane	Stimulating subtropical capital city experience	Plenty to see and do, relaxed fresh outdoors	75
Gold Coast	Beach and excitement, nightlife and entertainment	Exciting, fast-paced, fun	70
Sunshine Coast	Beach and relaxaion	Relaxed, simple, the way things used to be	90
Whitsunday Islands	Aquatic playground	Relaxed, fresh, friendly, vibrant, natural	75

Sources: Adapted from Scott et al. (2000)

Questions

1. Explain the potential differences in positioning a destination rather than a *THE* product belonging to a single company.

2. Explain why Queensland might need a number of sub-brands and explain their relationship to the umbrella brand.

Once an organization has decided how it wants to position itself relative to its competitors, it adapts its *marketing mix* to achieve such a differentiation. The marketing mix comprises those variables that an organization can control which stimulate consumer demand. Traditionally marketers have viewed the marketing mix as being concerned with the *Four Ps* of:

- Product;
- Promotion;
- Price; and
- Place (distribution).

However, it is common for those managing in service industries to also include three further aspects and it is sometimes labelled the Services Marketing Mix, as shown in Figure 6.2. In this way, the importance of these three further aspects of marketing in service setting is recognized.

These further *Three Ps* are:

- Personnel;
- Physical environment; and
- Processes.

A full consideration of the services marketing mix is beyond the scope of this text since the issues are concerned with more detailed implementation issues often dealt with by marketers. For a more detailed discussion of marketing mix issues in *THE* contexts see for example McKercher (1995); Allen *et al.* (2005); Hudson (2008); and Middleton *et al.* (2009).

Here we will, however, consider the *product* since achieving a balance between products at different stages of development can be viewed as a strategic issue affecting resource allocation, cash flow and risk.

Products

Product definition

Having considered markets we turn our attention to products.

Much of the strategic management literature is concerned with products and markets and the terminology *product–market* strategy is often used.

Figure 6.2 The services marketing mix

> ### DEFINITION/QUOTATION
>
> According to Kotler and Keller a product is:
>
> > Anything that can be offered to a market for attention, acquisition or consumption that might satisfy a want or a need. It includes physical objects, services, persons, places, organizations and ideas.
> >
> > Kotler and Keller (2012:347)

Importantly of course it is the sale of the product which provides sales revenue for the company. If a consumer buys a package holiday from one tour operator and is satisfied with that holiday, or has had a good experience of an event or at a particular venue, then he or she may decide to book again with the same company in the future. Therefore the company must pay careful attention to all facets of the product to make sure that it lives up to consumers' expectations and leads to brand and/or company loyalty.

When thinking about *THE* products it must be recognized that the 'product' does not just include the actual holiday or travel that is purchased, the visit to the tourist attraction, festival or event.

The product is in fact all those elements that make up the experience enjoyed by the customer. Of importance in product–market strategy is how the product features might be enhanced in a way that is valued by customers and that consequently they are willing to pay for. To do this it can be useful to consider the product's features and benefits at a number of levels. Different suggested approaches can give a different number of levels, but Kotler and Keller (2012:348) recommend that marketers (and strategists) recognize the product as being made up of five levels:

- the core product;
- the generic product;
- the expected product;
- the augmented product; and
- the potential product.

1. *The core product* is the main benefit which the customer gains when purchasing the product.

   For example – when a holidaymaker goes on a European holiday to Majorca, the core product may be one representing rest and relaxation whereas the core product for a holidaymaker going to Vietnam might be somewhat different. In this instance the core product might be to explore a newly developed international tourist destination.

2. *The generic product* is a basic version of the product. It refers to the features of the product that are purchased.

   For example – a visit to a festival might include travel arrangements to and from the festival, accommodation at the festival and 'add-ons' such as excursions to local attractions and vouchers to use at local restaurants. All the standard features that comprise the trip to the festival, including the brochure or promotional material, are part of this generic product.

3. *The expected product* represents a set of attributes and conditions that buyers normally expect and agree to when purchasing a product.

   For example – customers might normally expect certain features at the self-catering apartments which might form a part of the package arrangements they book at their holiday destination, such as clean rooms, bed linen, towels, plumbing fixtures, hanging space for clothes, a quiet location and privacy.

4. *The augmented product* goes beyond the customer's expectations to provide something extra and desirable.

For example – the levels of service provided by staff in a travel or concert booking agency, those in a call centre who arrange the booking, or the way in which particular companies deal with customer complaints provide examples of the augmented product level. The way in which these and other services are delivered can 'add value' to the product sold and can often distinguish one company's product offering from others.

Kotler views this augmented level as being the level at which most competition takes place, in the increasingly competitive market now faced by companies. To be successful in business, companies have to continually review their products (and crucially in *THE* contexts, the way in which they are delivered) so as to ensure they are superior to competitors.

However, each augmentation costs the organization resources in terms of time or money, and consequently questions must be asked as to whether customers will pay enough to cover the extra costs involved. Augmented benefits soon become expected benefits.

For example – en-suite rooms have moved from being the exception to the norm in most international standard hotels in the last forty years and more recently internet connectivity has increasingly become the norm.

Similarly what is contained in the expected product in one market may be in the augmented product in another.

For example – air conditioning might be a bonus in a temperate climate, but a necessity in tropical or desert climates. Short-haul airline passengers may tolerate cramped seating conditions in return for lower prices, whereas this is less likely to be the case with long-haul passengers.

This means that competitors have to continually search for still further features and benefits to add to their products. Sometimes, after a period of rivalry where competitors try to compete by adding more and more features and cost, a market segment emerges for a basic, stripped-down, low-cost version that just supplies the expected benefits.

For example – the emergence of the low-cost airline sector (e.g. Air Asia, easyJet and Ryanair) and budget hotel brands (e.g. Formula 1, Etap and Premier Inn) in recent years can be seen in this way.

5. *The potential product* includes all the augmentations and transformations that the product might ultimately undergo in the future. Whereas the augmented product describes product features included in today's product, the potential product represents the possible evolution of the product. Successful companies will therefore manage and evaluate their products very carefully. They will appreciate that some additional benefits must be provided to attract customers in competitive markets. Farsighted companies will therefore put much effort into research and development because the product with most potential is the product likely to be successful in tomorrow's markets.

All companies need to decide on an optimum number of different products to offer consumers:

For example – should the tour operator offer only inclusive air tours to Greece, or should packages also be developed for Cyprus and Turkey? Should the travel agent specialize in high-value cruise and long-haul specialized products, or products that will have more of a mass-market appeal?

The organization, however, must not only consider the present situation since consumer tastes change, tourist destinations go out of favour as new resorts are developed, and competing events and festivals are continually being developed. The organization must therefore also consider the future situation and specifically: which new products could be launched onto the market and when should they be launched?

The answers to these questions will depend upon factors such as:

- the resources available to the business;
- the market segments to be targeted; and
- the needs of the consumers.

Controlling the company's range of products, the so-called *product portfolio*, and phasing in new products as established ones decline is an important function of a strategic manager as distinct from the marketing manager who also has to take decisions concerning the features that will be included in each product. Such strategic decisions have also led to the development of a number of concepts and models, some of which are discussed in the following sections and are also summarised by, for example, Brownlie (1985) and Fleisher and Bensoussan (2003).

The product life cycle

The product life cycle concept is based on the analogy of living things, in that they all have a finite life. All products would be expected to have a finite life, whether it is long or short. The life cycle can operate at an individual product level, or a product type, or at a product class level, where arguably a market life cycle would be a more appropriate title.

At individual product level, the product life cycle is a useful tool in product planning, so that a balance of products is kept in various stages of the life cycle.

KEY CONCEPT

The human life cycle metaphor for products

The concept of life cycle does not just apply to humans (or animals); it also applies to products, tourist destinations, festivals and events. Human beings undergo a life cycle that has a huge bearing, not just on our biological changes, but also on behaviour and products often move through a similar cycle.

We undergo introduction when we are conceived and grow inside our mothers. After birth, we begin to grow – a process that continues until, after puberty, we reach our full height and weight. Our maturity phase is the longest. For most people, it will last from our mid-teens until the time when our faculties begin to fail us, perhaps in our sixties or seventies. When we reach old age, we begin to decline. Our eyesight may begin to deteriorate, we slow down and we may lose some of our intellectual sharpness. Finally, when decline has run its course, life is no longer viable, and we die.

At the product class level, we can use the product life cycle concept to analyse and predict competitive conditions and identify key issues for management. It is conventionally broken into a number of stages as shown in the diagram. We shall explore the key issues posed by the different stages.

Each stage of the product life cycle (Figure 6.3) has different implications for aspects of the organization and the way in which it manages its products. Specifically managers need to be aware of the changing impact on costs, competitors, objectives and cashflow – as products move through the life cycle. Figure 6.3 shows the life cycle and summarizes the main implications of these aspects.

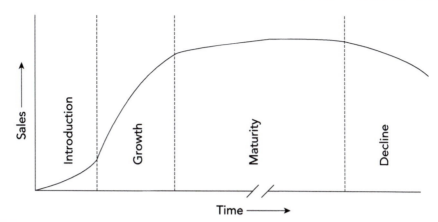

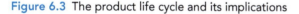

	Introduction	Growth	Maturity	Decline
Costs	Highest costs per customer	High costs per customer	Low costs per customer	Low costs per customer
Competitors	None or few	Few	Maximum number of competitors	Declining number of competitors
Product objectives	High product awareness and trial – need to explain nature of innovation	Maximum market share before too many competitors arrive	Maximize profit while defending market share and motivate customers to switch brand	Reduce expenditure and milk the brand Cost control is vital
Cash flow	Likely to be negative as launch costs are not covered by sales	As sales grow negative cash flow turns to a positive cash flow	Maximum positive cash flow as product has become established which allows surplus cash to be invested in other products	Strong cost controls enable positive though diminishing cash surpluses to be achieved

Figure 6.3 The product life cycle and its implications

The introduction stage

The introduction stage follows the product's initial development. It is consequently new to the market and will be bought by *innovators,* a term used to describe a small proportion of the eventual market. The innovators may not be easy to identify in advance and there are likely to be high launch and marketing costs. Because operational (or production) volumes are likely to be low, because it is still at a 'pilot' stage, the operational cost per unit will be high.

The *price elasticity of demand* will strongly influence whether the product is introduced at a high 'skimming' price or a low 'penetration' price.

Price skimming is appropriate when the product is known to have price inelastic demand such as with new exclusive resort developments or a first-class cabin provided by an airline serving a new destination.

Price penetration is appropriate for products with price elastic demand and when gaining market share is more important than making a fast recovery of development costs. A low-cost airline launching a new route or a budget hotel operator launching in a new city provide examples of such products.

KEY CONCEPT

Price elasticity of demand

Demand represents the quantity of a product buyers are willing and able to buy at a particular price over a specified period of time.

Demand to an economist is not quite the same as 'want'. Everyone might want to travel on a luxury round-the-world cruise, but not everyone has the ability to pay for it. Other things being equal we would expect the quantity of services demanded to be inversely proportional to its price. In other words if the price is increased, lower quantities would be demanded and vice versa.

The important concept of *price elasticity of demand* measures the responsiveness of demand to a change in price – some services are very responsive while others may be less so. In making pricing decisions it is very important to understand just how responsive demand is to price changes if revenue is to be maximized.

The main factors affecting price elasticity of demand in relation to *THE* products are likely to be:

- *The availability of substitutes* – The greater the degree of competition (and hence the availability of substitutes) the more elastic (responsive) demand is likely to be. *For example*, there are many festivals throughout Europe, particularly in the Summer months, and competition between them is strong whereas the number of airlines operating on particular routes is often very limited.

- *The time period* – Over a prolonged period consumers' demands are likely to be more elastic. *For example* if the price of holidays from Northern Europe to Spain increases relative to those of Greece, in the short term demand may not alter very much (since arrangements and bookings have been made), but over a longer period consumers are likely to switch demand to Greece. In other words the price elasticity of demand for Greece is likely to increase over time.

- *Proportion of income* – The higher the proportion of a consumer's income that a particular product takes up, the higher the price elasticity of demand is likely to be. *For example*, in purchasing a trivial item like a pencil a consumer is likely to be less concerned about the price than with an expensive purchase such as an airline flight or attendance at a concert.

- *Luxury vs. necessity* – Those seeking luxury are generally willing and able to pay for it and consequently the price elasticity of demand is likely to be lower for luxury products.

- *Business vs. Pleasure* – Business travellers are likely to be less price-sensitive than leisure travellers since they value time and reliability and consequently price elasticity of demand is likely to be lower.

Adapted from Evans (2002)

Pioneer companies (those who are first to the market with a particular product) are often forced, or sometimes willingly seek, to sell the product idea to an existing brand, and the early promotion may help competitors who enter the market later with *me too* versions of the product idea.

Entering the market at an early stage is usually risky. Not only will the company be likely to incur a negative cash flow for a period, but also many products fail at this stage. Against this risk is the prospect of increasing market share in the new product area faster than the 'me toos' and consequently achieving so-called *first mover* advantage.

First mover advantage occurs when the first product becomes the established provider and establishes a *barrier to entry* for subsequent entries to the market.

First mover advantage: Dubai and Singapore

A first mover advantage can be simply defined as a firm's ability to be better off than its competitors as a result of being first to market in a new product category (Suarez and Lanzolla, 2005). It is useful to distinguish between durable first-mover advantages, which improve a firm's market share or profitability over a long period, and those that are short-lived. Although no advantage lasts forever, firms that succeed in building durable first-mover advantages tend to dominate their product categories for many years, from a market's infancy until well into its maturity.

Coca-Cola in soft drinks and Hoover in vacuum cleaners unmistakably demonstrate both the value and longevity of early success (Suarez and Lanzolla, 2005). Those products that follow on behind trying to catch up and copy those with first mover advantage are often described as 'me too' products.

The growth of air transport networks and deregulation have allowed small places with relatively small populations like Singapore and Dubai to become major international tourism destinations and transportation hubs. Both Singapore and Dubai have managed to divert a significant number of passengers who stop in either of those cities on long-haul routes between Europe, Asia and the Southwest Pacific (Lohmann et al., 2009).

In both cases integrated and complex networks have been developed and both have enjoyed success both as hubs and through their respective airlines: Emirates and Singapore Airlines. Hubs were transformed into destinations by the complementary interaction of attractions, transport and accommodation sectors. Both used shopping 'paradises' to persuade visitors to stay.

Singapore and Dubai have both enjoyed first mover advantages in terms of the model they have adopted, but other countries have similar geographical features that may gradually erode this. Regional rivals Kuala Lumpur (Malaysia) and Bangkok (Thailand) enjoy similar locational advantages and are now endeavouring to challenge Singapore as the premier hub of the region (Bowen, 2000). Abu Dhabi (UAE) and Doha (Qatar) and their respective airlines, Etihad and Qatar Airways, are growing and provide competition to Emirates and Dubai (Lohmann et al., 2009).

Questions

1. Explain what is meant by *first mover advantage* and a *me too* strategy citing examples of both you are familiar with from *THE*.

2. Consider what advantages Singapore and Dubai might be able to exploit in developing *first mover* advantage.

The growth stage

During the growth stage, sales for the market as a whole increase and new competitors typically enter to challenge the pioneer for some of the market share. The competitors may develop new market segments in an attempt to avoid direct competition with the established pioneering market leader.

The market becomes profitable, cash flow becomes positive and the funds generated can be used to offset the development and launch costs. This is an important time to win market share, since it is easier to win a disproportionate share of new customers than to later get customers to switch brands. As new market segments emerge, key decisions will need to be made as to whether to follow them or stay with the original.

The maturity stage

Maturity is reached when a high proportion of people who will eventually purchase a product have already purchased it once. It is likely to be the longest stage, but depending on the market this could range from days or weeks to many decades or even centuries. It is important at this stage either to have achieved a high market share or to dominate a special niche in the market. It can be expensive and risky to achieve large market share changes at this time, so some companies prefer to concentrate their competitive efforts on retaining existing customers and competing very hard for the small number of new customers appearing. In this phase it is likely that large positive cash flows are being generated which can be reinvested in new products or in products at an earlier stage of their evolution.

In order to maintain and protect their position in a mature market, companies have to be vigilant in detecting changes taking place. In response to changes organizations have to be ready to modify or improve products and how customers perceive them and to undertake product repositioning.

The decline stage

It is part of product life cycle theory that all markets will eventually decline and therefore companies have to be ready to move to new markets where decline is felt to be inevitable, or to be ready with strategies to extend the life cycle if this is felt to be feasible. Appropriate extension strategies could include developing new uses for the product, finding new users and repositioning the product to gain a presence in the parts of the market that will remain after the rest of the market has gone. Even where markets have reached an advanced stage of decline, there may remain particular segments that can be profitable for organizations able to anticipate their existence and dominate them.

Companies that succeed in declining markets usually adopt a 'milking' strategy where investment is kept to a minimum and any market share that may be left by competitors that have left the market because of the decline is taken up. There is a certain recognition that death will come eventually and thus any revenues that can be made in the interim are something of a bonus.

The Tourism Area Life Cycle (TALC)

The ideas of the product life cycle have been applied in a tourism destination context through the Tourism Area Life Cycle (TALC). The TALC model has become one of the most cited and frequently used models in the tourism literature, having been applied in various parts of the world and in various contexts (see for example Almeida and Correia, 2010: Madeira; Diedrich and García-Buades, 2009: Belize; Whitfield, 2009: conference management; Garay and Cànoves, 2011: Catalonia, Spain; and Kozak and Martin, 2012: managing for profit).

Borrowing from the classic business literature on life cycles of products, with strong links to other spatial economic models, Butler argues that destinations can be viewed as products, and that their pattern of development closely mirrors the classic life cycle curve (Butler, 2009). According to TALC (see for example Butler, 1980, 2000, 2009; and Ma and Hassink, 2013) destinations go through a similar evolution to that of products, but visitor numbers are substituted for product sales. Destinations move from evolution (similar to introduction in the PLC) through involvement, development and consolidation (similar to growth in the PLC) before reaching stagnation (similar to maturity in the PLC). Like the PLC, decline will inevitably follow unless actions are taken which result in rejuvenation of the destination.

The shape of the curve, the length of each stage and the length of the cycle itself are variable.

For example – Cooper *et al.* (1998:114) point to 'instant' resorts such as Cancun in Mexico or time-share developments that move almost immediately to growth. In contrast, well-established resorts such as Scarborough on England's east coast have taken three centuries to move from exploration to rejuvenation.

Criticisms of the product life cycle

The product life cycle (and its application to *THE* contexts in the form of the Tourism Area Life Cycle) appears to be both widely understood and widely used (Greenley and Bayus, 1993) and Fleisher and Bensoussan (2003) provide a useful overview of the concept and its application. Nevertheless, some important criticisms of it have been made and it is important in using concepts of this type that they are not used uncritically and are combined with other corroborating evidence. Whilst it is easy to go back into history and demonstrate all the features of the concept, it is hard to forecast the future and in particular hard to forecast turning points. Not to try to do so at all, however, would seem to avoid confronting hard strategic issues.

Another criticism is that life cycles may sometimes not be inevitable as dictated by the market, but created by the ineptitude of management. If management assume that decline will come, they will take the decision to reduce investment and advertising in anticipation of the decline. Not surprisingly, decline does come, but sooner than it otherwise would have done had the investment not been withdrawn.

Moutinho (2000:143) details several criticisms of the concept in a tourism context. The Tourist Area Life Cycle decline relates to visitor numbers exceeding capacity levels at the destination, but Moutinho points out that capacity is a notoriously difficult concept to operationalize as it is possible to envisage different forms of capacity threshold. Physical, environmental and psychological capacity may vary and it may be possible to 'manage' capacity.

S-curve (technology life cycle analysis)

In arguing for a different approach which incorporates the role of technology changes, Brown (1991) states that 'marketing literature abounds with "S" curves to depict processes which start slowly, then gradually gather pace until they move into fast growth, which continues until saturation is approached, when growth slows down and finally plateaus' the most important of which is the PLC. A major difficulty in implementing that in reality is that the PLC rarely assumes a smooth predictable curve; there are often discontinuities in the curve. Product markets rarely develop as a single homogeneous unit, rather they develop as a series of segments (Brown, 1991) because of the impacts derived from the introduction of new technology.

Business history contains many examples of the enormous impact the introduction of new technology and innovation can have, such as the rapid displacement of mechanical cash registers by electronic cash registers during the 1970s. Similarly several examples can be cited in relation to the *THE* sectors.

For example – the introduction of jet aircraft from the 1950s and the introduction of the Boeing 747 ('Jumbo' Jet) in the 1970s had transformational impacts on the airline industry. Similarly, the development of the internet from the 1990s has had enormous repercussions for all industries but perhaps none more so than for travel and event intermediaries such as travel agents and booking agencies. The widespread diffusion of the internet allows customers to deal directly with travel companies and event organizers rather than going through an intermediary allowing so-called *disintermediation* to take place. The internet has also allowed customers to gain far greater ability to quickly compare prices.

S-curve analysis integrates technological change into strategic planning. It accomplishes this by plotting the effort expended into a product or process technology and the resulting return, the rationale being that every technology has a natural limit to the benefits it can generate. At some point increasing research and development expenditure will result in in a decreasing rate of productivity growth (Fleisher and Bensoussan, 2003).

Figure 6.4 illustrates the possible effects of distribution of *THE* products through traditional brochures and through online distribution. The figure indicates that online distribution has established itself as a more effective means of distribution, though brochure distribution remains important.

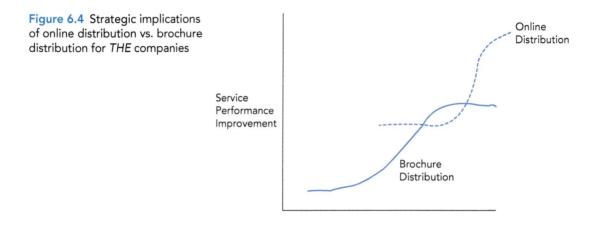

Figure 6.4 Strategic implications of online distribution vs. brochure distribution for *THE* companies

The existence of more effective or efficient technologies frequently results in the existence of multiple S-curves as shown in Figure 6.4. Rivals operating on S-curves above and to the left of the firm's current S-curve will be competitively superior in that they may have lower costs, higher quality or increased differentiation. Since this superior performance can be achieved; the challenge for managers becomes not whether to make a move but when. Switching technologies can be expensive and often involves new skills and processes.

Achieving this transition to a new technology is very difficult for most firms and timing is of utmost importance. To make the transition too early, before the marketplace is ready to embrace the new technology, is a costly mistake. Leaving the transition too late risks falling behind competitors and may make it very difficult to catch up the ground which has been lost.

SHORT CASE ILLUSTRATION

Introducing new technology: Boeing's 'Dreamliner'

Replacing older, less fuel-efficient, long-haul aircraft such as the Boeing 747 with more modern fuel-efficient aircraft such as the Boeing 787 ('Dreamliner') may move an airline forward technologically and it provides a public relations opportunity for the airline and manufacturer. However, it is also expensive and requires extensive training and development work. Furthermore, it is not without risks in terms of proving a new aircraft type.

The technical difficulties (mainly with batteries) encountered by the Dreamliner after its launch illustrates the point. Two Japanese carriers, All Nippon Airlines (ANA) and Japan Air Lines (JAL), were early purchasers in 2012 of the Dreamliners and began flying the fuel-efficient aircraft to cities such as Boston and San Jose, California, that wouldn't be profitable with larger planes.

However, in early 2013 a four-month global suspension of 787 services was ordered by regulatory authorities after lithium-ion batteries overheated on two different planes, with one of them catching fire while the aircraft was parked. Such episodes severely dent public confidence and lead to severe operating difficulties for all the early adopting airlines which included Ethiopian Airlines, Qatar Airways, Air India and United Airlines.

Nevertheless, in a bid to show it was back on track after the technical issues with the jetliner, Boeing announced in June 2013 at the Paris Air Show that it was launching a new version of the Dreamliner, with over 100 orders worth about $30 billion for the innovative fuel-efficient airliner.

New product development

The importance of new products

Change in society, markets, economies and society has led to a shortening of life cycles and this has intensified the need for most organizations to innovate in terms of the products that they offer. New products can provide the mechanism whereby further growth can take place. Increasing competition, often itself coming from new or modified products, means that innovation is frequently not an option, but a necessity for many companies operating in all sectors.

However, totally new products are in reality quite rare, though they may be labelled as 'new' for marketing purposes. Actually, many products promoted as 'new' have evolved from existing product offerings or are merely 'new' to a particular market segment, such as a particular geographical territory

Thus 'newness' can vary from restyling, or minor modification such as the introduction of restyled promotional brochures or new aircraft liveries to producing products that are *new to the world* that lead to new markets being created, such as the creation of a new genre of music and the events which stem from it.

For example – though blessed with beautiful scenery, superb beaches and a tropical climate the Caribbean country of Haiti has in recent years attracted only the most intrepid of international tourists. Lack of infrastructure, political turmoil and earthquakes have all had their impacts. However, matters are beginning to change and a new international market is being created as international tour operators such as Canada's 'Transat' begin to feature the destination which offers a value-for-money destination. A further boost to the country's international tourism aspirations was provided when the US Department of Defense announced during 2014, the removal of the country from its list of 'danger zones'.

The higher the degree of newness, the more likely it is that major gains in sales and profits may be made, but at the same time, the risks of incurring high costs and market failure are also increased. A single new product failure, if big enough, could lead to the financial failure of an organization. It is generally accepted that a very large proportion of new products fail, although precise quantification is impossible as many new products may be kept on the market despite not meeting their original objectives.

Organizations are faced with a dilemma in the management of new product development: in that it is essential for successful development, but is also fraught with risks. The successful management of the dilemma is often to produce a large number of new product ideas, most of which will never reach the market because they have been weeded out by an appropriate screening process.

New product idea generation

Ideas for new products can come from many sources. The greater the range of sources used, the more likely it is that a wide range and large number of new ideas will be produced (Sowrey, 1990).

IDEAS FROM CUSTOMERS

For most organizations the most important source of new ideas will be from their customers. Obtaining ideas from customers is a good way of ensuring that products are generated as a result of 'market pull'. This means that there will be a market for the products that result because they are specifically requested by the customers. Surveys and focus groups can help to produce ideas. The more straightforward approaches may give ideas for improvements, but more subtle approaches may reveal new needs.

Von Hippel (1978) showed that a very successful approach for new ideas in industrial B2B markets was to work with lead customers (respected, technically advanced buyers) to overcome their particular problems and then to use the resulting new products to sell to other customers. Sometimes the products may require modification for the other customers at some cost. The modified products that ensue then have unique value for these customers who are then willing to pay for the enhanced product features provided. Thus the product enjoys the benefits of price inelasticity of demand.

OTHER SOURCES OF IDEAS

It is impossible to construct a comprehensive list of sources of new product ideas but the following have proved themselves to be useful in the past:

- intermediaries such as advertising agencies, legal firms and property agents (who sometimes have their 'finger on the pulse' of market requirements);
- consultants (who may carry out market research on a company's behalf);
- universities and other academic institutions;
- competitors (where an organization copies a competitive product);
- suppliers (who may have devised a way to use a component or material);
- employees, sometimes through 'employee idea' schemes;
- distributors and agents for the product.

Screening

Once ideas for new products have been generated, a company must then sift through them to develop only those with genuine potential – a process known as *screening*. As far as possible, the screening process has to attempt to avoid two potential types of errors:

- GO errors, where products are developed that ultimately fail, or do not meet objectives; and
- DROP errors, where ideas are abandoned that would ultimately have succeeded.

GO errors are recognizable, at least by the organization that makes them, but most DROP errors are unrecognised because the project has not gone ahead (unless of course a competitor makes a success of an idea that has been abandoned).

In practice, screening is normally a multi-stage process, with at least some kind of review at several points. Since risks may be high, and organizational politics may play a part, it is usually recommended that in at least one of the stages a formal process is undergone where the idea is evaluated against predetermined objective criteria.

Development

The stages in development will vary according to the nature of the product and the work required to develop a new version, but it is important to include stages of the screening process before activities that involve the commitment of large amounts of finance and human and marketing resources, and it would not make sense to spend large amounts in developing a new product without producing evidence that there would be some demand for it. Stages in the process are typically as follows:

- initial appraisal;
- detailed business analysis and investment appraisal;
- technical development;
- market testing;
- launch.

A traditional view of the development process is that one stage should precede another. With increasing competition, reducing time to market has become very important in many industries. To reduce the time to market, some of the activities may go on at the same time, sometimes known as *parallel processing*. This puts a premium on good communications in the company between functions such as operations, finance and marketing.

To avoid the delays and complications that might be involved in handing a project from one function in the organization to another, multi-disciplinary teams sometimes known as *venture teams* may be created and in some circumstances the team may be given the new product to manage when it is on the market. If such a team is created, it is likely that more senior management will make the GO or DROP decisions to avoid the risk of the bias of an enthusiastic but optimistic team taking over.

In some areas of *THE* such as the development of new hotels, resort development, buying cruise liners or new aircraft, and the creation of visitor attractions; new product development requires significant capital investment. Consequently it is common to carry out a feasibility study prior to deciding whether to go ahead in order to test the viability of the proposed project.

For example – Swarbrooke (1995) identified a nine-stage feasibility study process when assessing the viability of a visitor attraction. The stages are summarised in Figure 6.5.

Key points arising from the feasibility study should include:

- assessing the *penetration factor* i.e. predictions of the proportion of people in each market segment who may visit the attraction;

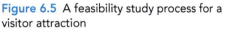

Figure 6.5 A feasibility study process for a visitor attraction

- analysis of where the visitors will come from, when they will come and how much they are likely to spend; and
- analysis of capital costs, estimated likely income and estimation of the breakeven level of visitors.

Product portfolio theory

What is a portfolio?

The notion of a portfolio exists in many areas of life, not just for products. Underpinning the concept is the need for a business to spread its opportunities and risks. A broad portfolio signifies that a business has a presence in a wide range of product and market sectors. Conversely, a narrow portfolio implies that the organization only operates in a few or even one product or market sector.

A broad portfolio offers the advantage of robustness in that a downturn in one market will not threaten the whole company. Against this advantage is the problem of managing business interests that may be very different in nature – the company may be said to lack strategic focus. Organizations operating with a very narrow portfolio (i.e. just one segment) can often concentrate wholeheartedly upon its segment but it can become vulnerable if there is a downturn of demand in the one segment it serves.

The Boston Consulting Group (BCG) matrix

The Boston Consulting Group (BCG) matrix offers a way of examining and making sense of a company's portfolio of product and market interests (see Fleisher and Bensoussan, 2003:Ch. 4). As with other models and matrices used in strategic analysis (of which there are many), the BCG matrix is a simplifying tool. It selects one parameter – relative market share – as an indicator of the strength of the competitive position and another parameter – market growth – as indicating the potential and attractiveness of the market (Morrison and Wensley, 1991).

A key point of the matrix is that market share and market growth provide approximations of the company's ability to generate cash. Cash flow is important in that it represents the most important determinant of a company's ability to develop its product portfolio. Cash generated by successful products can be utilized in developing new products.

Also implicit in the use of the matrix are the benefits to be gained from the *experience effect* (Henderson, 1984). It is recognized that companies (as with people) carry out their activities more efficiently with greater experience. Lessons are learned and adjustments to processes and systems are made. The experience effect is linked to market share through a virtuous cycle (Hooley and Saunders, 1993) as shown in Figure 6.6.

Figure 6.6 The experience effect

The virtuous cycle demonstrates the impact of the experience effect in that:

- a company with high market share gains more experience than its competitors;
- the experience results in lower costs;
- the lower costs mean that, at a given price, the company with the highest market share has the highest profits;
- the company with the highest profits or contributions from sales has more to spend on research and development or marketing, which allows it to maintain its high market share.

For example – applying this cycle for example to a tour operator in its dealings with hoteliers:

- A high market share enables the tour operator to have greater experience of dealing with hoteliers than its competitors.
- The experience represented by the large market share allows the tour operator to be able to reassure the hoteliers that large volumes will be sold so that high occupancy rates can be achieved.

- As a consequence of the high volumes, lower room rates will be paid by the tour operator (than by its competitors) to the hotelier.
- The lower costs enable the tour operator with the highest market share to achieve the highest profits.
- The tour operator with the highest profits has more to spend on research and development or on marketing, which allows it to maintain its high market share.

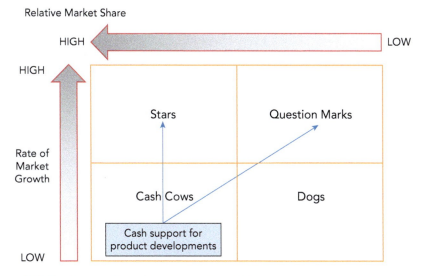

Figure 6.7 The Boston Consulting Group (BCG) Matrix

A large empirical study, the Profit Impact of Market Strategy (PIMS), provides further justification for the BCG approach. Perhaps the most important finding from the PIMS study is that there is a strong correlation between a high market share and the level of profitability (Buzzell, 2004). Thus a high market share is not an end in itself but something that is desirable since it leads (on average) to higher returns being achieved.

The BCG matrix is used to analyse the product range with a view to aiding decisions on how the products should be treated in an internal strategic analysis. Figure 6.7 shows the essential features of the Boston matrix.

Using the BCG matrix

CASH COWS

A product with a high market share in a low growth market is normally both profitable and a generator of cash. Profits from this product can be used to support other products that are in their development phase. Standard strategy would be to manage conservatively, but to defend strongly against competitors. Such a product is called a cash cow because profits from the product can be *milked* on an ongoing basis.

These are products associated with high positive cash flows and consequently can be used to support *stars* and selected *question marks*, as indicated by the arrows in Figure 6.7.

DOGS

A product that has a low market share in a low growth market is termed a *dog* in that it is typically not very profitable. To cultivate the product to increase its market share would incur cost and risk, not least because the market it is in has a low rate of growth. Accordingly, once a dog has been identified as part of a portfolio it is often discontinued or disposed of.

More creatively, opportunities might be found to differentiate the dog and obtain a strong position for it in a niche market. A small market share product can be used to price aggressively against a very large competitor as it is expensive for the large competitor to follow suit.

The matrix does not have an intermediate market share category, but there are large numbers of products that have a large market share, but are not market leaders. They may be the biggest profit earners for the companies that own them. They usually compete against the market leader at a disadvantage that is slight, but real. Management need to make very efficient use of marketing expenditure for such products and to try to differentiate from the leader. They should not normally compete head on, especially on price, but attempt to make gains if the market changes in a way that the leader is slow to exploit.

These are products associated with modest positive or negative cash flow.

STARS

Stars have a high market share of a rapidly growing market and therefore rapidly growing sales. They may be the sales manager's dream, but they could be the accountant's nightmare, since they are likely to absorb large amounts of cash, even if they are highly profitable. It is often necessary to spend heavily on advertising and product improvements, so that when the market slows these products become cash cows. If market share is lost, the product will eventually become a *dog* when the market stops growing.

These are products associated with modest positive or negative cash flow.

QUESTION MARKS

Question marks are aptly named as they create a dilemma. They already have a foothold in a growing market, but if market share cannot be improved, they will become dogs. Resources need to be devoted to winning market share, which requires bravery for a product that may not yet have large sales, or the product may be sold to an organization in a better position to exploit the market. These products will be high users of cash because they are trying to establish themselves in a growth market.

These are products associated with large negative cash flow.

In summary, portfolio management is concerned with balancing products and hence cash flow so that one category of products can support the development of other categories; risks can thereby be diminished and, specifically, companies should be looking to develop question marks into stars and stars into cash cows.

Table 6.6 summarises the strategic implications of using the BCG Matrix.

Using the terminology that is usually applied to the matrix portfolio management is concerned with:

- *milking* surplus cash generated by cash cows;
- using the cash generated in *maintaining* stars and *investing* in selected question marks; and
- *withdrawal* from dogs (if profitable niche positions cannot be established) or *harvesting* them if profitable niches can be established.

Limitations of the BCG matrix

Accurate measurement and careful definition of the market are essential to avoid mis-diagnosis when using the matrix. Critics, perhaps unfairly, point out that there are many relevant aspects relating to products that are not taken into account, but it was never claimed by the Boston Consulting Group that the process was a panacea, and covered all aspects of strategy.

Above all, the matrix helps to identify which products to push or drop and when. It helps in the recognition of windows of opportunity, and provides strong evidence against simple rules of thumb for allocating resources to products. However, the information needed to apply the matrix might be difficult and time consuming to obtain and to update and some *THE* managers might feel that the effort is not worthwhile.

Composite portfolio models

The limitations of the BCG matrix have given rise to a number of other models that are beyond the scope of this text. A leading example is the General Electric Matrix (see Fleisher and Bensoussan, 2003: Ch. 5).

Table 6.6 Using the BCG Matrix in strategic planning

Business category	Market share thrust	Business profitability	Investment required	Net cash flow
Stars	Hold/increase	High	High	Around zero or slightly negative
Cash cows	Hold	High	Low	Highly positive
Question marks A	Increase	None or negative	Very High	Highly negative
Question marks B	Harvest/divest	Low or negative	Divest	Positive
Dogs	Harvest/divest	Low or negative	Divest	Positive

Source: Adapted from Hax and Majluf (1983)

Whilst the Boston matrix is intended for products, but may be used for strategic business units that are fairly homogenous, the General Electric Matrix is mainly applied to strategic business units such as the subsidiaries of a holding company.

The model rates *market attractiveness* as high, medium or low and *competitive strength* as strong, medium or weak. Strategic business units are placed in the appropriate category, and although there is no automatic strategic prescription, the position is used to help devise an appropriate strategy.

Market attractiveness criteria will be set by the user and could include factors such as: market growth, profitability, strength of competition, entry/exit barriers, legal regulation, etc. Competitive strength could include factors such as: technological capability, band, image, distribution channel links, operational capability and financial strength. The flexibility to include as many variables as required is useful, but could lead to over-subjectivity. Most users of the model recommend that the variables be given a weighting to establish their relative importance, which will, in turn, reduce the potential for bias. In practice, managers tend to be aware that the tool is likely to be used as a basis for resource allocation and, consequently, they may attempt to influence the analysis in the favour of their own product or strategic business unit.

The analysis gives rise to a three-by-three matrix as shown in Figure 6.8.

Each of the cell positions has associated strategic implications:

- Cell A – The company would invest strongly in these products or SBUs as it offers an attractive strategic position where distinctive capabilities providing competitive strength can be harnessed in an attractive market.
- Cell B – The company could be aggressive and attempt to build strength in order to challenge competitors, or it could build selectively.

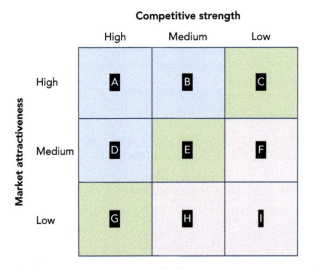

Classification	Strategic thrust
☐ High overall attractiveness (A, B and D)	Invest/grow
☐ Medium overall attractiveness (C, E and G)	Selectively improve/defend
☐ Low overall attractiveness (F, H and I)	Harvest/divest

Figure 6.8 The GEC matrix

- Cell C – There is a real dilemma, in that there is the difficulty of competing well against stronger competitors. The most plausible options would be to divest as the opportunity might be attractive to others, or to specialize around selected niches where some strength could be built.
- Cell D – Indicates investment and maintenance of competitive ability.
- Cells E and F – Indicate risk minimization and prudent selective choices for investment and expansion.
- Cells G and H – Indicate management of a mature or declining market in order to maximize earnings.
- Cell I – Could require divestment or minimizing investment in order to maintain the product or SBU as a going concern.

Extreme care is required in the judgements that place products or strategic business units into any one category and the model does not directly take into account synergies between different products or SBUs. However, importantly, the model does represent a means of relating competencies (of the organization) to the external environment. Consequently the model can be viewed as taking SWOT analysis, covered in Chapter 9, a stage further.

THINK POINTS

- Distinguish between price skimming and penetration strategies.
- Explain what is meant by a product portfolio.
- Explain the importance of cash flow to an understanding of the BCG matrix.
- Explain the major benefits and potential difficulties of using the BCG and GEC matrices.

SMALL BUSINESS FOCUS

Many of the marketing and product aspects considered in this chapter can be applied to small THE businesses in a similar way that they can be applied to larger businesses. In many cases though the concepts were developed primarily for large-scale businesses often with a number of products or strategic business units and many of the textbook examples used also relate to such organizations. Studies have shown that marketing in an SME context frequently works in different ways. Marketing SMEs is often characterised by:

- a focus on sales and promotion;
- a lack of formal marketing plans;
- the importance of the owner/entrepreneur in making marketing decisions;
- the importance of personal contacts with customers and potential customers; and
- the role of innovation and flexibility in continually adapting products to meet customer requirements.

The marketing function (if it exists) in many SMEs relates primarily to sales and promotions only, a perception which has grown from the ability of SMEs to obtain sales without planning their marketing activities (Stokes, 2000; Carson, 1990). There is frequently a lack of formal structure and conventional marketing concepts, which can be misinterpreted as not recognising marketing's importance (O'Dwyer et al., 2009).

However, as O'Dwyer et al. (2009) point out, much of the literature on SME marketing identifies the presence of a form of marketing which is unique to small firms (Stokes, 2000; Carson, 1993), since the role of entrepreneurs and innovation are of central importance and consequently SMEs frequently adapt general marketing concepts, practices and theories to suit their own purposes (Carson, 1993), while maintaining a process focus and concentrating on incremental innovations (Miles and Darroch, 2006).

Central to SME marketing is the continual development of the experiential knowledge of the entrepreneurs gained by doing business (Grant *et al.*, 2001). Thus, to a certain extent, the marketing characteristics of an SME are often derived from the experiential knowledge of the owner/manager and the firm's characteristics, such as a distinctive managerial style, independence, ownership, having limited resources, and the scale and scope of operations (Carson and McCartan-Quinn, 1995).

These characteristics combine to form an inherently innate method of doing business for SME owner/managers, which enables them to focus on achieving competitive advantage through added value marketing initiatives. Traditionally some marketing approaches concentrate on the marketing mix: the traditional marketing paradigm of the 4Ps (product, price, place and promotion) or the 7Ps adopted by service marketing (product, price, place, promotion, people, process and physical evidence). However, Stokes (2000) argues that the entrepreneurs, who are often central to SME decision-making, stress the importance of promotion and word-of-mouth. Such entrepreneurs often identify one of the unique selling points of their business as the nature of their personal contact with customers and stress that their focus is on the four Is (information, identification, innovation and interaction) (Stokes, 2000).

Palmer (2011:274–8) produces an overview of the potential marketing advantages that small businesses might experience enabling them to exploit being small and to achieve competitive advantages. To Palmer the competitive advantages may lie in three areas:

- Small businesses often exhibit greater adaptability than larger companies. Larger companies tend to be burdened by slower decision making processes and become more risk averse as they grow.
- In many *THE* service environments there are comparatively small economies of scale available to allow larger organizations to become more efficient and dominate the market. Despite the inexorable rise of technology and the growth of international brands this may explain why there are still many independent travel intermediaries; event management companies, tour operators and accommodation providers.
- Small businesses, often driven by an entrepreneurial owner/manager, tend to be good innovators. The internet opened up many opportunities for entrepreneurs to establish new business formats. The travel agency presents an example, since it was largely smaller businesses that were the first to innovate with web-based sales facilities and the larger chains were slower to adapt and set up their own internet facilities (Palmer, 2011). This was partly perhaps because setting up web-based activities presented a potential threat to other parts of their businesses such as the capital that had been invested in setting up physical travel agency branches.

Many larger businesses are primarily concerned with developing their brand and its values. In smaller businesses the emphasis may switch to developing a personal reputation, expressed through consistency and providing particular levels of service. The growth of boutique hotels (with under 50 rooms and having individualized design and service) illustrates this point. The growth of such hotels, 'may appeal to segments of buyers that seek the experience of surprise, rather than the monotony of standardised branded chain output' (Palmer, 2011:277).

Independent hotels are also often able to compete and prosper by not using their own brand but by linking it to the brand of marketing consortia (such as Best Western, Small Luxury Hotels of the World and Consort Hotels). Accommodation providers and other SMEs may also be able to leverage additional marketing benefits in particular geographical areas by effectively utilizing networking and clustering opportunities to group together for collective advantage (Novelli et al., 2006).

CHAPTER SUMMARY

The chapter dealt with issues concerned with defining and analysing markets for THE managers. It explained how splitting markets up into segments could be used as a competitive tool, and investigated different ways in which market segments might be chosen. The concept of the augmented product was considered as a tool to examine how features and benefits might be produced to provide a competitive edge.

The product life cycle showed how a number of strategic issues might be anticipated at different stages, and the management of the product portfolio dealt with the management of a whole product range. Aspects of product innovation were viewed by examining the processes of new idea generation and new product screening.

Finally the chapter considered the concept of a portfolio of products at different stages of development. Two models, namely the BCG and GEC matrices, were outlined. These provide means by which the portfolio of products might be analysed and provide a potential basis for the allocation of resources.

REFERENCES

Allen, J., W. O'Toole, R. Harris and I. McDonnell (2005) Festival and Special Event Management, Queensland: John Wiley & Sons Australia.

Almeida, A. and A. Correia (2010) 'Tourism Development in Madeira: An Analysis Based on the Life Cycle Approach', Tourism Economics, 16 (2): 427–41.

Bonoma, T. V. and B. P. Shapiro (1983) Segmenting the Industrial Market, Lexington, Mass.: Lexington Books.

Bowen, J. (2000) 'Airline Hubs in Southeast Asia: National Economic Development and Nodal Accessibility', Journal of Transport Geography, 8 (1): 25–41.

Brown, R. (1991) 'The S-Curves of Innovation', Journal of Marketing Management, 7 (2): 189–202.

Brownlie, D. (1985) 'Strategic Marketing Concepts and Models', Journal of Marketing Management, 1 (1–2): 157–94.

Butler, R. (2009) 'Tourism in the Future: Cycles, Waves or Wheels?' Futures, 41 (6): 346–52.

Butler, R. W. (1980) 'The Concept of the Tourist Area Life Cycle of Evolution and Implications for Management', The Canadian Geographer, 24 (1): 5–12.

—— (2000) 'The Resort Cycle Two Decades On', in B. Faulkner, G. Moscardo and E. Laws (eds.), Tourism in the 21st Century: Lessons from Experience, London: Continuum, pp. 284–99.

Buzzell, R. D. (2004) 'The PIMS Program of Strategy Research: A Retrospective Appraisal', Journal of Business Research, 57 (5): 478–83.

Carson, D. (1990) 'Some Exploratory Models for Assessing Small Firms' Marketing Performance: A Qualitative Approach', European Journal of Marketing, 234 (11): 8–51.

—— (1993) 'A Philosophy for Marketing Education in Small Firms', Journal of Marketing Management, 9: 189–204.

Carson, D. and McCartan-Quinn, D. (1995) 'Non-Practice of Theoretically Based Marketing in Small Business: Issues Arising and Their Implications', Journal of Marketing Theory and Practice, 3 (4): 24–31.

Chang, R. C., J. Kivela and A. H. Mak (2011) 'Attributes That Influence the Evaluation of Travel Dining Experience: When East Meets West', Tourism Management, 32 (2): 307–16.

Clifton, W. (2013) 'The Global Hotel Industry: Big, Beautiful and Branded? Part Two', Global Hotel Research Limited. Available online at http://www.ehotelier.com/hospitality-news (accessed 4 June 2013).

Cooper, C., J. Fletcher, D. Gilbert, R. Shepherd and S. Wanhill (1998) *Tourism Principles and Practice*, 2nd edn, Harlow: Longman.

Crawford-Welch, S. (1994) 'The Development of Courtyard by Marriott', in R. Teare, J. A. Mazanec, S. Crawford-Welch and S. *Marketing in Hospitality and Tourism: A Consumer Focus*, London: Cassell, pp. 184–96.

Crittenden, V. L., W. F. Crittenden and D. F. Muzyka (2002) 'Segmenting the Business-to-Business Marketplace by Product Attributes and the Decision Process', *Journal of Strategic Marketing*, 10 (1): 3–20.

Dev, C. S., M. S. Morgan and S. Shoemaker, S. (1995) 'A Positioning Analysis of Hotel Brands: Based on Travel-manager Perceptions' *The Cornell Hotel and Restaurant Administration Quarterly*, 36 (6), 48–55.

Diedrich, A. and E. García-Buades (2009) 'Local Perceptions of Tourism as Indicators of Destination Decline', *Tourism Management*, 30 (4): 512–21.

Evans, N. G. (2002) 'Travel and Tourism Economics', in R. Sharpley (ed.), *The Tourism Business: An Introduction*, Sunderland: Business Education Publishers, pp. 367–96.

—— (2012) 'Tourism: A Strategic Business Perspective', in T. Jamal and M. Robinson (eds.), *The Sage Handbook of Tourism Studies*, Thousand Oaks, Calif.: Sage, pp. 215–34.

Fleisher, C. S. and B. E. Bensoussan (2003) *Strategic and Competitive Analysis: Methods and Techniques for Analysing Business Competition, 2002*, Upper Saddle River NJ: Prentice Hall.

Fyall, A. and B. Garrod (2005) *Tourism Marketing: A Collaborative Approach*, Bristol UK: Channel View Publications.

Gallarza, M. G., I. G. Saura and H. C. García (2002) 'Destination Image: Towards a Conceptual Framework', *Annals of Tourism Research*, 29 (1): 56–78.

Garay, L. and G. Cànoves (2011) 'Life Cycles, Stages and Tourism History: The Catalonia (Spain) Experience', *Annals of Tourism Research*, 38 (2): 651–71.

Gibson, L. D. (2001) 'Is Something Rotten in Segmentation?' *Marketing Research*, 13 (1): 20–5.

Gonzalez, A. M. and L. Bello (2002) 'The Construct "Lifestyle" in Market Segmentation: The Behaviour of Tourist Consumers', *European Journal of Marketing*, 36 (1/2): 51–85.

Goodman, M. (2013) 'Hotels' Mr Smooth Learnt All the Tricks from His Dad, Interview with IHG Hotels Chief Executive', *The Sunday Times*, 7 April.

Grant, K., A. Gilmore, D. Carson, R. Laney and B. Pickett (2001) 'Experiential Research Methodology: An Integrated Academic-Practitioner "Team" Approach', *Qualitative Market Research: An International Journal*, 4 (2): 66–75.

Greenley, G. E. and B. L. Bayus (1993) 'Marketing Planning Decision Making in UK and US Companies: An Empirical Comparative Study', *Journal of Marketing Management*, 9 (2): 155–72.

Hax, A. C. and N. S. Majluf (1983) 'The Use of the Growth-Share Matrix in Strategic Planning', *Interfaces*, 13 (1): 46–60.

Henderson, B. D. (1984) 'The Application and Misapplication of the Experience Curve', *Journal of Business Strategy*, 4 (3): 3–9.

Hollensen, S. (2010) *Marketing Management: A Relationship Approach*, Harlow: Pearson Education.

Hooley, G. J. and J. Saunders (1993) *Competitive Positioning: The Key to Marketing Strategy*, London: Prentice Hall International.

Horner, S. and J. Swarbrooke (1996) *Marketing Tourism, Hospitality and Leisure in Europe*, London: International Thomson Business Press.

Hudson, S. (2008) *Tourism and Hospitality Marketing: A Global Perspective*, Thousand Oaks, Calif.: Sage.

Jonk, G., M. Handschuh and S. Niewiem (2008) 'The Battle of the Value Chains: New Specialized Versus Old Hybrids', *Strategy and Leadership*, 36 (2): 24–9.

Kalafatis, S. P., M. H. Tsogas and C. Blankson (2000) 'Positioning Strategies in Business Markets', *Journal of Business and Industrial Marketing*, 15 (6): 416–37.

Kay, J. (1995) *Foundations of Corporate Success*, Oxford: Oxford University Press.

Kolb, B. (2012) *Tourism Marketing for Cities and Towns Using Branding and Events to Attract Tourists*, Oxford: Butterworth Heinemann.

Kotler, P. R., D. H. Haider and I. Rein (1993) *Marketing Places*, New York: Free Press.

Kotler, P. and K. L. Keller (2012) *Marketing Management*, 14th edn, Harlow: Pearson Education.

Kotler, P. R., J. T. Bowen and J. Makens (2013) *Marketing for Hospitality and Tourism*, 6th edn. Harlow: Pearson.

Kozak, M. and D. Martin (2012) 'Tourism Life Cycle and Sustainability Analysis: Profit-Focused Strategies for Mature Destinations', *Tourism Management*, 33 (1): 188–94.

Litvin, S. W. (2006) 'Revisiting Plog's Model of Allocentricity and Psychocentricity . . . One More Time', *Cornell Hotel and Restaurant Administration Quarterly*, 47 (3): 245–53.

Lohmann, G., S. Albers, B. Koch and K. Pavlovich (2009) 'From Hub to Tourist Destination: An Explorative Study of Singapore and Dubai's Aviation-Based Transformation', *Journal of Air Transport Management*, 15 (5): 205–11.

Ma, M. and R. Hassink (2013) 'An Evolutionary Perspective on Tourism Area Development', *Annals of Tourism Research*, 41: 89–109.

Mayock, P. (2013) 'Marriott CEO Shares Moxy Update', available online at http://www.hotelnewsnow.com/Article/10644/Marriott-CEO-shares-Moxy-update (accessed 19 June 2013).

McKercher, B. (1995) 'The Destination-Market Mix: A Tourism Market Portfolio Analysis Model', *Journal of Travel and Tourism Marketing*, 4 (2): 23–40.

Middleton, V. T., A. Fyall, M. Morgan and A. Ranchhod (2009) *Marketing in Travel and Tourism*, London and New York: Routledge.

Miles, M. P. and J. Darroch (2006) 'Large Firms, Entrepreneurial Marketing Processes and the Cycle of Competitive Advantage', *European Journal of Marketing*, 40 (5/6): 485–501.

Mitchell, V. W. and D. F. Wilson (1998) 'Balancing Theory and Practice: A Reappraisal of Business-to-Business Segmentation', *Industrial Marketing Management*, 27 (5): 429–45.

Morgan, N., A. Pritchard and R. Pride (2012) *Destination Branding*, London and New York: Routledge.

Morrison, A. and R. Wensley (1991) 'Boxing Up or Boxed In? A Short History of the Boston Consultancy Group Share/Growth Matrix', *Journal of Marketing Management*, 7 (2): 105–29.

Morritt, R. and A. Weinstein (2012) *Segmentation Strategies for Hospitality Managers: Target Marketing for Competitive Advantage*, London and New York: Routledge.

Moutinho, L. (2000) 'Strategic Planning', in L. Moutinho (ed.), *Strategic Management in Tourism*, Wallingford UK: CABI, pp. 259–82.

Novak, T. P. and B. MacEvoy (1990) 'On Comparing Alternative Segmentation Schemes: The List of Values (LOV) and Values and Life Styles (VALS)', *Journal of Consumer Research*, 17 (June): 105–9.

Novelli, M., B. Schmitz and T. Spencer (2006) 'Networks, Clusters and Innovation in Tourism: A UK Experience', *Tourism Management*, 27 (6): 1141–52.

O'Dwyer, M., A. Gilmore and D. Carson (2009) 'Innovative Marketing in SMEs', *European Journal of Marketing*, 43 (1/2): 46–61.

Palmer, A. (2011) *Principles of Services Marketing*, Maidenhead: McGraw-Hill.

Park, J. Y. and S. S. Jang (2012) 'Psychographics: Static or Dynamic?' *International Journal of Tourism Research*, 16 (4): 351–4.

Pike, S. (2012) 'Destination Positioning Opportunities Using Personal Values: Elicited through the Repertory Test with Laddering Analysis', *Tourism Management*, 33 (1): 100–7.

Pike, S. and R. Mason (2011) 'Destination Competitiveness through the Lens of Brand Positioning: The Case of Australia's Sunshine Coast', *Current Issues in Tourism*, 14 (2): 169–82.

Pike, S. and C. Ryan (2004) 'Destination Positioning Analysis through a Comparison of Cognitive, Affective and Conative Perceptions', *Journal of Travel Research*, 42 (4): 333–42.

Plog, S. C. (1974) 'Why Destination Areas Rise and Fall in Popularity', *Cornell Hotel and Restaurant Quarterly*, 14 (4): 55–8.

Powers, T. L. and J. U. Sterling (2008) 'Segmenting Business-to-Business Markets: A Micro-Macro Linking Methodology', *Journal of Business and Industrial Marketing*, 23 (3): 170–7.

Preston, C. A. (2012) *Event Marketing: How to Successfully Promote Events, Festivals, Conventions and Expositions*, Hoboken NJ: John Wiley & Sons Inc.

Reid, R. D. and D. C. Bojanic (2009) *Hospitality Marketing Management*, Hoboken NJ: John Wiley & Sons Inc.

Robertson, M. and K. M. Wardrop (2011) 'Events and the Destination Dynamic: Edinburgh Festivals, Entrepreneurship and Strategic Marketing' in Yeoman, I., Robertson, M., Ali-Knight, J., Drummond, S., & McMahon-Beattie, U. (eds.), *Festival and Events Management*, Abingdon UK: Routledge: 115–29.

Sahin, S. and S. Baloglu (2011) 'Brand Personality and Destination Image of Istanbul, Anatolia', *An International Journal of Tourism and Hospitality Research*, 22 (1): 69–88.

Scott, N., N. Parfitt and L. Laws (2000) 'Destination Management: Co-operative Marketing: A Case Study of the Port Douglas Brand', in B. Faulkner, G. Moscardo and E. Laws (eds.), *Tourism in the 21st Century: Lessons from Experience*, London: Continuum, pp. 198–221.

Smith, W. R. (1956) 'Product Differentiation and Market Segmentation as Alternative Marketing Strategies', *The Journal of Marketing*, 21 (1): 3–8.

Sowrey, T. (1990) 'Idea Generation: Identifying the Most Useful Techniques', *European Journal of Marketing*, 42 (5): 20–9.

Stokes, D. (2000) 'Putting Entrepreneurship into Marketing: The Processes of Entrepreneurial Marketing', *Journal of Research in Marketing and Entrepreneurship*, 2 (1): 1–16.

Suarez, F. and G. Lanzolla (2005) 'The Half-Truth of First-Mover Advantage', *Harvard Business Review*, 83 (4): 121.

Swarbrooke, J. (1995) *The Development and Management of Visitor Attractions*, Oxford: Butterworth-Heinemann.

Tkaczynski, A. and S. R. Rundle-Thiele (2011) 'Event Segmentation: A Review and Research Agenda', *Tourism Management*, 32 (2): 426–34.

Tkaczynski, A., S. R. Rundle-Thiele and N. Beaumont (2009) 'Segmentation: A Tourism Stakeholder View', *Tourism Management*, 30 (2): 169–75.

Tsiotsou, R. H. and R. E. Goldsmith (2012) 'Target Marketing and Its Application to Tourism', in R. H. Tsiotsou and R. E. Goldsmith (eds.) *Strategic Marketing in Tourism Services*, Bingley: Emerald, pp. 3–16.

Usakli, A. and S. Baloglu (2011) 'Brand Personality of Tourist Destinations: An Application of Self-Congruity Theory', *Tourism Management*, 32 (1): 114–27.

Von Hippel, E. (1978) 'Successful Industrial Products from Customer Ideas', *Journal of Marketing*, 42 (1): 39–49.

Walsh, D. (2013) 'Rite of Passage to India: Children's Activity Camp Hits Expansion Trail', *The Times*, 18 February, p. 11.

Whitfield, J. (2009) 'The Cyclical Representation of the UK Conference Sector's Life Cycle: The Use of Refurbishments as Rejuvenation Triggers', *Tourism Analysis*, 14 (5): 559–72.

Winston, W. and D. J. Cahill (2013) *How Consumers Pick a Hotel: Strategic Segmentation and Target Marketing*, London and New York: Routledge.

Yeoman, I., M. Robertson, J. Ali-Knight, S. Drummond and U. McMahon-Beattie (eds.) (2012) *Festival and Events Management*, London and New York: Routledge.

WEBSITES

www.tq.com.au
www.thetravelcorporation.com
www.ehotelier.com
www.globalhoteldata.com
www.hotelnewsnow.com
www.moxyhotels.com

FURTHER READING

Reference	Focus
Aswood G. and H. Voogd (1994) 'Marketing of Tourism Places: What Are We Doing?', in M. Uysal (ed.), *Global Tourist Behaviour*, New York: Haworth Press, 5–20.	Product positioning Tourism Destinations
Baloglu, S. and D. Brinberg (1997) 'Affective Images of Tourism Destinations', *Journal of Travel Research*, 35 (4): 11–15.	Product positioning Tourism Destinations
Bigné, E., J. Gnoth and L. Andreu (2008?) 'Advanced Topics in Tourism Market Segmentation', in A. Woodside and M. Drew (eds.), *Tourism Management: Analysis, Behaviour and Strategy*, Wallingford UK: CABI, pp. 151–73.	Segmentation Tourism
Chen, C. C. and Y. H. Lin (2012) 'Segmenting Mainland Chinese Tourists to Taiwan by Destination Familiarity: A Factor-Cluster Approach', *International Journal of Tourism Research*, 14 (4): 339–52.	Segmentation Tourism China Taiwan

Cole, S. (2009) 'A Logistic Tourism Model: Resort Cycles, Globalization and Chaos', *Annals of Tourism Research*, 36 (4): 689–714.	Product life cycle Tourism Globalization
Dimanche, D. F., D. M. E. Havitz and D. D. R. Howard (1993) 'Consumer Involvement Profiles As a Tourism Segmentation Tool', *Journal of Travel and Tourism Marketing*, 1 (4): 33–52.	Segmentation Tourism
Govers, R., F. M. Go and K. Kumar (2007) 'Promoting Tourism Destination Image', *Journal of Travel Research*, 46 (1): 15–23.	Product positioning Tourism Destinations
Harris, M. (1988) 'Economical Positioning', *Cornell Hotel and Restaurant Administration Quarterly*, 31 (2): 97–115.	Product positioning Hospitality Hotels
Jang, S. and L. A. Cai (2002) 'Travel Motivations and Destination Choice: A Study of British Outbound Market', *Journal of Travel and Tourism Marketing*, 13 (3): 111–33.	Travel motivation Tourism
Kruger, M., M. Saayman and A. Saayman (2009) 'Sociodemographic and Behavioral Determinants of Visitor Spending at the Klein Karoo National Arts Festival', *Event Management*, 13 (1): 53–68.	Segmentation Festivals South Africa
Kruger, M., M. Saayman and S. Ellis (2011) 'Segmentation by Genres: The Case of the Aardklop National Arts Festival', *International Journal of Tourism Research*, 13 (6): 511–26.	Segmentation Festivals South Africa
—— (2010) 'Expenditure-Based Segmentation of Visitors to the Tsitsikamma National Park', *Acta Commercii*, 10 (1): 137–49.	Segmentation Tourism South Africa
Li, X. R., F. Meng, M. Uysal and B. Mihalik (2013) 'Understanding China's Long-Haul Outbound Travel Market: An Overlapped Segmentation Approach', *Journal of Business Research*, 66 (6): 786–93.	Segmentation Tourism China
Park, D. B. and Y. S. Yoon (2009) 'Segmentation by Motivation in Rural Tourism: A Korean Case Study', *Tourism Management*, 30 (1): 99–108.	Segmentation Tourism Korea
Park, S. and D. Y. Kim (2010) 'A Comparison of Different Approaches to Segment Information Search Behaviour of Spring Break Travellers in the USA: Experience, Knowledge, Involvement and Specialisation Concept', *International Journal of Tourism Research*, 12 (1): 49–64.	Segmentation Tourism USA
Prayag, G. (2012) 'Paradise for Who? Segmenting Visitors' Satisfaction with Cognitive Image and Predicting Behavioural Loyalty', *International Journal of Tourism Research*, 14 (1): 1–15.	Segmentation Tourism
Walmesley, D. and M. Young (1998) 'Evaluative Images and Tourism: The Use of Personal Constructs to Describe the Structure of Destination Images', *Journal of Travel Research*, 36 (winter): 65–9.	Product positioning Tourism Destinations

CASE LINKAGES

Case 2	Tourism Queensland
Case 3	Ryanair
Case 4	Hyatt Hotels
Case 5	Days Inn
Case 6	Reed Exhibitions
Case 7	Thomas Cook

Part **3**

Analysing the external environment and SWOT

Introduction

External analysis

The analysis of the internal environment (which provides the analytical underpinning for the Strengths and Weaknesses of the SWOT) was considered in Part 2 of this book.

Part 3 of the book turns to the analysis of the *external environment* facing *THE* organizations. The analysis in the subsequent chapters provides a rigorous underpinning for the 'Opportunities' and 'Threats' components of the SWOT. In some ways this form of analysis can be viewed as being more complicated than internal analysis since by definition it includes everything that is happening outside *THE* organizations' control. Since such analysis potentially covers a vast array of factors the problems lie in deciding the relevant factors to include and in categorising them in a useful and meaningful way.

Thus Chapters 7 and 8 are concerned with developing concepts and frameworks that help organize material appropriately and help in understanding what is occurring outside the organization concerned. Chapter 9 brings together the outcomes of the Internal Analysis (covered in Chapters 3, 4, 5 and 6) and the External Analysis (Chapters 7 and 8) in the form of a SWOT.

Study progress:

Part 1	Part 2	Part 3			Part 4	Part 5
Strategy and the tourism, hospitality and events contexts	Analysing the internal environment	Analysing the external environment and SWOT			Strategic selection	Strategic implementation and strategy in theory and practice
Introduction and Chapters 1 and 2	Chapters 3 3, 4, 5 and 6	Chapter 7 The macro context	Chapter 8 The micro context	Chapter 9 SWOT analysis	Chapters 10, 11 and 12	Chapters 13, 14 and 15

Purposes of external analysis

We can view external analysis on two levels:

First, *Macro-environment* (sometimes called the *far, broad* or *general environment*) contains a number of factors that affect not only an organization itself, but also all others in the industry. Most strategy textbooks use the STEP (or PEST) approach. In this book in recognition of the key influence of environmental influences (in terms of the built and natural environments) in *THE* contexts the STEP framework is widened to STEEP.

STEEP – The socio-demographic, technological, economic, environmental and political factors are certainly beyond an individual organization's control, although in some cases an organization may be able to exert some influence over some of the factors. Consequently strategic management rests upon an organization's ability to cope with any changes in the macro-environment through the successful formulation and implementation of appropriate strategies. The macro-environment is considered in Chapter 7.

Second, the Micro (or sometimes termed *near* or *competitive*) environment is the sphere in which the organization interacts most often – usually on a day-to-day basis. Any changes in the micro-environment can affect a *THE* organization very quickly and sometimes dramatically. In the case of most organizations, the micro-environment comprises influences from the competitive environment – its industry and markets. In Chapter 8 two models are discussed for making sense of these important strategic influences – Porters' Five Force Model and the Resource or Core Competence based model.

SWOT analysis

Chapter 9 provides the culmination of the analytical phase by bringing together and summarizing the results of the internal and external analyses in the form of a SWOT. The SWOT provides a position statement of where the organization is at the present time. Having understood the present position of the *THE* organization the SWOT provides a firm platform for going on to consider the future in terms of the strategic options to be pursued.

Part 4 will go on to consider the formulation, evaluation and selection of strategic options, which are derived in a logical and robust way from the analysis carried out.

Chapter

The external environment for tourism, hospitality and event organizations

The macro context

Introduction and chapter overview

Tourism, hospitality and events entities – whether hotels, tour operators, travel agencies, event managers, etc. – function as open systems in that they interact with, respond to, and are affected by their external environment (Coulter, 2002; Jogaratnam and Law, 2006). Thus having an understanding of the external environment is of critical importance to most managers. Gaining such an understanding is sometimes termed *environmental scanning* or *horizon scanning*, but here we will refer to it as macro-environmental analysis (see for example Fleisher and Bensoussan, 2003:Ch. 17).

The most widely used technique for analysing the macro-environment is to divide it into its constituent parts and here we use the terminology of *STEEP* analysis. STEEP analysis divides the influences in the macro-environment into five categories:

- Social
- Technological
- Economic
- Environmental
- Political.

It is worth noting that in some texts the STEEP acronym is replaced by STEP with environmental influences omitted. In other texts the STEP acronym is turned around and presented as PEST or sometimes PESTEL (explicitly adding Environmental and Legal categories to the acronym). However the framework for analysis is essentially the same. It is this popular framework which is explained and explored in this chapter.

After studying this chapter, readers should be able to:

- explain what is meant by the macro-environment;
- explain Ginter and Duncan's mechanisms of carrying out macro-environmental analysis;
- describe the components of each of the five STEEP influences and be able to apply them to relevant *THE* contexts;
- explain how the STEEP factors are interlinked and interrelated in *THE* contexts.

The macro-environment

What is the macro-environment?

The macro-environment refers to the broad environment outside an organization's industry and markets.

It is generally beyond the control and influence of the individual organization but can have significant impact on the micro-environment (industry and market) in which the organization operates. The macro-environment is sometimes referred to as the *far* or *remote* environment because it tends to exert forces from outside the organization's sphere of influence and the forces are usually beyond control.

Changes in the macro-environment can be of immense importance to an organization in that (amongst other important aspects) they can

- bring about the birth or death of an entire industry;
- make markets expand or contract;
- determine the level of competitiveness within an industry.

It is therefore essential that *THE* managers are alert to actual and potential changes in the macro-environment and that they seek to anticipate the potential impacts on their industry and markets.

Ginter and Duncan (1990) identify the potential benefits of macro-environmental analysis as:

- increasing managerial awareness of environmental changes;
- increasing understanding of the context in which industries and markets function;
- increasing understanding of multinational settings;
- improving resource allocation decisions;
- facilitating risk management;
- focusing attention on the primary influences on strategic change; and
- acting as an early warning system, providing time to anticipate opportunities and threats and devise appropriate responses.

In many ways analysis of the macro-environment is more difficult than internal analysis since it involves *everything* that occurs outside the organization.

The problems when dealing with such a vast amount of information are:

- assessing what should be included;
- assessing what should be left out;
- determining how the information should be organized in a rational and meaningful way.

There are no simple rules governing the contents and presentation of macro-environmental analysis as Richard Lynch makes clear in the quotation below.

> ### DEFINITION/QUOTATION
>
> There are no simple rules governing an analysis of the organization. Each analysis [of the macro-environment] needs to be guided by what is relevant for that particular organization.
>
> Lynch (2000:109)

Thus, though analytical frameworks can be suggested for sorting and organizing pertinent information, the key issues are likely to be highly specific to each organization's circumstances.

Conducting macro-environmental analysis

For Ginter and Duncan (1990) macro-environmental analysis involves:

- *Scanning* macro-environments for warning signs and possible environmental changes that will affect the organization;
- *Monitoring* environments for specific trends and patterns;
- *Forecasting* future directions of environmental changes; and
- *Assessing* current and future trends in terms of the effects such changes would have on the organization.

Limitations of macro-environmental analysis

We should be careful to note that macro-environmental analysis has its limitations and pitfalls.

At its root, the macro-environment can be extremely complex and at any one time there may be conflicting and contradictory changes taking place. The pace of change in many macro-environmental situations is increasing and becoming more turbulent and unpredictable as discussed by, for example, Chakravarthy (1997) and Mason (2007). This degree of uncertainty has, to some extent, cast some doubt over the value of carrying out a macro-environmental analysis at all. By the time that an organization has come to terms

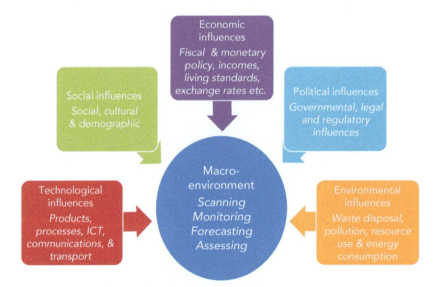

Figure 7.1 The main features of STEEP analysis.

with one major change in the macro-environment, another change often occurs that requires even more attention and action.

Accordingly, those managers that are concerned with strategic analysis must:

- be aware of the limitations and inaccuracies of macro-environmental analysis;
- carry out the analysis or update it continuously (because it changes so frequently);
- constantly seek to improve sources of information and techniques for its analysis;
- use the information as one source of organizational learning; and
- use the information to inform future strategy.

Notwithstanding these points, macro-environmental analysis is a valuable mechanism for increasing the strategic awareness of managers.

STEEP analysis

Overview of the STEEP influences

The complexity of the macro-environment makes it necessary to divide the forces at work into the five broad categories we have already encountered (see Figure 7.1). It is important to remember that the five categories are interrelated and constantly interact with each other.

In the process of STEEP analysis (sometimes called STEP or PEST analysis) it is therefore important to explore and understand the relationships between the forces at work. It is equally important to identify the relative importance of the influences at work for the organization, its industry and its markets. Finally, because of the uncertainty of the effects of macro-environmental change on the micro-environment, it is essential that a range of possible outcomes of the changes are identified and considered.

In carrying out a STEEP analysis it should be pointed out that some of the factors may be generic in that they affect all industrial sectors, whilst others are specific to *THE* or a particular sector. Peattie and Moutinho (2000) provide a review of some of the major environmental influences in travel and tourism using an extended framework, which they term SCEPTICAL analysis. In this case the acronym stands for *Social, Cultural, Economic, Physical, Technical, International, Communications and infrastructure, Administrative and institutional*, and *Legal and political* factors.

Other texts such as Costa (1995), Okumus (2004), Tum and Norton (2006) and Clarke and Chen (2007) also give some interesting insights in discussing the key macro-environmental factors affecting the *THE* sectors.

In her analysis, Auliana Poon (1993) pointed to the radical changes occurring in the travel and tourism industry. Poon viewed a 'new tourism' which is developing to replace the 'old tourism' based on mass tourism. The five key forces (*consumers, technology, production, management* and *frame conditions*) which had served to create mass tourism in the first place were themselves changing to create the new tourism.

Figure 7.2 summarizes some of the changes Poon observed that were taking place.

Some texts use the STEP or PEST acronym, thereby omitting explicit recognition of the environmental influences but considering them as part of the other influences. The approach adopted here however is to explicitly recognize the central importance of environmental influences in *THE* contexts by considering them under a separate heading. It is clearly the case that there can be few industries where the interdependence between the physical environment and economic activity is so clearly visible (Peattie and Moutinho, 2000). In their analysis Fleisher and Bensoussan (2003:Ch. 17) use the term *ecological*, but here the term *environmental* is preferred denoting that the analysis involves not just the ecological (natural environment) but also involves the *built environment*.

Figure 7.2 Old and new tourism compared

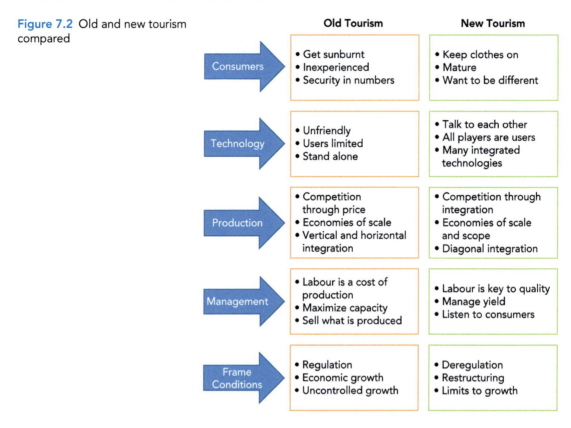

	Old Tourism	New Tourism
Consumers	• Get sunburnt • Inexperienced • Security in numbers	• Keep clothes on • Mature • Want to be different
Technology	• Unfriendly • Users limited • Stand alone	• Talk to each other • All players are users • Many integrated technologies
Production	• Competition through price • Economies of scale • Vertical and horizontal integration	• Competition through integration • Economies of scale and scope • Diagonal integration
Management	• Labour is a cost of production • Maximize capacity • Sell what is produced	• Labour is key to quality • Manage yield • Listen to consumers
Frame Conditions	• Regulation • Economic growth • Uncontrolled growth	• Deregulation • Restructuring • Limits to growth

---

THINK POINTS

- Explain the meaning of the term 'macro-environment'.
- Explain how the business, micro-environment and macro-environment relate to each other.
- Explain the stages in a macro-environmental analysis.

Using the STEEP analysis

How to carry out a STEEP analysis

Before looking at the individual elements of the STEEP analysis it is useful to consider how we might use the framework. What sort of information do we need to consider with each of the framework's element and how might the information be used?

The analysis is generally considered as falling into four stages.

- *Scanning and monitoring* the macro-environment for actual or potential changes in social, technological, economic and political factors.
- *Assessing the relevance and importance* of the changes for the market, industry and business.
- *Analysing each of the relevant changes* in detail and the potential relationships between them.
- *Assessing the potential impact* of the changes on the market, industry and business.

What to analyse

When managers carry out a STEEP analysis as part of a strategic analysis (and the same is true of students examining a case study) they would normally examine how each factor might impact upon:

- *The internal parts of an organization* – the effects of STEEP factors on the organization's core competencies, strategies, resources, value system and the organization's functional areas (operations, marketing, human resources and finance).
- *An organization's markets* – the effects of STEEP factors on product markets (e.g. market size, structure, segments, customer needs and wants, etc.) and the resource markets for human resources, financial resources, etc.
- *The industry in which the organization competes*– the effects of STEEP factors on the five competitive forces (buyer power, supplier power, threat of entry, threat of substitutes, competitive rivalry – see Chapter 8).

In the following sections the component parts of STEEP are considered systematically. The potential influences on any particular organization at any time is vast and is very dependent on the individual context of the organization (its location, sector, size, etc.). The approach adopted here is to discuss some of the generic factors and to provide illustrations of some specific factors by using the airline sector throughout for purposes of illustration (for consistency) together with some further examples and further reading from other sectors.

Socio-demographic influences

Analysis of the social environment is concerned with understanding the potential impacts of society and social changes on a business, its industry and markets.

For most analyses, analysis of the social environment will require consideration of:

- *social culture* (values, attitudes and beliefs) – the impact on demand for products and services, attitudes to work, savings and investment, ecology, ethics, etc.;
- *demography* – the impact of the size and structure of the population on the workforce and patterns of demand;
- *social structure* – the impact of attitudes to work and products and services.

SOCIAL CULTURE

The culture of countries in which a business operates (which was considered in Chapter 4) can be of particular importance. The culture of a country consists of the values, attitudes and beliefs of its people, which will affect the way that they act and behave (or, put simply, its 'personality'). There are important cultural differences between all countries. Culture can affect consumer tastes and preferences, attitudes to work, attitudes to education and training, attitudes to corruption and ethics, attitudes to credit, attitudes to the social role of a business in society and many other things.

DEMOGRAPHY

Demographic trends are similarly important. Demography is the social science concerned with the charting of the size and structure of a population of people. The size of the population will obviously be a determinant of the size of the workforce and the potential size of markets. Just as important will be the structure of the population. The age structure will determine the size of particular segments and also the size of the working population. The size and structure of the population will constantly be changing and these changes will have impact on industries and markets.

SOCIAL STRUCTURE

Social structure is strongly linked to demography and refers to the ways in which the social groups in a population are organized. There are a number of ways of defining social structure such as by socio-demographic groupings by age, sex, location, population density in different areas, etc. The social structure will affect people's lifestyles and expectations and so will strongly influence their attitudes to work and their demand for particular products and services.

Among the most important general changes in recent years in the social environment have been in people's attitudes to the natural environment. Increasing awareness of the problems caused by pollution and the exhaustion of non-renewable resources have caused travel and tourism organizations to rethink (in many cases) the way that they produce their products and the composition of the products themselves. Similarly, changes in social structure (upward mobility), lifestyle (increased leisure) and demography (ageing populations in developed countries) have significantly altered many market and industry structures.

SHORT CASE ILLUSTRATION

Socio-demographic influences: The airline sector

A number of demographic factors point towards a greater use of air travel. These factors include:

- an increasing proportion of the population being relatively healthy and prosperous;
- increasing numbers of retired people;
- a decline in average family size;
- greater international mobility of labour;
- increasing amounts of paid holidays; and
- larger numbers of double income families.

All the factors listed point to higher usage of air services. Leisure travel (which accounts for about 80 per cent of trips) has grown more rapidly than business-based travel.

Other factors that might be considered are lifestyle trends and attitudes of society towards air travel and associated airport development. An increasingly mobile society where people take safe, reliable and affordable air transportation for granted is challenged by a critical society which assesses the contribution of air travel to air and noise pollution (Holloway and Humphries, 2012). This dichotomy in which the competing needs and interests of airline stakeholder groups need to be considered represents a challenge to airlines, regulators and governments.

One study (Oyewole, 2001) of the airline industry found that gender, occupation, education and marital status have an important influence on satisfaction with airline services.

Questions

1. Explain why an understanding of socio-demographic influences might be important for airline managers.
2. What sort of demographic factors might lead to greater air travel in the future?

Technological influences

Analysis of the technological environment involves developing an understanding of the effects of changes in technology on all areas of a business and its activities, including:

- products and services;
- operational processes;
- information and communications;
- transport and distribution; and
- society, politics and economics.

Developments in information and communications technology (ICT) – like the development of personal computers, laptops and tablets, networks, satellite, cable and digital communications, the internet, and mobile phone applications – together with rapid advances in software have all contributed to revolutionizing the way that business is conducted in many industries.

Activities are now better co-ordinated and research and development is sped up, thus making businesses more flexible and responsive. Many activities previously carried out by middle layers of managers, which often involved collating and analysing data from operational activities and reporting to senior managers, can now be more effectively carried out using ICT solutions.

For example – many companies in *THE* (as in other industries), such as British Airways and Thomas Cook, have cut costs through reducing the numbers of people employed, particularly at middle levels of the organization, in a process referred to as *de-layering*.

Similarly, changes in transport technology have revolutionized business and have changed societies and cultures. It is possible to transport tourists and business people, as well as materials, components and products, with far greater speed and at much lower cost as a result of developments in road, rail, sea and air transport. These improvements in transport have also increased the total amount of personal and business travel that people undertake leading to profound societal changes both in tourist 'exporting' and 'importing' regions. Increasing wine consumption and more varied culinary tastes in many countries are responses (at least in part) to wider participation in international travel.

As a consequence it is important that organizations monitor changes in the technologies that can affect their operations or their markets. In most industries, organizations must be flexible and be ready to innovate and to adopt new technologies as they come along. The way in which (and the extent to which) organizations do or do not employ the latest technology can be an important determinant of its competitive advantage.

SHORT CASE ILLUSTRATION

Technological influences: Airline sector

The Computer Reservation Systems (CRS) such as Sabre, developed by American Airlines, are powerful tools of travel marketing technology. The systems developed largely in the 1960s and 1970s (with airlines in the forefront) have attained global reach and hence they are now often referred to as Global Distribution Systems (GDS). GDS have emerged over several decades as a central feature of electronic commerce in travel providing virtual real-time connectivity between thousands of suppliers of travel inventory (airlines, hotels, car rental, tour operators, cruise lines, etc.) and hundreds of thousands of retail sellers of travel products (Sismanidou *et al.*, 2009).

GDS progressively consolidated their position to only four major systems, namely Sabre, Amadeus, Galileo and Worldspan (the two latter now both acquired by Travelport, Inc. but operated separately from Travelport's Atlanta data centre). Allied to the use of GDS are the Revenue Management Systems that have been developed. These systems, which utilize the CRS accumulated databases, allow for the yield realized to be optimized by varying prices and altering the mix between classes of tickets that are issued.

The emergence of the Internet in the mid-1990s forced airlines to reshape their distribution strategy in order to boost their competitiveness (Buhalis, 2004).The emergence of internet search and booking engines (such as Expedia, Travelocity and ebookers), together with the sophisticated databases which have been compiled, allow for diversified distribution and communication channels to be utilized thus creating new opportunities for airline marketing.

In relation to the aircraft themselves, technological innovations continue to drive costs down and influence route structures. The 380 (Megaliner) developed by Airbus Industries, for example, has a capacity of some 550 passengers with operating costs about 17 per cent lower than the Boeing 747 (Brown, 2001). Route patterns and airport infrastructures are two aspects that have had to change in response to the aircraft's introduction. Additionally a number of smaller jet aircraft models with twin fuel-efficient lean-burn engines are being introduced and further such developments are planned.

For example, the long-haul wide-body aircraft Airbus A350 is being developed by the European company Airbus. The aircraft is designed to carry 270 to 475 passengers up to 15,000 km. In this segment the A350 will compete with the American Boeing's 787 (Dreamliner). Such aircraft allow the airlines to consider introducing routes which were previously considered to be unviable.

Questions

1. Explain the ways in which airline product distribution has changed in recent years.
2. Explain the changes taking place regarding aircraft types and assess the impact of the changes on airline route networks.

Economic influences

Analysis of the economic environment will centre on changes in the macro-economy and their effects on business and consumers. It is important to remember that because governments intervene (to varying extents) in the operation of all countries' economies, many factors classed as political in this chapter will have important economic implications.

Broadly speaking, the regulation of a national economy is brought about by two key policy instruments – fiscal policy and monetary policy. These policy instruments, alongside influences from international markets, determine the economic climate in the country in which a business competes. From these, a number of other, vital economic indicators 'flow' and it is these that organizations experience – either for good or ill.

KEY CONCEPT

Fiscal and monetary policy

Fiscal policy is the regulation of the national economy through the management of government revenues and expenditures. Each fiscal year, a government raises so much in revenues (such as through taxation) and it spends another amount through its various departments (such as on health, education, defence, etc.). The government is able to influence the economic climate in a country by varying either or both of these sides of the fiscal equation.

Monetary policy is the regulation of the national economy by varying the supply and price of money. Money supply concerns the volume of money (in its various forms) in the economy and the 'price' of money is the base rate which determines the interest rate that banks and other lenders charge for borrowings.

In the UK for example, the Chancellor of the Exchequer (a government minister) is in charge of fiscal policy whilst monetary policy is overseen by the Monetary Policy Committee of the Bank of England.

When the effects of fiscal and monetary pressure work themselves out in the economy, they can affect any or all of the following economic factors:

- economic growth rates (the year-to-year growth in the total size of a national economy, usually measured by gross domestic product);
- levels of income in the economy;
- levels of productivity (i.e. output per worker in the economy);
- wage levels and the rate of increase in wages;
- levels of inflation (i.e. the year-to-year rise in prices);
- levels of unemployment;
- balance of payments (a measure of the international competitiveness of one country's economy against its international competitor countries); and
- exchange rates (the exchange value of one currency against another).

Economic growth, exchange rates, levels of income, inflation and unemployment will all affect people's ability to pay for products and services and hence affect levels and patterns of demand. Similarly, levels of productivity, wage levels, levels of inflation, and exchange rates will affect costs of production and competitiveness. All of these indicators must be monitored in comparison to those faced by competitors abroad to provide indications of changes in international competitiveness.

SHORT CASE ILLUSTRATION

Economic influences: Airline sector

Aviation is a dynamic industry that continuously adapts to various market forces. Key economic market forces that impact the airline industry are fuel prices, economic growth and stage of economic development.

Air travel demand has closely mirrored the cyclical pattern shown by gross domestic product (GDP) figures in that it responds to cyclical upswings and downswings. However air travel growth has far exceeded GDP growth over most periods.

Air travel has always been a strongly cyclical business. Periods of 7 to 9 per cent annual growth of global consolidated passenger traffic alternate with years of slower rising, or declining, demand

(Franke and John, 2011). The industry has reliably returned to its long-term growth rate of approximately 5 per cent per year and Boeing expect such long-term trends to continue (albeit spread unevenly across the regions of the globe) in their forecast through to 2032.

The airline industry also has a high level of fixed costs and consequently average load factors and revenue measures per passenger are crucial in maintaining profitability. Load factors are measured systematically and are studied carefully by airline managers. The major measures are shown in Table 7.1 below:

Table 7.1 Economic influences – airline sector

Measure	Description
RPK – *Revenue Passenger Kilometre*	Measure of passenger traffic = Number of paying passengers × kilometres flown
ASK – *Available Seat Kilometre*	Measure of passenger capacity = Number of seats × kilometres flown
FTK – *Freight Tonne Kilometre*	Measure of freight traffic = Freight tonnes carried × kilometres flown
LF – *Load Factor*	Measure of capacity utilization = RPK / ASK

Furthermore fuel and aircraft prices are major expenditure items subject to fluctuations and the international orientation of the industry means that movements in foreign exchange rates can have major effects upon industry profitability. The post-2008 global recession has taken its toll on airlines' finances but most airlines learned lessons from the events of 2001/2003 (following 9/11) and reacted very quickly by grounding considerable capacity for the short term (Franke and John, 2011).

Questions

1. Why is airline travel so cyclical?

2. Explain the ways in which airlines assess their performance.

Environmental influences

The environmental influences here refer to the influence of concerns for the physical environment (both the natural environment and the built environment) on *THE* organizations. In recent years increasing concerns about ecology and 'green issues' has been an important social trend, which has changed attitudes towards the effects of products and operational processes on the environment. Issues such as global climate change, ozone depletion, deforestation, extinction of species, soil erosion, desertification, acid rain, toxic wastes, water and noise pollution have become important concerns with regard to the natural environment (Peattie and Moutinho, 2000).

To such concerns regarding the natural environment might be added others concerning the built environment such as traffic and airport congestion, deteriorating buildings and historic sites, poor urban planning and visually intrusive buildings. The problems and issues identified have certain unifying characteristics in that they:

- all have international dimensions;
- are not exclusively related to tourism, hospitality and events, but nevertheless have important implications for managers in *THE* sectors amongst others.

Whereas thirty years ago most consumers showed little concern for the long-term effects of products and processes on the natural environment, today people are increasingly aware of the need to protect it. Following various developments such as the publication of the Brundtland Report in 1987 (WCED, 1987) and the Earth Summit in Rio de Janeiro in 1992 there has been increasing commitment to the principles of sustainable development in many industries including *THE*. The term 'sustainable development' was used by the Brundtland Commission, which coined what has become the most often-quoted definition of sustainable development:

> **DEFINITION/QUOTATION**
>
> Sustainable development:
>
> > Development which meets the needs of current generations without compromising the ability of future generations to meet their own needs.
> >
> > World Commission on Environment and Development (1987)

This has led to pressure on governments to introduce legislation and other measures to control pollution and limit emissions. The combined desire of consumers for products which are themselves environmentally friendly and which have been produced by 'green' methods has resulted in the realization by business organizations that there are profits to be made by being 'environmentally friendly' or at least appearing to be so.

For example – international car rental firm Avis, founded in 1946 by Warren Avis, astutely anticipated post-war trends in travel. Starting with three cars in Detroit, Avis is today a global brand, with over 5,200 rental locations in more than 165 countries. Avis was the first car rental company to launch a Corporate Social Responsibility Policy in 1997, and claims to have been a 'Carbon Neutral' Operation since 2000.

> **SHORT CASE ILLUSTRATION**
>
> **Environmental programme as a source of competitive advantage: Scandic Hotels**
>
> Scandic Hotels, with its headquarters in Stockholm, Sweden, is the leading hotel brand in Scandinavia. The environmental programme which is central to the brand's promotional activity provides a source of competitive advantage for Scandic in a region where consumers are traditionally highly environmentally conscious. The hotel groups' pioneering environmental programmes have also been discussed in the academic literature (see for example Bohdanowicz et al. (2005) and Bohdanowicz and Zientara (2008).
>
> The group, which employs some 7,500 people, has 160 hotels of which 133 are in the Scandinavian countries with others located around Europe. The brand, which positions itself as offering 'value for money', places great emphasis on continual competence development of employees at all levels of the organization and on its environmental programme.
>
> Scandic's environmental programme was launched in 1994 following consultation with staff and the hotel has won numerous awards. The programme involves the continuing education of all employees and includes initiatives such as:

- The introduction in 1995 of eco-rooms, which are 97 per cent recyclable. More recently, the company has also developed 'eco-hotels' in which the entire construction of the hotels is guided by environmental principles. To date, more than 8,000 eco-rooms and six eco-hotels have been built;
- The achievement of 'Swan' certification for a number of hotels. The Swan is the official eco-label in Scandinavia and verifies that the hotels have met stringent environmental standards; and
- The abolition of individual soap and shampoo packages in 1994 reduced emissions of soap and shampoo by 40 metric tonnes and eliminated 10 million packages annually.
- In 2000 Scandic also introduced, following staff consultation, a community involvement programme called 'Scandic in Society' which aims to define the company's role in society by engaging in local issues which are important to each community in which Scandic hotels are located. Through such a programme the company aims to demonstrate its corporate citizenship and contribute to societal changes and improvements.

www.scandic-hotels.com

Questions

1. Explain the ways in which Scandic make their environmental programme into a central part of their competitive offering.

2. What risks might there be for the company in taking such a prominent environmental stance?

The issues of the sustainability of tourist destinations, hotels, events and attractions has been widely addressed in *THE* academic literature over recent years by authors such as Hawkins and Holtz (2001), Timur and Getz (2009) and Buckley (2012). A number of authors have also traced the environmental impacts of particular sectors of *THE*.

For example – Getz (2009) discusses the need for public sector involvement in successful and sustainable planning for festivals and events; while Hsieh (2012) analyses the environmental management policies and practices of 50 hotel companies as disclosed on their corporate websites. Graham (2013) traces environmental policies and practices at a number of airports including Oslo, Manchester, London Heathrow and Amsterdam.

Cartwright and Baird (1999), in tracing the environmental impacts of cruising, report on the ways in which attempts have been made to reduce the polluting effect of cruise ships. The traditional method of removing rubbish from ships was to dump it overboard. Now such practices are outlawed and large fines are imposed on shipping companies found guilty of such pollution partly in response to consumer pressures. A modern cruise ship such as P&O's Oriana contains four sewage plants so that as much rubbish as possible is retained and disposed of safely into containers at ports. There is also a worldwide ban on the discharge of fuel oil into the sea (Cartwright and Baird, 1999).

SHORT CASE ILLUSTRATION

Environmental influences: Airline sector

Environmental concerns in the airline sector include:

- the effects of noise;
- the air pollution caused by aircraft emissions; and
- the impacts of developing airport and ground transportation infrastructure.

Public tolerance of aircraft noise has been diminishing in spite of the reduction in noise levels due to the development of less noisy aircraft types (Graham, 2013). The problems associated with aircraft noise have led to ever more stringent and sophisticated noise abatement measures being introduced at most major airports. Some of these gases emitted by aircraft in flight, primarily carbon dioxide and water vapour, are greenhouse gases which contribute to global warming and climate change. However, it is thought that aviation's contribution to global human-made carbon dioxide emissions amounts to only around 2 per cent of the total (Graham, 2013). The environmental impacts caused by the airline sector and initiatives to deal with these impacts is well documented in academic literature (see for example Lynes and Andrachuk (2008) and Cowper-Smith and de Grosbois (2011).

The infrastructure of creating airports and ground transportation to support airlines has often proved controversial. Thus the agreement to proceed with a fifth terminal for London's Heathrow Airport was secured only after ten years of public consultations whilst Manchester Airport proceeded with building a second runway in the face of strong lobbying by environmental pressure groups.

Questions

1. Explain why airline managers need to take account of environmental concerns.
2. Consider which stakeholder groups are likely to be influential when making decisions about airport infrastructure projects.

Political, governmental, legal and regulatory influences

The political environment is defined as that part of the macro-environment, which is under the direct control, or influence of, the government. Governments have direct control or influence over:

- *Legislation and regulation* – this covers laws that influence employment, consumer protection, health and safety at work, contract and trading, trade unions, monopolies and mergers, tax, etc..
- *Economic policy* – particularly over fiscal policy. Governments usually set policy over the levels of taxation and expenditure in the country.
- *Government-owned businesses* – nationalized industries. Some governments retain control over key strategic industries (such as airlines) and the way in which these are controlled can have 'knock-on' effects to other parts of the economy.
- *Government international policy* – government intervention to influence exchange rates, international trade, etc.

The objectives that a government may have towards the regulation of business will depend in large part upon the political leaning of the governing party. Most governments have, however, sought to construct policy over a number of key areas of business activity.

- control of inflation (to improve international competitiveness);
- promotion of economic growth and investment;
- control of unemployment;
- stabilization of exchange rates;
- control of balance of payments;
- control of monopoly power, both by businesses and trade unions;

- provision of public and merit goods like health, education, defence, etc.;
- control of pollution and environmental protection;
- redistribution of incomes (to varying degrees);
- consumer protection;
- regulation of working conditions; and
- regulation of trade.

To varying degrees, all businesses will be affected by political influences. Accordingly, it is important for managers to monitor government policy to detect changes early so as to respond effectively.

Another important aspect of the political environment is *political risk* and its potential effects on business. Political risk is particularly important in international business. Whilst western Europe and North America are comparatively politically stable, other parts of the world like Eastern Europe, South America, sub-Saharan Africa and parts of the Middle East, Central Asia and North Africa have undergone periods of instability. It is therefore necessary to monitor closely the political situation in these areas when trading with them, as the political risks are large. Even in more stable areas, political uncertainty can be higher at, for example, election times or when other political crises arise.

SHORT CASE ILLUSTRATION

Political influences: Airline sector

The political environment of the airline sector has been characterized by an extended network of national and international rules and regulations, many of which date back to the Chicago Convention of 1944 and the Bermuda Agreement of 1946. Based on the acknowledgement of the sovereignty of nations over their airspace, and of the equal right for every nation to participate in air travel, the so-called five freedoms of the air were established:

- First Freedom – The right to fly over another country without landing;
- Second Freedom – The right to make a landing for technical reasons (e.g. refuelling) in another country without picking up/setting down revenue traffic;
- Third Freedom – The right to carry revenue traffic from your own country (A) to the country (B) of your treaty partner;
- Fourth Freedom – The right to carry traffic from country B back to your own country A; and
- Fifth Freedom – The right of an airline from country A to carry revenue traffic between country B and other countries such as C or D on services starting or ending in its home country A. (This freedom cannot be used unless countries C or D also agree.)

Doganis (2005)

The five freedoms were followed by a complex web of bilateral inter-governmental agreements that allowed national governments involved to maintain control over national interests related to air travel. A more liberal approach is reflected in the so-called open-skies agreements granting carriers of the states involved unlimited access to the routes between airports in these states. The concept of open skies reflects a development of major importance for the airline industry: liberalization unfolding around the globe (Doganis, 2005).

In the USA (which accounts for over 40 per cent of the world's airline industry) the strict regulations governing the domestic air travel market were swept away by the Airline Deregulation Act of 1978. The act abolished regulations specifying which carriers were allowed to fly on particular routes and controls on air fares. After deregulation many new carriers entered the market (and many subsequently folded). Some of the newer carriers such as Southwest, JetBlue and Frontier are now substantial entities in their own right, operating low-cost operating models. But most of the largest carriers – such as United which merged with Continental American which merged with US Airways and Delta which merged with Northwest – survived but undoubtedly competition in the US domestic market has increased.

Subsequently similar deregulation has occurred in Europe, albeit with a different approach towards its implementation due to the complexity of the European Union's fragmented political landscape. Consequently a step-by-step process towards liberalization took place which culminated in 1997 (Hanlon, 2007).

Other parts of the world have followed with similar policies of deregulation. Another major trend among European and other governments is the privatization (in whole or in part) of former state-owned carriers such as British Airways, Air France and Lufthansa.

Questions

1. Explain the reasons why the political environment for the airline sector is different from any other industry.
2. Consider the effect that deregulation in various parts of the world has had on the airline sector.

The relationships between the STEEP influences

The example of environmental influences

A temptation when carrying out a STEEP analysis is to think of each influence as separate when in fact they are often interlinked. The effects of environmental influences on organizations provide an example.

For example – the environmental concerns themselves (such as the use of water resources for golf course developments or the building of a visually intrusive hotel in a scenic area) are issues to be dealt with within the environmental category of the STEEP analysis. However such concerns might also involve social, political and technological factors in the analysis.

Thus, in the simple example of the golf course or visually intrusive hotel development above, environmental concerns raised by the developments might lead to social factors (increased awareness) which impact on political factors (legislation and regulation) and the two forces together have might produce technological change (products and processes which are less damaging to the environment).

Accordingly, a macro-environmental analysis should recognize the ways in which the five STEEP factors might be linked to each other in addition to the individual factors by themselves.

THINK POINTS

- Discuss the argument that suggests that turbulence and uncertainty render analysis of the macro-environment less useful.
- Explain the importance of sustainability to macro-environmental analysis in *THE* contexts.
- Explain why it is important to recognize the linkages between the STEEP elements.

Understanding the external environment is important for all businesses, but from a managerial perspective the primary differentiating factor between the internal and external environment (considered in Chapters 3–6) is control. Whereas managers have some degree of control over the internal environment this is rarely the case with regard to the external environment. However, large organizations may in some cases have some influence over the external environment or they can protect themselves against the dangers posed.

Larger organizations may, for example, be able to:

- switch investment from one country to another;
- influence government policy;
- use financial instruments to 'hedge' against interest rate and oil price movements; and
- diversify their product portfolios so a hostile external environment for one set of products may be offset by a benign environment in another.

However, SMEs are far more limited in that they rarely are able to have any meaningful degree of influence over the external environment, cannot easily switch investment and have far more limited access to the financial and commodity markets (or do so at far greater cost) leaving them more exposed. Furthermore, SMEs usually have a more limited product range meaning that weak performance in one area cannot be offset by strong performance in another.

In their study of tourism sector small business performance Morrison and Teixeira (2004) highlight the weak power position within the tourism sector of individual SME units. One major change in the external environment such as, an increase in interest rates, an economic recession or a catastrophic event at an event or destination could have a profound effect on any business but for SMEs operating in *THE* sectors such changes can (and often do) result in business failure.

Thus it is key to survival and business success for SMEs to scan their external environment and understand possible scenarios since uncertainty is always involved as discussed by Oreja-Rodríguez, and Yanes-Estévez, (2007) in their study of Spanish hotels.

It is necessary to think through the implications of each possible scenario and how the business might position itself to respond. However, by their nature, SMEs have more limited human, physical and financial resources. Furthermore, SMEs often focus on allocation of resources to achieve their maximum short-term advantage, which frequently leaves them to respond to external influences as they occur rather than taking a proactive approach (McAdam, 2000). Some evidence suggests that the majority of small firms do not utilize the traditional tools and techniques of strategic planning (Meers and Robertson, 2007).

Tools and models aim to clarify complex issues and Banham (2010) introduces her 'Degrees of Turbulence' model to assist owner/managers of SMEs in understanding the externalities that impact their business operations. This represents an attempt to simplify and systemize external environmental scanning for smaller businesses using a numerical scoring system to gauge the relative turbulence of the environment.

CHAPTER SUMMARY

Analysis of the macro-environment is primarily concerned with providing insight into the future facing an organization. The complexity and turbulence of the environment make prediction of the future problematic.

Analysis, however, informs managers in their strategic decision-making. The complexity of the external environment is simplified by breaking it down into the smaller social, technological, economic, environmental, and political components. These environments can then be analysed for their potential effects on the business and its micro-environment. The process of macro-environmental analysis must be continuous to cope with the pace of change.

REFERENCES

Banham, H. C. (2010) 'External Environmental Analysis for Small and Medium Enterprises (SMEs)', *Journal of Business and Economics Research*, 8 (10): 19–30.

Bohdanowicz, P., B. Simanic and I. Martinac (2005) 'Environmental Training and Measures at Scandic Hotels, Sweden', *Tourism Review International*, 9 (1): 7–19.

Bohdanowicz, P. and P. Zientara (2008) 'Corporate Social Responsibility in Hospitality: Issues and Implications. A Case Study of Scandic', *Scandinavian Journal of Hospitality and Tourism*, 8 (4): 271–93.

Brown, S. F. (2001) 'How to Build a Really Big Plane', *Fortune*, 5: 76–82.

Buckley, R. (2012) 'Sustainable Tourism: Research and Reality', *Annals of Tourism Research*, 39 (2): 528–46.

Buhalis, D. (2004) 'eAirlines: Strategic and Tactical Use of ICTs in the Airline Industry', *Information and Management*, 41(7), 805–25.

Cartwright, R. and C. Baird (1999) *The Development and Growth of the Cruise Industry*, Oxford: Butterworth Heinemann.

Chakravarthy, B. (1997) 'A New Strategy Framework for Coping with Turbulence', *Sloan Management Review*, 38 (2): 69–82.

Clarke, A. and W. Chen (2007) *International Hospitality Management*, London and New York: Routledge.

Costa, J. (1995) 'An Empirically-Based Review of the Concept of Environmental Scanning', *International Journal of Contemporary Hospitality Management*, 7 (7): 4–9.

Coulter, M. K. (2002) *Strategic Management in Action*, Englewood Cliffs, NJ: Prentice Hall.

Cowper-Smith, A. and D. De Grosbois (2011) 'The Adoption of Corporate Social Responsibility Practices in the Airline Industry', *Journal of Sustainable Tourism*, 19 (1): 59–77.

Doganis, R. (2005) *The Airline Business*, 2nd edn, London and New York: Routledge.

Fleisher, C. S. and B. E. Bensoussan (2003) *Strategic and Competitive Analysis: Methods and Techniques for Analyzing Business Competition*, Upper Saddle River, NJ: Prentice Hall.

Franke, M. and F. John (2011) 'What Comes Next After Recession? Airline Industry Scenarios and Potential End Games', *Journal of Air Transport Management*, 17 (1): 19–26.

Getz, D. (2009) 'Policy for Sustainable and Responsible Festivals and Events: Institutionalization of a New Paradigm', *Journal of Policy Research in Tourism, Leisure and Events*, 1 (1): 61–78.

Ginter, P. M. and J. Duncan (1990) 'Macroenvironmental Analysis for Strategic Management', *Long Range Planning*, 23 (6): 91–100.

Graham, A. (2013) *Managing Airports: An International Perspective*, 4th edn, Oxford: Butterworth Heinemann.

Hanlon, J. P. (2007) *Global Airlines: Competition in a Transnational Industry*, London and New York: Routledge.

Hawkins, D. E. and C. Holtz (2001) 'Environmental Policies and Management Systems Related to the Global Tourism Industry', in S. Wahab and C. Cooper (eds.), *Tourism in the Age of Globalisation*, London and New York: Routledge.

Holloway, J. C. and C. Humphries (2012) *The Business of Tourism*, 9th edn, Harlow: Pearson.

Hsieh, Y. C. J. (2012) 'Hotel Companies' Environmental Policies and Practices: A Content Analysis of Their Web Pages', *International Journal of Contemporary Hospitality Management*, 24 (1): 97–121.

Jogaratnam, G. and R. Law (2006) 'Environmental Scanning and Information Source Utilization: Exploring the Behavior of Hong Kong Hotel and Tourism Executives', *Journal of Hospitality and Tourism Research*, 30 (2): 170–90.

Lynch, R. (2000) *Corporate Strategy*, 2nd edn, Harlow: Pearson Education.

Lynes, J. K. and M. Andrachuk (2008) 'Motivations for Corporate Social and Environmental Responsibility: A Case Study of Scandinavian Airlines', *Journal of International Management*, 14 (4): 377–90.

Mason, R. B. (2007) 'The External Environment's Effect on Management and Strategy: A Complexity Theory Approach', *Management Decision*, 45 (1): 10–28.

McAdam, R. (2000) 'The Implementation of Reengineering in SMEs: A Grounded Study', *International Small Business Journal, London*, 17 (3): 305–23.

Meers, K. A. and C. Robertson (2007) 'Strategic Planning Practices in Profitable Small Firms in the United States', *The Business Review*, 7 (1): 302–7.

Morrison, A. and R. Teixeira (2004) 'Small Business Performance: A Tourism Sector Focus', *Journal of Small Business and Enterprise Development*, 11 (2): 166–73.

Okumus, F. (2004) 'Potential Challenges of Employing a Formal Environmental Scanning Approach in Hospitality Organizations', *International Journal of Hospitality Management*, 23 (2): 123–43.

Oreja-Rodríguez, J. R. and V. Yanes-Estévez (2007) 'Perceived Environmental Uncertainty in Tourism: A New Approach Using the Rasch Model', *Tourism Management*, 28 (6): 1450–63.

Oyewole, P. (2001) 'Consumer's Socio-Demographic Characteristics and Satisfaction with Services in the Airline Industry', *Services Marketing Quarterly*, 23 (2): 61–80.

Peattie, K. and L. Moutinho (2000) 'The Marketing Environment for Travel and Tourism', in L. Moutinho (ed.), *Strategic Management in Tourism*, Wallingford: CAB International, pp. 17–37.

Poon, A. (1993) *Tourism Technology and Competitive Strategies*, Wallingford: CAB International.

Sismanidou, A., M. Palacios and J. Tafur (2009) 'Progress in Airline Distribution Systems: The Threat of New Entrants to Incumbent Players', *Journal of Industrial Engineering and Management*, 2 (1): 251–72.

Timur, S. and D. Getz (2009) 'Sustainable Tourism Development: How Do Destination Stakeholders Perceive Sustainable Urban Tourism?' *Sustainable Development*, 17 (4): 220–32.

Tum, J. and P. Norton (2006) *Management of Event Operations*, London and New York: Routledge.

World Commission on Environment and Development (1987) *Our Common Future*, Oxford: Oxford University Press.

WEBSITES

www.boeing.com
www.scandic-hotels.com

FURTHER READING

Reference	Focus
Cooper, C. (2008) *Tourism: Principles and Practice*, Harlow: Pearson Education.	Tourism External analysis
Everett, J. and J. Watson (1998) 'Small Business Failure and External Risk Factors', *Small Business Economics*, 11 (4): 371–90.	SMEs External analysis Risk
Moscardo, G. (2007) 'Analyzing the Role of Festivals and Events in Regional Development', *Event Management*, 11 (1–2): 1–2.	Economic environment Festivals and events
Sectors, E. (1997) 'Strategic Uncertainty and Environmental Scanning: The Case for Institutional Influences on Scanning Behavior', *Strategic Management Journal*, 18 (4): 287–302.	Environmental scanning Uncertainty
Stoffels, J. D. (1994) *Strategic Issues Management: A Comprehensive Guide to Environmental Scanning*, Oxford: Pergamon Press.	Environmental scanning Uncertainty
Teo, P. (2002) 'Striking a Balance for Sustainable Tourism: Implications of the Discourse on Globalisation', *Journal of Sustainable Tourism*, 10 (6): 459–74.	Tourism Sustainability

CASE LINKAGES

Case 1	Strategic alliances in the airline industry
Case 2	Tourism Queensland
Case 5	Days Inn

Chapter **8**

The external environment for tourism, hospitality and event organizations

The micro context

Introduction and chapter overview

In the introduction to Part 3 we encountered the idea that an organization's external environment comprises two strata – the macro-environment and the micro-environment. We considered the macro-environment in Chapter 7 (using the STEEP framework) and in this chapter we turn to an analysis of the micro-environment.

The micro-environment comprises those influences that the organization experiences frequently. For most businesses, it concerns the industries in which they operate. Within this arena businesses may compete with each other or, in some circumstances, collaboration may be more appropriate. We discuss two models for industry analysis in this chapter. We then go on to discuss the scope of collaborative behaviour, before considering the way in which competitors in an industry fall into strategic groups.

LEARNING OBJECTIVES

After studying this chapter, readers should be able to:

- distinguish between micro and macro level external analyses;
- explain the importance of industry and market analysis with regard to *THE* sectors;
- describe the construction and application to *THE* of Porter's five forces framework;
- explain the limitations of Porter's five forces framework;
- define and distinguish between competitive and collaborative behaviour in industries;

- assess and explain the limitations of the resource-based model of industry analysis;
- define strategic groups and be able to apply the concept in industry analysis for *THE* sectors.
- explain the meaning of Critical Success Factors and distinguish them from Key Performance Indicators.

Industries and markets

The importance of industry and market identification

Some strategic management texts wrongly use the terms *industry* and *market* interchangeably. Kay (1995) points out that to confuse the two concepts can result in a flawed analysis of the competitive environment and, hence, in flawed strategy. Modern organizations, such as *vertically integrated* travel companies, may operate in more than one industry (or industrial sector) and in more than one market.

For example – Tui plc, a vertically integrated European travel group, operates in the airline, travel intermediary (tour operator and travel distribution), accommodation and cruising sectors of the travel industry and has major markets in Scandinavia, Continental Europe, the UK and North America. Each industry (or industrial sector) and market will have its own distinctive structure and characteristics which will have particular implications for the formulation of strategy.

KEY CONCEPT

Industry and market

Industries produce goods and services – the *supply side* of the economic system.

Markets consume goods and services that have been produced by industries – the *demand side* of the economic system.

Industries are centred on the supply of a product or service while markets are concerned with demand. It is important, therefore, to understand and analyse both industries and markets to assist in the process of strategy selection.

It is sometimes difficult to define a particular industry precisely. Porter (1980) defines an industry as a group of businesses whose products are close substitutes, but this definition can be inadequate because some organizations and industries produce a range of products for different markets. The importance of identifying the industry setting successfully and understanding its implications is examined by Rumelt (1991) and McGahan and Porter (1997).

STRATEGY IN PRACTICE

Ways of understanding markets, industries and strategic groups in strategy

Kay (1995) considers the differences between markets, industries and strategic groups. A core competence (or distinctive capability) becomes a competitive advantage only when it is applied in a market, an industry or a strategic group.

Competitive advantage is a relative term in that an organization can enjoy a competitive advantage by reference to other suppliers to the same market, other organizations in the same industry, or other competitors in the same strategic group. Demand factors determine the market, while supply factors determine the industry.

By way of example Kay cites Eurotunnel and P&O Ferries. Both serve the same market as they represent alternative options customers might choose in order to cross the English Channel between France and the UK.

However they are in very different industries in that one is a shipping company whilst the other is the manager of a large infrastructure project. The strategic group is viewed as the competitive battleground and is determined by classifying companies with similar strategies. Thus Lufthansa and British Airways are part of the same strategic group, Southwest Airlines, a low cost airline operating only domestic services in the USA would be in a different strategic group.

It is important for organizations to identify the relevant market, industry and strategic group and to understand that they are not the same. In the 1980's Bass, then Britain's largest brewer, viewed the prospects for the beer market as being unexciting and redefined its core business as being concerned with leisure. The company bought Horizon Travel, a leading tour operator, as spending time in pubs and going on holiday were correctly seen as alternative ways of spending leisure time and competed for the same share of consumer's expenditure.

However, the skills of brewing were quite different from those required to provide package holidays and the acquisition was unsuccessful. The business was subsequently sold to the Thomson Travel Group (now part of Tui plc). Bass failed to realize that there is indeed a *leisure market* but there is not a *leisure industry*.

Kay (1995)

Thus while an industry is centred upon producers of a product or service, a market is centred on customers and their requirements (needs and wants). A particular market consists of a group of customers with a specific set of requirements, which may be satisfied by one or more products. Analysis of a market will therefore involve gaining understanding of customers, their requirements, the products which satisfy those requirements, the organizations producing the products and the means by which customers obtain those products (distribution channels).

As well as selling their products in markets, businesses also obtain their resources (labour, materials, equipment, land, etc.) in markets – referred to as *resource markets*. Additionally, most businesses are interested in markets for substitute products and they will also be keen to investigate new markets for their products.

The relationship between a business organization, its industry and markets

Analysis of its industry and markets allows an organization to:

- identify other industries where it may be able to deploy its core competencies;
- understand the nature of its customers and their needs;
- identify new markets where its core competencies may be exploited (see Chapter 3 for a discussion of core competencies);
- identify threats from existing and potential competitors in its own and other industries;
- understand markets from which it obtains its resources.

Analysis of the competitive environment (industry and market) is important to the development of an organization's future strategy, as is analysis of the macro-environment (covered in Chapter 7) and internal analysis (which was the subject of Part 2 of this book). The industry and market context will play an important role in shaping an organization's competencies and core competencies.

The core competencies of a business must continually be reviewed in relation to:

- changing customer needs;
- competitors' competencies; and
- other market opportunities.

Industry analysis

What is industry analysis?

Industry analysis aims to establish the nature of the competition in the industry and the competitive position of the business. Industry dynamics, in turn, are affected by changes in the macro-environment (see Chapter 7).

For example – ageing populations in many developed countries have significantly affected the demand for tourism products with the growth in cruising, escorted coach tours and long-stay holidays being but three industry responses to the trend.

THINK POINTS

- Using examples from *THE*, define and distinguish between an *industry* and a *market*.
- What is the purpose of industry analysis?
- Explain using examples from *THE* what is meant by the term *strategic group* and distinguish how it is different from an industry.

There is a danger that industry analysis can be seen as a 'one off' activity but like all components of the strategic process, it should be undertaken on an on-going basis. The industry analysis framework developed by Porter (1980) is the most widely used and is explained in this section.

KEY CONCEPT

Micro- and macro-environments

The most commonly used frameworks for analysing the external business environment distinguish between two levels or strata of environmental influence.

The micro (or near) environment is that which immediately surrounds a business, the parts of which the business interacts with frequently and over which it may have some influence. For most purposes we can identify competitors, suppliers and customers as comprising the main constituents of this layer of the environment.

The macro (or far) environment comprises those influences that can affect the whole industry in which a business operates. The macro-environment comprises influence arising from political, economic, socio-demographic and technological factors. The nature of these factors normally means that individual businesses are unable to influence them – strategies must usually be formulated to cope with changes in the macro-environment.

Porter's five forces model of industry analysis

Models that become widely accepted and utilized are generally simple and easy to recall. Such is the case with Porter's widely used 'Five Forces' model of industry analysis. Furthermore the concept has been widely applied and critiqued in the *THE* academic literature (see for example Lee and King, 2006; Benson and Henderson, 2011; and Tavitiyaman *et al.*, 2011).

Porter (1985) developed a framework for analysing the nature and extent of competition within an industry. He argued that there are five competitive forces which determine the degree of competition within an industry. Understanding the nature and strength of each of the five forces within an industry assists managers in developing the competitive strategy of their organization. The five forces are:

• the threat of new entrants to the industry;
• the threat of substitute products;
• the power of buyers or customers;
• the power of suppliers (to businesses in the industry); and
• rivalry among businesses in the industry.

By determining the relative 'power' of each of these forces, an organization can identify how to position itself to take advantage of opportunities and overcome or circumvent threats. The strategy of an organization may then be designed to exploit the competitive forces at work within an industry.

Before considering the detailed aspects of the five forces framework a number of points should be noted about the framework:

• Although originally developed with commercial businesses in mind the framework can provide valuable insights for most organizations, destinations or attractions.

• When using Porter's framework it is important to identify which of the five forces are the key forces at work in an industry. In many cases it transpires that one or more of the five forces prove to be 'key forces' and the strategic analysis must focus on these if it is to use the framework fruitfully.

• The dynamic nature of the competitive environment (meaning that it is constantly changing) means that the relative strength of the forces in a particular industry will change over time. It is therefore important that the five forces analysis is repeated on a regular basis so as to detect such changes before competitors and allow an early adjustment of strategy.

• Before any conclusions can be drawn about the nature of competition within an industry each of the five forces must be analysed in detail.

• The framework should be based at the level of the strategic business unit (SBU) rather than at the level of the entire organization. That is when considering the five competitive forces facing an organization it is not the entire organization that should be considered (except where the organization is

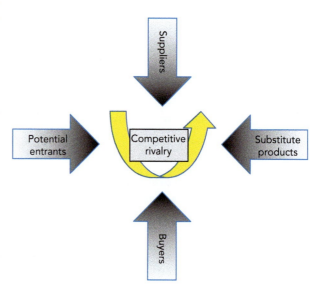

Figure 8.1 Porter's five forces framework (adapted from Porter, 1985).

simple and consists of one SBU only) but the forces should be considered in relation to constituent SBU's. This is because individual organizations may be diverse in their markets and operations.

For example – a vertically integrated travel company such as Tui (which we cited as an example previously) operates tour operations, travel agents, online distribution, accommodation, an airline and cruise ships. In each of these sectors the company faces different sets of competitors, suppliers and substitutes and also faces varying regulatory processes. An airline might compete simultaneously in several different arenas such as long haul, domestic and European. In each of these the airline might target different target groups such as leisure, business and freight and face a different set of competitors. Thus the competitive forces are different in each of its chosen competitive arenas.

- The five forces are not independent of each other with pressures from one competitive force having the potential to trigger off changes in the other forces.

For example – potential new entrants to a market finding their route to be blocked may find new routes to the market by bypassing traditional distribution channels using agents or intermediaries and sell directly to consumers. Most airlines following the low-cost model, such as easyJet, Air Asia or Southwest Airlines, do not commonly use distribution through intermediaries such as travel agents and do not feature prominently on GDS systems. Instead tickets are normally sold directly to consumers (largely through the internet) thereby cutting out the intermediaries and the commission which would ordinarily have been paid to them. Thus the bargaining power of one set of buyers (the travel agents) was reduced by the introduction of a new market entrant whilst the bargaining power of another set (consumers) was increased as a result of increased competition provided by the new entrant.

Each of the five forces will be discussed in turn in the context of various forms of travel and tourism organization.

Force 1: The threat of new entrants to the industry

The threat of entry to an industry by new competitors depends upon the 'height' of a number of entry barriers. Barriers to entry can take a number of forms.

THE CAPITAL COSTS OF ENTRY

The size of the investment required by a business wishing to enter the industry (or industry sector) will be an important determinant of the extent of the threat of new entrants. The higher the investment required, the less the threat from new entrants is likely to be. The lower the required investment, the greater the threat. In some areas of *THE,* such as the building of a hotel or a visitor attraction, starting a cruise line or launching an airline, the capital costs are clearly quite high.

However, in some situations it might be possible to avoid or defer some capital costs by separating ownership from the management of the assets or by leasing or franchising. Separating ownership and management is common in the hotel sector where a property company may own the physical assets but a hotel operator manages the hotel. Leasing aircraft and ships is common in the airline and cruising sectors and allows high up-front costs to be spread out over a period of time.

In other areas of *THE* such as starting a tour operator, a travel agency, an internet intermediary or an event management company, the capital costs might be relatively low since they do not normally require the purchase of expensive assets.

BRAND LOYALTY AND CUSTOMER SWITCHING COSTS

If the companies in an industry produce differentiated products and services and customers are loyal to particular brands, then potential new entrants will encounter resistance in trying to enter the industry. Brand loyalty will also be an important factor in increasing the costs for customers of switching to the products of new competitors.

For example – in some instances, tourism destination products are able to fully differentiate their products. There is only one Louvre art gallery in Paris where the Mona Lisa can be viewed and the Emperor Penguin can only be viewed (except in captivity) in extreme southern latitudes. Similarly there is only one Glastonbury rock festival held in Somerset, UK, in the early summer each year.

SHORT CASE ILLUSTRATION

Brand loyalty: Hong Kong Dragon Boat Festival

It all started in 1976 when Hong Kong fishermen participated in an international dragon boat race (there was one foreign team – from Japan) off the north eastern coast of Hong Kong island. From such humble beginnings the event sparked an explosion of worldwide interest in dragon boat racing and transformed an ancient Chinese folk ritual into a modern international sport.

The races have now become established as an annual international event. In June 2013, over 5,000 athletes representing more than 200 teams from all over the world competed in the Hong Kong International Dragon Boat Races, with Hong Kong's iconic skyline as the backdrop.

By definition the 'Hong Kong' Dragon Boat Races cannot be staged elsewhere. A tradition is formed over many years and a brand backed by business sponsorship becomes established with loyalty amongst the sport's participants and supporters built up.

www.discoverhongkong.com

Questions

1. Explain how the building of a brand has established a barrier to entry in this case.
2. Provide another example from your knowledge of *THE* of a brand becoming established to create a barrier to entry.

Thus customers cannot switch to new entrants if they want to experience these attractions or events.

However, in many cases *THE* consumers are driven by price and exhibit little brand loyalty. Thus consumers may switch from existing tour operators, travel agents, hotel groups, events and attractions and airlines to new entrants on the basis of a more competitive offering. In some cases, however, switching costs are imposed through customer loyalty schemes such as the Frequent Flyer and Guest Loyalty programmes operated by airlines, hotels and other suppliers. These programmes (such as American Airlines' AAdvantage; Air France-KLM's Flying Blue; and Hilton's HHonors and Accor Group's Le Club Accorhotels) represent powerful incentives for *THE* consumers to remain loyal to particular brands.

ECONOMIES OF SCALE OR SCOPE AVAILABLE TO EXISTING COMPETITORS

If existing competitors are already obtaining substantial economies of scale it will give them an advantage over new competitors who will not be able to match their lower unit costs of production.

For example – a new entrant offering package holidays to Spain from the major European markets (Germany, the UK and Scandinavia) would face strong competition from large entrenched operators such as Tui, Kuoni and Thomas Cook. These operators often have long-standing arrangements with accommodation suppliers in Spain and other Mediterranean destinations. Given their ability to contract bed spaces in bulk, they are able to negotiate highly favourable terms that may not be available to a smaller new entrant.

KEY CONCEPT

Economies of scale and scope

Economies of scale and economies of scope are widely used terms in the academic literature. They are conceptually similar (and often the term economies of scale is used loosely to denote both concepts) but they are different in detail.

Economies of scale for an organization primarily refers to reductions in the average cost (cost per unit) associated with increasing the scale of operations for a single product type.

Economies of scope for an organization refers to lowering the average cost for a firm in producing two or more products.

For example – an airline operating to a single destination may be able to achieve *economies of scale* by operating a larger aeroplane as business increases since it will probably have lower operating costs per passenger. Similarly if further routes are added to the airline network *economies of scope* may occur since the costs of maintenance, sales and marketing, check in staff, etc. may be shared by several routes thus bringing average costs per passenger down.

ACCESS TO INPUT AND DISTRIBUTION CHANNELS

New competitors may find it difficult to gain access to channels of distribution, which will make it difficult to provide their products to customers or obtain the inputs required.

For example – in the case of the tour operator cited previously, such is the shortage of some categories of accommodation in some destinations that existing operators have sometimes contracted all the available capacity, thereby excluding new entrants to access to the necessary inputs. Furthermore the existing large tour operators have established distribution channels (such as travel agents, call centres and the internet) in their major markets which they have developed over the years in order to provide the most cost efficient means of distribution. A new entrant would require heavy investment in order to secure such access.

THE RESISTANCE OFFERED BY EXISTING BUSINESSES

If existing competitors choose to resist strongly it will make it difficult for new organizations to enter the industry.

For example – if existing businesses are obtaining economies of scale it will be possible for them to undercut the prices of new entrants because of their cost advantage. In some cases, existing competitors may make price cuts or increase marketing expenditure in order to deter new entrants. It has sometimes been claimed that such *predatory* pricing behaviour has been undertaken by the established 'full-service' airlines in order to deter new low-cost carriers (see for example: Forsyth *et al.*, 2006; Hanlon, 2007; Fageda *et al.*, 2011).

If barriers to entry make it difficult for new competitors to enter the industry then this will limit the amount of competition within it. As a result, competitors within the industry will attempt to seek to strengthen the barriers to entry by cultivating brand loyalty, increasing the costs of entry and 'tying up' input and distribution channels as far as is possible.

Conversely potential new entrants will lobby for the removal or reduction of such barriers in order to allow them to enter the industry and compete for business. In other words they will try to make the industry *contestable* as it is sometimes termed.

GOVERNMENT REGULATION

In some situations new competitors are prevented from entering the market by government or inter-governmental regulation of the *THE* sectors.

For example – provision of accommodation and services for tourists by organizations is strictly regulated within the internationally renowned national parks of the USA such as Yellowstone and Yosemite. This is in marked contrast to the largely unregulated position outside the parks.

The institutional environment plays a very important role in regulating competition, particularly in transition countries such as China.

For example – in China, the hotel sector has been open to foreign investment for over two decades and has a diversified ownership structure, whereas the travel services sector has been dominated by government-owned firms and relatively closed to foreign investment (Qu *et al.*, 2005).

Government intervention is a typical characteristic of the institutional environment in these transition countries, Wang and Xu (2011) argue. In such circumstances the government intervenes not only in the formulation of investment policy, but also in its implementation and even in firms' operations, particularly those of state-owned enterprises. A variety of approaches, including the provision of favourable land, tax and financing policies, have been adopted to attract tourism investment (Wang and Xu, 2011).

Force 2: The threat of substitute products

A substitute can be regarded as something which meets the same needs as the product of the industry.

For example – an individual wishing to cross the English Channel between England and France can choose to travel by cross-channel ferry or by the train service using the channel tunnel. These products all provide the benefit to the customer of crossing to France, despite the fact the ferry and rail services are provided by different industries.

The extent of the threat from a particular substitute will depend upon two factors.

THE EXTENT TO WHICH THE PRICE AND PERFORMANCE OF THE SUBSTITUTE CAN MATCH THE INDUSTRY'S PRODUCT

Close substitutes whose performance is comparable to the industry's product and whose price is similar will be a serious threat to an industry. The more indirect the substitute, the less likely the price and performance will be comparable. Since most *THE* products are of relatively high cost and the expenditure is usually seen as a luxury rather than a necessity, the products will compete for disposable income with other high-cost items such as cars and 'white goods' (refrigerators and washing machines).

THE WILLINGNESS OF BUYERS TO SWITCH TO THE SUBSTITUTE

Buyers will be more willing to change suppliers if switching costs are low or if competitor products offer lower price or improved performance. This is also closely tied in with the extent to which customers are loyal to a particular brand. The more loyal customers are to one supplier's products (for whatever reason) then the threat from substitutes will be accordingly reduced.

> ### KEY CONCEPT
>
> **Switching costs**
>
> One of the key strategic manoeuvres in maintaining customer loyalty is to increase the cost – to the customer – of changing to a new supplier. If switching costs are high, then customers will have an economic disincentive to switch and hence will tend to stay with the existing supplier. For direct substitutes, switching costs may be increased by customer loyalty schemes or promotional offers to existing customers.
>
> For indirect substitutes there are likely to be higher actual or perceived switching costs, since the benefits derived from say a holiday or attendance at a festival are very different from those derived from buying say a new washing machine, yet they both compete for a share of consumers' disposable income.

Competitors in an industry will attempt to reduce the threat from substitute products by improving the performance of their products, by reducing costs and prices, and by differentiation.

> ### KEY CONCEPT
>
> **Direct and indirect substitutes**
>
> There are very few products for which there is no substitute. A substitute can be defined as a product that offers substantially equivalent benefits to another. This criterion – that of receiving equivalent benefits – can be met in two ways: directly and indirectly.
>
> Direct substitutes are those that are the same in substance. Direct substitutes may simply be competitive brands or competing destinations. Singapore Airlines, Malaysia Airlines and Thai Airways are direct competitors for air services to and from south east Asia, whilst Amsterdam, Paris and London are directly competing destinations in the European international short-break market.
>
> Indirect substitutes are those that are different in substance but which can, in certain circumstances, provide the same benefit. Thus international air travel and teleconferencing are different in substance but can provide similar benefits in certain circumstances. If a meeting is required to discuss new product ideas the two indirect substitutes should be considered. If however the purpose of the business trip is to meet potential suppliers or view new hotel or event facilities it is unlikely that teleconferencing would provide an adequate substitute.

Force 3: The bargaining power of buyers

The extent to which the buyers (customers) of a product exert power over a supplying organization depends upon a number of factors. Broadly speaking, the more power that buyers exert, the lower will be the transaction price. This has obvious implications for the profitability of the supplier. The factors that affect the relative power of buyers include:

THE NUMBER OF CUSTOMERS AND THE VOLUME OF THEIR PURCHASES

The fewer the buyers and the greater the volume of their purchases, the greater will be their bargaining power. A large number of buyers each acting largely independently of each other and buying only small quantities of a product will be comparatively weak.

For example – the major cruise lines operating in the Caribbean (of which there are relatively few) have power over the many competing small Caribbean island destinations when deciding on their cruise schedules and negotiating port charges. On the other hand, individual travellers will have limited bargaining power when dealing with large cruise lines since there are many such customers but relatively few cruise lines.

THE NUMBER OF BUSINESSES SUPPLYING THE PRODUCT AND THEIR SIZE

If the suppliers of a product are large in comparison to the buyers, then buying power will tend to be reduced. The number of suppliers also has an effect – fewer suppliers will tend to reduce the bargaining power of buyers as choice and the ability to 'shop around' is reduced.

For example – individual airlines wanting to serve London, and wanting to serve the lucrative business market in particular, are faced with a difficult situation. The three largest London airports (Heathrow, Gatwick and Stansted) are no longer owned and operated by a single company, BAA plc, as they were until 2013, when BAA plc relinquished control of Gatwick and Stansted. Nevertheless, Heathrow is by far the largest, has the greatest number of business clients and has the most connectivity with other destinations. This gives the London Heathrow airport operator a strong position when negotiating landing rights with airlines.

SWITCHING COSTS AND THE AVAILABILITY OF SUBSTITUTES

If the costs of switching to substitute products are low (because the substitutes are close in terms of functionality and price), then customers will be accordingly more powerful.

For example – customers would not normally be financially penalized for moving their business from one Spanish resort to another, or for moving a concert from one venue to another (unless contractually bound).

It should be borne in mind that buyers are not necessarily those at the end of the supply chain. At each stage of a supply chain, the bargaining power of buyers will have a strong influence upon the prices charged and the industry structure.

For example – in the supply chain for hotel rooms at a particular destination the buyers include individual business and leisure customers, tour operators, travel intermediaries (such as travel agencies and internet comparison sites), airlines and other transportation groups, and event promoters. The amount of power which each buyer exerts can differ substantially. Those buyers which can buy in bulk and provide the accommodation provider with guaranteed occupancy levels will be able to exert far greater pressure on the hotels in question than individual customers.

In summary, the relative power of buyers is likely to be most powerful when:

- there are few of them and they purchase large quantities;
- there are a large number of suppliers;
- the size of the buyers is large relative to the size of the suppliers;
- switching costs for buyers from one product supplier to another are low;
- substitute products are available; and
- switching costs between suppliers is low.

When the opposite conditions apply then buyers will be weak.

Force 4: The bargaining power of suppliers

Organizations must obtain the resources that they need to carry out their activities from resource suppliers. These resources fall into the four categories we have previously encountered: human, financial, physical and intellectual.

Resources are obtained in resource markets where prices are determined by the interaction between the organizations supplying a resource (suppliers) and the organizations from each of the industries using the particular resource in question. It is important to note that many resources are used by more than one industry. As a result, the bargaining power of suppliers will not be determined solely by their relationship with one industry but by their relationships with all of the industries that they serve.

The major factors determining the strength of suppliers are:

THE UNIQUENESS AND SCARCITY OF THE RESOURCE THAT SUPPLIERS PROVIDE

If the resources provided to the industry are essential to it and have no close substitutes then suppliers are likely to command significant power over the industry. If the resource can be easily substituted by other resources, then its suppliers will have little power.

For example – it is for this reason that people with rare or exceptional skills can command higher salaries than lesser-skilled people. The music artist or sports team represents the talent appearing at a concert festival or major sports event, for instance. The power of the personal or team brand is such that they provide the principal *unique selling point* (USP) for the event. Consequently the artist or members of the sports team command high salaries since the event depends directly on their participation for its success.

Similarly the limited number of aerospace suppliers gives them considerable power. The worldwide suppliers of large jet aircraft are limited to two (Boeing of the USA and Airbus, a collaboration between France, Germany and Spain with participation by the UK) whilst the large-scale suppliers of jet engines are limited to four (General Electric and Pratt and Whitney of the USA, Rolls Royce of the UK and SNECMA of France).

HOW MANY OTHER INDUSTRIES HAVE A REQUIREMENT FOR THE RESOURCE?

If suppliers provide a particular resource to several industries then they are less likely to be dependent upon one single industry. Thus, the more industries to which they supply a resource, the greater will be their bargaining power.

For example – in some of the most developed accommodation markets such as London, Dubai and New York, hotels often find it difficult to recruit an adequate supply of staff as they have to compete for labour with many other industries. Consequently staff members are frequently supplied from foreign countries with lower wage rates and/or higher unemployment levels.

SWITCHING COSTS BETWEEN SUPPLIERS

In some cases switching between suppliers may be difficult and costly. Close working relationships may have been built up over a protracted period of time so that any new supplier would not have the necessary knowledge or experience required or systems and services may have been tailored towards the requirements of a particular supplier.

For example – an airline which operated an all-Boeing fleet of aircraft would find it difficult to switch quickly to supply from Airbus since pilots would have been trained for Boeing aircraft, capacity would have been calculated using Boeing seat configurations, engineers would have been trained to maintain Boeing aircraft and spares would have been bought for the Boeing aircraft.

Conversely, the costs of switching for an event management company in moving the concert they are organizing and promoting in a particular city from one venue to another may be very low.

THE NUMBER AND SIZE OF THE RESOURCE SUPPLIERS

If the number of organizations supplying a resource is small and the number of buyers is large, then the power of the suppliers over the organizations will be greater in any industry. If the suppliers are small and there are a large number of them, they will be comparatively weak, particularly if they are small in comparison to the organizations buying the resource from them.

For example – most of the suppliers of food and services to an international hotel group such as Sheraton are weak because they are small in comparison to the hotelier. Hotel groups will have a number of suppliers at their various locations and are able to switch suppliers if necessary to gain lower input costs or higher quality.

In summary, suppliers to an industry are likely to be most powerful when:

- the resource that they supply is scarce;
- there are few substitutes for it;
- switching costs are high;
- they supply the resource to several industries;
- the suppliers themselves are large;
- the organizations in the industry buying the resource are small.

When the opposite conditions apply then suppliers will be weak.

Force 5: The intensity of rivalry among competitors in the industry

Businesses within an industry will compete with each other in a number of ways. Broadly speaking, competition can take place on either a price or a non-price basis.

- Price competition involves businesses trying to undercut each other's prices, which will, in turn, be dependent upon their ability to reduce costs of production.
- Non-price competition will take the form of branding, advertising, promotion, additional services to customers and product innovation.

In some sectors of *THE* competitive rivalry is fierce, while in others it is less intense or even non-existent since oligopolies or monopolies are formed.

For example – the competition amongst upscale hotels in Las Vegas, USA, has been intense over recent years (see short case illustration below). A building boom during the 1990s and early years of the 2000s was followed by economic slowdown after 2008, which affected occupancy rates and led to heavy discounting of room rates.

This can be contrasted with rail services in many countries such as France, Italy, Germany, Malaysia and China where state-controlled enterprises hold monopoly (or near monopoly) positions.

SHORT CASE ILLUSTRATION

Competitive rivalry: Las Vegas hotel occupancy rates

It may be a cliché to say so but Las Vegas, Nevada, is unlike any other city in America. From its humble origins as a small desert town with a few hotels and saloons that served the workers who built the nearby Hoover Dam, the town has mushroomed, constantly adding hotels and attractions. Older hotels like the Dunes and the Sands were demolished to make room for the new properties. People travel to Las Vegas for business, with convention business having increased markedly in recent years, and for leisure, driven by gaming and high-quality entertainment.

The Las Vegas Convention and Visitors Authority (LVCVA) gathers a variety of data that is used to measure the health and growth of the economic engine that drives the Las Vegas economy. In 2012 some 39.7 million visited the town, but the Las Vegas hotel market is intensely competitive and continually seeking ways to attract additional visitors through price incentives, refurbishment of existing facilities and new building and through adding attractions.

Nevertheless overall occupancy rates have fallen from their 2007 peak as the economic recession following the 2008 banking crisis took its toll as shown in Figure 8.2.

The overall occupancy rate for 2012 of 84.4 per cent is still high by most standards, but occupancy rates vary enormously between high weekend demand and lower occupancy rates during the week. Variable occupancy rates in turn lead to highly elastic pricing structures. Prices usually rise in Las Vegas at weekends and fall during the intervening period, in marked contrast to most city-based accommodation markets, which exhibit higher rates during the week to cater for business demand.

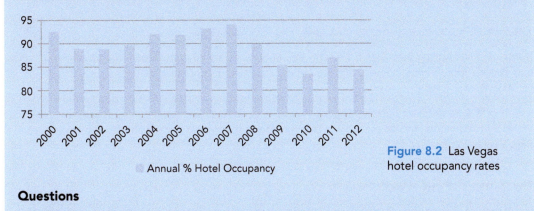

Annual % Hotel Occupancy

Figure 8.2 Las Vegas hotel occupancy rates

Questions

1. Explain the pattern of demand for hotel accommodation in Las Vegas and contrast it with most other city markets.
2. Contrast the competitive rivalry in Las Vegas with a state-controlled railway company.

In highly competitive markets companies engage in regular and extensive monitoring of key competitors.

Four examples might be:

- examining price changes and matching any significant move immediately;
- examining any rival product change in great detail and regularly attempting new initiatives in one's own organization;

- watching investment in new competing operations; and
- attempting to poach key employees.

In Figure 8.1 it can be seen that the other four forces point inwards towards this fifth force.

This representation is intentionally to remind us that the strength of this force is largely dependent upon the contributions of the other four that 'feed' it. However there are also some conditions within the industry itself that may lead specifically to a higher degree of competitive rivalry. These specific factors include the following:

THE RELATIVE SIZE OF COMPETITORS

When competitors in a sector are of roughly equal size there is a possibility that rivalry is increased as the competing companies try to gain a higher degree of market dominance but profits fall as a result of this increased rivalry.

Conversely in situations where there is a dominant organization, there may be less rivalry (and consequently higher levels of profitability) because the larger organization is often able to stop or curtail moves by smaller competitors.

For example – in relation to Macao, Sheng (2011) argues that there has been local underinvestment and a large influx of foreign labour, and in such circumstances large transnational enterprises may make their profits at the expense of local businesses. As a consequence Sheng maintains that it is the government's responsibility, China in the case of Macao, to regulate foreign investment in a way that is conducive to sustainable development.

THE NATURE OF COSTS IN INDUSTRY SECTORS

If sectors of an industry have high fixed costs in that they are capital intensive, rivalry amongst competitors may become more intense as price-cutting becomes a way of filling capacity.

For example – in the cruise sector and amongst hotels, tour operators, event managers and airlines, discounting is commonplace during the period close to departure, when the accommodation is required or the event is scheduled to take place. This is as a result of the inherent perishability of the product and the high level of fixed costs.

THE MATURITY OF THE MARKETS SERVED

If the market is mature and thus only growing slowly competition is likely to be more intense than a market that is still growing vigorously. This is because in a mature market the only way for an organization to achieve higher sales is by taking market share from competitors and consequently rivalry is increased. In markets which are still growing vigorously, however, new opportunities are opening up for organizations and thus sales can be increased without taking market share from competitors.

THE DEGREE OF BRAND LOYALTY OF CUSTOMERS.

If customers are loyal to brands then there is likely to be less competition and what competition there is will be non-price. If there is little brand loyalty then competition will be more intense.

For example – cruise passengers, for instance, have traditionally been very loyal to a particular cruise line and even to their preferred ship whereas North European package tourists taking Mediterranean holidays have shown themselves to be willing to switch brands freely lured by a high level of price competition. Such brand loyalty is closely linked to a further factor that of differentiation.

THE DEGREE OF DIFFERENTIATION

Where products can be easily differentiated rivalry is likely to be less intense whereas where differentiation is difficult rivalry is likely to be more intense.

For example – continuing the example from above, it is relatively easy to differentiate a cruising product through the type, size, quality and crew of a ship. By contrast, with regard to a package holiday to the Mediterranean, tour operators may use similar types of aircraft, accommodation, ground-handling agents and distribution channels, and offer the same destination choice. Consequently in such cases, the opportunities to differentiate their product offerings are more limited.

GOVERNMENT REGULATION

The degree of government regulation will have an influence over the extent of competitive rivalry in a sector. The international airline industry was traditionally heavily regulated with governments taking direct roles in setting inter-governmental agreements in order to exert control.

For example – international air travel between many countries has been regulated through a complex web of bilateral treaties negotiated between the governments at either end of air routes, and although much deregulation has taken place, many restrictions still remain. Similarly, in the UK the government acting through the Civil Aviation Authority's Air Travel Organisers' Licence (ATOL) system seeks to control the capacity of air inclusive tour operators. In both these cases rivalry might be more intense if government regulation ceased to exist.

By contrast government controls over the international hotel sector are rare other than through normal planning restrictions.

THE HEIGHT OF EXIT BARRIERS

The height of exit barriers (the ease with which organizations can leave the sector) will have an impact upon competitive rivalry. Where high capital costs have been incurred as with the purchase of aircraft, cruise liners or the construction of hotels or visitor attractions, it may be difficult to exit from these sectors, as these assets cannot easily be put to other uses and may be difficult to sell particularly in times of economic downturn. Consequently overcapacity may persist in such sectors for a period of time leading to increased rivalry between competitors.

For example – issues in relation to over-capacity in some Asian hotel markets such as Hong Kong and Shanghai are discussed by Tsai and Gu (2012) and Zheng and Gu (2011) respectively, while Lee and Jang (2012) assess potential overcapacity issues in US lodging provision.

A high degree of rivalry will usually reduce the potential profitability of an industry and may lead to innovations which serve to stimulate consumer demand for the *THE* products being offered. In recent years, many sectors of *THE* have become more competitive as the result of the influence of several factors including:

- technology advances;
- government deregulation;
- government privatization;
- economic slowdown in many economies;

- removal of restrictions on foreign travel; and
- removal of limits on supply.

For example – the competition amongst European tour operators to secure hotel rooms and self-catering accommodation rooms at prime Spanish resorts; the competition between European cities as short-break destinations; the growth of Dubai as a tourist destination; the increasingly crowded schedule of European summer music festivals; and the increased competition in the air travel market between Europe and North America are all examples of increasingly competitive sectors of *THE*.

THINK POINTS

- Explain how Porter's five forces framework works as a tool of industry analysis.
- What are the limitations of the five forces framework?
- Using examples from *THE*, explain what *entry barriers* are and the link between their 'height' and the likely profitability of an industry.

The five forces framework and profitability – a summary

As has been discussed, a relationship can be established between an organization's position in respect to the five forces and its potential profitability. Table 8.1 summarizes how the five forces can help to determine company and industry profitability.

Table 8.1 Porter's five forces and profitability – a summary (after Campbell *et al.*, 2002:141)

Force	Profitability likely to be higher if there is/are:	Profitability likely to be lower if there is/are
Bargaining power of suppliers	Weak suppliers	Strong suppliers
Bargaining power of buyers	Weak buyers	Strong buyers
Threat of new entrants	High entry barriers	Low entry barriers
Threats from substitute products	Few possible substitutes	Many possible substitutes
Competitive rivalry	Little rivalry	Intense rivalry

Limitations of the five forces framework

Porter's five-force framework represents a good starting point for the understanding of competitive forces and has obvious value as a tool for managers seeking a better understanding of such forces. However, the framework is subject to several important limitations. The major limitations of the framework are as follows.

IT IMPLIES THAT SUPPLIERS, BUYERS AND COMPETITORS ARE THREATS

The framework is built on the premise that suppliers, buyers and competitors represent threats that need to be tackled. However some organizations have built successful strategies on the basis of building close working relationships with suppliers, buyers and competitors.

Collaborative (or cooperative) strategy has become an important part of the overall *THE* competitive landscape and takes a number of forms involving aspects such as strategic and marketing alliances; partnering, networking and clustering. In various ways all these activities (see Chapter 11) separate organizations, or parts of them, work together for mutual benefit and in many cases public and private sectors work together in so-called public–private partnerships.

This facet of strategy for *THE* organizations has generated a broad literature having been discussed by a number of authors on subjects relating to:

- Airlines: Kleymann and Seristö (2001); Evans (2001a); Morrish and Hamilton (2002); Hanlon (2007); and de Man *et al.* (2010).
- Travel intermediaries: Evans (2001b).
- Tourism and hospitality: Crotts *et al.* (2000); Go and Appelman (2001); Chathoth and Olsen (2003); Fyall and Garrod (2005); Pansiri (2008); Ramayah *et al.* (2011); and Cabiddu *et al.* (2013).
- Public–private partnerships: Hall (1999); and Bramwell and Lane (2000).
- Events and attractions: Long (2000); Aas *et al.* (2005); and Stokes (2006).
- Destinations: Wang and Fesenmaier (2007); and Wang *et al.* (2012).

IT CLAIMS TO ASSESS INDUSTRY PROFITABILITY

Porter (1980) argues that the framework makes it possible to assess the potential profitability of a particular industry. While there is some evidence to support this claim, there is also strong evidence to suggest that company-specific factors are more important to the profitability of individual businesses than industry factors (Rumelt, 1991).

IT IMPLIES THAT THE FIVE FORCES APPLY EQUALLY TO ALL COMPETITORS IN AN INDUSTRY

In reality, the strength of the forces may differ from business to business. The framework implies that if, for example, supplier power is strong then this will apply to all the businesses in the industry. In fact, supplier power may differ from business to business in the industry. Larger businesses will face less of a threat from suppliers than will smaller ones. Similarly, businesses with strong brand names will be less susceptible to buyer power and substitutes than those with weaker brands.

Notwithstanding the criticisms, Porter's five forces analysis has been influential and is widely applied. As with other simplifying models it has to be applied carefully and critically and should be used as one form of evidence to be used in conjunction with others.

The short case illustration below applies Porter's five forces analysis to the European airline industry.

SHORT CASE ILLUSTRATION

Forces driving competition: The European airline industry

New Entrants

- relatively high entry barriers
- high capital costs for start-ups
- well-established brands
- some examples of tacit government support for national 'flag carriers'
- shortages of airport take-off and landing slots at some major airports
- corporate jets, low cost carriers, and regional airlines challenging larger more established airlines.

Buyers

- decreasing customer loyalty
- airline frequent flyer programmes
- greater choice on some routes
- complicated and confusing fare structures
- competition from charter carriers on some routes
- consolidation amongst travel intermediaries
- increasing consumer use of price comparison sites.

Substitutes

- development of high-speed trains across Europe;
- extensive motorway network for car usage;
- new telecommunication technologies such as teleconferencing.

Suppliers

- *oligopoly* of aircraft and aircraft engine suppliers;
- oligopoly of aircraft leasing companies;
- local monopolies of infrastructure providers (airports and surface transport);
- national monopolies and under capacity of air traffic control providers and air space.

Rivalry among competitors

- Varies on different routes but increasing generally.
- Increasing price competition and continuing quality and service competition.
- Extensive use of CRS systems and increasing use of internet distribution.
- Sophisticated yield management systems in widespread use enabling price discrimination to take place.
- Collaboration through strategic alliances and code-sharing.
- Charter, regional and new low-cost entrants providing increased competition.
- Established carriers adding to service quality or dropping service features to compete with new entrants.
- Market liberalization during the 1990s and continuing privatization of state-owned airlines.
- Failure of some established national flag carrier airlines (Swissair and Sabena) led to re-birth as fully commercial concerns.

Air transport is only one example of the various sectors in which industry leaders are facing increased competition from low-cost companies (Ryans, 2008:xiii). However, Casey (2010:176) suggests that the advent of low-cost air travel has ushered in one of the biggest revolutions in tourism and travel since the package holiday's arrival half a century earlier. Indisputably low-cost airlines (LCAs) have contributed to changing how people travel, the geography of air services and competition between airlines and between cities or regions (Fageda *et al.*, 2011).

The nature of competition has changed in recent years as market liberalization has enabled LCAs to enter the market. New operational practices, lower service levels, internet distribution and the operation of a single aircraft type keep costs at low levels in a manner pioneered by Southwest Airlines in the USA. The LCA model started in Europe in 1995. Irish airline Ryanair's Michael O'Leary visited Southwest in 1991 and adapted its model a few years later (Creaton, 2005). Subsequently easyJet was launched as an LCA in 1995 and many others have followed.

Today, LCAs can be found in many areas worldwide including Asia–Pacific, Maghreb, Middle East, South America and even some countries in Sub-Saharan Africa (Francis *et al.*, 2006; Macário and Reis, 2011; Albers *et al.*, 2010; Zhang *et al.*, 2008; Fageda *et al.*, 2011). In 2010, there were an estimated 94 LCAs worldwide carrying 650 million passengers – 23.5 per cent of total passengers (Fageda *et al.*, 2011) – though it can be argued that the distinction between LCAs and full-service airlines is breaking down in many regions (as full-service airlines cut costs), making the differentiation between the two increasingly difficult.

The newer entrants to the European airline industry have induced new demand for air travel among the population and new city pairings previously thought not to be viable have emerged. An environment of deregulation and privatization has resulted in a more open market but congestion at several major airports, air traffic control limitations, and strong entrenched airlines, sometimes benefitting from tacit government support have limited competition on some routes. The turbulent environment has placed a high degree of pressure on airlines to adapt in order to survive. As a sign of adaptation the formation of strategic alliances has become a defining characteristic of the global air transport sector.

Questions

1. Outline the factors leading to the rise of low-cost airlines.
2. How has the intensity of competitive rivalry changed in recent years in the European airline industry?
3. Comment on why it might be useful to apply Porter's Five Forces model in situations like the European Airline industry.

The competitive analysis of nations or regions

Porter's Five Forces Analysis was developed during the 1980s and has proved to be highly influential in providing a framework for the analysis of a wide variety of organizations, including those in the public and not-for-profit sectors.

In a later work, Porter (1990) develops his ideas relating to competition and relates them to countries in trying to explain why some nations are more competitive than others and some regions within countries are also more competitive than others. For a full discussion of the contribution of this framework to strategic thinking see: Stonehouse *et al.* (2007:Ch. 5).

Tourism greatly contributes to wealth creation as it did to Spain in the 1960s and 1970s, to Greece since the early 1970s and to Turkey since the mid-1980s (Wahab and Cooper, 2001). Porter developed his 'Diamond' analysis to assess the competitive advantage of nations or regions. The Diamond represents a framework consisting of four factors which individually and through the linkages between them can be used to assess the degree to which a country or region enjoys a relative competitive advantage.

The four factors are:

1. factor conditions (physical resources, human resources, capital resources, infrastructure and knowledge resources);

2. market structures, organization and strategies;

3. demand conditions; and

4. related and supporting industries.

In addition Porter identified two further factors: *government* (which can influence any of the four factors) and *chance events* (which can shift competitive advantage in unpredictable ways).

In Porter's analysis each of these factors should be analysed and the relative strengths or weaknesses evaluated. An important aspect of Porter's work relates to the importance of *clusters*. Clusters are geographic concentrations of interconnected companies and institutions in a particular field. They encompass an array of linked industries and other entities, which are important to competition. The best-known international examples that are often cited include the cluster of technology companies south of San Francisco in California's Silicon Valley and Tennessee's music industry cluster centred on Nashville (See Porter *et al.*, 2012); but many other examples exist around the world.

In *THE* sectors clustering clearly takes place in terms of supplying the needs of visitors at destinations and many *THE*-oriented companies and ancillary services tend to cluster around transport hubs, particularly airports.

For example – London's Gatwick airport in the UK and nearby towns such as Crawley host a growing cluster of travel-related firms. These companies include: loyalty scheme provider The Air Mile Travel Company; tour operators British Airways Holidays, Citalia and First Choice (part of Tui plc), and Kuoni; and electronic travel intermediary ebookers. Companies such as these benefit from access to a hub airport, ease of access to London as an international business and professional centre; access to airline partners; and access to an experienced pool of labour.

Clustering also takes place in various sectors of *THE*, though the phenomenon and its implications has not been widely investigated in the academic literature. However, Novelli *et al.* (2006) consider clustering of tourism SMEs in a UK context while Jackson (2006) and Jackson and Murphy (2006) consider destination clustering in Australian and Chinese contexts respectively. In his study Hawkins (2004) considers the sustainability of business opportunities for tourism businesses clustering around a network of world heritage sites in Indonesia.

The short case illustration below demonstrates the importance of clustering in the context of the Italian meetings and conventions sector.

SHORT CASE ILLUSTRATION

Clustering: Italian meetings and conventions

The meetings, incentive travel, conventions, and exhibitions (MICE) industry is one of the fastest growing segments of *THE* today, both in a global and country-specific context (Kim *et al.*, 2003). Though it is difficult to define precisely it is clear that it is growing steadily in many countries. Kim *et al.* (2003) and Kim and Chon (2009), for instance, report the increased importance of MICE to the South Korean economy.

Bernini (2009) investigated the clustering of the convention industry in Italy. In 2004, it was estimated that Italian convention turnover was worth approximately US$28 billion to the Italian economy or about 26 per cent of the total turnover produced by the tourism and hospitality industry.

The study identifies a number of clusters of convention activity. Preeminent amongst these are the two 'capital' clusters of Rome and Milan and a further cluster of eight 'leading convention towns' which are Venice, Turin, Rimini, Genoa, Bologna, Naples, Palermo and Florence. Given Italy's cultural and artistic heritage a further cluster of minor arts cities such as Verona and Siena is also identified as being important.

Rome and Milan are the two largest Italian cities and represent the national and business capitals respectively and hence have many ancillary services for convention delegates such as hotel accommodation, restaurants and international airports. Both cities have about 220 convention-oriented firms which represent about 43 per cent of the national total. Bernini (2008:884) states that 'these clusters are the result of the co-location of complementary firms, not involved in the same activity, which benefit from the network membership and alliance dynamics'.

Questions

1. If you were managing a company running conventions in Rome or Milan, what specific benefits might you hope to gain through clustering and are there likely to be any drawbacks?
2. What other examples can you cite of clustering in *THE* sectors and do you think clustering of such activities is likely to be more or less important in the future?

Thus where such clusters can be identified a mutually supportive set of enterprises exists that compete and collaborate in such a way that may give rise to competitive advantage being established. The short case illustration below illustrates the importance of clustering to hotels.

SHORT CASE ILLUSTRATION

Clustering of hotels: Premier Inn

The advantages of clustering have long been recognized by leading hotel groups. Many such groups concentrate their development efforts on particular geographical territories so as to focus management expertise and to obtain economies of scale and scope. Many hotel groups, for instance, have regional or area managers whose responsibilities cover the overall activities of several hotels within a group. Clustering in this way is rather different from the clustering involving numerous companies clustering for mutual benefit; in these sorts of cases clustering is done largely to achieve operating efficiencies or so-called *economies of scope*.

Whitbread plc, for example, uses the advantages of clusters in developing its Premier Inn brand which has grown quickly to become Britain's largest hotel chain. In an investor presentation in March 2013, the company demonstrated the advantages of clustering. At that time there were 656 Premier Inn hotels arranged into 110 clusters. In Manchester for example the 14 Premier Inn hotels in the area are arranged into three clusters: Manchester Trafford, Manchester City and Manchester North.

By clustering in this way opportunities are provided for:

- managerial expertise to be shared between hotels;
- associated costs shared between several sites rather than just one;
- staff to follow a clear career progression;
- standardization to be facilitated between sites;

- the pooling of consumables procurement and administration; and
- processes (e.g. staff training and hiring) to be streamlined within the cluster.

www.whitbread.co.uk

Questions

1. Explain how the clustering involved in the Premier Inn case is different to conventions in Italy in the previous case illustration.
2. What factor might inhibit working in clusters for a group of hotels and could clustering work on a basis other than geography?

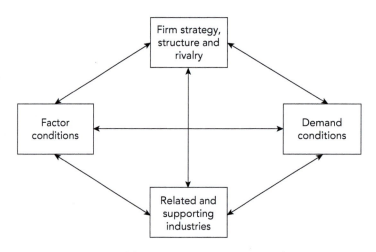

Figure 8.3 Porter's Diamond Analysis of the competitive advantage of nations

The Porter Diamond is shown in Figure 8.3.

The Diamond analysis of Michael Porter has been widely applied in *THE* settings (see for example: Enright and Newton, 2004; Hawkins, 2004; Jackson, 2006; Jackson and Murphy, 2006; Hong, 2009; Ribes *et al.*, 2011; and Porter *et al.*, 2012).

For example – in their paper, which is based on earlier work, Wahab and Cooper (2001) discuss Porter's Diamond in a tourism context and apply the analysis to Egypt. The authors conclude that whilst Egypt clearly has great potential as a tourist destination, some of the potential had (at the time of writing) still to be realized and that consequently the country had not yet reached a position of comparative advantage.

The strategy in practice example below outlines some of the steps a tourist destination area might take in practice in order to achieve a competitive advantage over rivals.

STRATEGY IN PRACTICE

Improving the competitiveness of a tourist destination

A list of guidelines for improving the competitiveness of a tourist destination were produced by Smeral (1998) building on the work of Porter (1990) and also reported by Wahab and Cooper

(2001). The guidelines include factor conditions (which are background considerations) but of specific importance to the tourism sector are: market structures, organization and strategies; demand conditions; and government.

Market structures, organization and strategies:

- Image-building within the context of global competition.
- Aggressive and innovative marketing to foster growth and expansion of tourism's value added through special interest motivations.
- Information coordination and intensification of knowledge pertaining to a destination's strengths and weaknesses within a competitive environment at the international, national and regional levels.

Demand conditions:

- Expanding the destination's share of quality tourism movement from primary, secondary and opportunity markets offering them quality facilities and services.
- Reducing demand seasonality through strategies aiming at guaranteeing a steady flow of tourist traffic from various markets.
- Enhancing tourist receipts by concentrating mostly on higher spending tourist arrivals.
- Encouraging repeat visitors through offering them diversified attractions separately presented or in combined forms.
- Holistically oriented local, regional and national policy.

Government:

- Encouragement of systematic and continuous research into tourism market trends, demand changes and innovations in leisure and tourism activities.
- Serious and systematic control of and guidance to the travel and tourism industries to keep total quality at its most appropriate to face global competition.
- Improving academic and professional education and intensifying quality training in tourism to meet industry requirements.
- Eliminating 'red tape' and avoiding all administrative hurdles including any conflict or overlapping of jurisdictions.
- Ameliorating environmental quality.
- Proactive management of change.

Smeral (1998), also reported by Wahab and Cooper (2001)

An alternative approach to competitive and collaborative analysis

Competitive and collaborative arenas

It is not always the case that businesses in an industry compete with each other – they might, from time to time, have reasons to collaborate. Accordingly, in some 'arenas' businesses compete whilst in others they may work together.

At the root of this understanding is the fact that organizations and industries are open systems – they interact with many environments. The 'arenas' in which the organization operates are described below.

- *The industry* – the industry within which the organization currently deploys its resources and competencies in producing products.
- *Resource markets* – the markets from which the organization, its competitors and other industries obtain their resources.
- *Product markets* – markets where the organization sells its products. These can be subdivided into:
  - markets for the organization's products
  - markets for substitute products
  - new markets to which the organization may be considering entry.
- *Other industries* – where businesses possess similar competencies to those of the organization. Such industries are important for two reasons:
  - the business may be considering entry to them
  - organizations in these industries are potential competitors who may enter the business's industry and markets.

Each of these arenas must be analysed as they directly affect an organization's competitive positioning and hence its chances of outperforming competitors.

The competitive and collaborative arena framework builds upon Porter's five forces framework but explicitly recognizes that the competitive environment is divided into four separate but interrelated arenas.

THINK POINTS

- Explain the concept of Porter's Diamond Analysis in relation to nations or regions.
- Using examples from *THE* explain what is meant by *clustering* and assess its usefulness for *THE* organizations.
- Define and distinguish between competition and collaboration.

A resource-based approach to environmental analysis

Limitations of existing frameworks of analysis

This chapter has so far concentrated on explaining the traditional strategic management frameworks employed in the analysis of the competitive environment.

The resource-based approach to strategic management, which is particularly associated with the work of Jay Barney in the early 1990s (Barney, 1991) and more recently was assessed by Barney *et al.* (2011) emphasizes the importance of core competencies in achieving competitive advantage. In doing so it employs a different approach to analysis of the competitive environment since several limitations (Fleisher and Bensoussan, 2003:Ch. 6) were identified with the existing frameworks in that they:

- Do not sufficiently integrate external and internal analysis.
- Pre-suppose that businesses are naturally competitive and not collaborative in their behaviour.
- Tend to emphasize product and service markets rather than those where organizations obtain their resources.
- Do not adequately recognize the fact that organizations themselves may alter their own competitive environments by their competence leveraging and building activities (see the Key Concept in Chapter 2).

- Do not adequately recognise the fact that organizations currently outside a company's industry and market may pose a significant competitive threat if they possess similar core competencies and distinctive capabilities.

- Similarly do not recognize that the leveraging of existing competencies and the building of new ones may enable businesses to compete outside their current competitive arenas.

The resource-based framework

A resource-based framework for analysis of the business and its competitive environment is shown in Figure 8.4. Analysis is divided into five interrelated areas:

- the organization;
- its industry;
- product markets (existing markets, markets for substitutes, potential new markets);
- resource markets; and
- other industries.

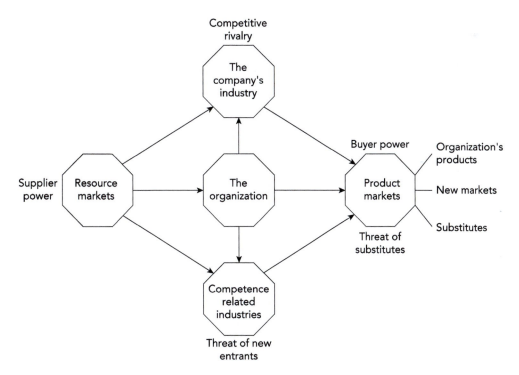

Figure 8.4 The resource-based model of strategy

(*Note:* competence-related industries are those where businesses possess similar competencies to those of competitors.)

The significance of each area is considered overleaf.

The organization

The organization concerns the configuration of the internal value chain, its competencies, resources and core competencies and is discussed in Part 2 of this book (particularly in Chapter 2).

The organization's industry

The organization's industry consists of the business and a group of companies producing similar products, employing similar capabilities and technology.

Analysis of the industry therefore examines over time (for each player in the industry):

- the skills and competencies of the competitors;
- the configuration of value-adding activities;
- the technologies employed;
- the number and relative size of competitors in the industry;
- the performance of competitors (particularly in financial terms);
- the ease of entry to and exit from the industry; and
- the strategic groupings (see later in the chapter for a discussion of this concept).

This analysis will assist the organization in gaining greater understanding of its core competences, its major competitors and their core competences, and competitive and collaborative opportunities and threats.

Product markets

Product markets are those where businesses deploy their competences and sell their products and services. A business may operate in one or more product markets. In addition, a business will be interested in understanding markets to which it is considering entry on the basis of its core competences and also markets for substitute products. Each of these markets will have its own characteristics and each market can be analysed in terms of:

- customer needs and motivations;
- unmet customer needs;
- market segments and their profitability;
- the number of competitors to the market and their relative market shares;
- the number of customers and their relative purchasing power;
- access to distribution channels;
- potential for collaboration with customers;
- ease of entry;
- potential for competence leveraging; and
- need for new competence building.

In commercial (for-profit) settings, unless an organization's products and services are sold at a profit the business will ultimately fail. Market-driven businesses, which set out to meet existing customer needs, anticipate their currently unmet needs and actually seek to shape the needs of their customers are likely to be the most successful.

Thus, when companies have products which have leading positions in their identified markets they are likely to be most successful. An example of a market-leading product which competes partly on the basis of its sustainable practices is provided by the Peruvian company Inkaterra which is illustrated below.

SHORT CASE ILLUSTRATION

Market leading products: Inkaterra, Peru

Inkaterra has pioneered and promoted sustainable tourism in Peru and at the same time operated a profitable business model. The successful coexistence of profitable commercial activities funding scientific research brought it to international prominence in 2012 with the award of the prestigious World Travel and Tourism Council (WTTC) Tourism for Tomorrow World Conservation Award.

Founded in 1975 Inkaterra is a for-profit tourism company that actively supports scientific research and biodiversity conservation and hosts over 65,000 tourists each year. The company, which employs over 500 staff mainly drawn from local towns and villages, operates five hotels in the area of Machu Picchu (which was declared a UNESCO World heritage site in 1983) and the Madre de Dios area of the Amazon rainforest in southern Peru. The Inca settlement of Machu Picchu which dates from the 15th century is a highly sensitive site because of environmental degradation which has been monitored by the World Monuments Fund.

Since its inception an outstanding guest experience along with a commitment to conservation and local community benefit have been driving forces in the company's growth and development. Sustainable tourism principles and practices are used to facilitate the increased understanding among travellers of the biodiversity and cultural heritage of the Andes and the Amazon of Peru.

With the establishment of The Inkaterra Association (ITA), focused solely on biodiversity research, a model partnership was formed between a for-profit tourism company and a non-profit research organization. Funding for scientific study of rare fauna and flora as well as educating national and international tourists about Peru's diverse tropical ecosystems and wildlife has been provided. Projects include: sequestering over 3 million tons of carbon dioxide within the rainforest in the Inkaterra Ecological Reserve (monitored with the University of Leeds, UK since 1989); a Rescue Centre for endangered 'Spectacled Bears'; and the restoration of many acres of rare native cloud forest. Inkaterra hotels also practise environmentally friendly operations, including state-of-the-art irrigation systems utilizing rain and grey water, and closed-pit composting and recycling which together with other measures provide a dedicated 100 per cent carbon-neutral hotel stay for guests.
www.inkaterra.com; www.wttc.org; www.wmf.org; www.whc.unesco.org, Sloan et al. (2013).

Questions

1. Consider why Inkaterra might be considered to be a market-leading product.
2. Consider the sustainability of Inkaterra's business model.

Market subgroups

An important part of understanding the market is identifying subgroups within the market that share common needs.

Such shared characteristics will cause specific customer groups to have different needs and to act and behave differently to other customer groups (or *segments*). Fundamentally, segmentation means subdividing the total market into customer sub-groupings, each with their own distinctive attributes and needs.

Customer groups are commonly segmented according to demographic variables (or 'people dividers') like age, sex, occupation, socio-economic grouping, race, lifestyle, buying habits and geography (i.e. where they live). When customers are other businesses they can be grouped by the nature of the business, organization type and by their size.

Each segment is then analysed for its size and potential profitability, for customer needs and for potential demand, based on ability and willingness to buy. Segmentation analysis assists in the formulation of strategy by identifying particular segments and consumer characteristics that can be targeted.

The concept of market segmentation is discussed in greater depth in Chapter 6.

Customer motivations

Once market segments have been identified, they must be analysed to reveal the factors that influence customers to buy or not buy products. It is particularly important to understand factors affecting customer motivations like:

- sensitivity to price;
- sensitivity to quality; and
- the extent of brand loyalty.

Differences in customer motivations between market segments can be illustrated by reference to the market for air travel. The market can be segmented into business and leisure travel. Customers in each group have very different characteristics and needs.

For example – business travellers are not particularly price-sensitive, but are sensitive to standards of service, to scheduling, and to availability of connections. Leisure travellers on the other hand are generally much more price-conscious and are less sensitive to scheduling and connections.

Market research has an important role to play in building understanding of customer needs so that they can be targeted by appropriate product or service features.

Potential new markets are those where the product or service bought by customers is based upon similar competencies to those of the organization or where customer needs are similar to those of customers in the business's market. If conditions are favourable the organization may consider using its current competences to enter new markets. Of course it may also have to build new competencies in order to be able to meet new customer needs.

Resource markets

Resource markets are those markets where organizations obtain finance, human resources, materials, equipment, services, etc. It is evident that businesses will normally operate in several such markets, each with its own characteristics, depending upon the company-specific resources that are required. Resource markets can be analysed in terms of:

- number of actual and potential resource suppliers;
- size of suppliers;
- supplier capabilities and competencies;
- potential for collaboration with resource suppliers;
- access by competitors to suppliers;
- the nature of the resource and the availability of substitutes.

By analysing each of its resource markets, the managers of a business can identify the extent of competition that they face from suppliers of resources, the competition that they face from other competitors using the same resources and the potential for collaboration with suppliers (if appropriate).

Competence-related industries

Other industries comprising businesses possessing similar competencies and which often produce products or services, which are substitutes for those of the business in question must also be analysed. This analysis is necessary for three reasons in that the organization may:

- face a threat from other competitors possessing similar competencies, which may seek to enter its industry and markets;
- be able to enter industries where competencies are similar to those, which it already possesses; and
- be able to enter the markets currently served by competitors in the competence related industry.

Competence-related industries can be analysed for:

- Key competencies of the businesses in the industry.
- The number and size of the businesses in the industry.
- The threat from competitors in such industries who may leverage their competencies to enter the markets of the business.
- Opportunities for the business to leverage its existing competencies and build new ones in order to enter competence-related industries and their markets.
- Substitutability of the products of the industry for those of the business – how close the substitute product is to satisfying the same consumer demands as the business's product or service.

A summary of the resource-based model

The competence-/resource-based model is more complex than the five forces framework, but offers a more comprehensive analytical framework in that it enables an organization to:

- Establish the extent of competition within its own industry and market.
- Assess the threat of competition from competitors in industries where similar competencies to their own are employed.
- Identify other markets it may be able to enter by leveraging its existing competencies and by adding new ones.

Once adapted, the framework enables managers to understand:

- The nature of competition within the industry and markets (both product and resource) in which they operate.
- The threat from competitors in other industries.
- Potential opportunities in new industries and markets.

> **THINK POINTS**
>
> - What is a resource market?
> - Explain how the resource based model aids the understanding of industry analysis.
> - Compare and contrast Porter's Five Forces model with the resource-based view of Industry analysis and assess the usefulness of both.

Strategic group analysis

What are strategic groups?

A business can rarely confine its analysis to the level of the industry and markets in which it operates. It must also pay particular attention to its closest competitors which are known following as its *strategic group* (Porter, 1980). Strategic groups cannot be precisely defined but they consist of organizations:

- possessing (or potentially possessing) similar competencies;
- serving customer needs in the same market segment; and
- producing products or services of similar quality.

Such analysis (see for example Söllner and Rese, 2001; Fleisher and Bensoussan, 2003; Gursoy *et al.*, 2005; and Short *et al.*, 2007) allows the managers of a business to compare its performance to that of its closest competitors in terms of profitability, market share, products, brands, customer loyalty, prices and so on. In this way managers are able to *benchmark* the performance of their organization against their closest rivals. It is important that the closest rivals are identified carefully.

For example – although the five-star Ritz Hotel in Paris's Place Vendôme and a small guesthouse in rural France both provide the same service (providing accommodation and dining for guests) and hence are technically competitors, they operate in quite different strategic groups.

They are unlikely to appeal to the same customers (or will at least appeal to the same customers but at different times) and their products, distribution channels, identities and prices are quite different. The Ritz strategic group (that grouping of hotel operators that compete with each other directly) will include other luxury hotels in Paris and key world capitals, whereas the rural French guesthouse strategic group will include other guesthouses in rural France.

Strategic group analysis (sometimes called competitive group analysis) is an interesting way of analysing the competitive structure in an industry and assessing the positioning of key competitors. By plotting how the major organizations in an industry (or a sub-sector within it) compete along two competitive dimensions, managers start to understand the relative position of their company and its products or services relative to major competitors.

There are three steps involved in the analysis and graphical representation of strategic groups:

- Identify the important competitive dimensions in an industry, taking into account the information you have available. Competitive dimensions are the specific factors the firms are using to compete within the industry. The competitive dimensions might include factors such as quality (perceived or actual), price, geographical scope or typical customer types.
- Construct two-dimensional plots of the competitive dimensions.
- Analyse the firm's position relative to competitors.

SHORT CASE ILLUSTRATION

Strategic group analysis: Wyndham Hotel Group

Many companies produce informative, revealing and analytical prentations for investors which are usually available online. Though such presentations need to be viewed critically, (since they are designed to attract investors and present the organization in the most favourable light), they nevertheless give valuable insights into:

- the organization's financial position;
- the strategic thinking of its management; and
- the position of the organization relative to competitors.

Wyndham Hotel Group, headquartered in New Jersey, USA, is one of the world's largest and most diverse hotel companies with approximately 7,380 hotels worldwide. Wyndham Worldwide, which forms a coherent portfolio of hospitality-focused businesses, was formed in 2006 when the diversified Cendant corporation was broken up into four separate businesses following financial irregularities.

The company is one of the world's leading diversified providers of travel-related products and services for businesses and individual consumers, with leading brands in lodging franchising; vacation ownership; and vacation rentals and exchange. Hotel Brands include Wyndham, Travelodge, Days Inn, Howard Johnson and Ramada and brands such as RCI, Hoseasons and Canvas Holidays in its rentals and exchange division.

The company's presentation to investors portrays the company; as shown in Figure 8.5, as befitting from its diversified income streams (from its three divisions) which deliver high levels of cash flow which, it contends, enable it to deliver superior growth. The strategic group analysis, adapted from its presentation below, shows the company in relation to five other (unnamed) lodging groups.

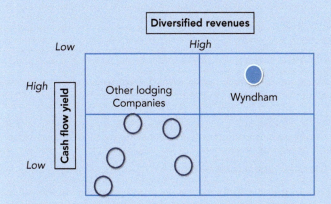

Figure 8.5 Wyndham hotel group presentation

Questions

1. Consider why diversified revenues and cash flow yields are important measures for Wyndham to use in comparison with competitors.
2. Consider what other measures for strategic group analysis might have been used in this case?

Competitor profiling

The strategic group analysis potentially enables an organization to identify its key competitors in a way that is easily communicated to both internal and external stakeholder groups.

A useful further step is to profile these key competitors in order to gain a more detailed insight as to:

- how and where the competitors might pose a *threat*; or
- under what circumstances might collaboration be sought, and thereby *opportunities* realized.

This sort of analysis is very useful in providing a detailed analysis of each competitor, but caution needs to be exercised in interpreting the information gathered.

Industries and competitors are dynamic as opposed to static and the competitors an organization faces have an interest in providing forward information that is not too useful to their rivals. Thus the information gathered often represents mainly historical data that is in the public domain (as with the Whitbread illustrative case below). Information based on future proposed changes to strategy for competitor organizations is usually much harder to obtain because it is likely be highly *commercially sensitive*.

Such an analysis might be carried out using the following headings:

- Overview
- Objectives
- Resources
- Past record of performance
- Current Products and services
- Present strategies.

The short case illustration below applies competitor profiling to the UK based hospitality company Whitbread plc.

SHORT CASE ILLUSTRATION

Competitor profiling: Whitbread plc

A hotel operator seeking to expand in the UK hotel market would need to profile existing key competitors.

One of these would certainly be Whitbread plc, which has developed the leading brand of 'lodge' hotels that offer modern value-for-money accommodation with few added extras but consistent and reliable standards. The company is traded on the London stock market and is a constituent member of the FTSE 100 index of the UK's largest companies.

Overview: The UK Company Whitbread plc was a major brewer founded in the middle of the nineteenth century. The end of the twentieth century and the start of the twenty-first marked a watershed in the company's history, as Whitbread sold its breweries and then exited its pubs and bars business. After several decades of diversification, during which the beer and pubs giant branched out into new markets, Whitbread refocused its business on the growth areas of hotels, restaurants and health and fitness clubs. The reinvention of Whitbread as a leading UK hospitality business naturally coincided with the end of the brewing and pub-owning tradition which Samuel Whitbread had begun over 250 years earlier. Today Whitbread can be viewed as the UK's biggest hospitality company, employing over 40,000 people with the leading lodge hotel brand and coffee shop operating brands: Premier Inn and Costa respectively.

Objectives: The priorities, on behalf of shareholders, are to grow the business and to achieve annual improvements in the return on their capital. The business is focused on growth sectors of the UK leisure market – lodging, eating out and coffee consumption. The company has stated objectives by 2018 of:

increasing the number of UK Premier Inn rooms by 45 per cent by 2018 to around 75,000;

doubling the system-wide sales of Costa to £2 billion.

Resources: The company in 2012/13 had a turnover of about £2.0 billion million with profits before tax standing at approximately £355 million representing a return on capital approaching 14 per cent. Approximately 40,000 people are employed by the company of which about 29,000 are employed by the company's hotel and restaurant businesses.

Past record of performance: The company has consistently recorded growth in its levels of profitability over recent years having risen in each trading year from £239 million in 2009/10 to £411.8 million in 2013/14 (before tax and amortization) despite difficult trading conditions in its core UK market. The repositioning of the company some years ago to move away from brewing to focus on three core areas (hotels, restaurants and coffee shops) in which it possesses strong brands has shown consistent results.

Current Products and Services: In the hotel sector the company has hitherto concentrated its efforts on its Premier Inn brand which with about 650 hotels and 51,000 rooms is the UK's leading hotel operator. Exploratory market testing has taken place in the Middle East and India where the group has four and two hotels respectively. The Premier Inn brand has grown significantly in recent years where distressed property values caused by the economic downturn have provided opportunities to expand quickly in a cost-effective manner.

Present strategies: The company is trying to achieve its stated objectives through a strategy which has fours stated facets:

- *Winning teams* – building highly engaged teams, through recruitment, investing in training and offering appropriate rewards.
- *'Customer heartbeat'* – putting the customer at the heart of all the company's actions through the people delivering services and through investing in the estate.
- *Profitable growth* – delivered through selective investment in Premier Inn brand and organic growth in Costa in domestic and selected international markets while maximizing group synergies through a focus on delivering a consistently good customer experience in a service and people intensive environment and utilizing central property expertise.
- *'Good together'* – the company aims to be a force for good in our communities focusing on Teams and Community involvement, customer wellbeing and care for the environment.

Categorization and analysis by author based on Whitbread plc
Annual Report and Accounts, 2012/13 available at www.whitbread.co.uk

Questions

1. Consider what you would regard as Whitbread's Strengths and Weaknesses if you were a manager at a competing hotelier.
2. Consider why a competitor might not want to rely too heavily in its decision making on the competitor profiling tool of analysis alone.

Industry and market critical success factors

In any industry and its associated markets, there will be certain factors, which are of fundamental importance to the success of the businesses operating within that competitive environment. These are known as critical success factors (CSFs – see the Key Concept in Chapter 4). Competitive analysis allows managers to identify CSFs. A business must ensure that its competencies and core competencies directly address these CSFs.

CSFs differ between individual industries and markets. In the pharmaceutical industry CSFs will be in the areas of research and development and production. For *THE* organizations, however, CSFs are likely to lie in areas such as the reputation of the brand, service excellence, product range, product features, distribution and innovation.

The concept of 'success factors' is attributed to Ronald Daniel of the international management consultancy firm McKinsey and Company, writing in 1961. The concept was developed further into 'critical success factors' by Rockart (1979).

Critical success factors (CSFs) can be viewed as those elements that are vital for a strategy to be successful. Thus a critical success factor drives the strategy forward and makes the strategy successful, hence the use of the word 'critical'.

CSFs have been applied broadly in various *THE* contexts with a large academic literature having emerged which applies the concept to all sectors of *THE*. See for example: Lade and Jackson (2004) and Andersson and Getz (2009) – festivals and events; Brotherton (2004) and Avcikurt *et al.* (2011) – hospitality; Getz and Brown (2006), Haven-Tang *et al.* (2007), Baker and Cameron (2008) and Hughes and Carlsen (2010) – tourism and tourist destinations.

The short case illustration below uses the work of Getz (2004) to illustrate the specific CSFs found to be important in relation to Canadian destination marketing organizations.

SHORT CASE ILLUSTRATION

CSFs: Canadian destination marketing organizations

Getz (2004) undertook research in order to gain a better understanding of the nature and competitive importance of bidding for events by destination marketing organizations in Canada, with emphasis on identifying critical success factors for winning bids. Data were collected on the goals and nature of the event-bidding process from convention and visitor bureaux in Canada.

The study found that Canadian bureaux were very active in bidding on a diverse range of events, especially meetings, conventions, political events and sports events. Most bureaux encouraged and assisted other local organizations to make bids for themselves and concentrated on major events with city-wide economic impacts.

In this context the most important critical success factors for winning bids were found to be:

- strong partners;
- excellent presentations; and
- treating each bid as a unique process.

Many respondents in the study also felt their destination needed bigger and better facilities and more marketing/bidding resources.

Questions

1. Why might Getz's research be useful for the Canadian Destination Marketing Bureaux to consider in formulating their strategies for future development?

2. Consider the CSFs for another aspect of *THE* you are familiar with.

Sometimes confusion exists about the distinction between CSFs and another popular term in strategy, namely *Key Performance Indicators* (KPIs).

THINK POINTS

- Using relevant examples from *THE*, explain the concepts of *Strategic Group Analysis* and *Competitor Profiling*.
- Explain what is meant by *KPIs* and *CSFs* and comment on their usefulness in managing *THE* organizations.
- Using relevant examples from *THE* explain what the limitations of *Competitor Profiling* might be.
- Explain the links between industry analysis and *CSFs*.

Whereas CSFs are concerned with those factors or elements without which the strategy would not be successful, KPIs represent a measurement tool. They are measures that quantify management objectives and enable the measurement of strategic performance.

For example – whereas the KPI is a measure of progress towards a goal or objective, CSFs allow the strategy to be successful by, for instance, attracting new customers through putting measures in place to attract those customers:

- KPI = Sales rise 10 per cent each year over a five-year period.
- CSF = Installation of a new Customer Relationship Management (CRM) system and enhanced booking functionality on website (and, indirectly, influencing and acquiring new customers through customer satisfaction).

SMALL BUSINESS FOCUS

In the previous chapter it was pointed out that large organizations may in some cases have some influence over the external environment or they can protect themselves against the dangers posed. This statement has validity, both for the macro level of external analysis, but also for the micro or competitive level as discussed in this chapter.

Unlike large firms, which have some chance of shaping or influencing their competitive environment (at least to some degree), smaller organizations generally have little choice but to accept the competitive environment in which they operate (Haberberg and Rieple, 2001:499). The smaller company has to focus on minimizing the harmful consequences (as best they can) and adapting to the circumstances.

In order to react to the competitive environment it is necessary for the smaller business first to understand it. Consequently analysis of some sort is of great importance to smaller businesses, just as it is to larger businesses, so that they are able to react quickly and effectively to competitive threats.

It is vital for small business to understand who they are really competing against. This is not always as obvious as it may sound. To understand who the *real* competitors are and the type of competitive threat that they pose will require a focus on the particular arena in which competition takes place and may need the adaptation of relevant tools and techniques.

There are generally two possibilities with regard to identifying key competitors (Lasher, 1999:66). The most important competitors may be those companies that are identified as the:

- leaders in the segments targeted; or
- companies that are in some sense close.

Close competitors might be those competitors which are close geographically or might be close in a different sense.

For example, close competitors might be competing for the same suppliers, distribution channels or offering similar product features.

Thus, when dealing with smaller companies the scope of the analysis carried out needs to be considered carefully. Establishing the relevant scope of analysis may help identify whom the key competitors might be. Furthermore, the tools and techniques of competitive analysis outlined in this chapter may need to be modified for the circumstances.

For example – a large international restaurant chain or hotel company in its analysis of competitors might take a global view of competition and compare itself in the main to other international branded chains.

However, a single family-owned restaurant or hotel may be more concerned with the local town in which it operates. Hence the boundaries of the analysis are largely established as the boundaries of the town itself (though there needs to be some recognition that consumers are mobile and can switch to a different town). Therefore the relevant competitors may include the international branded chains but may also include other smaller restaurant or hotel businesses operating in their vicinity.

The single family business (of which of course there are many in *THE*) may not have the competitive advantages of the branded chain elsewhere, but in their particular town they might be able to compete very effectively. This effective competition provided by the independent business might be on the basis of characteristics such as: location, pricing or reputation for good service.

A *Strategic Group Analysis* and *Competitor Profiling* could help in this situation, in that they may aid the hotelier or restaurateur in identifying the key competitors in the industry. The scope of the analysis, however, in this case would not be on the industry regionally, nationally or even internationally, but would be based on the town in which the hotel or restaurant is situated.

To continue the example, a Strategic Group Analysis could be carried out on the basis of the two attributes of price and location for a single family-owned hotel business in the town as shown in Figure 8.6.

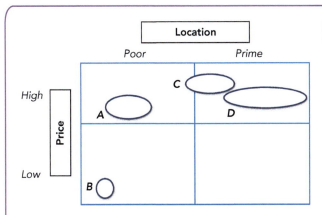

Figure 8.6 Strategic group analysis for hotels in a particular town

In Figure 8.6 four Strategic Groups are identified:

A. midscale branded chain hotels with moderate prices in poor-to-moderate locations;

B. budget branded chain hotels with low prices in poor locations;

C. upscale branded hotels with high prices in moderate locations; and

D. independent hotels with moderate-to-high prices in prime locations

It is assumed that the independent family-run hotel in question is in Group D and is, like others in the group, well established and this has enabled it to have a prime location, unlike the newer branded arrivals in town. The location enables the independent hotels to charge higher prices than would otherwise be the case, enabling the independent hotel in question within this group to compete effectively in this particular town.

Following on from the strategy group analysis, a competitor profiling exercise could be carried out by the independent family-run hotel in order to gain a deeper understanding of the competitive positioning of each identified competitor.

In this way some of the tools of analysis covered in this chapter are adapted to the relevant circumstances and scope of a smaller company. In different circumstances this type of analysis might be adapted and applied to:

- A small event management company specializing in particular types of events, such as leadership development courses or firework displays.
- A tour operator specializing in a particular market niche, such as selling holidays to a specific set of Greek islands that the company knows well.

This chapter has also covered different ways in which smaller companies can group together in order to protect themselves against larger competitors. One such way is through *clustering* together with similar companies so that a city or area becomes known for certain specialisms. Smaller companies can also gain protection through collaboration and networking (which was touched upon in this chapter) and will be covered in greater detail in Chapter 11.

CHAPTER SUMMARY

Analysis of the micro-environment or competitive analysis is intended to increase managers' understanding of the industry and markets in which their business operates. The process begins with a clear identification of those industries and markets and their key characteristics. The process then allows managers to develop a detailed picture of the industry in which they operate, the markets for their products, the markets where they obtain their resources, their strategic grouping, markets that they may wish to enter in the future, and industries with related competencies.

This analysis will enable managers to identify:

- critical success factors in their industry and markets;
- needs and opportunities for competence building and leveraging; and
- the potential for collaboration with suppliers, distributors, customers and competitors.

REFERENCES

Aas, C., A. Ladkin and J. Fletcher (2005) 'Stakeholder Collaboration and Heritage Management', *Annals of Tourism Research*, 32 (1): 28–48.

Albers, S., C. Heuermann and B. Koch (2010) 'Internationalization Strategies of EU and Asia-Pacific Low Fare Airlines', *Journal of Air Transport Management*, 16 (5): 244–50.

Andersson, T. and D. Getz (2009) 'Tourism as a Mixed Industry: Differences between Private, Public and Not-for-Profit Festivals', *Tourism Management*, 30 (6): 847–56.

Avcikurt, C., H. Altay and M. O. Ilban (2011) 'Critical Success Factors for Small Hotel Businesses in Turkey: An Exploratory Study', *Cornell Hospitality Quarterly*, 52 (2): 153–64.

Baker, M. J. and E. Cameron (2008) 'Critical Success Factors in Destination Marketing', *Tourism and Hospitality Research*, 8 (2): 79–97.

Barney, J. (1991) 'Firm Resources and Sustained Competitive Advantage', *Journal of Management*, 17 (1): 99–120.

Barney, J. B., D. J. Ketchen and M. Wright (2011) 'The Future of Resource-Based Theory Revitalization or Decline?' *Journal of Management*, 37 (5): 1299–315.

Benson, A. M. and S. Henderson (2011) 'A Strategic Analysis of Volunteer Tourism Organisations', *The Service Industries Journal*, 31 (3): 405–24.

Bernini, C. (2009) 'Convention Industry and Destination Clusters: Evidence from Italy', *Tourism Management*, 30 (6): 878–89.

Bramwell, B. and B. Lane (eds.) (2000) *Tourism Collaboration and Partnerships: Politics, Practice and Sustainability*, Bristol: Channel View Publications.

Brotherton, B. (2004) 'Critical Success Factors in UK Budget Hotel Operations', *International Journal of Operations and Production Management*, 24 (9): 944–69.

Cabiddu, F., T. W. Lui and G. Piccoli (2013) 'Managing Value Co-creation in the Tourism Industry', *Annals of Tourism Research*, 42: 86–107.

Campbell, D., G. Stonehouse and B. Houston (2002) *Business Strategy: An Introduction*, Oxford: Butterworth Heinemann.

Casey, M. (2010) 'Low Cost Air Travel: Welcome Aboard?' *Tourist Studies*, 10 (2): 175–91.

Chathoth, P. K. and M. D. Olsen (2003) 'Strategic Alliances: A Hospitality Industry Perspective', *International Journal of Hospitality Management*, 22 (4): 419–34.

Creaton, S. (2005) *Ryanair: How a Small Irish Airline Conquered Europe*, London: Aurum.

Crotts, J. C., D. Buhalis and R. March (2000) 'Introduction: Global Alliances in Tourism and Hospitality Management', *International Journal of Hospitality and Tourism Administration*, 1 (1): 1–10.

Daniel, D. R. (1961) 'Management Information Crisis', *Harvard Business Review*, 39 (5): 111–20.

de Man, A. P., N. Roijakkers and H. De Graauw (2010) 'Managing Dynamics through Robust Alliance Governance Structures: The Case of KLM and Northwest Airlines', *European Management Journal*, 28 (3): 171–81.

Enright, M. J. and J. Newton (2004) 'Tourism Destination Competitiveness: A Quantitative Approach', *Tourism Management*, 25 (6): 777–88.

Evans, N. (2001a) 'Collaborative Strategy: An Analysis of the Changing World of International Airline Alliances', *Tourism Management*, 22 (3): 229–43.

—— (2001b) 'Alliances in the International Travel Industry: Sustainable Strategic Options?' *International Journal of Hospitality and Tourism Administration*, 2 (1): 1–26.

Fageda, X., J. L. Jiménez and J. Perdiguero (2011) 'Price Rivalry in Airline Markets: A Study of a Successful Strategy of a Network Carrier against a Low-Cost Carrier', *Journal of Transport Geography*, 19 (4): 658–69.

Fleisher, C. S. and B. E. Bensoussan (2003) *Strategic and Competitive Analysis: Methods and Techniques for Analysing Business Competition, 2002*, Upper Saddle River NJ: Prentice Hall.

Forsyth, P., J. King and C. Lyn Rodolfo (2006) 'Open Skies in ASEAN', *Journal of Air Transport Management*, 12 (3): 143–52.

Francis, G., N. Dennis, S. Ison, I. Humphreys, M. Aicken (2006) 'Where Next for Low Cost Airlines? A Spatial and Temporal Comparative Study', *Journal of Transport Geography*, 14 (2): 83–94.

Fyall, A. and B. Garrod (2005) *Tourism Marketing: A Collaborative Approach* (vol. XVIII), Bristol UK: Channel View Publications.

Getz, D. (2004) 'Bidding on Events: Identifying Event Selection Criteria and Critical Success Factors', in *Journal of Convention and Exhibition Management*, 5 (2): 1–24.

Getz, D. and G. Brown (2006) 'Critical Success Factors for Wine Tourism Regions: A Demand Analysis', *Tourism Management*, 27 (1): 146–58.

Go, F. M. and J. Appelman (2001) 'Achieving Global Competitiveness in SMEs by Building Trust in Interfirm Alliances', in S. Wahab and C. Cooper (eds.), *Tourism in the Age of Globalisation*, London and New York: Routledge, pp. 183–97.

Gursoy, D., M. H. Chen and H. J. Kim (2005) 'The US Airlines Relative Positioning Based on Attributes of Service Quality', *Tourism Management*, 26 (1): 57–67.

Haberberg, A. and A. Rieple (2001) *The Strategic Management of Organisations*, Harlow UK: FT Prentice Hall.

Hall, C. M. (1999) 'Rethinking Collaboration and Partnership: A Public Policy Perspective', *Journal of Sustainable Tourism*, 7 (3–4): 274–89.

Hanlon, J. P. (2007) *Global Airlines: Competition in a Transnational Industry*, London and New York: Routledge, pp. 262–77.

Haven-Tang, C., E. Jones and C. Webb (2007) 'Critical Success Factors for Business Tourism Destinations: Exploiting Cardiff's National Capital City Status and Shaping Its Business Tourism Offer', *Journal of Travel and Tourism Marketing*, 22 (3–4): 109–20.

Hawkins, D. E. (2004) 'Sustainable Tourism Competitiveness Clusters: Application to World Heritage Sites Network Development in Indonesia', *Asia Pacific Journal of Tourism Research*, 9 (3): 293–307.

Hong, W. C. (2009) 'Global Competitiveness Measurement for the Tourism Sector', *Current Issues in Tourism*, 12 (2): 105–32.

Hughes, M. and J. Carlsen (2010) 'The Business of Cultural Heritage Tourism: Critical Success Factors', *Journal of Heritage Tourism*, 5 (1): 17–32.

Jackson, J. (2006) 'Developing Regional Tourism in China: The Potential for Activating Business Clusters in a Socialist Market Economy', *Tourism Management*, 27 (4): 695–706.

Jackson, J. and P. Murphy (2006) 'Clusters in Regional Tourism an Australian Case', *Annals of Tourism Research*, 33 (4): 1018–35.

Kay, J. (1995) *Foundations of Corporate Success*, Oxford: Oxford University Press.

Kim, S. S. and K. Chon (2009) 'An Economic Impact Analysis of the Korean Exhibition Industry', *International Journal of Tourism Research*, 11 (3): 311–18.

Kim, S. S., K. Chon and K. Y. Chung (2003) 'Convention Industry in South Korea: An Economic Impact Analysis', *Tourism Management*, 24 (5): 533–41.

Kleymann, B. and H. Seristö (2001) 'Levels of Airline Alliance Membership: Balancing Risks and Benefits', *Journal of Air Transport Management*, 7 (5): 303–10.

Lade, C. and J. Jackson (2004) 'Key Success Factors in Regional Festivals: Some Australian Experiences', *Event Management*, 9 (1–2): 1–2.

Lasher, W. R. (1999) *Strategic Thinking for Smaller Businesses and Divisions*, Oxford: Blackwell.

Lee, C. F. and B. King (2006) 'Assessing Destination Competitiveness: An Application to the Hot Springs Tourism Sector', *Tourism and Hospitality Planning and Development*, 3 (3): 179–97.

Lee, S. K. and S. S. Jang (2012) 'Re-examining the Overcapacity of the US Lodging Industry', *International Journal of Hospitality Management*, 31 (4): 1050–8.

Long, P. (2000) 'After the Event: Perspectives on Organizational Partnerships in the Management of a Themed Festival Year', *Event Management*, 6 (1): 45–59.

Macário, R. and V. Reis (2011) 'Low Cost Airlines: Strategies and Reaction Patterns', in R. Macário and E. Van

De Voorde (eds.), *Critical Issues in Air Transport Economics and Business*, London and New York: Routledge, pp. 51–74.

McGahan, A. M. and M. E. Porter (1997) 'How Much Does Industry Matter, Really?', *Strategic Management Journal*, 18 (Summer Special Issue): 15–30.

Morrish, S. C. and R. T. Hamilton (2002) 'Airline Alliances , Who Benefits?' *Journal of Air Transport Management*, 8 (6): 401–7.

Novelli, M., B. Schmitz and T. Spencer (2006) 'Networks, Clusters and Innovation in Tourism: A UK Experience', *Tourism Management*, 27 (6): 1141–52.

Pansiri, J. (2008) 'The Effects of Characteristics of Partners on Strategic Alliance Performance in the SME Dominated Travel Sector', *Tourism Management*, 29 (1): 101–15.

Porter, M. E. (1980) *Competitive Strategy: Techniques for Analysing Industries and Competitors*, New York: Free Press.
—— (1985) *Competitive Advantage*, New York: Free Press.
—— (1990) *The Competitive Advantage of Nations*, Basingstoke: Macmillan.

Porter, M. E., M. Bernard, R. S. Chaturvedi, A. Hill, C. Maddox and M. Schrimpf (2012) 'Tennessee Music Cluster: Microeconomics of Competitiveness', Harvard Business School Presentation, May 2012.

Qu, R., C. Ennew and M. Thea Sinclair (2005) 'The Impact of Regulation and Ownership Structure on Market Orientation in the Tourism Industry in China', *Tourism Management*, 26 (6): 939–50.

Ramayah, T., J. W. C. Lee and J. B. C. In (2011) 'Network Collaboration and Performance in the Tourism Sector', *Service Business*, 5 (4): 411–28.

Ribes, J. F. P., A. R. Rodriguez and M. S. Jiménez (2011) 'Determinants of the Competitive Advantage of Residential Tourism Destinations in Spain', *Tourism Economics*, 17 (2): 373–403.

Rockart, J. F. (1979) 'Chief Executives Define Their Own Data Needs', *Harvard Business Review*, 57 (2): 81–93.

Rumelt, R. P. (1991) 'How Much Does Industry Matter?', *Strategic Management Journal*, 12 (3): 167–85.

Ryans, A. (2008) *Beating Low-Cost Competition: How Premium Brands Can Respond to Cut-Price Rivals*, Chichester: John Wiley & Sons.

Sheng, L. (2011) 'Foreign Investors Versus Local Businesses: An Urban Economics Model for Tourist Cities', *International Journal of Tourism Research*, 13 (1): 32–40.

Short, J. C., D. J. Ketchen, T. B. Palmer and G. T. M. Hult (2007) 'Firm, Strategic Group and Industry Influences on Performance', *Strategic Management Journal*, 28 (2): 147–67.

Sloan, P., W. Legrand and C. Simons-Kaufmann (2013) 'Social Entrepreneurship and Cultural Tourism in Developing Economies', in M. Smith and G. Richards (eds.), *Routledge Handbook of Cultural Tourism*, London and New York: Routledge, pp. 236–42.

Smeral, E. (1998) 'The Impact of Globalization on Small and Medium Enterprises: New Challenges for Tourism Policies in European Countries', *Tourism Management*, 19 (4): 371–80.

Söllner, A. and M. Rese (2001) 'Market Segmentation and the Structure of Competition: Applicability of the Strategic Group Concept for an Improved Market Segmentation on Industrial Markets', *Journal of Business Research*, 51 (1): 25–36.

Stokes, R. (2006) 'Network-Based Strategy Making for Events Tourism', *European Journal of Marketing*, 40 (5/6): 682–95.

Stonehouse, G., D. Campbell, J. Hamill and T. Purdie (2007) *Global and Transnational Business: Strategy and Management*, Chichester, UK: John Wiley & Sons.

Tavitiyaman, P., H. Qu and H. Q. Zhang (2011) 'The Impact of Industry Force Factors on Resource Competitive Strategies and Hotel Performance', *International Journal of Hospitality Management*, 30 (3): 648–57.

Tsai, H. and Z. Gu (2012) 'Optimizing Room Capacity and Profitability for Hong Kong Hotels', *Journal of Travel and Tourism Marketing*, 29 (1): 57–68.

Wahab, S. and C. Cooper (2001) 'Tourism, Globalisation and the Competitive Advantage of Nations', in S. Wahab and C. Cooper (eds.), *Tourism in the Age of Globalisation*, London and New York: Routledge, pp. 3–21.

Wang, C. and H. Xu (2011) 'Government Intervention in Investment by Chinese Listed Companies That Have Diversified into Tourism', *Tourism Management*, 32 (6): 1371–80.

Wang, Y. and D. R. Fesenmaier (2007) 'Collaborative Destination Marketing: A Case Study of Elkhart County, Indiana', *Tourism Management*, 28 (3): 863–75.

Wang, Y., J. Hutchinson, F. Okumus and S. Naipaul (2012) 'Collaborative Marketing in a Regional Destination: Evidence from Central Florida', *International Journal of Tourism Research*, 15 (3): 285–97.

Zhang, A., S. Hanaoka, H. Inamura and T. Ishikura (2008) 'Low-Cost Carriers in Asia: Deregulation, Regional Liberalization and Secondary Airports', *Research in Transportation Economics*, 24 (1): 36–50.

Zheng, T. and Z. Gu (2011) 'Overcapacity in Shanghai's High-End Hotel Sector: Analysis Based on an Inventory Mode', *Journal of Convention and Event Tourism*, 12 (4): 253–70.

WEBSITES

www.inkaterra.com
www.lvcva.com
www.whc.unesco.org
www.whitbread.co.uk
www.wyndhamworldwide.com
www.wmf.org
www.wttc.org
www.discoverhongkong.com

FURTHER READING

Reference	Focus
Flagestad, A. and C. A. Hope (2001) 'Strategic Success in Winter Sports Destinations: A Sustainable Value Creation Perspective', *Tourism Management*, 22 (5): 445–61.	Competitive advantage Tourism Sport
Gomezelj, D. O. and T. Mihali (2008) 'Destination Competitiveness: Applying Different Models, the Case of Slovenia', *Tourism Management*, 29 (2): 294–307.	Competitive advantage Tourism destinations Slovenia
Hjalager, A. M. (2000) 'Tourism Destinations and the Concept of Industrial Districts', *Tourism and Hospitality Research*, 2 (3): 199–213.	Clusters Tourism Hospitality
Jackson, J. and P. Murphy (2002) 'Tourism Destinations as Clusters: Analytical Experiences from the New World', *Tourism and Hospitality Research*, 4 (1): 26–52.	Clusters Tourism
Kim, B. Y. and H. Oh (2004) 'How Do Hotel Firms Obtain a Competitive Advantage?' *International Journal of Contemporary Hospitality Management*, 16 (1): 65–71.	Competitive advantage Hotels
Lee, M. J. and K. J. Back (2005) 'A Review of Economic Value Drivers in Convention and Meeting Management Research', *International Journal of Contemporary Hospitality Management*, 17 (5): 409–20.	Clusters Conventions
Saxena, G. (2005) 'Relationships, Networks and the Learning Regions: Case Evidence from the Peak District National Park', *Tourism Management*, 26 (2): 277–89.	Clusters Tourism UK
Tinsley, R. and P. Lynch (2001) 'Small Tourism Business Networks and Destination Development', *International Journal of Hospitality Management*, 20 (4): 367–78.	Clusters Tourism SMEs

CASE LINKAGES

Case 1	Strategic alliances in the airline industry
Case 2	Tourism Queensland
Case 4	Hyatt Hotels
Case 5	Days Inn

SWOT analysis for tourism, hospitality and event organizations

Introduction and chapter overview

The previous chapters have covered the internal analysis of organizations (Chapters 3–6) and the external environment which organizations face (Chapters 7 and 8).

It is important to bring all the analytical work together in one place so as to provide a summary and to provide a firm foundation for the next stage – formulating strategy. This work provides an opportunity to summarize the previous analysis in the form of a SWOT.

SWOT analysis (sometimes referred to as TOWS analysis) is an acronym where the letters stand for *strengths*, *weaknesses*, *opportunities* and *threats*. The analysis has become a major analytical tool and has become firmly established in the literature. Although it is the most widely used technique for summarizing the results of the various types of analysis described in the previous chapters, it nevertheless can be implemented in various ways. Consequently different approaches are suggested in the many texts which cover this analytical technique, but here a simple, structured and logical approach is suggested.

The chapter first covers the general principles of SWOT analysis before going on to consider how the analysis should be implemented.

LEARNING OBJECTIVES

After studying this chapter, you should be able to:

- recognize the way in which SWOT has been applied in various *THE* contexts;
- explain what is meant by SWOT analysis;

- understand the coherent and logical sequence that exists between the SWOT presentation and detailed internal and external analyses;
- describe how a SWOT should be constructed;
- consider the way in which points can be presented in a SWOT;
- apply the SWOT analysis principles appropriately in *THE* settings;
- understand the relationship between the SWOT analysis and strategic formulation.

SWOT analyses in tourism, hospitality and events

SWOT analysis has been widely applied in *THE* settings. It has been applied not only to organizations operating in the sectors of *THE*, but has also often been applied to destinations and individual events.

Karadakis *et al.* (2010), for example, produced a SWOT in which the mega sporting event of the Athens Olympics was analysed and Bardolet and Sheldon (2008) produced a SWOT comparing tourism in the Balearic Islands with Hawaii and found that there are many common factors. It has also been applied at the micro level (such as an individual hotel or a particular event) and at the macro level covering, say, an entire country or region or a group of hotels.

In applying SWOT analysis it is argued below that:

- strengths and weaknesses are normally factors which are internal to the organization, destination, etc. and can therefore be controlled by managers; whereas
- opportunities and threats are factors which are external to the organization and consequently are beyond managers' control.

However, in applying SWOT in *THE* settings it is very important to recognize that *THE* organizations, destinations, festivals and events rely very heavily on the resources that are available.

For example – the Mediterranean climate of southern Spain cannot be replicated in northern Europe; the grandeur of the Grand Canyon cannot be moved. Similarly the success of the annual Salzburg Festival of classical music (which was first held in the Austrian city in 1877), to some degree depends on the fact that the famous composer Wolfgang Amadeus Mozart was born there. Conversely, the unpredictable summer climate of northern Europe might be viewed as a weakness in trying to attract international summer visitors.

Thus, tourism, hospitality and events often rely very heavily on resources which are natural or which cannot be easily replicated or moved elsewhere. Although such resources are clearly *not* controlled by individual managers, they represent key factors that are given to managers and are underlying strengths (or possibly weaknesses). As such they can be viewed as internal to the analysis rather than external because they are integral to success or failure.

Many SWOTs applied in *THE* settings will thus cite climatic, geographical or social factors as strengths or weaknesses. These are resources which are relied upon and consequently it is argued it is legitimate to consider them as strengths or weaknesses rather than opportunities or threats.

For example – in their comparison of the Balearic and Hawaiian archipelagos, Bardolet and Sheldon (2008) cite 'the attractive climate' as a strength common to both destinations. It is clearly the case that the climate is a key part of the attraction in both cases and that this is an underlying resource upon which the destinations rely. However, it is also the case that managers in the two examples do not control the climate but they do rely on the nature of the climatic resources as an underlying strength which supports tourism, hospitality and events; and the associated businesses involved in the two archipelagos.

The short case illustration below demonstrates the use of the SWOT technique in relation to the destination of Macau.

SHORT CASE ILLUSTRATION

SWOT analysis applied to Macau

Macau, which lies on the western side of the Pearl River Delta, is one of the two special administrative regions of the People's Republic of China (PRC), the other being Hong Kong. The territory's economy is heavily dependent on gambling and tourism, but also includes manufacturing.

The sustainability of tourism development has become a leading issue of Macao in recent years. While the industry has grown dramatically over the last decade, such an issue has been expanding in importance in line with the growing contribution the industry makes to the territory's economy as a whole. With a population of about 500,000 and a land area of only 27.3 square kilometres, visitor arrivals have grown enormously and the increasing significance of the tourism industry has given rise to discussions regarding social and economic consequences.

Macao is a city with a blending of eastern and western cultures, has a mixture of Euro-Asian architecture and attracts large numbers of international tourists. Tourism employs approximately a third of the territory's workforce and generates about 40 per cent of the territory's gross domestic product (GDP).

Table 9.1 SWOT analysis applied to Macau

Strengths	Weaknesses
The unique historical background and Sino-Portuguese cultural features	Limited natural resources for tourism development
Glamorous events take place all year around.	The average length of stay of visitors is short at about one day
Simplified entry procedures to southern China with most visitors not requiring a visa in advance	A shortage of qualified local workers for its continuing tourism development
Excellent transportation infrastructure	

Opportunities	Threats
Macao's application for UNESCO World Heritage site status (subsequently granted)	Adversely affected by external shocks such as the Asian Financial Crisis and SARS outbreak
The economic relationship with Mainland China has been getting much closer	Many tourists arrive by air from Taiwan, the 'Mainland-Taiwan' issues may affect these decisions to visit or use Macao for transit
MICE tourism has been developing and could be a new source of tourism growth in the future	Countries such as Australia, South Korea, Laos and Malaysia have increasingly competed with Macao in the gaming market
	Posssible relaxation of gambling restrictions in mainland China

Source: Adapted from Pao (2004).

Macao is renowned as a gaming centre and indeed Macao is the world's largest centre for such activity. However, the tourism industry also comprises hotel and catering businesses, recreational activities and MICE activities. MICE (meetings, incentives, conventions and exhibitions) is a commonly used term which broadly covers the arrangement of symposiums, seminars, exhibitions, expositions, trade fairs, incentive events and cultural and sport events.

Questions

1. Explain the underlying logic behind presenting a *SWOT* in this case.
2. From a managerial point of view what is the fundamental difference between *strengths* and *weaknesses* on the one hand and *opportunities* and *threats* on the other?

General principles

The strengths and weaknesses are based on the internal analysis of an organization (which was covered in Chapters 3 to 6) and the opportunities and threats are based on the analysis of the environment which is external to the organization (which was covered in Chapters 7 and 8).

The key distinguishing characteristic between the strengths and weaknesses on the one hand and the opportunities and threats on the other is the degree of *control* that managers may have.

In many *THE* contexts (as noted in the previous section) the normal principles may be varied slightly in that underlying resources upon which the organization, destination, festival event, etc. rely (but which are clearly beyond the control of managers) may be considered as strengths or weaknesses. This is because they are given factors which remain in place largely unaltered.

With the internal strengths and weaknesses managers can exert control whereas with regard to the opportunities and threats managers may in certain circumstances have some influence but they will not be able to control such factors.

For example – if an organization has a strong balance sheet (a strength) this will have resulted from managerial decisions or if the organization is seen as being over-staffed (a weakness) managers can address the issue through reducing staff numbers. However, changing government policies; product changes by competitors; or a war breaking out (all of, which might produce opportunities or threats to an individual organization, depending on the circumstances) are beyond the control of organizational managers.

KEY CONCEPT

SWOT

SWOT is the key technique for presenting the results of strategic analysis. It provides a platform for going on to formulate the strategy for the future. The strengths and weaknesses should normally be based upon the internal analysis of the organization whilst the opportunities and threats should be based upon an analysis of the organization's external environment.

An important differentiator between the internal and external environments is control. Whereas managers can control the internal environment through the decisions they make, they cannot control the external environment.

Although it is very common in practice to begin the process of formulating strategy by asking the participants in a rather informal way to draw up a SWOT for their organization, such a process represents a limited use of the technique. It is however, useful for getting the participants to become quickly and fully engaged in the process of strategy formulation (Finlay, 2000). It can also help identify the wide range of factors which might warrant further more detailed investigation.

THINK POINTS

- Explain why is it necessary for a SWOT analysis to be based on other types of analysis?
- Explain how SWOT fits into the overall strategic management process.
- What is the major difference for managers when considering strengths and weaknesses on the one hand and opportunities and threats on the other?
- Explain why it is sometimes necessary to vary the general principles of a SWOT in *THE* contexts?

The final SWOT presented should though be based on a thorough, wide-ranging, detailed audit and assessment of an organization and its environment (Haberberg and Rieple, 2001). In this way points presented are evidence based and consequently can be fully justified. Thus the SWOT should be seen primarily as representing the end point of the analytical stage (rather than the starting point) in which findings can be presented in a clear, concise manner but which nevertheless are grounded in a robust framework of analysis.

It is useful to summarize what the SWOT is and is not:

- The SWOT represents a *position statement* stating where the organization is now in relation to its environment.
- The SWOT should clearly follow from a robust analysis of the internal and external environment.
- The strengths and weaknesses of the SWOT are normally based on the internal analysis of the organization's environment over which managers have control.
- The opportunities and threats of the SWOT are normally based on the external analysis of the environment facing the organization over which managers (normally) have no control.
- The strengths and opprtunities represent factors which help the organization acheve its objectives.
- The weaknesses and threats are factors which may prevent the organization from achieving its objectives.
- The SWOT is not the strategy itself and should not involve making statements about what should be done in the future.
- The SWOT provides a firm platform for planning for the future of the organization i.e. formulating the strategy which is the next stage in the strategic process.

SWOT Implementation

The SWOT is often presented in a table. Figure 9.1 shows a SWOT and its underlying logic.

The task of managers with regard to each element can be summarized as:

- *strengths* – build or protect so that they continue to be strengths;
- *weaknesses* – address so that they become strengths in the future or they are eliminated;
- *opportunities* – position the organization so that it is able to selectively take advantage of the opportunities available;

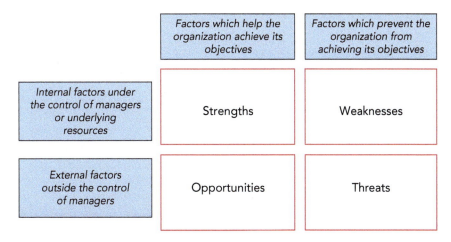

Figure 9.1 The logic of SWOT analysis

- *threats* – position the organization so that the threats are removed or that they are understood and the organization is protected from their impacts.

The SWOT should have a strategic focus in that it concentrates on those factors, which have:

- a major impact on past performance;
- a major impact on future performance; and
- distinguish the organization from its competitors.

In presenting the SWOT table a number of rules should be followed:

- *Avoid detail* – Too much detail should be avoided in presenting the SWOT, so that the key points can be clearly seen. Keep each point short and to the point so that an overview can quickly be gained. The detailed justifications for the points presented in the table should be presented separately.

- *Must have strategic focus* – The SWOT is a tool of strategic management and therefore the points presented in the SWOT must be strategic in nature rather than operational or tactical.

- *Points are often relative rather than absolute* – Many of the points presented in the SWOT may be relative rather than absolute and consequently a matter of some judgement. Thus it is difficult to say at exactly when a high level of financial *gearing* becomes a weakness or when a share of a particular market, load factors, occupancy levels or ticket sales become strengths.

- *Hard facts and softer factors are both important* – The SWOT should not concentrate solely on 'hard' facts (such as financial measures or market growth statistics) that can be measured or proven. Softer factors such as organizational culture or the leadership skills exhibited by managers may be more difficult to measure, but they are nevertheless important for organizational performance.

- *Strategic points should be prioritised and combined* – The most important points should be shown first and points that are not key or strategic in nature should be excluded. In some cases it may be necessary to combine points to make one large, overarching point. For instance, if a SWOT is partly based on a financial analysis of an organization, which indicates a strong financial position, the SWOT should not have individual points on high level of profitability, low gearing, adequate liquidity, etc. for to do so would confuse the presentation. The point presented in the SWOT should be that the organization has a strong financial position. The justification for making such a point would be provided by the assessments relating to profitability, gearing liquidity and so on.

- *Clear presentation* – The presentation should be specific, avoid blandness but be realistic in its assessment.

Two common errors in producing a SWOT are outlined below.

> ### DEFINITION/QUOTATION
>
> **Common errors with SWOT analysis**
>
> In his analysis of the problems of presenting a valid SWOT Richard Lynch (2012:305) recognizes two common errors:
>
> - 'Probably the biggest mistake that is commonly made in *SWOT* analyses is to assume the analysis is bound to be "correct" because it contains every conceivable issue and is truly comprehensive'. This is not the case; 'it merely demonstrates a paucity of real thought and a lack of strategic judgement about what is really important for that organization'.
> - 'Another common error is to provide a long list of points, but little logic, argument and evidence. A short list with each point well-argued is more likely to be convincing'.

In order to keep the SWOT focused it is suggested that a maximum of six points should be presented under each of the SWOT headings. However, it might be the case that in some circumstances the overriding importance of certain points mean that far fewer than six points are presented.

If, however, there are a larger number of points presented, it must be questioned as to whether all the points mentioned are truly strategic, or whether some of the points represent different aspects of the same issue and therefore could be combined.

> ### THINK POINTS
>
> - Explain the underlying logic which supports SWOT analysis.
> - Describe the major rules which should be followed when presenting a SWOT.
> - Describe some of the common errors which are made when presenting a SWOT.

In Table 9.2 a number of issues are presented for possible inclusion in a SWOT presentation. It should be noted that this list is indicative since the issues will vary enormously depending upon individual circumstances. John Argenti (1968), one of the early writers on strategy, famously compared the points in a SWOT to elephants: you're looking for strategic elephants; they are a rare species; they are large but sometimes difficult to spot; they can be difficult to turn around; do not develop more than six strategic elephants (for each category of the SWOT).

Table 9.2 Some possible factors in a SWOT analysis

Internal	
Strengths	Weaknesses
Market dominance	Market share weakness
Core strengths	Few core strengths and low on key skills
Economies of scale and scope	Equipment with higher costs than competition
Low-cost position	Weak finances and poor cash flow
Leadership and management skills	Management skills and leadership lacking
Financial and cash resources	Poor organizational structure

Internal	
Strengths	**Weaknesses**
Operational ability and age of equipment Innovation processes and results Organizational structure Reputation Differentiated products Good balance of products Product or service quality	Low quality and reputation Products not differentiated Dependent on few products Products in mature or declining PLC stages Low market share

External	
Opportunities	**Threats**
New markets and segments New products Diversification opportunities Market growth Competitor weaknesses Strategic space Demographic and social change Change in political and economic environment New take-over or partnership opportunities Economic upturn International growth	New market entrants Increased competition Pressure from customers and/or suppliers Substitutes Low market growth Economic cycle downturn Technological threat Change in political or economic environment Demographic change New international barriers to trade Environmental impacts of activities New destinations or events

Source: Adapted from Lynch (2012:304).

SMALL BUSINESS FOCUS

Small businesses in *THE* sectors have significant hurdles to overcome in successfully competing with larger businesses, but they may also have some advantages. The SWOT must represent a realistic appraisal for the SMEs which honestly represents the true position relative to the larger organizations, destinations, events, etc. which are engaged in the competitive arena.

As Palmer (2011:275) points out small businesses are often associated with a bundle of positive attributes such as: friendliness; flexibility; originalilty; and, individuality. Conversly, big businesses may be associated with negative connotations such as being: impersonal; inflexible; standardized; and lacking a 'human dimension'.

However there are also a number of potential factors which may inhibit small business performance which need to be recognized and their impact appraised. Morrison and Teixera (2004), for example, list a number of such potential obstacles which are shown in Table 9.3.

In constructing a SWOT for a smaller *THE* organization, event or destination it might be useful to compile a simple checklist which is probably far more focused on individual characteristics of the owner/manager than they are likely to be in larger businesses. However, as with all SWOTs, it should be based on robust analysis of all the relevant factors taking into account both qualitative and quantitative data as appropriate.

Table 9.3 Obstacles to small firm business performance in tourism

Obstacle focus	Obstacle description
Internal: owner manager	Lack of ambition, vision
	Lack of inclination to increase production or operations
	Constrained resources to address gaps in managerial competencies
	Perceptions that enterprise development would negatively impact on product/service quality
	Anti-business 'hobbyist' approach to running the business
	Protecting quality of lifestyle
Internal: business	Multi-skilling in every category of staff is needed
	Limited resources and capacity available to narrow skill gaps
	Physical constraints curtail expansion
External	Weak power position within the industry sector and markets as an individual unit
	High dependency on *externalities* (external costs or benfits beyond the control of the organization)

Source: Adapted from Morrison and Teixera (2004)

The following checklist might be useful in such circumstances. The questions should be asked of the organization but also of the leader/manager since in many smaller businesses they have a pivotal role.

Strengths – Concerned with the attributes of the owner/manager and the business which could help the business achieve its objectives.

- What do you do well?
- What are your unique skills and competencies?
- What expert or specialized knowledge do you possess?
- What experience do you have?
- What do you do better than your competitors?
- What are your most profitable areas of business?

Weaknesses – Concerned with the lack of attributes of the owner/manager and the business which may hinder the business in achieving its objectives.

- In what areas do you need to improve?
- What resources do you lack?
- What parts of your business are not very profitable?
- Where do you need further education, training and/or experience?
- What costs you time and/or money?

Opportunities – Concerned with the external opportunities which may help you achieve your objectives.

- In what ways could you do more for your existing customers or clients?
- How can you use technology to enhance your business?
- Are there new target audiences you have the potential to reach?
- Are there related products and services that provide an opportunity for your business?

Threats – Concerned with the external threats which may hinder you in achieving your objectives.

- What is the balance of power between your organization and suppliers and customers?
- What are the strengths of your biggest competitors?
- What are your competitors doing that you are not?
- What is happening in the economy?
- What is happening in the industry and markets you are involved with?

CHAPTER SUMMARY

SWOT is a tool that is widely used and understood by students and managers. It should represent a solid foundation for moving on to strategic formulation but care has to be taken in implementing the SWOT so as to ensure it is not bland, and is fully supported by the evidence that is available. However, as Haberberg and Rieple (2001) point out in their comprehensive treatment of the subject area the SWOT analysis should not be viewed as the start of the analysis. Instead, 'in order to arrive at a proper SWOT appraisal, other analyses need to be carried out first'.

This is the approach that is taken in this chapter with the SWOT representing the culmination of the internal and external analyses described in Chapters 3–8. Thereby a rigorous analysis of the current situation provides a solid and defensible platform from which to move forward towards the formulation of strategy focusing on the future position.

SWOT analysis has been widely applied in *THE* settings with examples cited in the references and further reading. These examples span all parts of *THE* and range from micro SWOT analyses of individual hotels or one-off events, through the application to individual organizations and the adaptation of the technique to areas, regions – and in some instances entire countries.

REFERENCES

Argenti, J. (1968) *Corporate Planning: A Practical Guide*, London and New York: Routledge.

Bardolet, E. and P. J. Sheldon (2008) 'Tourism in Archipelagos: Hawai'i and the Balearics', *Annals of Tourism Research*, 35 (4): 900–23.

Finlay, P. (2000) 'Strategic Management: An Introduction to Business and Corporate Strategy', Harlow: Pearson Education.

Haberberg, A. and A. Rieple (2001) *The Strategic Management of Organizations*, Harlow: Pearson Education.

Karadakis, K., K. Kaplanidou and G. Karlis (2010) 'Event Leveraging of Mega Sport Events: A SWOT Analysis Approach', *International Journal of Event and Festival Management*, 1 (3): 170–85.

Lynch, R. (2012) *Corporate Strategy*, 6th edn, Harlow: Pearson Education.

Morrison, A. and R. Teixeira (2004) 'Small Business Performance: A Tourism Sector Focus', *Journal of Small Business and Enterprise Development*, 11 (2): 166–73.

Palmer, A. (2011) *Principles of Services Marketing*, 6th edn, Maidenhead: McGraw-Hill.

Pao, J. W. (2004) 'Recent Developments and Prospects of Macao's Tourism Industry', *AMCM Quarterly Bulletin*, 13 (October): 79–95.

FURTHER READING

Reference	Focus
Akca, H. (2006) 'Assessment of Rural Tourism in Turkey Using SWOT Analysis', *Journal of Applied Sciences*, 6 (13): 2837–9.	SWOT Tourism Turkey
Akova, O., M. Sarıışık and D. Dönmez [[Q: 2011]] Strategies for Tourism Industry under the Global Economic Crisis: A Swot Analysis of Turkish Tourism. Paper presented to the International Conference on Eurasian Economies, Bishkek, Kyrgyzstan, available at www.eecon.info/ accessed 8th September 2014.	SWOT Tourism Turkey
Buhalis, D. and C. Cooper (1998) 'Small and Medium Sized Tourism Enterprises at the Destination', in E. Laws, B. Faulkner and G. Moscardo (eds.), *Embracing and Managing Change in Tourism: International Case Studies*, London and New York: Routledge, pp. 324–46.	SWOT Tourism SMEs
Carlsen, J. and T. D. Andersson (2011) 'Strategic SWOT Analysis of Public, Private and Not-for-Profit Festival Organisations', *International Journal of Event and Festival Management*, 2 (1): 83–97.	SWOT Festivals Private public partenships
Helms, M. M. and J. Nixon (2010) 'Exploring SWOT Analysis: Where Are We Now? A Review of Academic Research from the Last Decade', *Journal of Strategy and Management*, 3 (3): 215–51.	SWOT Research
Hill, T. and R. Westbrook (1997) 'SWOT Analysis: It's Time for a Product Recall', *Long Range Planning*, 30 (1): 46–52.	SWOT Critique
Jolliffe, L., H. T. Bui and H. T. Nguyen, H. T. 'The Buon Ma Thuot Coffee Festival, Vietnam: Opportunity for Tourism?' in J. Ali-Knight, M. Robertson, A. Fyall and A. Ladkin (Eds), *International Perspectives of Festivals and Events: Paradigms of Analysis*, San Diego CA: Elsevier, pp. 125–38.	SWOT Festivals Vietnam
Lee, T. H. and R. T. Liu (2011) 'Strategy Formulation for the Recreational Areas of Central Taiwan: An Application of SWOT (Strengths, Weaknesses, Opportunities, Threats) Analysis', *Journal of Hospitality Management and Tourism*, 2 (3): 38–47.	SWOT Tourism China
Long, J. Z., and Zhu, H. (2007) 'An Application of Tows Method in the Strategy Planning of Regional Tourism – A Case Study of An'shan', *Human Geography*, 1.	SWOT Tourism China
Narayan, P. K. (2000) 'Fiji's Tourism Industry: A SWOT Analysis', *Journal of Tourism Studies*, 11 (2): 15–24.	SWOT Tourism Fiji
Sarıışık, M., O. Turkay and O. Akova (2011) 'How to Manage Yacht Tourism in Turkey: A SWOT Analysis and Related Strategies', *Procedia: Social and Behavioral Sciences*, 24: 1014–25.	SWOT Tourism Turkey
Sharpley, R. (2002) 'The Challenges of Economic Diversification through Tourism: The Case of Abu Dhabi', *International Journal of Tourism Research*, 4 (3): 221–35.	SWOT Tourism Abu Dhabi
Stevenson, H. H. (1989) 'Defining Corporate Strengths and Weaknesses', in D. Asch and C. Bowman (eds.), *Readings in Strategic Management*, Basingstoke: Macmillan in Association with the Open University, pp. 162–76.	SWOT

Weihrich, H. (1982) 'The TOWS Matrix: A Tool for Situational Analysis', *Long Range Planning*, 15 (2): 54–66.	SWOT
Yoo, J. J. E. (2005) 'Development of the Convention Industry in Korea', *Journal of Convention and Event Tourism*, 6 (4): 81–94.	SWOT Conventions Korea
Yu, L. and G. Huimin (2005) 'Hotel Reform in China: A SWOT Analysis', *Cornell Hotel and Restaurant Administration Quarterly*, 46 (2): 153–69.	SWOT Hotels China

CASE LINKAGES

Case 1	Strategic alliances in the airline industry
Case 2	Tourism Queensland
Case 4	Hyatt Hotels
Case 5	Days Inn

Part **4**

Strategic selection

Introduction

The previous three parts of this book have been concerned with an introduction to the subject matter and establishing the *THE* context, followed by chapters which studied strategic analysis both internally and externally. This culminated in the bringing together of available information (from the analyses) in the form of a SWOT. This establishes the current position based on a rigorous examination of the information and data available. This is a necessary prerequisite for moving on to consider the options available to *THE* organizations for future development and making choices between these and selecting those most appropriate.

In Part 4 we turn towards the future by considering the strategic choices *THE* organizations have to make. Strategic selection is concerned with making the decisions about an organization's future and the way in which it needs to respond to the many pressures and influences identified in the analysis studied in the previous chapters.

Study progress:

Part 1	Part 2	Part 3	Part 4			Part 5
Strategy and the tourism, hospitality and events contexts	Analysing the internal environment	Analysing the external environment and SWOT	Strategic selection			Strategic implementation and strategy in theory and practice
Introduction and Chapters 1 and 2	Chapters 3, 4, 5 and 6	Chapters 7, 8 and 9	Chapter 10 Competitive strategy and strategic direction for tourism, hospitality and event organizations	Chapter 11 Strategic methods for tourism, hospitality and event organizations	Chapter 12 Strategic evaluation and selection	Chapters 13, 14 and 15

Specifically strategic selection is concerned with three stages:

- *formulating* options for future development (Chapters 10 and 11);
- *evaluating* between available options (Chapter 12);
- *selecting* which options should be chosen (Chapter 12).

Many *THE* organizations are complex in terms of the scope and scale of their operations and in the way that they are managed. The nature of the industry is such that many such organizations may:

- be operating internationally;
- comprise many different departments or divisions;
- have operations that are geographically scattered;
- have a large centralised head office or a small head office with dispersed authority.

As a result of this complexity it is common to distinguish between various levels of strategic choice, although textbooks often vary in their definition and scope of these levels. Three levels of organizational strategy are discernible:

Corporate level strategy
The overall purpose and scope
of an organization.

Business level strategy
How to compete successfully
in certain markets.

Operational level strategy
Detailed implementation issues. How
corporate and business level strategies
can successfully be put into practice.

Figure P4.1 The levels of strategy

- *corporate* level;
- *business* level;
- *operational* level.

The main focus of this text is on the business and operational levels.

However, it should be noted at the outset that the boundaries between the levels are often unclear, particularly in smaller organizations where frequently the levels will effectively merge together.

Figure P4.1 shows the three levels of strategy as a hierarchy.

Corporate level strategy is concerned with the overall purpose and scope of an organization.

This level of strategy might include the broad determination of which business areas or geographical areas the organization might want to be involved with. Clearly this area of strategic choice is thus closely involved with the organization's mission and its manifestation in the form of a mission statement. This level of strategy is usually determined by the most senior levels of the organization i.e. the Board of Directors and the Chief Executive Officer (CEO).

The short case illustration below provides an example of Corporate Level Strategy for a major UK Brewer and pub owner.

SHORT CASE ILLUSTRATION

Corporate level strategy for a major UK brewer and pub owner

During the 1990s Bass plc (once the UK's largest brewer and bar operator), sold its brewing interests and most of its pubs. The proceeds raised from these disposals were used to invest in hotels primarily through the purchase of the Holiday Inn and Inter Continental chains.

This was clearly a corporate level decision to entirely refocus the business, which culminated in 2001 with the renaming of the company as Six Continents plc, and subsequently as InterContineatal Hotels Group plc (IHG Group). The name change reflected the fact that the company had been transformed from a largely UK based brewer into a global hotel operating company.

www.ihg.com

Questions

1. Explain the differences between *corporate* and *business* level strategy.

2. Why might this case be regarded as an example of *corporate* level strategy?

Whilst transformational changes (such as the one outlined above) occur from time-to-time they tend to be far less common than the business level decisions that organizations continually need to make. The focus of this part of the text is thus primarily at the business level of strategy.

Business level strategy is concerned with how to compete successfully in certain markets.

The focus at this level is not normally upon the entire organization (as in corporate level strategy), except in the case of smaller organizations. Instead this level of strategy focuses on breaking the entire organization down into its constituent parts i.e. its *strategic business units* (SBUs). This level of strategy will also be the concern of the Board of Directors and the CEO, but it will also usually involve other managers who are responsible for the individual SBUs. The concerns at this level of strategy include:

- How can *advantage* over competitors be achieved?
- Which *products or services* should be developed and in which markets should they be sold?
- What *methods* can be used to achieve competitive advantage and to develop products and services?

These three concerns of business level strategy are addressed by *strategic formulation* of strategies by considering:

- The basis on which competition takes place – *Competitive Strategy*.
- The direction in which development should take place – *Strategic Direction*.
- The methods by which development should be achieved – *Strategic Methods*.

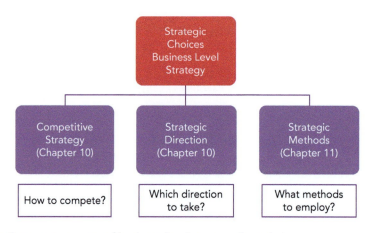

Figure P4.2 The three components of business level strategy formulation

These three aspects of strategic formulation will be covered in subsequent chapters. Competitive strategy and strategic direction are considered in Chapter 10 while strategic methods are discussed in Chapter 11.

Figure P4.2 shows the elements that need to be considered in strategic formulation and how they all form part of the business strategy.

Once strategic options for the future have been *formulated* (identified) it is necessary for them to be *evaluated* and the most appropriate strategies should be selected and formulated. The evaluation and selection of strategies are considered in Chapter 12.

Operational level strategy – is concerned with the more detailed implementation issues relating to how the proposed corporate and business level strategies can successfully be put into practice.

The concern here is how the changes arising from the adoption of corporate and business level strategies can be managed effectively and on the detailed decisions that have to be made in each area of the organization to implement the higher order decisions. This level of strategy will usually involve most managers and many other employees in organizations.

These issues are considered in Part 5 of this text.

10

Competitive strategy and strategic direction for tourism, hospitality and event organizations

Introduction and chapter overview

Fundamentally strategic management is concerned with achieving sustainable competitive advantage in the future. To achieve such a situation any organization is faced with identifying strategic options for future development, evaluating them and selecting those that the organization considers most likely to be successful.

Strategic Options

Strategic selection is concerned with:

- *formulation* of strategic options;
- *evaluating* the available options;
- *selecting* the options most likely to lead to strategic success.

This chapter and Chapter 11 are concerned with the formulation of strategy, and Chapter 12 goes on to consider evaluating the available options and selecting between them.

Competitive strategy, strategic direction and strategic methods

Formulating *business strategy* is concerned with three primary issues:

- *Competitive strategy* – the basis on which competition will take place.
- *Strategic direction* – which direction for development will be taken.
- *Strategic methods* – how will the development be achieved, i.e. which methods will be adopted.

Competitive strategy and strategic direction will be considered in this chapter and strategic methods will be considered in Chapter 11. How an organization evaluates the various strategic options available (in relation to these three aspects) and chooses between them is the subject matter for Chapter 12.

Business strategy and corporate strategy

An important point is that the focus of strategy at this level, often referred to as 'business' strategy, is not, normally, upon the entire organization, except where the organization is small in size. In business strategy the concern is usually with breaking the entire organization down into its constituent parts, i.e. its strategic business units (SBUs).

The concerns at this level of strategy include:

- how can advantage over competitors be achieved? (*competitive strategy*);
- which products or services should be developed and in which markets should they be sold? (*strategic direction*);
- what methods of development should be adopted? (*strategic methods*).

When considering the entire organization it is usually referred to as *corporate* strategy. However, the division between the business level and corporate levels of strategy can be slightly difficult to discern. In SMEs they are often effectively the same, since being small in scale the SME often only has a single SBU since it may operate in a single market with a single product.

Also, and importantly, although the focus here is on the business level – i.e. the level of the SBU – at some stage the organization as a whole must bring the strategies of the individual SBUs together. Since resources are finite the organization is unlikely to have the resources available to develop each SBU at the same rate and some will offer higher returns than others. Thus choices have to be made at the *corporate* level between the competing demands of the individual SBUs.

How competitive advantage can be achieved

The study of strategic management offers several explanations of how competitive advantage can be achieved and sustained. This chapter focuses on two of the major explanations of competitive advantage:

- competitive positioning;
- core competence.

The *competitive positioning* approach is based largely upon Porter's generic strategy framework (Porter 1980, 1985).

The *core competence* or *resource-based approach* explains competitive advantage in terms of the development and exploitation of an organization's core competencies (see Chapter 3).

A third approach, the *relational approach*, recognizes that many resources critical to an organization's success can come from outside the organization. Consequently the importance of inter-firm working (in the form of alliances, joint ventures franchising arrangements, etc.) is stressed. This approach is considered in Chapter 11 as part of *strategic methods*. Kim and Oh (2004) provide a useful summary and critique of the three approaches in a *THE* context.

These three approaches can be viewed as being complementary and mutually enriching rather than mutually exclusive.

The chapter ends with a discussion of the general mechanisms that organizations employ to grow and develop in order to sustain and develop their competitive advantage, i.e. *strategic directions*. We use the Ansoff Matrix as a starting point for this discussion.

After studying this chapter, you should be able to:

- understand various *THE* contexts in which competitive strategy and strategic directions have to be considered;
- explain the concept of competitive advantage;
- describe and evaluate Porter's generic strategy framework;
- describe and evaluate the strategy clock and Poon's tourism competitive strategy concepts;
- explain the concept of hybrid strategy;
- explain the role of core competencies and distinctive capabilities in building competitive advantage;
- explain the role of the value chain in linking core competencies and generic strategies;
- identify the strategic direction available to organizations;
- identify where core competences and strategies can be exploited;
- understand how the concepts and models discussed can be applied to *THE* contexts;
- provide illustrative examples from *THE* organizations of competitive strategy and strategic directions.

Strategy formulation in *THE* contexts

As stated previously business strategy is concerned with addressing three key issues:

- how can advantage over competitors be achieved? (*competitive strategy*);
- which products or services should be developed and in which markets should they be sold? (*strategic direction*);
- what methods of development should be adopted? (*strategic methods*).

These issues are of fundamental importance in any industry, not just in the sectors of *THE*. However, the strategic options which are formulated in order to address these issues and the strategy which is developed to take the organization forward will vary according to the circumstances of the particular industry concerned.

In other words, in formulating strategy managers must consider the wider external environmental factors affecting organizations operating in the industry or parts of it. Some texts refer to these factors as the *frame conditions*.

Frame conditions can be viewed as being those conditions operating in the organization's commercial environment that frame (or influence) strategic decision making for a particular organization.

The frame conditions represent the major changes or trends occurring in an industry or parts of it that managers must be aware of and take into account when formulating their strategies. The frame conditions may affect all organizations or only those operating in a particular sector, sub-sector or geographical location.

Table 10.1 summarizes some of the major frame conditions affecting *THE*. It should be stressed that this is not an exhaustive list, but instead is indicative of the sort of issues that might be considered. It could well be that in certain contexts these are not the major frame conditions that need to be considered, but that others are considered more important. It could also be that some of the issues represented in Table 10.1 manifest themselves in a different way or are relevant for different sectors in different ways than those indicated in the table.

The key point is that in formulating valid strategic options that are capable of achieving competitive advantage, managers operating in *THE* must seek to identify and understand the major changes that have occurred and continue to affect their sector of the industry. The analysis chapters of this book (Chapters 3–9) considered some of the issues as examples, but Table 10.1 summarizes them and groups them together for the first time in this book. While the issues presented are not necessarily unique to *THE*, they are certainly issues that have been important in many parts of *THE* worldwide over recent years.

The sectors and sub-sectors are consistent with the conceptualization of *THE* considered in Chapter 2 and shown diagrammatically in Figure 2.3.

This figure indicates that *THE* comprises six sectors:

- hospitality;
- attractions;
- destination organizations;
- travel organizers;
- events; and
- transport.

Competitive strategy

Competitive strategy is concerned with the bases on which a strategic business unit (SBU) might achieve competitive advantage in its chosen market or markets.

For *THE* organizations in the private sector competitive advantage is clear:

> **Organizations need to compete with the competitors in their particular sector in order to gain customers and to achieve profitability for the benefit of the business owners.**

For organizations which are often publicly funded or in the public sector – such as tourist offices, museums and art galleries, historic monuments, or publicly funded festivals and events, (or public–private partnerships) – competitive advantage is also important, though slightly less clear and expressed in different terms: the concern in these cases is with an equivalent issue. Here the concern can be expressed in terms of the bases on which the organization chooses to sustain the quality of its services within agreed budgets or, as it is often expressed, how it provides 'best value'. These organizations, attractions, events and festivals need to be able to demonstrate that they are competitive in such circumstances because they usually need to compete with other publicly funded activities (such as health, education and social services) for a finite stock of resources. Furthermore they have to compete with other locations offering similar attractions, festivals and events, etc.

THINK POINTS

- Explain the meaning of *frame conditions*.
- Explain why it is necessary for *THE* managers to have a good understanding of the most relevant frame conditions.
- Provide an example of a frame condition relevant to a sector of *THE* you are familiar with which is not included in Table 10.1, but you think is of importance to future development.

Table 10.1 Summary of the major frame conditions affecting *THE*

Frame condition	Comments	Main sectors affected
Collaboration	Collaborating between various companies in *THE* has expanded through various types of strategic alliances, joint ventures, franchising etc., with companies attempting to gain advantages of economies of scale and scope.	Transport: Airlines Hospitality: Hotels
Cost cutting	The commercial environment has been getting ever more competitive as the economic weakness in the world economy of recent years has combined with lower barriers to entry, pressure on public financing, privatization and deregulation. Companies have responded by focusing on cost base by measures such as 'downsizing' (making the business smaller) and 'outsourcing' (buying in inputs rather than providing them internally).	All sectors
Cruising	The growth of cruising in parts of the world in recent years has exceeded the growth of tourism generally.	Transport: Shipping Hospitality: On-board services
Deregulation and privatization	Markets have been deregulated and public companies have been privatized in parts of *THE* as governments have been under financial pressure not to provide financial support for *THE* activities.	Transport: Airlines, railways, airports Destination organizations: National, regional and local tourist offices, Tourism associations
Emerging outbound tourist markets	Many countries such as China, Japan, Mexico, Indonesia and Malaysia are developing large outbound tourism markets.	Transport: Airlines Travel organizers: tour operators, retail and business travel agents, Internet intermediaries Destination organizations: National, regional and local tourist offices, Tourism associations
Emerging tourism destinations	Many countries such as China, India, Vietnam, Tanzania and the Philippines have shown rapid growth in international tourism arrivals. Existing and new built and natural attractions have been marketed.	Transport: Airlines, bus/coach operators Hospitality: Hotels and other accommodation providers Travel organizers: tour operators, retail and business travel agents Destination organizations: National, regional and local tourist offices, Tourism associations Attractions: Museums, art galleries, parks and gardens etc.

	Description	Sectors
Eventful cities	Many cities (and regions) around the world have focused on events such as festivals and conferences as a key part of their economic development and tourism strategies.	Transport: Airlines, Railways, Airports Attractions: Museums, Art galleries, Heritage sites, Event venues Events: Event management companies, Sport and cultural events, Festivals Destination organizations: National, regional and local tourist offices, Tourism associations Hospitality: Hotels, restaurants and other accommodation providers
Growth of all inclusive	All-inclusive resorts and hotels have grown in popularity as consumers have sought pricing certainty, quality assurance and controlled environments.	Transport: Airlines Hospitality: Hotels Travel organizers: tour operators
Industry structural changes	There has been a great deal of structural changes and industry consolidation in parts of THE. Many organizations have become part of vertically and/or horizontally integrated structures while others have diagonally integrated using common technology platforms.	Transport: Airlines, airport, cruise lines Travel organizers: tour operators, retail and business travel agents, Internet intermediaries Hospitality: hotels and other accommodation providers Events: Event management companies
International event management	Events (and the companies which organize and manage them) has been a highly fragmented business field, dominated by domestic providers. Recent years have seen the emergence of some large diversified companies with international capabilities which add to what is already a highly competitive sector with low barriers to entry.	Events: Event management companies, sporting events, concerts and performances, festivals, exhibitions, conferences. Destination organizations: National, regional and local tourist offices, Tourism associations Attractions: Museums art galleries, parks and gardens etc.
Internationalization	Many companies have grown, merged and formed alliances to move from domestic orientation and to increase their international presence.	Transport: Airlines Hospitality: Hotels Travel organizers: tour operators, internet comparison sites Events: Event management companies
Low-cost competitors	Companies have emerged which focus their competitive stance on cutting out additional product features and concentrating on cutting costs wherever possible.	Transport: Airlines
Public-private partnerships	In many countries public funding for THE has been curtailed and public authorities have wanted to involve private sector expertise and attract private capital investment.	Transport: Airlines, Railways, Airports Attractions: Museums, Art galleries, Heritage sites, Event venues Events: Event management companies, Sport and cultural events, Festivals Destination organizations: National, regional and local tourist offices, Tourism associations

Table 10.1 continued

Frame condition	Comments	Main sectors affected
Technology: disintermediation	Technology has had affected many parts of *THE* in many ways but perhaps the most important changes have been the growth of the Global Distribution Systems (GDS) and the internet. The internet has allowed disintermediation to take place on a large scale, i.e. consumers can buy tourism, hospitality and event products directly from suppliers from their computers and mobile devices with no need for an intermediary.	Transport: Airlines, railways Travel organizers: tour operators, retail and business travel agents, Internet intermediaries Events: Event management companies, Sport and cultural events, Festivals Hospitality: Hotels and other accommodation providers
Technology: resource substitution and resource re-location	Many parts of *THE* are highly labour-intensive which tends to be an expensive resource. It is also difficult to ensure consistent quality standards are met. Computer and communications technology have been utilized to replace labour with technology or to relocate labour resources to where they are provided at lower cost. For example, call centres have been replaced by interactive websites for booking and price comparison, self-checking-in is now common at airports and electronic information points are available at tourist sites. At the same time call centres and other functions have been relocated in many cases from 'western' countries to countries such as India and the Philippines (known as 'offshoring') or sometimes to low-labour-cost localities in the same country (known as 'near-shoring').	Transport: Airlines, railways, airports and railways stations Travel organizers: tour operators, retail and business travel agents, Internet intermediaries Events: Event management companies, Sport and cultural events, Festivals Hospitality: Hotels and other accommodation providers Destination organizations: National, regional and local tourist offices, Tourism associations
Technology: transportation	Transport technology is continually developing with new aircraft types being developed, cruise ships becoming larger and more sophisticated, more high-speed railways being built and increasing infrastructure such as road and airport capacity in many parts of the world.	Transport: Airlines, Railways, Airports, road, bus/coach
Value accommodation	The fastest growing part of the hotel market in many markets has focused on branded, value-based chains of budget hotels.	Hospitality: Hotels

Michael Porter's generic strategies

Introduction

Perhaps the oldest and best-known explanation of competitive advantage is given by Porter in his *generic strategy* framework which was first developed during the 1980s. Although this framework has been increasingly called into question in recent years, it still provides useful insights into competitive behaviour. The framework and its limitations are considered in this section. Perhaps its main use is that it provides a framework that has an intrinsic logic which forces managers to think about the underlying basis upon which they are attempting to compete.

According to Porter (1985) competitive advantage arises from selection of the generic strategy which best fits the organization's competitive environment and then organizing value adding activities to support the chosen strategy. There are three main alternatives:

- *Differentiation* – creating a customer perception that a product is superior to those of competitors so that a premium price can be charged.
- *Cost leadership* – being the lowest-cost producer of a product so that above-average profits are earned even though the price charged is not above average.
- *Focus* – utilizing either a differentiation or cost leadership strategy in a narrow profile of market segments (possibly just one segment).

Organizations that fail to make a strategic decision to opt for one of these strategic stances are in danger of being *stuck in the middle* (to use the Porter's terminology). In other words the organization, in failing to decide, tries to both be the cost leader and the differentiator, achieves neither and in the process confuses consumers.

Porter argues that an organization must make two key decisions on its strategy:

- Should the strategy be one of differentiation or cost leadership?
- Should the scope of the strategy be broad or narrow?

The possible orientations that result are shown diagrammatically in Figure 10.1

In other words, an organization must decide whether to try to gain competitive advantage by:

- differentiating its products and services and selling them at a premium price; or
- producing its products and services at a lower cost than its competitors.

Higher profits can be made by adopting either approach.

	Competitive advantage	
	Low cost	*Differentiation*
Broad scope – targets whole market	Cost leadership	differentiation
Narrow scope – targets only one segment	Cost focus	Differentiation focus

Competitive scope (vertical axis label)

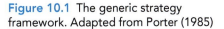

Figure 10.1 The generic strategy framework. Adapted from Porter (1985)

Figure 10.2 A simplified understanding of cost and differentiation strategies (Note: price = full costs plus profits).

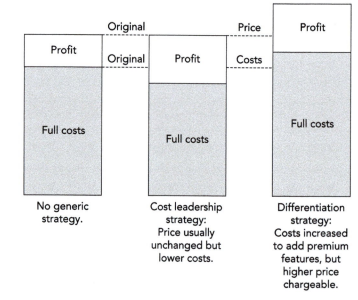

No generic strategy.

Cost leadership strategy: Price usually unchanged but lower costs.

Differentiation strategy: Costs increased to add premium features, but higher price chargeable.

An organization must also decide whether to:

- target the whole market with its chosen strategy; or
- target a specific segment or niche of the market.

Figure 10.2 shows a diagrammatic representation of differentiation and cost leadership.

With the cost leadership strategy an organization charges the same price as the initial level, but derives higher profits by cutting its costs. In the case of differentiation, an organization is able to charge a premium price (because it offers features consumers are willing to pay for), while maintaining costs at their initial level thereby achieving higher levels of profitability.

Cost leadership strategy

A cost leadership strategy is based upon a business organizing and managing its value adding activities so as to be the lowest cost producer of a product or service within an industry.

There are several potential benefits of a cost leadership strategy for a business in that it:

- Can earn higher profits by charging a price equal to or even below that of competitors because its costs are lower.
- Provides the possibility of increasing both sales and market share by reducing price below that charged by competitors (assuming that the product's demand is price elastic in nature).
- Allows the possibility to enter a new market by charging a lower price than competitors.
- Can be particularly valuable in a market where consumers are price sensitive.
- Creates an additional *barrier to entry* for organizations wishing to enter the industry.

Value chain analysis is central to identifying where cost savings can be made at various stages in the value chain and its internal and external linkages (see Chapter 3).

A successful cost leadership strategy is likely to rest upon a number of organizational features. Attainment of a position of cost leadership depends upon the arrangement of value chain activities.

Examples of how costs savings might be achieved include the following:

- Reducing costs by copying rather than originating product design features. *For example* – a tour operator, hotel company or event promoter might copy the design and functions of an existing website developed by competitors so that development costs are minimized.

- Using less expensive resource inputs. *For example* – many low-cost airlines (such as easyJet, Ryanair and Air Berlin in Europe; Air Asia, Lion Air and JetStar in Asia/Pacific; and Frontier Air, Jet Blue and Gol in the Americas) and event organizers, amongst others in *THE*, have substituted expensive labour for technology. Telephone sales agents have been replaced by internet sales, which offer far cheaper sales and are facilitated by the simplicity of the underlying product.

- Producing products with 'no frills', thus reducing labour costs and increasing labour productivity. *For example* – the low-cost airlines such as those mentioned above have generally taken away free meals from their products thereby reducing costs.

- Achieving economies of scale by high-volume sales perhaps based on advertising and promotion or allowing high fixed costs of investment in modern technology to be spread over a high volume of output. *For example* – the growth of the internet has transformed the intermediation process between consumers and companies providing products and services in *THE* during the last twenty years or so. Several large global players (mainly American based) have emerged. These include Ticketmaster a subsidiary of Live Nation Inc. in relation to events; and Travelocity (a subsidiary of global distribution system company Sabre), Orbitz and European-based ebookers in relation to tourism and hospitality products. Expedia Inc. below illustrates the rise of these intermediaries.

SHORT CASE ILLUSTRATION

Achieving economies of scale through technology: Expedia, Inc.

In 1996, a small division within Microsoft launched online travel booking site Expedia.com, which gave consumers a revolutionary new way to research and book travel. Three years later, Expedia was sold, becoming a publicly traded company

InterActive Corporation's (IAC) acquired a controlling interest in Expedia in 2002 and Expedia subsequently grew quickly as synergies with the parent company's other travel holdings were realized and the technology platforms were developed. The company also acquired other leading travel brands, including online travel sites Hotels.com and Hotwire; and traveller reviews and opinions site TripAdvisor.

In 2005, IAC sold its travel businesses under the name Expedia, Inc., and since that time Expedia, Inc. has evolved into what is today the world's largest online travel company and parent company to a global portfolio of leading consumer brands. In 2011 Expedia, Inc. sold TripAdvisor Media Group and retained its successful travel transaction brands.

Expedia, Inc.'s corporate headquarters are located in Bellevue, Washington USA, with offices throughout the Americas, Europe, and Asia-Pacific regions. Expedia, Inc. employs over 12,000 employees worldwide across its network of brands, including approximately 2,845 employees of eLong, Inc., a Chinese subsidiary.

The brands that comprise Expedia, Inc. operate sites localized for more than 150 travel booking sites in more than 70 countries. Investment in technology, shared resources amongst a number of brands and acquisitions has enabled Expedia to obtain economies of scale and achieve market leadership.

www.expediainc.com

Questions

1. Explain the reasons why Expedia has been able to grow into a market leading position.

2. Consider the main competitive threats faced by an intermediary such as Expedia.

- Using high-volume purchasing to obtain discounts for bulk-buying of resource inputs such as accommodation or transportation requirements. *For example* – Tui and Thomas Cook have grown to preeminent positions in European tour operations, allowing the two companies to demand lower prices for resource inputs (such as hotels and other accommodation) than might be available to smaller competitors.

- Locating activities in areas where costs are low or government help, such as grant support, is available. *For example* – UK airline British Airways has located call centres at peripheral locations in the UK such as Newcastle and Glasgow where abundant fairly cheap labour is available and where government aid in the form of tax savings are available for incoming investors. Other *THE* companies use *outsourcing* to site call centres in countries such as India and the Philippines where labour costs are lower.

- Obtaining *experience curve* economies (see the Key Concept in Chapter 3). *For example* – the operator of an established theme park may be able to operate the park with lower costs than a new entrant since they might have more experience of staff scheduling and training, minimizing power costs, purchasing new rides, waste disposal, pricing, maintenance and employing specialist staff. The case of Merlin Entertainments Group below illustrates the point.

SHORT CASE ILLUSTRATION

Experience curve effects: Merlin Entertainments Group

Merlin Entertainments is a UK entertainment group which operates about 100 attractions in 22 countries with well-known international brands such as Madame Tussauds, Legoland, and Sealife centres as well as theme parks such as Alton Towers in the UK and Gardaland in Italy.

One feature of the company is its ability to deliver development needs completely in-house. This capacity enables it to have the experience and ability to deliver projects on time, on budget and to the required specification. In 2012 for instance, the company worked on 29 major projects in nine countries, investing capital in excess of £120m.

One of these developments was in Kansas City where an entertainment cluster has been developed which comprises a Sea Life Aquarium and a Legoland Discovery Centre. The development was successfully delivered on budget in 18 months from site negotiation to opening.

www.merlinentertainments.biz

Questions

1. Explain how *experience curve* effects might work to the benefit of Merlin.

2. Consider other examples from *THE* where you consider *experience curve* effects may aid an organization in competing successfully.

- Standardising products or resource inputs. *For example* – Holiday Inn is able to franchise its concept internationally to franchisees because it is has operating procedures, brand attributes, training practices, financial controls and technical support that are fairly standardized throughout the world. Similarly,

Southwest Airlines is able to achieve economies in maintenance, purchasing and crew training because it operates only one aircraft type (albeit in various versions): the Boeing 737. It is the world's largest user of this aircraft type.

Perhaps no industrial sector exemplifies the adherence to the principles of cost leadership more than the airline sector as outlined in the short case illustration below.

SHORT CASE ILLUSTRATION

Cost leadership: The airline industry

The growth of so-called low cost airlines, which commenced with the birth of Southwest Airlines in 1971 and was facilitated by US Airline deregulation from the 1970s onwards, has been one of the major developments in global *THE*. Highly regulated airline markets were progressively deregulated in many countries following the US initiative and this spawned many new low-cost startups around the world. Many of the startups quickly failed due to competition from existing carriers, poor financing or failure to adhere to the low-cost principles; but many have prospered and grown into substantial carriers.

Doganis (2001) estimated that the cost advantage of the low-cost carriers at the time of writing was of the order of 40–50 per cent. Though some of the cost advantages have probably been eroded subsequently as full-service airlines (such as British Airways, Cathay Pacific and United) have adopted some of the cost-saving measures pioneered by the low-cost airlines or developed low-cost subsidiaries, the low-cost airlines still strive for cost leadership by cutting out product features which are not valued and by making operations highly efficient.

Table 10.2 Cost leadership: the airline industry

	Attribute	Characteristics
Product	Fare	Low, simple and unrestricted
	Frequency	High
	Network	Point to point
	Connections	No
	Distribution	Call centres, internet, ticketless
	Class	Single class
	Seat Comfort	High-density seating
	Food	No meals or free alcoholic drinks. Snacks and soda can be purchased
	Seat Assignment	No
Operations	Aircraft Fleet	Single type
	Aircraft Use	High capital productivity >12 hours
	Airports	Secondary and uncongested
	Airports Turnaround	20–30 minutes
	Sector Length	Short 400 miles
	Staff	High labour productivity. Competitive salaries

Alamdari and Fagan (2005) summarized the primary features of the original low-cost model pioneered by Southwest Airlines.

As Alamdari and Fagan point out, some of the airlines (such as Ryanair in Europe) have based their business models fairly rigidly on Southwest's fundamental low-cost principles. However, increasingly other low-cost airlines have emerged 'that adhere to Southwest's fundamental principle of undercutting the incumbent or the alternative carrier on price while attempting to differentiate their services from those of their competitors'.

While there are many variations of the low-cost model, and indeed Southwest Airlines has itself deviated at least in part from some of its original principles, some of the features of the low-cost model are rarely altered; particularly the focus on point-to-point services, short sector lengths, high aircraft usage rates and short airport turnaround times.

Questions

1. Explain the main features of the cost leadership model exemplified in this case.
2. Explain the factors which led to the rise of low-cost airlines and consider the competitive threats such airlines might face in their future development.

A cost leadership strategy, coupled to low price, is best employed in a market or segment where demand is *price elastic* (see Key Concept below).

Under such circumstances sales and market share are likely to increase significantly thus increasing economies of scale, reducing unit costs further, so generating above average profits. Alternatively, if a price similar to that of competitors is charged accompanied by advertising to boost sales, similar results will be obtained.

KEY CONCEPT

Price elasticity of demand

We encountered price elasticity of demand in Chapter 6 and here we further emphasize its importance in underpinning strategic pricing decisions. Economists use the term price elasticity to describe the extent to which the volume of demand for a product is dependent upon its price. The coefficient of elasticity is expressed in a simple equation.

Ep (price elasticity) = percentage change in quantity/percentage change in price.

The value of Ep tells us the price responsiveness of the product's demand. If for any given price change Ep is greater than −1, it means that the change in price has brought about a higher proportionate change in volume sold. This relationship between price change and quantity is referred to as price elastic demand.

Demand is said to be price inelastic if the quantity change is proportionately smaller than the change in price (resulting in an Ep of less than −1). The larger the value of Ep, the more price elastic the demand and conversely, the nearer Ep is to 0, the more price inelastic the demand.

The price elasticity of demand (the value of Ep) is dependent upon the nature of the market's perception of a product.

Products tend to be relatively price elastic if the market sees a product as unnecessary but desirable, as in the case of many leisure oriented *THE* products and services or say chocolate. Products will tend to have relatively price inelastic demand if the customer perceives a need for a product rather than a want. The demand for many business oriented *THE* products or services or most pharmaceutical products often exhibit relative price inelasticity of demand.

Differentiation strategy

A differentiation strategy is based upon persuading customers that a product is superior in some way to that offered by competitors. Differentiation can be based on premium product features or simply upon creating consumer perceptions that a product is superior. The major benefits to a business of a successful differentiation strategy are that:

- its products will command a premium price;
- demand for its product will be less price elastic than demand for competitors' products;
- above-average profits can be earned;
- it creates an additional barrier to entry to new businesses wishing to enter the industry.

A business seeking to differentiate itself will organize its value chain activities to help create differentiated products and to create a perception among customers that these offerings are worth a higher price.

Differentiation can be achieved in several ways by:

- Creating products which are superior to competitors by virtue of design, technology, performance, etc.

  For example – over the last few years the demand for cruises has been growing quickly around the world and the types of customers have been changing in that more families and younger customers are being attracted in addition to the traditional older age group clientele.

  Consequently the major cruise lines have responded by adding tonnage but also attempting to differentiate their ships in various ways. The Royal Caribbean cruise line (www.royalcaribbean.com) for instance has targeted the family market with its two 'Oasis' class ships which are amongst the largest passenger ships afloat. The ships' features include: a five-deck high Boardwalk outdoor area running down the middle of the ships which feature lush tropical gardens; a sloped-entry beach pool with surf simulators; a zip wire; and a youth zone featuring a science lab and computer gaming.

SHORT CASE ILLUSTRATION

Differentiation using technology: The Edinburgh Festival

Although often referred to as The Edinburgh Festival, the festival has developed into a vast and complex series of six summer festivals flowing through hundreds of venues and offering thousands of events. The festivals, which include the original Edinburgh International Festival, the Edinburgh International Film Festival and the Edinburgh Festival Fringe (the world's largest such event), run between June and August each year attracting performers and audiences from around the world. Although largely organized separately, taken together they constitute a vital part of Edinburgh's economy and international image.

Edinburgh's festival season was initiated with the birth of the International Festival in the post-war Britain of 1947 'to provide a platform for the flowering of the human spirit'. The festivals developed of course at a time before the internet, when programmes were all on paper, days were planned weeks in advance and there were far fewer such events competing for attention and custom.

Today's summer experience is very different with the vast array of events and activities and the need to compete, requiring technology as a key point of differentiation. The Edinburgh Festival's free GPS-enabled app is an important part of the technology supporting the event. It covers all the festivals and includes useful features such as allowing customers to:

- Locate events close to their present location.
- Keep track of events and plan future attendance.
- Be alerted to events nearby or starting soon.
- Access user-generated reviews.
- Read the 'Festival Buzz', which tracks shows being most discussed online.
- Read 'iFringe', that collects together a diverse number of independent professional reviewers such as FringeGuru and Edinburgh Spotlight in one place for quick reference.
- Contact others with 'FestAfriend' which links up with others interested in the same shows.

www.edinburghfestivals.co.uk

Questions

1. Explain the main ways in which The Edinburgh Festival is *differentiating* itself from competitors through the use of technology.

2. In what other ways might similar festivals choose to *differentiate* themselves from competitors?

- Offering a superior level of service.

  For example – an upscale hotel chain such as Hong Kong-based Mandarin-Oriental (www.mandarinoriental.com), which operates hotels largely in Southeast Asia and major American and European cities, attempts to differentiate itself by offering a very high level of service. This is achieved, in part, by having a very high ratio of staff to guests.

- Having access to superior distribution channels.

  For example – a multiple chain of travel agents, which has been established for some time, may have been able to develop a network of branches in prime retail locations (especially important in the retail sector). Although internet distribution has been increasingly important, retail travel agents remain important in many countries, offering as they often do: advice; competitive pricing; convenient locations; financially protected products and the ability to put different elements of a 'package' together. To accumulate suitable sites at competitive rates would take some time and considerable expense for a newcomer to the sector. By way of an example, Trailfinders plc (www.trailfinders.com) has operated since 1970 and currently operates from 27 retail premises in the UK and Ireland. The company has built up a reputation for dealing with long-haul independent travellers and has won numerous awards. The company tends to employ agents who have themselves travelled extensively.

- Creating a strong brand name through design, innovation, advertising, loyalty programmes and public relations.

  For example – the development by American Airlines of the world's largest frequent flyer programme (AAdvantage) creates loyalty for its brand among passengers. The promotional scheme launched in 1981 has some 67 million members. Though many of its features have been copied by other airlines the size of its membership together with the route flexibility offered by the airline's extensive network and those of its partners, which include British Airways, provide competitive strength. Nevertheless competitive pressures have led the airline to liberalize rules over the years, to develop partnerships with hotels and car rental companies, and to offer promotions.

- Distinctive or superior product promotion.

  For example – the *'It's More Fun in the Philippines'* campaign developed for the Philippines Department of Tourism (www.itsmorefuninthephilippines.com) has won numerous advertising industry awards. The campaign initiated in 2012 used social media to enlist the help of the Filipino public in creating the campaign, thus enabling the limited marketing budget to be multiplied enormously. The campaign went viral within hours of its official launch, with Filipinos using the 'It's more fun' theme to express their own feelings on the web in numerous imaginative ways. It helped drive visitors to the country to a record number of tourist arrivals in 2012 and for the country to outperform its competitors in the region.

A differentiation strategy is likely to necessitate emphasis on innovation, design, research and development, awareness of particular customer needs and marketing. To say that differentiation is in the eyes of the customer is no exaggeration. It could be argued that it is often brand name, brand values or a logo which distinguishes one product from another, rather than real product superiority. The case of W hotels below demonstrates how a hotel company has used design and branding to create a differentiated product.

A differentiation strategy is employed in order to reduce *price elasticity of demand* for the product so that its price can be raised above that of competitors without reducing sales volume, so generating above-average profits.

The case of W hotels demonstrates differentiation in practice.

SHORT CASE ILLUSTRATION

Differentiation using design and innovation: W hotels

Although they vary greatly, the term 'boutique hotel' has usually been used to describe full-service smaller hotels, with luxury facilities in interesting settings. The individual hotels are distinctive and often reflect the nature of the neighborhoods in which they are located.

Boutique hotels began appearing in the 1980s in major cities like London, New York and San Francisco. The term is often attributed to New York hoteliers Ian Schrager and Steve Rubell when they opened their New York hotel, Morgans, in 1984. The growth of such hotels can be viewed as a reaction against the standardization of many hotels which form part of a chain and a recognition that younger customers were more design conscious.

Many international hotel chains have reacted to this trend by launching boutique brands of their own. For example, Intercontinental Hotel Group operates about 60 hotels using its Indigo boutique brand while Marriott launched its Moxy boutique hotel brand during 2013.

W Hotels is Starwood's luxury boutique hotel brand which is generally targeted at a younger clientele than its other brands which include Westin, Sheraton and Le Meridien. It was launched in 1998 with the W New York, and the brand has since expanded with over 50 hotels and resorts around the world.

Though the hotels vary in their size and types of locations, they have a common theme of minimalist stylish decor and informal names for categories of rooms and public areas. For example the lobbies of all the hotels are known as the 'Living Room'. W hotels attempt to include the letter W wherever possible – the swimming pool is known as 'Wet', the concierge is known as 'Whatever Whenever', the laundry bag is known as 'Wash' and so on.

http://www.starwoodhotels.com/whotels/

Questions

1. Explain the main elements of W hotels' *differentiation* strategy.
2. Consider the factors which could threaten the continued development of the chain in using such a *differentiating* strategy.

Focus strategy

A focus strategy is aimed at a segment of the market for a product rather than at the whole market. In the case of SMEs, since they are small in scale they almost certainly have to operate a focus competitive strategy in order to compete.

With a focus strategy, a particular group of customers are identified on the basis of age, income, lifestyle, sex, geography, and other distinguishing demographic characteristics or on the benefits sought from travel and tourism products. Within the segment a business employs either a cost leadership or a differentiation strategy.

The major benefits of a focus strategy are that it:

- requires a lower investment in resources compared to a strategy aimed at an entire market;
- allows specialization and greater knowledge of the segment being served; and
- makes entry to a new market simpler and less costly.

A focus strategy will require:

- identification of a suitable target customer group which form a distinct market segment;
- identification of the specific needs of that group;
- establishing that the segment is sufficiently large to sustain the business;
- establishing the extent of competition within the segment;
- production of products to meet the specific needs of that group; and
- deciding whether to operate a differentiation or cost leadership strategy within the market segment.

Focus strategies can be developed in *THE* in a range of different circumstances by:

- Focusing on a particular group of buyers.

  For example – Contiki Tours (www.contiki.com), now a subsidiary of London-based The Travel Corporation, market their coach-based holidays to customers in many parts of the world. The company, founded in the 1960s by a New Zealander as a safe and secure means for Australians and New Zealanders to see Europe, now offer tours which combine activities and sightseeing in North America, Asia, Australia and New Zealand and Europe. All tours are targeted at a single demographic sub-group, namely the 18–35 age group.

- Specializing in particular geographic destinations.

  For example – Sunvil Holidays (www.sunvil.co.uk), a specialist UK-based tour operator, was founded and is still owned by an entrepreneur from a Greek Cypriot background. Although it has now diversified

Table 10.3 Key features of generic competitive strategies

	Differentiation	Cost leadership	Focus
Aim	Ability to charge a premium price	To be lowest cost supplier	Either to charge a premium price or to be lowest cost supplier in particular segments of the market
How	Superior product/service Advertising and promotion Branding Distribution channels Different locations Customer care Technology Licences/regulation	High volume sales Economies of scale New technology High productivity Low cost inputs Low distribution costs Low location costs	As for differentiation or cost leadership, applied to particular segments
Strategy entails	Changed perception Higher price than rivals Quality Innovation	Price equal to or below rivals Acceptable quality Advertising to sell high volume	Segments and consumer needs Choose differentiation or cost leadership strategy for a segment or niche
When to use	Price insensitive Established position in the market	Price sensitive market Market entry	For firms not large enough to target whole market Firms possessing specialist skills

into other areas, the company is able to compete with larger rivals in the market for holidays to Cyprus by utilizing in-depth knowledge of the destination and a network of contacts; and a loyal customer base.

- Catering for the benefits sought by a particular group of buyers or a particular product.

  For example – Meeting Magic (www.meetingmagic.co.uk) is an event management company established in 1999 based in Marlow, UK, which, as its name suggests, specializes in organizing and facilitating effective meetings. The meetings can range from small groups (e.g. leadership team strategic meetings) through to large groups or conferences and the techniques employed include using graphical representation to develop and communicate strategy.

Many organizations use a focus strategy to enter a market before broadening their activities into other related segments.

Table 10.3 provides a summary of the key features of generic competitive strategies.

Criticisms of Porter's generic strategy framework

A critical evaluation of the framework

In recent years Porter's generic strategy framework has been the target of increasing criticism and discussion of its limitations (see for example Hendry, 1990; Gurau, 2007; and Poon, 1993 in a *THE* context).

At least six limitations of Porter's model have been identified.

A business can apparently employ a successful 'hybrid' strategy without being 'stuck in the middle'.

Porter argued that a business must choose between a differentiation and cost leadership strategy. To be 'stuck in the middle' between the two, he argued, will result in sub-optimal performance.

There is evidence to suggest, however, that some companies with lower than industry average costs can nevertheless sell their products on the basis of differentiation. That is, they employ a combined or 'hybrid' strategy. The effects of innovations or economies of scale may allow a successful hybrid strategy to be employed.

For example – an airline flying a new fuel-efficient aircraft type may achieve the benefits of cost leadership and differentiation simultaneously. The new aircraft type differentiates the airline in the eyes of potential customers and the fuel effieciency allows lower costs than competitors to be achieved.

The case of Singapore Airlines below illustrates this situation.

SHORT CASE ILLUSTRATION

Pursuing a 'hybrid' competitive strategy: Singapore Airlines

It could be argued that none of Porter's categories should be regarded as alternatives and that in reality to categorise competitive strategy in this way is simplistic and possibly misleading. However it does in a clear and simple way force managers to seriously consider the basis on which they are competing and to adjust their competitive strategy if it is necessary to do so.

Some authors have argued that it is possible to achieve cost leadership and differentiation at the same time (without being 'stuck in the middle') in a so-called hybrid or dual strategy. Heracleous and Wirtz (2010) for example argue that Singapore Airlines might be a successful example of such a strategy.

SIA has combined the supposedly incompatible strategies of differentiation – which it pursues through service excellence and continuous innovation – and cost leadership. The airline is well known for its quality having won numerous awards including the World's Best Airline award from *Condé Nast Traveller* and Skytrax's Airline of the Year. What is less well known is its cost leadership.

Using International Air Transport Association data, Heracleous and Wirtz analysis of the years 2001 to 2009 show that SIA's costs per available seat kilometre (ASK) were just 4.58 cents. This compared with costs for full-service European airlines of 8 to 16 cents, for U.S. airlines of 7 to 8 cents, and for its Asian competitors of 5 to 7 cents.

One reason for this cost leadership performance lies in the age of its fleet. SIA has invested heavily in its aircraft. For instance, in 2009 its aircraft were 74 months old, on average, less than half the industry average of 160 months, which triggers a virtuous cycle:

Because mechanical failures are rare, fewer take-offs are delayed, more arrivals are on time, and fewer flights are cancelled.

New planes are also more fuel-efficient and need less repair and maintenance.

Consequently the planes are able to spend more time flying and thus earning revenue. In 2008 the airline averaged 13 hours flying per day versus the industry average of 11.3 hours.

Finally customers of course tend to like newer planes thereby boosting sales.

Heracleous and Wirtz (2010)

Questions

1. Explain why Singapore Airlines might be considered to be pursuing a *hybrid competitive strategy* in this case.
2. Consider other examples of a *hybrid* strategy from your knowledge of *THE* organizations and consider whether such a position is sustainable.

A successful hybrid strategy will be based upon a conscious decision by senior managers to combine differentiation with price and cost control. Under such circumstances a business can be successful. When a business slips into the situation unconsciously it can still be regarded as being 'stuck in the middle' and is less likely to be successful.

Cost leadership does not, in and of itself, sell products.

Buying decisions are made upon the basis of desirable product features or upon the price, not on the basis of the unit cost itself, which may not be known by consumers.

Differentiation strategies can be used to increase sales volumes rather than to charge a premium price.

Porter's work does not consider the possibility that a business employing a differentiation strategy might choose not to charge a premium price, but rather to increase sales and market share by foregoing the premium price for an introductory period. This criticism, however, does not fundamentally undermine Porter's thinking.

Price can sometimes be used to differentiate.

Porter does not consider the possibility that price may be used to differentiate a product. Mintzberg *et al.* (1995) argue that price – along with image, support, quality and design – can be used as the basis of differentiation.

A 'generic' strategy cannot give competitive advantage.

It is evident that in order to outperform competitors a business must do things better and differently from them. The word 'generic' could be construed to imply that Porter is arguing that there are general recipes by which competitive advantage can be achieved. This, however, is not the case. Porter's framework is merely a framework by which competitive strategies can be grouped to assist in understanding and analysis.

The resource/competence-based strategy has arguably superseded the generic strategy framework.

The resource-based approach argues that it is the core competencies of the individual business which give it competitive advantage and not generic strategies. In fact the two approaches do not preclude each other. The relationships between the two approaches are discussed in a later section of this chapter.

Despite the limitations that are outlined above, Porter's generic strategy framework continues to be widely used by practitioners and academics, perhaps for the following reasons:

- it has an underlying logic that can be easily understood;
- it has been widely disseminated and applied in textbooks and academic papers;
- it forces managers to consider seriously the underlying basis on which they are trying to compete.

Despite the criticisms, Porter's work can, in modified form, constitute the basis of a useful framework for categorizing and understanding sources of competitive advantage.

One such approach is the Strategy Clock framework developed by Faulkner and Bowman (1995) and reported by Johnson *et al.* (2011).

The strategy clock framework

The strategy clock framework develops and adds to Porter's original model and consequently some aspects are open to similar criticisms.

However, it is a more sophisticated approach that recognizes and deals with some of the criticisms of Porter and in particular recognizes that in certain circumstances a 'hybrid' combined strategy can be successful.

The model is shown in Figure 10.3 and is followed by brief explanations of the categories used.

In concluding this section it is possible to say that the extent of differentiation, price and cost control will depend upon the nature of the market in which the business is operating. In markets where consumers show a preference for quality then the emphasis is less on price and costs; whilst in markets where demand is price sensitive the emphasis will be on keeping both price and costs as low as possible. Of course, organizations may also seek to shape customer attitudes by advertising and promotion so as to modify market conditions.

Competitive strategies for *THE* – Poon's framework

The approaches to competitive strategy outlined in this chapter up to this point have not been developed in a *THE* context specifically, although the approaches can be applied to the industry. Poon (1993), conscious of the limitations and criticisms levelled at the approach of Porter, developed a rather different approach, which, she argues, takes into account the realities of *THE*. Although developed in a tourism and hospitality context, the points Poon expresses are, arguably, just as applicable to events management settings.

The key realities identified by Poon are:

- The service-orientation of the industry and its need to focus on the quality of service delivery which in turn is inextricably linked with the development of human resources.
- The increasing sophistication of travel and leisure consumers.
- The industry-wide diffusion of information technology.
- The radical transformation of the industry, which requires continuous innovation to ensure competitive success is achieved.

In order to successfully respond to these industry realities Poon postulates that travel and tourism organizations need to apply four principles in developing their competitive strategies:

- put customers first;
- be a leader in quality;

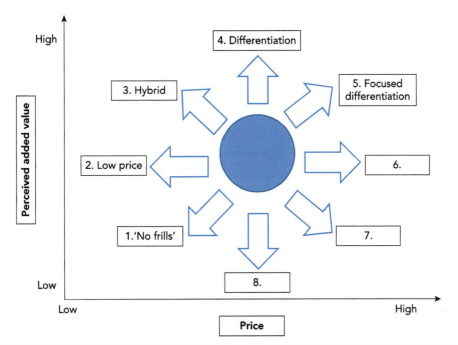

Segment	Needs/risks
1. **'No frills'**	Likely to be segment specific
2. **Low price**	Risk of price war and low margins; need to be cost leader
3. **Hybrid**	Low cost base and reinvestment in low price and differentiation

4. **Differentiation**
   (a) Without price premium
   (b) With price premium
	Perceived added value by user, yielding market share benefits
	Perceived added value sufficient to bear price premium

5. **Focused differentiation**	Perceived added value to a particular segment warranting price premium
6. **Increased price/standard value**	Higher margins if competitors do not follow; high risk
7. **Increased price/low value**	Only feasible in monopoly position
8. **Low value/standard price**	Loss of market share

Figure 10.3 The strategy clock

- develop radical innovations; and
- strengthen the organization's strategic position within the industry's value chain.

The principles of competitive success in *THE* (according to Poon) are outlined in Figure 10.4.

Figure 10.4
The principles of
competitive success
in *THE*

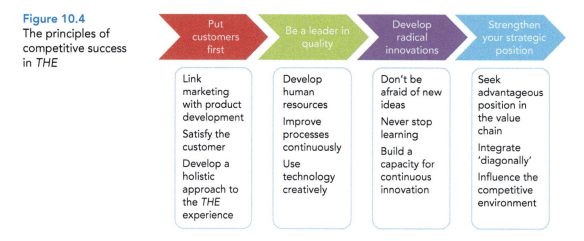

Competence-based competitive advantage

The generic strategy model is not the only one that seeks to provide an explanation of the sources of competitive advantage. The *competence* or *resource-based model* emphasizes that competitive edge stems from attributes of an organization known as *competencies* or *capabilities*, which distinguishes it from its competitors allowing it to outperform them (see Chapter 3).

Core competence and distinctive capabilities

Chapter 3 explained the ways in which internal analysis makes it possible to better understand core competencies by a process of deconstructing them into the component resources and competencies, which act as their foundation.

This chapter builds upon this analysis to explore the ways in which existing competencies can be extended and new ones cultivated. It goes on to examine how and where these core competencies can be exploited so as to acquire and prolong competitive advantage.

Much of the recent attention to the concept of *core competence* which is based upon the work of Prahalad and Hamel (1990) and Stalk *et al.* (1992), who advocate the idea of competing on the basis of *capabilities*; and Kay (1995), who advances the idea that competitive advantage is based upon *distinctive capabilities*.

Core competencies

Perhaps the best-known explanation of core competence is that provided by Prahalad and Hamel.

DEFINITION/QUOTATION

Core competence

Core competencies are the collective learning of the organization, especially how to co-ordinate diverse production skills and integrate multiple streams of technologies.

(Prahalad and Hamel, 1990)

Prahalad and Hamel specify three tests to be applied in the identification and development of core competence. A core competence should:

- equip a business with the ability to enter and successfully compete in several markets;
- add greater perceived customer value to the business's products and services than that perceived in competitor's products; and
- be difficult for competitors to imitate.

According to Prahalad and Hamel there are many examples of a core competence resulting in competitive advantage. Universal WorldEvents (below) by specializing in one industry and fully understanding its requirements has been able to build and sustain a core competence as the basis for its competitive advantage.

SHORT CASE ILLUSTRATION

Core competence: Universal WorldEvents

The events management sector is extremely fragmented. Low barriers to entry, few regulatory requirements and growing demand have meant that the sector has become extremely competitive and many companies in the sector appear to offer the same range of services. Consequently it is a competitive advantage if a company can identify its core competence and successfully promote this to build up a reputation and capability which can be sustained. One such company is Universal WorldEvents (www.universalworldevents.com).

Universal WorldEvents is a full service global event management company which has been delivering meetings and events since the 1970s. Over 300 employees are located in a network of offices which has been built up across the UK, Mainland Europe, the US and Asia. During 2013 the company managed more than 1,750 meetings and events in 57 countries, looking after almost 140,000 delegates.

The company plans, researches, delivers and evaluates every element of an event. From the destination, venue, programme, method of message delivery, content of presentations, team building and social activities. This combination of services is not unusual for event management organizations and does not represent the application of a core competence. Unlike many events where public relations opportunities are maximised, Universal WorldEvents has to work in a different way.

The core competence of Universal WorldEvents lies in its specialism and how this is applied through the company's orientation. The company specializes in the healthcare sector working with 16 of the leading 20 pharmaceutical companies in the world. This is a complex and highly regulated environment where there is often a need for specialist medical or pharmaceutical knowledge. It is also an environment where discretion and the need for both commercial and patient confidentiality are vitally important.

The experience, knowledge of the key market players, specialist healthcare knowledge and reassurance that there is an understanding of the sensitivity of the environment are clearly of great importance. However, as with most such companies, it is the employees that are vital in delivering the service to the required standards. Hence, the company conducts staff compliance training for all operational staff and has a Medical Director to ensure there is full knowledge of all guidelines that need to be complied with on an international basis.

www.universalworldevents.com

Prahalad and Hamel argue that competitive advantage is likely in practice to be based on a very limited number of competencies. These competencies will allow managers to produce new and unanticipated products and to be responsive to changing opportunities because of operational skills and the harnessing of technology.

Given the turbulent business environment in many sectors of *THE*, such adaptability is essential if competitive advantage is to be built and sustained. It is also argued that in some cases the true competitive advantage lies in the way in which core competencies are combined rather than in the core competence itself.

Distinctive capabilities

Kay (1993) has taken the concept of capability, initially identified by Stalk *et al.* (1992), to develop a framework which explains competitive advantage in terms of what he defines as *distinctive capability* (see also Chapter 3). This idea of distinctive capability has much in common with that of core competence in that it views competitive advantage as being dependent upon unique attributes of a particular business and its products.

According to Kay (1993), distinctive capability results from one or more of the following sources.

- *Architecture* – The unique network of internal and external relationships of an organization which produces superior performance. These can be unique relationships with suppliers, distributors or customers which competitors do not possess. Equally, the unique relationships may be internal to the business and based upon the way that it organizes its activities in the value chain.

- *Reputation* – This stems from several sources including superior product quality, characteristics, design, service and so on.

- *Innovation* – The ability of the business to get ahead and stay ahead of competitors depends upon its success in researching, designing, developing and marketing new products. Equally it depends upon the ability of the business to improve the design and organization of its value-adding activities.

- *Strategic assets* – Businesses can also obtain competitive advantage from assets like natural monopoly, patents and copyrights which restrict competition.

Core competence, distinctive capability and competitive advantage

So what do the concepts of *core competence* and *distinctive capability* add to our understanding of competitive advantage?

1. They provide us with insight into how an organization can build attributes which can deliver superior performance.

2. They inform the process of determining where such competence and capabilities can be exploited.

3. A core competence becomes competitive advantage when it is applied in a particular market or markets.

The process of building new core competencies or extending existing ones must take into account the following considerations:

- *Customer perceptions* – Competencies, capabilities and products must be perceived by customers as being better value for money than those of competitors. The organization's reputation (although difficult to measure) can be particularly important in this regard.

- *Uniqueness* – Core competencies must be unique to the organization and must be difficult for competitors to emulate. Similarly there must be no close substitutes for these competencies.

- *Continuous improvement* – Core competencies, products and services must be continuously upgraded to stay ahead of competitors. Product and process innovation are particularly important.

- *Collaboration* – Competitive advantage can result from the organization's unique network of relationships with suppliers, distributors, customers and even competitors. There is the potential for 'multiplier effects' resulting from separate organization's complementary core competences being combined together.

- *Organizational knowledge* – Competencies must be based upon organizational knowledge and learning. Managers must improve the processes by which the organization learns, builds and manages its knowledge.

Knowledge management as a source of competitive advantage

Particularly in service organizations, knowledge has come to be regarded as the *prime* source of competitive advantage (Lynch, 2012: 266) and a vast literature has developed on the subject and on the related concept of *the learning organization* (see for example, Stonehouse and Pemberton, 2000).

In *THE* contexts, studies in hospitality (Hallin and Marnburg, 2008) and tourism (Shaw and Williams, 2009) both acknowledge the importance of knowledge management, while claiming that *THE* has been slow in its recognizing its importance and adopting it in practice.

Nevertheless, Hallin and Marnburg (2008) recognize that many somewhat anecdotal examples exist of knowledge management practice particularly in relation to hotels and cite Accor Hotels in Germany and Hilton International as examples.

In events management settings, it can be argued that it is frequently the way in which companies use and manage the knowledge available to them that is the source of their sustainable competitive advantage. Universal Worldevents (used as an illustrative example above) derives its competitive advantage fundamentally from the way in which it utilizes its knowledge of the healthcare sector and shares this knowledge through its dispersed global network employees.

For example – The Hilton University (www.lms.hilton.com/) is a well-established corporate university, which supports all the brands in the hotel group. The University approach is developing a learning culture for Hilton Hotels by encouraging and offering a consistent approach to training for team members at all levels using e-learning technology (Baldwin-Evans, 2006). Hilton International emphasizes knowledge-sharing and on-the-job mentoring in respect to competency development of its members. The company introduced in 2002 a new innovative e-learning system that is highly cost-effective and can advance generic skills in terms of communications and customer service (Hallin and Marnburg, 2008)

> **KEY CONCEPT**
>
> **Knowledge and organizational learning**
>
> There has been an ever-increasing interest in knowledge as a strategic asset in recent years and more specifically the potential for an organization to generate competitive advantage on the basis of its knowledge assets.
>
> Knowledge to an organization can be defined as:
>
> > a shared collection of principles, facts, skills, and rules.
> >
> > (Stonehouse and Pemberton, 1999)
>
> Knowledge can be either explicit or implicit. The former is tangible, being clearly stated and consisting of details which can be recorded and stored. Implicit or tacit knowledge, which can be equally important, is often unstated, based on individual experience and, therefore, difficult to record and store (Demarest, 1997).
>
> Knowledge is not static but is dynamic and consequently much has been written on the ability of organizations to successfully use information as it evolves and changes and to learn from it. The 'learning organization', as it is termed, is particularly associated with the work of Argyris (1992) and Senge (1997).
>
> Stonehouse and Pemberton (1999) maintain that in today's highly competitive environment it is not only the way in which organizations learn from the knowledge they have, but also the way in which certain organizations 'learn about learning' that makes them likely to be the most competitively successful. Learning about learning creates an organizational context that both nurtures new knowledge and exploits its existing knowledge assets (Pemberton and Stonehouse, 2000).

Sustainable competitive advantage

It is a worthy cause for *THE* organizations to strive to achieve a competitive advantage. However, if the position cannot be maintained over a period of time then it may not be worth the effort and investment that are necessary to achieve such a position in the first place.

Sustainable competitive advantage will have been achieved:

> *When an organization receives a return on investment that is greater than the norm for its competitors and when this enhanced return persists for a period long enough to alter the relative standing of the organization among its rivals.*
>
> *(Finlay, 2000)*

Sustainability depends on three factors:

- *Durability* – No advantage is sustainable for ever, as competitors will seek to imitate it. Reputation has the potential, however for providing long-lasting advantage as the standing of well-known long lasting market leaders such as British Airways, Tui and American Express testifies.

- *Transparency* – The harder it is for outsiders to understand how an organization does what it does the harder it will be for imitators.

  For example – Walt Disney has long been admired for the way in which the company successfully manages and operates its theme parks and builds value from the animated characters it has created. Competitors have found it difficult to exactly replicate the successful formula.

- *Replicability* – Once a rival has understood the competencies needed to copy a rival, they will need to obtain the resources necessary to replicate the rival's product. If the resources are freely available in markets then this might not pose a problem but in some circumstances they may be limited.

  For example – airport take-off and landing slots, hotel rooms in popular resorts, specialist staff such as pilots, access to airline routes and access to distribution channels are all examples of resources which might be restricted for some reason.

The VRIO framework

The preceding sections considered some of the considerations for assessing core competencies. However, perhaps what has been lacking so far is a mechanism for testing the competitive resources.

Jay Barney provided such a mechanism in his VRIO framework which is explained in his co-written textbook (Barney and Hesterly, 2011). The sequential decision-making approach advocated by Barney questions each resource or capability in terms of its:

- *Value* – The resource or capability must have value if it is to allow the organization to choose a strategy which exploits opportunities available or responds to threats from competitors.
- *Rarity* – If the resource or capability is widely available to others it will not provide a basis for competitive advantage and superior returns on investment.
- *Imitability* – If the resource or capability can be easily imitated or copied competitors will do so and so competitive advantage may be achieved temporarily but will not be sustainable.
- *Organizational capability* – An organization needs to be able to organize itself in such a way that it is capable of exploiting the resource or capability which it has identified as valuable, rare and incapable of being imitated.

The VRIO framework is summarized in Table 10.4.

Table 10.4 The VRIO framework for testing competitive resources

Is a resource or capability...					
Valuable?	Rare?	Costly to imitate?	Capable of being exploited by the organization?	Competitive implications	Comparative economic performance to be expected from the resource
No	–	–	No	Competitive disadvantage	Below normal
Yes	No	–	Yes/No	Competitive parity	Normal
Yes	Yes	No	Yes/No	Temporary competitive advantage	Above normal
Yes	Yes	Yes	Yes	Sustained competitive advantage	Above normal

Source: Adapted from Barney and Hesterley (2011)

Core competence, generic strategy and the value chain – a synthesis

How the different approaches 'agree'

It has been argued (see for example Heene and Sanchez, 1997) that the resource or competence-based approach is largely incompatible with the competitive positioning or generic strategy approach advocated by Porter (1980, 1985).

Mintzberg *et al.* (1995) however, make the case that the two approaches are in many respects complementary rather than mutually contradictory. Perhaps the best way of illustrating the linkages between the approaches is through the value chain of the organization.

As competitive advantage is based upon the unique approach of the individual organization to its environment, it is not possible to identify a one-for-all prescription, which will guarantee superior performance in all situations. Both the competitive positioning and the resource-based approach, however, provide frameworks, which allow broad sources of competitive advantage to be categorized for the purposes of analysis and development of future strategy.

Table 10.5 Possible relationships between generic strategies and core competencies in relation to the value chain

Value chain activity	Areas of competence associated with differentiation strategies	Areas of competence associated with cost/price based strategies
Primary activities		
Inbound logistics	Control of quality of inputs	Strict control of the cost of inputs. Tendency to buy larger volumes of standard inputs.
Operations	Control of quality of output, raising standards	Lowering operational costs and achieving high-volume operations
Marketing and sales	Sales (and customer relations) on the basis of quality technology, performance, reputation, outlets, etc.	Achieving high-volume sales through advertising and promotion
Outbound logistics	Ensuring efficient distribution	Maintaining low distribution costs
Service	Adding to product value by high-quality and differentiated service	Minimal service to keep costs low
Support activities		
The business's infrastructure	Emphasis on quality	Emphasis on efficiency and cost reduction
Human resource development	Training to create a culture and skills which emphasize quality, customer service, product development	Training to reduce costs
Technology development	Developing new products, improving product quality, improving product performance, improving customer service	Reducing production costs and increasing efficiency
Procurement	Obtaining high-quality resources and materials	Obtaining low cost resources and materials

A differentiation strategy, for example, will be likely to be dependent upon core competencies in areas of the value chain like design, marketing and service. Similarly a cost or price-based strategy may well require core competencies in value chain activities like operations, procurement and perhaps in marketing. It is much less likely that a cost leader will have core competencies based on design and service.

Possible relationships between core competencies, generic strategies and the value chain are shown in Table 10.5.

THINK POINTS

- Outline the criticisms that have been made of Porter's generic strategy.
- Explain the factors which might make the *sustainability* of competitive advantage more likely citing examples from *THE* you are familiar with.
- Explain the *VRIO* concept and how it works.

Where to exploit core competencies and strategies

As core competencies and business strategies are developed, it is necessary to decide where they can be exploited. Core competencies and strategies can be targeted at existing customers in existing markets or it may be possible to target new customers in existing markets. Alternatively it may be possible to target new customers in new markets. These markets may be related to markets currently served by the organization or they may be unrelated markets. The organization may also consider employing its competencies in a new industry.

These decisions on where to deploy core competencies are concerned with:

- Determining the *strategic direction* of the organization (which is considered in the following section).
- Once this decision has been made then decisions must be made on the strategic *methods* to be employed in following the chosen strategic direction (which is considered in Chapter 11).

The process of exploiting existing core competencies in new markets is known as *competence leveraging* (Hamel and Prahalad, 1992).

The notion here is that operating strategically is not just about how resources are allocated (between competing demands) but how effectively they are utilized. Some organizations are able to achieve better results than others by utilizing similar resources more effectively. In other words, competitively successful organizations are able to find less resource intensive ways of achieving their goals and objectives or to use the commonly used phraseology 'they get more bang for their buck'.

For example – Lynch (2012:164) cites the case of Walt Disney. For many years after the founder's death the company continued to make good films and developed the California Disneyland theme park and later the Disney World theme parks focused on the Disney characters. It was only in the 1980s that the company leveraged its resources in fully exploiting its core competence (the cartoon characters it had created) by moving heavily into merchandizing, hotels, cruises and publishing.

Generally existing resources can be leveraged in five ways as shown in Table 10.6.

In order to enter new markets it is often necessary for the organization to build new core competencies, alongside the existing core competencies, which are being leveraged, so as to satisfy new customer needs. The identification of customer needs to be served by core competencies is based upon analysis of the organization's competitive environment using the resource-based framework developed in Chapter 3.

Table 10.6 Leveraging existing resources

Leveraging existing resources	Comments
Concentration	Concentrating resources on the key objectives of the organization and targeting those in particular which will add the most value.
Conservation	Using every part of the resources, perhaps by avoiding waste or duplication or recycling resources with the aim of exploiting the entire resource available to the organization.
Accumulation	Exploiting all the accumulated skills and knowledge available to an organization and combining them effectively. It may involve buying in the necessary experience, skills and knowledge when necessary.
Complementarity	Blending together resources and capabilities from different parts of the organization by, for example, ensuring that the operational and sales and marketing activities of the organization work effectively together.
Recovery	Ensuring that resources generate cash as quickly as possible thus achieving benefits sooner rather than later.

Source: Adapted from Lynch (2012) based on Hamel and Prahalad (1992).

The remainder of this chapter considers the alternative strategic directions, which an organization can pursue. The methods, which can be employed in following these strategic directions, are considered in Chapter 11.

Strategic directions

Introduction

Just as every product or business unit must determine an appropriate competitive strategy in order to achieve an enhanced competitive position relative to rivals so every organization must also decide upon its attitude towards growth or alternative *directions* of strategic development. That is, should the direction taken be to expand, cut back or continue operations unchanged?

As with the other key business-level decisions (relating to the competitive stance and strategic methods), decisions related to strategic direction are usually taken at the strategic business unit or product level, since conditions in one part of the organization may be different from those in another part.

For example – a vertically integrated travel company might want to expand its airline activities whilst at the same time reducing the size of its tour operations because of the market conditions pertaining to these two parts of the business. In this case there might be over-capacity in tour operating but under-capacity in airline capacity.

An events management company might want to expand in one area of its business dealing with clients from a growing business sector while at the same time shrinking other parts of the business which are doing less well.

An international hotel company may see excellent opportunities to expand in certain countries because of an expanding economy but at the same time need to contract in others because of say a poor regulatory environment making the business less viable.

At the overall organizational (or 'corporate') level however, managers must also be mindful of the overall *balance* between the directions taken by individual business units since available resources will be finite. Necessary resources may not be available to invest in all aspects of the organization simultaneously so that resources may be taken from one area to invest in another area in order to allow it to develop and grow. These principles of selective investment and growth are consistent with the thinking embodied in the *Product Life Cycle* and *portfolio models* (such as the Boston Consultancy Group matrix) which were explained in Chapter 6.

In general terms three orientations are possible with regard to directional strategy:

- *growth strategies* – expanding the activities of the SBU;
- *stability strategies* – maintaining the activities of the SBU;
- *retrenchment strategies* – reducing the activities of the SBU.

Having chosen the general orientation (such as growth), the management of an organization can then choose more specific strategies. Growth, for example, can be broken down according to Igor Ansoff (1987) into four distinct categories. We will now turn to consider briefly the three strategic directions of growth, stability and retrenchment.

Growth – Igor Ansoff's product–market framework

The most commonly used model for assessing the possible strategic *growth* directions an organization can follow (which is also commonly cited in the marketing literature), is the *Ansoff Matrix* shown in Figure 10.5. This matrix which has two variables (products and markets) shows potential areas where core competences and generic strategies can be deployed.

There are four broad alternatives:

- *market penetration* – increasing market share in existing markets utilizing existing products;
- *market development* – entering new markets and segments using existing products;
- *product development* – developing new products to serve existing markets;
- *diversification* – developing new products to serve new markets.

It should be emphasized that the matrix is related to the level of risk that managers are prepared to accept. Entering new markets or producing new products present areas of risk since many new products fail and managers will not have precise knowledge of market conditions when they enter new markets.

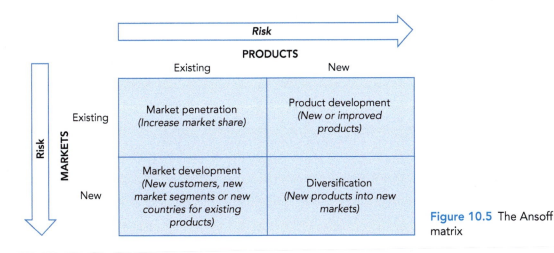

Figure 10.5 The Ansoff matrix

Thus the lowest risk option is market penetration since this option represents known markets and known products. Diversification on the other hand represents the highest risk category, because the organization will be entering new markets with new products. The arts in the UK (see short case illustration) provide an illustration of how Ansoff's Matrix can be applied.

SHORT CASE ILLUSTRATION

Applying the Ansoff Matrix: The arts in the UK

Though classical music is a somewhat imprecise term, the word 'classical', when used to describe a musical style, is used by Western popular culture to distinguish this kind of music from jazz, rock, or other contemporary styles. Classical music audiences have been broadly static in the UK between the mid-1980s and 2003, with classical music attendances during the period being in the range of 11–13 per cent of the population in any given year during the period.

Increasing participation in the arts (of which classical music is a part) has been a stated objective of UK governments and classical music has to compete for public funding alongside other art forms. Hence there is perceived need to develop audiences. Audience development is a planned process which involves building a relationship between an individual and the arts. It is an activity which is undertaken specifically to meet the needs of existing and potential audiences.

Barlow and Shibli (2007), argue that the Ansoff Matrix provides a logical framework for evaluating strategies designed to impact on customers (audience) and products (programmes) in the arts. The matrix provides a clear conceptualization of products and markets which is easily understood and provides a firm basis for managerial decision making.

Applying the Ansoff Matrix to audience development has the following implications:

- *Market penetration* – Increasing the frequency of attendance and attracting back lapsed attenders.
- *Product development* – New programmes offered to existing audiences.
- *Market development* – Attracting new people for the first time to the existing programme.
- *Diversification* – Introducing a new programme for a new audience.

In applying the matrix to classical music the authors point out that different positions within the matrix require different strategies. For example, in the case of market development free or low-cost 'taster sessions' and the provision of information and reassurance may be appropriate strategies. Alternatively, pursuing a market penetration strategy may require different strategies such as providing incentives for existing concert-goers to attend more often through reduced prices for regular attendance.

Barlow and Shibli (2007)

Questions

1. Explain the concept of the *Ansoff Matrix* and how it relates to this case.
2. Explain what the underlying purpose of applying models (such as the *Ansoff Matrix*) to cases like this when considering future strategy.

Market penetration

The main aim of a market penetration strategy is to increase market share using existing products within existing markets. This may involve taking steps to enhance existing core competencies or building new ones. Such competence development may be intended to improve service or quality so as to enhance the reputation of the organization and differentiate it from its competitors. Equally, competence development may be centred on improving efficiency so as to reduce costs below those of competitors.

Mature or declining markets are more difficult to penetrate than those which are still in the growth phase, which provide more opportunities. In the case of a declining market, the organization may also consider the possibility of retrenchment or withdrawal so as to redeploy resources to more lucrative markets.

Market penetration is likely to be appropriate when:

- the existing market has growth potential;
- other competitors are leaving the market;
- the organization can take advantage of its acquired experience and knowledge in the market; and
- the organization is unable for some reason (such as lack of resources or regulatory restrictions) to enter new markets.

When a business's current market shows signs of saturation then it may wish to consider alternative directions for development.

SHORT CASE ILLUSTRATION

The Concept Premier Inns: market penetration

The concept of 'value' or 'budget' hotels has taken root in the UK over the last 20 years. The growth of the largest brands in the budget sector: Premier Inns and Travelodge has been rapid. The hotels often located at convenient roadside locations, airports and city centres, offer good quality standardized rooms, capable of accommodating a family at a reasonable price. The growth of these hotels has placed pressure on older properties and on the 'bed and breakfast' establishments.

The market leader in the UK is Premier Inn owned by the quoted UK hospitality group Whitbread plc which also owns the Costa Coffee brand. Unlike Costa Coffee (which Whitbread is expanding rapidly into international markets), the company has to date almost exclusively chosen to consolidate its lead position in the UK through *market penetration* with its Premier Inn brand. The company has tested international markets notably India, UAE and Ireland, but has yet to commit sizeable resources to these markets.

Table 10.7 Market penetration: Premier Inns

Hotel group	No. of hotels	No. of rooms (thousands)
Premier Inn	649	52
Travelodge	517	38
Holiday Inn Express	126	15
Ibis	57	8
Jurys Inn	25	6
Days Inn	57	4
Ramada Encore	18	2

The brand has grown, quickly targeting some 500 local markets and operated almost 650 hotels in mid-2013 to achieve its leadership position in its competitive set as shown in Table 10.7.

Notwithstanding its current leadership position Premier Inn continues to view opportunities for further penetration of the market in the UK and has set an ambitious growth target of growing by about 45 per cent and reaching 75,000 rooms by 2018.

www.whitbread.co.uk/

Questions

1. Explain the rationale of expanding through market penetration for Whitbread plc's Premier Inn brand
2. Consider why Whitbread is choosing only to invest very cautiously in foreign markets for its Premier Inn brand at present.

Market development

Market development is based upon entry to new markets, employing essentially unchanged products (although they may be modified in detail).

The new markets may be new geographical areas or new segments of existing markets. In either case this strategic option attempts to attract new customers for the existing range of products or services. The key to success in market development is the transferability of the product as it is *repositioned* in new markets.

For example – McDonald's fast food restaurants have advanced inexorably from country to country, masterminded from its suburban Chicago headquarters. It has done so with only relatively minor amendments to the overall product concept in order to take into account national cultural differences and purchasing habits. In France for instance, alcohol is served in its restaurants in contrast with most other countries where it is not sold.

Entering new markets is likely to be based upon leveraging existing competencies but may also require the development of new competencies (see the Key Concept in Chapter 3 for a definition of leveraging). Entering new segments of existing markets may require the development of new competencies, which serve the particular need of customers in these segments.

Internationalization and globalization are commonly used examples of market development. It is likely that an organization will need to build new competencies when entering international markets to deal with linguistic, cultural, logistical and other potential problems.

Market development is likely to be appropriate when:

- the existing market has no growth potential;
- regulatory or other restrictions prevent an increase in an organization's market share in its current market;
- other geographic markets or market segments offer good growth potential; and
- existing products are easily transferable.

The major risk associated with market development is that it centres on entry to markets of which the organization's managers may have only limited experience and consequently costly mistakes may be made.

Market development: Holidaybreak plc

Holidaybreak plc. was founded in 1973 as Eurocamp Travel Limited – a family-run business, based in Cheshire, UK, offering camping holidays in Brittany, France. From modest beginnings the business grew steadily benefiting from the growing interest in France as a holiday destination. In the early eighties, mobile homes and destinations outside France were added to the product range. The eighties were years of innovation and growth as the UK market to France expanded rapidly and the company's Eurocamp brand took over leadership of the camping sector.

In 1984 the Eurocamp brand was launched on the Dutch market followed by Germany in 1988. Since the floatation of the company on the London Stock Exchange in 1991 the business has continued to develop and the corporate name was changed from Eurocamp to Holidaybreak plc. to reflect the diversity of the company's expanding activities.

In recent years the marketing reach of the Eurocamp brand has been extended into several new territories, notably Switzerland, Belgium, Denmark and more recently Poland, Sweden and Austria, whilst customers have increasingly opted for mobile-home rather than tent accommodation.

The Holidaybreak group, of which the Eurocamp brand is an important part, was acquired by the Indian travel group Cox and Kings in September 2011. The combination of Holidaybreak and Cox and Kings provides the company with renewed market development opportunities internationally. The existing Eurocamp products can be offered to Cox and Kings' customers in India, the rest of Asia and the Oceania region.

www.Holidaybreakplc.co.uk

Questions

1. Explain the *market development* that Holidaybreak has undertaken in recent years.

2. Explain the core competence that Holidaybreak is able to leverage across multiple markets.

Product development

Product development centres on the development of new products for existing markets.

As with the previous two growth directions, the intention is to attract new customers, retain existing ones and to increase market share. Providing new products will be based upon exploiting existing competencies but may also require that new competencies are built (such as in product research and development).

Product development offers the advantage to a business of dealing with customer needs of which it has some experience because they are within its existing market. In a world of shortening product life cycles, product development has become an essential form of strategic development for many organizations.

Product development is likely to be appropriate when:

- an organization already holds a high share of the market and could strengthen its position by the launch of new products;
- the existing market has good potential for growth providing opportunities of good economic returns for new product launches;
- customer preferences are changing and they are receptive to new product ideas or new destinations; and
- competitors have already launched their own new products.

Although when mentioning product development 'new' products are considered, it is possible to consider new products in several different ways.

There are very few products which are totally new. Holidays to the moon might be such an example. Many so-called new products are actually variations on existing products or products that are new to a particular organization. Thus new products might be:

- Completely new to a particular organization as for example when a tour operator launches an airline or an events management company that organizes music festivals adds exhibitions and meetings to its product portfolio.

- Developments of additional lines of existing products as for example when tour operators launch new destinations or a hotel group 'extends' its well-established brand from roadside locations to city centres as Premier Inn (above) in the UK did in recent years.

- Creations of differing quality versions of the same product as for example when British Airways added an additional airline class in 2000 for those paying 'full economy' (as opposed to discounted fares) when it launched its premium economy class an innovation which has subsequently been copied by many airlines.

Introducing new products is however highly risky because many new products fail. There are a number of factors which could reduce the risks of failure.

New products should:

- have a market focus;
- build on existing core competencies;
- involve cross disciplinary teams in their development; and
- involve good internal communications so that all within the organization are kept informed.

SHORT CASE ILLUSTRATION

Product development: Club Med

In 1950 with Europe at peace, Frenchman Gilbert Trigano together with Gérard Blitz a Belgian bought some American army surplus tents and camp beds, set them up in a pinewood on the Spanish island of Majorca and called the enterprise Club Mediterranean. The idea was a success from the start. Holiday camps were not new. In Britain Billy Butlin's camps had provided cheap refuges from rainy summers.

It was Trigano who developed the Club Med product into a profitable business. During his four decades with Club Med, bungalows and hotels were added with the soft comforts of home. Staff were hired to do the chores and Club Med establishments spread throughout the world. Club Med became a messenger of France's perceived high standards in food, wine, language and fashion.

In the 1990s, the Club's fortunes declined as competitors copied its concepts and holidaymakers demanded more sophisticated offerings. Philippe Bourguignon, former CEO of EuroDisney, came in as CEO with a diversification strategy which involved launching gyms, bars, night clubs and a budget version of the village but it was not successful.

During the early part of the new century driven by the changing expectations of its customers and another CEO Henri Giscard Estaing the company has returned to develop its core product:

holiday villages. Peripheral activities were sold, and new investors were found (the company's largest shareholder is now China's Cheung Kong Holdings). The villages moved upscale to the 4- and 5-star brackets and were aimed firmly at families seeking activities in beautiful locations. It has invested heavily in renovating its villages, closed non-performing villages and is expanding into China.

The brand has regained its success by discarding non-core activities, investing heavily in product development and specifically targeting the family market which accounts for approximately 70 per cent of its clientele.

www.clubmed-corporate.com/

Questions

1. Explain the *product development* that Club Med has undertaken and the reasons why it had to adopt this option.
2. Explain the reasons why a company such as Club Med discards its 'non-core' activities.

Diversification

Diversification involves growth achieved through new products sold in new markets.

Since it involves both markets and products which are new to the organization and of which managers have no experience, this is viewed as the option entailing the most risk. Despite the risk there will be situations where this represents the most sensible option to choose.

Diversification can be achieved by developing in a number of directions (which will be discussed in subsequent sections) and by utilizing a number of different methods (which will be discussed in the following chapter).

Figure 10.6 summarizes the directions and methods of diversification available to managers.

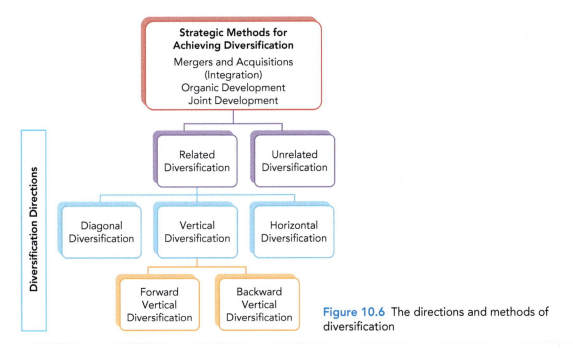

Figure 10.6 The directions and methods of diversification

The underlying reason usually advanced by managers for diversification is synergy. Synergistic benefits are created when value is created through diversification. In essence synergy is concerned with the whole being worth more than its constituent parts, which has sometimes been expressed in strategy texts as the '2 + 2 = 5 effect'.

DEFINITION/QUOTATION

Synergy

Synergy refers to the benefits gained where activities or assets complement each other so that their combined effect is greater than the sum of the parts.

Johnson *et al.* (2011:238)

In other words the value created from controlling (or owning) various parts of the value chain is greater than when they were controlled separately because the individual elements support each other. As Lynch (2012:319) points out though the concept is relatively easy to understand it is rather more difficult to analyse and measure precisely. The topic has also received a great deal of attention in the strategic management academic literature and the breadth of the research was reviewed by Purkayastha *et al.* (2012).

More specifically, diversification is likely to be an appropriate strategic option when the organization concerned:

- has current products and markets which no longer provide an acceptable financial return;
- has underutilized resources and competencies;
- wishes to broaden its portfolio of business interests across more than one product/market segment;
- wishes to make greater use of any existing distribution systems in place, thus diluting fixed costs and increasing returns;
- wants to derive the benefits of economies of scope;
- wants to spread risks; and
- has a need to even out the cyclical effects in a given sector.

KEY CONCEPT

Economies of scope

Economies of scope are the extra cost savings that are available as a result of separate products or services sharing the same facilities or resources.

Thus for example, by combining two organizations may be able to share certain activities such as sales and marketing, purchasing, financial management, etc. in order to derive *economies of scope*.

Related diversification occurs when:

The products and/or markets share some degree of commonality with existing ones. This 'closeness' can reduce the inherent risks (since managers are dealing with both new markets and new products) associated with diversification. In practice, related diversification usually means growth into similar industry sectors or *forward* or *backward* in an organization's existing supply chain.

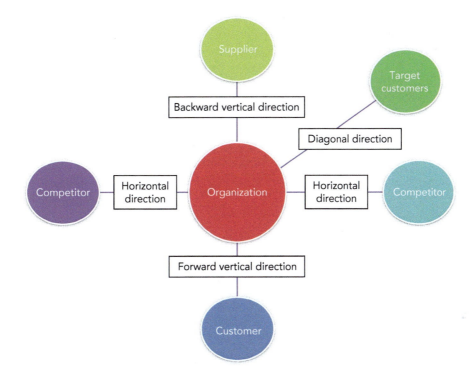

Figure 10.7 Patterns of related diversification

Related diversification (sometimes termed *concentric* diversification) can follow four main patterns as shown in Figure 10.7.

Vertical backward diversification occurs when an organization seeking to operate in markets from which it currently obtains its resources (i.e. extending the value chain in an *upstream* direction).

For example – an event management company gaining a controlling stake in an event venue such as a concert theatre or a tour operator developing a hotel chain or an airline would be examples of vertical backward diversification.

Upstream diversification (as it is sometimes termed) provides greater control over supplies of resources. The benefits of vertical backward diversification are that:

- supplies are guaranteed;
- the costs of supplies are internalized i.e. brought within the organization's control;
- supplies may be denied to competitors or made more expensive to acquire;
- the portfolio of activities is broadened giving protection against risk; and
- potential problem areas with regard to supplies are identified and dealt with quickly.

Vertical forward diversification occurs when an organization seeks to operate in markets currently served by its customers or distributors (i.e. extending the value chain in a *downstream* direction).

For example – an event management company or a tour operator developing a distribution network such as a chain of agents or call centres would be an example of vertical forward diversification in that companies are taking control of aspects of their distribution and customer services.

This form of diversification gives an organization closer contact with customers and can give significant marketing advantages in that it gives an organization market intelligence that might not be forthcoming when dealing through an intermediary such as an independently owned chain of agents.

THINK POINTS

- Distinguish between market development and product development citing examples you are familiar with from *THE*.
- Explain what is meant by forward and backward vertical diversification.
- Explain the four quadrants of the Ansoff matrix in relation to the risks incurred.

The benefits of vertical backward diversification are that:

- guaranteed outlets are provided for products to be distributed;
- the costs of distribution are internalized and can therefore be controlled;
- distribution outlets are denied to competitors;
- information is gathered regarding consumer purchasing behaviour both for the organization's own products and for competing products; and
- the portfolio of activities is broadened giving protection against risk.

Note: Vertical diversification should not be confused with *vertical integration*, which concerns mergers or takeovers (acquisitions) in order to integrate existing organizations. That is a further decision regarding the *method* of diversification to be employed (See Chapter 11 on strategic methods).

For example – rather than purchase an existing agency chain, the event management company or tour operator (featured in the previous two examples) might choose to develop such a chain for themselves from scratch or to work cooperatively with another company through an alliance or other arrangement.

Horizontal diversification involves an organization entering complementary or competing markets.

For example – a tour operator working with or taking over another tour operating organization; an airline or hotel strategic alliance when two or more airlines or hotels work in a complementary manner to achieve common objectives; or two event management companies in different countries working together to achieve wider geographical coverage for mutual benefit would all be examples of horizontal diversification.

Note: In a similar fashion to vertical diversification above, *horizontal diversification* should not be confused with *horizontal integration*, which is the merger with or takeover (acquisition) of a competitor. Diversification may be achieved by integrating a competitor that had been acquired but it might also be achieved through joint developments (such as alliances) or by developing internally (see Chapter 11 on strategic methods).

The benefits of horizontal diversification are that:

- market share is increased;
- greater purchasing power leads to more favourable rates being negotiated with suppliers and distributors;
- economies of scale are derived from the enlarged organization;
- opportunities to increase market share are denied to competitors; and
- competitors may become collaborators.

Related diversification has the benefit of leveraging existing competencies as well as requiring the building of some new competencies. In other words, it draws upon existing organizational knowledge as well as requiring the building of some new skills and knowledge.

Service-based companies experience particular problems when growing due to the nature of the product. In particular the intangibility of the product and the inseparability of production and consumption lead to difficulties in targeting new segments which Carman and Langeard (1980) discuss. However, service-based companies such as those in *THE* may also have particular advantages that allow their core competencies to be leveraged in related areas, but in a different way from the horizontal and vertical axes considered so far in this chapter.

Poon (1993), refers to this fourth pattern of related diversification: that of *diagonal diversification*. This form of diversification (common in service industries) utilizes a common platform of information utilizing technology to target a group of customers with a closely related set of products.

For example – Banks use their customer databases to target their customers with offers of insurance, mortgages, financial planning services and possibly travel products.

In a similar way Saga, a UK company that developed travel products for the over-55 age categories, has more recently targeted its customers with a range of financial services. Another example would be provided by American Express, the American financial services and travel group which is involved in travel-related and financial services. Many of its sales in leisure travel are to its American Express charge-card holders.

Diagonal diversification offers the following benefits:

- It allows organizations to get close to their customers and lower costs for each product by sharing overheads across several product categories.
- It allows organizations to benefit from economies of scope and systems savings.
- It is cheaper for one organization to produce a combination of services rather than for many organizations to produce each separately.

Diagonal diversification is illustrated in Figure 10.8

Unrelated diversification (sometimes termed *conglomerate* diversification) occurs when growth takes place in product and market areas that are completely new and with which the organization has no previous experience. The lack of experience in these products and markets serves to increase the potential risks.

Unrelated diversification carries greater risk than related diversification as it involves producing new products for markets with which the organization is unfamiliar. Businesses tend to take this option when

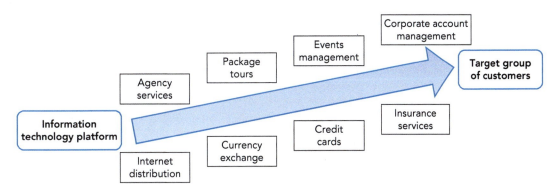

Figure 10.8 Diagonal diversification in *THE*

they see serious restrictions on growth potential in their existing markets, and in related markets, or when they see significant opportunities for growth in new market areas. In addition, there are potential financial and risk bearing economies of scale, opportunities to build on existing competencies and the possibility of synergy.

Unrelated diversification is far less common than related diversification in publicly quoted companies. The synergies between unrelated businesses are more difficult to achieve, although shared technology is one way in which they might be achieved. In the past stock markets have found such conglomerates difficult to value resulting in the so-called *conglomerate discount*.

In this way conglomerates can trade at a discount to the overall individual value of their businesses. The conglomerate discount arises because such companies are difficult to understand and they straddle several business sectors, so that they are difficult to compare with other companies. In addition investors who try to reduce risk by having a diversified portfolio of investments can achieve the necessary diversification they seek by simply purchasing multiple stocks in various business categories. Thus the experience of quoted conglomerates has often been that the whole is worth less than the sum of its parts and pressure from investors builds up to split the company so that the value embedded in its constituent parts can be realized.

However, unrelated diversification is still common among private companies (which do not require stock market quotations) and is still very popular in certain countries. Such conglomerate groups of companies are common for example in many Asian countries such as China, India, Malaysia, Thailand and Indonesia; a point that goes unrecognized in many Western-oriented texts. The short case illustration below provides an example of one such conglomerate.

SHORT CASE ILLUSTRATION

Hutchison Whampoa is an investment holding company based in Hong Kong which can trace its origins back to 1863. It is one of the largest companies listed on the Hong Kong Stock Exchange. The group (which is 49.97 per cent owned by another Hong Kong conglomerate the Cheung Kong Group) has a diverse array of holdings. The holdings are from a range of industries which can be viewed as unrelated. The activities include:

- ports and related services;
- property and hotels;
- retail;
- energy, infrastructure, investments and others;
- telecommunications; and
- video delivery solutions.

Part of its diverse activities include the Harbour Plaza Hotel Management company based in Hong Kong, which is jointly owned with another Hong Kong 'conglomerate' Cheung Kong Holdings and managed as part of the Hutchison Property and hotel division. Diversification into hotels occurred when the Hotel Group was established in 1997 to focus on the development and operations of hotel businesses world-wide. The company currently manages 10 hotels in Hong Kong, and Mainland China trading as Harbour Plaza, Harbour Grand Hotels and Rambler Hotels.

www.hutchison-whampoa.com

Questions

1. Consider the reasons why conglomerates such as Hutchison Whampoa remain as successful business forms in many countries.
2. Although the businesses contained within the Hutchison Whampoa appear to be largely unrelated there may be advantages of being part of a diverse group. Explain what these advantages might be.

Stability strategies (maintain the activities of the SBU)

An organization's SBUs may choose stability over growth by continuing current activities without any significant change in direction. Stability strategies are not the same as 'doing nothing', for to remain stable actions have to be taken to defend the current market position from competitors. There may be several reasons for opting for such a strategic direction:

- The current environment is hostile or unpredictable making investment required for growth unattractive.
- A balance has to be maintained in the organization so that finite resources have to be deployed in other SBUs which provide greater opportunities.
- A position of maturity has been reached where further growth is difficult and emphasis is placed on defending the current position.
- Many small business owners opt for this strategy as they are happy with their position having found a niche that they understand and which they are able to defend.

Stability strategies can be very useful in the short-to-medium term but can be dangerous in the longer term as competitors start to make inroads into market share.

Wheelen and Hunger (1998) identify three variants of stability:

- *Pause/proceed with caution* – Is an opportunity to rest and reflect before continuing a growth or retrenchment strategy. It represents a deliberate attempt to make only incremental improvements until the environment changes. Such a strategy may be the result of excessive growth in the past, which has led to pressures on the organization, or from the need to stabilize after a period of decline.
- *No change* – Is a decision to do nothing new, choosing to continue current operations for the foreseeable future. Returns are adequate in the current position so why put these returns at risk by going after growth?
- *Profit* – Is a decision to do nothing new in a worsening environmental position but instead to act as though the organization's problems are only temporary. The profit strategy attempts to support profits when an organization's sales are declining by reducing investment and reducing unnecessary expenditure i.e. squeezing out costs to increase margins.

Retrenchment strategies (reduce the activities of the SBU)

An organization's SBU may pursue a retrenchment strategy when it is in a weak competitive position and the environment remains hostile for the alternative stability or growth strategies.

For example – in the period following the 9/11 terrorist attacks in America, travel companies around the world chose to reduce the scale of their operations in response to the severe drop in demand. AerLingus, the Irish airline, which relies on the Trans-Atlantic trade (which was particularly badly hit) for about 70 per cent of its revenues, scaled back large parts of its operations in the wake of the attacks and looked for potential partners and sought additional sources of finance. In the poor trading conditions which continued for several years following the attacks two national 'flag carrier' airlines – Swissair and the Belgian airline Sabena – both went bankrupt.

Wheelen and Hunger (1998) identify four variants of retrenchment:

- *Turnaround* – Emphasizes the improvement in operational efficiency when an organization has problems which whilst serious are not critical (see for example Solnet *et al.*, 2010, for a discussion of turnaround in relation to hotels and tourism). Analogous to a weight reduction diet, Pearce and Robbins (1994) view such a strategy as a two-stage process involving contraction followed by consolidation. Contraction is the initial effort to 'stop the bleeding' with general cutbacks in size and costs followed by consolidation which implements a programme to stabilize the now leaner organization.

- *Captive company* – Involves giving up independence in return for security whereby management offers the company to one of its largest customers to ensure survival. The customer guarantees the survival of the company by offering a long-term contract.

- *Sell out/divestment* (see also strategic methods chapter) – If an organization or SBU is in a weak competitive position it may choose to retrench through selling the entire organization or divesting those SBUs that are in a weak position in order to provide finance for those that are stronger.

- *Bankruptcy/liquidation* – Occurs when the organization finds itself in a very poor competitive position with few prospects. Bankruptcy (sometimes called administration) involves giving up the management of the company to the courts in return for some settlement of the corporation's obligations. The court appointed managers would attempt to keep the organization going as a 'going concern'. By contrast liquidation is the termination of the organization when it is too weak to be sold to others as a going concern and any assets are sold in order to pay as much as possible to the organization's creditors.

The illustration below provides an example of a turnaround at the Holiday Inn Hotel group.

SHORT CASE ILLUSTRATION

Turnaround: Holiday Inn Hotels

The international hotel brand Holiday Inn (part of the IHG Group) has expanded rapidly around the world in the last few decades largely through franchising, but the growth path has not always been smooth.

American entrepreneur Kemmons Wilson opened the first Holiday Inn hotel in 1952 in Memphis, Tennessee, after he returned from a family holiday discouraged over the lack of family and value-oriented lodging. Children stayed free, and the hotel offered a swimming pool, air conditioning, and restaurant on the property. Telephones, ice, and free parking were standard as well. Although commonplace today, these services were revolutionary at the time and set a standard for the hotel industry.

What Holiday Inn then proceeded to do, which had not been done before, was to standardize the style of the motels and hotels and franchise the concept to other business owners. Holiday Inns spread quickly first in the USA and subsequently to other parts of the world. However, as with any brand it has to be kept fresh and relevant and it became increasingly clear by the early years of the century that the 'legacy' brand had become tired with many older properties. Other hotel chains had overtaken Holiday Inn and sales were under pressure.

Consequently, in 2007 the company launched an ambitious $1 billion rebranding initiative for its 60-year-old brand, the largest ever undertaken by a hotel chain. By 2011, Holiday Inn had removed nearly 1,200 underperforming Holiday Inn and Holiday Inn Express hotels and added 1,500 new ones and a new logo and brand attributes were developed and rolled out across the network.

Rating company, J.D. Power and Associates awarded the brand top spot in customer satisfaction for the mid-scale, full-service category in North America. Holiday Inn and Holiday Inn Express brands have subsequently experienced significant RevPar (Revenue per available room) growth since the turnaround strategy was put into place.

www.IHG.com and various newspapers

Questions

1. Explain why Holiday Inn had to launch its turnaround strategy.
2. Identify and explain the main elements of Holiday Inn's turnaround strategy.

Strategic directions, risk and balance

There are risks associated with all forms of strategic development. In relation to the strategic directions of development the risks are:

- Smallest when development is largely based upon existing core competencies and when it takes place in existing markets.
- Greatest when development requires entry to unrelated markets.

Whether or not the risks are worth taking will depend upon the current position of the organization and the state of its markets and products. Entry to new markets, whether related or unrelated, will depend upon the business's assessment of the opportunities in new markets compared to opportunities in its existing markets.

A *THE* organization may also need to consider the issue of 'balance' in relation to the decisions it makes regarding strategic direction. Since a business only has access to a finite pool of resources it will need to make choices about how the resources are deployed. Although it might want to target growth in all its SBUs it may not have sufficient resources and it may not be sensible to simultaneously target growth in all parts of the business.

Thus a business may go for growth in parts of its business where opportunities appear to be greatest and returns appear to be higher. At the same time the business may target stability or retrenchment in other parts of the business where there are fewer opportunities and returns are lower.

In this way a business with a number of SBUs considers the balance of products and markets investing finite resources in those which offer the greatest returns. However, since the internal environment of organizations and the external environment faced by *THE* organizations are dynamic rather than static the directions taken by each SBU may change over time.

For example: Decisions as to when to grow may be influenced by the economic performance of countries which usually run in economic cycles of strong and poorer rates of growth or by the political climate. Consequently, investment of finite resources in a particular foreign subsidiary may be restricted when the economy of that country is performing poorly or when there is political instability, because the opportunities do not present attractive financial returns. When the economy of the country recovers or political stability returns, the company concerned may resume a growth strategy for that SBU by investing in that particular foreign subsidiary.

Thus the European travel group, Thomas Cook, long-established in Egypt, sold most of its investments in Egypt during summer 2013. The company judged that the political instability and poorly performing economy prevented it from achieving attractive financial returns. In other words it was retrenching from one of its SBUs in order to deploy its finite resources in other parts of the business offering more attractive returns.

THINK POINTS

- Explain why organizations do not always want to grow and outline the alternatives.
- Explain why there are relatively few conglomerates operating as public companies quoted on the world's stock markets.
- Outline the advantages of organizations having a balanced portfolio of products in relation to the levels of risk incurred.

SMALL BUSINESS FOCUS

Background

This chapter has considered two of the three key issues in strategic formulation relating to *competitive strategy* and *strategic direction*. The chapter has also considered the frame conditions which underpin decision making in *THE*. In all three aspects considered, there are important implications for smaller businesses.

The business strategy academic literature is heavily weighted towards larger, diversified companies which are often multi-national companies (MNCs). Such companies will have multiple SBUs. These companies, by definition, have some degree of diversity, and this facet gives them some degree of protection against risk since one SBU may not be trading well but another might be so one can support the other. This focus in the literature on larger companies is natural because more information on them is publicly available. It is also because, as Mathur and Kenyon 2001:5) point out:

> vexing management problems do not arise to anything like the same extent in smaller businesses. However, the competitive issues of strategy are just as critical for even the one-person business.

Smaller companies, SMEs, do not have the same level of protection against business uncertainties, since they are not likely to have SBUs but instead the whole company is likely to be focused on a single product or a limited range. This has implications both for the competitive strategy and for the strategic direction that smaller *THE* businesses might choose to take.

Competitive strategy for tourism, hospitality and events SMEs

With regard to competitive strategy and Porter's generic strategy alternatives in particular, it is likely that most SMEs in *THE* will have to compete on the basis of a *Focus* competitive strategy. The focus might be based on cost leadership, or more likely on differentiation, as cost leadership is normally difficult for SMEs to achieve, since their scale precludes them from reaping the benefits of economies of scale or scope.

In the often highly fragmented sectors in which *THE* companies operate, a focus (often termed *niche*) strategy provides a position that can be defended. This is because a particular niche has

Table 10.8 The advantages and disadvantages of niche strategy

Niche strategy: potential advantages	Niche strategy: potential disadvantages
Supplier becomes a specialist in serving the needs of customers in a particular niche	Notable success in the niche could lead to its growth and the niche becomes an attractive segment for new entrants
Expertise and knowledge may make it very difficult for others to compete	Niche has to be large enough to warrant attention but not so large that other entrants will be attracted
Newcomers discouraged from entering niche because of incumbent's expertise	Larger competitors can bring additional resources which smaller firms cannot hope to match
If the niche is small there is little incentive for larger companies to enter	The niche loses its attraction to customers for some reason or becomes unavailable.
Niche buyers may have relatively little power because there are few suppliers	Niche buyers gain power as other niches elsewhere or with a better offer become available

Source: Partly adapted from Lasher (1999:100)

been developed where expertise, customer service or location can be exploited, which are not easily accessible by larger companies.

For example – a long-established family-owned hotel or restaurant might have the best location at a destination; the event manager can offer a highly personalized service based on local knowledge and the tour operator specializing in particular types of activity-based holidays is able to sell on the basis of employing highly specialized staff with appropriate experience.

The potential advantages and disadvantages of adopting such a niche strategy for smaller *THE* companies are summarized in Table 10.8.

Strategic direction for tourism, hospitality and events SMEs

In relation to strategic direction the smaller scale of operations can be both an advantage and a disadvantage. On the one hand smaller enterprises can quickly adjust their direction in response to changes in the micro- or macro-environment.

Their size means that they are likely to be:

- more responsive to customer demands;
- more flexible and adaptive since they do not have multiple SBUs and multiple markets to consider; and
- quicker and more decisive at decision-making, aided by their *flatter* structures often with a single leader (see Chapter 12).

However, SMEs in *THE* (as in other industries) are also extremely vulnerable to external environmental shocks over which they have no influence. Whilst larger organizations might have some protection against adverse external factors through the diversity of their operations and the size of their reserves, SMEs tend to have no such protection.

Consequently, decisions on when and how to grow, or alternatively to go for stability or retrenchment, have to be taken very carefully. A poor decision could prove extremely costly as it could destroy the entire enterprise, as opposed to just a part of it for a larger diversified company.

This factor appears to weigh very heavily in the minds of many owner managers. There is some evidence from *THE* contexts (see for example Goulding *et al.*, 2005; Bosworth and Farrell, 2011) that many entrepreneurs in reality do not try to maximize profitability, an assumption usually made in economics, but instead are satisfied at lower levels. Since profits can be seen as the reward for taking risks this implies a risk-averse strategy being adopted by many owner managers of smaller firms. Bosworth and Farell, for instance, report income *satisficing* behaviour amongst tourism and hospitality businesses of rural Northumberland, UK.

The notion of *satisficing* is a behaviour linked to the behavioural theory of the firm associated with the work of Cyert and March (1963). In this view of the firm (which often applies to smaller companies) a critical level of profit is achieved by firms; thereafter, priority is attached to the attainment of other goals as the owners are satisfied with the levels of profit that have been achieved.

Tourism, hospitality and events frame conditions for SMEs

The early part of this chapter discussed frame conditions for *THE* which were summarized in Figure 10.1. All companies need to think carefully about the frame conditions affecting their own companies and the relevant details will vary in each individual set of circumstance according to the location of the company; the markets it is involved with; the nature of its products; and the scale and scope of its operations.

This last factor is relevant here. The view taken of frame conditions will be different for smaller companies as opposed to their larger counterparts. We could go through the list produced in Figure 10.1 and possibly add some additional frame conditions particularly pertinent to SMEs. However, we will take one example; that of internationalization.

For example – though many SMEs in *THE* operate internationally (because of the nature of their products and markets) few will be involved with internationalization, which involves a wider commitment to international activities (see Chapter 14). However, that is not to say that the topic is not important to SMEs. This is because even if they themselves are not at the stage of development where international activities are being developed, larger companies they have to compete with will be. Thus, for instance, an event management company could suddenly find that the particular domestic market niche that the company has developed is being challenged by a foreign-based competitor for market share.

CHAPTER SUMMARY

In formulating strategy for future development three key issues are considered: competitive strategy; strategic directions and strategic methods. The first two of these are considered in this chapter with strategic methods being considered in the subsequent chapter.

In considering the formulation of strategy, managers in *THE* need not only consider the three key issues outlined above, but also consider the relevant context in which they are operating. Thus there are a number of 'frame conditions' which represent the major changes and trends that are apparent in *THE* sectors.

The essence of competitive advantage is the ability to outperform competitors.

Whilst it is difficult to identify the source or sources of an organization's competitive advantage precisely, it is possible to place potential sources of competitive advantage into broad categories which assist in the analysis of a business and in the formulation of its future strategies.

Porter's generic strategy framework, modified and enlarged upon by the Strategy Clock which includes the concept of hybrid strategies, is useful in appraising the roles of differentiation, price and cost in achieving competitive advantage. Poon presents an interesting view of competitive strategy in a travel and tourism context. The core competence and distinctive capability frameworks offer a means of evaluating the part played by a business's resources, competencies, relationships, reputation, innovation and assets in delivering competitive edge. It is the way in which the business configures and manages its value-adding activities, which forms the link between core competencies and generic strategies. Core competencies and generic strategies can be exploited in existing and new markets.

The strategic direction of the organization determines the nature of product and market development and the Ansoff matrix provides a simple and widely used way of conceptualizing the direction of growth. There may also be times when an organization judges it is not the right time to grow, and stability or retrenchment are considered as alternative directions of development.

In Chapter 11 the third key issue of strategic formulation is considered; namely the strategic methods that will be employed.

REFERENCES

Alamdari, F. and S. Fagan (2005) 'Impact of the Adherence to the Original Low Cost Model on the Profitability of Low-Cost Airlines', *Transport Reviews*, 25 (3): 377–92.

Ansoff, I. (1987) *Corporate Strategy*, London: Penguin.

Argyris, C. (1992) *On Organizational Learning*, Oxford: Blackwell.

Baldwin-Evans, K. (2006) 'Hilton Highlights Link between Staff Loyalty and E-learning', *Human Resource Management International Digest*, 14 (1): 36–8.

Barlow, M. and S. Shibli (2007) 'Audience Development in the Arts: A Case Study of Chamber Music', *Managing Leisure*, 12 (2–3): 102–19.

Barney, J. (1991) 'Firm Resources and Sustained Competitive Advantage', *Journal of Management*, 17 (1): 99–120.

Barney, J. B. and W. S. Hesterly (2011) *Strategic Management and Competitive Advantage*, 4th edn, Upper Saddle River NJ: Pearson Education.

Bosworth, G. and H. Farrell (2011) 'Tourism Entrepreneurs in Northumberland', *Annals of Tourism Research*, 38 (4): 1474–94.

Carman, J. M. and E. Langeard (1980) 'Growth Strategies for Service Firms', *Strategic Management Journal*, 1 (1): 7–22.

Cyert, R. M. and J. G. March (1963) *A Behavioral Theory of the Firm*, Englewood Cliffs, NJ: Prentice Hall.

Demarest, M. (1997) 'Understanding Knowledge Management', *Long Range Planning*, 30 (3): 374–84.

Doganis, R. (2001) *The Airline Business in the 21st Century*, London and New York: Routledge.

Faulkner, D. and C. Bowman (1995) *The Essence of Competitive Strategy*, London: Prentice Hall.

Finlay, P. (2000) *Strategic Management: An Introduction to Business and Corporate Strategy*, Harlow: Pearson Education.

Goulding, P. J., T. G. Baum and A. J. Morrison (2005) 'Seasonal Trading and Lifestyle Motivation: Experiences of Small Tourism Businesses in Scotland', *Journal of Quality Assurance in Hospitality and Tourism*, 5 (2–4): 209–38.

Gurau, C. (2007) 'Porter's Generic Strategies: A Re-interpretation from a Relationship Marketing Perspective', *The Marketing Review*, 7 (4): 369–83.

Hallin, C. A. and E. Marnburg (2008) 'Knowledge Management in the Hospitality Industry: A Review of Empirical Research', *Tourism Management*, 29 (2): 366–81.

Hamel, G. and C. K. Prahalad (1989) 'Strategic Intent', *Harvard Business Review*, 67 (3): 63–78.

—— (1992) 'Strategy as Stretch and Leverage', *Harvard Business Review*, 71 (2): 75–84.

Heene, A. and R. Sanchez (eds.) (1997) *Competence-Based Strategic Management*, New York: John Wiley.

Hendry, J. (1990) 'The Problem with Porter's Generic Strategies', *European Management Journal*, 8 (4): 443–50.

Heracleous, L. and J. Wirtz (2010) 'Singapore Airlines' Balancing Act', *Harvard Business Review*, 88 (7/8): 145–9.

Johnson, G., R. Whittington, K. Scholes and S. Pyle (2011) *Exploring Strategy: Text and Cases*, Harlow: Financial Times Prentice Hall.

Kay, J. (1995) *Foundations of Corporate Success*, Oxford: Oxford University Press.

Kim, B. Y. and H. Oh (2004) 'How Do Hotel Firms Obtain a Competitive Advantage?' *International Journal of Contemporary Hospitality Management*, 16 (1): 65–71.

Lasher, W. R. (1999) *Strategic Thinking for Smaller Businesses and Divisions*, Oxford: Blackwell.

Lynch, R. (2012) *Strategic Management*, 6th edn, Harlow: Pearson Education.

Mathur, S. S. and A. Kenyon (2001) *Creating Value: Successful Business Strategies*, 2nd edn, London and New York: Routledge.

Mintzberg, H., J. B. Quinn and S. Ghoshal (1995) 'The Strategy Process: Concepts, Contexts and Cases', Englewood Cliffs, NJ: Prentice Hall.

Pearce II, J. A. and D. K. Robbins (1994) 'Retrenchment Remains the Foundation of Business Turnaround', *Strategic Management Journal*, June: 313–23.

Pemberton, J. D. and G. H. Stonehouse (2000) 'Organizational Learning and Knowledge Assets: An Essential Partnership', *The Learning Organization*, 7 (4): 184–94.

Poon, A. (1993) *Tourism Technology and Competitive Strategies*, Wallingford: CAB International.

Porter, M. E. (1980) *Competitive Strategy: Techniques for Analysing Industries and Competitors*, New York: Free Press.

—— (1985) *Competitive Advantage*, New York: Free Press.

Prahalad, C. K. and G. Hamel (1998) 'The Core Competence of the Corporation', *Harvard Business Review*, Reprinted in S. Segal-Horn (ed.), *The Strategy Reader*, Oxford: Blackwell in association with the Open University, 1st edn, pp. 220–33.

Purkayastha, S., T. S. Manolova and L. F. Edelman (2012) 'Diversification and Performance in Developed and Emerging Market Contexts: A Review of the Literature', *International Journal of Management Reviews*, 14 (1): 18–38.

Senge, P. M. (1997) 'The Fifth Discipline', *Measuring Business Excellence*, 1 (3): 46–51.

Shaw, G. and A. Williams (2009) 'Knowledge Transfer and Management in Tourism Organizations: An Emerging Research Agenda', *Tourism Management*, 30 (3): 325–35.

Solnet, D. J., N. Paulsen and C. Cooper (2010) 'Decline and Turnaround: A Literature Review and Proposed Research Agenda for the Hotel Sector', *Current Issues in Tourism*, 13 (2): 139–59.

Stalk, G., P. Evans and L. E. Shulmann (1992) 'Competing on Capabilities: The New Rules of Corporate Strategy', *Harvard Business Review*, March/April: 57–69.

Stonehouse, G. H. and J. D. Pemberton (1999) 'Learning and Knowledge Management in the Intelligent Organization', *Participation and Empowerment: An International Journal*, 7 (5): 131–44.

Wheelen, T. L. and J. D. Hunger (1998) *Strategic Management and Business Policy: Entering 21st Century Global Society*, Reading, Mass.: Addison-Wesley.

—— (2002) *Strategic Management and Business Policy*, 8th edn, Upper Saddle River, NJ: Prentice Hall.

WEBSITES

www.clubmed-corporate.com

www.contiki.com

www.edinburghfestivals.co.uk

www.expediainc.com/

www.lms.hilton.com/

www.itsmorefuninthephilippines.com

www.mandarinoriental.com

www.merlinentertainments.biz/

www.meetingmagic.co.uk

www.starwoodhotels.com/whotels/

www.sunvil.co.uk

www.trailfinders.com

www.universalworldevents.com

www.whitbread.co.uk/

www.holidaybreakplc.co.uk

www.hutchison-whampoa.com
www.royalcaribbean.com

FURTHER READING

Reference	Focus
Altinay, M. and H. A. Biçak (1998) 'Competitive Strategies for the Tourism Sector of a Small Island State: The Case of North Cyprus', *Journal of Vacation Marketing*, 4 (2): 136–44.	Competitive strategy Tourism Hospitality North Cyprus
Andersson, T. D. and D. Getz (2008) 'Stakeholder Management Strategies of Festivals', *Journal of Convention and Event Tourism*, 9 (3): 199–220.	Competitive strategy Festivals
—— (2009) 'Tourism as a Mixed Industry: Differences between Private, Public and Not-for-Profit Festivals', *Tourism Management*, 30 (6): 847–56.	Competitive strategy Festivals Public sector
Avci, U., M. Madanoglu and F. Okumus (2011) 'Strategic Orientation and Performance of Tourism Firms: Evidence from a Developing Country', *Tourism Management*, 32 (1): 147–57.	Competitive strategy Tourism Turkey
Buhalis, D. (2000) 'Marketing the Competitive Destination of the Future', *Tourism Management*, 21 (1): 97–116.	Competitive strategy Tourism Technology
Buhalis, D. and C. Cooper (1998) 'Competition or co-operation? Small and Medium Sized Tourism Enterprises at the Destination', in E. Laws, B. Faulkner and G. Moscardo (eds.) *Embracing and Managing Change in Tourism: International Case Studies*, London and New York: Routledge, 324–46.	Competitive strategy Tourism SMEs
Claver-Cortés, E. and J. Pereira-Moliner (2007) 'Competitiveness in Mass Tourism', *Annals of Tourism Research*, 34 (3): 727–45.	Competitive strategy Tourism Tourist destinations
Cooper, C. (2006) 'Knowledge Management and Tourism', *Annals of Tourism Research*, 33 (1): 47–64.	Knowledge management Tourism
Crouch, G. I. and J. R. Ritchie (1999) 'Tourism, Competitiveness and Societal Prosperity', *Journal of Business Research*, 44 (3): 137–52.	Competitive strategy Tourism
Cunill, O. M. (2006) *The Growth Strategies of Hotel Chains: Best Business Practices by Leading Companies*, London and New York: Routledge.	Strategic direction Growth Hotels
Dimmock, K. (1999) 'Management Style and Competitive Strategies among Tourism Firms in the Northern Rivers', *Tourism Management*, 20 (3): 323–39.	Competitive strategy Tourism Australia
Evans, M. R., J. B. Fox and R. B. Johnson (1995) 'Identifying Competitive Strategies for Successful Tourism Destination Development', *Journal of Hospitality and Leisure Marketing*, 3 (1): 37–45.	Competitive strategy Tourism Tourism destinations
Garrigós-Simón, F. J., D. P. Marqués and Y. Narangajavana (2005) 'Competitive Strategies and Performance in Spanish Hospitality Firms', *International Journal of Contemporary Hospitality Management*, 17 (1): 22–38.	Competitive strategy Hospitality Spain

Getz, D. (2002) 'Why Festivals Fail', *Event Management*, 7 (4): 209–19.	Competitive strategy Festivals Competitive failure
—— (2004) 'Bidding on Events: Identifying Event Selection Criteria and Critical Success Factors', *Journal of Convention and Exhibition Management*, 5 (2): 1–24.	Competitive strategy Festivals Critical success factors
—— (2009) 'Policy for Sustainable and Responsible Festivals and Events: Institutionalization of a New Paradigm', *Journal of Policy Research in Tourism, Leisure and Events*, 1 (1): 61–78.	Competitive strategy Festivals Events
Go, F. M. and P. Welch (1991) 'Competitive Strategies for the International Hotel Industry', Special Report, Economist Intelligence Unit.	Competitive strategy Hotels
Hede, A. M. (2008) 'Managing Special Events in the New Era of the Triple Bottom Line', *Event Management*, 11 (1–2): 1–2.	Competitive strategy Events
Jönsson, C. and D. Devonish (2009) 'An Exploratory Study of Competitive Strategies among Hotels in a Small Developing Caribbean State', *International Journal of Contemporary Hospitality Management*, 21 (4): 491–500.	Competitive strategy Hotels Caribbean
Klemm, M. and L. Parkinson (2001) 'UK Tour Operator Strategies: Causes and Consequences', *International Journal of Tourism Research*, 3 (5): 367–75.	Competitive strategy Tourism Tour operators
Kozak, M. and M. Rimmington (1999) 'Measuring Tourist Destination Competitiveness: Conceptual Considerations and Empirical Findings', *International Journal of Hospitality Management*, 18 (3): 273–83.	Knowledge Management Festivals Events
Lade, C. and J. Jackson (2004) 'Key Success Factors in Regional Festivals: Some Australian Experiences', *Event Management*, 9 (1–2): 1–2.	Competitive strategy Tourism Tourist destinations
Lawton, T. C. (2002) *Cleared for Take-Off: Structure and Strategy in the Low Fare Airline Business*, Farnham, UK: Ashgate.	Competitive strategy Festivals Critical success factors
Lawton, T. C. and S. Solomko (2005) 'When Being the Lowest Cost Is Not Enough: Building a Successful Low-Fare Airline Business Model in Asia', *Journal of Air Transport Management*, 11 (6): 355–62.	Competitive strategy Airlines Cost leadership
Malighetti, P., S. Paleari and R. Redondi (2009) 'Pricing Strategies of Low-Cost Airlines: The Ryanair Case Study', *Journal of Air Transport Management*, 15 (4): 195–203.	Competitive strategy Airlines Cost leadership
Markides, C. C. and P. J. Williamson (1994) 'Related Diversification, Core Competences and Corporate Performance', *Strategic Management Journal*, 15 (2): 149–65.	Competitive strategy Airlines Cost leadership
Martín, J. C. and C. Román (2010) 'Airlines and Their Focus on Cost Control and Productivity', in R. Macário, and E. Van de Voorde (eds.), *Critical Issues in Air Transport Economics and Business*, Abingdon, UK and New York: Routledge, pp. 29–51.	Diversification Core competencies Corporate performance
Mathews, V. E. (2000) 'Competition in the International Hotel Industry', *International Journal of Contemporary Hospitality Management*, 12 (2): 114–18.	Competitive strategy Airlines Cost leadership

Mehmetoglu, M. and K. A. Ellingsen (2005) 'Do Small-Scale Festivals Adopt Market Orientation as a Management Philosophy?' *Event Management*, 9 (3): 119–32.	Competitive strategy Hospitality Hotels
Melian-Gonzalez, A. and J. M. Garcia-Falcon (2003) 'Competitive Potential of Tourism in Destinations', *Annals of Tourism Research*, 30 (3): 720–40.	Competitive strategy Fesivals Strategic directions
Neha, S., R. Pradeep and H. Clark (2007) 'Knowledge Mapping for Safe Festivals and Events: An Ontological Approach', *Event Management*, 11 (1–2): 71–80.	Competitive strategy Tourism Tourist destinations
Ottenbacher, M. C. (2007) 'Innovation Management in the Hospitality Industry: Different Strategies for Achieving Success', *Journal of Hospitality and Tourism Research*, 31 (4): 431–54.	Competitive strategy Hospitality Knowledge and Innovation
Phillips, P. A. (1999) 'Hotel Performance and Competitive Advantage: A Contingency Approach' *International Journal of Contemporary Hospitality Management*, 11 (7): 359–65.	Competitive strategy Hospitality Hotels
Porter, M. E. (1996) 'From Competitive Advantage to Corporate Strategy: Managing the Multibusiness Company', in M. Goold, M. and K. Luchs (eds.) *Strategic Issues for Diversified Groups*, New York: Routledge, pp. 285–314.	Competitive strategy Competitve advantage SBUs
Stokes, R. (2008) 'Tourism Strategy Making: Insights to the Events Tourism Domain', *Tourism Management*, 29 (2): 252–62.	Strategy formulation Tourism Events
Swart, K. (2005) 'Strategic Planning: Implications for the Bidding of Sport Events in South Africa', *Journal of Sport Tourism*, 10 (1): 37–46.	Strategy formulation Events South Africa
Wahab, S. (1996) 'Tourism Development in Egypt: Competitive Strategies and Implications', *Progress in Tourism and Hospitality Research*, 2 (3–4): 351–64.	Competitive strategy Tourism Egypt
Wahab, S. and C. Cooper (2001) 'Tourism, Globalisation and the Competitive Advantage of Nations', *Tourism in the Age of Globalisation*, London and New York: Routledge, pp. 3–21.	Competitive strategy Tourism Destinations
Wernerfelt, B. (1984) 'A Resource-Based View of the Firm', *Strategic Management Journal*, 5 (2): 171–80.	Strategy formulation Resource based view
Whitla, P., P. G. Walters and H. Davies (2007) 'Global Strategies in the International Hotel Industry', *International Journal of Hospitality Management*, 26 (4): 777–92.	Competitive strategy Hospitality Hotels
Wilkinson, P. F. (1989) 'Strategies for Tourism in Island Microstates', *Annals of Tourism Research*, 16 (2): 153–77.	Competitive strategy Tourism Island states
Wong, K. K. and C. Kwan (2001) 'An Analysis of the Competitive Strategies of Hotels and Travel Agents in Hong Kong and Singapore', *International Journal of Contemporary Hospitality Management*, 13 (6): 293–303.	Competitive strategy Tourism Hotels Singapore and Hong Kong

CASE LINKAGES

Case 2	Tourism Queensland
Case 3	Ryanair
Case 4	Hyatt Hotels
Case 5	Days Inn
Case 6	Reed Exhibitions
Case 7	Thomas Cook

11

Strategic methods for tourism, hospitality and event organizations

Introduction and chapter overview

This chapter and the preceding chapter (Chapter 10) are concerned with the formulation of strategy; with the following chapter (Chapter 12) being concerned with evaluating the available options and choosing between them.

The previous chapter considered two aspects of strategic formulation, namely *competitive strategy* and *strategic direction*. This chapter considers the third aspect: *strategic methods* – how will the development be achieved, i.e. which methods will be adopted.

In Chapter 10 we considered two approaches to competitive advantage that have been developed in the academic literature: the *competitive positioning* approach and the *core competence* or *resource-based* approach.

This chapter briefly discusses a third approach – the *relational approach* – which recognizes that many resources critical to an organization's success can come from outside the organization. Consequently, this approach stresses the importance of inter-firm working in the form of business structures such as alliances, joint ventures, franchising arrangements and management contracts, all of which have become common in *THE* contexts.

The decision as to which method of strategic development to adopt is critical to the success of strategy. We have encountered the idea of growth as one of the main business objectives. The variety of methods used for development will be considered, together with a critical appraisal of the success or failure of these methods.

The chapter considers first internal (or organic) growth and then discusses the various mechanisms of external development: mergers and acquisitions and various forms of joint development involving various types of collaborative arrangements. Finally, the chapter looks at 'downsizing' strategies such as demergers.

After studying this chapter, readers should be able to:

- Define and distinguish between internal and external methods of business development and to provide relevant *THE* examples.
- Describe and provide illustrations of the various types of merger and acquisition.
- Explain the motivations behind mergers and acquisitions and the reasons why they succeed or fail.
- Describe what is meant by the various forms of joint development such as strategic alliances and assess with relevant *THE* examples why organizations enter into them.
- Compare and contrast the circumstances in which the various methods might be used in the constituent parts of *THE*.
- Explain what is meant by a disposal and describe why, at times, *THE* organizations might pursue this pathway.

Alternative strategic methods

Having considered the direction of development and aspects of competitive strategy in the previous chapter, we can now turn to a consideration of the strategic methods which can be employed to achieve the strategic objectives that have been set. In determining the methods by which strategic development will take place the management of *THE* organizations are faced with making a choice between three basic options. These are to:

- Develop internally (or organically as it's often called) utilizing existing available resources.
- Merge with/acquire other companies or allow the company to be acquired by another company.
- Develop through joint development with other organizations by making some form of collaborative arrangement.

The three strategic methods are shown diagrammatically in Figure 11.1.

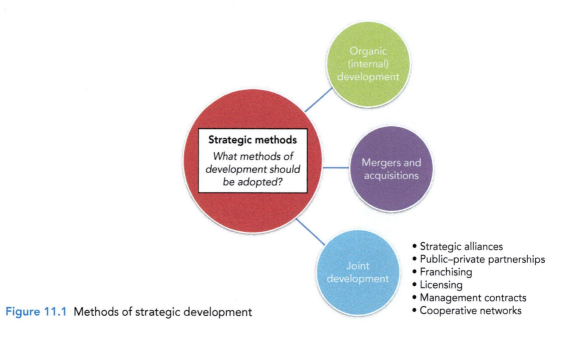

Figure 11.1 Methods of strategic development

Many organizations use each of the alternative strategic options in different circumstances. The same company may, for instance, choose to grow organically in one market, acquiring another company in a second market and form a collaborative venture in a third market in recognition of the differing market characteristics that exist.

The different methods have associated advantages and risks and the choice between the methods may vary at different points of the economic cycle.

Strategic methods in *THE* contexts

Organizations operating in *THE* have to make a choice between the various methods available to them and a full range of strategic methods are used by them. Franchising, management contracts, strategic alliances and public–private partnerships are particularly characteristic of the sectors of *THE*, though the methods are not evenly represented in all sectors as shown later in Table 11.6. These characteristic forms of joint development are discussed fully later in the chapter.

Throughout the chapter *THE* examples of strategic methods in practice are highlighted and these are summarized in Table 11.1.

THINK POINTS

- Using examples from *THE*, define and distinguish between internal and external business growth.
- Describe and distinguish between the three conceptual approaches to strategic management which have been introduced in this text.

Table 11.1 A summary of illustrative cases of strategic methods used by *THE* organizations highlighted in this chapter

Strategic method	*THE* examples	Comments
Organic development	MSC Cruise Line	Swiss cruise line expands through the development of two vast new cruise ships
	Frankfurt Messe	German exhibition organizer expands around the world
	Marriott International inc.	Global US based hotel corporation develops a new brand – Courtyard
	Accor Hotels	French global hotel group expands mainly through organic growth
Mergers and acquisitions (M&A)	International Airlines	Consolidation of airlines through mergers following partial deregulation
	Reed Exhibitions	Event manager develops into world leader through acquisition
	Carnival and Star Cruise Lines	Two cruise lines contest the takeover of Norwegian Cruise line
	US Airlines and Online Retailers	Airline names disappear and powerful online retailers are created by M&A
	European Tour Operators	Mergers of vertically integrated tour operators cleared by regulators

Table 11.1 continued

Strategic method	*THE* examples	Comments
Joint development		
Strategic alliances and joint ventures	Global Distribution Systems (GDS)	Joint venture companies formed to develop major GDS systems
	International Airlines	Major international airlines group together to form three strategic alliances
	Virgin, Emirates and Etihad	Airlines choose not to join strategic alliances to maintain independence
	Hilton Worldwide	Two independent Hilton companies form a strategic alliance which develops into a merger
	Carlson Redizor Hotel	A good 'strategic fit' between hotel partners developing a strong alliance
Public–private partnerships (PPP)	Colorado Convention Center and SMG	City and state join with major event company SMG to develop and manage a major event venue
	Busan International Film Festival	PPP in Korea develops a major international event to attract visitors
	Baltimore Inner Harbour	PPP redevelops run-down waterfront with attractions, event, hotels and infrastructure
	Marketing Birmingham	British industrial city uses PPP to enhance facilities and attractions and attract visitors
Franchising	Yum! Brands and Enterprise Holdings	International growth through franchising for fast food and car rental companies
	Holiday Inn Hotels	Large hotel chain acts as the model others follow for growth
	Royal Host Inc.	Royal Host expands Travelodge chain in Canada through a master franchise agreement
Management contracts	Skywest	American regional airlines operating services under management contracts
Cooperative networks	Best Western	The world's largest hospitality consortium allows individual properties to compete internationally
Retrenchment		
Divestment	Thomas Cook plc	A vertically integrated tour operator sells businesses to reduce debt
Management buy-out	Icelolly.com	Travel price comparison website is bought by its management

Organic (internal) growth

The commonest mechanism of growth

Organic growth is the most straightforward mechanism of business growth. Most companies have used internal growth as their main method of growth at some time and so its 'popularity' is obvious. The essential feature of organic growth is the reinvestment of previous years' profits in the existing business, together with finance provided by shareholders and banks. By increasing capacity (by, say, offering a larger number of holidays for sale, increasing the number of hotel rooms or managing a larger number of events), the organization takes on more employees to cope with the extra demand. In so doing, turnover increases and so does the capital (balance sheet) value of the business.

Organic growth is common during the early stages of corporate development as companies build markets and develop new products. It is also a common method of growth where access to capital markets might be restricted as with public sector organizations. Large companies may also use this method alongside external growth to consolidate market position.

For example – the introduction of an additional cruise ship by a cruise line or the building of an additional hotel by a hotel group are examples of organic growth. Earlier years' retained profits, possibly enhanced by additional funding provided by banks or shareholders, are channelled into the development and the organization benefits from the increased market share and increased turnover. MSC Cruises is a division of a Swiss shipping company with headquarters in Geneva and is the fourth largest cruise operator in the world, after Carnival Corporation and plc, Royal Caribbean Cruises and Norwegian Cruise Line. When two ships each weighing almost 140,000 tonnes (the MSC Divina and MSC Preziosa) entered service in 2012 and 2013 the cruise line was able to significantly increase passenger capacity and its market share.

The case of Frankfurt Messe below illustrates an organization that has grown quickly by utilising organic growth to achieve a considerable scale of operations.

SHORT CASE ILLUSTRATION

Organic growth: Frankfurt Messe event management organization

Germany, being a manufacturing and trading nation, has a long tradition of organizing international trade fairs and exhibitions, the origins of which date back several hundred years in some cases. Consequently Hannover, Hamburg, Düsseldorf, Munich, Berlin and Frankfurt all have extensive modern exhibition spaces which rank amongst the world's largest. Berlin, for example, hosts ITB Berlin which rivals London's World Travel Market as the world's largest event focusing on the travel and hospitality industries and their suppliers.

In 1585, a small group of Frankfurt merchants put the request to the town council to establish a regular exchange in the form of trade fairs. Frankfurt has considerable advantages as a trading centre situated as it is at the heart of European trading routes. Modern day trade fairs were reestablished after the second world war and grew steadily in the post-war years as Frankfurt established itself as Germany's preeminent financial centre (as the home of the German and European Central Banks and Germany's leading commercial banks) and also crucially as Germany's leading hub airport – a position it retains to this day.

In the post-war period the Messe Frankfurt organization was established to organize and manage trade fairs. The Messe (Market) Frankfurt organization is a public sector body which is 60 per cent owned by the City of Frankfurt and 40 per cent by the state government of Hesse. The growth is partly attributable to the application of the Messe Frankfurt business model.

The increasing diversity of the products on offer quickly created a trend towards greater specialization of trade fairs. This was reflected in the 'Frankfurt principle'. Individual product groups which had previously been represented in the comprehensive multi-sector trade fairs for the consumer goods industry were further developed to create independent industry events. Thus Frankfurt created market leading trade fairs in industry sectors such as automotive, textiles, books, music, lighting and paper.

From a fairly small base in post-war Germany, Messe Frankfurt has grown to become one of the world's leading exhibition end events management organizations – a position it has achieved largely through organic growth. In 2012 109 trade fairs were organized, attracting over 1.5 million visitors. The company has been able to leverage its expertise through international events and although its centre of gravity will remain in Frankfurt, crucially 68 of the events in 2012 were organized in foreign locations, which the company delivered through a network of 28 global subsidiaries. The international expansion of Messe Frankfurt, particularly in emerging markets, is an important part of the company's strategy for future development.

www.messefrankfurt.com

Questions

1. What are the advantages and possible limits of the Frankfurt Messe business model?

2. What sort of competitive threats might Frankfurt Messe face?

The potential advantages and disadvantages of organic growth over other methods of development are summarized in Figure 11.3.

Many large companies have used this method extensively in reaching their present size, but few have used the method exclusively.

For example – the Marriott hotel corporation developed its Courtyard hotels concept organically during the 1990s, from the drawing board through to its current international market penetration in major business cities (Crawford-Welch, 1994).

Table 11.2 The potential advantages and disadvantages of pursuing organic growth

Potential advantages	Potential disadvantages
Usually a lower risk option in that the increase in capacity remains fully under the control of the existing management thereby avoiding the risks of dealing with other organizations is avoided.	Usually a slower mechanism compared to external growth methods where the 'bolting on' of a new company or co-operation with other organizations is a faster route to growth than gradual growth by internal means.
Core competencies can usually be exploited and existing expertise, experience and knowledge can be capitalized upon.	Relying on the competencies and resources of a single organization may lead to shortages and might mean that important opportunities are not exploited.
The potential problems associated with the integration of differing organizational cultures are avoided.	
Disruption to cash flows is likely to be less than in the case of mergers or acquisitions and to a lesser extent with the various forms of joint development. Other methods of development often require large up-front payments whereas organic development allows investment to be spread over time.	

This method tends to be chosen in circumstances where:

- suitable partners for joint development are unavailable;
- merger or acquisition is prevented on the grounds of cost, unavailability of suitable targets or regulatory disapproval;
- access to capital is limited to pursue alternative methods;
- directors want to maintain control; and
- the necessary resources and competencies are available internally.

The case of Accor (below) shows how this large hospitality company has primarily used organic growth, coupled with targeted acquisitions, to drive growth.

SHORT CASE ILLUSTRATION

Organic growth: Accor Hotels

The French group Accor, with its headquarters in Paris, is one of the world's largest hoteliers. The brands it operates under various contractual arrangements include: Sofitel, Mercure, Pullman, Novotel and Ibis.

In 2012, Accor opened more than 30,000 rooms (210 hotels) around the world. The group followed mixed methods of strategic development in that it primarily grew through organic growth which was supplemented by targeted acquisitions. The group added some 8,000 rooms through the acquisition of the Mirvac group of hotels in Australia and New Zealand and Grupo Posadas in South America. Both acquisitions are in high-growth hospitality markets and in both cases hotels have been rebranded to trade under the group's upscale and midscale brands such as Sofitel, Pullman, Novotel and Mercure.

However, the majority of Accor's growth in 2012 has come from organic growth of its brands targeted at emerging hospitality markets and this trend is set to continue.

To take full advantage of the dynamic growth in emerging markets, which is being led by a fast-rising middle class in search of travel and leisure opportunities, most of the 2012 room openings were concentrated in Asia-Pacific and Latin America, with the BRIC countries (Brazil, Russia, India and China) accounting for nearly one third of the total.

This powerful regional dynamic was particularly apparent for the group in China, India, Brazil and Indonesia, a trend which is likely to continue as shown by Table 11.3 below.

Table 11.3 Accor's emerging markets: growth achieved largely organically

| | Current portfolio | | Pipeline through to 2016 | |
	Hotels	Rooms	Hotels	Rooms
China	127	31,000	Nearly 100	20,000
India	19	3,694	42	8,000
Indonesia	56	11,300	54	10,000
Brazil	173	27,612	100	16,000

Source: Table constructed by the author from Accor's Annual Report 2012, accessed at www.accor.com

Questions

1. Why do you think Accor has chosen mainly to grow organically?

2. What are the potential disadvantages to Accor of this form of growth?

External mechanisms of growth: mergers and acquisitions (M&As)

Definitions

It is difficult to open the business press without encountering details of a proposed or progressing merger or acquisition. The term *merger* is however sometimes replaced in such text with the word *takeover* or *acquisition*. The same news story may use all three terms as though the words meant the same thing. It is also common in the media and elsewhere for the terminology *M&A* to be used as a shortened umbrella term covering all such activity.

For the purposes of a strategy text such as this, it is important to clarify the main terms generally used in connection with this process:

Merger: the shareholders of the organizations come together, normally willingly, to share the resources of the enlarged (merged) organization, with shareholders from both sides of the merger becoming shareholders in the new organization.

The international airline industry, for example, has undergone a period of rapid consolidation over the last ten to 15 years involving a number of mergers (particularly in North America). This merger activity is briefly described in the short case illustration below.

SHORT CASE ILLUSTRATION

Mergers in the international airline industry

The US Airline Deregulation Act of 1978 introduced airlines operating in the USA to a new world of competitive threats and opportunities. The key change, whereby price-regulating power was removed from the Civil Aeronautics Board (CAB), enabled airlines to increase the variety of fares offered and the frequency by which fares were changed (Evans, 2001a). The changes which the act brought forward led to the entry into the market of low-cost carriers such as Southwest Airlines and Frontier and eventually led to industry consolidation in the USA. Later deregulation in Europe has also led to some consolidation in Europe and elsewhere.

Established 'legacy' carriers in the USA had extensive networks operating hub-based networks and generally had high-cost bases and low and variable levels of profitability. The high costs and the frequent economic downturns in the sector frequently led to the major airlines incurring heavy losses and several, such as American and US Airways, have been close to bankruptcy. One response to these pressures has been the consolidation of the US air market which dates back to 2005 with the merger of US Airways and America West followed by Delta merging with Northwest in 2010 (keeping the Delta name) and United merging with Continental in 2012 (keeping the United name). American Airways and US Airways completed a merger during 2013 retaining the American Airways name and with US airways leaving the Star Alliance and joining the OneWorld alliance as part of American Airways.

Thus 'the large eight airlines of ten years ago are on course to become the big four (including Southwest), with reduced competition meaning that the remaining players have greater pricing power – the ability to raise fares after years of slashing ticket prices during market share grabs' (Parker, 2013a).

Elsewhere in the world, consolidation has been less extensive though important mergers have taken place in Europe and Latin America:

- Air France merged with KLM Royal Dutch Airlines in 2004 to form Air France KLM;
- The International Airlines Group was formed in 2011 by a merger of British Airways and Spanish carrier Iberia;
- Lufthansa acquired Swiss in 2005 and Austrian Airlines in 2009;
- Latam Airlines is the result of the merger in 2012 between LAN Airlines of Chile and TAM Airlines of Brazil.

While the level of market concentration means that much of the consolidation has probably already taken place, in Europe Parker (2013a) argues that there is a case for more mergers because there are still too many carriers.

Evans, 2001a; Parker, 2013a and various newspaper articles

Questions

1. What factors favoured consolidation in the international airline industry?
2. Why do many airlines historically have low and variable profit levels?

Acquisition: a 'marriage' of unequal partners with one organization buying and subsuming the other party. In such a transaction the shareholders of the target organization cease to be owners of the enlarged organization unless payment to the shareholders is paid partly in shares in the acquiring company. The shares in the smaller company are bought by the larger.

Reed Exhibitions below provides an example of an acquisition.

SHORT CASE ILLUSTRATION

Acquisitions: Reed Exhibitions

Reed Exhibitions is a subsidiary of the UK- and Dutch-owned publishing and communications business Reed Elsevier plc which is based in London. The business has grown rapidly in recent years despite the challenging economic environment and with revenues of about £850 million it accounts for about 14 per cent of Reed Elsevier's group revenues.

Although comparisons are difficult and industry boundaries are not easily determined in what is a highly fragmented industry, Reed Exhibitions is a leading events management business and the market leader in exhibitions with about 5 per cent of world markets. Key products include London's World Travel Market which has also spread to subsidiary locations.

Today Reed Exhibitions, like most large businesses, has a mix of strategic methods as evidenced by the 2012 Reed Elsevier Annual Report which states that the exhibition business:

. . .is focused on driving organic growth by leveraging its global sector expertise, by developing new events and by building out its technology platforms. It is also shaping the portfolio through a combination of strategic partnerships and selective acquisitions in high growth sectors and geographies as well as withdrawal from markets and industries with lower growth prospects.

However, the key transformational episode in the business's rise to its leading industry position came in 2000 when the company acquired Miller Freeman Europe. With operations in France, Germany, Italy, Spain and Scandinavia, major events which were acquired included Batimat, the world's leading building exhibition (held annually in Paris), and Alimentaria international trade fairs focusing on food and drink.

The acquisition of what was at the time the leading pan-European trade exhibition organizer catapulted the company into the world's leading exhibition organizer, a position it has retained. In the decade since, there has been a strategic shift in emphasis towards the growth markets of China, Latin America, Russia and the Middle East, fuelled by joint venture partnerships. In China, for example, Reed has created eight joint venture companies which bring together the global resources of Reed with local partners which have local market knowledge access and expertise. The first of these companies established in 2003 was Reed Huayin (Shanghai), which is a joint venture with the Huayin Media Group, the leading media and information provider for the Chinese printing and packaging industry.

Reed Elsevier Annual Report 2012, accessed at www.reedelsevier.com/

Questions

1. What are the methods that Reed Exhibitions has used to grow?

2. Why might the methods used have changed at different periods in its development?

Takeover: technically the same as an acquisition, but the term is often taken to mean that the approach of the larger acquiring company is unwelcome from the point of view of the smaller target company. The term *hostile takeover* describes an offer for the shares of a target public limited company, which the target's directors reject. If the shareholders then accept the offer, despite the recommendation of the directors, the hostile takeover goes ahead.

For example – In 2000, Carnival Corporation of the USA, the world's largest cruising company, and Star Cruises contested ownership of the Norwegian Cruise Line. Star, which was founded as an associate of the Genting Group of Malaysia with its corporate headquarters in Hong Kong, and Carnival both tried to take over the Norwegian Cruise Line based in Miami. After an expensive and hard-fought battle Star succeeded in resting control of the takeover target.

The effects of mergers and acquisitions

Whichever of these routes (mergers, takeovers or acquisitions) is taken, the result is a larger and usually more financially powerful company. There are cases, however, where the purchasing company pays too much to acquire another company or where the high financing costs cannot be serviced satisfactorily. In these cases the purchasing company is left financially weakened and may be subject to be taken over by another company.

The word *integration* is the collective term used to describe these growth mechanisms.

One of the consequences of M&A activity is that many of the well-known 'names' of the past have disappeared, while some of today's best-known companies are relatively young in their current form.

For example – in the North American airline industry, well-known names with long histories such as Northwest, Continental and America West have ceased to exist in the last ten years or so. By way of contrast, online global travel retailer Expedia traces its roots as a Microsoft subsidiary only to 1996 before it was sold by the company in 1999. Both companies retain their headquarters in suburban Seattle.

KEY CONCEPT

Combined market value

All public limited companies have a market value. Market value equals the number of shares on the stock market (the *share volume*) multiplied by the share price. It is taken to be a good indicator of the value of a company because it accounts for the company's asset value plus the 'goodwill' that the market attaches to the share. It follows that the combined market value of a merger or acquisition is the two companies' values added together. It is an indication of what the company will be valued at after the integration goes ahead.

A common misunderstanding surrounding the integration process is that two organizations always come together in their entirety. In practice, much integration is the result of one organization joining with a divested *part* of another. That is to say that one company has made a strategic decision to withdraw from an industry or market in an attempt to maximize the value of the resources it no longer wants (i.e. an unwanted part of the previous company structure) and sells them to another company.

The reasons why companies *demerge* and sell subsidiaries in non-core elements is addressed later in this chapter.

THINK POINTS

- Define and distinguish between internal and external business growth.
- Using examples from *THE*, define and distinguish between a merger and an acquisition.
- Summarize the reasons why a business might seek to pursue external rather than internal growth.

Synergy – the main objective of mergers and acquisitions

Synergy was introduced in Chapter 10. Synergistic benefits can arise from both organic (internal) developments, by deploying organizational resources more effectively, or externally through M&As or joint development.

The over-riding purpose served by integration is that of synergy. Integration can be said to be synergistic when the *whole is greater than the sum of the parts*, often expressed as we noted in Chapter 10 as '2+2=5'. If the integration is to achieve synergy, the 'new' company must perform more efficiently than either of the two parties would have done had they remained separate. Interestingly, in describing the strategic alliance between Rezidor and Carlson Hotel groups (discussed later in the chapter) the companies utilize similarly poor arithmetic in describing the benefits of their alliance as the '1+1=3' effect.

On a simple level, we can conceptualize synergy using a human example. A car rally team of two enables the team to win a race if they work together with one driving and one navigating. If the two were to work separately, then each person would have to drive and navigate at the same time.

Synergy is measured in terms of increased added value. Kay (1995:145) makes the point that 'value is added, and only added, [in an integration] if distinctive capabilities or strategic assets are exploited more effectively. A merger adds no value if all that is acquired is a distinctive capability which is already fully exploited, as the price paid will reflect the competitive advantage held'.

Accordingly, integrations that do not enable the 'new' organization to produce higher profits or consolidate a stronger market position are usually deemed to have been relatively unsuccessful. Why failures sometimes occur is discussed in a subsequent section.

The motivations for mergers and acquisitions

Though synergy is often cited as the over-riding purpose for external growth achieved through integration, there are a number of more detailed potential reasons for pursuing such a strategic method. Table 11.4 presents a summary of these motivations.

The precise nature of the integration selected will depend upon the specific objectives being pursued. If, for example, market share is the objective, then it is likely that a company will seek a suitable horizontal

Table 11.4 A summary of the motivations for mergers and acquisitions

M&A motivation	Comments
Increase market share	Increase pricing power in an industry.
As means of entering a new market	Possibly to offset the effects of decline in current markets or to broaden the portfolio of markets in which sales are generated.
Reduce competition	Purchasing a competitor or a potential competitor.
Gain control of valuable assets	Purchasing and controlling assets such as brand names, pieces of intellectual property like patents, access rights, e.g. development land for new hotels or take-off and landing slots at crowded airports.
Gain preferential access	Purchasing 'downstream' assets to gain preferential access to distribution channels or 'upstream' assets by purchasing a supplier to gain preferential access to inputs.
Broaden product range	Purchasing another business to exploit more market opportunities and to spread risk.
Develop new products	Acquiring a business may be a faster way of developing new products than by research and development carried out internally.
Gain access to new technologies	New operational or information technologies may reduce costs, increase quality or increase product differentiation.
Gain economies of scale	Combining two companies may result in economies in areas such as purchasing, human resources and marketing.
Make productive use of underused resources	Resources such as finance sitting in bank accounts or staff not working effectively might lead to greater productivity being achieved.
'Asset strip'	The practice of breaking up an acquired company and recovering more than the price paid by selling the parts separately.
Enhance corporate reputation	Appropriate if the existing company name has been associated with an alleged misdemeanour.

integration. On the other hand, a vertical integration would be more appropriate if supply or distribution concerns are uppermost amongst a company's threats.

External growth achieved through integration is usually expensive and it therefore has significant financial resource implications, not to mention sizeable bills presented by lawyers and investment bankers who are inevitably brought in to advise on the process. Accordingly, it is entered into for specific strategic purposes that cannot be served through the normal progression of organic development.

There are also often significant challenges facing managers in integrating the merged businesses. These managerial challenges for moving the merged company forward successfully might include:

- designing an effective organizational structure;
- deciding where operations and head offices should be located;
- successfully integrating policies, processes and procedures;
- creating or modifying organizational cultures so that the two parts work together harmoniously;
- ensuring that marketing and branding of the two parts are aligned;
- planning the cash flow so that merger costs can be successfully serviced.

Potential problems and success factors with mergers and acquisitions

The fact that mergers and acquisitions are undoubtedly popular as methods of business growth may lead us to conclude that they are always successful. In practice, this is not always true. A number of studies have analysed the performance of companies after integrations and the findings are not very encouraging (see for example Kay, 1995 and Tuch and O'Sullivan, 2007).

These studies found that many corporate 'marriages' failed to work and sometimes ended in divorce, or that a combined company failed to add value for the company's owners (its shareholders). Of those that did survive, Tuch and O'Sullivan (2007), in a review of empirical research on the impact of acquisitions on firm performance, found that, in the short run, acquisitions have at best an insignificant impact on shareholder wealth, while in the long-run performance analysis reveals overwhelmingly negative returns.

There are a number of reasons – 'failure factors' – why integrations might not work. History has shown that mergers and acquisitions work best when the initiator company follows a number of intuitively fairly obvious 'rules'. They are designed to offset the failure factors which have been identified. Accordingly, the importance of detailed information gathering before the integration and careful analysis of the information cannot be over emphasized.

Table 11.5 presents a summary of the potential failure and success factors for mergers and acquisitions.

Government policy and integrations

Government policies on mergers and acquisitions may contribute to some integration failures. Many countries worldwide have adopted policies and legal underpinning providing for merger control. National or sometimes supranational competition agencies, such as the European Union or the US Federal Trade Commission, are often empowered to consider the competitive implications of allowing larger mergers to proceed.

Such measures are adopted so as to prevent anti-competitive consequences of over-concentration of power as a result of mergers and acquisitions. The relevant authorities are usually concerned with asking whether the concentration will impede successful competition.

Table 11.5 A summary of potential failure and success factors for mergers and acquisitions

Potential failure factors for mergers and acquisitions	Potential success factors for mergers and acquisitions
Lack of research into the circumstances of the Target Company (and hence incomplete knowledge). Failure in this aspect (often termed 'due diligence' by accountants) can result in some nasty surprises after the integration.	Identification of a suitable 'target' candidate with whom to merge or acquire. Preparation for an approach should involve a detailed evaluation of the target company's competitive position. This would typically comprise a survey of its profitability, its market share, its product portfolio, its competitiveness in resource markets, etc.
Cultural incompatibility between the two parties.	Consideration being given to the compatibility of the two companies' management styles and culture. Because integrations often involve the merging of the two boards of directors, it is usually important that the directors from the two companies are able to work together. In addition, the cultures, if not identical in character, should be capable of being brought together successfully.
Lack of communication within and between the two parties.	The possibility of a successful marriage between the two *corporate structures* (see the discussion of this in Chapter 10). If one is, for example, very tall and centralized and the other is 'fatter' and decentralized, problems may occur in attempting to bring the two together.
Loss of key personnel in the target company after the integration.	Retaining key personnel. If the target company has key personnel (say a key manager or a distinctive research capability resident within a number of uniquely qualified scientists) then measures should be taken to ensure that these key people are retained after the integration. This can often be achieved by holding contractual talks with these people before the integration goes ahead.
Paying too much for the acquired company and hence over-exposing the acquiring company to financial risk.	The initiating company ensuring that the price paid for the target is realistic. A key calculation of any investment is the return made on it and this is usually measured as the profit before interest and tax divided by the price paid for it. It follows that the return on investment (as a percentage) will depend upon the price paid for the target company. The valuation of a company is a complex accounting calculation, which depends on the balance sheet value, the prospects and performance of the company, and the value of its intangible assets (such as its brands, patents, etc.).
Assuming that growth in a target company's market will continue indefinitely. Markets can fall as well as rise and future trends may not follow past patterns.	The price paid for the target company should take likely market trends into account. This is often done through so-called 'scenario planning'. This involves analysing various scenarios which model market movements in various circumstances. This enables the buying company to buy the target company which will provide an appropriate return even if the market falls.

Control of mergers and acquisitions: The example of the European Union (EU)

The European Union provides an example of the way in which individual governments (or governments acting collectively in this case) attempt to regulate and control mergers and acquisitions.

European competition regulations are provided for in The Treaty of Rome, 1957 (the primary legislation of the EU), in the form of two 'articles' that regulate integration between companies resident within two or more EU states. Both articles are designed to stimulate competition between companies in member states. They can be used by authorities within the EU to influence the behaviour of business that may seek to enter into integrations that may reduce competition in a market. One of these, Article 86, refers particularly to mergers and acquisitions.

Article 86 is designed to prohibit the abuse of a dominant market position (i.e. a high market share). It does not prohibit monopoly as such, but seeks to ensure that large business do not use their power against consumer and competitor interests. This indirectly acts against large companies seeking to acquire a high market share by integration.

The administrative part of the EU, the European Commission, has the responsibility to implement Article 86. If the annual turnover of the combined businesses exceeds specified thresholds in terms of global and European sales, the proposed merger must be notified to the European Commission, which must examine it. Below these thresholds, the national competition authorities in the EU Member States may review the merger. Mergers are approved if they are found not to impede successful competition. If it is found that the merger will impede competition it is either rejected or approved with conditions.

THINK POINTS

- Explain the reasons why mergers and acquisitions sometimes go wrong.
- Explain the measures an organization should take to increase the probability of success of a merger or acquisition.
- Providing examples, explain why public authorities try to regulate mergers and acquisitions.

The short case illustration relating to consolidation of European tour operators below illustrates examples of mergers that were approved by the EU, albeit in one of the cases cited, subject to conditions being met.

SHORT CASE ILLUSTRATION

Merger control: European tour operators

The European outbound tour operator sector underwent a period of consolidation during the first decade of this century. The highly fragmented sector experienced a large number of both horizontal and vertical mergers and acquisitions and two major pan-European groups emerged.

Both groups emerged in the middle of 2007 and both the mergers were approved (albeit with conditions in the case of Tui).

Thomas Cook Group plc is a British global travel company listed on the London Stock Exchange. It was formed on 19 June 2007 by the merger of the German Thomas Cook AG (itself the successor to the long established British group, Thomas Cook and Son) and MyTravel Group plc.

TUI Travel PLC is an international leisure travel group listed on the London Stock Exchange. It was formed in September 2007 by the merger of British tour operator, First Choice Holidays plc, and the Tourism Division of Germany-based TUI AG, which owns 56.4 per cent of the company.

The European Commission while approving both mergers did so in the case of Tui on the condition that it sold its Irish subsidiary Budget Travel.

The EU is normally wary of approving deals that reduce the number of big market operators to just two (Buck and Blitz, 2007). However, in its findings on the Thomas Cook merger with MyTravel plc, the Commission acknowledged that the travel market had changed substantially since it reviewed and blocked the planned merger of MyTravel (then known as Airtours) and First Choice in 1999.

The development of the internet has provided consumers with access to a large spectrum of travel sites, it said, including online tour operators but also search engines and comparison websites.

www.tuitravelplc.com; www.thomascookgroup.com; and Buck and Blitz (2007)

Questions

1. Why might regulators have been concerned about the competitive impact of the mergers?

2. What competitive changes in the marketplace may have led to the mergers being approved?

The relational approach to strategic management

As Rumelt (1991) testifies in a much-cited article, strategy is concerned fundamentally with explaining differential firm performance.

In searching for sources of differential performance or competitive advantage, two prominent views have emerged

- the competitive positioning approach; and,
- the core competence or resource-based approach.

These two perspectives focus on those resources that are housed within the firm and have certainly contributed to how firms achieve competitive advantage. In an influential article, Dyer and Singh (1998) introduce a third view:

- The relational approach

The relational approach recognizes that a firm's critical resources may extend beyond firm boundaries. The main aspects of this approach are summarized well by De Wit and Meyer (2010: Ch. 7) and their approaches are contrasted and applied in a hospitality context by Kim and Oh (2004).

The central thesis expounded by Dyer and Singh is that a pair or network of firms can develop relationships that result in sustained competitive advantage.

In studying strategy, while competition between single firms is still the main focus of attention, various ways of joint development nevertheless provide opportunities to create and sustain competitive advantage. Because firms may exist as parts of larger networks of relationships with buyers, suppliers and competitors, competitive advantage can be achieved either through an exchange relationship or through the joint contribution of the specific partners (Dyer and Singh, 1998).

Organizations do not operate in isolation, as is perhaps implied by the two approaches considered previously, but instead interact with other organizations to achieve common goals. When two or more organizations move beyond a mere transactional relationship and work jointly towards a common goal they form an alliance, partnership or network (De Wit and Meyer, 2010:158), the details of which we will consider in the subsequent sections.

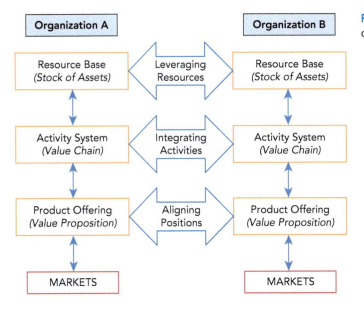

Figure 11.2 Inter-organizational cooperative objectives

The ways in which organizations work together vary enormously in terms of their complexity, long-term sustainability and the level of commitment. However at the heart of the involvement is the understanding that working together in a co-operative manner can lead to objectives being achieved which could not be achieved by a single organization working alone. Specifically, working cooperatively may lead to objectives being attained in relation to resources, activities and products as indicated by De Wit and Meyer (2010) in Figure 11.2.

The three approaches are put into context and contrasted in a *THE* setting by Kim and Oh (2004). As Kim and Oh point out the three approaches are not mutually exclusive but instead emphasize different important aspects of strategy in achieving competitive advantage and adopt an integrated approach. They argue that to achieve long-term profitability and growth firms should:

- Adapt themselves to the rapidly changing environment (Porter's competitive positioning)
- Continually develop new resources such as market-based resources (resource-based approach); and
- Build strong relationships with customers, suppliers, and other companies selling in the same markets (the relational approach).

Thus an integrated approach to strategy is called for which draws on the three strands of thought. The challenge then for managers is not to choose one approach over another, since they are not like opposing armies in a battle, but rather to seek the advantages of the different perspectives and blend them together in an effective synthesis.

External mechanisms of growth – Joint development

Introduction

Joint development is where two or more organizations work together to share resources and activities to pursue common strategic objectives.

This method of development has been increasingly popular over recent years and is very common amongst *THE* organizations seeking help and support from other organizations. Companies within the airline, hospitality and travel organizer sectors of the industry – in particular and between these sectors (with ancillary services such as car rental often also involved) – are increasingly favouring joint development achieved through so-called collaborative strategy as their chosen means of growth. Public sector bodies involved in events, tourism and hospitality and wider aspects of public policy are also favouring joint development by working with the private sector in so-called public–private partnerships. It is clear that collaborative arrangements of various types have become an increasingly important strategic method of development in *THE*, although statistical data is often lacking.

Indeed, Dev *et al.* (1996) assert that throughout the 1980s and 1990s joint development in *THE* increased until the position was reached in the early 1990s at which most of the world's major airline, hotel and car rental firms were linked by a web of cross-shareholdings, joint ventures, and joint sales and service arrangements.

Joint development is sometimes viewed as a 'hybrid' method of strategic development since it does not imply full integration like mergers and acquisitions or the 'go-it-alone' approach implied by organic development. Instead it represents a middle way, involving co-operation with partners. Whilst this method of development has its own specific advantages and disadvantages, it is also a method that is favoured in some cases because of the drawbacks with the alternative methods:

- *Organic development* – Increasingly complex environments have meant that organizations often cannot develop adequately through using their own resources and competencies alone. In such circumstances organic development is often slow and companies are not able to achieve the required scale of operations (or cannot achieve the scale quickly enough) in order to compete effectively with international competitors.
- *Mergers and take-overs* – This method might also be viewed as having serious drawbacks or may be prevented in some cases by regulatory restrictions, lack of appropriate targets or insufficient financing. This method is expensive, entails some loss of control and has often led to a loss of value for the combined company rather than value creation (Tuch and O'Sullivan, 2007).

Joint development involves companies working co-operatively as opposed to competing with each other and *collaborative* strategy (or co-operative strategy as it is often termed) has become an important focus of strategic management (both in practice and conceptually) in recent years. Thus collaborative strategies involve organizations working with rivals or other related companies to the mutual benefit of both [or all] organizations (Lynch, 2012:208).

In rapidly globalizing world markets, collaborative strategy is often viewed as the engine driving companies that are deficient in certain competencies, resources or assets, to link together with other companies in a similar predicament in order to derive jointly the competitive advantages they lack on their own.

Recent years have seen the rapid rise of collaborative strategy as a favoured strategic option. The point is highlighted by Faulkner (1995) when he argues that collaborative (co-operative) strategy had become the counterpart of competitive strategy as a key strategic management tool. The famous Japanese management guru Kenichi Ohmae (1989) observes in comparing commercial organizations with the foreign policies of national governments that companies are learning what nations have always known; 'in a complex, uncertain world filled with dangerous opponents, it is best not to go it alone'.

Categorizing various forms of joint development

There are various ways in which joint development takes place involving differing levels of co-operation between the parties involved.

In categorizing these collaborative agreements theoretical bases have been advanced. Contractor and Lorange, (1988), who have written extensively on this subject, for instance, view inter-organizational collaboration in terms of the degree of interdependency between the parties involved.

Faulkner (1995) categorizes collaborative relationships in relation to their degree of integration ranging from markets to hierarchies.

- In a *hierarchy* a central authority governs internal relationships and has the formal power to coordinate strategy and solve inter-departmental disputes (De Wit and Meyer, 2010:165).
- In a *market* relationships between firms are non-hierarchical, as they interact with one another without any explicit or dispute settlement mechanism (De Wit and Meyer, 2010:165).

Between the two extremes a range of inter-organizational forms exist with ascending levels of integration.

Strategic alliances and joint ventures represent the most integrated form of inter-organizational collaboration. Any further integration represents a single corporate form subject to fully integrated decision making. At the other end of the spectrum of inter-organizational collaboration are co-operative networks. Figure 11.7 illustrates Faulkner's categorization of inter-organizational forms.

There are many inter-organizational forms which can be developed between the extremes of hierarchies and markets. Todeva and Knoke (2005), for example identify 13 basic forms of inter-organizational relations appearing in the theoretical and research literatures.

Joint development in *THE*

Here we will focus on those aspects of joint development of most relevance to *THE*, namely:

- strategic alliances and joint ventures
- public–private partnerships
- franchising
- management contracts
- cooperative networks.

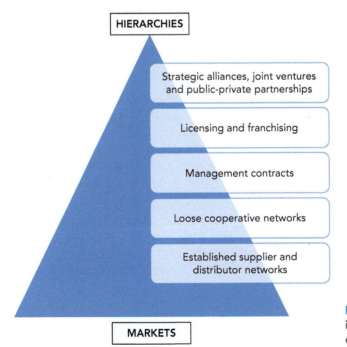

Figure 11.3 A categorization of inter-organizational forms of joint development

Table 11.6 Focus of inter-organizational activity in *THE*

	Transport	Hospitality	Attractions	Destination organizations	Travel organizers	Events
Strategic alliances	✓	✓	✓		✓	
Public–private partnerships			✓	✓		✓
Franchising		✓			✓	
Management contracts	✓	✓	✓			
Cooperative networks		✓	✓	✓	✓	✓

There are many examples of the inter-organizational forms listed in the sectors which constitute *THE*. However, the examples are not evenly spread throughout the *THE* sectors.

As Table 11.6 indicates the focus of inter-organizational forms differs in the six constituent sectors we identified in Chapter 2 (Figure 2.2). Thus, for example, strategic alliances are particularly prevalent with regard to transport, hospitality and travel organizers, while public–private partnerships are a particular feature of attractions, destination organizations and events.

Strategic alliances

Defining and Categorizing Strategic Alliances

A large academic literature has emerged discussing strategic alliances since Harvard academic Rosabeth Moss Kanter's influential contributions were published in the 1990s (Kanter, 1990 and 1994). The various aspects of strategic alliances such as their categorization, reasons for their formation, partner selection, success and failure factors are summarized by Ireland *et al.* (2002) and Kale *et al.* (2002) and in *THE* contexts by Evans (2001a, b). Even though their failure rate is high, the number of alliances being formed is growing because they have the potential to create value (Ireland *et al.*, 2002).

While many analysts regard strategic alliances as recent phenomena, inter-organizational linkages have existed since the origins of the firm as a production unit (Todeva and Knoke, 2005). The literature is far from clear as to just what constitutes a 'strategic alliance' and many definitions have emerged such as French (1997) and Glaister and Buckley (1996). There is some consensus that strategic alliances represent a high level of collaboration between partner organizations and that alliances form a subset of collaborative activity that excludes a number of other forms of inter-firm co-operation that are *not* alliances (Glaister and Buckley, 1996).

Most writers would agree that the term strategic alliance applies largely (though not exclusively) to 'horizontal' inter-organizational relationships between companies engaged in similar types of activity at the same level. Thus, in categorizing strategic alliances, most writers would exclude buyer–seller relationships, sub-contracting, franchising, management contracts and licensing, where to some degree the parties involved may have opposing goals and the relationships are 'vertical' between organizations along the channel of distribution.

A common understanding of strategic alliances is cited from the academic literature provided by Yoshino and Rangan (1995:5). The authors provide three criteria that should be satisfied in identifying strategic alliance. Thus Yoshino and Rangan state that a strategic alliance involves:

- at least two partner firms that remain legally independent after the alliance is formed;

- sharing of benefits and managerial control over the performance of assigned tasks;

- making continuing contributions in one or more strategic area, such as technology or products.

These three criteria imply that strategic alliances create inter-dependence between autonomous economic units, bringing new benefits to the partners in the form of intangible assets, and obligating them to make continuing contributions to their partnership (Todeva and Knoke, 2005).

Different alliance forms represent different approaches that partner firms adopt to control their dependence on the alliance and on other partners. The strategic alliance forms that result are also associated with different legal forms, which enable firms to control the resources allocation and the distribution of benefits among the partners.

Bennett (1997) writing in an airline context, for example, distinguishes between 'tactical' alliances, which are loose forms of collaboration that exist to gain marketing benefits, and 'strategic' alliances, which are characterized by being longer and wider in their scope and level of commitment. Thus the many code-sharing agreements that proliferate among the world's airlines can be viewed as tactical rather than strategic, since they are limited in their scope.

A strategic alliance also involves, in some cases, a demonstration of commitment by way of *equity swaps* by which the partner companies purchase minority equity stakes in each other thereby having a vested interest in ensuring the financial success of partners.

The distinction between *joint ventures* and *strategic alliances* is one of emphasis rather than fundamental distinguishing characteristics. A joint venture normally implies joint ownership of assets by the parties involved, the formation of separate independent operating companies for the management of the shared activities, and collaboration on a relatively narrow range of activities. In practice the distinction between the two terms is often blurred. The Global Distribution Systems are examples of Joint Ventures and they provide an illustration below.

SHORT CASE ILLUSTRATION

Joint ventures: Global distribution systems

The major computer reservation systems that have developed were (in most cases) examples of joint ventures. The major world-wide systems now generally termed Global Distribution Systems enable automated transactions between vendors and booking agents to provide travel-related services to the end consumers. The major GDS operators are:

- Sabre
- Amadeus
- Worldspan
- Galileo.

Sabre, based in Dallas, Texas, owes its origins to American Airlines which developed the system until it was sold by the airline in 2000.

The other three major GDS systems were all developed by consortia of airlines which traded as separate joint-venture companies until they were sold by their respective airlines.

Worldspan and Galileo, although they both continue to trade separately, are part of the TravelPort corporation based in Atlanta, Georgia. Worldspan was developed by Delta Airlines, Northwest Airlines (now merged with Delta) and the now defunct TWA. Galileo was operated as a joint venture between a number of European airlines including British Airways, KLM and Aer Lingus.

Amadeus, based in Madrid, Spain, was developed and operated by another joint venture company owned by a consortium of European airlines including Air France, Lufthansa, SAS and Iberia until it became an independent company in 2005.

There are also a number of smaller, more regionalized GDS providers including Abacus. The company, which is based in Singapore, unlike the global suppliers outlined above, continues to operate as a joint venture company. It is owned by a consortium of leading Asian airlines including All Nippon Airways, Cathay Pacific, China Airlines, Eva Airways, Garuda Indonesia, Philippine Airlines, Malaysia Airlines, Royal Brunei Airlines, and Singapore Airlines.

In addition to GDS suppliers there are hundreds of Alternative Distribution System (ADS) channels that are operating. These can be viewed as 'hybrid distribution' mechanisms as they provide web-based visibility while gaining their information from the major GDS systems. These suppliers include well-known names such as Travelocity, Expedia and e-Bookers and Opodo. (which was itself owned by Amadeus until it was sold in 2011).

www.abacus.com.sg; www.amadeus.com; www.travelport.com; www.sabre.com.

Questions

1. Why might joint ventures be the favoured method for developing GDS systems?
2. What competitive threats might affect further growth of GDS and how might they respond?

Strategic alliances in *THE*

The formation of strategic alliances has been evident in many industries including pharmaceuticals, vehicle manufacture and chemicals. This process has been replicated in the international travel industry where they have come to form a central feature of the developing industrial structure, particularly in relation to hospitality companies and transport companies.

Many writers including Bennett (1997), Evans (2001a and 2001b), Chathoth and Olsen (2003) and Oum *et al.* (2000 and 2004) have pointed to the high level of activity in the field of *THE* alliance formation particularly in relation to airline and hospitality companies.

However, the alliances differ in:

- their motives;
- their scope;
- their structures,
- their objectives; and
- the ways in which they are managed.

The motivations for forming strategic alliances in *THE* are numerous and complex. It is clear, however, that in recent economic history *THE* has been characterised by the emergence of many alliances, some of which have subsequently failed and new realignments of companies have been forged. Long-standing 'natural' alliances between travel companies and accommodation providers which saw the ownership of hotels by railway, shipping and airline company interests as a means of extending their reach into new markets have been replaced by other arrangements as inter-company and inter-modal competition has increased (Garnham, 1996).

Many examples of alliances exist in the airline and hotel sectors, although many fall short of being 'strategic' in the true sense, but are more 'tactical' in their orientation, focusing primarily on marketing and information technology collaboration rather than wider collaboration.

In distinguishing between three levels of alliance on the basis of short-term, medium-term or long-term (strategic) relationships, Dev and Klein (1993) argue that in such a hierarchy of relationships, partners often progress from the simple short-term relationships through to complex strategic relationships, but that only at the strategic level do alliances offer companies the ability to respond to the pressures of global competition and illiquidity. Potential benefits from such strategic ways of working together they argue accrue from:

- enhanced market coverage both geographically and by segment;
- greater economies of scale in advertising, sales, distribution and purchasing; and
- complementary strengths in operations and marketing.

THINK POINTS

- Explain what is meant by a 'strategic alliance' and how does it differ from a merger?
- Using relevant examples explain why *THE* organizations seek to form strategic alliances.
- Explain the difference between a strategic alliance and a joint venture?

The short case below illustrates how airlines are attempting to gain the advantages of operating through strategic alliances.

SHORT CASE ILLUSTRATION

Strategic alliances: International airlines

The airline industry has long been characterized by agreements between pairs of airlines on particular routes. These 'bilateral' agreements are particular to the routes in question, change quite regularly and are limited to particular aspects of the airlines' operations.

Strategic alliances go much further than these bilateral code-sharing agreements because agreements are 'strategic' in nature in that they:

- involve several airlines;
- are wide-ranging in their scope including various aspects of activities; and
- are long-lasting in their impact on the airlines involved.

Many of the world's international airlines now belong to one of the three major strategic alliance groupings: Star Alliance, Oneworld and SkyTeam.

In each case the constituent airlines are trying to derive the advantages of working collaboratively as part of the strategic alliance.

These advantages for the airlines might include cost reductions or enhanced revenue from sharing:

- sales offices;
- maintenance and operational facilities;
- airport lounges;
- coordinating schedules thereby increasing load factors and avoiding flight duplication;
- aircraft purchasing; and
- marketing.

The benefits for the traveller might include:

- the ability to gain access to a wider network;
- easier transfers between airlines; and
- the sharing of loyalty programme incentives.

The long case study 'Strategic alliances in the airline sector' in Part 6 provides more detail on the three airline strategic alliance groupings.

www.staralliance.com; www.skyteam.com; www.oneworld.com

Questions

1. What are the differences between strategic alliances and code-share arrangements?

2. What factors have led to airlines forming strategic alliances?

A conceptualization of the collaborative process for international airlines

Figure 11.4 provides a conceptual model of the strategic management processes involved in the formation of strategic alliances using the airline sector as an example, though it could be adapted for other THE sectors.

It is argued (Evans 2001a) and consistent with the structure of this text, that a four-stage process takes place:

- The strategic analysis of the internal organizational and external environmental 'drivers', which act as the underlying motivating reasons for alliance formation is carried out.
- Alternative strategic options are postulated and evaluated and the option of strategic alliance formation (either with or without equity) participation is chosen.
- Implementation issues have to be considered including the choice of appropriate partners and issues relating to the structure and scope of the alliance.
- The strategic alliance is evaluated against selected criteria purporting to measure the success of the alliance. The evaluation of the alliance is fed back into the analytical phase so that any changes based upon experience can be incorporated.

Motivations for strategic alliance formation

A number of studies have sought to identify the underlying motivations for the formation of strategic alliances – for example Glaister and Buckley, 1996 and Bennett, 1997 – and it is generally accepted that some types of external drivers need to be present.

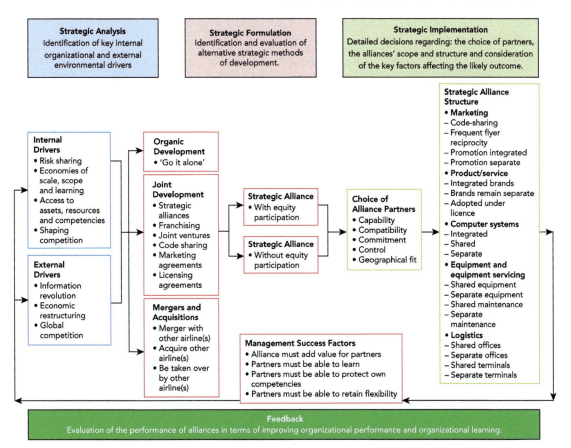

Figure 11.4 Conceptualization of the collaborative strategy process for international airlines

Child and Faulkner (1998) suggest that there are six key external driving forces and four key internal needs acting as motivational forces in the formation of alliances:

External driving forces for alliance formation can be considered to be:

- turbulence in world markets and high economic uncertainty;
- the existence of economies of scale and/or scope as competitive cost-reducing agents;
- the globalization or regionalization of a growing number of industries;
- the globalization of technology;
- fast technological change leading to ever increasing investment requirements; and
- shortening product life cycles.

Internal needs for alliance formation are to:

- achieve economies of scale and learning with one's partner;
- get access to the benefits of the other firms' assets, such as, technology, market access, capital, operational capacity, products or personnel;
- reduce risk by sharing it, notably in terms of capital requirements, but also in respect of research and development expenditure; and

- help 'shape' the market, i.e. increased scale provides more power to set prices and influence how the market operates.

The nature of the internal needs and external drivers will of course vary between industries and industry sectors, and the emphasis may alter in different markets and may shift over time.

Potential difficulties with strategic alliances

Despite the surge in their popularity, international strategic alliances are often viewed as inherently unstable organizational forms. It has been noted by Porter and Fuller (1986), for instance, that alliances involve significant costs in terms of co-ordination, reconciling goals with an independent entity and creating competitors. These associated costs serve frequently to make alliances transitional rather than stable organizational forms and therefore rarely can they be viewed as a sustainable means of creating competitive advantage. The failure rate associated with alliance arrangements is high, often resulting in significant costs to one or both parties concerned. This high failure rate has been reported in a number of studies. Bleeke and Ernst (1991), for instance, in their study of cross-border alliances found that some two thirds had run into serious managerial or financial trouble within the first two years resulting in a high rate of failure.

In a *THE* context strategic alliances, it can be argued, are often a second best option, often necessary only as result of regulatory and legal restrictions, which frequently make mergers and acquisitions problematic.

In the airline sector where strategic alliances are commonplace, the strategic importance that many governments attribute to airlines means that there are legal restrictions on foreign ownership. In the United States foreign investors are restricted to 25 per cent ownership while in the European Union the figure is 49 per cent. Thus in both these cases (which are replicated in many other countries) a controlling stake in airlines is denied to foreign investors. Thus in the airline sector where full ownership of companies by foreign based nationals is often prohibited, and which is often characterized by a high degree of consumer loyalty to 'national champions', alliance formation has in many cases been viewed as the only viable market entry mechanism, at least in the short-to-medium term.

Such organizational structures can hardly be viewed as models of business efficiency and long-term sustainability therefore must be questionable. Thus alliances, it can be argued, are rarely stable sustainable entities, for they commonly represent the only viable market entry mechanism when regulatory and other barriers to entry effectively block other market entry modes (such as full acquisition). Additionally many of the alliances that are formed appear in a constant state of flux altering their shapes, sizes and partners in response to changes in the competitive environment: with partners being added or dropped and partners falling out amongst themselves.

One further point to note is that alliances can fail *not* because of the partners' failure to agree on substantive points but on the contrary; the alliance leads to the delivery of a high degree of collaboration and agreement between the partners. In cases where the results of successful collaboration are apparent, partners may be forced towards merging their activities providing regulatory and legal restrictions do not stand in the way. The case of Hilton Hotels (see illustrative case) illustrates this facet of strategic alliances.

Collaboration, though often financially beneficial, nevertheless may imply that the partners are operating sub-optimally, since the need for communication and management duplication imposes higher cost levels. The airline alliances have elaborate committee structures so that their member airlines' views are represented. Such structures are often viewed as over-bureaucratic, expensive and leading to slow decision making.

Though there is some inherent instability in the airline alliances which have been mentioned, it should be noted that the alliances themselves have been operating for over 20 years, albeit aided by the regulatory

SHORT CASE ILLUSTRATION

Strategic alliances: Hilton strategic alliance develops into a full merger

Hilton is one of the most recognized brands in international hospitality, but the brand has not always been unified. Two arms of Hilton – Hilton Hotels Corporation of the USA and Hilton Hotels International, based in the UK – were separated under different ownership in 1964; some 45 years after Conrad Hilton opened the first hotel to bear his surname in Chicago. Thus there were two separate, fully independent companies operating hotels under the Hilton name – the American branch operating largely in North America and the British branch mainly operating Hilton hotels elsewhere in the world. From the time of the split, the relationship between the two chains bearing the Hilton name was frequently acrimonious and had never been close.

The situation, which was confusing to consumers and failed to fully capitalize on a strong brand, was clearly not an optimal way of operating. In 1996 both chains appointed chairmen committed to capitalizing fully on the strength of the Hilton brand which resulted in an agreement during 1997 to form a wide-ranging strategic alliance between the two chains, covering a joint reservations system (boosted by $100 million spending on new technology), the extension of HHC's loyalty rewards to Hilton International, the adoption of joint brand identities including a new logo and joint marketing campaigns.

While the strategic alliance improved the operational efficiency of the brand and worked well, the logical extension of the co-operation was full integration. This was achieved in 2005 when Hilton Hotels Corporation acquired the British chain Hilton International for £3.3 billion. Subsequently the company was sold to private equity group Blackstone during 2007 for $26 billion, just as the economy was moving into recession, saddling the group with $20 billion of debt. Blackstone's investment eventually paid off when the group was floated on the New York stock market in 2013.

www.hiltonworldwide.com

Questions

1. What are the factors which led to the two parts of Hilton merging?

2. What are the difficulties that might have be been encountered after the two parts merged?

---

restrictions described. It should also be noted that though the three major alliance groupings mentioned (together with several other smaller groupings) are important in the airline sector, there are also many other airlines that have yet to join any of the alliances or which have chosen not to do so.

In particular the low-cost carriers which have proliferated around the world have developed independent models which do not involve alliance membership. Some other well-known airlines (particularly the fast-growing Middle East airlines) have deliberately chosen not to join strategic alliances, choosing to remain independent as a deliberate part of their strategic development.

For example – UK-based Virgin and the fast-growing United Arab Emirates' airlines of Emirates and Etihad based in Dubai and Abu Dhabi respectively have chosen not to join the alliance groupings. In November 2013, the Financial Times quoted Tim Clark, Emirates President, saying that 'It was within our DNA to chart our own destiny'. Instead, amongst other actions, the airline has negotiated a wide-ranging code-sharing agreement with Australia's Qantas. Etihad Airlines, though, in rejecting alliance membership, has pursued a different strategy in that it has purchased minority stakes in five airlines, including Air Berlin, Germany's second-largest carrier (Parker, 2013b).

Partner selection in strategic alliances

Despite the evident instability demonstrated by many alliances, there may be ways in which companies can form and manage alliances to ensure a longer life expectancy and a higher degree of stability. Although there are, no doubt, many complex reasons for alliance failures, many writers such as Kanter (1994) and Medcof (1997) agree that poor initial selection of alliance partners is a key variable.

Medcof (1997), for instance, postulates that the first imperative in partner selection is to ensure that the proposed partner represents a good *strategic fit*, that is the weaknesses of one partner are complemented by the strengths of the other partner and vice versa.

Four criteria have been proposed by Brouthers *et al.* (1995) for when partners are deemed to be a good strategic fit and to determine whether a proposed partnership is likely to be workable at an operational level. These criteria, referred to conveniently as the 'four Cs', are *complementary skills; cooperative cultures; compatible goals;* and *commensurate levels of risk.*

- The *complementary skills* criterion questions whether the prospective partners have the ability to successfully carry out their respective roles in the alliance.

Managers should form alliances only with firms that fulfil a specific need and that can contribute to the overall strength of the alliance. Without the addition of new skills, expertise or market access, there is little incentive for the respective companies to work together.

- The *cooperative cultures* criterion concerns the ability of the partners to work together effectively.

The criterion therefore relates to the respective corporate cultures of the partner organizations and to the working relationships between staff and management at the partners. Managers must look for opportunities to learn from partners and be sensitive to different cultural norms in different settings.

For example – in the case of the strategic alliance that was agreed between Carlson and Rezidor (see illustrative case below) both companies shared strong Scandinavian roots and had successfully worked closely together before a formal strategic alliance was agreed in 2012.

- The *compatible goals* criterion concerns the willingness of partners to commit resources, effort and know-how to an alliance.

In a worst-case scenario a partner might expend only the minimum effort required to keep the alliance alive whilst opportunistically leaving others to bear the brunt of the responsibilities and at the same time receiving know-how and market intelligence from alliance partners. Strategic objectives should be fulfilled through the alliance which could not have been fulfilled without the alliance being in place. In some cases one partner may be dominant thereby suppressing the aspirations of others. In other cases a dominant partner may ensure the effectiveness of the alliance owing to that partners' superior expertise or market position. The key question in this regard is whether the system of control which the alliance puts in place allows all partners to achieve their strategic objectives.

- The *commensurate levels of risk* criterion concerns the appropriate balance between partners in the alliance and between risks contained within the alliance and those sheltered from it.

A strategic alliance in which one member company is taking a disproportionate share of the financial and/or operational risks is unlikely to be sustainable. In many cases alliances are formed to reduce risks, but while reducing some risks they may produce risks of their own. For example the alliance may reduce exposure to political uncertainties but increase the risks of giving away corporate competencies or financial pressures brought about by the financial weaknesses of a partner.

- What might an organization do to ensure that its strategic alliance is successful?
- Explain the difference between a strategic and a tactical alliance?
- Explain why partner selection is so important in strategic alliances and what factors should be considered.

An important example of strategic alliances relating to hotels – the Carlson Rezidor Hotel Group – below illustrates some of the points made in the preceding sections.

SHORT CASE ILLUSTRATION

Strategic alliance involving equity participation: Carlson Residor

The Carlson group of travel companies is a large diversified travel group based in Minneapolis which owns significant brands including TGI Friday restaurants and a majority stake in Carlson Wagonlit Travel, a global leader in business travel management. The group also owns the Radisson brand which it has developed outside North America, largely through a strategic alliance with the Rezidor Hotel Group.

When Scandinavian Airways (SAS) decided to sell off the hotel group it had developed in 2006 a public company quoted on the Stockholm stock exchange was born. Carlson, which had long cooperated with SAS, bought a 50.3 per cent controlling stake in Rezidor and entered into a strategic alliance with Rezidor which continues to develop strongly. The Carlson Rezidor Hotel Group was launched in January 2012 as a strategic alliance between Rezidor and Carlson.

Through a number of joint activities, Carlson Rezidor aim to globally align their core brands and to reach more than USD400 million in incremental revenue as well as a RevPAR index increase of more than nine points by 2015. Within the strategic alliance, Rezidor is also employing a strategy of increasingly moving to an asset-light business model to enhance earnings. The proportion of hotels in differing categories is shown in Table 11.7 below.

Table 11.7 Hotel co-operation as a strategic alliance

	Franchised	Managed	Leased
2006	26%	43%	31%
2013	22%	54%	24%

The particular asset-light model favoured by Rezidor involves moving from franchised and leased properties towards a portfolio of mainly managed assets as the table shows. The rationale for this strategic choice is that leases are viewed as highly profitable but volatile; franchises provide stable income but with lower potential margins; whereas, managed properties are likely to give the highest returns over time.

www.rezidor.com, www.carlson.com

Questions

1. What are the advantages of Carlson-Rezidor forming a strategic alliance?
2. What factors might lead to the Carlson-Rezidor alliance being sustainable?

Public–private partnerships

Another form of joint development common in *THE* is what are often referred to as *public–private partnerships* and are a response to the nature of the industry. Though Long (1997) writes in a tourism context his observation is equally valid for hospitality and events when he states that 'the fragmented nature of the tourism industry comprised, in most areas, of large numbers of small to medium-scale enterprises, together with a wide range of interest groups from public sector agencies to community groups in destinations, is increasingly recognised'.

As a response to the fragmentation and range of public sector, private sector and community stakeholder groups, various types of arrangements are widespread in many countries to bring the interests together through collaborative arrangements in the form of public–private partnerships.

These public–private partnerships take many forms and often are related to achieving a set of wide-ranging objectives, which include tourism, hospitality and events organizations, but may also include many other types of organizations. Often the public–private partnerships are involved in a broader process of urban development or urban renewal which may have important tourism, hospitality and events components but also involve other elements such as housing, offices, retail developments and transport infrastructure.

In general terms, however, such partnerships normally involve:

- The *public sector* providing the policy and planning framework, and infrastructure provision together with some financial incentives.
- The *private sector* being involved in providing some or all of the financial resources and managerial competencies.

One way in which public–private partnerships are facilitated lies in the provision of event venues and facilities to attract visitors which in turn attract other investment in the form of hotels, restaurants and other activities. The Colorado Convention Center, illustrated below, provides an example of such a partnership.

SHORT CASE ILLUSTRATION

Public–private partnerships: Managing event venues: The Colorado Convention Centre

The USA has a number of large property management companies with sizeable international operations which specialize in event venues. However, unlike its major competitors such as AEG, Live Nation and Nederlander Organization, which generally own or lease their properties, SMG specializes in managing publicly owned facilities. Founded in 1977, Pennsylvania based SMG is now a venue management group with operations concentrated in North America but with further operations in Europe and Asia. One example of a public–private partnership involving SMG's private sector expertise is located in Denver, Colorado.

Built in 1990, the Colorado Convention Center and nearby Bellco theatre are top economic engines driving Colorado's economy. The Convention Center hosts over 400 events annually and is owned by the City and County of Denver but operated under contract by SMG, in a public–private partnership. The partnership is similar to numerous examples operating around the world in that public authorities provide infrastructure, but bring in specialist private sector competencies to manage the facilities.

www.smg.com, www.denver.org

Questions

1. What competencies and resources are provided by the public and private sectors in this case?

2. What motivates public authorities to form PPPs such as the one in Denver?

Public–private partnerships have become common in *THE* in several diverse ways as, for example, in:

- the development or regeneration of many cities;
- providing and managing music, exhibition and conference venues;
- organizing festivals and events for the benefit of both residents and tourists; and
- financing and managing costly infrastructure such as railways, airports, toll highways and hotels.

Public sector involvement in tourism and the visitor economy including hospitality and events is commonplace and brought about by a variety of factors (Heeley, 2001). These include the need to:

- regulate private sector activities;
- provide non-remunerative infrastructure and superstructure;
- remove obstacles to more effective private sector performance;
- redress market failures; and
- provide industry leadership and promotion.

Increasingly, though, it has been recognized in many countries – in terms of government spending (at national, regional and local levels) – that spending on tourism, hospitality and events rates low down in the order of priorities. Such spending is often relatively insignificant both in scale and in terms of need when compared with spending on, say, health, defence, social welfare and education; hence the need to attract private capital.

THE, is however recognized by governments as a significant and growing contributor to revenues both directly and indirectly. Visitors directly contribute to the economy but also contribute through secondary spending by *THE* organizations which spreads to other industries and by providing positive images of destinations thereby indirectly contributing to attracting other commercial activities.

Thus the underlying rationale for public–private partnerships is that the government at various levels want to maintain an interest in *THE* (for the reasons stated above), but in many cases would like to limit its financial contribution and involve private-sector finance and competencies. In many cases public-sector contributions to infrastructure (such as airport and road building) are often used as *pump-priming* to *lever* larger private-sector financial contributions.

The Busan International Film Festival below is an example of public and private sectors working together to create a major international event.

SHORT CASE ILLUSTRATION

Public–private partnerships: Busan International Film Festival

The Busan International Film Festival (BIFF) was inaugurated in South Korea's second largest city. It has subsequently expanded to become one of Asia's largest film festivals, alongside festivals such as those held in Shanghai and Tokyo, the Hong Kong International Film Festival and the International Film Festival of India held annually in Goa. BIFF has grown steadily and in recent years has attracted in excess of 200,000 visitors to the event held in October each year.

As with many other large public events around the world, one of the driving forces behind the success of the festival is the active public–private partnership which supports it. BIFF relies on 'the strength and determination of institutional and governmental support and funding' (Teo: 118).

Financed by Busan's Municipal Authorities, the Korean Ministry of Culture, Sports and Tourism, as well as the Korean Film Council, BIFF has benefited from a political stability that allows the festival to avoid entering into complex budgetary arrangements with sporadic funders and sponsors. Yet, although the active involvement of local and state government ensures constancy and solidity, BIFF still also benefits from the financial endorsement and support of private companies, local banks and universities.

This public–private partnership has proved extremely effective in terms of providing stability for the festival and the necessary financial resources to a provincial Korean festival to achieve and maintain allow international competitiveness.

www.biff.kr and Teo (2009)

Questions

1. Why might a PPP be effective in these circumstances?

2. What other methods might be appropriate for developing such an event?

A feature of the past 40 years has been the creation of 'hybrid' public–private sector mechanisms that have been premised on the public sector letting go of some or all of its traditional intervention and leadership accountabilities (Heeley, 2001).

In a later article Heeley (2011) cites the cases of a number of European cities including: Oslo, Lausanne, Dublin, Barcelona, Vienna and Prague which have established public–private partnerships to facilitate the development of the visitor economy that *THE* activities facilitate. In the USA many examples of real estate developments being facilitated by public–private partnerships focused on the provision of visitor attractions, convention facilities, restaurants, hotels and event venues are evident.

One such example is the case of Baltimore Inner Harbour (see below), which has developed for over forty years through various public–private partnership arrangements (the details of which have changed over the years).

SHORT CASE ILLUSTRATION

Public–private partnerships: Baltimore Inner Harbour; a model for waterfront redevelopment

One case of public–private partnerships in action with tourism, hospitality and events very much at its heart that is often quoted is the case of Baltimore Inner Harbour (see for example Kostopoulou, 2013). Baltimore is the blueprint many other cities have studied and adapted to specific circumstances.

Toronto and Boston also started their waterfront redevelopment projects at about the same time in the late 1970s and subsequently many other US cities such as San Francisco, Seattle and Cleveland as well as several European port cities such as Barcelona, Genoa and Cardiff have followed this lead (Jauhiainen, 1995). The lessons from such redevelopment have also been applied in a Chinese setting by Xu and Yan (2000).

In the case of Baltimore Inner Harbour, an historic but rundown waterfront has been transformed through a partnership now coordinated by the Baltimore Waterfront Partnership (www.waterfront-partnership.org). The development is multi-faceted and includes tourist attractions such as the National Aquarium and Maryland Science Center, and the nearby Baltimore Convention Center and Hyatt Regency Baltimore Hotel. These leisure- and business-focused attractions have acted as 'magnets' to attract further investment and many other hotels, housing schemes and restaurants have been developed in the area.

After 40 years of development it has been argued that further investment is needed to improve and extend facilities and an Inner Harbour 2.0 plan has been proposed which includes the provision of a footbridge linking the two sides of the harbour.

Jauhiainen (1995), Xu and Yan (2000); Kostopoulou (2013); www.waterfrontpartnership.org.

Questions

1. What direct and indirect benefits does Baltimore hope to achieve from its PPP?

2. Why does the public sector not carry out such development on its own?

In the UK these joint development initiatives were pioneered by Plymouth in 1978 with the formation of the Plymouth Marketing Bureau. Many British cities such as Birmingham, Liverpool, Glasgow, Sheffield, Cardiff and Manchester followed in the 1990s. In these cases and in subsequent British examples such normal visitor and convention bureaux activities, i.e. tourism, were supplemented by the related fields of city imaging and festivals management (Heeley, 2001). Subsequently the partnerships were often given wider powers to provide an integrated approach to *THE* as well as inward investment and economic development activities.

THINK POINTS

- Explain the objectives that public and private sectors hope to gain from PPPs?
- What types of development in *THE* are involved with PPPs?
- Why might PPPs prove unsuccessful in some circumstances?

Birmingham's re-emergence in recent years as 'Marketing Birmingham' (shown below) illustrates this integrated approach to *THE*, inward investment and economic development.

SHORT CASE ILLUSTRATION

Public–private partnerships: Marketing Birmingham

Birmingham is an industrial city in the English midlands at the centre of a conurbation of about 2.5 million. The city is famed for its varied manufacturing base and grew to its prominent position during the industrial revolution, but would not be thought of as a 'traditional' visitor destination unlike its nearby historic counterpart, Stratford-upon-Avon.

However, during the economic downturn the city has been hit hard and has turned to attracting increasing numbers of business and leisure visitors as a way of increasing economic activity. This it has done by relying on its central position, selling events often staged at large publicly funded venues and through the activities of a public–private partnership – *Marketing Birmingham*.

Marketing Birmingham is the city's strategic marketing bureau and operates the city's leisure and business tourism programmes *Visit* and *Meet Birmingham* as well as the inward investment programme *Business Birmingham*. The public–private partnership's vision is one in which the city is 'a thriving economic hub and a pleasure to visit time and again. A city that's proud of its story and confident of its future'. Its objectives are to:

- attract investment into Birmingham and surrounding areas – the Black Country and Solihull – and to create jobs;
- increase the value and volume of the visitor economy by helping to diversify and promote its offer;
- deliver significant economic impact by attracting major events and conferences to the area, in line with sectors being targeted for inward investment; and
- strengthen the image and profile of Birmingham as an investment and visitor destination.

Marketing Birmingham is funded by the public and private sectors, including Birmingham City Council, European Regional Development Funding and some 400 local companies. Overall responsibility for the company's progress and governance rests with the Board of Directors, which brings together high-profile figures from both the public and private sectors.

The International Convention Centre (ICC), which comprises 11 purpose-built conference halls, was opened in 1991 having been funded from a number of sources including Birmingham City Council, the Birmingham Chamber of Commerce and European Regional Development Fund (ERDF). The opening of such a venue together with other venues, such as the adjacent Birmingham Symphony Hall and the National Exhibition Centre in the Birmingham suburbs, has enabled Birmingham to host major international events and to build its visitor economy. Birmingham's visitor economy has grown by 10 per cent in six years resulting in a record number of visitors and spending in 2012 when 33.8 million visitors contributed £5.1 billion to the local economy. One of the major contributors to this growth has been the role of the International Convention Centre (ICC) which is situated in the centre of the city.

For example, Birmingham and the (ICC) have won the international bid to host the annual Royal College of Obstetricians and Gynaecologists (RCOG) World Congress in 2016. The three-day international conference is expected to bring more than 2,000 delegates, speakers and exhibitors to the region from nearly 70 countries, boosting the local visitor economy by £2.8 million. Meet Birmingham, the city's official business tourism programme, played a key role in securing the prestigious congress with support from the ICC, which will host the event from 20–22 June 2016.

Adapted from www.marketingbirmingham.com, Edwards and Taylor (2012).

Questions

1. What are the management and governance issues that might arise in such a PPP?
2. Could the same approach be easily transferred to other cities?

Franchising

Franchising is a method involving two parties: the *franchisor* and the *franchisee*.

In return for gaining access to the brand attributes, image, marketing and other support from the franchisor, such as systems and training, the franchisee usually takes a substantial portion of the financial risk (providing the capital investment) and pays fees to the franchisor. Since it involves another party providing the financial resources, it has often proved to be a fast method of expanding for many hotels, restaurants and car hire companies, amongst others.

Franchising is one of the most popular methods of growth in parts of *THE*. Leading industry and ancillary service brands such as Avis and Hertz (car rental companies), Marriott, Holiday Inn, Choice and Radisson (hotels); and McDonald's, Burger King and KFC (fast food outlets) have expanded primarily by pursuing the franchise method. The illustrative case below involving fast food and car rental firms illustrates the speed at which companies can grow when they have established a strong brand by adopting this method.

SHORT CASE ILLUSTRATION

International growth through franchising: Fast foods and car rental

It is not a well-known name, but it is likely that Yum! Brands is familiar to most of this book's readers through its products. Yum! is a fast food provider based in Louisville Kentucky which owns the worldwide rights to well-known brands including KFC, Pizza Hut and Taco Bell. The company formed in 1997 as the result of a sale of PepsiCo's fast food division is a 'Fortune 500' company which is quoted on the New York Stock Exchange and has revenues in excess of $12.5 billion.

Enterprise Holdings is one of America's largest privately held companies. The company, with annual revenues in excess of $18 billion is based in St Louis Missouri and traces its origins to the late 1950s. Enterprise holdings control three of the world's leading vehicle rental franchises: Enterprise, Alamo and National.

In both these cases, a substantial scale and internationally diversified scope of operations have been built relatively quickly. It is unlikely that such scale and scope could have been achieved as quickly if the companies concerned had to rely on their own financial resources. The scale of capital investment required would have been massive and the inherent risks involved would probably have deterred potential investors.

Instead the risks and capital investment were largely dispersed among the many franchisees spread around the world. The franchises investing their own capital were incentivized to grow the businesses and were able to apply local market knowledge while being able to rely on the support offered by strong internationally recognized brands.

www.yum.com and www.enterpriseholdings.com

Questions

1. Why have American companies been particularly successful in using this form of growth?
2. Why has franchising been so prevalent in certain parts of *THE* including fast food, car rental and hotels but not in others?

In capital-intensive parts of *THE* requiring a big financial up-front outlay to establish facilities or in smaller start-up businesses, franchising provides an opportunity for organizations to lower the risks and the level of investment to expand. Thus, this method of growth is particularly prevalent amongst hotel organizations, travel intermediaries and ancillary services such as restaurants and car hire companies, but examples are also to be found amongst airlines and festival and event management companies. It is the case that many small *THE* businesses have been established by becoming franchisees of larger businesses with strong brands.

In the past a number of airlines including British Airways, Lufthansa and Air France have made franchising an important element of the strategic methods they have employed. The method has, however, become less important amongst airlines as acquisitions, industry consolidation, strategic alliances and code-sharing agreements have often taken their place.

There are still some examples in the airline sector, such as Sun Air (www.uk.sun-air.dk), operating as a British Airways franchise, and Air Nostrum (www.airnostrum.es), operating as an Iberia franchise. These two airlines operate regional services from bases in Denmark and Spain respectively.

Nowhere in the commercial field has franchising been more evident than amongst the leading international hotel groups. Progressively most of the largest chains to some degree have followed this strategic method which was pioneered by Holiday Inn during the 1950s (see the illustrative case below). The big international hotel groups operate so-called 'asset-light' business models, having sold most of their real estate assets to concentrate on brand growth through managing and franchising their hotels.

SHORT CASE ILLUSTRATION

Franchising: Holiday Inn Hotels

In 1952 an American entrepreneur named Kemmons Wilson opened the first Holiday Inn hotel in Memphis, Tennessee, after he returned from a family holiday discouraged over the lack of family- and value-oriented lodging. Children stayed free, and the hotel offered a swimming pool, air conditioning, and restaurant on the property. Telephones, ice, and free parking were standard as well. Although commonplace today, these services were revolutionary at the time and set a standard for the hotel industry.

The company became a pioneer of franchising and rapidly expanded the Holiday Inn system primarily through utilizing this method of strategic growth. The brand was almost literally rolled out across the USA, following the U.S. interstate highway system's growth across the country. On the heels of this domestic success, the brand soon found investor interest in Europe and Asia, becoming the largest single hotel brand in the world. By the late 1980s, the Holiday Inn brand could be found in many parts of the world.

In 1990, IHG plc (then known as Bass plc), which has its corporate headquarters in London, acquired Holiday Inn and moved the hotel headquarters from Memphis to Atlanta in the summer of 1991. Atlanta offered the corporate infrastructure, worldwide transportation access and international presence which was felt was necessary for the company to succeed as a global business. Holiday Inn, together with its complementary brands which include Holiday Inn Express, Crowne Plaza and Intercontinental Hotels, has grown (predominantly through franchising) into a vast international hotel grouping. The IHG plc annual review (2012) reported the following key statistics:

Table 11.8 Holiday Inn Hotels

IHG Group plc. – key facts	
Hotels	4,602
Franchised hotels	3,934 (85.5%)
Managed hotels	658 (14.3%)
Owned and leased hotels	10 (0.2%)
Operating profit:	
Americas	$486 million
Asia, Middle east and Africa	$88 million
Europe	$115 million
'Greater China'	$81 million

Go and Pine (1995) suggest that the franchise strategy pursued by Holiday Inn 'is among the greatest success stories in US Business'. In operating franchises Holiday Inn sought to apply strict operating standards and supplied franchisees with almost everything apart from the land upon which the hotel would be built, in order to ensure that there were 'no surprises' (Nickson, 1997).

www.ihgplc.com; *Go and Pine (1995); Nickson (1997).*

Questions

1. What might the potential difficulties be for a franchisor such as Holiday Inn?
2. What might be the potential difficulties for a Holiday Inn franchisee?

The franchise method can vary in its detailed implementation. It may involve a fairly simple arrangement whereby one franchisee develops one unit or a single territory from the franchisor. Many Avis or McDonald's franchisees for example operate one or a limited number of franchise locations.

A more complex arrangement may exist when a large company purchases a *master franchise* from the franchisor, which gives the company exclusive rights to the franchise name for a region or country.

For example – Royal Host Inc. is a Canadian diversified hospitality company which is quoted on the Toronto Stock Exchange and is based in Halifax, Nova Scotia. The company is involved in hotel investment, management and franchising.

Among other activities Royal Host owns the master franchise for the Travelodge brand in Canada. The Travelodge brand is owned in North America by Wyndham Worldwide though a separately owned company trades under this name in the UK (www.travelodge.co.uk), where it is the second largest chain. Under its Master Franchise agreement with Wyndham, Royal Host owns and operates the Travelodge Canada franchise business which currently comprises over 90 hotels across nine Canadian Provinces and Territories. It is Canada's third largest hotel chain.

Although hospitality franchise agreements resemble strategic alliances, in that two parties work collaboratively, they are dissimilar in terms of the attainment of allying partners' objectives and development of inter-firm relationships through resource sharing, as explained below.

Table 11.9 Summary of the advantages and disadvantages of franchising

	Advantages	Disadvantages
Franchisor	Low capital costs	Returns may be capped
	Ability to use brand strength to expand quickly	Some loss of control of the brand
	Use franchisee's local market knowledge and entrepreneurial abilities	Having to consider the interests of the franchisees as a stakeholder group
		Need to scrutinize the structure, organization and financial viability and capabilities of the franchisee
Franchisee	Lower risk than going it alone	Fees and part of profits paid to the franchise holder
	Support from a major company	Risk that franchise quality deteriorates or the franchisor withdraws it
	Exclusive rights to a brand in a particular territory	

In a hospitality franchise agreement, although the two firms involved typically share assets, the risk exposure is not equally shared. The franchisor is exposed to lower risks than the franchisee, who meets the infrastructural requirements of the agreement. The franchisor meets the product, technology, marketing and training aspects of the agreement for a fixed and/or variable fee. Although the variable component of the fee changes with the level of sales, the reduced risk exposure is balanced by the fee's fixed component.

On the other hand, the franchisee's return depends purely on the cash flow generated by the franchise operation. The franchisor usually has the upper hand in the agreement. Consequently, these types of contracts do not create parity in the agreement between the franchisor and franchisee.

The reasons for the popularity of franchising for the franchisor and franchisee and possible disadvantages are summarised in Table 11.9.

Management contracts

Management contracts are a popular joint development method of international growth particularly in the hospitality and airline sectors but also in some cases in relation to attractions and venues.

A management contract is an arrangement under which operational control of an enterprise is vested by contract in a separate enterprise which performs the necessary managerial functions in return for a fee.

The distinction between management contracts and franchising lies in the fact that management contracts involve not just selling a method of carrying out activities and the support of an established brand, as with franchising or licensing, but involve actually carrying out these activities. A management contract can involve a wide range of functions, such as:

- operation of a facility;
- reservation, ticketing and operating systems;
- management of human resources;
- accounting and financial control;
- sales and marketing services; and
- training.

In the case of accommodation, where management contracts are very common, utilizing this method the ownership of the physical asset (the hotel or other accommodation) is separated from its management. The management contract is thus an agreement between a hotel owner (or other form of accommodation) and a hotel operating company, by which the owner employs the operator as an agent to assume full responsibility for the management of the property (Olsen *et al.*, 1991).

As an agent, the operator usually pays, in the name of the owners, all property and operating expenses from the cash-flow generated through operations, retains its management fees and remits surpluses, if any, to the property owner. The property owner on the other hand usually provides the hotel land, building furniture, furnishings equipment and working capital, while also assuming full legal and financial responsibility for the hotel (Olsen *et al.*, 1991).

Many well-known upscale international hotel chains (such as Sheraton, Sofitel, le Meridien, Marriott, Hilton International, Hyatt, Radisson, Nikko and Shangri-La) have successfully utilized this method of expansion. Large international food-service companies such as Compass, Sodexo, and Aramark, based in UK, France and USA respectively have also used this method. These companies (and many others), through being awarded management contracts, have expanded their diverse catering operations internationally to include transport facilities, sport and entertainment venues, and corporate premises.

For the operating company the management contract:

- allows rapid expansion to take place;
- allows easy market penetration; and
- involves little or no capital investment.

The operating company is therefore not prone to speculative risks associated with falling property prices (and also does not benefit from rises in property values). In some cases the operating company will, however, invest some of its own capital in the project alongside the property developer. The operating company also has an agreed rate of return built into its contractual terms.

The principal disadvantage of the management contract for the operating company is the insecurity associated with this method. From time to time the management contracts come up for renewal. It is usual for the workings of the relationship to be reviewed and its success judged at this time. In practice a change in the operating company is quite common, so that when the management contract is renewed the company operating a hotel under a management contract might change from say le Meridien (a Starwood brand) to Hyatt.

There are also a number of the world's airlines which operate feeder or so-called 'regional' services for other carriers. In the world's largest aviation market, the USA, this arrangement is particularly common with a number of airlines competing to operate feeder services into the main hubs of the large international carriers. These airlines generally operate on fixed-price management contracts. Many of these airlines operate most of the functions of a full airline but fly in the colours of the so-called 'legacy' airlines (such as American, Delta and United Airlines) and coordinate their schedules accordingly.

THINK POINTS

- Providing *THE* examples explain the differences between growth achieved through franchising and management contracts.
- Outline the benefits and potential difficulties of franchising for both the franchisor and the franchisee.
- Why has franchising been so successful as a growth method for *THE* and ancillary services?
- Why might PPPs prove unsuccessful in some circumstances?

This system of management contracts among airlines is illustrated by the case of Skywest Inc. below.

SHORT CASE ILLUSTRATION

Management contracts: Skywest Inc.

Though it is a major transport company in its own right with well over 400 aircraft, Skywest Inc. is not well known to consumers. Like other airlines such as Republic Airways and Mesa Air operating similar models, it generally operates through management contracts entered into with other airlines.

Its operating divisions of Utah-based SkyWest Airlines and Atlanta-based ExpressJet provide air passenger services with approximately 4,000 daily departures to destinations in the United States, Canada, Mexico and the Caribbean. Most flights are operated for the 'regional' brands of major US carriers: Delta Connection, United Express and American Eagle and it uses the systems and brand identities of these airlines in operating its services.

The services are managed through long-term, fixed-fee code-share agreements. Among other features of these fixed-fee management contracts the Skywest's partners generally reimburse the company for specified direct operating expenses (including fuel) and pay a fee for operating the aircraft. Such an arrangement provides benefits for both Skywest and its partners. For Skywest it has a relatively stable revenue stream, has access to a strong brand and has an incentive to reduce costs so as to increase operating margins. For the partner airline for which it operates, an extensive and complex regional network is provided at a competitive agreed cost.

www.inc.skywest.com

Questions

1. What are the advantages for major airlines of sub-contracting services to SkyWest through management contracts?
2. What are the risks and benefits for SkyWest?

Co-operative networks

Various types of co-operative networks or consortia have been developed in *THE*.

These networks and consortia are most evident in *THE* in two ways:

- The hospitality sector (where the method is most frequently evident) is characterized by a high degree of fragmentation with a large number of individual or family-owned enterprises. These independently operated businesses face increasing competitive pressures from hotel chains operating branded products which enjoy marketing economies and sophisticated systems.

- *Referral networks* have been formed whereby many of the world's major airlines, hotels, car rental firms, event venues, tour intermediaries and ancillary suppliers are linked by a web of arrangements. These arrangements involve consumers being cross-referred from one supplier to other 'preferred' suppliers in the supply chain. In such circumstances there is an inference that consumers will find that the preferred suppliers are leaders in their offerings or that they are able to offer preferential financial terms.

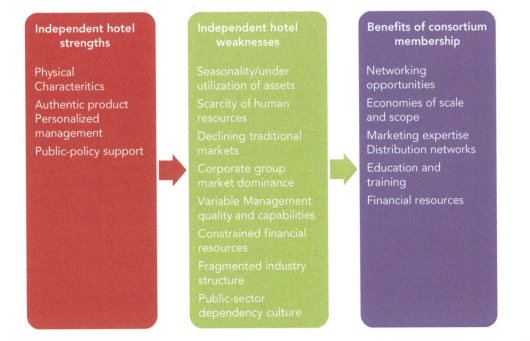

Figure 11.5 The benefits of consortium membership for independent hotels (adapted from Morrison, 1994)

Hospitality consortia

In response to the threats of competing in arenas increasingly dominated by large companies, individually operated hotel and accommodation businesses have increasingly joined together in networks or consortia. By doing so they are attempting to achieve the marketing, branding, and systems advantages of larger rivals whilst maintaining their independence. In return for the payment of a fee the individual hotel receives a range of benefits. In categorizing hotel consortia Fyall and Garrod (2005: 261) point out that the consortia vary in terms of the degree of commitment, control, co-operation involved and in the organizational formality. They also vary in terms of the financial commitments that are undertaken by their members.

The strengths and weaknesses of independent hotels and the benefits they hope to derive from joining a consortium are summarised in Figure 11.5.

Many consortia have been established in specific parts of the world and some such as Best Western, Relais and Châteaux and Small Luxury Hotels of the World have gained widespread international coverage. Consortia have also been formed which involve smaller chains of hotels (rather than individual properties) allowing the chains to maintain their brand attributes and to compete effectively with larger internationally diversified brands.

SHORT CASE ILLUSTRATION

Hospitality consortium: Best Western

Best Western traces its origins back to 1946 when it began as an informal referral system among member hotels in California. It has subsequently grown from its Phoenix, Arizona, base to a presence in over 100 countries representing over 4,000 properties making it one of the world's largest branded chains.

The business model operated by Best Western is that it operates as a non-profit membership association with each member voting on aspects of the association in a way similar to a marketing co-operative. Best Western provides marketing support, reservations systems and a unified brand identity in return for less. The hotels are allowed to keep their independent identity though they are required to use Best Western signage and systems and to identify themselves as Best Western hotels. In the US there are many smaller chains of Best Western hotels which are owned by the same management, though this is less common elsewhere.

Best Western offers members the potential advantage of retaining their independence while at the same time providing the benefits of a full-service, international lodging affiliation offering a global reservations system, marketing, advertising, purchasing, training and quality standards.

Adapted from www.bestwestern.com.

Global Hotel Alliance (GHA) brings together mainly mid-to-upscale brands from around the world. Unlike Best Western it represents smaller chains of hotels which maintain their individual branding. The consortium represents brands such as ParkRoyal, Pan Pacific and Marco Polo which have properties across Asia Pacific; and Kempinski Hotels, a luxury brand with properties across Europe, Asia and Africa and Leela, which is represented at key locations across India.

Best Western provides a well-known example of a hospitality consortium which has grown to a worldwide presence.

Referral networks

These arrangements involve consumers being cross-referred from one supplier to other 'preferred' suppliers in the supply chain, usually in a vertical or diagonal supplier relationship. These networks have proliferated in *THE* to such an extent that most hotel and airlines have suppliers that are favoured partners to which they are referred, though such arrangements are less common in other parts of *THE*.

In such circumstances there is an inference that consumers will find that the preferred suppliers are leaders in their offerings or that they are able to offer preferential financial terms. The arrangements frequently involve loyalty schemes. It is common for there to be reciprocity between airline and hotel frequent flyer and loyalty schemes whereby points earned on own scheme can be credited as points in the other. Since the advent of the internet there have been changes. It was common for airlines to refer to a limited number of hotel partners with which they had a contractual or occasionally equity-owning relationship. This is less common now as airlines often utilize internet intermediaries such as Expedia or Tripadvisor on their sites so as to provide a greater range of choices.

Some of the preferred supplier arrangements for selected airline and hotels are summarized in Table 11.10

Methods of strategic development: a comparison

Clearly each of the strategic development methods outlined in the preceding sections – organic growth, mergers and acquisitions, and joint development – have certain inherent advantages and disadvantages associated with them.

Internal development, for instance, may be relatively slow, while choosing an alliance partner which does not have complementary competencies can be problematic. Merging and takeovers can be expensive and evidence shows that in many cases this method fails to add value to the enlarged group.

Table 11.10 Preferred suppliers for selected airlines and hotels

Selected airline examples	Focus of operations	Preferred car rental suppliers	Preferred hotel suppliers
Aer Lingus	Europe and North America	Hertz	No clear preferred supplier
easyJet	Europe	Europcar	No clear preferred supplier
Jet star	Asia Pacific	Avis and Budget	No clear preferred supplier
South West	North America	Alamo, Avis, Budget, Dollar, Hertz, National Thrifty	No clear preferred supplier
United Airlines	Worldwide	Hertz and Avis	No clear preferred supplier
US Airways	Worldwide	Enterprise, Alamo and National	No clear preferred supplier

Selected hotel examples	Focus of operations	Preferred car rental suppliers	Frequent flyer programmes
Accor	Worldwide	Europcar	Most leading international airlines, excluding US Airline programmes
Best Western	Worldwide	Alamo, Avis, Budget, National	Star Alliance members, Air France/KLM; and most leading US Airline programmes
Hilton	Worldwide	Alamo and National	Most leading international airlines, including US Airline programmes
Mandarin Oriental	Asia Pacific	No clear preferred supplier	Most leading international airlines, excluding US Airline programmes
Marco Polo	Asia Pacific	No clear preferred supplier	Most leading international airlines, excluding US Airline programmes
Marriott	Worldwide	Hertz	Most leading international airlines, including US Airline programmes
Pan Pacific	Asia Pacific	No clear preferred supplier	Most leading international airlines, excluding US Airline programmes

Sources: Company websites

Companies operating in *THE* have to make a choice between the various methods available to them. The decision as to which method to adopt will be influenced by both internal and external factors including the competitive, economic and regulatory environment faced by the company, the availability of finance and other resources. The methods chosen may also depend on the relative strength of the organization, timing and the balance of its portfolio of activities. The choices are complex and will change over time.

Taking the accommodation sector as an example and hotels in particular development can be carried out by franchising; management contracts and owning or leasing property achieved by organic growth or mergers and acquisitions.

Table 11.11 gives a comparison between development through franchising, management contracts and owning or leasing hotels as summarized by the leading international group IHG. In the case of building up portfolios of owned and leased properties, some may have been built up organically whilst others may

Table 11.11 A comparison of franchising, management contracts and managing or leasing hotels

	Franchised	Managed	Owned and Leased
Brand ownership	IHG	IHG	IHG
Marketing and Distribution	IHG	IHG	IHG
Staff	Third party	IHG usually provides General Manager as a minimum	IHG
Hotel ownership	Third party	Third party	IHG
IHG Capital	None	Low/none	High
IHG Income	Fee % of rooms revenue	Fee % of total revenue plus % of profit	All revenues and profits

Source: www.IHG.com

have been acquired through mergers and acquisitions. In either case the hotel group has to provide capital which makes expansion costly and sometimes (in the case of organic development) relatively slow.

In practice the decisions made by major international hotel groups can vary quite considerably. Notwithstanding these differences there has been a significant shift towards the speed of development possible with so-called 'asset-light' business models. These models of development favour franchising and management contracts as opposed to ownership and leasing.

Figure 11.6 demonstrates how selected international hotel groups have developed using different methods. Whilst for example Wyndham Worldwide and IHG have grown largely through franchising, Accor has a portfolio where franchised, managed and owned or leased properties are far more in balance.

Johnson *et al.* (2011), drawing on the work of Dyer *et al.* (2004) and Yin and Shanley (2008), attempt to summarize four key variables that can aid managers in choosing between acquisitions, alliances and organic development.

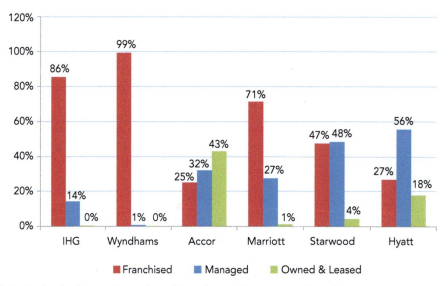

Figure 11.6 Methods of growth employed by selected international hotel groups

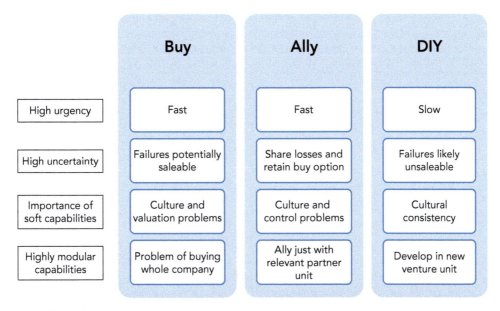

Figure 11.7 Buy, ally or DIY matrix

The 'Buy, Ally or DIY (do it yourself)' matrix produced by Johnson *et al.* is shown as Figure 11.7.

The Buy, Ally or DIY uses four variables:

- *Urgency* – In developing a business, mergers and acquisitions can be a relatively quick method of growth. Organic growth, on the other hand, since it involves everything having to be provided from the organization's own resources and capabilities, is normally a somewhat slower method of growth.

  For example – it is unlikely that TUI would have been able to develop its tour operating business from a mainly German base to a pan-European giant without two strategic moves; the purchase in 2000 of Thomson (Britain's largest tour operator at the time) and the subsequent merger with another large quoted UK tour operator, First Choice Holidays in 2007, transformed the group.

- *Uncertainty* – If there is a high degree of uncertainty alliances offer flexibility in that if successful there is potential to move on to a full merger whereas failures are shared between partners thereby limiting losses. Acquisitions offer the chance of a resale even if the venture is not successful, since the assets have attracted a bid in the past thereby demonstrating potential. A failed organic development might have to be written off since the unit concerned has never been subject to a market valuation.

- *Capabilities* – So-called 'soft' capabilities, such as people and skills, are much harder to value and replicate than 'hard' capabilities such as equipment and machinery.

Most *THE* acquisitions involve a large component of soft capabilities since they are human-resource-intensive activities, often with a strong reliance on brand values. Soft capabilities are also more difficult to control. Consequently organizations need to be cautious with acquisitions or when entering into joint ventures because of these potential difficulties. On the other hand organic development in this respect can be less risky. By developing organically an organization can ensure that these soft capabilities are developed in a culturally consistent manner using acquired knowledge and experience.

- *Modular Capabilities* – The extent to which the capabilities being sought by an organization are 'modular' will have an impact on the favoured method. If the capabilities are distributed in particular divisions or SBUs of the proposed partners then an alliance or joint venture is likely to be favourable. Such an arrangement would mean that one venture could link just with the relevant parts of the partner leaving each to run the rest of their businesses independently. An acquisition could involve acquiring the whole company including parts of no interest which have to be subsequently sold, possibly at a loss. Organic development can also be favoured in these circumstances since the new business can be developed as a distinct and separate division which avoids the involvement of the entire organization.

The choice between the three alternative methods is at times restricted by regulations, available finance and available opportunities. Nevertheless, the matrix shown in Figure 11.7 is a valuable tool in focusing managers on the possible options which might be available for their organizations.

Methods of retrenchment

What is retrenchment?

We should not assume that business strategies are always designed to cause business growth. There are times when organizations may wish to become smaller, i.e. to retrench. As with growth strategy, retrenchment (size reduction) can be achieved through various methods. Retrenchment can be achieved by:

- organic reduction (by winding down operations in specific product areas);
- divestment or demerger – the opposite of acquisitions and mergers;
- disengagement with partners involved in joint development.

Demergers and divestments (which together are referred to as *disposals*) involve taking a part of a company and selling it off as a 'self-contained' unit with its own management, structure and employees in place. The unit may then be sold on to a single buyer (for whom it will be an acquisition) or it may be floated on the stock market as a public limited company.

Disposals occur when parent organizations wish to offload a part of their structure that is no longer in line with their core activity. They can take the form of *divestments, demergers, equity carve-outs or management buy-outs.*

Reasons for disposal

There are a number of reasons why a company may elect to dispose of a part of its structure. The most prominent reasons for disposing of part of a company may include:

- under-performance (e.g. poor profitability), possibility due to poor synergy;
- a change in the strategic focus of the organization meaning some parts are no longer required;
- poor medium-to-long-term prospects;
- it is an unwanted subsidiary of an acquired company;
- the need to raise capital to reinvest in core areas or to increase liquidity in the selling company;
- the belief that it would be more productive if it were owned by another company;
- being used as a tactic to deflect a hostile takeover bid; and
- being part of a process of 'asset stripping' – the process of breaking a company up into its parts and selling them off for a sum greater than that paid for the whole.

Shareholders and disposals

The most common method of corporate disposal is a 'private' transaction between two companies, which is intended to be of benefit to both parties. The seller gains the funds from the transaction and is able to focus on its core areas. The buyer gains the product and market presence of the disposal, which, in turn, will be (we assume) to its strategic advantage.

Disposals are designed to create synergy to the shareholders in the same way as are integrations. We should not lose sight of the fact that business organizations are owned by shareholders and it is the role of company directors (as the shareholders' agents) to act in such a way that shareholder wealth is maximized. If this can be achieved by breaking a part of the company off, then this option will be pursued.

Thomas Cook group has made a number of divestments in recent years as part of its debt reduction strategy, as illustrated below.

SHORT CASE ILLUSTRATION

Divestment: Thomas Cook plc

November 2013 saw the European Thomas Cook plc travel group announce its first full year profits since 2010. The group is involved in a recovery which involves staff cutbacks, closing a large number of shops and selling what it regards as non-core assets. Revenues for the group were slightly higher at £9.3bn, while earnings before interest and tax, though still small at £13m, compared favourably with a loss of £170m in the previous year.

In March 2013 Thomas Cook plc announced that it would sell off its heavily loss-making North America travel businesses to Red Label Vacations for £3.4 million. The sale of Thomas Cook Canada and Thomas Cook USA, which includes the tour operator Sunquest and the 60-branch My Travel retail chain in Canada, represents the sale of a part of the business which lost almost £40m in the previous year.

The sale represented the first since a new chief executive (Harriet Green) was appointed in May 2012. She launched a new strategy of bringing down debt levels at the group by selling 'non-core' assets. Subsequently assets in India, Egypt and Lebanon among others were sold as part of this strategy and a 'sale and leaseback' deal was agreed for some of its aircraft fleet.

Newspapers – various.

Questions

1. Why is Thomas Cook engaged in divestments?

2. Why do you think Thomas Cook has decided to sell these particular assets?

Other methods of disposal

In addition to divestments and demergers, two other disposal methods are noteworthy.

Equity carve-outs

Equity carve-outs are similar to demergers insofar as the spin-off company is floated on the stock exchange. However in this form of disposal, the selling company retains a shareholding in the disposal, with the balance of shares being offered to the stock market. In this respect, equity carve-outs can be seen as a semi-disposal – part of the disposal is kept, but not as a wholly owned subsidiary.

Management buy-outs

A management buy-out (MBO) is said to have occurred when a company which a parent company wishes to dispose of is sold to its current management. MBOs are often a mutually satisfactory outcome when the disposal candidate is unwanted by its parent but when it has the possibility of being run successfully when the existing management have the requisite commitment and skills.

SHORT CASE ILLUSTRATION

MBO: Icelolly.com

Travel price comparison website Icelolly.com completed a £17 million management buyout led by its chief executive officer Dave Clayton in September 2013. The buyout of the Bradford-based company (UK) was backed by Palatine (a Private Equity company) and the investment allows it to continue to invest in its online network and infrastructure. The original founding partners in the business exited the business as part of the buy-out.

Travel companies were early adopters of ecommerce and more and more consumers are research-ing travel related products online. The Icelolly.com holiday price comparison website, founded in 2005, offers around 40 million holiday packages from over 50 UK-based tour operators. The business also trades as an online travel agent via a series of brands, as well as selling advertising space via its site traffic and email database.

www.travelmole.com; www.icelolly.com

Questions

1. What advantages are there in an MBO for Icelolly.com and its founders?
2. For what reasons do managers want to undertake an MBO?

The advantages of MBOs can be summarised as follows.

- The selling parent company successfully disposes of its non-core business and receives a suitable price for it, which it can then re-invest in its main areas of activity.
- The divested organization benefits from committed managers (who become its owners). When the management team find themselves personally in debt as a result of the buy-out (having had to find the money for the purchase), their motivation and commitment tends to be maximized. In many MBOs, some of the capital for the purchase is provided by venture capital companies.
- If part of the MBO capital is met by the company's existing employees, the organization benefits from

the commitment of people who have part-ownership and who therefore share in the company's success through dividends on shares and through growth in the share price.

SMALL BUSINESS FOCUS

This chapter has indicated that there is a great deal of consolidation occurring in all parts of *THE*. As the world's large *THE* groups consolidate they are deriving the benefits from economies of scale and scope and concentrate resources so that they can acquire the latest technology and expertise. In doing so strong internationally recognized brands are being developed for more sophisticated and demanding customers. This growth of the large brands has been achieved by a mix of methods which vary in different parts of *THE*.

However, the consolidation should not be over-emphasized. Although the big brands are expanding their market shares, the sectors which constitute *THE* for the most part are highly fragmented. Accommodation, events management, travel intermediaries, attractions and venues, festivals and exhibition organizers still have many smaller companies operating as a result of relatively low barriers to entry and the emphasis on personal service. One of the world's largest branded hotel companies, Marriott, estimates its world market share to be only 4 per cent for example.

Unlike large firms, which have some chance of shaping and controlling the environment in which they operate, SMEs have limited resources and consequently have little option but to take whatever the environment throws at them (Haberberg and Rieple, 2001:499). In such circumstances the methods for strategic development SMEs adopt may be limited and they may need to gain protection from predatory larger competitors. Thus mergers and acquisitions may in many circumstances not be possible as they are expensive, access to finance is often difficult for SMEs and they often end in failure.

In many cases then the only options available are likely to be organic development and some sort of joint development. Many SMEs succeed through organic growth in *THE* because they have found a particular niche that they can exploit or because they can provide competitive service delivery that is appropriately personalized. Indeed though it is usually assumed that most businesses want to pursue growth and profitability objectives this may not necessarily be the case with regard to some SMEs operating in *THE* sectors. Several researchers (see for example, Getz and Petersen, 2005) have identified the prominence of lifestyle motives among tourism and hospitality business owners that may preclude them from pursuing growth and profitability at the expense if their lifestyle objectives.

Some of the difficulties encountered by SMEs are in part overcome through aspects of collaboration, which has been viewed through the importance of networks and clusters (Morrison et al., 2004). Joint development has become particularly prevalent as a means of expansion for SMEs and this chapter has looked at several means by which SMEs can develop, such as by franchising and by joining marketing consortia.

Franchising has been particularly important as a growth method for hotel groups, although Alon et al. (2012) found that hotels are significantly different from retail and business services franchises. Franchising-related costs are highest in terms of the required capital investment for hotels – they have proved to be increasingly important for growth in this sector. Total investment required by Choice Hotels International ranges from $2.3 to $14.6 million and Hilton $53.4 to $90.1 million, to give two examples. By contrast, most other service franchising industries require less than $1 million start-up costs.

The high capital requirement raises considerable risks for smaller companies, but most academic studies have considered the advantages of this method from the franchisor perspective. Only a few studies (such as Xiao *et al.*, 2008 and Brookes and Altinay, 2009) have studied this aspect of strategic management from an SME perspective, i.e. from the viewpoint of the franchisee. Brookes and Altinay in a European hotel context found that in selecting partners, franchisees valued factors such as the ability to retain control of assets; a perception of mutual value and risk; the similarity of organizational values and culture; and the perception of a fair deal. In a study of potential Chinese hotel franchisees, Xiao *et al.* (2008) found that hotel chains that have strong brand awareness, supportive centralized reservation systems, and offer relatively high returns on investment at relatively low franchise fees are likely to be most attractive.

CHAPTER SUMMARY

This chapter has considered the various methods of strategic development that are available to *THE* managers and considered a third approach to strategic management – the relational approach.

Organic growth is arguably the most common form of strategic development, as most organizations use it on an ongoing basis. It is therefore difficult to quantify the degree of internal development taking place at any time. The action which creates one organization from two is known as integration. Whilst there are many logical reasons for organizations to select this method of development, research evidence has suggested that its success rate is not particularly high. Integrations are unsuccessful for many reasons but mainly due to a lack of research into the target company and its environment.

Various types of joint development such as strategic alliances and franchises have been considered. These are collaborative relationships between organizations, which fall short of full merger which are particularly important in many *THE* contexts. The various forms of alliance can range from informal to highly formalized agreements and their success often depends on the commitment of both parties to achieving the objectives of the alliance.

There are times at which *THE* organizations need to opt not for growth but have to be more defensive in opting for retrenchment. There are various ways in which this can be carried out which include disposal, equity carve-outs and management buy-outs.

BIBLIOGRAPHY

Alon, I., L. Ni and Y. Wang (2012) 'Examining the Determinants of Hotel Chain Expansion through International Franchising', *International Journal of Hospitality Management*, 31 (2): 379–86.

Bennett, M. M. (1997) 'Strategic Alliances in the World Airline Industry', *Progress in Tourism and Hospitality Research*, 3 (3): 213–23.

Bleeke J. and D. Ernst (1991) 'The Way to Win in Cross-Border Alliances', *Harvard Business Review*, 69 (6): 127–35.

Brookes, M. and L. Altinay (2011) 'Franchise Partner Selection: Perspectives of Franchisors and Franchisees', *Journal of Services Marketing*, 25 (5): 336–48.

Brouthers, K. D., L. E. Brouthers and T. J. Wilkinson (1993) 'Strategic Alliances: Choose Your Partners', *Long Range Planning*, 28 (3): 18–25.

Buck, T. and R. Blitz (2007) 'Mytravel Merger Approved', *Financial Times*, 5 May.

Chathoth, P. K. and M. D. Olsen (2003) 'Strategic Alliances: A Hospitality Industry Perspective', *International Journal of Hospitality Management*, 22 (4): 419–34.

Child, J. and D. Faulkner (1998) *Strategies of Cooperation: Managing Alliances, Networks and Joint Ventures*, Oxford: Oxford University.

Contractor, F. and P. Lorange (1988) 'Why Should Firms Cooperate? The Strategy and Economic Basis for

Cooperative Ventures', in F. Contractor and P. Lorange (eds.), *Cooperative Strategies in International Business*, Lexington, Mass.: Lexington Books, pp. 3–30.

Crawford-Welch, S. (1994) 'The Development of Courtyard by Marriott' in R. Teare, J. A. Mazanec, S. Crawford Welch and S. Calver (eds.), *Marketing in Hospitality and Tourism: A Consumer Focus*, London: Cassell, pp. 184–96.

De Wit, B. and R. Meyer (2010) *Strategy Synthesis: Resolving Strategy Paradoxes to Create Competitive Advantage: Text and Readings*, Andover: Cengage.

Dev, C. S. and S. Klein (1993) 'Strategic Alliances in the Hotel Industry: The *Cornell Hotel and Restaurant Administration Quarterly*, February, 43–5.

Dev, C. S., S. Klein and R. A. Fisher (1996) 'A Market-Based Approach for Partner Selection in Marketing Alliances', *Journal of Travel Research*, 35 (1): 11–17.

Dyer, J. H. and H. Singh (1998) 'The Relational View: Cooperative Strategy and Sources of Interorganizational Competitive Advantage', *Academy of Management Review*, 23 (4): 660–79.

Dyer, J. H., P. Kale and H. Singh (2004) 'When to Ally and When to Acquire', *Harvard Business Review*, 82 (7–8): 108.

Edwards, S. and L. Taylor (2012) 'The Exportation of Event Expertise: Taking Best Practice to International Markets in the MICE Sector', in N. Ferdinand and P. J. Kitchin (eds.), *Events Management: An International Approach*, London: Sage, 303–14.

Evans, N. (2001a) 'Collaborative Strategy: An Analysis of the Changing World of International Airline Alliances', *Tourism Management*, 22 (3): 229–43.

—— (2001b) 'Alliances in the International Travel Industry: Sustainable Strategic Options?' *International Journal of Hospitality and Tourism Administration*, 2 (1): 1–26.

Faulkner, D. (1995) *Strategic Alliances: Cooperating to Compete*, New York: McGraw-Hill.

French, T. (1997) 'Global Trends in Airline Alliances', *Tourism Analyst*, 4: 81–101.

Fyall, A. and B. Garrod (2005) *Tourism Marketing: A Collaborative Approach*, Bristol UK: Channel View Publications.

Garnham, B. (1996) 'Alliances and Liaisons in Tourism: Concepts and Implications', *Tourism Economics*, 2 (1): 61–77.

Getz, D. and T. Petersen (2005) 'Growth and Profit-Oriented Entrepreneurship among Family Business Owners in the Tourism and Hospitality Industry', *International Journal of Hospitality Management*, 24 (2): 219–42.

Glaister, K. W. and P. J. Buckley (1996) 'Strategic Motives for International Alliance Formation', *Journal of Management Studies*, 33 (3): 301–32.

Go, F. M. and R. Pine (1995) *Globalization Strategy in the Hotel Industry*, London and New York: Routledge.

Haberberg, A. and A. Rieple (2001) The Strategic Management of Organizations, Harlow: Pearson Education.

Haspeslagh, P. and D. Jemison (1991) *Managing Acquisitions: Creating Value through Corporate Renewal*, New York: Free Press.

Heeley, J. (2001) 'Public-Private Sector Partnerships in Tourism', in A. Lockwood and S. Medlik (eds.), *Tourism and Hospitality in the 21st Century*, Oxford: Butterworth-Heinemann, pp. 273–83.

—— (2011) 'Public: Private Partnership and Best Practice in Urban Destination Marketing', *Tourism and Hospitality Research*, 11 (3): 224–9.

Ireland, R. D., M. A. Hitt and D. Vaidyanath (2002) 'Alliance Management as a Source of Competitive Advantage', *Journal of Management*, 28 (3): 413–46.

Jauhiainen, J. S. (1995) 'Waterfront Redevelopment and Urban Policy: The Case of Barcelona, Cardiff and Genoa', *European Planning Studies*, 3 (1): 3–23.

Johnson, G., R. Whittington and K. Scholes (2011) *Exploring Strategy: Text and Cases*, 9th edn, Harlow: Financial Times Prentice Hall.

Kale, P., J. H. Dyer and H. Singh (2002) 'Alliance Capability, Stock Market Response and Long-Term Alliance Success: The Role of the Alliance Function', *Strategic Management Journal*, 23 (8): 747–67.

Kanter, R. M. (1990) *When Giants Learn to Dance*, New York: Simon & Schuster.

—— (1994) 'Collaborative Advantage: The Art of Alliances', *Harvard Business Review*, 72 (4), 96–108.

Kay, J. (1995) *Foundations of Corporate Success: How Business Strategies Add Value*, Oxford: Oxford University Press.

Kim, B. Y. and H. Oh (2004) 'How Do Hotel Firms Obtain a Competitive Advantage?' *International Journal of Contemporary Hospitality Management*, 16 (1): 65–71.

Kostopoulou, S. (2013) 'On the Revitalized Waterfront: Creative Milieu for Creative Tourism', *Sustainability*, 5 (11): 4578–93.

Long P. E. (1997) 'Researching Tourism Partnership Organizations: From Practice to Theory to Methodology', in P. E. Murphy, *Quality Management in Urban Tourism*, London: John Wiley & Sons, pp. 235–52.

Lynch, R. (2012) *Strategic Management*, Harlow: Pearson.

Medcof, J. W. (1997) 'Why Too Many Alliances End in Divorce', *Long Range Planning*, 30 (5): 718–32.

Morrison, A. J. (1994) 'Marketing Strategic Alliances: The Small Hotel Firm', *International Journal of Contemporary Hospitality Management*, 6 (3): 25–30.

Morrison, A., P. Lynch and N. Johns (2004) 'International Tourism Networks', *International Journal of Contemporary Hospitality Management*, 16 (3): 187–202.

Nickson, D. (1997) 'Research: "Colorful Stories" or Historical Insight? A Review of the Auto/Biographies of Charles Forte, Conrad Hilton, J. W. Marriott and Kemmons Wilson', *Journal of Hospitality and Tourism Research*, 21 (1): 179–92.

Ohmae, K. (1989) 'The Global Logic of Strategic Alliances', *Harvard Business Review*, 67 (2): 143–54.

Olsen, M. D., S. Crawford-Welch and E. Tse (1991) 'The Global Hospitality Industry of the 1990s', in R. Teare and A. Boer (eds.), *Strategic Hospitality Management*, London: Cassell, pp. 213–26.

Oum, T. H., J. H. Park and A. Zhang (2000) Globalization and Strategic Alliances: The Case of the Airline Industry, Bingley UK: Emerald.

Oum, T. H., J. H. Park, K. Kim and C. Yu (2004) 'The Effect of Horizontal Alliances on Firm Productivity and Profitability: Evidence from the Global Airline Industry', *Journal of Business Research*, 57 (8): 844–53.

Parker, A. (2013a) 'Consolidation: Concentration of Carriers Puts Collapse on Europe Agenda', *Financial Times*, 16 June.

—— (2013b) 'Gulf Carriers Destabilise Alliances', *Financial Times*, 14 November.

Porter, M. E. and M. B. Fuller (1986) 'Coalitions and Global Strategy', in M. E. Porter (ed.), *Competition in Global Industries*, Boston, Mass.: Harvard Business School Press, pp. 315–43.

Rumelt, R. P. (1991) 'How Much Does Industry Matter?' *Strategic Management Journal*, 12 (3): 167–85.

Teo, S. (2009) 'Asian Film Festivals and Their Diminishing Glitter Domes: An Appraisal of PIFF, SIFF and HKIFF', in R. Porton (ed.), *Dekalog 3: On Film Festivals*, London: Wallflower, pp. 109–21.

Todeva, E. and D. Knoke (2005) 'Strategic Alliances and Models of Collaboration', *Management Decision*, 43 (1): 123–48.

Tuch, C. and N. O'Sullivan (2007) 'The Impact of Acquisitions on Firm Performance: A Review of the Evidence', *International Journal of Management Reviews*, 9 (2): 141–70.

Xiao, Q., J. W. O'Neill and H. Wang (2008) 'International Hotel Development: A Study of Potential Franchisees in China', *International Journal of Hospitality Management*, 27 (3): 325–36.

Xu, Y. J. and X. P. Yan (2000)' Waterfront Tourist Development: The North American Experience and Its Application to China', *Economic Geography*, 20 (1): 99–103.

Yin, X. and M. Shanley (2008) 'Industry Determinants of the "Merger Versus Alliance" Decision', *Academy of Management Review*, 33 (2): 2473–91.

Yoshino, M. M. Y. and U. S. Rangan (1995) *Strategic Alliances: An Entrepreneurial Approach to Globalization*, Cambridge Mass.: Harvard Business Press.

WEBSITES

www.abacus.com.sg/

www.accor.com/

www.aerlingus.com/

www.amadeus.com/

www.bestwestern.com/

www.biff.kr/

www.carlson.com/

www.easyjet.com/

www.enterpriseholdings.com/

www.gha.com/

www.hiltonworldwide.com/

www.icelolly.com/

www.ihgplc.com

www.jetstar.com/

www.mandarinoriental.com/

www.marcopolohotels.com/
www.marketingbirmingham.com/
www.marriott.com/
www.messefrankfurt.com/
www.oneworld.com
www.panpacific.com
www.rezidor.com
www.reedelsevier.com
www.relaischateaux.com
www.royalhost.com
www.sabre.com
www.skyteam.com
www.slh.com
www.southwest.com
www.staralliance.com
www.thomascookgroup.com
www.travelmole.com
www.travelport.com
www.tuitravelplc.com
www.united.com
www.usairways.com
www.waterfrontpartnership.org
www.wyndhamworldwide.com
www.yum.com

FURTHER READING

Reference	Focus
Alamadari, F. and P. Morell (1997) 'Airline Alliances: A Catalyst for Regulatory Change in Key Markets', *Journal of Air Transport Management*, 3 (1): 1–2.	Strategic alliances Airlines Airports
Albers, S., B. Koch and C. Ruff (2005) 'Strategic Alliances between Airlines and Airports: Theoretical Assessment and Practical Evidence', *Journal of Air Transport Management*, 11 (2): 49–58.	Strategic alliances Airlines Market regulation
Alon, I., L. Ni and Y. Wang (2012) 'Examining the Determinants of Hotel Chain Expansion through International Franchising', *International Journal of Hospitality Management*, 31 (2): 379–86.	Franchising Hotels
Altinay, L. (2006) 'Selecting Partners in an International Franchise Organization', *International Journal of Hospitality Management*, 25 (1): 108–28.	Public-private partnerships Tourism Festivals
—— (2007) 'The Internationalization of Hospitality Firms: Factors Influencing a Franchise Decision-Making Process', *Journal of Services Marketing*, 21 (6): 398–409.	Franchising Hospitality Partner selection
Andersson, T. D. and D. Getz (2009) 'Tourism as a Mixed Industry: Differences between Private, Public and Not-for-Profit Festivals', *Tourism Management*, 30 (6): 847–56.	Franchising Hospitality Partner selection

Beamish, P. W. and A. C. Inkpen (1995) 'Keeping International Joint Ventures Stable and Profitable', *Long Range Planning*, 28 (3): 26–36.	Joint ventures Competitive advantage
Chen, J. J. and I. Dimou (2005) 'Expansion Strategy of International Hotel Firms', *Journal of Business Research*, 58 (12): 1730–40.	Franchising Hotels Korea
Cho, M. (2004) 'Factors Contributing to Middle Market Hotel Franchising in Korea: The Franchisee Perspective', *Tourism Management*, 25 (5): 547–57.	Strategic alliances Tourism Hospitality
Connell, J. (1997) 'International Hotel Franchise Relationships: UK Franchisee Perspectives', *International Journal of Contemporary Hospitality Management*, 9 (5/6): 215–20.	Franchising Hotels UK
Crotts, J. C., D. Buhalis and R. March (2000) 'Introduction: Global Alliances in Tourism and Hospitality Management', *International Journal of Hospitality and Tourism Administration*, 1 (1): 1–10.	Marketing destinations Events Collaborative strategy
Davidson, R. and T. Rogers (2012) *Marketing Destinations and Venues for Conferences, Conventions and Business Events*, London and New York: Routledge.	Strategic alliances Competitive advantage
Doz, Y. and G. Hamel (1998) *Alliance Advantage*, Cambridge Mass.: Harvard Business School Press.	Public-private partnerships Visitor bureaux Canada
Getz, D., D. Anderson and L. Sheehan (1998) 'Roles, Issues and Strategies for Convention and Visitors' Bureaux in Destination Planning and Product Development: A Survey of Canadian Bureaux', *Tourism Management*, 19 (4): 331–40.	Public-private partnerships Tourism Sustainability
Graci, S. (2013) 'Collaboration and Partnership Development for Sustainable Tourism', *Tourism Geographies*, 15 (1): 25–42.	Mergers and acquisitions
Haleblian, J., C. E. Devers, G. McNamara, M. A. Carpenter and R. B. Davison (2009) 'Taking Stock of What We Know about Mergers and Acquisitions: A Review and Research Agenda', *Journal of Management*, 35 (3): 469–502.	Franchising Hotels China
Heung, V., H. Zhang and C. Jiang (2008) 'International Franchising: Opportunities for China's State-Owned Hotels?' *International Journal of Hospitality Management*, 27 (3): 368–80.	Strategic alliances Tourism
Hill, T. and R. N. Shaw (1995) 'Co-marketing Tourism Internationally: Bases for Strategic Alliances', *Journal of Travel Research*, 34 (1): 25–32.	Strategic alliances Airlines Competitive advantage
Iatrou, K. and F. Alamdari (2005) 'The Empirical Analysis of the Impact of Alliances on Airline Operations', *Journal of Air Transport Management*, 11 (3): 127–34.	Franchising Hospitality
Ingram, H. (2001) 'Franchising Hospitality Services', *International Journal of Contemporary Hospitality Management*, 13 (5): 267–8.	Strategic methods Franchising Hotels
Mason, J. C. (1993) 'Strategic Alliances: Partnering for Success', *Management Review*, May, 10–15.	Strategic alliances Competitive advantage

Morrish, S. C. and R. T. Hamilton (2002) 'Airline Alliances: Who Benefits?' *Journal of Air Transport Management*, 8 (6): 401–7.	Strategic alliances Airlines Competitive advantage
Olsen, M. D. (1993) 'International Growth Strategies of Major US Hotel Companies', *Travel and Tourism Analyst*, 3: 51–64.	Strategic methods Hotels Growth strategies
Oum, T. H. and A. Zhang (2001) 'Key Aspects of Global Strategic Alliances and the Impacts on the Future of Canadian Airline Industry', *Journal of Air Transport Management*, 7 (5): 287–301.	Strategic alliances Airlines Canada
Pansiri, J. (2005) 'Pragmatism: A Methodological Approach to Researching Strategic Alliances in Tourism', *Tourism and Hospitality Planning and Development*, 2 (3): 191–206.	Strategic alliances Tourism Hospitality
Park, J. H. and A. Zhang (2000) 'An Empirical Analysis of Global Airline Alliances: Cases in North Atlantic Markets', *Review of Industrial Organization*, 16 (4): 367–84.	Strategic alliances Airlines North America
Pine, R., H. Q. Zhang and P. Qi (2000) 'The Challenges and Opportunities of Franchising in China's Hotel Industry', *International Journal of Contemporary Hospitality Management*, 12 (5): 300–7.	Franchising Hotels China
Preble, J. F., A. Reichel and R. C. Hoffman (2000) 'Strategic Alliances for Competitive Advantage: Evidence from Israel's Hospitality and Tourism Industry', *International Journal of Hospitality Management*, 19 (3): 327–41.	Strategic alliances Hospitality Israel
Shaughnessy, H. (1995) 'International Joint Ventures: Managing Successful Collaborations', *Long Range Planning*, 28 (3): 10–17.	Joint ventures Competitive advantage
Stafford, E. R. (1994) 'Using Co-operative Strategies to Make Alliances Work', *Long Range Planning*, 27 (3): 64–74.	Joint development Strategic alliances Competitive advantage
Stiles, J. (1994) 'Strategic Alliances: Making Them Work', *Long Range Planning*, 27 (3): 133–7.	Strategic alliances Competitive advantage
Sudarsanam, P. S. (1995) *The Essence of Mergers and Acquisitions*, Englewood Cliffs, NJ: Prentice Hall.	Mergers and Acquisitions
World Tourism Organization (1996) *Towards New Forms of Public-Private Sector Partnerships: The Changing Role, Structure and Activities of National Tourism Administrations, a Special Report for the World Tourism Organization*, Madrid: World Tourism Organization.	Public-private partnerships Tourism
—— (2003) *Co-operation and Partnerships in Tourism: A Global Perspective*, Madrid: World Tourism Organization.	Public-private partnerships Tourism
Zajac, E. J. (1998) 'Commentary on "Alliances and Networks" by R. Gulati', *Strategic Management Journal*, 19 (4): 319–21.	Strategic alliances Network theory
Zapata, M. J. and C. M. Hall (2012) 'Public–Private Collaboration in the Tourism Sector: Balancing Legitimacy and Effectiveness in Local Tourism Partnerships. The Spanish Case', *Journal of Policy Research in Tourism, Leisure and Events*, 4 (1): 61–83.	Public-private partnerships Tourism Spain

CASE LINKAGES

Case 1	Strategic alliances in the airline industry
Case 4	Hyatt Hotels
Case 5	Days Inn
Case 6	Reed Exhibitions
Case 7	Thomas Cook

12

Strategic evaluation and selection for tourism, hospitality and event organizations

Introduction and chapter overview

Important decisions are never easy. In order to ensure that we make the right choice in any given situation, we must first of all be in possession of all relevant information. This is the purpose of the strategic analysis stage – to ensure that the management of a *THE* organization is fully aware of the internal strengths and weaknesses, and of the external opportunities and threats.

The next stage in making an important decision is to be aware of *all* of the options available and to make a choice between them following a process of evaluation. In Chapters 10 and 11 various options were considered, relating to the key strategic issues facing *THE* organizations:

- *Competitive strategy* – how can advantage over competitors be achieved?
- *Strategic directions* – which products or services should be developed and in which markets should they be sold?
- *Strategic methods* – what methods of development should be adopted?

The most obvious choice is not necessarily the *right* one. Indeed, the whole concept of 'right' and 'wrong' may itself be difficult. There may be some options (following an evaluative process) which may be obviously wrong. They just do not make any sense when they are evaluated and the organization's current situation is considered.

However, there may be several options that are considered to be equally 'right', or the evaluation leads to conflicting signals being given. In such circumstances managers have to make a judgement based on the information they have available. Since we are talking about options for *future* strategic development, it is only after a period of time elapses that the judgement can be assessed and a definitive view can be established as to whether the correct option was in fact chosen.

Following the generation of options, the next stage is to evaluate each option using consistently applied criteria. The purpose of evaluation is to ensure that all options are assessed with equal thoroughness. Finally, strategic selection involves actually making a decision based upon the evaluation of the options. In other words a choice is made between the various competing options.

This chapter considers each of these stages in turn in relation to the key strategic decisions about strategic development.

LEARNING OBJECTIVES

After studying this chapter you should be able to:

- describe the nature of strategic options in relation to *THE* organizations;
- explain the key areas that strategic development decisions concern;
- describe the three criteria that are applied to strategic options;
- understand the financial and non-financial tools and techniques that can be used to evaluate strategic options;
- understand examples of the ways in which *THE* organizations have utilized evaluation in choosing their strategies and be able to identify the issues involved in relation to *THE* organizations;
- understand the differences between a prescriptive and emergent approach to strategy;
- explain the limitations of an 'emergent' approach to strategy when it comes to strategic evaluation and selection.

Identifying strategic options

The nature of strategic options

At the start of this chapter we must remind ourselves of what makes a decision *strategic* in nature as opposed to one that is *operational*. We encountered these terms in Chapter 1 in the context of the nature of strategic objectives and in the Introduction to Part 4.

Strategic decisions are taken at the highest level of an organization. They concern decisions on how the whole organization broken down into its constituent SBUs will be positioned in respect to its product and resource markets, its competitors and its macro influences. Accordingly, the options at the strategic level are those that offer solutions to the 'big questions' in this regard.

Operational-level decisions are those that are concerned with how the internal parts of the organization should be configured and managed so that they can achieve the strategic objectives.

The 'big questions' that are considered in strategic selection usually concern three major areas, all of which are discussed in detail elsewhere in this text.

- Decisions on *competitive strategy* (see Chapter 10).
- Decisions on products and markets relating to the *direction* of development (see Chapter 10).
- Decisions on *methods* of development (see Chapter 11).

In most cases an organization will need to make continual decisions on all of these matters. We should not lose sight of the fact that the strategic process is just that – a process. Strategic selection is no more of a 'once for all' activity than either strategic analysis or strategic implementation. For organizations that exist in rapidly changing environments, decisions on strategic options will be required on a continual basis, hence the importance of ensuring we have a good grasp of the issues that are discussed in this chapter.

Competitive strategy decisions

Decisions over the organization's competitive or generic strategy (as discussed in chapter 10) are important not only because they define the organization's competitive position, but also because they will determine the way that the internal value chain activities are configured (see Chapters 3 and 10).

If the company elects to pursue a differentiation strategy, for example, the implications of this will be felt in all parts of the organization. The culture and structure will need to be configured in such a way that they support the generic strategy and the product features and quality will also reflect it. Similarly, the way that the organization sources and configures its resource base will need to support the strategy.

The same issues will be considered if a cost-driven strategy is chosen, although the way in which the internal activities are configured will be somewhat different.

Direction of development – product and market decisions

The questions over *which products* and *which markets* are extremely important because they can determine not only the levels of profitability, but also the survival of the organization itself. It is likely that strategy will involve a change in the SBU or company's size. You will recall that in Chapter 10 three strategic options were considered:

- growth;
- stability;
- retrenchment.

If 'stability' is the chosen option this does not mean that nothing should be done, since to do so would invite competitors to enlarge their own market shares. In such circumstances market share may be fiercely defended through such measures as pricing, promotional offers or increased levels of efficiency. Furthermore even if the market share remains stable if the market as a whole is growing then the size of the overall business will increase; to use the analogy of a cake, your own organization's slice of the cake may remain constant, but the overall size of the cake is growing.

If retrenchment is the chosen option, decisions have to be made concerning which product or market areas should be reduced, sold off or withdrawn.

In cases where growth is the chosen strategic option that the organization will pursue (see Chapter 10), decisions have to be taken about the direction of growth. These strategic choices arise from Igor Ansoff's (Ansoff, 1987) framework and should not be confused with Porter's generic strategies (Porter, 1985). Ansoff's generic growth strategies concern whether growth will involve new or existing markets and products (see Chapter 6).

There are a number of further product and market decisions that are normally required.

Market categories

First, decisions must be made about the categories of markets that the business will be involved with. The organization will have to reach decisions on geographic coverage, international exposure and the benefits and risks that relate to such such options (see Chapter 14).

Product features

Second, decisions must be made on the features that the product will possess. The mix of product benefits that a product will possess will not only strongly affect costs, but also the position that the product will assume in the market. We encountered Kotler's (1997) five 'levels' of product features (or 'benefits') in Chapter 6 and the inclusion or omission of any of these will have a strong bearing upon any proposed strategy.

Product and market portfolios

Third, product and market decisions must include a consideration of portfolio (see Chapter 6). The extent to which the products and markets are focused or spread can be very important. A broad portfolio (presence in many product market sectors) offers the advantages of the ability to withstand a downturn in one sector and to exploit opportunities that arise in any of the areas in which the business operates. Conversely, a narrow portfolio enables the organization's management to be more focused and to develop expertise in its narrower field of operation.

Life cycle considerations

The final consideration to be made for products and markets concerns their life cycle positions. It is perhaps intuitively obvious to say that products or markets that are approaching late maturity or are in decline should be of particular concern, but there is also a need to produce new products or develop new markets on an ongoing basis. Products in late maturity or in decline can produce medium-to-high levels of positive cash flow. New products on the other hand in the introductory or early growth phases often produce negative cash flows. Thus mature and declining products can release financial resources which can be invested in new products which can then in time move up the PLC towards maturity (see Chapter 6).

Strategic Method Decisions

The third area for which strategic business level decisions are required relates to the methods or mechanisms that are to be used (see Chapter 11). A basic choice exists between:

- internal (organic) development;
- mergers and acquisitions; and
- joint development such as alliances and franchising.

The choice has important implications for the:

- *resources* that are required;
- degree of *control* over future strategic decisions;
- *speed* with which a change in the position of the SBU could be achieved; and
- need to *re-configure* the internal value chain of the organization.

For example – a tour operator has decided that its future growth method should be that of organic growth achieved through adding destinations to the existing range that it serves.

In making the decision the company's managers would be cognizant of the fact that this method usually produced slower growth than alternatives (since resources are provided by one organization only). Either alternative (some form of joint development or a merger or acquisition) would involve a *step change* in size and produce speedier growth. However, the organization's managers would also be aware that internal growth retains full control within the existing organization with no control being ceded to other organizations. That is, the existing managers would continue to control the company including subsequent decisions about strategy.

Applying evaluation criteria

When considering which course of action to pursue, it is normally the case that a number of options present themselves to an organization's top management. In order to ensure that each option is fairly and equally assessed, a number of criteria are applied.

KEY CONCEPT

Prescriptive strategy

This text is primarily concerned with prescriptive strategy which takes the view that a rational, evidence-based analaysis of the environment will reveal options which will deliver the strategy. The options revealed in this way have then to be evaluated and choices are made to select the options most likely to produce a successful outcome. Since the choice is based on logic and evidence, proponents of prescriptive strategy would argue that it is more likely to be successful than alternatives.

Emergent strategy, on the other hand, reflects the fact that sometimes strategy is not derived from a formal planned approach (as implied above) but instead emerges from many sources, in many different ways.

In reality in most real-world situations strategy is probably derived from both sources as Mintzberg and Waters (1985) argue; that 'realized' strategy is the product of both deliberate planning (prescriptive strategy) and also emerges in an unplanned way (emergent strategy).

For each option, three criteria are applied – each option is questioned. In order to 'pass', the option must usually receive an affirmative answer to each criterion. In some texts various acronyms are introduced to describe the criteria such as RACES (as described by Haberberg and Rieple, 2001), SCARE and CARES which usually stand for Resources, Acceptable, Consistent, Effective and Sustainable, which are considered in the order required by the acronym.

Here another widely used scheme is the SFA framework of:

- suitability
- feasibility
- acceptability.

Thus each strategic option should be considered in relation to the three criteria by considering whether the strategic option is suitable, feasible, acceptable and enables competitive advantage to be achieved as summarized in Table 12.1.

The process of evaluation is an integral part of the overall strategy process as indicated in Figure 12.1.

Suitability

Suitability is concerned with assessing whether the strategy is capable of enabling the organization to achieve its strategic objectives.

A strategic option is suitable if it will enable the organization to actually achieve its strategic objectives. If it will in any way fall short of achieving these objectives, then there is no point in pursuing it and the option should be discarded.

Table 12.1 Summary of the criteria used for evaluation

Criteria	Key issues
Suitability	Does the proposed strategy: exploit *opportunities* in the environment and avoid or address the *threats*; capitalize on an organization's *strengths* and avoid or address the *weaknesses*; address the expectations of stakeholder groups.
Feasibility	Is the proposed strategy possible: in relation to the organization's internal culture, capabilities and resources; in relation to the organization's external stakeholders.
Acceptability	Does the proposed strategy deliver performance: outcomes which are acceptable to the organization's stakeholders; which is superior to the current situation; which is better than competitors.

Figure 12.1 The strategic evaluation process

For example – if an events management organization has set one of its strategic objectives 'to spread its market portfolio by gaining a presence in selected foreign markets', then the option of increasing the company's investment in its domestic market would clearly be unsuitable.

The suitability of options must be assessed not only in relation to the objectives that have been set but also in relation to the SWOT. The SWOT itself is of course the culmination of a number of analytical tools and techniques such as STEEP; five forces and value chain; and the cultural web.

THINK POINTS

- Explain where strategic evaluation and selection fit into the strategic process.
- Describe the three criteria that can be used to evaluate strategic options.
- In relation to the direction of development outline the main product-market decisions which are required?

Options might be regarded as suitable when they:

- Exploit *opportunities* in the environment and avoid or address the *threats;*
- Capitalize on an organization's *strengths* and avoid or address the *weaknesses;* and
- Address the expectations of stakeholder groups.

It is also important to recognize cases where strategic options may be unsuitable:

- There may be options that are more suitable so that suitability might be seen in relative terms and the various options ranked according to their suitability.
- There is a need for internal consistency in the choice of options. The choice of competitive strategy (such as cost leadership or differentiation), the development direction (such as market development or diversification) and the development method (internal, acquisition or joint development) need to work together as a 'package'.

SHORT CASE ILLUSTRATION

Suitability: Foreign airline access to US markets

The airline market in the USA is by far the world's largest accounting for over 40 per cent of world demand. However, despite airline deregulation which took place in the 1970s and 1980s restrictions on foreign ownership of airlines still apply. Like many governments the US has historically restricted foreign ownership so as to protect its domestic companies in the belief that it is strategically important for the country to have a strong domestic industry. The restrictions have limited foreign investment and prevent foreign carriers from entering the market.

For example, British Airways, a subsidiary of IAG Group, has long been reported to have sought a merger partner in the USA. At various times talks have been held with American Airlines and US Airways. However, a non-American airline seeking to grow through market penetration is restricted in its choice of strategic method. The foreign ownership restrictions prevent the purchase of an American airline or the development of airlines by foreign-based companies. Thus if British Airways or any other airline wanted to achieve its stated strategic objective of US airline market penetration it would have little option but to do so through developing joint development opportunities such as through alliance relationships to develop its position in this vitally important market. This is what has actually happened in that cooperation with American Airlines takes place through the OneWorld Alliance.

Thus in this example if an option of US acquisitions was proposed by managers it would not be 'suitable' since it would not be capable of achieving the strategic objective.

Questions

1. Explain the issue of suitability highlighted by this case.
2. What are the advantages and possible disadvantages to the country placing restrictions on foreign ownership imposed in this example?

Table 12.2 presents some examples of why some options might be regarded as suitable in terms of specific directions or methods of development (considered in Chapters 10 and 11).

Screening

Having applied the suitability criterion a further stage might be interjected in some cases – that of *screening*.

If certain options are clearly unsuitable it makes little sense going through the time, effort and expense involved in applying the further criteria. Consequently, at the screening stage a decision is made as to

Table 12.2 Some examples of suitability

Strategic option	Why this option might be suitable in terms of:		
	Environment	Competencies and resources	Examples from *THE* (used in in this text)
Directions			
Retrenchment	Withdraw from declining markets Maintain market share	Identify and build on strengths through continued investment and innovation	Holiday Inn Hotels
Market penetration	Gain market share for advantage	Exploit superior resources and competencies	Premier Inns
Product development	Exploit knowledge of customer needs	Exploit expertise in developing new or improved product offerings	Premier Inn British Airways Club Med
Market development	Current markets saturated New opportunities for: Geographical spread; Entering new segments; or. New uses for existing products	Exploit current product portfolio Exploit current competencies	McDonald's fast food restaurants Holidaybreak plc
Diversification	Current markets saturated or declining	Exploit core competencies in new arenas	A tour operator developing a hotel chain An event management company gaining a control of an event venue American Exprerss Saga Hutchison Whampoa
Methods			
Organic development	First in field providing *first mover* advantage Cautious controlled development Partners or acquisitions not available or not suitable	Building on own competencies Learning and competence development	MSC Cruise Line Frankfurt Messe Marriott International inc. Accor Hotels
Merger/ acquisition	Speed of development Alter supply/demand balance Improved ratios	Acquire competencies Scale and scope economies	International Airlines Reed Exhibitions Carnival & Star Cruise Lines US Airlines & Online Retailers European Tour Operators

Methods			
Joint development	Speed Required for market entry Industry norm	Complementary competencies Learning from partners	Global Distribution Systems International Airlines Virgin, Emirates and Etihad Hilton Worldwide Carlson Redizor Hotel Colorado Convention Center and SMG Busan International Film Festival Baltimore Inner Harbor Marketing Birmingham Yum! Brands and Enterprise Holdings Holiday Inn Hotels Royal Host Inc. Skywest Best Western
Retrenchment			Thomas Cook plc Icelolly.com

Source: Adapted from Johnson *et al.* (2011:365)

whether it is worth continuing with the further stages of evaluation or if certain options should be disregarded at this stage of evaluation owing to their unsuitability.

The case of the Kenes Group, an event management company which organizes scientific conferences worldwide, illustrates why screening might be necessary.

SHORT CASE ILLUSTRATION

Screening: International growth for Kenes events management company

The management of events is a very diverse field and is highly fragmented with many small businesses operating. Like an advertising agency, a football team or a small travel agency, events management companies often rely very heavily on the competencies of a small group of highly skilled people as their main source of competitive advantage. Consequently such organizations have to plan their growth carefully so that they do not over-burden their key resource.

The Kenes Group focuses on providing international congress organization services from its headquarters in Geneva, Switzerland and regional and national offices in key business locations around the world. Founded in 1965, Kenes is an industry leader in organizing medical and scientific conferences and is a member of the international trade bodies ICCA (the International Congress and Convention Association) and IAPCO (the International Association of Professional Congress Organizers).

Although large in its chosen specialist field there are many competitors and the company has to consider the suitability of international expansion carefully before proceeding. As the company's website points out, 'we only establish regional and national offices if it makes sense for our clients and if we can ensure that the Kenes quality, mission and values will be upheld by the regional and local partners we know and trust'.

Clearly a company such as the Kenes Group is pursuing a strategic objective which involves spreading its market portfolio by gaining a presence in selected foreign markets. Though geographically widely spread, its current executive offices – providing global coverage through regional offices – nevertheless exclude a presence in some key countries such as Brazil, China, Russia and Indonesia.

In such a case the management needs to consider its financial and human resources carefully and the relative attractiveness of market opportunities before expanding into new countries and it might be the case that a screening process takes place to determine which countries provide the best opportunities.

www.kenes-group.com

Questions

1. Explain why a screening process might be beneficial in this case when assessing international expansion?

2. What factors might it be useful for Kenes to take into account when considering opening new international offices?

For example – in the previous section an example was given of an events management company. The company had set one of its strategic objectives 'to spread its market portfolio by gaining a presence in selected foreign markets'.

To continue this example, it might be the case that when the management considered its financial and human resources, being a relatively small company, it was felt that it only had sufficient resources to expand into one new country at a time. Initially it had considered that six countries might be possible contenders for the first expansion. A simple screening process (such as shown in the table below) might help the company in question to decide which country offered the best opportunities in the first instance.

In this example, the six countries are ranked from 1–6 (with 1 being the most attractive) on four measures. The measures chosen might vary according to circumstances, but taking these measures into account three countries (B, C and E) appear 'suitable' and worthy of further evaluation. Country B for example appears to be an attractive market of a good size. The company is well placed to exploit the market in terms of its competencies, but unfortunately the regulatory and general business environment only appear to be moderately favourable (compared to options C and E).

Table 12.3 A screening process based on ranking alternative options

	Country A	Country B	Country C	Country D	Country E	Country F
Market size	4	2	1	6	3	5
Market attractiveness	3	1	2	5	4	6
Company competencies	6	2	3	4	1	5
Regulation and business environment	4	3	2	5	1	6
TOTAL	17	10	8	20	9	22

Thus in this case a screening process by which six alternatives were ranked has allowed three options to be 'screened out', allowing three (options B, C and E) to go forward for further evaluation.

Table 12.3 is a simple screening process based on ranking alternative options. Though conceptually simple, it relies heavily on the strength of the underlying analysis. The ranking of the options should be based on a solid analysis of the available evidence, otherwise the screening and the ranking on which it depends will have no validity. To assess the market attractiveness, for instance, requires a sound understanding of the dynamics of the particular market in question. This will perhaps be based on Porter's Five Forces framework which was covered in Chapter 9 and other relevant analytical tools and techniques.

Feasibility

Feasibility is concerned with assessing whether the strategy is capable of working in practice.

A strategic option might be considered to be suitable but it is found that it is not possible – in other words the option is not feasible. When evaluating options using this criterion, it is likely that the options will be feasible to varying degrees. Some will be completely unfeasible, others might be feasible, whilst others still are definitely feasible.

The extent to which an option is feasible will accordingly depend in practice upon two areas:

First the culture, competencies and resources, which are *internally controlled* by the organization. An organization might not have the culture, competencies or resources, which are necessary to carry out the options. A deficit in any of the key resource areas (physical resources, financial, human and intellectual) will present a problem at this stage of evaluation. If an option requires capital that is unavailable, human skills that are difficult to buy in, land or equipment that is equally difficult to obtain or a scarce intellectual resource, then it is likely to fail the feasibility criteria.

SHORT CASE ILLUSTRATION

Feasibility: Access to scarce resource at London's Heathrow Airport

Take off and landing slots are rights allocated to an airline by an airport or government agency granting the slot owner the right to schedule a landing or departure at a particular time. Usually they are referred to as a 'pair of slots' to denote the right to both take off and land.

London's Heathrow Airport, one of the world's leading international airports, has been working at or close to capacity for a number of years. The pairs of slots are a scarce resource, as they are at many busy airports around the world. The rights of airlines to operate the slots generally lie with those airlines which have operated at the airport for a protracted length of time operating so-called *grandfather rights*. Although most airlines did not originally pay for the slots, but inherited them through historically operating from the airport, they protect them and rarely sell them.

Since the inherited rights are rarely relinquished by airlines, the allocated slots have gained a commercial value and can be traded between airlines. In 2008, for example, Continental Airlines (now part of United Airlines) paid $209m for four pairs of slots, while in early 2013, Etihad paid $70m for three slot pairs from Jet Airways of India. Ironically, Etihad acquired the slots not to use them but to gain an equity stake in Jet, which has leased the slots back from Etihad.

Many airlines would like to establish a presence at Heathrow, a key international transit hub, some in preference to using London's second largest airport, Gatwick. However the airlines are prevented from doing so by the lack of slots coming onto the market or their cost when they do so.

Consequently, whilst establishing a presence at Heathrow might be a *suitable* aspect of a growth strategy, for an airline, it would not be *feasible*. This is due to the deficit in a key resource area i.e. the failure to gain access to the physical resource of Heathrow.

www.headforpoints.com

Questions

1. Explain the difference between 'suitability' and 'feasibility' illustrated by this case.

2. What options might be feasible for an airline seeking to expand operations focused on London?

Table 12.4 A ten-point checklist on internal feasibility

Internal issue	Key questions
Capital investment required	Do we have the funds?
Projection of cumulative profits	Is it sufficiently profitable?
Working capital requirements	Do we have enough working capital?
Tax liabilities and dividend payments	What are the implications, especially on timing?
Number of employees	Are there sufficient or too many employees? In the case of redundancy, what are the costs associated with this?
New technical skills required, new operational equipment required	Do we have the skills? Do we need to recruit or hire temporarily some specialists?
New products and how are they to be developed	Are we confident that we have a portfolio of fully tested new products? Are they breakthrough products or merely catch-up on our competition?
Amount and timing of marketing investment and expertise required	Do we have the funds? When will they be required? Do we have the specialist expertise such as, advertising and promotions agency teams to deliver our strategic options?
The possibility of acquisition, merger or joint venture with other organizations and the implications	Have we fully explored other strategic options that would bring their own benefits and problems?
Communication of ideas to all those involved: how will this be done?	Will we gain the commitment of the managers and employees affected? Who are required to implement the required changes?

Source: Adapted from Lynch (2012:381)

The checklist shown as Table 12.4 indicates some of the key internal feasibility issues to consider.

The second area that needs to be considered with regards to feasibility relates to the consideration of competitive reactions and other considerations which are *external* to the organization. Specifically, the acceptance of customers and suppliers, competitive reactions and necessary approvals from government or regulatory bodies needs to be considered.

SHORT CASE ILLUSTRATION

Feasibility: Chinese budget hotel brands' fight for market share

After learning and absorbing international practices, China's domestic hotel firms developed rapidly after 1990. Not only are these domestic firms growing in size, but many have strategically positioned themselves in different market segments. Chinese domestic branded budget chains developed prominently with a race to roll out their brands across the country to gain so-called *first mover* advantage and secure a large market share. To do so rests partly on their ability to raise capital from overseas equity markets.

One such example (Gu *et al.*, 2012) is that of Home Inn, a budget hotel chain joint venture by Capital Tourism Corporation and CTrip (China's largest online travel agent) formed in 2002. The US$109 million the company raised from its initial public offering (IPO) from the NASDAQ exchange in New York during 2006 was invested in its aggressive expansion. The finance enabled the company to compete effectively with Jin Jiang Inn, China's leading budget hotel chain.

However another Chinese budget hotel chain, 7 Days Inn, followed the development model, by following what is sometimes referred to as a *me too* strategy in strategy texts. During 2009 it raised US$111 million through a New York Stock Exchange IPO. The company is currently ranked as one of the top five budget chain hotels in China. Its quick ascent to the top rank of budget hotel operators following its founding in 2005 was attributed to its ability to raise capital from an overseas equity market.

Thus Home Inn used a particular funding method in order to expand rapidly. In pursuing this growth, however, the hotel chain would have had to consider whether it would be *feasible* for other operators to pursue a similar strategy. As it turned out it was feasible for another chain to adopt a *me too* strategy and gain finance in a similar way in order to fund its expansion plans.

Gu et al. (2012)

Questions

1. Explain why an organization such as Home Inn should consider the reactions of competitors in considering *feasibility*.

2. Explain what is meant by *first mover advantage* and a me-too strategy in relation to this illustrative case.

The checklist shown as Table 12.5 indicates some of the key external feasibility issues to consider.

Table 12.5 A four-point checklist on external feasibility

External issue	Key questions
Customers	How will our customers respond to the strategies we are proposing?
Competitors	How will our competitors react? Do we have the necessary resources to respond?
Suppliers	Do we have the necessary support from our suppliers?
Government	Do we need government or regulatory approval? How likely is this?

Source: Adapted from Lynch (2012:382)

Acceptability

Acceptability is concerned with assessing the expected performance outcomes of a strategy to determine whether they are likely to be acceptable to stakeholders.

In considering expected performance it is useful to make an assessment following Johnson *et al.* (2011: 371), on what can be termed the 'three Rs of acceptability':

- Reactions of stakeholders
- Returns
- Risks.

In assessing the strategy for acceptability it is sensible to consider all of the three Rs.

Consequently the acceptability of a chosen strategy is often determined by using a range of analytical financial and non-financial tools such as those described later in the chapter. A strategic option is acceptable if those who must agree to the strategy accept the option. This raises an obvious question – who are those who agree that the option is acceptable?

Reaction of stakeholders

We encountered the concept of stakeholders in Chapter 1. The extent that stakeholders can exert influence upon an organization's strategic decision making rests upon the two variables: power and interest (see Chapter 1).

Stakeholders that have the highest combination of both the ability to influence (power) and the willingness to influence (interest) will have the most *effective* influence. Where two or more stakeholder groups have comparable influence, the possibility of conflict over acceptability will be heightened (see the easyJet illustrative case below). In most cases, the board of directors will be the most influential stakeholder. It is also important to consider the commitment from managers and employees. If important members of the organization are not committed to the strategy it is unlikely to be successfully implemented.

SHORT CASE ILLUSTRATION

Acceptability of stratetgic options: easyJet

EasyJet plc is a British airline based at London Luton Airport. The airline was launched in 1995 as part of the easyGroup conglomerate by Cypriot businessman Sir Haji-loannou with two 'wet leased' aircraft and was floated on the London Stock Exchange in November 2000. Subsequently easyJet has grown rapidly as consumers took to the variant of the low-cost model pioneered by Southwest Airlines in the USA which the airline operates. It has grown through organic growth, acquisitions and by developing new operating bases across Europe. In 2012, easyJet carried over 50 million passengers and is the second-largest low-cost carrier in Europe behind Ryanair.

Although he subsequently stepped down from the easyJet board, Haji-loannou and his family remain the largest shareholders with 36.5 per cent of shares. He has repeatedly clashed with easyJet's board over plans to buy over 130 new Airbus aircraft arguing that such rapid expansion of the fleet (from its level in 2013 of about 200 aircraft) was unsustainable and that instead more of the money should go to shareholders in dividends. The easyJet board however has argued that growth and fleet renewal were essential to maintain easyJet's strong European market position.

Rankin (2013) and www.corporate.easyjet.com

Returns

We learned in Chapter 1 that one of the key objectives in strategy is to create competitive advantage. This criterion asks a simple question of any strategic option – what is the point of pursuing an option if it isn't going to result in superior performance (compared to competitors) or higher than average profitability? In other words, a strategic option would fail this test if it were likely to only result in the business being 'ordinary' or average in relation to the industry or sector norm.

This is particularly important when considering product options. For example, if a new product option is forecast to receive an uncertain reception from the market, we might well question the point of the launch at all. It would be unlikely to result in competitive advantage for the business.

How do we know if competitive advantage is likely to be achieved in the future as a result of implementing the chosen strategy? Of course we cannot be certain since we are dealing with forecasts of the future rather than measurements of the past, but the answer lies in the *returns* that are likely to be received.

In the commercial sector this normally relates primarily to the *financial* returns that are likely to be received as a result of implementing the strategy. For non-commercial activities the returns may be assessed in a rather different way. In these circumstances we are more likely to be concerned with the benefits that are received relative to the costs that are incurred to achieve these benefits (so-called cost–benefit analysis).

Financial tools for evaluating returns

In the evaluation and selection stage, a number of 'tools' are available to managers that may assist in deciding upon the most appropriate option. Not all of them will be appropriate in every circumstance and some are used more widely than others. They are used to explore the implications of the options so that the decisions that are made are based upon the best possible information.

Accountants or financial analysts are usually very involved in strategic evaluation and selection because of their expertise in understanding the financial implications of the possible courses of action. Some of the tools involved can be quite complicated, so a detailed discussion of their workings is beyond the scope of this book. However, it is extremely important that the decision makers (who may or may not be financial specialists) have an understanding of the financial principles involved in order to make sound judgements, hence the need to cover the issues and principles here.

The reader is referred to more specialized texts which cover this material in greater depth, for example Horner (2013) is a good starting point for non-financial specialists while Arnold (2012) gives more detailed general coverage. Scholes *et al*. (1998) consider financial decisions specifically in a public sector strategic management context. Specialist *THE* texts which cover this material and place it into a relevant contextual framework include DeFranco and Lattin (2006).

There are two key areas of financial decision making we will consider namely: cash flow forecasting and methods of investment appraisal.

Cash flow forecasting

One of the most straightforward financial tools available to managers is cash-flow forecasting – sometimes called funds-flow analysis. Many businesses fail not because they fail to be profitable but because they run out of cash. Such a situation means that a company becomes *insolvent* in that they are unable to pay their bills as they become due.

A business may have substantial assets such as cruise ships, aircraft and buildings, but creditors such as suppliers, staff and the government, cannot be paid using these as they need to be paid in cash. Assets such as buildings and transport equipment etc. can of course be sold for cash but this cannot happen easily or quickly so they are not liquid but are *illiquid* assets.

A company may also be making a profit (or capable of making a profit) in the future, but creditors are concerned not with the company's profitability (since this will be paid to shareholders or retained by the company), but with receiving the cash which they are due in a timely manner. If this does not occur the creditors might take action to recover the amounts they are due and this might include trying to *liquidate* the company and realising the value of its assets by selling them.

Essentially, cash-flow forecasting involves a forecast of:

- the expected revenues from an option;
- the costs that will be incurred, derived from the product of the revenues and costs, the net cash inflows or outflows.

For most options, the forecast will be broken down into monthly 'chunks' and a statement will be constructed for each month in which cash outflows and inflows are shown, together with opening and closing bank balances. The closing bank balance in one month (as shown in Table 12.6) is carried forward (c/f) and becomes the opening balance brought forward (b/f) in the following month.

The purpose of the forecast is that it allows for potential problems and solutions to be identified. If the same procedure is carried out for each option, the most favourable can be identified or suggestions can be made in order to improve the forecast cash position.

Analysis of the cash flow forecast should prompt certain questions (which were also previously considered in relation to the Interjet example shown as Table 5.6 in Chapter 5). These questions include:

- How easily predictable are the cash flows?
- How seasonal or cyclical are the cash flows?
- Can the company keep within its borrowing limits?
- Is the company generating enough cash to ensure its survival?

Table 12.6 A simplified cash flow forecast

	Mth 1	Mth 2	Mth 3
Revenue	500	400	400
Expenditure	−400	−1000	−500
Net	100	−600	−100
Bal. B/f	200	300	−300
Bal. C/f	300	−300	−400

- Does the company require further credit facilities?
- How long does it take customers to pay the company?
- How quickly does the company pay suppliers and others?
- To what extent are payments *business critical* i.e. critical to the company's successful on-going trading?

Cash flow forecasts may show up real potential problems. Failure to address them could potentially result in insolvency (the failure to pay bills as they become due). The inherent volatility of cash flows of many *THE* companies caused by factors such as seasonality and economic cycles has led to the failure of many *THE* companies. These companies may have been profitable but cash flow issues have resulted in their insolvency because creditors have refused to provide additional credit to maintain the companies as *going concerns*.

It is imperative that managers have a good insight into future cash flow patterns, and if problems foreseen they have a set of planned actions to address them. Managers need to be able to convince banks and other creditors that their investments are safe and that credit should not be withdrawn.

Thus, there are a number of actions a company may wish to consider to alleviate perceived cash flow problems that the forecast shows for particular options including:

- postponing capital expenditure;
- accelerating cash inflows;
- postponing or reducing cash outflows;
- selling non-core assets;
- negotiating new lines of credit or extending existing lines;
- leasing rather than buying equipment;
- tightly controlling costs such as salaries;
- prioritising 'business critical' expenditure over other expenditure;
- phasing payments so that they are paid when seasonal cash inflows are at their highest.

Figure 5.6 shows an example of a cash flow forecast for a (fictional) tour operator, Interjet, which experiences seasonal cash flow difficulties.

As with many *THE* businesses the resulting cash-flow forecast shows large seasonal fluctuations, which managers have to be aware of and take active steps to ensure that the difficulties are not insurmountable and are managed appropriately.

The Interject Example (Table 5.6) shows forward projections of cash-flow and is intended to highlight a number of problems which can be identified and which require managerial actions to be planned such as those identified above. Clearly without actions being taken the company in the example will experience future problems and crucially will exceed its overdraft limit from Month 6 to Month 11. Without renegotiation of these facilities the company faces a potential position of insolvency as it will have no funds available to pay its bills as they become due.

It is not possible to categorically to predict whether the collective actions that the company might take would be successful in the case of Interjet, since this is s simplified example. Some important information is not given, such as the attitude of the bank towards the company with regard to its planned overdraft limit. However careful consideration of the case can provide some suggested actions which could help.

For example, some aspects of the company's capital budget may be considered vital to the company's on-going success, but other aspects may be far less vital and could be postponed or cancelled altogether. Similarly, the amount of credit given by the company to its customers (debtors) compared to the amount of credit the company receives from its creditors might be considered. Other actions might also be considered by the company to alleviate its difficulties.

Questions:

1. Explain what is meant by the term insolvency and how it can occur despite a company being profitable.
2. Provide an example of a THE company you are familiar with which has failed owing to its insolvency and explain the underlying reasons why this might have occurred.
3. Advise the Board of Interjet (Figure 5.6) on the forecast cash flow difficulties it is facing and when they are likely to occur.
4. Advise the Board of Interjet of the actions that managers might take to alleviate its difficulties.

Investment appraisal – introduction

An investment, at its simplest, is some money put up for a project in the expectation that it will enable more money to be made in the future. The additional money over and above the original investment is termed the *return on investment*. There is often a strong time element to investment appraisal techniques because the returns on the investment may remain for several years or even decades. It is for this reason that a factor is often built in to the calculation to account for the *time value of money* (see Key Concept below).

KEY CONCEPT

The time value of money

Generally a sum of money received now is preferable to the same sum of money received at some point in the future.

The reason for this time preference is the *time value* of money and not because of inflation or risks – though both are important. In most developed and developing economies inflation has caused the value of money to diminish over time. Even if there were no inflation and there was an absolute certainty that the amount of money would be returned, the time preference for money would still hold true.

The explanation lies in the concept of opportunity cost. If a sum is received immediately, rather than some time in the future, it can be invested in some way and yield a rate of return. Thus the difference between present and future receipt is the cost of the investment opportunity foregone.

Because future inflows of cash are less desirable than present inflows, they must be discounted at a rate of interest so that the current and future inflows of cash are equalized.

There are thus two key questions surrounding investment appraisal which are:

- *How much* will the organization make against each investment option?
- *When* will the organization receive its return on investment?

Investment appraisal – investment appraisal methods

Key measures of *acceptability* are the *returns* that are likely to accrue from specific options and the *risks* of potential losses. Returns are based upon forecasts. What risks arise if the forecast returns turn out to be inaccurate?

A common method of assessing the financial acceptability of strategic options is through the application of *investment appraisal* techniques. Various methods of investment appraisal can be used. We will briefly consider the principles involved with the five most common methods below. These are:

- Payback method
- Breakeven analysis
- Accounting rate of return
- Net present value (NPV)
- Internal rate of return (IRR) } Discounted cash flow (DCF) methods

Payback method

The first and most obvious thing that managers want to know about any investment is the *payback period*. This is the time taken to repay the investment – the shorter the better. If, for example, an investment of £1,000,000 is expected to increase returns by £100,000 a month, then the payback period will be ten months.

In practice, payback periods are rarely this short and it is this fact that makes investment appraisal calculations a bit more complicated. When the effects of inflation are taken into account, the returns on an investment can be eroded over time. Consequently, accountants include a factor to account for the effects of inflation, usually on a 'best-guess' basis. The payback method can be justified on the grounds that it represents a simple, quick screening process.

However it can be criticized in that it ignores the so-called 'time value of money' and also ignores inflows after the payback period.

Breakeven analysis

Breakeven analysis is concerned with finding the point at which the total revenue from a project is equal to the total costs incurred.

The analysis (see for example Glautier and Underdown, 2001:Ch. 31) is directed towards finding the *tipping point* (breakeven point) beyond which revenue exceeds the total costs, i.e. the variable and fixed costs combined. As such it rests on a number of assumptions including:

- costs can be easily attributed between fixed and variable elements;
- fixed costs are constant;
- fixed costs can be allocated to particular products; and
- it is possible to predict the volume of sales at various prices.

Nevertheless breakeven analysis is widely understood and can easily be communicated around organizations so that employees know the sales levels which must be achieved to attain profitability of operations. It is extremely important in many aspects of *THE* for companies to know their breakeven points.

Thus breakeven analysis is a useful and widely used tool but needs to be treated with some caution since it rests on a number of assumptions and it is in itself variable. Managers should of course be concerned not just with the breakeven point that is calculated but in affecting it in such a way that the breakeven point is brought down. In other words the measure of capacity (such as the load factor, occupancy rate etc.,) that is used at which breakeven is reached is lowered. In order to do this managers have to look closely at their costs in order to ensure that they are minimized.

For example – an airline or a coach operator measures their load factors meticulously because they are 'proxy' measures of their profitability. A certain load factor is reached beyond which profitability is achieved and the further revenues over and above this *tipping point* add directly to the margins being achieved. Similarly a hotel operator, restaurant or venue operator will measure room occupancy rates, covers served and tickets sold for similar reasons. Most companies will have a view on the level at which the breakeven is achieved and pass this onto employees particularly those involved in achieving sales.

Accounting rate of return (ARR)

The ARR is as its title implies an accounting measure. It is calculated in three steps:

- take average annual inflows over project life;
- deduct depreciation on the initial outlay; then
- divide result by the average investment over the period.

The ARR can be justified (like the payback method) on the grounds that it represents a simple, quick screening process but it can also be criticized in that it ignores the time value of money.

Discounted cash flow (DCF) methods

The two main DCF methods (*net present value* and *internal rate of return*) are considered superior but more complicated than Payback, Breakeven and ARR because such methods consider the timing of cash flows – *the time value of money*.

The time value of money is based on the notion that organizations or individuals need to be compensated for foregoing the use of money for a period of time if, for example, it has been invested in a project.

Such methods are based on the concept of compound interest in reverse. For example, if interest rates are 10% and a certain investment promises to pay $100,000 in one year's time, the amount we would need to invest now is:

$$\frac{\$100,000 \times 100}{110} = \$90,900.$$

$90,900 *now* is equivalent to $100,000 received in one year. It is the *present value* of $100,000.

Net present value (NPV)

NPV is the value obtained by *discounting* the forecast cash inflows and outflows of a project at a chosen *acceptable* rate of return and taking the net total. An acceptable rate of return is the rate that the stakeholders would think is acceptable relative to other comparable investments.

The present value of the inflows and outflows can be found by applying a discount factor from published tables. For example, the discount factor applied after one year at the rate of 10 per cent is 0.9091, 0.8264 after two years, etc. That is, each US dollar is worth 0.9091 after one year, 0.8264 after two years, etc. Thus NPV involves the following steps:

1. Find the present value of the project's cash inflows (using discount rate tables).
2. Find the present value of the project's cash outflows (using discount rate tables).
3. If 1 minus 2 is positive then the investment is worthwhile; if it is negative the project or option should be rejected.

Internal rate of return (IRR)

The goal with this method is to find the interest rate at which inflows exactly equal outflows – where NPV = 0. Where IRR is higher than the rate deemed to be an acceptable level of return then the option should be considered as financially viable.

For example – if 10 per cent is viewed as an acceptable rate of return and IRR is calculated to be 15 per cent then the project would be deemed to be viable.

The steps to find IRR are as follows:

1. Select an acceptable interest rate as a rate of return.
2. Discount the present and future cash inflows and outflows at this rate.
3. If the result of this step is *not* zero, return to step 1 and select a different interest rate.
4. Continue until the result is zero, i.e. the interest rate at which NPV = zero has been found. This is the IRR of the project.
5. If the IRR exceeds the target rate of return which has been set then the investment should go ahead.

NPV and IRR compared

Although IRR is easier to understand because it is expressed as a percentage, whereas NPV is an amount, NPV is normally considered superior because:

1. NPV is easier to calculate.
2. IRR ignores the relative size of the investments being considered.
3. IRR rates are non-additive, i.e. the rates from two or more projects cannot be added together.
4. In some circumstances there may be more than one IRR.

Limitations of the financial tools

The limitations of the financial tools rest on the problem of the unpredictability of the future. We learned in Chapters 7 and 8 that the macro- and micro-environments can change, sometimes rapidly. Accordingly the actual returns that an organization makes on an investment may not always be what were expected.

In making investment decisions there is a need to consider the effects of inflation: the increase in price of goods and services over a period of time.

A distinction can be made between anticipated and unanticipated inflation. Anticipated inflation can be taken into account by investment appraisal models whereas unanticipated inflation is one of a number of sources of uncertainty (Samuel *et al.*, 1995). The investment analysis is only a tool in helping to make decisions and ultimately a judgement has to be made since uncertainty will always exist when forecasting the future.

Thus when the analysis is complete investors may require a so-called risk premium over and above the investment return to compensate them for the degree of uncertainty (including inflation) that they judge to be involved. In forecasting the level of inflation for net present value calculations, the presence of inflation would erode the purchasing power (what the cash sums would buy) but would not alter the relative attractiveness of competing projects (Samuel *et al.*, 1995). In major economies such as those in Western Europe, North America, Japan and Australia, the level of inflation has historically been relatively stable at between 2 and 10 per cent, with an occasional 'shock' such as in the mid 1970s when in the UK, for example, it reached 24 per cent.

Table 12.7 NPV worked example of two hotel projects (part 1)

		Hotel Project A Rio De Janeiro US$ million	Hotel Project B Sao Paulo US$ 000s
Outlay period	0	(15,000)	(15,000)
Inflow period	1	7.000	2,000
	2	5,000	3,000
	3	4,000	7,000
	4	4,000	10,000

Table 12.8 NPV worked example of two hotel projects (part 2)

Period	Project A	Project B	Present value at 10%	Project A	Project B
0	−15,000	−15,000		−15,000	−15,000
1	7,000	2,000	0.9063	6,344	1,813
2	5,000	3,000	0.8203	4,102	2,461
3	4,000	7,000	0.7441	2,976	5,209
4	4,000	10,000	0.6756	2,702	6,756
Total				1,124	1,238

In other parts of the world, however, problems with the supply of goods and the value of currency can lead to much higher inflation levels which have occasionally exceeded 100 per cent a year. A presumption of low and stable inflation will therefore tend to encourage investment rather than high and unpredictable inflation which will discourage investment or require a large risk premium to be paid to investors as compensation for the increased levels of perceived risk.

Tables 12.7 and 12.8 show a simplified fictitious example which compares two hotel projects.

Consider the case of a (fictitious) hotel company considering an investment in a new Brazilian hotel to open in 2015, before the Rio de Janeiro Olympic Games in 2016.

The hotelier has the option of either building the hotel in Rio which would enable the company to gain good levels of occupancy at high room rates shortly after opening or to open in Brazil's business capital Sao Paulo, which may give more even returns over a longer period.

In this case it is necessary to determine which project is preferable assuming:

- the company only has available funding for one of the projects;
- a discount rate of 10 per cent; and
- NPV provides the most effective means of investment appraisal since it considers the time value of money.

In the tables above the cash flows are discounted by a factor contained in published present value tables contained in many textbooks.

In this case:

- Both projects achieve a positive NPV so both are worthwhile.
- Project B is preferable since it provides a higher NPV, though it has a slightly longer payback period.

Non-financial tools for evaluating returns

Financial evaluation of strategic options is very important, but for most organizations, other tools can also provide useful information. These may require financial information as an input and so they should be seen not as an alternative to financial analyses, but an addition to it. They enrich the information enabling management to select the best strategic option.

Cost–benefit analysis

Cost–benefit analysis applies to almost every area of life, not just strategic evaluation and selection. The cost–benefit concept suggests that a money value can be put on all costs and benefits of a strategy, including tangible and intangible returns to people and organizations proposing the project. Each option will have a cost associated with it and will be expected to return certain benefits. If both of these can be quantified in financial terms, then the cost–benefit calculation will be relatively straightforward. The problem is that this is rarely the case.

The major benefit of such analysis is that it forces managers to be explicit about the various factors which influence strategic choice, so that even if people disagree about the valuations contained in the analysis, the material is brought out into the open and the merits of the various arguments can be compared (Johnson et al., 2011:379)

The costs of pursuing one particular option will have a number of elements. Any financial investment costs will be easily quantifiable. Against this, the cost of not pursuing the next best option needs to be taken into account – the *opportunity cost*. There may also be a number of social and environmental costs which are much harder to attach a value to.

The same problems apply to the benefits. In addition to financial benefits, an organization may also take into account social benefits and others such as improved reputation or improved service. Intangible benefits are very difficult to attach a value to for a cost–benefit analysis as they can take a long time to work through in increased financial performance.

Whilst it is difficult to quantify non-financial benefits, it is usually possible after some calculations have been made and often negotiations and research amongst the interested parties. Certainly the technique is commonly used to assess the acceptability of strategic options, particularly in the public sector (see for example Scholes and Johnson, 2001) and in cases where development involves public–private partnerships. The technique has also been quite widely used in THE settings, particularly in relation to major infra-structural projects such as for transport developments and also in relation to the staging of festivals and events. See for example Dwyer (1993) for a description of the method applied to tourism and hospitality, and Mules and Dwyer (2005) and Dwyer et al. (2000) who apply the concept to events and conventions respectively.

The problems with this evaluative technique though are that:

- Some of the 'measures' that are used are in fact subjective judgements and consequently open to challenge.
- There is no agreed methodology and in reality the term covers a range of approaches.
- In many cases there are issues about knowing just where the analysis should stop.

For example – in considering a major new airport development for a city it would seem appropriate that the increased costs of noise and emission pollution and congestion for the city should be costed. However, aircraft emissions are thought to be partly responsible for the global warming phenomena. Consequently, should the costs associated with global warming arising from increased air transport movements also be factored into the calculations or is this aspect too remote from the project under consideration?

> ### KEY CONCEPT
>
> #### Social costs and benefits
>
> All organizations have an impact upon the societies that are in their locality or that are affected by their products or activities. As we argued in Chapter 2 that *THE* often has a profound social impact in the home location, at destinations and in transit between the two. Although the term *social* is a bit nebulous, it is generally taken to mean the effect of the condition being evaluated on employment, social well-being, health, chemical emissions, pollution, aesthetic appearance, charitable societies, etc.
>
> A strategic option will have an element of social cost and social benefit. We would describe a social cost as a deterioration in any of the above – an increase in unemployment, higher levels of emissions, pollution, declining salaries, etc. Conversely, a social benefit will result in an improvement in the condition of society – increasing employment, cleaner industry, better working conditions, etc.

Impact analysis

When a strategic option may be reasonably expected to have far-reaching consequences in either social or financial terms, an impact study may be appropriate. Essentially, this involves asking the question: If this option goes ahead, what will its impact be upon. . .?

The aspects that might be impacted upon will depend upon the particular circumstances of the option. The impacts are widely discussed in *THE* contexts by authors such as Mathieson and Wall (1982), Mules (2000) and Archer (1996). Andersson and Lundberg (2013) point out that impact analysis of festivals and events has been a central theme in event studies for decades. In their paper the authors study a three-day music event in Sweden, propose a model for measuring impacts from a sustainability perspective and develop a common monetary metric which could be applied in different settings.

As with cost–benefit analysis, impact analysis really describes a range of approaches because the type of analysis, the sort of questions which are asked and the measures which are important are highly context-specific. In other words the underlying principles may be the same but the detail will vary in the cases of say a hotel development, an infrastructure project or in the case of the impact of festivals and events.

For example – with regard to a proposed development of a new theme park, the impact study might typically take into account the development's implications for:

- Local employment.
- Primary and secondary levels of spending to be generated and *leakages* from the local economy.
- The effect of the development on other businesses.
- The capacity of the local infrastructure such as road and rail services but also utilities such as water and sewerage, waste disposal, gas and electricity.
- The environmental impact on the local flora and fauna and the effects of noise pollution.
- The aesthetic impact of the development on the local community.

In many cases an impact study will be an intrinsic part of the cost–benefit calculation and it suffers from the same limitations – that of evaluating the true value of each thing that may be impacted.

SHORT CASE ILLUSTRATION

Evaluation: the Olympic bidding process for the Tokyo 2020 Olympic Games

The Olympic Games is the world's biggest sporting event and cities have to bid against each other in a highly publicized bidding process. The bids have to go through a careful evaluation process before the successful city is chosen. Though the terminology is not used the evaluation involves a series of stages which in essence involve suitability, screening, feasibility and acceptability.

Suitability – Each competing country has a National Olympic Committee (NOC). The NOC coordinates any possible bid from the country it represents and assesses the suitability of the bid. At this stage the bid may be withdrawn because it is not deemed to be suitable and therefore unlikely to succeed, but if it passes this hurdle the NOC formally passes the bid onto the International Olympic Committee for further scrutiny. Cities such as Prague (Czech Republic), Saint Petersburg (Russia) and Toronto (Canada) considered making bids for the 2020 Olympic Games, but they did not do so. Rome (Italy) was to submit a bid to the IOC but the Italian Government subsequently withdrew its support and the bid was withdrawn.

Screening – Following submission of their bids the 'applicant cities' are required to answer a questionnaire covering themes of importance to a successful Games organization. This allows the IOC to analyze the capabilities and the strengths and weaknesses of the potential host cities as well as assess the risks involved. Following a detailed study and ensuing reports, the IOC Executive Board selects the cities that are qualified to proceed to the next phase. At this screening stage some cities are screened out and cannot proceed. In the bidding process for the 2020 Olympic Games, Baku (Azerbaijan) and Doha (Qatar) were rejected at this stage and did not proceed.

Feasibility – At the candidature stage the accepted 'candidate cities' submit a second questionnaire in the form of an extended, more detailed candidature questionnaire which includes detailed financial and operational details and impact assesssments. The reports are carefully studied by the IOC Evaluation Commission. The members of the Commission make four-day inspection visits to each of the candidate cities, where they check details of the bid. The results of its inspections are passed to IOC members up to one month before the electing IOC Session. Three cities were considered for selection to host the 2020 games at this stage: Istanbul (Turkey), Madrid (Spain) and Tokyo (Japan).

Acceptability – The acceptability of the bids is the responsibility of members of the IOC who each have one vote. Voting continues in rounds eliminating cites until a city with an overall majority is chosen. Thus in its meeting on 7th September 2013 held in the neutral city of Buenos Aires (Argentina), Tokyo was chosen to host the 2020 Summer Olympic Games.

www.olympic.org

Questions

1. Explain why the Olympic Games goes through this structured evaluation process.
2. What stakeholders other than the IOC members may have a view on the 'acceptability' of the Olympic bids?

Risk

The third 'R' of acceptability relates to risk and uncertainty.

Most decisions about strategy are made under conditions of some uncertainty – for who can predict the future with any degree of certainty when the environment is complex and rapidly changing? There is clearly then a risk that the outcome will turn out differently from what was planned.

Thus we need to have a framework for considering what would happen to the organization if the assumptions which underpin the strategy turn out to be wrong and what risks this might entail. All organizations encounter risks, some of which are fairly generic in nature – such as financial risks associated with interest rates – and others which are quite specific to each individual business situation.

It is important that managers:

- identify the major risks that the organization encounters;
- attempt to understand the nature of the risks identified and how they are likely to change; and
- plan their strategy in such a way that enables them to manage and deal with the risks.

No business can eliminate risk and since the level of returns is usually correlated with risk, it may be that it is sensible to take on some risk which could be avoided. By doing so managers have the opportunity of maximizing returns, but it is important that a balanced assessment is made that the relative risks and returns are considered. It is also necessary that the risks are 'owned' by particular identified managers and directors so that they are tracked, the changing implications are monitored and steps are taken to manage the risks appropriately. These steps may include:

- Just recognizing the risk exists in the knowledge that good returns are being received.
- Having a portfolio approach so that a risk in one part of the business is balanced by non-risky aspects elsewhere.
- Taking active measures to control risks such as through hedging, working collaboratively with partners or off-laying the risk to suppliers of customers.

The type of risks a large *THE* business may encounter is illustrated by the case of Live Nation, shown below.

SHORT CASE ILLUSTRATION

Risk analysis: Live Nation

Live Nation Entertainment, Inc. based in Beverly Hills, California, claims to be the largest live entertainment company in the world and operates five main areas associated with live entertainment events: promoting music events, operating venues, ticketing services (such as Ticketmaster), sponsorship and advertising sales, and artist management and services.

All businesses encounter risks and it is important managers of those businesses identify the risks and understand the implications if adverse circumstancs arise. As part of its annual reporting the company analyses in detail the business and financial risks it encounters. Some of the business risks identified by the company are summarised in Table 12.9.

Table 12.9 Business risks: Live Nation

Our business:

Is highly sensitive to public tastes and is dependent on our ability to secure popular artists and other live music events

Depends on relationships between key promoters, executives, agents, managers, artists and clients

Faces intense competition in the live music, ticketing and artist services industries

Is seasonal and our results of operations vary from quarter to quarter and year over year

Depends, in significant part, on entertainment, sporting and leisure events and factors adversely affecting such events could have a material adverse effect

Operates in international markets in which we have limited experience and which may expose us to risks not found in doing business in the United States

Is subject to exchange rates which may cause fluctuations in our results of operations that are not related to our operations

May be unsuccessful in our future acquisition endeavours, if any, which may have an adverse effect on our business

May not be able to adapt quickly enough to changing customer requirements and industry standards

Encounters the risk of personal injuries and accidents in connection with our live music events, which could subject us to personal injury or other claims

Is dependent upon our ability to lease, acquire and develop live music venues

Depends in part on the promotional success of our marketing campaigns

Could encounter poor weather adversely affects attendance at our live music events, which could negatively impact our financial performance

Source: Live Nation (2012)

Questions

1. Explain why a company like Live Nation needs to identify the risks it is subject to.

2. In what general ways might managers respond to the risks identified in a case such as Live Nation?

Scenario planning and sensitivity analysis

The uncertainties of the future, as we have seen, make any prediction inexact. Whilst an organization can never be certain of any sequence of future events, scenario planning (or 'what if?' analysis, as it is sometimes called) and its variant, sensitivity analysis, can give an idea of how the outcome would be affected by a number of possible disruptions. For a general discussion of this technique see for example Saltelli *et al.* (2000) and Fleisher and Bensoussan (2003); and for a context-specific discussion see for example Yeoman and McMahon-Beattie (2005) in their application of the technique to Scottish tourism and hospitality.

The development of computerized applications such as spreadsheets has made this activity easier than it used to be. A financial model on a spreadsheet that makes a number of assumptions such as revenue projections, cost forecasts, inflation rate, etc., can be modified to instantly show the effect of, say, a 10 per cent increase in costs or a higher-than-expected rate of inflation. This is designed to show how sensitive the cash flow is to its assumptions – hence the name.

For example – an airline might produce a projection of future earnings on the basis that the average price it would have to pay for its jet fuel requirements, a major constituent of airline costs, is US$150 per barrel (a barrel is 42 US gallons or roughly 159 litres). The airline obviously is unable to control the price of this key input and indeed has no accurate means of forecasting it. Consequently, when forecasting its future earnings the airline might regard it as a prudent step to produce alternative scenarios which ask the 'what if?' question. The scenarios might suppose that:

- A major war breaks out or the Organization of Petroleum Exporting Countries (OPEC) restricts supplies thereby increasing jet fuel prices by 20 per cent.
- Surplus supplies of jet fuel become available as a result of lower demand for air services leading to jet fuel prices falling by 20 per cent.

Having produced the scenarios and calculated the impact of the events on the cost of jet fuel the airline would factor the costs into its overall calculations. As a result the airline might be able to produce a central or base earnings forecast based on the $150 per barrel price, but would also have knowledge of the effect an increase or decrease in fuel costs would have on overall profitability.

In other words the *sensitivity* of earnings to fuel price changes would have been assessed. In some cases the analysis might go a stage further by applying weightings to the scenarios. Thus the airline might be fairly confident about its central assumption and assign a 50 per cent weighting, i.e. its assessment of the situation is that there is a 50 per cent chance of the central assumption of $150 being realized. Similarly, the company might assess the situation and feel that if the central case is not borne out then a rise is more likely than a fall and consequently 30 per cent and 20 per cent weightings are assigned to the rising and falling fuel price scenarios respectively.

SHORT CASE ILLUSTRATION

Sensitivity analysis: Air New Zealand

Companies frequently assess the sensitivity of their earnings to major changes in their annual report and accounts and other company documents. This serves to warn investors and other stakeholders of the potential volatility of earnings. It also informs the stakeholders that managers are aware of the risks and of the steps they might be taking (such as hedging) to deal with the risks identified.

To return to an example used in Chapter 5 of Air New Zealand, in its annual report identifies a number of risks and analyses the sensitivity of earnings to price changes. The Air New Zealand annual report (Air New Zealand, 2012:31) states that 'the sensitivity analyses are hypothetical and should not be considered predictive of future performance' and that 'the sensitivities to specific events or circumstances will be counteracted as far as possible through strategic management actions'.

The report identifies key sensitivities relating to foreign currency; liquidity; equity investment prices; interest rates and jet fuel prices. In relation to jet fuel prices, for example, the report estimates that in 2013 a US$20 increase or decrease would have positive or negative impact of approximately NZ$33 million. This represents a substantial portion of the airlines net profits which in 2013 amounted to approximately NZ$182 million. In order to alleviate this risk the management hedges a large part of its exposure to fuel price movements through the use of financial instruments.

Air New Zealand (2012)

Questions

1. Explain why Air New Zealand is concerned about jet fuel prices.
2. Explain what is meant by sensitivity analysis and consider in what circumstances it might be useful to *THE* organizations.

Qualitative variables can also be analysed. If an option has a high dependency upon the availability of a key raw material or the oversight of a key manager, a 'what if?' study will show the effect that the loss or reduction in the key input would have.

Strategic evaluation in emergent strategies

In Chapter 1 and elsewhere we encountered the idea that business strategies can be either prescriptive (or deliberate) or emergent (we return to this concept in more detail in Chapter 15). This is to say that some strategies are planned in advance, often following a rational sequence of events – prescriptive strategies. Others are not planned in this way and are said to be emergent – they result from an organization's management following a consistent pattern of behaviour. A planned prescriptive approach can imply excessive formality, inflexibility and an over-reliance on analysis. Indeed, in a well-known article on strategy Lenz and Lyles (1989) argue that too much analysis can stifle innovation and lead to 'paralysis' (a lack of action). However, in a prescriptive approach at least managers and other stakeholders can be assured that strategic options have been formulated, evaluated and chosen based on evidence.

This distinction is important when it comes to strategic evaluation. Companies that employ the deliberate model are likely to use the criteria and the tools above whilst those that prefer the emergent model are less likely to do so explicitly. This is not to say, however, that the analytical process cannot form a part of an intelligent manager's intuitive thinking.

It is here that one of the potential limitations of emergent strategy becomes apparent. If an organization follows a deliberate process with its systematic and sequential events, then it can be more certain that all possible options have been identified and evaluated before the most appropriate one is selected. An organization using an intuitive emergent approach that relies upon patterns of behaviour cannot be certain that the best option is taken throughout the decision-making process. It might get it right – but it might not.

The contrary argument for emergent strategy is that in today's rapidly changing environments organizations must be flexible, adaptive and move quickly when required. A deliberate approach can militate against these actions in that it infers a more orderly, planned approach, which is time-consuming and may stifle innovation and creativity. With a great deal of uncertainty, product innovation leading to rapid market changes and an ever-more competitive environment, emergent approaches have become popular in the academic literature.

Henry Mintzberg's research findings first developed during the 1980s (Mintzberg and Waters, 1985) have often emphasized the importance of emergent strategy, which arises informally at any level in an organization as an alternative or complement to deliberate strategy. His much-cited work 'The rise and fall of strategic planning' presents a critique of planned (prescriptive) approaches and emphasizes the need for a more emergent form of strategy. Other writers such as Ackermann and Eden (2014) take the emergent theme a stage further when they emphasize the 'making' of strategy as a highly inclusive and action-oriented activity. The academic debates and the main features of emergent strategy and its implications for decision making are well articulated by Lynch in Chapters 5, 7 and 11 (2012).

Realistically, in planning most organizations probably adopt a 'hybrid' approach that lies somewhere between the two extremes, in order to try to obtain the advantages of a planned approach without losing the possible innovation and flexibility that might be evident in a more emergent approach. Stakeholders such as shareholders and banks tend to force many organizations down a prescriptive (deliberate) route of strategic formulation. This is because in making investment decisions they want to see evidence that the organization has considered its strategy carefully and considered alternatives based on analysis of the evidence.

However, there has undoubtedly been recognition that strategic formulation cannot be static. In contemporary, fast-moving markets, which value creativity and innovation and where barriers to entry have been removed or lowered, organizations have to maintain flexibility so as to compete effectively. Recognizing the advantages of more emergent approaches to strategic formulation also has particular relevance for SMEs since, for reasons we will consider below, they can gain competitive advantage over larger competitors in fast-moving markets through innovation.

The preceding discussion emphasizes the fact that strategy is not a once-only activity – the organization determines its strategy and then implements it. Instead, whichever end of the prescriptive–emergent continuum an organization chooses as the basis for strategy formulation it must be viewed as a 'process'. The process requires continual monitoring of the implementation of the strategy, feedback provided to managers and adjustments made when necessary. The implementation issues relating to strategy will be covered in the next part of this book.

THINK POINTS

- Explain the differences between the main investment appraisal techiques.
- What are the limitations of a cost–benefit analysis?
- Explain the limitations that emergent strategies may have in the strategic evaluation stage.
- What are the possible limitations of a cost–benefit analysis?
- Explain the limitations that emergent strategies may have in the strategic evaluation stage.
- Explain why a screening stage is often inserted between suitability and feasibility in strategic evaluation.
- Explain what is meant by the three Rs of acceptability?
- Assess the limitations that emergent strategies may have at the strategic evaluation stage.

SMALL BUSINESS FOCUS

There is some evidence that though most organizations view strategy and strategic planning as highly important, many organizations do not use the tools and techniques of evaluation outlined in this chapter (despite the advantages in delivering rigour). This is particularly true of SMEs. Stonehouse and Pemberton (2002), building on the work of Glaister and Falshaw (1999), for example, state that 'only a limited set of tools are deployed by small, medium or large organizations, though there is evidence that larger organizations are more likely to take a more structured approach and utilise the tools'. The authors also identified a short-term outlook in relation to the business planning of the companies they surveyed.

Notwithstanding the lack of formal use of the strategic tools and techniques, many SMEs have to produce regular business plans in order to satisfy the banks and shareholders which finance them. This forces them to take a planned prescriptive approach to strategy albeit sometimes rather short-to-medium-term in its outlook. But there is also a need for SMEs to continually innovate to stay ahead of competitors (which are often larger) and the theme of innovation is something that is particularly stressed in the literature relating to emergent approaches to strategy.

There is a body of research which argues that SMEs in fast moving markets enjoy particular advantages over more established competitors largely due to their ability to innovate and adapt quickly, operating in a more emergent manner. Although this literature mainly relates to technology companies (see for example Christensen *et al.*, 1998) it can be argued that the markets in many parts of *THE* also represent such fast-moving markets and thus place a high dependence on innovation. Thus innovation is a key driver in many SMEs in *THE*, and a driver which can provide a strong position relative to larger competitors. See for example Prentice and Andersen (2003), Hjalager (2002 and 2010) and Sundbo *et al.* (2007).

In discussing innovation in tourism, Sundbo *et al.* (2007) conclude that tourism firms, hotels, restaurants and transport have been seen to be among the most innovative while Prentice and Andersen (2003) point out that it is Edinburgh's reputation for innovation in relation to the arts that underpins its success as a multi-festival city. There are a number of examples of quite rapid market changes which have often transformed the competitive landscape in *THE* such as:

- the growth of low-cost airlines;
- rapidly segmenting markets for cruising;
- the growth of individually styled boutique hotels;
- the proliferation of new and more specialized festivals; and
- the 'discovery' of new travel destinations.

The rapid market changes are encouraged by lower barriers to entry and the desire of *THE* consumers for products which provide consumers with experiences which are 'new', 'exciting', 'challenging' and 'different'. Such products are often also driven by style, fashion branding and status.

THE organizations providing such products are often relatively new and innovative SMEs benefiting from *first mover* (or *early mover*) advantage. Equally by its very nature the openness of the tourist sectors make it easy for enterprises to observe what others are doing, with the result that SMEs may be able to get a 'free ride' on the investments, ideas and successes of others (Hjalager, 2002). In adopting a so-called *me too* strategy, SMEs are able to adapt, extend and provide niche versions of products provided by larger companies. In some cases innovative SBUs of larger companies, operating relatively independently of the parent company, have been innovative or have been quick to follow the innovations of SMEs (as with the boutique brands of the larger hotel chains).

Lynch (2012: 188), in describing what he terms 'strategy dynamics in fast-moving markets', argues that when industries are subject to rapid change then there are two issues facing leading established organizations. As a consequence opportunities are presented to SMEs and new competitors.

The two issues identified by Lynch are:

- *The sunk cost effect* – Organizations which have already committed substantial resources may be reluctant to change. These represent resources sunk into technologies or products and while the sunk costs have already been spent, nevertheless they will influence strategic thinking and may inhibit change on the part of larger companies.
- *The replacement effect* – Existing large companies have less incentive to innovate than SMEs and new entrants. This is because the existing companies already enjoy market dominance and therefore innovation would not enhance their position but just replace one technology or product innovation with another. SMEs on the other hand have incentive to innovate since they can gain market share and later market dominance by doing so.

Figure 12.2 provides a diagrammatic representation showing the opportunities available to SMEs as a result of the strategy dynamics of fast-moving markets.

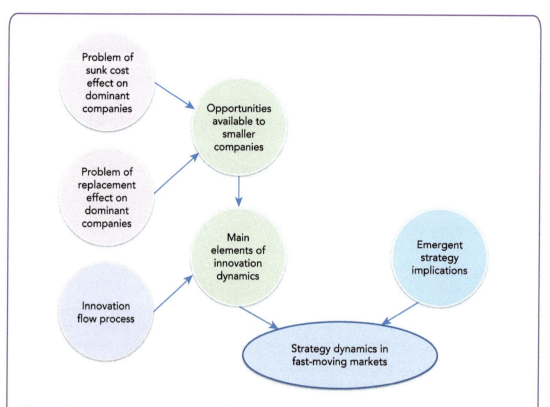

Figure 12.2 Exploring the dynamics of fast-moving markets

For example – the operator of a hotel chain may have invested heavily in spreading the attributes of the hotel brand around its network. Customers grow accustomed to these attributes and a certain expectation and brand loyalty develops. However, over time the hotels may become 'tired' or old-fashioned and are overtaken by newer more fashionable brands. Without refreshment and innovation the older brand gets left behind as others benefit from being more innovative. The Holiday Inn brand when it was introduced in the 1950s was seen to set new standards for midscale hotels. However, by the turn of the century newer brands had caught up and a far more segmented market faced the brand. Consequently a major (largely successful) revamp of the brand has taken place in recent years.

CHAPTER SUMMARY

The process of choosing strategic options is concerned with evaluating and selecting the best options. Options are considered in relation to the three key aspects of strategy:

- Competitive strategy
- Strategic directions
- Strategic methods.

Each option is considered in turn using three overarching criteria:

- Suitability
- Feasibility
- Acceptability.

The acceptability phase is concerned with assessing options in relation to three Rs:

- Reactions of stakeholders
- Returns
- Risks.

A number of financial and non-financial tools and techniques can be used to evaluate the 'acceptability' of each option before the most favourable one is chosen. Finally, the chapter considered the risks inherent in an emergent strategy approach when it comes to strategic evaluation and considered the potential advantages SMEs might have in fast-moving markets which might exist in parts of THE.

Having chosen strategic options, organizations are faced with the issues involved in implementing the chosen strategy. This is the subject area of the next part of the book.

BIBLIOGRAPHY

Ackermann, F. and C. Eden (2014) *Making Strategy: The Journey of Strategic Management*, 2nd edn, London: SAGE.

Air New Zealand (2012) *Air New Zealand Annual Report*, available at www.airnewzealand.com (accessed March 2014).

Ambrosini, V., G. Johnson and K. Scholes (eds.) (1998) *Exploring Techniques of Analysis and Evaluation in Strategic Management*, Harlow: Prentice Hall.

Andersson, T. D. and E. Lundberg (2013) 'Commensurability and Sustainability: Triple Impact Assessments of a Tourism Event', *Tourism Management*, 37: 99–109.

Ansoff, I. (1987) *Corporate Strategy*, London: Penguin.

Archer, B. H. (1996) 'Economic Impact Analysis', *Annals of Tourism Research*, 23 (4): 704–7.

Arnold, G. (2005) *Corporate Financial Management*, London: Pearson Education.

Arnold, G. (2012) *Corporate Financial Management*, 5th edn, Harlow: Pearson.

Brown, D. O. and F. A. Kwansol (1999) 'Using IRR and NPV Models to Evaluate Societal Costs of Tourism Projects in Developing Countries', *International Journal of Hospitality Management*, 18 (1): 31–43.

Christensen, C. M., F. F. Suárez and J. M. Utterback (1998) 'Strategies for Survival in Fast-Changing Industries', *Management Science*, 44 (12-Part-2): S207–S220.

DeFranco, A. L. and T. W. Lattin (2006) *Hospitality Financial Management*, New York: John Wiley & Sons.

Dwyer, L. and P. Forsyth (1993) 'Assessing the Benefits and Costs of Inbound Tourism', *Annals of Tourism Research*, 20 (4): 751–68.

Dwyer, L., R. Mellor, N. Mistilis and T. Mules (2000) 'A Framework for Assessing Tangible and Intangible Impacts of Events and Conventions', *Event Management*, 6 (3): 175–89..

Eden, C. and F. Ackermann (2013) *Making Strategy: The Journey of Strategic Management*, London: Sage.

Fleischer, A. and D. Felsenstein (2000) 'Support for Rural Tourism: Does It Make a Difference?' *Annals of Tourism Research*, 27 (4): 1007–24.

Fleisher, C. S. and B. E. Bensoussan (2003) *Strategic and Competitive Analysis: Methods and Techniques for Analyzing Business Competition*, Upper Saddle River, NJ: Prentice Hall.

Getz, D., T. Andersson and J. Carlsen (2010) 'Festival Management Studies: Developing a Framework and Priorities for Comparative and Cross-Cultural Research', *International Journal of Event and Festival Management*, 1 (1): 29–59.

Glaister, K. W. and J. R. Falshaw (1999) 'Strategic Planning: Still Going Strong?', *Long Range Planning*, 32 (1): 107–116.

Glautier, M. W. E. and B. Underdown (2001) *Accounting Theory and Practice*, London: Pearson.

Gu, H., C. Ryan and L. Yu (2012) 'The Changing Structure of the Chinese Hotel Industry: 1980–2012', *Tourism Management Perspectives*, 4: 56–63.

Haberberg, A. and A. Rieple (2001) *The Strategic Management of Organizations*, Harlow: Pearson Education.

Hjalager, A. M. (2002) 'Repairing Innovation Defectiveness in Tourism', *Tourism Management*, 23 (5): 465–74.

—— (2010) 'A Review of Innovation Research in Tourism', *Tourism Management*, 31 (1): 1–12.

Horner, D. (2013) *Accounting for Non-Accountants*, London: Kogan Page.

Johnson, G., R. Whittington and K. Scholes (2011) *Exploring Corporate Strategy*, 6th edn, Hemel Hempstead: Prentice Hall.

Kotler, P. (1997) *Marketing Management Analysis, Planning, Implementation and Control*, 9th edn, Englewood Cliffs, NJ: Prentice Hall International.

Lenz, R. T. and M. A. Lyles (1989) 'Paralysis by Analysis: Is Your Planning System Becoming Too Rational?' in D. Asch and C. Bowman (eds.), *Readings in Strategic Management*, London: Macmillan, 57–70.

Lindberg, K., T. D. Andersson and B. G. Dellaert (2001) 'Tourism Development: Assessing Social Gains and Losses', *Annals of Tourism Research*, 28 (4): 1010–30.

Lynch, R. (2012) *Corporate Strategy*, 6th edn, Harlow: Pearson Education.

Mathieson, A. and G. Wall (1982) *Tourism: Economic, Physical and Social Impacts*, London and New York: Longman.

Mintzberg, H. and J. A. Waters (1985) 'Of Strategies, Deliberate and Emergent', *Strategic Management Journal*, 6 (3): 257–72.

Mules, T. (2000) 'Globalisation and the Economic Impacts of Tourism', in B. Faulkner, G. Moscardo and E. Laws (eds.), *Tourism in the 21st Century: Lessons from Experience*, London: Continuum, pp. 312–27.

Mules, T. and L. Dwyer (2005) 'Public Sector Support for Sport Tourism Events: The Role of Cost-Benefit Analysis', *Sport in Society*, 8 (2): 338–55.

Owen, G. (1998) *Accounting for Hospitality, Tourism and Leisure*, 2nd edn, Harlow: Longman.

Porter, M. E. (1985) *Competitive Advantage*, New York: Free Press.

Prentice, R. and V. Andersen (2003) 'Festival as Creative Destination', *Annals of Tourism Research*, 30 (1): 7–30.

Rankin, J. (2013) 'Easyjet: Allocated Seating Attracts Older Passengers and Boosts Profits', *The Guardian*, 19 November.

Rumelt, R. P. (2003). 'Evaluating Business Strategy', in H. Mintzberg, J. B. Quinn and S. Ghoshal, *The Strategy Process*, 4th edn, Harlow UK: Pearson, 80–7.

Saltelli, A., K. Chan and E. M. Scott (eds.) (2000) *Sensitivity Analysis (vol. 134)*, New York: Wiley.

Samuels, J., F. Wilkes and R. Brayshaw (1995) *Management of Corporate Finance*, 6th edn, London: Chapman & Hall.

Scholes, K. and G. Johnson (eds.) (2001) *Exploring Public Sector Strategy*, London: FT.

Scholes, K., G. Johnson and V. Ambrosini (1998) *Exploring Techniques of Analysis and Evaluation in Strategic Management*, Harlow: Pearson Higher Education.

Stonehouse, G. and J. Pemberton (2002) 'Strategic Planning in SMEs: Some Empirical Findings', *Management Decision*, 40 (9): 853–61.

Sundbo, J., F. Orfila-Sintes and F. Sørensen (2007) 'The Innovative Behaviour of Tourism Firms: Comparative Studies of Denmark and Spain', *Research Policy*, 36 (1): 88–106.

Yeoman, I. and U. McMahon-Beattie (2005) 'Developing a Scenario Planning Process Using a Blank Piece of Paper', *Tourism and Hospitality Research*, 5 (3): 273–85.

WEBSITES

www.corporate.easyjet.com

www.headforpoints.com/

www.kenes-group.com/

www.olympic.org

www.airnewzealand.com

www.livenationentertainment.com

FURTHER READING

Reference	Focus
Brown, D. O. and F. A. Kwansol (1999) 'Using IRR and NPV Models to Evaluate Societal Costs of Tourism Projects in Developing Countries', *International Journal of Hospitality Management*, 18 (1): 31–43.	Investment appraisal Tourism Hospitality
Dwyer, L., A. Gill and N. Seetaram (eds.) (2012), *Handbook of Research Methods in Tourism: Quantitative and Qualitative Approaches*, Cheltenham UK: Edward Elgar Publishing	Research Methods Tourism
Dwyer, L., R. Mellor, N. Mistilis, and T. Mules (2000) 'A framework for assessing tangible and intangible impacts of events and conventions', *Event Management*, 6 (3): 175–89.	Cost-benefit analysis Evaluation framework Events and conventions
Fleischer, A., and D. Felsenstein (2000) 'Support for rural tourism: does it make a difference?' *Annals of Tourism Research*, 27 (4), 1007–24.	Cost-benefit analysis Tourism
Getz, D., T. Andersson and J. Carlsen (2010) 'Festival management studies: developing a framework and priorities for comparative and cross-cultural research', *International Journal of Event and Festival Management*, 1 (1): 29–59.	Cost-benefit analysis Evaluation framework Festivals
Lindberg, K., T. D. Andersson and B. G. Dellaert (2001) 'Tourism development: Assessing social gains and losses', *Annals Of Tourism Research*, 28 (4): 1010–30.	Cost-benefit analysis Tourism
Rumelt, R. (1980) 'The Evaluation of Buisness Strategy' in W. F. Glueck (ed.), *Business Policy and Strategic Management*, New York: McGraw Hill.	Evaluation Strategy
Williams, A. and E. Giardina (1993) *Efficiency in the Public Sector: The Theory and Practice of Cost-Benefit Analysis*, London: Edward Elgar.	Cost-benefit analysis Public sector

CASE LINKAGES

Case 4	Hyatt Hotels
Case 5	Days Inn

Part **5**

Strategic implementation and strategy in theory and practice

Introduction

The previous part of this book was concerned with formulating the options available to *THE* organizations for future development, evaluating the options and selecting between these options.

In Part 5 we turn towards strategic implementation before a consideration of strategic management trends in theory and practice. Once a tourism, hospitality or events management organization has selected the most appropriate strategic options, the organization must consider a number of key issues related to actually putting the proposed strategy into practice.

As ever the danger can lie in this more detailed level of strategic management. However well thought out the strategy may be, if sufficient thought is not given to the ways in which it should be *implemented* and appropriate actions follow, it is unlikely that the strategy will prove to be successful.

Study progress:

Part 1	Part 2	Part 3	Part 4	Part 5		
Strategy and the tourism, hospitality and events contexts	Analysing the internal environment	Analysing the external environment and SWOT	Strategic selection	Strategic implementation and strategy in theory and practice		
Introduction and Chapters 1 and 2	Chapters 3, 4, 5, and 6	Chapters 7, 8, and 9	Chapters 10, 11 and 12	Chapter 13 Strategic implementation for tourism, hospitality and events	Chapter 14 International and global strategies for tourism, hospitality and events	Chapter 15 Strategy and tourism, hospitality and event organizations: theory and practice

The word 'implementation' perhaps implies that it is a 'one-off' process with the strategy being implemented then left alone. This is not the case. Strategic management should be viewed as an on-going process for lessons learned (both successes and failures) from the implementation stage can provide feedback into the analysis phase. The external and internal environments of THE organizations are constantly changing so that such organizations need to continually re-evaluate environments. Changes in these may require modifications to the chosen strategies and consequently revisions to the ways in which they are implemented.

In this part of the book a number of the most important issues connected with strategic implementation are considered.

Resources – Implementation requires a reconfiguration of the *THE* organization's resource base. Does the organization have the inputs it needs in terms of finance, people, physical inputs and intellectual assets to carry out the strategy, and how should these resources be configured? If not how will the resources be obtained (Chapter 13).

Communication and Coordination – In order to be successful all parts of the organization need to be aware of the overall strategy and its implications. It is likely that in most organizations the corporate objectives will be cascaded through the organization so that objectives and operational plans are set for all functional areas and SBUs (Chapter 13).

Structure and Culture – A *THE* organization will need to bring its structure and culture into such a position that they facilitate a successful outcome. It may be that the structure and culture are not initially supportive for the strategic changes the organization is trying to implement. In such a situation the organization will need to instigate the requisite changes (Chapter 13).

Leadership and Change – Implementation of strategy invariably involves change. This will affect employees' roles and responsibilities, may mean redundancies or additional appointments and external stakeholders such as shareholders will also be implicated. Change can be a difficult managerial challenge requiring strong leaders. While some may welcome proposed changes others may resist thus risking the efficient implementation of the strategy. Different approaches may be adopted by leaders and managers according to the circumstances (Chapter 13).

Internationalization – THE represents inherently international sectors of industry, with consumers crossing international borders and usually relatively low barriers preventing international growth for companies. In such circumstances it is important to consider the approach of organizations to internationalization. International strategy is considered in Chapter 14.

At the end of a book on strategic management for tourism, hospitality and events it is apposite to stand back and consider the changing nature of the subject matter. Thus the book concludes in Chapter 15 with a brief overview of present and future trends in the study of strategic management and what impact this might have on managers operating in *THE*.

Having studied the concepts, tools and techniques of strategy, readers might be left to ask how exactly should a strategy be prepared and presented in a practical sense? Chapter 15 concludes the book with a consideration of guidelines which might be considered in presenting strategy so that it can be clearly articulated to others and understood by them.

Chapter 13

Strategic implementation for tourism, hospitality and events

Introduction and chapter overview

Strategic implementation is concerned with the issues considered necessary for the successful execution of strategy. In other words this is the 'strategy in action'.

In a prescriptive strategic process, strategic implementation would be carried out only after an organization has gathered sufficient information on its internal and external environments (this being the purpose of strategic analysis) and after it has undertaken the process of the formulation, evaluation and selection of the most appropriate strategic options (see Chapter 12).

This chapter will discuss the difficulties of the strategic implementation phase, as identified in the literature, before going on to consider key areas which managers of strategic change need to consider. Finally a tool to coordinate, manage and measure strategic implementation is considered.

In order to successfully carry out a strategy, an organization must consider several key areas. The organization must consider how the strategy will:

- be resourced;
- impact on the culture, structure and internal systems of the organization;
- necessitate change and the leadership and management implications of making the changes; and
- be communicated to staff and translated for all parts of the organization.

This chapter discusses each of these matters in turn. Throughout this text it has been emphasized that strategy (whether in its prescriptive or emergent forms) should *not* be viewed as a one-off exercise, but instead as a continual process. As part of this process it has also been emphasized that feedback is required on how successful the strategy is so that it can be modified if necessary.

This raises the question: how do you know if the strategy is successful or not? As a result of this potential difficulty, the strategic implementation phase of strategy is often closely linked with measuring organizational success. In this way organizations have ways of understanding to what degree the strategic measures they are implementing are successful or not.

Various tools and techniques have been developed to help managers to:

- implement strategy in a consistent manner across their organizations;
- measure organizational success; and
- provide feedback and tracking to inform any amendments to the strategy which may be required.

The best known of these tools is the Balanced Scorecard which will be considered towards the end of the chapter as a way of integrating and coordinating the strategic implementation process.

LEARNING OBJECTIVES

After studying this chapter you should be able to:

- describe where implementation fits into the strategic process;
- understand how the characteristics of *THE* might have an impact on the implementation process;
- explain the role of resource planning in strategic implementation;
- explain how and why corporate culture plays an important part in implementation;
- understand the link between structure and strategy;
- evaluate the essentials of change management;
- assess the management and leadership styles necessary to implement changes;
- explain the use of the Balanced Scorecard as a tool to be used in strategic implementation; and
- provide examples of implementation issues being addressed in *THE* contexts.

Implementation and the strategic process

Implementation is the system-wide action taken by firm members aimed at accomplishing formulated strategies (Hahn and Powers, 2010).

Most people intuitively understand that a lot of information is required before any big decision is made.

For example – consumers wouldn't normally buy most *THE* products, say a holiday, a hotel booking or attendance at a festival (all relatively expensive purchases) without investigating the attractions of the destination, hotel or event and usually finding out something about the company providing the service before purchasing. Buying, say, a pencil would not warrant such analysis since it would usually represent a small proportion of the buyers' income.

In the same way, an organization would be risking a great deal if it were to pursue a strategic option without first carrying out a detailed analysis of its internal and external environments.

Put simply, successful strategy selection and implementation relies upon the pre-supposition that the organization has carried out a meaningful strategic analysis and is consequently aware of its internal strengths and weaknesses and its external opportunities and threats. Without being 'armed' with this information, the company cannot be certain that the chosen strategy would be the correct choice.

It is not surprising perhaps, since it is more geared towards action and less conceptual in nature, that the implementation phase of strategy has received relatively less academic attention than the analysis and formulation phases (Kaplan and Norton, 2001:1; Evans, 2005; Hahn and Powers, 2010). It has also been argued that the so-called 'quality gurus', such as Tom Peters (Peters and Waterman, 2004), largely abdicated responsibility for delineating patterns of implementation which are coherent (Morris and Haigh, 1996). Other authors make important contributions by pointing to the difficulties inherent in the implementation phase (Epstein and Manzoni, 1998) or by calling for a re-assessment of the difficulties inherent in the process (Lorange, 1998).

However, the fact that successful implementation is key to a successful strategy has long been recognized. Several authors (see for example Ghoshal and Bartlett, 1999; Miller, 2001) point to the lack of successful strategic implementation as an issue affecting many businesses. In their study Bartlett and Ghoshal (1987: 12) point out that the issues involved did not relate to a poor understanding of environmental factors or an inappropriately strategic intent. Instead the authors report that 'without exception [the organizations in the study] knew what they had to do; their difficulties lay in how to achieve the necessary changes'. Miller *et al.* refer to the 'implementation gap' in arguing that 'organizations are slower to change and more difficult and expensive to develop than strategies are to prepare'.

Consequently, given its importance in the successful delivery of outcomes, the strategic implementation phase has started to attract more attention in recent years. See for example, Okumus (2003), Evans (2005) and Hahn and Powers (2010).

Aspects of strategic implementation

In order to successfully put into practice (implement) a strategy, an organization will need to consider three aspects:

1. *Resources* – how should the strategy be resourced?

This relates to the way in which the organization will obtain the requisite finance, human resources (usually in the form of appropriately skilled employees), the physical resources such as equipment and buildings, and intellectual or 'intangible' resources. All parts of the organization need to be aligned so that all parts are working towards a common vision, aim and objectives. In doing so detailed decisions about obtaining and utilizing resources have to be made so as to ensure that resources are used effectively and waste and duplication are avoided.

2. *Configuration* – how should the culture and structure of the organization be configured to 'fit' the proposed strategy?

In the previous point we stressed that all parts of the organization need to be aligned so that the strategy can successfuly achieve its vision, aim and objectives. However, since all parts of the organization need to contribute to its successful implementation, it is necessary that the structure of the organization and the organizational culture are fit for purpose so that there are no impediments to success. This is not always the case and in many instances the structure has to be amended and the culture changed so that there is a so-called 'strategic fit'.

3. *Change* – how should the changes arising from the strategy be managed and led?

Implementing strategy invariably involves changes to aspects of the organization and how it positions itself. To successfully implement change, managers need to consider what type of change is envisaged and how it might be managed and led.

Thus strategic implementation is involved with making detailed decisions regarding three key aspects of strategy relating to: resources; configuration and change.

When these decisions have been made it is vital (since all parts of the organization need to be aligned for successful implementation), that a further issue is considered. This relates to the disseminatinon and coordination of the strategy. Some research suggests that many strategies are well perceived but poorly

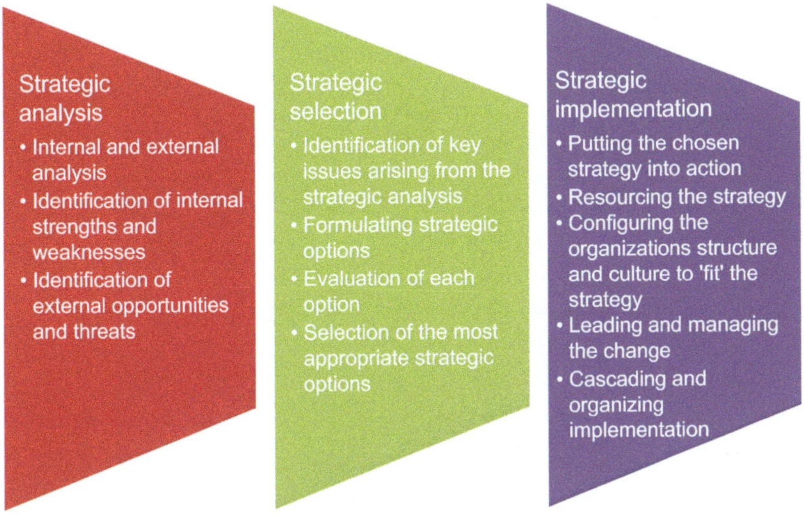

Strategic analysis

- Internal and external analysis
- Identification of internal strengths and weaknesses
- Identification of external opportunities and threats

Strategic selection

- Identification of key issues arising from the strategic analysis
- Formulating strategic options
- Evaluation of each option
- Selection of the most appropriate strategic options

Strategic implementation

- Putting the chosen strategy into action
- Resourcing the strategy
- Configuring the organizations structure and culture to 'fit' the strategy
- Leading and managing the change
- Cascading and organizing implementation

Figure 13.1
The linear-rational (prescriptive) strategic process

executed and Jones (2008) in his book which focuses on communicating strategy reports on reseraach which suggests less than 10 per cent of employees actually understand their firms' strategy.

Thus crucial questions arise as to:

- How should the strategy be spread throughout the organization (or 'cascaded' as it is often termed)?
- How should the implementation be coordinated effectively, in a practical way?

This involves:

- communicating the strategy effectively;
- coordinating the implementation of the strategy consistently and effectively; and
- measuring the success of the strategy so that modifications can be made if necessary.

Thus the strategy must be communicated and disseminated. As part of this process a detailed strategy may be developed for each part of the organization – such as marketing, finance, personnel and strategic business units – since successful implementation normally involves all elements being aligned with specific objectives. Effectively organizing strategic implementation is a major managerial task and in this chapter we will consider one widely adopted means of managing this process – The Balanced Scorecard.

Figure 13.1 indicates how the implementation of strategy relates to the other major components of strategy: *strategic analysis* and *strategic selection* (formulation, evaluation and selection).

Implementation in *THE* contexts

The underlying premise of this book is that strategic management in tourism, hospitality and events management contexts is different in that there are certain characteristics in these sectors that managers need to consider. In Chapter 2 and elsewhere in the book we discussed these characteristics. Five of them, it was argued, were common in most service industry contexts and a further six, while not necessarily unique to tourism, hospitality and events management were nevertheless particularly prominent in these contexts.

The 11 characteristics and examples of the managerial implications that arose because of these characteristics were summarised in Table 2.2. The characteristics have particular relevance for the way in which strategy is implemented in tourism, hospitality and events management organizations. Specifically managers in these sectors need to consider the characteristics in relation to:

- how resources are allocated and deployed;
- how the organization is configured in terms of its culture and structure; and
- how the process of change (implied by strategic implementation) is managed.

Tables 13.1 and 13.2 build upon the characteristics summarized in Table 2.2. These tables summarize some of the specific services (Table 13.1) and *THE* issues (Table 13.2) facing managers. The figures also consider how managers might respond in relation to resources, configuration of structure and culture, and managing change (which are covered in the subsequent sections of this chapter).

Table 13.1 Strategic implementation in relation to service product characteristics

Service product – characteristics			
Characteristic	Implementation issues: *Resources*	Implementation issues: *Configuration*	Implementation issues: *Change*
Intangibility Products cannot be tested or sampled	Physical and virtual marketing materials must be of a high standard Effective distribution of the products is essential Tangible additions to the product often important	*Structure* – Front-line sales force must be well-trained and able to sell the product attributes competently *Culture* – Delivering excellent service is of utmost importance to all employees	Building brand loyalty difficult and time consuming and brand switching is common. Therefore managers must devote resources to positioning and building brands and recognize and manage risks to the brand
Inseparability Production and consumption take place at the same time	Often no opportunity to store resources so they must be available in the right quantities and location when required	*Structure* – Front-line staff must be trained and empowered to satisfy customer demands *Culture* – 'Getting it right first time' or rectifying mistakes when they happen quickly and satisfactorily *Culture* – Empowerment of staff within specified boundaries so that lapses can be overcome	Must ensure high customer service levels are maintained Font-line staff are carefully selected, well trained and have the appropriate skills and aptitude for customer service roles
Perishability Products cannot be stored	Supply is often fixed in the short to medium term so pricing and other promotional methods used to affect demand	*Structure* – Need for flexibility so that appropriate responses to rapid environmental changes can be implemented *Structure* – Flatter structures favour rapid decision making and information flows *Culture* – Avoiding waste and cutting costs is a key driver	Need performance monitoring systems to avoid wasting resources and plan resource deployment Must carefully monitor sudden changes in demand and supply and re-deploy resources accordingly

Service product – characteristics			
Characteristic	Implementation issues: *Resources*	Implementation issues: *Configuration*	Implementation issues: *Change*
Heterogeneity Products are not identical	Staff vital in delivering excellent services so must recruit and retain good staff, train them well, ensure rewards are well targeted and take measures to ensure they are well motivated Stress differentiation between own products and competitors	*Structure* – Ensure that structure enables information from front-line staff quickly reaches company decision makers *Culture* – Staff are a key part of the product and service quality is of utmost importance *Culture* – Staff are empowered to make decisions	Listening to and understating the customer; anticipating customer needs; and giving a high priority to customer satisfaction important Manage the heterogeneity in such a way that the differences are valued by the customer, but that high quality standards are maintained *throughout*
Ownership Customers use services rather than own them	Building loyalty difficult but promotional activities, excellent staff and loyalty schemes should be aligned towards building it	*Structure* – Front-line and back-office staff must act as if customers are owners of the product *Culture* – Strong and explicit organizational values important in building staff and customer loyalty *Culture* – Despite lack of ownership quality of 'after-sales' service vital for repeat bookings	Ensure loyalty schemes are well targeted and offer vale for money for customers and the organization Develop a relationship with customers through PR, promotion and organizational image so that customers feel like they 'own the product'

Table 13.2 Strategic implementation in relation to tourism, hospitality and events management characteristics

Tourism, hospitality and events – characteristics			
Characteristic	Implementation issues: *Resources*	Implementation issues: *Configuration*	Implementation issues: *Change*
High cost product Often a relatively expensive purchase	Provide opportunities to sample, test or compare the product Ensure resources are deployed on product features valued by the customer and for which they are willing to pay	*Structure* – All levels of the organization are required to take responsibility for excellent service delivery and product enhancement *Culture* – Continuous improvement and innovation are encouraged so that products and service levels keep ahead of competitors	Continually evaluate product offering so that it is correctly positioned in the market Ensure pricing and product information is updated and accurate Build trust with customers through relationship building

Table 13.2 continued

Tourism, hospitality and events – characteristics			
Characteristic	Implementation issues: *Resources*	Implementation issues: *Configuration*	Implementation issues: *Change*
Seasonality Products often have very seasonal demand patterns	Flexible resourcing so that there is availability when required but resources can be discarded when not required Extensive use of part-time and volunteer workers Seasonal cash-flows and foreign currency receipts and payments are carefully managed	*Structure* – Flexibility and clarity to accommodate seasonal workers and ensure they are well managed *Culture* – Inclusivity so that part-time voluntary and staff do not feel excluded and they are aware of organizational norms and requirements	Manage change in demand and supply balance carefully so that resources are available when required and waste in their deployment is avoided Pricing effectively matches seasonal variations so that revenues are maximized Take action to extend the season or minimize its impacts
Ease of entry/exit Often relatively low barriers to entry	Resources often need to be deployed flexibly to respond quickly to competitive threats Need to focus on cost base because otherwise lower cost competitors will enter the market and undercut New competitors can quickly emerge so important to establish position in market through differentiation and/or price Many opportunities for innovative SMEs if they have the necessary resources available Raise the height of barriers for new entrants if possible, by gaining access to resources which are denied to others such as a resort, hotel or concert venue	*Structure* – Must not be over bureaucratic so that it is capable of responding quickly to new vigorous competitors *Culture* – Develop an 'open' culture where employee ideas and innovations are encouraged and incentivized appropriately *Culture* – If there is relative ease of entry and exit develop a culture which constantly assesses whether correct markets are being targeted and correct products are being offered	Products and innovations can often be easily replicated so need to seek niches, specialisms. product features brand or pacing points which can be defended Innovative SMEs can effectively compete if they utilize technology, design, service quality or a particular niche effectively

Tourism, hospitality and events – characteristics			
Characteristic	Implementation issues: *Resources*	Implementation issues: *Configuration*	Implementation issues: *Change*
Interdependence The sub-sectors of *THE* are closely linked	Seek opportunities to share resources with collaborating organizations, suppliers and customers	*Structure* – Ensure there is a 'strategic-fit' between structures of collaborating organizations *Culture* – Work with organizations with compatible vision and values	Ensure partners and suppliers have goal alignment Communicate and share information effectively with partners, suppliers and customers Coordinate strategic planning effectively
Impact on society *THE* has a high impact on society	Use natural resources in an environmentally responsible way SMEs can compete effectively with larger companies by deploying resources in such a way which emphasizes their 'green' credentials	*Structure* – A decentralized structure might allow for local manners to be more sensitive to local impacts and make necessary adjustments *Culture* – There might be a need to devise a strategy taking into account not only central headquarter issues but also local cultures, styles, values and expectations.	*THE* is unique among service industries in its impact. Managers in *THE* must be sensitive to this issue and emphasize the corporate responsibility of their organization Managers must be aware of changing consumers who recognize the impacts of their consumption and attempt to work with responsible suppliers New forms of tourism are creating additional opportunities and challenges which managers need to research, understand and design and deliver targeted products
External shocks Prone to external shocks, beyond managers' control	Risks vs rewards are carefully assessed and resources deployed accordingly Portfolio of products and markets spreads risks Assets protected where possible e.g. through insurance, spreading their location and 'asset-light' operations	*Structure* – Flexibility important so response can be speedy and effective *Structure* – All employees must know how their specific role fits in and how they should respond *Culture* – Safety and security of customers is not an objective but an absolute value and cannot be compromised	Risks are identified and contingency plans in place Managers must have understanding of their role in unexpected circumstances Scenario planning helps organization prepare contingency plans Financial risks such as foreign exchange, and interest rates and fuel prices, should be assessed and managed

Implementation – resources

Resources – the key inputs

The successful management of a strategy is likely to depend on the management of many resource areas. (Johnson *et al.*, 2011:386). In the same way that people and animals need the inputs of air, food, warmth, etc., organizations also need inputs in order to function normally. Economics textbooks would refer to these inputs as the *factors of production*.

They fall into four broad categories:

1. *physical resources* – land, buildings, plant, equipment, etc.;
2. *financial resources* – share and loan capital required for development and expansion;
3. *human resources* – obtaining the requisite number of appropriately skilled employees;
4. *intellectual or 'intangible' resources* – non-physical inputs that may be necessary in some industries such as databases, legal permissions, brand or design registration, contacts, etc. (see Hall, 1992).

In most instances *THE* organizations must obtain resource inputs in competitive markets. Even in instances where *THE* organizations are in public control they have to compete for resources with other publicly funded activities such as education and health. This means that they must compete with other organizations for the best people, the cheapest finance, the best locations for development, etc.

For example – a retail travel agent setting up a new branch in a town will want to ensure that they occupy a site that has a large number of people passing the shop window (or 'footfall' as retailers often refer to it). Other retailers may also want to gain access to such a site so the travel agent may have to compete for this scarce resource, thus bidding up the price. At some point the price (in the form of rent) may become too great in relation to the expected revenues, so decisions have to made as to how much can be afforded.

Thus all of these inputs have a cost attached to them and so careful planning for resource requirement is usually a key calculation in strategic implementation.

Matching strategy with resources

Once a strategic option has been settled upon (following the strategic selection stage), management attention turns to assessing the resource implications of the strategy. The extent to which the resource base needs to be adjusted will, of course, depend upon the degree of change that the proposed strategy entails.

Broadly speaking, resource planning falls into three categories:

- Some strategies, particularly those that are not particularly ambitious, require *few changes* in the resource base. They may require, for example, a *slight* increase in financing to fund modest expansion or the recruitment or retraining of some human resources to meet a skill shortage in one or two areas. Conversely of course, a few changes in strategy may require the disposal of some assets or a slight reduction in the human resource base.

- Some strategies require an *increase* in the resource base in order to facilitate a more substantial programme of growth. This usually entails two things: an internal reallocation of resources and the purchasing of fresh resource inputs from external suppliers. Internal reallocation entails reducing resource deployment in one area of the organization and moving it across to where it is needed, say by redeploying human resources or by selling some non-core activities to reinvest the money in the area of growth. New resources (from outside the organization) are obtained through the usual channels – from the job market, the real estate market, the financial markets and so on.

- Finally, some strategies involve a *reduction* in the resource base in order to successfully manage decline. If an organization finds, after a resource audit, that it has too many resources (say too many employees, too many aircraft, too many hotel properties in the wrong locations, etc.) then measures are put in place to carry out some reduction. Excess capital or physical resources can often be successfully reinvested in business areas that are in more buoyant markets whilst excess human resources must usually be released.

In order to successfully implement the chosen strategic options the resources available need to be carefully assessed through a process such as a resource audit. Though this might have been carried out as part of the strategic analysis stage, the implementation stage allows for the information to be 'tested' in detail with regards to the chosen option specifically rather than all available options.

An audit process can be used to make assessments of any or all of the resource inputs. In Chapter 4, we discussed in some depth the human resource audit, but the same procedures can be employed to audit financial, physical or intellectual resources.

The nature of an audit of any kind (including resource audits) is for the purpose of checking or testing. Resources are audited (or purposefully checked) for:

- *sufficiency* (is there enough for the purpose?);
- *adequacy* (is the condition, location, state, or quality of the resources adequate for the purpose?); and
- *availability* (are the required resources available at the time, price and in the quantities required?).

For example – an audit of a hotel group's chain of hotels (an example of physical resources) might take the form of assessing whether the number of rooms is *sufficient* for current needs and any planned expansion. This might be followed by an evaluation of its *adequacy* – the location of the hotels relative to customers and those of competitors; the state of repair and decoration of the hotels; and, the ability of the hotels to support the prevailing business (leisure, business, conferences etc.). Finally, if more resources are required or if development of the land or buildings is needed, *availability* is examined, either of additional property or land for development.

THINK POINTS

- Explain where implementation fits into the strategic process.
- Explain the major features of a resource audit.
- What key considerations might managers in *THE* contexts need to consider in the implementation phase of strategy?

The short case illustration below shows the approach outlined above extended to all the resource categories for a hotel chain and suggests the use of a 'traffic light' approach which highlights those aspects requiring particular managerial attention.

SHORT CASE ILLUSTRATION

Resource audit for a hotel group planning growth in East Asia

As part of its strategy a (hypothetical) hotel group may decide that it wants to expand into the fast growth market of East Asia. A resource audit will help establish the extent to which resources are likely to be in place to support the strategy.

An audit of the hotel group's chain of hotels in East Asia (an example of physical resources) might take the form of:

Assessing whether the number of rooms is *sufficient* for current needs and any planned expansion.

This might be followed by an evaluation of its *adequacy* – the location of the hotels relative to customers and those of competitors; the state of repair and decoration of the hotels; and, the ability of the hotels to support the prevailing business (leisure, business, conferences etc.).

Finally, if more resources are required or if development of the land or buildings is needed, *availability* is examined, either of additional property or of permissions for development.

A way of presenting the full resource audit is shown in the table below where all the resource categories on the vertical axis are assessed according to the sufficiency, adequacy, and availability criteria. The table uses a traffic light coding system in which:

Table 13.3 Resource audit

Resource category	Resource sufficiency	Resource adequacy	Resource availability
Physical resources	No, not sufficient. Additional hotels need to be built, acquired or managed in the specified region to meet the strategic objective that has been set	Hotels already in the group are adequate and performing well but require some updating in parts	Resources are being built by property developers throughout the region so that resources are available
Financial resources	A large amount of finance is supporting the rapid growth in these markets	Adequate finance is available form a range of sources including banks equity markets and government agencies at internationally competitive rates	Though hotels are being developed by property developers there is strong competition among international hotel groups to manage, own or lease these properties. Great care must be taken to select strong assets in good locations and not to over-pay for them
Human resources	There are many people who are seeking hotel careers	Though there are some skilled employees being trained by colleges and hotel groups, there is a major training requirement to provide employees with adequate skill levels and cultural awareness of the company	Employees are available at reasonable cost but there are some minor timing issues involved in bringing them into the group.
Intangible resources	The hotel group has strong brand recognition and established support systems	There is some need to adapt the brand and systems for local conditions	The brand and systems should be available when the other resources have been acquired or developed

- green meets the criteria;
- amber partly meets the criteria; and
- red does not at present meet the criteria.

The traffic light coding allows significant resourcing issues to be highlighted so that it can be easily communicated to stakeholders both internal and external to the organization. Thus in this case the sufficiency of physical resources, the adequacy of human resources and the availability of financial resources appear to be key resourcing issues to be addressed.

Questions

1. Explain why a resource audit is useful to the organization in this case illustration.
2. Why might a 'traffic light' approach to presentation be useful in considering an organization's resources?

Developing and controlling resources

Resources are developed and then controlled to ensure they meet the needs of the proposed strategy.

Financial planning

Financial planning takes the form of financing the proposed strategy (see Chapter 5 for a more detailed discussion of these issues). *Capital budgeting* concerns projecting the capital needs of a strategy. This is usually a relatively straightforward operation as costs can normally be forecast with some accuracy. Once the capital requirements are known, a plan is put in place to finance any shortfall. Whilst some strategies can be financed from retained profits (depending upon how much retained profit the company has), others are financed from external sources such as share (rights) issues, debt capital or the issuing of corporate bonds or debentures. The pros and cons of these approaches to financing are discussed in Chapter 5.

Human resource planning

Human resource planning (see Chapter 4) involves projecting the human capital required for the successful implementation of the proposed strategy. It would typically take the form of forecasts of both the *numbers* of people required and the types of *skills and abilities* that will be in demand. If a shortfall in either of these is identified, the 'gap' will be filled by one or more of the following.

- Training, retraining or staff development – to close the skills gap by developing existing employees.
- Appointing new employees – entering the labour market and competing with other employers for the requisite number of appropriately skilled employees.

Physical resource planning

Physical resource planning is slightly more complex than financial and human resource planning. The reason for this is that so many inputs fall into this category. We include in this category land, buildings, location, plant and equipment.

Some physical resources are more easily obtained than others. Most equipment is relatively easily obtained, unless the requirement is very specialized. However, careful planning may be necessary for some equipment needs require long lead times for their construction.

For example – a cruise line or an airline seeking to update its fleet with new ships or aircraft would need to plan a number of years in advance in order to secure delivery on a particular date.

Obtaining a particular location, land and buildings can be problematic. Businesses that have requirements for key locations and buildings of particular specificity expose themselves to the possibility of having to settle for second best if they are unable to effectively compete in these particular resource markets.

Some sectors of *THE* exemplify this competition for physical resources. The location of a travel retail outlet, a hotel, a visitor attraction or a festival will often be a key determinant in the success of the business. Successfully competing with competitors for prime locations will consequently be of paramount importance, especially when these locations are in short supply.

For example – Hong Kong has developed over the last two hundred years into a world-class business location, but land is a precious commodity since it has a comparatively small land area. This special Administrative Region of China has developed predominantly on Hong Kong island (where the Central Business District is located) and across the harbour in Kowloon on the Chinese mainland. On the island, especially in 'Central' (the central business district), the lack of suitable sites and the costs of development have forced most hotels to seek other locations. Banks and other financial institutions have been willing to pay very high prices for prime sites and consequently many of the new hotel developments have taken place in Kowloon, where development sites are more plentiful and where land costs are lower.

Similarly, when Hong Kong Disneyland Resort (Disney's fifth resort and its second in Asia) opened in 2005, it did so on the outlying island of Lantau where Hong Kong's International Airport, Chek Lap Kok, was also situated. By doing so the resort was able to obtain large amounts of land at moderate prices, but also to gain the advantages of rapid access to the city and adjacent international airport.

Intellectual resource planning

Intellectual resources – inputs that cannot be seen and touched – can be the most important resource inputs of all (see Chapter 1). Some proposed strategies have a requirement for a legal or regulatory permission, a database (say of key customers in a certain market segment) or experience of dealing with certain markets.

Implementation: configuration of culture and structure

Cultural suitability

We encountered the concept of organizational culture in Chapter 4. Strategic implementation usually involves making an assessment of the suitability of a culture to undertake the strategy. In the same way that human personalities differ in their readiness to undertake certain courses of action, so also some organizational 'personalities' differ.

In the context of implementation, culture is usually analysed for its suitability. If we consider human personalities, we can readily appreciate that not all personalities are equally suitable for all jobs or tasks.

Some people, for example, have a personality that is ready to embrace a new challenge and who take to change with vigour and excitement. They enjoy bungee jumping and parachute jumps. Other people prefer things not to change. They are conservative in nature and they would be likely to turn down the opportunity to engage in risky sports. These two personality types highlight the suitability contrasts that can exist.

In Chapter 4 we encountered three typologies of corporate culture. Handy (1993) identified four types of culture – power, role, task and person – while Hofstede (1980) in his Cultural Dimensions theory focused on international differences in relation to culture. Miles and Snow (1978) also identified four culture types by their reaction tendency and this is probably the more useful typology in this context.

Miles and Snow's typology and cultural postures

Miles and Snow's (1978) typology divides culture types according to how they approach strategy. These distinctions are important as they tell us how each culture type will react to different strategic options.

Miles and Snow identify four categories of organizational culture:

- *Defender* cultures are suitable for organizations that exist in relatively well-defined market areas and where improving the position in existing markets is the most appropriate strategic option (e.g. market penetration). The culture would feel uncomfortable with diversification or having to develop new markets. The values resident within defender cultures work well if markets are stable and relatively mature.

- *Prospector* cultures, in contrast to defenders, are continually seeking out new product and market opportunities. Accordingly, they often create change and uncertainty. The cultural norms within the culture are consequently more able to develop new markets and products.

- *Analyser* cultures exhibit features of both defenders and prospectors. They have developed a culture that is able to accommodate both stability (which defenders like) and instability (which prospectors have learned to adjust to). The culture can be formal in some circumstances and flexible and 'organic' in others.

- *Reactor* cultures can sometimes lack strategic focus and are consequently sometimes accused of being 'blown around' by changes in their environments. They do not innovate and tend to emulate the successes of competitors.

The purpose of examining Miles and Snow's typology

It is evident that the ability of cultures to undertake different strategic courses of action varies. It is likely, for example, that defender cultures and those like them would be less able to undertake a programme of radical change than, say, those which exhibit prospector characteristics.

Cultural differences between *the current culture* and *what is required* for a strategy is one of the most important aspects of strategic implementation. Incongruities between the two present a challenge to management in respect of either changing the culture or compromising on strategic objectives such that cultural change is required to a lesser extent. We will return to the nature of change – including cultural change – later in this chapter.

SHORT CASE ILLUSTRATION

Can culture be changed through learning: British Airways

A specific culture is something that every organization has, but it is difficult to define, explain and to change, though many writers have contributed their thoughts on the subject. With such inherent difficulties is it possible to change cultural norms through teaching employees so that they learn different approaches? It is difficult to answer this question definitively, but many companies have tried such cultural change programmes. One well-known example from the airline sector (albeit some time ago) relates to British Airways.

During the 1970s and 1980s the publicly owned British airline British Airways or 'BA' as it was commonly referred to had become synonymous with poor service. The common joke of the time was that BA stood for 'bloody awful'.

Despite difficulties in more recent years (in common with many international airlines) due to challenging economic circumstances, British Airways is often put forward as a successful example of cultural change. After the airline went public by floating on the stock exchange in 1987 a major cultural change programme was introduced which emphasized the service-led orientation of the business. Virtually the entire workforce of the time (37,000) was put through a two-day culture change training course entitled 'Putting People First'. Almost all of the airline's 1,400 managers went through a five-day version entitled 'Managing People First'. What separated this programme from most normal management training programmes was its size, the consistency with which it was applied throughout the organization to all grades of employees and the determination of senior management to drive the programme through.

The programme's emphasis was on instilling a new culture, but this ran alongside other changes. An appraisal scheme was introduced which measured not only what managers did but how they went about it and bonuses were introduced. An emphasis was also placed on informing staff of the competitive pressures facing the airline and on empowering staff to make decisions on their own initiative rather than being bound by inflexible rules.

Tushman and O'Reilly (1996)

Questions

1. Explain the main features of the cultural change programme adopted by BA after privatization.
2. Explain what you think the lessons to draw from BA's cultural change programme might be.

What is structure?

Organizational structure refers to the 'shape' of the organization.

The importance of structure to strategic success is intuitively easy to grasp by using the structure of a human body as a metaphor. Some people are naturally tall and broadly set, whilst others are naturally small and lithe. The skeletal and muscular structure of people is a major determinant of their suitability for certain sports – larger people may be better suited to tug-of-war or basketball teams, while smaller people may be better suited to running or competitive horse racing.

There is no such thing as 'the perfect structure' for an organization, since usually compromises have to be made in their design and often they are the result of ad-hoc growth where parts are added over time rather than planned from the outset. For a more detailed discussion of various structural types and their relative advantages and disadvantages, see for example Lynch (2012:Ch. 12).

However, what we are interested in is not a study of organizational structure in itself (interesting though this may be), but how it relates to the successful implementation of strategy.

In this context it is necessary to consider whether the proposed structure is capable of helping the organization achieve the objectives that have been set as part of its strategy. In this regard key issues include:

- How easy is it to change the structure when circumstances change?
- How efficient is the structure in ensuring that key information and decisions are disseminated appropriately?
- To what degree does the formal organization chart represent the way in which decision making really takes place?

Structure follows strategy?

In the strategic management literature a major debate, which is summarized by Galan and Sanchez-Bueno (2009), has taken place over many years regarding the relationship between the strategy and structure of organizations.

US economic historian Alfred Chandler (1962) based on studies of American companies argued that the structure is subordinate to and therefore should follow the formulation of strategy. To Hall and Saias (1980) however, the strategic opportunities available to an organization are partly the result of its existing organizational structure so that in some cases the strategy follows on from the structure.

In a widely quoted article Henry Mintzberg (1990:183) concludes that neither structure or strategy takes precedence and that both should be considered as part of an integrated system:

. . .that structure follows strategy as the left foot follows the right in walking. In effect, strategy and structure both support the organization. None takes precedence; each always precedes the other, and follows it, except when they move together, as the organization jumps to a new position. Strategy formation is an integrated system, not an arbitrary sequence.

The main issues in designing an organizational structure are concerned with:

- Division of labour – who does what?
- Source of authority – who has the right to tell others what to do?
- Relationships – how does the structure fit together?

In attempting to resolve the key design issues organizational structures tend to be described in terms of their:

- height
- width
- complexity.

In designing the structure of an organization these three issues are taken into account with a fourth design issue concerned with devising

- a method of division.

The 'height' of structures

Height refers to the number of layers that exist within the structure.

It is perhaps intuitively obvious that larger organizations are higher than smaller ones. The guide to how high an organizational structure should be depends upon the complexity of the tasks that a proposed strategy entails.

For example – contrast a small events management company with a diversified international travel group.

The small company involved in organizing and managing events is competing in one location with an easily identified number of competitors and a single set of product types. Customers probably value the direct communication with the decision makers in the company which is brought about by the lack of layers

Figure 13.2 The height of organizations

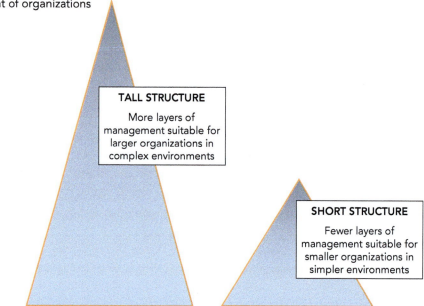

within the company. This scenario is much less complex than a multinational vertically and horizontally integrated travel company that competes in many national markets, in several product types and with a high dependence on innovation. In such circumstances there are likely to be a greater number of layers to the organization in order to facilitate its complex processes. Customers are likely to purchase the products on the basis of their attributes and are unconcerned about the internal structure of the organization they are dealing with.

Essentially, height facilitates the engagement of specialist managers in the middle of an organization who can oversee and direct the many activities that some larger organizations are involved in. Not all organizations have this requirement and it would be more appropriate for such organizations to have a flatter structure (see Figure 13.2).

The trend in recent years has been for organizations to become flatter as increasingly technology can provide information directly from the point of sale to the highest levels. Similarly technology permits communications from the highest level of the company to be quickly and widely disseminated amongst all staff at every level. This process is often known as *de-layering* and facilitates quicker decision making and faster communications between managers and operational employees who have to implement the decisions.

KEY CONCEPT

Tall and short structures

Tall structures involve more layers of specialist managers to enable the organization to coordinate a wider range of activities across different product and market sectors. It is more difficult for senior management to control and is obviously more expensive in terms of management overhead.

Shorter structures involve few management layers and are suitable for smaller organizations that are engaged in few products or market structures. They are cheaper to operate and facilitate a greater degree of senior management control.

The 'width' of structures

The 'width' of organizational structures refers to the extent the organization is centralized or decentralized.

A decentralized organizational structure is one in which the centre elects to devolve some degree of decision-making power to other parts of the organization. A centralized organization is one in which little or no power is devolved from the centre. In practice, a continuum exists between the two extremes along which the varying extents of decentralization can be visualized (see Figure 13.3).

As with the height of structures, there is a trade-off between the costs and benefits of width. The advantages of centralization are mainly concerned with the ability of the centre to maintain tighter direct control over the activities of the organization. This is usually more appropriate when the organization is smaller and engages in few product or market segments. Some degree of decentralization is advantageous when the organization operates in a number of markets and localized specialized knowledge is an important determinant of overall success.

The principal advantages of centralization and decentralization are summarized in Table 13.4.

Complexity of structure

The complexity of structure is usually taken to mean the extent to which the organization observes a formal hierarchy in its reporting relationships. Strict hierarchy is not always an appropriate form of organization, especially when it cannot be automatically assumed that seniority guarantees superior management skill.

In some contexts, formal hierarchy is entirely appropriate in implementing strategy. In others, however, allowing employees to act with some degree of independence can enable the organization to be more efficient. The use of matrix structures (discussed later in the chapter), for example, can result in the organization being able to carry out many more tasks than a formal hierarchical structure. Many companies go some way in this regard by seconding employees into special task forces or cross-functional teams that are not part of the hierarchical structure, and which act semi-independently in pursuit of their brief.

The matrix structure is quite common in larger companies where there is likely to be greater complexity. By way of contrast some organizations operate with little or even no formal structure. Many smaller companies operate in such a way believing that structures are not necessary and can impede creativity and teamwork.

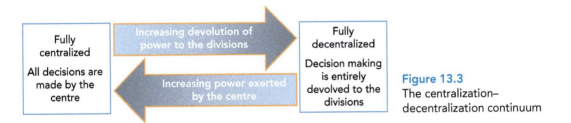

Figure 13.3
The centralization–decentralization continuum

Table 13.4 The advantages of centralization and decentralization

Advantages of centralization	Advantages of decentralization
Managers at centre maintain tight control	Can engage in a wider range of activities
Avoids problems of complex structures	Enables increased specialization
Communications quicker and cheaper	Can reduce time taken to make key decisions
Delegation risks avoided	Can develop and improve the skills of managers

For example – the events management sector is highly fragmented with a large number of very small localized companies operating and low barriers to entry (and exit). Some may have just a sole proprietor, or members of a single family carrying out all tasks, or have a few full-time employees with a larger number of part-time workers brought in to staff the event and then released. In such circmstances it is unlikely that there will be a formal structure and informality allows all attention to be focused on achieving the task at hand.

In this chapter we have discussed culture and structure separately, since they are in themselves complex organizational issues with a great deal of academic literature devoted to each.

However, they can also be viewed as being intrinsically linked in that the organizational structure that is adopted will have important implications for the culture that the organization wants to encourage and equally, if a particular culture is present that the organization wants to facilitate, it implies that a certain structural form will be favoured by the organization.

The close links between structure and culture are demonstrated in the short case illustration of easyJet below.

SHORT CASE ILLUSTRATION

Linkages between culture and structure: easyJet

Many *THE* companies explicitly feature their organizational culture in promotional materials in order to:

- attract new employees with appropriate skills and attitude;
- motivate and inform existing employees; and
- promote a positive image of the organization to external stakeholders.

The low-cost airline easyJet is one such company which promotes its company culture strongly. It also illustrates the strong linkages between culture and structure. The company stresses its informality, a casual dress code, and an open office layout, but as the quotation below demonstrates, a key part of the organizational culture at easyJet relates to the structure which it adopts.

On its website (www.easyjet.com) easyJet stresses that it has a 'strong culture' within the company that is 'individual and unique' rather than copying other companies in its sector. The following extract from the website illustrates the way in which the airline explicitly links its structure and facilities for its employees, to the culture it is trying to adopt when it states:

'It starts with a very flat hierarchy, which eliminates unnecessary and wasteful layers of management. To enable us to make travel affordable for our customers the working environment is functional, not luxurious'.

www.easyjet.com, accessed May 2014

Questions

1. Explain the main features of the easyJet culture and consider why these features might have been adopted.
2. What difficulties might easyJet encounter in relation to culture and structure as it continues to grow?

Methods of divisionalization

The fourth and final way of understanding how structure fits into strategic implementation is by considering how the parts of the organization are to be divided.

As with all of the other matters to be considered in structure, the method of division is entirely dependent upon the context of the company and its strategic position. It is a case of establishing the most appropriate divisional structure to meet the objectives of the proposed strategy.

Divisions are based upon the grouping together of people with a shared specialism. By acting together within their specialism, it is argued that synergies can be obtained both with and between divisions. In divisionalizing an organization the three previous factors (height, width and complexity) are underlying determinants which are taken into account.

There are five common methods of divisionalization. A company or group of companies can be divisionalized by:

- Functional specialism (typically, operations, HRM, marketing, finance, etc.).
- Geographic concentration (where divisions are regionally located and have specialized knowledge of local market conditions).
- Product specialism (where divisions, usually within multi-product companies, have detailed knowledge of their particular product area).
- Customer focus (where the company orientates itself by divisions dedicated to serving particular customer types, for example retail customers, industrial customers, etc.).
- Holding company (where a company owns various individual businesses and the holding company acts as an investment company overseeing its investments in individual businesses which can be wholly or partly owned but where the individual companies run largely autonomously).

In many cases, a 'hybrid' approach to divisionalization might be appropriate.

For example – a (hypothetical) vertically integrated travel company which provides tour operations, has an airline and which operates online and physical travel retailing with sales in the UK, Western Europe and North America might have a hybrid divisional structure. Such a structure might have geographical, product, and functional elements as shown in Figure 13.4. Each geographical region might have three product areas, which each have their own functional divisions.

A final common way of structuring an organization is the so-called 'matrix structure'.

Such a structure combines two forms of organization such as functional and geographic as shown in Figure 13.5. In such an organization there are dual lines of authority for employees – one vertical and the other

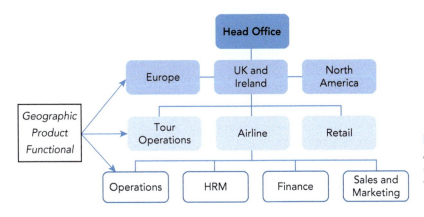

Figure 13.4
An example of a 'hybrid' divisional structure for a vertically integrated travel company

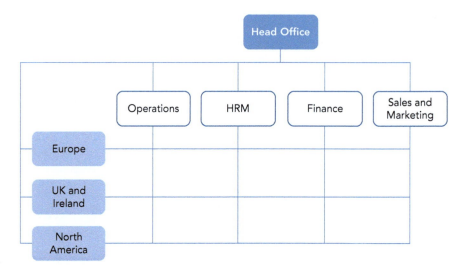

Figure 13.5 An example of a matrix organizational structure for an international travel company

vertical. In the example below there in relation to HRM, for instance, the organization may have an HRM Manager in each of its regions (Europe, UK and Ireland and North America). The managers will be reporting horizontally to the director for these geographical regions who will be responsible for all activities in the region, but they will also be responsible, vertically, to the HRM director who will be responsible for all HRM activities across the company. In this way the geographical director coordinates a team responsible for all activities in the region while the functional directors will coordinate all activities related to their specialisms across the company.

The advantages of such a structure are that it is likely to focus attention on key tasks and is adaptable. It also encourages team working. However, it is complex and can produce tensions between the different lines of reporting. Many larger *THE* organizations, such as international hotel chains, travel companies and airlines have versions of a matrix structure.

An organization is given definition and 'shape' by the formal structure it adopts since this orders the various tasks and relationships so that they are directed towards the fulfilment of the organization's objectives.

> **THINK POINTS**
>
> - Explain the advantages of centralization and decentralization in *THE* contexts.
> - In *THE* contexts why might a strict hierarchy not always be the most suitable structural arrangement?
> - What are the five major methods of divisionalization?

However, it is important to recognize that whatever structure is adopted, in all organizations there co-exists a pattern of informal relationships, communication and authority which is often termed the 'informal organization'. Each part of the organization, social group, working team or group of specialists may have its own customs, norms, authority structure and goals.

The informal organization may operate for or against the interests of the formal organization. Many organizations recognize and sometimes encourage the informal organization as a way of increasing productivity and team working. The informal organization can usefully:

- improve communication by means of 'the grapevine';
- coordinate the activities of individuals and groups;
- establish unwritten but practical ways of doing things; and
- provide ideas and enhancements.

Conversely the informal organization may absorb energy and time on unproductive activities.

KEY CONCEPT

Who is the boss in *THE* contexts?

The structures discussed in this section of the book appear to make it clear who 'the boss' is. It is normally the Chief Executive Officer (CEO) based at the organization's head office that is responsible to the Board of Directors.

However, there are some circumstances in *THE* where this might not be so evident. The role of specialists is important in many businesses, but in many aspects of *THE*, they are absolutely crucial to the successful on-going operation of the business and there are managerial implications which arise from this.

Take, for example, the pilot of an aircraft; the captain of a cruise ship; the stage manager at a concert or theatrical performance; or the head chef in the kitchen of a major hotel.

In all the examples cited, the people involved may not figure prominently in the organization chart depicting the structure of a particular organization, since there may be many pilots, captains, stage managers, chefs, etc. However, all have highly specialized skills that are crucial in service delivery. In the cases of the pilot and the ship's captain, their positions are supported by legal statutes, in that their primary responsibilities are for the safety of their aircraft or ship, and not aimed at boosting company profitability.

Consequently, when the CEO walks onto a plane or a ship, into the concert venue or the hotel kitchen, he or she could legitimately be told by the pilot, captain, chef, manager, etc. in recognition of their specialist skills and responsibilities:

'Outside you are "the boss" – but here, I am in charge.'

The implications of this apparent inversion of authority is that many organizations will have some key members of staff who are crucial in implementing the strategy successfully. The staff may have specialist knowledge or particular responsibilities (that determine their priorities) and implementing the strategy may not be their utmost priority. They might support the strategy but could also attempt to block it or ignore it.

Hence, it is important for senior managers in the organization to identify these individuals or groups and communicate with them appropriately to gather support for the changes that are required. This of course is not always easy and is not always successful. It is an aspect of the management of change (which is discussed in the next section).

In some *THE* contexts this informal organization extends to a consideration of who is in charge, i.e. 'who is the boss'? Though the organizational structure as shown in the organization chart may make it clear, the reality as indicated in the Key Concept above might be somewhat different, and organizational leaders must strive to communicate effectively with key groups of staff.

Implementation – managing and leading change

The need for change

At its simplest, strategy is all about change. In this chapter, we have encountered the importance of an organization's resource base, its culture and its structure. In order to bring about strategic repositioning (say in respect to products and markets), all of these may need to be changed.

Change can take different forms in different circumstances. For example, it can be viewed in four dimensions in that it might be:

- continuous or discontinuous;
- incremental or transformational;
- proactive or reactive; and
- broad or narrow in its scope.

Different organizations exhibit differing attitudes to change. We can draw a parallel here with different types of people. Some people are very conservative and configure their lives so as to minimize change. Such people will generally fear change and will resist it. Other people seem to get bored easily and are always looking for new challenges, jobs, and so on. Organizations reflect this spectrum of attitudes. It is here that we encounter the concept of *inertia*.

Inertia – identifying barriers to change

Inertia is a term borrowed from physics. It refers to the force that needs to be exerted on a body to overcome its state in relation to its motion. If a body is stationary then we would need to exert a force upon it to make it move. The size and shape of the body will have a large bearing upon its ablty to move – compare for example, the inertia of a football to that of a train.

In the same way, different organizations present management with varying degrees of inertia. Some are easy to change and others are much more reluctant. The willingness to change may depend upon the culture of the organization, its size, its existing structure, its product and/or market positioning and even its age (i.e. how long it has existed in its present form).

For most purposes, we can say that resistance to change on the part of employees can be caused by a number of attitudes. A number of studies in *THE* have reported resistance to change. See for example Okumus and Hemmington (1998) and Pechlaner and Sauerwein (2002). In a study of hotel managers in China, Singapore, Malaysia, and Hong Kong, Jogaratnam and Tse (2004) found that few hospitality managers have been used to the need to constantly innovate and influence change and that many managers are afraid to change.

Those affected by the change and resisting it may do so because they:

- *Lack understanding of the details* – They may not have had the reasons for the change explained to them or they may not be aware of how they will personally be affected. This particular barrier can normally be overcome relatively easily by management taking the requisite measures to close the information gap.
- *Lack trust* in respect to management.
- *Have a fear* – Particularly in respect to their personal position or their social relationships. They may fear that the proposed changes will adversely affect their place in the structure or the relationships they enjoy in the organization.
- *Have uncertainty about the future* – Attitudes to uncertainty vary significantly between people with some showing a much more adverse reaction to it than others.

Understanding change – Kurt Lewin's three-step model

Lewin (1947) suggested that organizational change could be understood in terms of three consecutive processes: unfreezing, moving and then refreezing as shown in Figure 13.6.

Figure 13.6 Lewin's model of change

Unfreezing (mobilization for change)

Unfreezing involves introducing measures that will enable employees to abandon their current practices or cultural norms in preparation for the change. In many organizations, little has changed for many years and unfreezing is necessary as a 'shaking-up' phase. The impetus for unfreezing can come from either inside or outside the organization itself. Changing market conditions, for example, sometimes give employees warning that change will be imminent. Internally, a management shake-up, a profit warning or talk of restructuring may bring about similar expectations.

Moving (movement to a new level)

Moving to the new level involves bringing about the requisite change itself. The time period given over to this phase varies widely. Structural change can usually be brought about relatively quickly. Changes in internal systems sometimes take longer (such as the introduction of new quality or information systems) whilst changing culture can take years.

Refreezing (sustaining change)

Refreezing is necessary to 'lock in' the changes and to prevent the organization from going back to its old ways. Again, we would usually take cultural changes to require more 'cementing in' than some other changes and some resolve might be required on the part of senior management to avoid slippage.

SHORT CASE ILLUSTRATION

Cultural change at easyJet and Ryanair

Ryanair and easyJet are two of the airlines which have spearheaded the low-cost airline revolution in Europe since the 1990s and both have grown rapidly to become established as substantial airlines.

The low-cost model, as its name implies, is built on cutting out unnecessary costs. Consequently, though variations have emerged, low-cost airline operations usually imply: cutting out additional product features, high aircraft utilization rates, point-to-point (as opposed to 'hub-and-spoke') routing, using a limited number of aircraft types, sales mainly derived online and fast airport turn-around. The airlines were also often cited for providing poor levels of customer service. In some cases the poor levels of service almost seemed to have become symbolic of the fact that the airline was doing everything possible to cut prices for passengers. If you want the advantages of low fares, this is the price you must accept.

In a 2002 interview (*The Times*, 2002), long-serving CEO and talisman for low-cost airlines, Michael O'Leary, said

Our customer service is about the most well-defined in the world. We guarantee to give you the lowest airfare. You get a safe flight. You get a normally on-time flight. That's the package. We don't and won't give you anything more on top of that.

But times are changing and competitive pressures on European short-haul routes have been intensifying. The so-called 'full service' airlines have responded in short-haul markets in many cases by: cutting costs; removing product features; or developing their own low-cost subsidiaries (such as IAGs Vueling and Iberia Express).

The low-cost airlines have had to adjust their own business models with regard to their culture and service standards to respond to their rejuvenated competitors. The *Financial Times* reported that 'customer service has become easyJet's own weapon, wielded against rivals in the highly competitive airline market' (Wild, 2013) as the company pushed ahead with a programme to transform the company's culture. 'While Ryanair was paring its core service to the bone, rival easyJet made some counterintuitive moves for a low-cost airline – offering flexible tickets and allocated seating to woo business travellers' (Topham, 2013).

The cultural change taking place at easyJet is facilitated through a major training programme. Staff are instructed on their ABC – attitude, behaviour and communication – and are being shown how unwitting actions make an impression on customers. Further initiatives to raise standards include an updated uniform and a 'customer charter'. The customer charter includes promises from many staff around the company to act as 'customer champions' to inform and inspire colleagues. Incentives for staff in buying into the revised organizational culture lie mainly in the form of pride in the company, winning your name on an aircraft, or becoming an ambassador for Unicef.

Two profit warnings during 2013 have also encouraged change at Ryanair aimed at taking a softer stance towards customers and attracting a greater number of business travellers. Changes include a recent re-launch of the website; a greater emphasis on major city airports in its route planning; a reduction in fines for lost boarding cards and charges for hold baggage; more refined advertising; and introduction of allocated seating. At the same time the airline has placed a greater emphasis on customer service and tellingly Michael O'Leary has removed himself as the spokesman for the airline.

The Times (2002); Wild (2013); Topham (2013); www.ryanair.com; www.easyjet.com.

Questions

1. Why is change necessary at easyJet and Ryanair?
2. What sort of difficulties might easyJet and Ryanair encounter in trying to change their organizational cultures?

Understanding the context of change

Being able to manage change effectively is key to organizational survival and this ability to change effectively is probably the Achilles' heel of even very successful companies (Holbeche, 2012:ix). In order to successfully lead and manage change it is first necessary to understand change conceptually. Here we present a summary but the subject matter is covered in detail by Balogun and Hailey, 2008; and Holbeche, 2012.

Before embarking on a programme of change, organizational leaders need to be aware of the context of change within the organization. Table 13.5 presents some key contextual factors that a *THE*

Table 13.5 Considering the context of change within organizations

Change – contextual factor	Primary issue
Time	How quickly is change required?
Scope	To what degree is change needed?
Preservation	What needs to be preserved when other aspects are changed?
Diversity	Will all parts of the organization be treated the same, or will there be room for diversity of approach?
Experience and capability	Does the organization have experience of change and the capability to carry it through the process?
Capacity	Are the resources required for change available?
Readiness	How willing and able to change are the people in the organization's consituent groupings?
Power	Do the organization's leaders have the necessary power to lead the required changes?

organization might need to consider before embarking on a programme of change as part of its implementation of strategy.

Understanding change – the urgency and nature of change

Organizations continually need to change and need to do so at a pace that is equal to or faster than the external environment in which they operate. If they fail to do so, so-called *strategic drift* occurs.

This occurs when an organization, even one that has enjoyed considerable success, responds too slowly to changes in the external environment and continues with the strategy that once served it very well. A well-known example that is often cited (though outside our focus) is that of Kodak, which in the context of film and photography failed to adapt its strategy to the rapid digitalization of the industry.

The case of the Calgary First Night Festival's demise illustrates the problems of strategic drift in the competitive world of festivals.

SHORT CASE ILLUSTRATION

Strategic drift: Calgary First Night Festival

Recent years have seen a huge increase in the number and range of festivals in countries around the world as localities, regions and countries compete for consumer spending. Successful festivals such as those in Edinburgh, Scotland, and Salzburg and Bregenz in Austria can be highly lucrative for their local economies both directly and indirectly through the enhanced image of the city that they engender.

However, the environment is highly competitive. The environment is competitive in two respects in that there are now many more festivals competing for public custom, but also the festivals have to compete for finite public and commercial financial resources. Many festivals are highly specialized and depend on public subsidy, volunteers and sponsorship for survival. Failure to keep pace with the changes in relation to these factors is an example of *strategic drift*.

Getz (2002) cites the example of the termination of the First Night Festival in the Canadian city of Calgary, which attracted up to 40,000 people for this paid-admission, non-alcoholic, family arts festival, which was held on new year's eve from 1985 through to 1995. Failure was attributed not to lack of interest but to other environmental factors:

Price restrictions were imposed which prevented the organizers from increasing their revenue;

An initial city grant was discontinued and put additional pressure on the event;

The festival was not eligible for ongoing funding from the Calgary Regional Arts Foundation, which otherwise supports local festivals; and

The volunteer festival directors were 'burnt-out' because of the constant fight for financial viability.

Thus failure to respond to the rapidly changing financial circumstances and an unsustainable leadership model implied that a strategic drift had taken place, i.e. the festival's rate of change failed to keep pace with the changing external environment.

Questions

1. What is meant by the term 'strategic drift' and how it is illustrated in this case?

2. What might the organizers of the festival have done to prevent failure in this case?

Two key aspects of change that managers need to determine relate to the urgency for the changes to be implemented and the nature of the change which needs to take place.

The pace at which change happens can usually be divided into one of two categories – step (often termed transformational) and incremental change. Incremental change (or incrementalism as it is often referred to) has become associated with the management learning process and is connected in particular with the work of Quinn (1989) and is assessed by Johnson (1988).

Figure 13.7 illustrates the two principal categories of change. As the terminology suggests, step change represents a major change implemented over a short period of time whereas incrementalism involves many small steps and learning as you proceed so that adjustments can be made as necessary. Quinn and Voyer (1998) suggest that there are two factors that determine which is the most appropriate.

- *How urgent the need for change is* – A market crisis will typically bring about an urgent need for rapid change whereas preparing for the introduction of a new legal regulation in five years' time will usually allow change to be brought about more slowly and perhaps more painlessly.

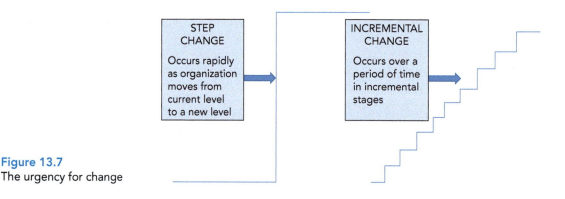

Figure 13.7
The urgency for change

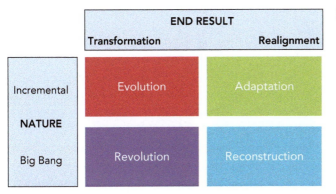

Figure 13.8 A model of types of change

- *How much inertia is evident within the organization's culture* – The time taken to unfreeze the inertia in some organizations will necessarily take longer than in others.

Step change offers the advantage of 'getting it over with'. It enables the organization to respond quickly to changes in its environment and hence enable it to conform to new conditions without lagging behind. Its disadvantages include the 'pain' factor – it may require some coercion or force on the part of management, which in turn may damage employee–management relationships.

Incremental changes offer the advantage of a step-by-step approach to change. For an organization with high inertia, it enables management to gain acceptance before and during the change process, and consequently, it tends to be more inclusive. The process is divided into a number of distinct phases and there may be periods of 'rest' between the phases. It would be an inappropriate technique to use in situations of rapid environmental change.

Balogun and Hailey (2008) usefully categorize types of change in four categories in their model of types of change shown as Figure 13.8.

In their model portraying types of change Balogun and Hailey (2008) divide change into four types, defined in two dimensions in terms of the:

- *end result of change* – i.e. the extent of the desired change; and
- *nature of the change* – i.e. the speed at which the changes will be implemented.

The four categories of change can be described in the following ways:

- *Adaptation* – is aimed at realigning rather than transforming the organization and is implemented slowly through staged initiatives.
- *Reconstruction* – is also aimed at realigning rather than transforming the organization but occurs in a more dramatic and fast manner.
- *Evolution* – is a transformational change implemented gradually through different stages and interrelated initiatives.
- *Revolution* – is fundamental transformational change occurring by simultaneous initiatives on many fronts, and often in a relatively short space of time. It is more likely (than evolution) to be forced on staff and reactive to rapidly changing market conditions.

The short illustrative case of the German Airline Lufthansa illustrates a strategic change process being implemented in the turbulent environment faced by airlines in recent years.

SHORT CASE ILLUSTRATION

Strategic change at Lufthansa

The German Airline Lufthansa with its main operating base at Frankfurt International Airport is the principal airline in a group of airlines which also includes Swiss and Austrian Airlines and low-cost carrier Germanwings. International airlines have had to become adept at managing change in response to rapid and fundamental environmental changes and highly volatile records of profitability.

Bruch *et al.* (2005) record that Lufthansa had shifted its shape successfully several times over the previous years since its spectacular turnaround from the brink of bankruptcy in 1991 (which is detailed by Bruch and Sattelberger 2000). 'The company became a master of managing strategic change despite the turbulent aviation market conditions prevalent from 1991 to 2004 by launching a series of major initiatives' (Bruch *et al.*, 2005:98).

The initiatives included a change programme 'D-Check' which was implemented throughout the airline from 2001 to 2004. The programme, which built on the lessons of three previous change programmes, involved many initiatives aimed at achieving cost savings. It enabled the organization to survive the airline financial crisis that emerged in the early years of the century far better than most competitors.

The latest manifestation of change implemented by Lufthansa is its SCORE programme which has a clearly defined goal: to sustainably boost earnings by EUR1.5bn by 2015. As with many such programmes, an acronym is used for ease of use and recall. In this case, SCORE represents five key aspects of Lufthansa's business:

- Synergies
- Costs
- Organization
- Revenue
- Execution.

SCORE, first implemented in 2012, represents a broad range of activities across all business segments and between them, in the group. They include a diverse range of projects, such as strengthening joint-purchasing, improving fuel efficiency, pooling and streamlining administrative functions or outsourcing them to more cost-effective sites, creating a more efficient IT structure, harmonizing the fleet and reviving loss-making European routes with the new Germanwings.

Early successes were visible and measurable with an earnings contribution of EUR 614 million attributable to the programme and enabling a further broad range of initiatives to be implemented during the second year of the programme in 2013. Group Chairman, Christoph Franz said: 'SCORE strengthens our core business segment and makes us less susceptible to external factors'.

Lufthansa (2012); Bruch and Sattelberger (2000); Bruch et al. (2005).

Questions

1. What problems might Lufthansa encounter in implementing its programme of change and how might these difficulties be overcome?

2. What are the main features of Lufthansa's change programme and why it is so important for the airline group?

The process of leading and managing the changes

Strong management and leadership of change are vital if the changes which are planned to be implemented are to be successful.

There are no generally accepted definitions of the terms 'management' or 'leadership'. In both cases many definitions have emerged in the academic and commercial literature and the meaning of both terms are subject to much debate. Hence in both cases the terms, their meaning and their application are subject to various interpretations.

Although in common usage the terms are often used interchangeably, care must be taken in distinguishing between the two concepts. Kotter (2001), for example, argues that leadership and management are two distinctive and complementary systems, each having its own function and its own characteristic activities, but both are necessary for complex organizations and vital to the successful implementation of strategic changes.

- *Management* is about planning, controlling, and putting appropriate structures and systems in place; whereas
- *leadership* has more to do with anticipating change, coping with change, and adopting a visionary stance.

Zaleznik (2004) also perceives a difference between management and leadership. Managers are seen as fairly passive people-centred operators intent on 'keeping the show on the road', whereas leaders seem to be more solitary, proactive, intuitive, emphatic and are attracted to situations of high risk where the rewards for success are great.

In summary, the difference between leadership and management is:

- *Leadership* is setting a new direction or vision for a group or for oneself that others follow, i.e. a leader is the spearhead for that new direction.
- *Management* controls or directs people/resources in a group according to principles or values that have already been established.

Management usually consists of people who are experienced in their field, and who usually possess a good technical knowledge. Their authority derives from the position they hold.

But what is leadership? There are almost as many definitions as there are commentators. Many associate leadership with one person leading.

However, four aspects stand out:

- To lead involves *influencing others*, and may derive from the position they hold or from other characteristics such as their personal qualities.
- Where there are leaders there are *followers*.
- Leaders seem to come to the fore when there is a *crisis or special problem*. In other words, they often become visible when an innovative response is needed.
- Leaders are people who have a clear idea of what they want to achieve and why. This is often described in terms of a *'vision'*.

Thus, leaders are people who are able to think and act creatively in non-routine situations – and who set out to influence the actions, beliefs and feelings of others. In this sense being a 'leader' is personal. It flows from an individual's qualities and actions. However, it is also often linked to some other role such as a manager or expert.

Hence there can be a lot of confusion. Not all managers, for example, are leaders; and not all leaders are managers. Leaders stand out by being different. They question assumptions and are suspicious of tradition and have a preference for innovation.

The study of leadership is not new. Interest in what makes effective leaders is one as long as history itself with many examples in the literature taken from the military field. Management by contrast is usually viewed as a more recent phenomenon linked to the development of modern industrial practices.

As Bass and Bass (2009) write:

> *The study of leadership rivals in age the emergence of civilization, which shaped its leaders as much as it was shaped by them. From its infancy, the study of history has been the study of leaders – what they did and why they did it.*

Kotter (1995) produces eight practical guidelines for leaders and managers seeking to transform their organizations. See Key Concept below.

KEY CONCEPT

Successfully transforming organizations

In stressing the need for strong effective leadership and management in organizations implementing programmes of change, Kotter argues that there are eight steps to successfully transform organizations:

- Establishing a sense of urgency
- Forming a powerful guiding coalition
- Creating a 'vision'
- Communicating the 'vision'
- Empowering others to act on the 'vision'
- Planning and creating short-term wins
- Consolidating improvements and producing still more change
- Institutionalizing new aproaches

Figure 13.9 Successfully transforming organizations

The process of actually leading and managing strategic change brings us to consider a number of managerial approaches and their appropriateness in various contexts.

Leadership and management approaches

Managers and leaders have different styles (approaches) that they adopt in implementing change in their organizations. It is true to say that there is no 'best' style of leading and managing strategic change (Johnson *et al.*, 2011: 473), but instead it is perhaps better to think of leaders needing to adjust the style they adopt according to the circumstances they encounter. This approach has become known as *situational leadership* following the work of Paul Hersey and Ken Blanchard during the 1970s, which is summarized and critiqued by Graeff (1997).

> ### THINK POINTS
> - What is inertia and how is it applied to organizational change?
> - Explain Lewin's three-step model of change.
> - Define and distinguish between step and incremental change.

Building on this adaptation of leadership style according to the circumstances, Balogun and Hailey (2008) argue that there are five styles that can be adopted each with associated advantages and disadvantages. The styles represent a continuum from coercion, in which change is forced on people, to education and delegation, in which change is delegated. Consequently each style may be more appropriate for adoption in some circumstances rather than others. This view is supported by the work of Pettigrew and Whipp (1991). Based on their research into a number of well-known British companies during the 1980s, Pettigrew and Whipp suggest that it may well also be the case that the style which is adopted by organizational leaders changes over time as the change programme is implemented and does (or perhaps does not) have the planned impact.

The five styles and their associated advantages and disadvantages identified by Balogun and Hailey are summarized in Table 13.6.

The role of the 'change agent'

Many writers have stressed the importance of the leadership role in successfully implementing change. See, for example, Howell and Higgins (1990) and Haberberg and Rieple (2001:Ch. 14). The individual or 'change agent' instigating change, may be the key manager (usually the Chief Executive or the Managing Director) within the organization or it may be that the organization brings in an external consultant for the duration of the process.

How the process of change is implemented and by whom is an interesting issue in itself. In the so-called *top-down* versus *bottom-up* discussion which has taken place in the academic literature over recent years, the role of top management is clearly important, whichever style they adopt and whether they lead the change themselves or bring in external consultants to do so.

However, Beer *et al.* (1990) found that change programmes that were directed by top management were quite likely to fail. The change programmes which were more likely to be successful were those that were started at the bottom of the organization and were driven by individuals or task groups who 'championed' specific aspects of change.

Beer *et al.* argue that top management's role in the change process is to support but not interfere with change, to create the climate for change to take place specifying the general direction of change and to communicate the successes and failures of the change process so that the lessons can be learned. Specifically, the authors recommend that the role of top management in a programme of change should be to:

- *mobilize commitment* to change through joint diagnosis and team efforts;
- *develop a shared vision* for change emanating from the task teams;
- *foster consensus* for the new vision by giving support and encouragement;
- *replace managers* who cannot work under the new system;
- *spread revitalization* to all departments without pushing from the top;
- *institutionalize change* through systems and procedures; and
- *monitor and adjust strategies* in response to problems.

Table 13.6 Styles of leading change

Style	Description	Advantages	Disadvantages
Education and delegation	Use small group briefings with people and explain things to them. The aim is to gain support for the change by generating understanding and commitment	Spreads support for change Ensures a wide base of understanding	Takes a long time If radical change is required, fact-based argument may not be enough to convince others of need to change Easy to voice support, then walk away and do nothing
Collaboration	Widespread involvement of the employees on decisions about what and how to change	Spreads not only support but 'ownership' of change by increasing involvement	Time consuming Little control (by senior management) over decisions made May lead to change outside original vision
Participation	Involvement of employees in 'how' to deliver the desired changes. May also include limited collaboration over aspects of the 'how' to change as opposed to 'what' to change	Again spreads ownership and support for change but with a more controlled framework Easier to shape decisions	Can be perceived as manipulation
Direction	Change leaders make the majority of decisions about what to change and how. Use of authority to direct change.	Less time consuming Provides a clear change direction and focus	Potentially less support and commitment and therefore proposed changes may be resisted
Coercion	Use of power to impose change	Allows for prompt action	Unlikely to achieve buy-in (by employees) except in a crisis

Source: Adapted from Balogun and Hailey (2008: 36)

The change agent approach in which an external person or team is brought in to implement change has been termed the 'champion of change' model. While an external person has the disadvantage that they do not know the context of the change or the personalities involved as well as an insider, there are a number of advantages in that:

- It provides a focus for the change in the form of a tangible person who becomes the personification of the process. A 'walking symbol' of change can act as a stimulus to change and can ensure that complacency is avoided.

- In many cases, the change agent will be engaged because he or she is an expert in his field. The person may have overseen the same change process in many other organizations and so is well acquainted with the usual problems and how to solve them.

- The appointment of a change agent sometimes means that senior management time need not be fully occupied with the change process. The responsibility for the change is delegated to the change agent and management thus gain the normal advantages of delegation. Accordingly, senior management are freed up to concentrate on developing future strategy.

Many management consultants vie for opportunities to advise organizations in implementing their strategies and have developed proprietary frameworks and systems to do so. One such external approach to implementing strategy is the 7-S model developed by the well-known international consultancy firm McKinsey. *In Search of Excellence* (2004), the best-selling book by McKinsey partners Tom Peters and Robert Waterman, introduced the mass business audience to the firm's 7-S model.

Whatever type of change is envisaged, the model can be used to understand how the organizational elements are interrelated, and so ensure that the wider impact of changes made in one area in terms of its impacts elsewhere is taken into consideration. The model, shown as Figure 13.10, is based on the notion that the seven elements (structure, strategy, systems, skills, style, staff and shared values) need to be aligned and mutually reinforcing so that the organization can perform well.

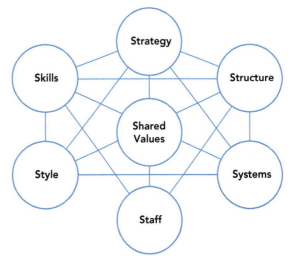

Figure 13.10 The McKinsey 7-S Framework

A methodology for communicating, coordinating and measuring strategic implementation

The need for a practical and coherent implementation technique

Measuring organizational success and implementing effective strategies for future success represent continuous challenges for managers, researchers and consultants (Evans, 2005). Against this background there is a continual striving to find a workable means of strategic implementation. Managers in a wide variety of industries are rethinking their performance measurement systems and means of strategic implementation.

One such means of implementation that is widely used is the Balanced Scorecard (BSC) which is covered in detail below.

Arguably, nowhere is the need for a consistent and coherent approach to strategic implementation more apposite than in the sectors of *THE*. A rapid switch from local and domestic competition to 'global' markets has taken place. In such markets large international companies strive to develop and implement strategies to ensure strategic success. At the same time, innovative companies have emerged encouraged by low barriers to entry and easing of regulatory restrictions. Increasing attention is being given to performance measurement and strategic implementation in many instances throughout *THE*.

This chapter has so far discussed various aspects of strategic implementation:

- *Resources* – how should the strategy be resourced?
- *Configuration* – how should the culture and structure of the organization be configured to 'fit' the proposed strategy?
- *Change* – how should the changes arising from the strategy be managed and led?

All of these aspects represent important dimensions of strategy implementation, but do not provide a detailed coherent framework within which managers can act. Two important issues arise:

- How should the strategy be spread (or *cascaded* as it is often termed) throughout the organization?
- How should the implementation (in a practical sense) be coordinated, managed and monitored?

Successful implementation of strategy involves all parts of an organization being successfully aligned to meet the strategic objectives that have been set as part of the strategic process. Thus, the strategy must be communicated and disseminated as part of this process. A detailed strategy may be developed for each part of the organization such as the marketing, finance operations and personnel functional areas and the strategic business units of the organization.

It is against the background of the need for a comprehensive implementation techniques that other approaches have been developed. The service profit chain (Heskett *et al.*, 1997) assesses the sources of profitability and growth in labour-dominated service firms and was discussed in Chapter 3. The service profit chain's purpose is to provide managers with a framework to help them manage by enabling them to focus on (predominantly) quantifiable measures that lead to financial performance measures. In this respect the model is similar to the Balanced Scorecard approach to strategy developed by Kaplan and Norton (discussed below). However, focusing as it does on the service delivery aspects of performance, the model is useful but does not represent an holistic approach to managing service based organizations (Evans, 2005).

Introduction to the Balanced Scorecard

Of all the frameworks for performance measurement and strategic implementation, it is the Balanced Scorecard (BSC) technique that has gained wide acceptance, particularly in the United States. A survey of its members by the American Institute of Public Accountants, for example, revealed that 43 per cent were utilising the technique (Maisel, 2001). Though not without its critics (see for example Norreklit, 2000), the success of BSC is evident and it is due perhaps not only to its intrinsic value to businesses, but also because the concept has been aggressively marketed.

The Balanced Scorecard was developed by Robert Kaplan (a Harvard professor) and a consultant David Norton in the early 1990s and resulted from their experiences in implementing strategic initiatives at several US corporations.

Kaplan and Norton identified two significant deficiencies in the implementation of strategic plans:

- *A measurement gap* – though most companies measure performance, most of the measurements used are historical looking backwards rather than focused on future success; and
- *A strategy gap* – many companies identified general plans, but in many cases they did not translate effectively into managerial actions. The authors claimed that many strategic initiatives had little real impact on the organization because they were not cascaded to managers and employers to use in their daily work.

BSC presents a technique for translating an organization's mission (embodied in its strategy) into more tangible measurable goals, actions and performance measures. The technique involves a range of measures (not only financial measures) since it has been argued that such measures alone are inadequate in evaluating a company's competitive position (Stalk *et al.*,1992). This is particularly true of the service sector, with its focus on human resources, intangible assets, and difficulties with regard to delivery of consistent product standards (Evans, 2005).

The BSC technique is documented in a number of papers in the 1990s and in greater detail in two books (see for example Kaplan and Norton, 1996 and 2001). The later works shifted the emphasis from a system of performance measurement towards a system for managing and implementing strategy, which is our focus here.

Many other authors have helped to disseminate the technique's features and a number of the studies have documented the technique in relation to the sectors of *THE* and to hotels and accommodation in particular.

See for example Doran *et al.* (2002); Evans (2005); Sainaghi, R. (2010); and, for case studies utilizing the technique, Denton and White (2000); and Huckestein and Duboff (1999).

Crucially the BSC approach can also be applied at different levels of an organization. Typically the total organizational Business Scorecard will be mapped and specified and then it will be replicated in modified form to each part of the organization, i.e. it can be applied with a common structure but specific and modified objectives, measures and targets to:

- the total organization;
- strategic business units;
- individual operational teams;
- individual members of staff.

In this way each part of the organization contributes to the achievement of a common set of objectives and targets and this can easily be seen by internal and external stakeholders.

Consequently BSC represents a methodology for implementation that:

- has a high degree of visibility and can easily be understood;
- can be easily and consistently communicated to staff and other stakeholders;
- offers a high level of consistency in its approach;
- can be 'cascaded' to all parts of the organization; and
- produces tangible and measureable outcomes so that the success (or otherwise) of strategic implementation can be assessed.

The Balanced Scorecard as a part of the strategy process

The process involves:

- identifying key components of operations;
- setting goals for them; and
- finding ways to measure progress towards their achievement.

Traditional financial measures, viewed as lagging indicators of performance, are balanced with non-financial measures, which are lead indicators and serve to drive future performance. The measures are not to be viewed merely as a collection of various metrics (Kaplan and Norton, 2001:11), but instead they are selected to show cause and effect in the implementation of the company's mission and organizational strategy.

An important preliminary step prior to choosing the scorecard goals and measures is to "map" the strategy in detail, a process that Kaplan and Norton (2001:69–131) describe in some detail.

A first stage in mapping the strategy is to understand where it fits into the overall management processes of an organization. To Kaplan and Norton (2001:72) strategy does not stand alone but it is one step in a logical continuum that moves an organization from a high-level mission statement to the work performed by individual 'front-line' and 'back office' employees.

Implied in this continuum is a causal link which starts with individual employees and through collective actions builds up to the achievement of the organizational mission. In this way strategy becomes embedded in the organization in that strategy becomes 'everyone's everyday job' (Kaplan and Norton, 2001:9) and as the title of their book makes plain – the organization becomes 'strategy focused'. BSC is an integral part of the continuum in that it is the technique which enables the strategy that has been formulated to be implemented and its progress monitored.

Figure 13.11 Strategy as a continuum involving BSC

Figure 13.11 provides a representation of strategy (that is consistent with the approach taken elsewhere in this book) which starts with the high level mission and ends with personal objectives for individual employees.

The understanding of strategy in the context of a continuum from the vision through to employees is demonstrated by the case of Amtrak (shown in the short illustrative case below) which utilizes BSC as part of its planning processes.

SHORT CASE ILLUSTRATION

BSC as a part of the continuum of strategy at Amtrak

Amtrak is a publicly funded railway service operated and managed as a for-profit corporation and began operations in 1971, providing intercity passenger train services in the United States.

The company's strategic plan for 2011–15 clearly shows the continuum of strategy from vision to individual employees in the context of a rail operator which is subject to external scrutiny, regulation and funding.

One critical piece of this strategy is implementing a Balanced Scorecard system. This strategic planning tool has become popular in private industry and government agencies (particularly in North America). Such a system (shown in Figure 13.12) turns Amtrak's strategic plan into action plans for departments and individual employees. Employee performance reviews and long-term financial plans will be driven by the strategic plan.

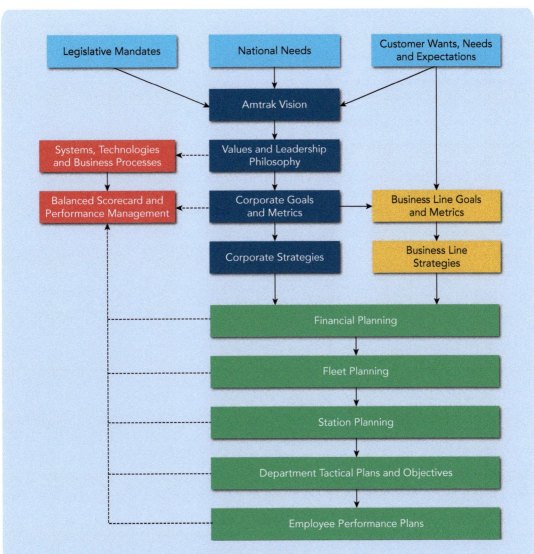

Figure 13.12 BSC as a part of the continuum of strategy at Amtrak

Questions

1. What is the continuum of the strategy process at Amtrak ?
2. Why might it be important to Amtrak to incude BSC as part of its strategic planning?

The Balanced Scorecard in practice

A typical scorecard normally includes four components:

- a financial perspective;
- an internal business perspective;
- a customer perspective; and
- an innovation and learning perspective.

The components as shown in Figure 13.13 should not be viewed in isolation but as an integrated model in which there are 'cause and effect' relationships. The authors argue (2001:76) that the BSC has a 'top-down' logic in starting with the financial outcomes, moving on to the customer outcomes that includes 'the value proposition' (which defines how the organization differentiates itself for customers), before moving on to business processes and the learning and growth infrastructure which are the drivers of change.

For each component the organization has to identify a number of:

- objectives (or goals);
- measures for gauging the degree of goal attainment;

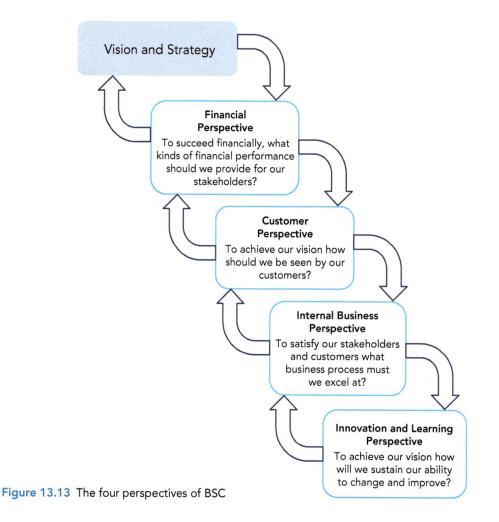

Figure 13.13 The four perspectives of BSC

- targets which identify progress towards achieving the goals; and
- initiatives (or priorities) within the period.

The cause and effect linkages of a strategy map are demonstrated in a tourism context in Figure 13.14. In this case the strategy map for the Canadian Tourism Commission shows the linkages which enable staff aligned with the strategy who eventually through the cause and effect linkages allow the CTC to achieve the mandate which it receives from the Canadian Government.

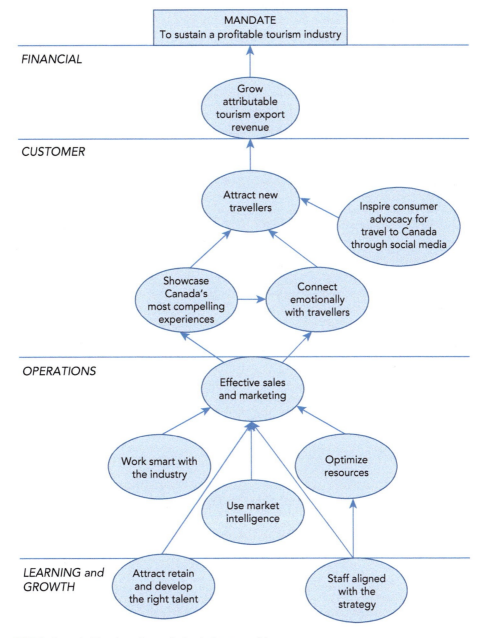

Figure 13.14 Canada Tourism Commission's Strategy Map

The purpose of the CTC's strategy map is to show the cause-and-effect relationships of our strategic objectives in a visual manner. It demonstrates how our organization creates value for the tourism industry, and aligns with our performance measurement framework as it mirrors the same perspectives as those found in our Balanced Scorecard.

(CTC, 2012)

CTC's Balanced Scorecard is consistent with its strategy map and is shown in the illustrative case below.

SHORT CASE ILLUSTRATION

BSC at the Canadian Tourism Commission

Based in Vancouver, British Columbia, the Canadian Tourism Commission (CTC), wholly owned by the Government of Canada, leads Canadian tourism marketing. To demonstrate that it was managing taxpayer money and creating value for Canada, the CTC decided to adopt the Balanced Scorecard as a strategic implementation tool in 2006.

CTC's ultimate goal is to grow tourism export revenue for Canada, and this goal is supported by two objectives and four priorities as articulated below. The targets CTC set for 2013 were to generate $547.9 million in tourism export revenue (i.e. new money flowing into Canada's economy) and $72.6 million in federal tax revenue, and create or maintain over 4,500 jobs in tourism businesses across Canada.

Table 13.7 BSC at the Canadian Tourism Commission

	Goals, objectives, measures and priorities	Targets
Financial	GOAL: Grow tourism export revenue for Canada in markets of highest return and where the Canada brand leads	
	MEASURES (Examples):	
	Attributable tourism export revenue from direct-to-consumer advertising	$423.9 million
	Attributable tourism export revenue from travel trade promotions	$64 million
	Attributable jobs created and/or maintained	4,439
	Attributable federal tax revenue leads	$72.6 million
Customer	OBJECTIVE 1: Generate demand for Canada's visitor economy	
	MEASURES:	
	Marketing campaign ROI	ratio 37 : 1
	Number of people converted	282,768
Operations	OBJECTIVE 2: Execute effective sales and marketing platforms to help Canadian businesses sell Canada now	
	MEASURE:	
	Partner satisfaction	65%
	PRIORITY:	
	Link sales and marketing plans to business insights and market research	Destination awareness 27%
	PRIORITY:	
	Enhance fundamentals that position Canada's tourism industry for growth	Country brand rank Top 5

	Goals, objectives, measures and priorities	Targets
Learning and growth	PRIORITY: Employee engagement index	65%

Source: Adapted from CTC (2012)

Questions

1. What benefits might CTC gain by using the BSC?
2. How is the BSC shown here related to the strategy map shown in Figure 13.14?

Balance Scorecard – potential difficulties

At each stage of the development of BSC as a tool for implementation it is necessary to be aware of potential difficulties which need to be overcome (Evans, 2005).

Evans (2005) identifies three key potential difficulties:

- *Mistaking data for useable information* – A balance needs to be achieved in having enough detail to be actionable, but only enough to be meaningful and that can be easily interpreted by managers.
- *Failing to establish causal linkages between scorecard components* – Kaplan and Norton (2001:69) argue that each measure of a balanced scorecard becomes embedded in a chain of cause-and-effect logic that connects the desired strategic outcomes with the drivers that will lead to the successful achievement of these outcomes. Thus, in this way the mapping of the BSC tells the story of the strategy in a way that is meaningful to stakeholders.
- *Failing to get the support of employees for the management system* – It is important that an understanding of strategy cascades down through an organization so that all employees are aware of strategic intent and the impact of operational activities upon its delivery. Such an understanding is more easily conveyed using a tool such as BSC, which clearly establishes causal links.

THINK POINTS

- Explain how the BSC framework can be utilized in strategic implementation.
- What are the four perspectives in a typical BSC?
- Explain why strategic mapping is important to the BSC process.

SMALL BUSINESS FOCUS

The fragmentation of many parts of *THE* and the consequent importance of SMEs has been outlined throughout this book. It is largely accepted that SMEs are different in many respects to larger companies, not least when it comes to issues of strategic implementation. In particular SMEs may be less inclined to operate formal planning systems and consequently be more likely to tend towards more emergent approaches to strategy, the role of the leader or entrepreneur may be more prominent and SMEs may lack the resources of their larger counterparts.

In summarizing previous research Garengo and Biazzo (2012) confirm these differences in that SMEs often:

- are operationally focused and lack formalized strategies;
- suffer from entrepreneurial behaviour where performance measures are considered constraints to change; and
- offer limited resources and managerial capacities fuelled by mainly implicit and context-specific knowledge.

The reality for many small firms is that short-term survival is more important than strategic planning say five years hence, since there appears to be an inverse relationship between the age of a business and its likelihood of failure. This is perhaps because by definition older firms have already demonstrated a successful capacity to adapt and develop and have built competencies and capabilities which allow this process to continue (Haberberg and Rieple, 2001:500).

Thus for many SMEs in *THE* there may be a number of difficulties when strategic implementation issues are considered. A specific but limited literature has emerged which considers the issues in *THE* contexts (see for example, Hwang and Lockwood, 2006; Kyriakidou and Gore, 2005). In studying smaller tourism businesses in New Zealand, Ateljevic and Doorne (2004) pointed to the difficulties smaller businesses have with regard to specialist labour resources. Not only are employees expected to be specialists (e.g. chef, receptionist, and guide) but they also require detailed understanding of the business and the dynamics of the industry sector.

Some of the key difficulties may relate to the availability of finance or appropriately skilled personnel; access to training programmes; and, regulatory environments favouring larger enterprises. A further difficulty may relate to entrepreneurs being involved in *THE* for the lifestyle it offers, rather than being motivated by growth and development of the enterprise.

Notwithstanding the difficulties outlined, the implementation phase of strategy is often easier and more successful in SMEs than in larger companies. This is often because the larger the company the greater the distance between the chief executive and front-line staff (Lasher, 1999:109) leading to lack of control and communication, or because of the direct involvement of the owner who sets the standards and style of the operation (Hwang and Lockwood, 2006).

Other factors which might make implementation of strategy more successful in SMEs include:

- *Complexity* – Less complex structures make it easier to direct communications and receive feedback.
- *Centralization* – Less likely to be decentralized due to their smaller scale so that management control is easier and usually quicker.
- *Cultural consistency* – Larger organizations often have sub-cultures and informal cultures operating in parts of the organization making it difficult to make changes in a consistent manner.
- *Leadership* – SMEs are often strongly associated with entrepreneurs or a small number of leaders, so it is clear where authority lies and decisions can be made quickly and decisively.

CHAPTER SUMMARY

The implementation of a selected strategy rests upon the successful management of a number of issues.

An organization must first ensure that sufficient resources are available and in place to implement the strategy. Deficits should be made good and once acquired, resources need to be configured to support the key value-adding activities.

The culture and structure need to be assessed for their suitability to undertake the strategy and must be changed as necessary. The chapter also considered the issues surrounding the management and leadership of change – usually an important part of managing the implementation of strategy.

Finally a framework (BSC) was suggested for actually managing and measuring the changes arising from implementing strategy in a practical sense.

REFERENCES

Ateljevic, J. and S. Doorne (2004) 'Diseconomies of Scale: A Study of Development Constraints in Small Tourism Firms in Central New Zealand', *Tourism and Hospitality Research*, 5 (1): 5–24.

Balogun, J. and V. H. Hailey (2008) *Exploring Strategic Change*, Harlow UK: Financial Times/Prentice Hall.

Bartlett, C. A. and S. Ghoshal (1999) *Managing across Borders: The Transnational Solution* (vol. II), Cambridge, Mass.: Harvard Business School Press.

Bass, B. M. and R. Bass (2009) *The Bass Handbook of Leadership: Theory, Research and Managerial Applications*, New York: Simon & Schuster.

Beer, M., R. Eisenstat and B. Spector (1990) 'Why Change Programs Don't Produce Change', *Harvard Business Review*, 68 (6), 158–66.

Bruch, H. and T. Sattelberger (2000) 'The Turnaround at Lufthansa: Learning from the Change Process', *Journal of Change Management*, 1 (4): 344–63.

Bruch, H., P. Gerber and V. Maier (2005) 'Strategic Change Decisions: Doing the Right Change Right', *Journal of Change Management*, 5 (1): 97–107.

Chandler, A. D. (1962) *Strategy and Structure: Chapters in the History of the American Industrial Enterprise*, Cambridge, Mass.: MIT Press.

Chesshyre, T. (2002) 'Interview with Michael O'Leary', *The Times*, 5 January.

CTC (2012) Canadian Tourism Commission Corporate Plan 2013–17, Available from www.en-corporate.canada.travel/ (accessed April 2014).

Denton, G. A. and B. White (2000) 'Implementing a Balanced Scorecard Approach to Managing Hotel Operations: The Case of White Lodging Services', *Cornell Hotel and Restaurant Administration Quarterly*, 41 (1): 94–107.

Doran, M. S., K. Haddad and C. W. Chow (2002) 'Maximising the Success of Balanced Scorecard Implementation in the Hospitality Industry', *International Journal of Hospitality and Tourism Administration*, 3 (3): 33–58.

Epstein, M. and J. F. Manzoni (1998) 'Implementing Corporate Strategy: From Tableaux De Bord to Balanced Scorecards', *European Management Journal*, 16 (2): 190–203.

Evans, N. (2005) 'Assessing the Balanced Scorecard as a Management Tool for Hotels', *International Journal of Contemporary Hospitality Management*, 17 (5): 376–90.

Galan, J. I. and M. J. Sanchez-Bueno (2009) 'The Continuing Validity of the Strategy-Structure Nexus: New Findings, 1993–2003', *Strategic Management Journal*, 30 (11): 1234–43.

Garengo, P. and S. Biazzo (2012) 'Unveiling Strategy in SMEs through Balanced Scorecard Implementation: A Circular Methodology', *Total Quality Management and Business Excellence*, 23 (1): 79–102.

Getz, D. (2002) 'Why Festivals Fail', *Event Management*, 7 (4): 209–19.

Ghoshal, S. and C. Bartlett (1987) 'Management across Borders: New Strategic Requirements', *Sloan Management Review*, 43: 1–17.

Graeff, C. L. (1997) 'Evolution of Situational Leadership Theory: A Critical Review', *The Leadership Quarterly*, 8 (2): 153–70.

Haberberg, A. and A. Rieple (2001) *The Strategic Management of Organizations*, Harlow UK: Financial Times/Prentice Hall.

Hahn, W. and T. L. Powers (2010) 'Strategic Plan Quality, Implementation Capability and Firm Performance', *Academy of Strategic Management Journal*, 9 (1): 63–81.

Hall, D. J. and M. A. Saias (1980) 'Strategy Follows Structure!' *Strategic Management Journal*, 1 (2): 149–63.

Hall, R. (1992) 'The Strategic Analysis of Intangible Resources', *Strategic Management Journal*, 13 (2): 135–144.

Handy, C. (1993) *Understanding Organizations*, London: Penguin.

Heskett, J. L., W. E. Sasser and L. A. Schlesinger (1997) *The Service Profit Chain*, New York: Simon & Schuster.

Hofstede, G. (1980) *Culture's Consequences: International Differences in Work-related Values*. Beverly Hills CA: Sage.

Holbeche, L. (2012) *Understanding Change*, London and New York: Routledge.

Howell, J. M. and C. A. Higgins (1990) 'Champions of Change: Identifying, Understanding and Supporting Champions of Technological Innovations', *Organizational Dynamics*, 19 (1): 40–55.

Huckestein, D. and R. Duboff (1999) 'Hilton Hotels: A Comprehensive Approach to Delivering Value for All Stakeholders', *Cornell Hotel and Restaurant Administration Quarterly*, August, 40 (4): 28–38.

Hwang, L. J. J. and A. Lockwood (2006) 'Understanding the Challenges of Implementing Best Practices in Hospitality and Tourism SMEs', *Benchmarking: An International Journal*, 13 (3): 337–54.

Jogaratnam, G. and E. C. Y. Tse (2004) 'The Entrepreneurial Approach to Hotel Operation Evidence from the Asia-Pacific Hotel Industry', *Cornell Hotel and Restaurant Administration Quarterly*, 45 (3): 248–59.

Johnson, G. (1988) 'Rethinking Incrementalism', *Strategic Management Journal*, 9 (1): 75–91.

Johnson, G. and K. Scholes (2011) *Exploring Corporate Strategy*, 6th edn, Hemel Hempstead: Prentice Hall

Johnson, G., R. Whittington and K. Scholes (2011) *Exploring Strategy: Text and Cases*, 9th edn, Harlow: Financial Times Prentice Hall.

Jones, P. (2008) *Communicating Strategy*, Farnham: Gower Publishing.

Kaplan, R. S. and D. P. Norton (1996) 'Using the Balanced Scorecard as a Strategic Management System', *Harvard Business Review*, 74 (January/February): 75–85.

— (2001) *The Strategy-Focused Organization*, Boston, Mass.: Harvard Business School Press.

Kotter, J. P. (1995) 'Leading Change: Why Transformation Efforts Fail', *Harvard Business Review*, 73 (2): 59–67.

Kotter, J. P. (2001) 'What Leaders Really Do?', *Harvard Business Review*, 79 (11), 85–98.

Kyriakidou, O. and J. Gore (2005) 'Learning by Example: Benchmarking Organizational Culture in Hospitality, Tourism and Leisure SMEs', *Benchmarking: An International Journal*, 12 (3): 192–206.

Lasher, W. R. (1999) *Strategic Thinking for Smaller Businesses and Divisions*, Oxford: Blackwell.

Lewin, K. (1947) 'Feedback Problems of Social Diagnosis and Action: Part II-B of Frontiers in Group Dynamics', *Human Relations*, 1 (2): 147–53.

Lorange, P. (1998) 'Strategy Implementation: The New Realities', *Long Range Planning*, 31 (1): 18–29.

Lynch, R. (2012) *Strategic Management*, 6th edn, Harlow: Pearson Education.

Maisel, L. S. (2001) *Performance Measurement Practices Survey*, New York: American Institute of Public Accountants.

Miles, R. E. and C. C. Snow (1978) *Organizational Strategy, Structure and Process*, New York: McGraw-Hill.

Miller, D. (2001) 'Successful Change Leaders: What Makes Them? What Do They Do That Is Different?' *Journal of Change Management*, 2 (4): 359–68.

Miller, S., D. Wilson and D. Hickson (2004) 'Beyond Planning: Strategies for Successfully Implementing Strategic Decisions', *Long Range Planning*, 37 (3): 201–18.

Mintzberg, H. (1990) 'The Design School: Reconsidering the Basic Premises of Strategic Management', *Strategic Management Journal*, 11 (3): 171–95.

Morris, D. S. and R. H. Haigh (1996) 'Overcoming the Barriers to TQM', in G.K. Kanji (ed.) *Total Quality Management in Action*, London: Chapman & Hall, pp. 92–101.

Moss Kanter, R. (1989) *The Change Masters: Innovation and Entrepreneurship in the American Corporation*, New York: Simon & Schuster.

Norreklit, H. (2000) 'The Balance on the Balanced Scorecard: A Critical Analysis of Some of Its Assumptions', *Management Accounting Research*, 11 (1): 65–88.

Okumus, F. (2003) 'A Framework to Implement Strategies in Organizations', *Management Decision*, 41 (9): 871–82.

Okumus, F. and N. Hemmington (1998) 'Barriers and Resistance to Change in Hotel Firms: An Investigation at Unit Level', *International Journal of Contemporary Hospitality Management*, 10 (7): 283–8.

Pechlaner, H. and E. Sauerwein (2002) 'Strategy Implementation in the Alpine Tourism Industry', *International Journal of Contemporary Hospitality Management*, 14 (4): 157–68.

Peters, T. J. and R. H. Waterman (2004) *In Search of Excellence: Lessons from America's Best-Run Companies*, New York: HarperCollins.

Pettigrew, A. and R. Whipp (1991) *Managing Change for Competitive Success*, Oxford UK: Wiley-Blackwell.

Quinn, J. B. (1989) 'Managing Strategic Change' in D. Asch and C. Bowman (eds.) *Readings in Strategic Management*, Basingstoke: Macmillan, 20–36.

Quinn, J. B. and J. Voyer (1998) 'Logical Incrementalism: Managing Strategy Formation', in H. Mintzberg, J. B. Quinn and S. Ghoshal (eds.), *The Strategy Process*, Englewood Cliffs, NJ: Prentice Hall.

Sainaghi, R., P. Phillips and V. Corti (2013) 'Measuring Hotel Performance: Using a Balanced Scorecard Perspectives' Approach', *International Journal of Hospitality Management*, 34: 150–9.

Schein, E. H. (1985) *Organizational Culture and Leadership*, San Francisco, Calif.: Jossey-Bass.

Stalk, G., P. Evans and L. E. Sgulman (1992) 'Competing on Capabilities: The New Rules of Corporate Strategy', *Harvard Business Review*, 70 (March/April): 57–69.

Topham, G. (2013) 'Ryanair: More Christmas Cheer, Less of the Bah, Humbug from Michael O'Leary', *The Observer*, 1 December.

Tushman, M. L. and C. A. O'Reilly (1996) *Winning through Innovation: A Practical Guide to Leading Organizational Change and Renewal*, Boston, Mass.: Harvard Business School Press.

Wild, J. (2013) 'Easyjet Blazes Trail on Customer Service', *Financial Times*, 23 December.

Zaleznik, A. (2004). 'Managers and Leaders. Are They Different? [originally published 1977]' *Harvard Business Review*, 82 (1), 74–81.

WEBSITES

www.easyjet.com
www.ryanair.com
www.amtrak.com
www.corporate.canada.travel
www.lufthansa.com

FURTHER READING

Reference	Focus
Atkinson, H. (2006) 'Strategy Implementation: A Role for the Balanced Scorecard?' *Management Decision*, 44 (10): 1441–60.	Strategy implementation Balanced Scorecard
Atkinson, H. and J. Brander Brown (2001) 'Rethinking Performance Measures: Assessing Progress in UK Hotels', *International Journal of Contemporary Hospitality Management*, 13 (3): 128–35.	Performance measurement Balanced Scorecard Hotels
Benson, A. M. and S. Henderson (2011) 'A Strategic Analysis of Volunteer Tourism Organizations', *The Service Industries Journal*, 31 (3): 405–24.	Balanced Scorecard Tourism Strategic Analysis
Brown, J. B. and B. McDonnell (1995) 'The Balanced Score-Card: Short-Term Guest or Long-Term Resident?' *International Journal of Contemporary Hospitality Management*, 7 (2/3): 7–11.	Balanced Scorecard Hospitalitty
By, R. T. (2005) 'Organizational Change Management: A Critical Review', *Journal of Change Management*, 5 (4): 369–80.	Managing change Strategic implementation
Cameron, K. S. and R. E. Quinn (2011) *Diagnosing and Changing Organizational Culture: Based on the Competing Values Framework*, San Francisco CA: Jossey Bass.	Cultural Change Hospitality
Cheong, W. L., C. H. Low and J. K. W. Sum (2001) 'Tourism in South Korea: A Performance Evaluation Model for Korea National Tourism Organization', doctoral dissertation, Nanyang Technological University, Nanyang Business School.	Balanced Scorecard Tourism Korea
Chon, K. S. and M. D. Olsen (1990) 'Applying the Strategic Management Process in the Management of Tourism Organizations', *Tourism Management*, 11 (3): 206–13.	Strategic implementation Tourism
Cruz, I. (2007) 'How Might Hospitality Organizations Optimize Their Performance Measurement Systems?' *International Journal of Contemporary Hospitality Management*, 19 (7): 574–88.	Performance measurement Hospitality

Davis, T. R. V. (1996) 'Developing and Employee Balanced Scorecard: Linking Frontline Performance to Corporate Objectives', *Management Decision*, 34 (4): 14–18.	Balanced Scorecard Performance measurement Cascading strategy
Dawson, M., J. Abbott and S. Shoemaker (2011) 'The Hospitality Culture Scale: A Measure Organizational Culture and Personal Attributes', *International Journal of Hospitality Management*, 30 (2): 290–300.	Organizational culture Hospitality
Doran, M. S., K. Haddad and C. W. Chow (2002) 'Maximizing the Success of Balanced Scorecard Implementation in the Hospitality Industry', *International Journal of Hospitality and Tourism Administration*, 3 (3): 33–58.	Balanced Scorecard Hospitality
Eden, C. and F. Ackermann (2013) *Making Strategy: The Journey of Strategic Management*, London: Sage.	Strategic implementation Strategy mapping
Harris, P. J. and M. Mongiello (2001) 'Key Performance Indicators in European Hotel Properties: General Managers' Choices and Company Profiles', *International Journal of Contemporary Hospitality Management*, 13 (3): 120–7.	Balanced Scorecard Performance measurement Hotels
Hede, A. M. (2008) 'Managing Special Events in the New Era of the Triple Bottom Line', *Event Management*, 11 (1–2): 1–2.	Events management Performance measurement Managing change
Kline, S. F., A. M. Morrison and A. S. John (2005) 'Exploring Bed and Breakfast Websites: A Balanced Scorecard Approach', *Journal of Travel and Tourism Marketing*, 17 (2–3): 253–67.	Balanced Scorecard Hospitality SMEs
Korir, J. and B. Imbaya (2013) 'Measuring Performance of Minor Event Management Ventures in Kenya', *Developing Country Studies*, 3 (3): 86–93.	Balanced Scorecard Events management Performance measurement
Min, H., H. Min and S. J. Joo (2008) 'A Data Envelopment Analysis-Based Balanced Scorecard for Measuring the Comparative Efficiency of Korean Luxury Hotels', *International Journal of Quality and Reliability Management*, 25 (4): 349–65.	Balanced Scorecard Hotel Korea
Mwaura, G., J. Sutton and D. Roberts (1998) 'Corporate and National Culture: An Irreconcilable Dilemma for the Hospitality Manager?' *International Journal of Contemporary Hospitality Management*, 10 (6): 212–20.	Organizational culture Change Hospitality National culture
Okumus, F. and N. Hemmington (1998) 'Barriers and Resistance to Change in Hotel Firms: An Investigation at Unit Level', *International Journal of Contemporary Hospitality Management*, 10 (7): 283–8.	Strategy implementation Hospitality
Okumus, F. and A. Roper (1999) 'A Review of Disparate Approaches to Strategy Implementation in Hospitality Firms', *Journal of Hospitality and Tourism Research*, 23 (1): 21–39.	Change Hospitality Hotels
Olson, E. M., S. F. Slater and G. T. M. Hult (2005) 'The Importance of Structure and Process to Strategy Implementation', *Business Horizons*, 48 (1): 47–54.	Strategy implementation Organizational structure
Park, J. A. and G. B. Gagnon (2006) 'A Causal Relationship between the Balanced Scorecard Perspectives', *Journal of Human Resources in Hospitality and Tourism*, 5 (2): 91–116.	Balanced Scorecard Tourism Hospitality

Pechlaner, H. and E. Sauerwein (2002) 'Strategy Implementation in the Alpine Tourism Industry', *International Journal of Contemporary Hospitality Management*, 14 (4): 157–68.	Strategy implementation Tourism
Phillips, P. and P. Louvieris (2005) 'Performance Measurement Systems in Tourism, Hospitality and Leisure Small Medium-Sized Enterprises: A Balanced Scorecard Perspective', *Journal of Travel Research*, 44 (2): 201–11.	Balanced Scorecard Tourism Hospitality SMEs
Pryor, M. G., D. Anderson, L. A. Toombs and J. H. Humphreys (2007) 'Strategic Implementation as a Core Competency: The 5Ps Model', *Journal of Management Research*, 7 (1): 3–17.	Strategy implementation Core competence
Reisinger, Y. and J. C. Crotts (2010) 'Applying Hofstede's National Culture Measures in Tourism Research: Illuminating Issues of Divergence and Convergence', *Journal of Travel Research*, 49 (2): 153–64.	National culture Tourism
Sainaghi, R. (2010) 'Hotel Performance: State of the Art', *International Journal of Contemporary Hospitality Management*, 22 (7): 920–52.	Performance measurement Hotels
Testa, M. R. (2002) 'Leadership Dyads in the Cruise Industry: The Impact of Cultural Congruency', *International Journal of Hospitality Management*, 21 (4): 425–41.	Organizational culture Leadership Cruising
—— (2004) 'Cultural Similarity and Service Leadership: A Look at the Cruise Industry', *Managing Service Quality*, 14 (5): 402–13.	Organizational culture Leadership Cruising
—— (2007) 'A Deeper Look at National Culture and Leadership in the Hospitality Industry', *International Journal of Hospitality Management*, 26 (2): 468–84.	Organizational culture Leadership Cruising
Thomas, R., M. Gable and R. Dickinson (1999) 'An Application of the Balanced Scorecard in Retailing', *The International Review of Retail, Distribution and Consumer Research*, 9 (1): 41–67.	Balanced Scorecard Service industry Retailing
Thomas, R., G. Shaw and S. J. Page (2011) 'Understanding Small Firms in Tourism: A Perspective on Research Trends and Challenges', *Tourism Management*, 32 (5): 963–76.	Tourism SMEs Strategic implementation
Watson, S. and N. D'Annunzio-Green (1996) 'Implementing Cultural Change through Human Resources: The Elusive Organization Alchemy?' *International Journal of Contemporary Hospitality Management*, 8 (2): 25–30.	Cultural change Hospitality

CASE LINKAGES

Case 2	Tourism Queensland
Case 3	Ryanair
Case 4	Hyatt Hotels
Case 5	Days Inn
Case 7	Thomas Cook

Chapter 14

International and global strategies for tourism, hospitality and events

Introduction and chapter overview

One of the most important considerations in the implementation of strategy is the extent to which the organization's activities are spread across geographical regions.

Some organizations are entirely domestically based, others operate in many countries, and others still operate in almost all regions of the world. This chapter is concerned with a discussion of the key issues surrounding the *why* and *how* questions:

- *Why* do organizations expand in this way?
- *How* do they go about it?

The *why* questions are covered in a discussion of the factors that drive increased internationalization. The *how* questions are answered in a discussion of the market entry options.

There is a growing interest in researching the internationalization process of service firms (see for example Blomstermo *et al.*, 2006) and a growing number of studies have focused on *THE*, and hotels in particular.

For example – Hjalager (2007) traces the stages that tourism goes through in the process of globalization and in doing so she points to the distinguishing characteristics of tourism which distinguish it from other sectors. Chen and Dimou (2005) investigate the main factors that influence the corporate development decision of international hotels with particular reference to franchising vs. management contracts. Both papers also provide thorough reviews of the relevant literature.

This chapter considers the decisions many organizations in *THE* need to make at some time during their development related to internationalization and globalization.

This chapter in considering the international and global dimensions of strategic development inevitably draws heavily on previous chapters. In particular it utilizes material from Chapter 10 (which considered the direction of development and competitive strategy) and Chapter 11 (which considered strategic methods). Though neither of these chapters specifically considered the strategic development of organizations in international or global contexts, nevertheless many such decisions (especially in inherently international sectors such as those of *THE*) involve international decision making. In this chapter we focus specifically on the international and global dimensions when it comes to implementing strategic decisions.

Both the terms internationalization and globalization are widely used both in 'every-day' language and also in the academic literatures related to business and *THE*. The terms are also often used interchangeably.

Here, the differences between the two terms as presented by the relevant academic literature are examined. Two frameworks developed by Yip and Porter to aid our understanding of the processes involved are presented and these models it is suggested can usefully be applied in *THE* contexts.

In considering international and global strategy many organizations consider whether to undertake operations themselves or 'outsource' activities to another company. Though such decisions do not always involve an international dimension, in *THE* decision making there is often an international dimension. Thus the topic of outsourcing is considered in this chapter and there is quite a large literature in *THE* (particularly related to hotels and airlines) which specifically relates to this topic.

The chapter also considers what is often described as market entry strategy. This is concerned in considering specifically

- What are the drivers (factors) underlying market entry?
- How should organizations seek to enter particular international markets?
- Which methods (modes) should be used to enter these markets?

The chapter presents a conceptualization (model) of market entry strategy which provides a useful way of understanding the various factors involved in considering market entry strategy and the linkages between them.

Though here internationalization, globalization and market entry strategy are presented separately they are aspects of the same set of issues. Thus the chapter concludes by considering the aspects holistically and using the hospitality sector as an exemplar of this approach.

It might be thought that since this topic area involves added complexity and risk for organizations, that it may not be a concern for SMEs. However, it is suggested this is not the case in many *THE* companies since they are inherently international in their orientation.

LEARNING OBJECTIVES

After studying this chapter, you should be able to:

- define and distinguish between internationalization and globalization;
- explain the factors that drive globalization;
- describe and demonstrate the application of Yip's framework for analysing the extent of globalization in an industry and market;
- explain the adaptation of Porter's generic strategy to global and international settings;
- apply internationalization and globalization concepts and frameworks to *THE* contexts;
- explain the major global strategy alternatives;
- explain the international market entry strategies; and
- apply market entry strategy and conceptualization to THE contexts.

Internationalization and globalization

What is the difference?

Business has been international since the days of the ancient Egyptians, Phoenicians and Greeks. Merchants travelled the known world to sell products manufactured in their home country and to return with products from other countries. Initially, international business simply took the form of exporting and importing.

The term *international* describes any business that carries out some of its activities across national boundaries, so clearly a large number of *THE* businesses are included in this categorization. Even smaller businesses are also often increasingly international in their outlook, taking advantage of lower entry barriers with respect to technology and deregulation and forming alliances and networks across borders giving rise to the term *born global* to describe their activities (see Sharma and Blomstermo, 2003). Public sector organizations are also increasingly having to compete internationally and having to make choices about outsourcing, international collaboration and tendering against foreign competitors for domestic contracts (Johnson *et al.*, 2011:265)

Globalization, on the other hand, is more than simply internationalization and has given rise to a vast literature in relation to business but also in relation to wider societal issues. Indeed globalization can be viewed as one of today's most controversial issues, and importantly (for our purposes) *THE* is at the same time both a central part of the process which causes of globalization and a part of the result. As Hjalager (2007:438) puts it:

> *travel and tourism are among the many causes and results of globalization processes.*

DEFINITION/QUOTATION

Internationalization and globalization

Globalization can be defined as the increasing integration of economies, societies, and civilizations. It includes, and goes beyond, the more simple internationalization defined as relations among and within nations. Globalization is a restructuring process that works across units and affects all aspects of human life: from capital flows, through political collaboration, to the flow of ideas. It also includes environmental pollution, criminal behaviour, disease and, ultimately, terror.

Hjalager (2007:437–8)

A large multinational company is not necessarily a 'global business'. In order for a business to become global in its operations, we would usually expect a number of important characteristics to be in place. Global organizations usually exhibit the characteristics outlined below:

- *Convergence of customer needs* – They take advantage of the increasing trend towards a convergence of customer needs and wants across international borders (Levitt, 1983) in many commercial segments such as: fast foods; soft drinks and beverages; accommodation; and travel intermediaries.

- *Globalized industries* – They compete in industries that are globalized. In some sectors, successful competition necessitates a presence in almost every part of the world in order to effectively compete in its global market.

- *Location of value-added activities* – They can, and do, locate their value-adding activities in those places in the world where the greatest competitive advantages can be gained. This might mean, for example, shifting (outsourcing) certain operations to a low-cost region.

- *Integration and co-ordination of activities* – They are able to integrate and co-ordinate their international activities between countries. The mentality of 'a home base, with foreign subsidiary interests' that has been so prevalent amongst traditional multinational companies is eroded in the culture of global businesses. They have learned to effectively manage and control the various parts of the business across national borders despite local cultural differences.

The development of an organization's global strategy, therefore, will be concerned with:

- global competencies;
- global sales and marketing; and
- global configuration and co-ordination of its value-adding activities (see the discussion of value adding in Chapter 3).

KEY CONCEPT

Multinational and transnational companies

The terms 'multinational' and 'transnational' are both commonly found in the business and *THE* literatures. The two terms are often used interchangeably, but here (following Stonehouse et al., 2007) it is argued that the difference between the two is one of emphasis on the degree of centralized control.

Both multinational and transnational companies share the feature that they are usually large and they have direct investments in one or more foreign countries. The foreign investments may be part-shareholdings, but are more usually wholly owned subsidiaries.

The difference is in the degree to which the foreign investments are co-ordinated. We tend to think of a *transnational* company as one that has a high degree of co-ordination in its international interests. It will usually have a strategic centre, which manages the global operation such that all parts act in accordance with a centrally managed strategic purpose.

The term *multinational company* is usually taken to mean an international company whose foreign interests are not co-ordinated (to a large degree) from a strategic centre.

Globalization of markets and industries

Market homogenisation

It was Levitt (1983) who first argued that changes in technology, societies, economies and politics are producing a 'global village'. By this he meant that consumer needs in many previously separate national markets were becoming increasingly similar throughout the world. It should be recognized that globalization is not without its critics. Douglas and Wind (1987), for example, critically examine the key assumptions underlying globalization and the underlying philosophy that a strategy of global products and brands is the key to success in international markets.

Segal-Horn (2004), argues that the globalization of services (including *THE*) is distinctive when compared to manufacturing. Market homogenization means that segments should be defined internationally. However, whereas in manufacturing this usually means identical products are produced in services (where standardization is more difficult) it does not usually mean providing the same product in all countries but offering 'local adaptations around a standardized core' (Segal-Horn 2004:424).

For example – in *THE* there are numerous examples of companies responding to market homogenization through what Segal-Horn describes as local adaptations around a single core. Fast food restaurants such as Burger King and McDonalds, hotel chains such as Holiday Inn and car hire companies such as Hertz and Avis exhibit such responses.

In assessing the viability of international strategies for services, emphasis is often placed on economies of scale and economies of scope (which are explained by, for example, Ghoshal, 2004). Indeed Segal-Horn asserts that many industries including travel and fast food now meet the criteria of a 'global industry' (as defined by Kobrin, 1991:18). A global industry in this definition is defined in terms of the significance of the competitive advantage of international operations arising mainly from the structural characteristics of scale economies and through technological intensity.

A categorization of some of the sources of competitive advantage derived from economies of scale and scope by service companies active internationally is shown as Table 14.1.

However, Segal-Horn also stresses the 'fuzzy' industry barriers as an important and distinctive aspect of international growth for many service providers and this facet certainly applies in *THE* contexts. Thus much of the growth has been across rather than within industry boundaries, e.g. retail/financial services; retail/leisure; leisure/travel; and travel/hospitality. Consequently, she argues that service industries should most appropriately be viewed not as discrete entities but instead as fuzzy sets of activities. This can be viewed as a similar notion to the diagonal integration which was discussed in Chapter 11, in that economies are gained by crossing the industry boundary.

For example – The American Express group is diversified both geographically and in relation to the range of its services and illustrates service growth within a fuzzy industry set of leisure/travel/financial services (Segal-Horn, 2004:425).

Table 14.1 Potential sources of economies of scale and scope in international services

Economies of scale	Economies of scope
Geographic networks	IT and shared information networks
Physical equipment	Shared learning and doing
Purchasing/supply	Product or process innovation
Marketing	Shared R&D
Logistics and distribution	Shared channels for multiple offerings
Technology	Reproduction formula for service system
Production resources	Range of services and service development
Management	Complementary services
Organization	Branding
Operational support	International franchising
Knowledge	Training
	Goodwill and corporate identity
	Culture
	Internal exploitation of economics
	Reduced transaction costs
	Know-how effects
	Privileged access to parent services

Sources: Segal-Horn (2004) and compilation from Normann (1984); Ghoshal (2004); and Enderwick (1989).

In summary, Segal-Horn (2004:425) emphasizes the importance of economies of scope (as well as scale), to the international growth of many service firms a view which is asserted in the quotation below.

DEFINITION/QUOTATION

Growth through wider scope

To generalize, 'Growth' for service firms may not involve a deepening of asset structure as in manufacturing companies, but a horizontal accretion of assets across different markets and different industries (i.e. scope).

Segal-Horn (2004:425)

Similarly, a discourse in areas of *THE* (particularly relating to tourism; visitor attractions; and festivals and events) has taken place that discusses issues of authenticity and sustainability in relation to the increasingly globalized pattern of economic development. See for example McCartney and Osti (2007); and Quinn (2005) in relation to festivals and events; and Teo (2002) for a discussion of the sustainability of tourism in the face of the pressures of globalization. McCartney uses the International Dragon Boat festival held in Hong Kong to illustrate the issues which arise. Paradoxically in relation to cultural events the increasing popularity (to global audiences) can also take away from the authentic experience, becoming more 'staged' as performances for visitors (McCartney and Osti, 2007).

However, it is now generally recognized that in some way most markets and industries are becoming more global in nature. While there is certainly still room for interpretation of what this actually means in practice we will examine some of the major implications of this trend for *THE* organizations.

Developments in technology and removal of regulatory barriers to make markets 'contestable' have increasingly enabled services to be spread throughout many countries. Furthermore, transport developments have not only made it easier to move products and materials between countries, but they have also resulted in a huge increase in the amount that people travel around the world. Such travel educates people to the products and services available in other countries and, on their return home, they often wish to have access to products and services from overseas. This trend has been reinforced by changes in information technology, particularly those related to the internet, cinema and television, which have been important in some aspects of cultural convergence.

The development of the World Trade Organization WTO (not to be confused with the other WTO – the World Tourism Organization) and its predecessor, GATT (the General Agreement on Tariffs and Trade), has resulted in huge reductions in the barriers to trade between countries since the Second World War. Rising income levels throughout many parts of the world have also given economic impetus to the development of global markets.

It is not only markets which are, in many cases, becoming more global. Industries are also becoming more global. The value chains of businesses in many industries span the globe.

For example – in the case of a diversified international tour operator, inputs in the form of tourist destinations may be sourced from many parts of the world with the supply from one country varying from year to year based on the costs of the destination relative to other competing destinations. The resulting changing expenditure patterns of tourists will have a profound direct and indirect effect on the local economies of the specific tourist destinations. Not only will spending patterns affect direct suppliers (such as restaurants, hotels, coach operators, airports, entertainment and event venues, tourist attractions and car hire firms), but indirect suppliers will also be affected. These might include garage services, food suppliers, laundry services, banking and retailing.

Global configuration of activities and outsourcing

Organizations concentrate certain of their activities in locations where they hope to obtain cost, quality or other advantages. Other activities, like distribution, are also often dispersed around the world. The way that a business configures its activities across national borders can be an important source of competitive advantage. The spread of an organization's value-adding activities around the world also means that there are important advantages to be gained from effective integration and co-ordination of activities.

In concentrating certain activities in certain locations around the world organizations have a key question to address: should we carry out the activities ourselves or should the activities be outsourced to specialist suppliers?

The main reasons for outsourcing include cost savings, a focus on core competencies, and flexibility in management (Hsu and Liou, 2013). Although cost savings are clearly a key driver in making the outsourcing decision, in their influential book, Hamel and Prahalad (1994) argue that companies which measure their competitiveness solely on the basis of price are actually contributing to the erosion of their core competencies. They assert that care must be taken to protect and nurture core competencies and consequently products and services, which are regarded as core competencies, should be produced internally.

DEFINITION/QUOTATION

Outsourcing

> Outsourcing is the contractual relationship between a client and a provider – the supplier of some service – by means of which the latter assumes the commitment to deliver that service to the former. Outsourcing is characterised by the fact that the service might be delivered internally within the client firm, but the latter achieves some benefit from outsourcing it
>
> Gonzalez *et al.* (2011)

Outsourcing (introduced in Chapter 3) has become one of the key restructuring tools for companies seeking to boost their growth and business performance (Mol, 2007), and it has been widely applied to sectors of *THE* particularly in relation to international hotel groups and airlines. Outsourcing has also been widely discussed in the academic literature in relation to these sectors see for example Lamminmaki (2005) and Espino-Rodrıguez and Padro´n-Robaina (2005) in relation to hotels; and Rieple and Helm (2008) and Hsu and Liou (2013) in relation to airlines.

Travel and tourism are different

Tourism, it can be argued is different from other services in at least one important respect. Tourism is highly visible as well as invisible in its impact and is capable of making profound societal and cultural changes, not only to host destinations but also to tourist 'exporting' areas (Evans, 2012: 221). However, we can distinguish between 'tourism' as a human phenomenon and the travel industry which facilitates the phenomenon.

The terms 'travel' and 'tourism' are both commonly used. In many circumstances they are interchangeable, or one or other of the terms is used to denote both travel *and* tourism. Indeed this book itself uses the term 'tourism' as a 'short-hand' expression, when really it relates to both travel and tourism.

The distinction between them may seem fine but it has an important implication when it comes to outsourcing.

There are of course many definitions of tourism but one commonly used definition defines tourism as: 'the temporary movement to destinations outside the normal home and workplace, the activities undertaken during the stay, and the facilities created to cater for the needs of tourists' (Mathieson and Wall, 1982:1).

Thus tourism can be viewed as a phenomenon that is essentially an activity engaged in by human beings. It includes the act of travel from one place to another, a particular set of motives for engaging in that travel and the engagement in activity at the destination (Tribe, 1997).

At the same time 'travel' can be viewed as a vast industry the growth of which has mirrored the dynamic growth of tourism as a human phenomenon. Viewed in this way tourism as an activity is destination specific – it cannot move. Sydney Harbour Bridge, The Great Wall of China or the Grand Canyon are rooted in a certain place and have to be visited at their location by tourists, i.e. they cannot be outsourced.

Thus there is a widespread assumption that tourism is an exception, an industry where global mechanisms and consequences do not come fully into play. Consequently it can be argued that tourism (as a phenomenon) cannot be 'outsourced' (Hjalager, 2007). This is due to the centrality of the 'sense of place' to tourism, and a large academic literature examines this facet (see for example Tsai, 2012, who studied the notion of place in relation to international tourists in Singapore). Tourists visit a particular place for the range of benefits offered and the benefits cannot be moved or outsourced.

However, by contrast 'travel' or more precisely the travel industry upon which tourism depends, is not constrained by place in the same way. Its activities can and are often outsourced and it is an option that managers must consider.

The same arguments about the sense of place and the immovability (or lack of outsourcing opportunities) can also be extended to hospitality and events – though arguably to a slightly lower degree.

For example, it is conceivable that The Wimbledon Tennis Championships, The Salzburg Music Festival, Hong Kong's famous Peninsula Hotel or The Paris International Air Show could be moved to another location. In doing so the essential characteristics of each (which depend in large part

> on their location) would be lost. The brand would be weakened and it would probably make little commercial sense to do so. Thus, in these cases certain aspects of the business (such as sales and marketing; 'back office' administrative functions and accounting) might be outsourced, but moving the entire product offering would be very difficult.

Though outsourcing does not necessarily involve outsourcing to a different country, in many cases or with certain functions (e.g. call-centres) it does, or domestic providers may have to bid against foreign-based providers. Outsourcing has given rise to its own specific terminology in terms of 'off-shoring' and 'near-shoring'.

- *Off-shoring* is generally taken to mean providing services in locations anywhere in the world where they can be delivered competitively through the use of technology.
- *Near-shoring* is generally taken to mean that services are located in locations either domestically or in a foreign country that is easily accessible. Near-shoring has become a recent trend as the pricing power of off-shoring destinations like China, India and the Philippines has decreased relatively due to climbing wages and fast economic growth.

The generally recognized disadvantages of outsourcing (Hsu and Liou, 2013) include:

- information security;
- loss of management control;
- staff morale problems; and
- labour union issues.

Other unanticipated problems may also occur which may serve to erode the supposed advantages attributed to outsourcing. Howells (1999) argues that many companies have found that outsourcing activities have introduced unexpected complexities, added costs and friction to the value chain, and can require more senior management attention and deeper management skills than initially anticipated.

SHORT CASE ILLUSTRATION

Outsourcing activities for airlines: Qantas

International airlines have experienced highly volatile trading conditions in recent years as high fuel prices, intense competition, economic recession and unexpected crises (such as 9/11) have affected their levels of profitability.

Assessing the relative costs or strategic benefits of outsourcing in the airline industry is therefore likely to be challenging (Rieple and Helm, 2008). The factors involved are complex; full information about costs is hard to gather and the circumstances being considered are dynamic rather than static. Nevertheless many airlines have considered outsourcing some of their activities (Al-Kaabi et al., 2007; Hsu and Liou, 2013) particularly in relation to maintenance, repair and overhaul (MRO), but also in relation to sales and marketing, ICT support and technical support.

Specialist companies such as Navitaire, (a wholly owned subsidiary of the major international management consultant Accenture), have emerged to aid airlines, and other companies in facilitating the outsourcing of some of their functions. Navitaire claims to have helped 70 airlines as their website points out:

It is more critical than ever to streamline operations without compromising service quality. Navitaire, a wholly owned Accenture subsidiary, can help airlines achieve high performance by assuming responsibility for many key processes, including reservations, Internet and direct distribution; flight operations and operations recovery; and revenue accounting. Navitaire provides industry-leading technology services to more than 70 of the world's airlines.

For example – Australian airline Qantas (which has a major code-sharing agreement with Emirates) has endured poor recent performance with an operating loss being recorded in 2013. Consequently the airline has focused strongly on its cost base and one of the operational moves it has made is to announce during 2013 that it was shutting its heavy maintenance base at Avalon Airport in the state of Victoria with the loss of up to 300 jobs. Although the airline continues to have maintenance facilities at Sydney and Brisbane it was reported (Creedy, 2014) that where the aircraft fleet sizes are small or sub-scale, like the Airbus A380, Qantas would carry out heavy maintenance at overseas providers such as Singapore, Hong Kong or UK, because it was not economic to carry out the work in Australia.

www.accenture.com/; www.qantas.com.au; *Al-Kaabi et al. (2007)*;
Creedy (2014); Rieple and Helm (2008); and *Hsu and Liou (2013).*

Questions

1. Explain the potential advantages of outsourcing to an airline such as Qantas?

2. What difficulties might Qantas need to overcome in implementing its outsourcing?

Internationalization and globalization – the approaches of Porter and Yip

There are several models which seek to explain the basis of international and global strategy. This chapter explains the frameworks developed by Porter (1986 and 1990) and Yip (1992).

- *Porter* – focuses on adapting the generic strategy framework to global conditions and the role of configuration and co-ordination of value-adding activities in securing global competitive advantage.

- *Yip* – develops the concept of Total Global Strategy based upon his globalization driver framework.

Although these are the models considered in this chapter, interested readers should consider reading the work of Bartlett and Ghoshal (1987 and 1989), Prahalad and Hamel (1985) and Stonehouse *et al.* (1999).

Mirroring the general business literature, there is also a large developing literature on globalization and its impacts on the development of *THE* sectors.

For example – Wahab and Cooper (2001) consider various aspects of tourism in relation to global issues while Hjalager (2007) reviews the literature on the topic and examines the stages tourism goes through in the process of globalization. There is a great deal of literature which focuses on the hotel and airline sectors in particular. Go and Pine (1995) and Whitla *et al.* (2007) contain conceptual and practical insights into the globalization issues facing hotels. Hanlon (2007) and Ramón-Rodríguez *et al.* (2011) outline the unique set of factors facing aviation in relation to international and global issues. The literature relating to internationalization and globalization of festivals and events is more sparse though Matheson *et al.* (2006) consider globalization in relation to Singapore festivals.

Multi-domesticity

Porter (1990) argues that industries can be either global or *multi-domestic*. Multi-domestic industries are those where competition in each nation is essentially independent. He gives the example of consumer banking (as opposed to investment banking) where a bank's domestic reputation and resources in one nation have tended to have little effect on its success in other countries. The international banking industry is, Porter agues, essentially a collection of domestic industries.

Global industries are those in which competition is global. The consumer electronics industry is a good example where companies like Philips, Sony, Apple, Siemens, LG and Panasonic compete in almost all countries of the world. The implication would appear to be that businesses should adopt a global strategy in global industries and a multi-local strategy in multi-domestic markets. Yet the situation is not so simple as this. Even markets like consumer banking are becoming more global. The trend is for most industries to become more global, but even within industries major differences may occur.

One way of viewing globalization is as a continuum from globalization through international to local or multi-domestic (as shown in Figure 14.1).

In *THE*, the large global distribution systems (such as Galileo, Amadeus and Sabre) have a global reach, whereas towards the other end of the continuum most retail travel agents and rail and bus operators might be viewed as towards the multi-domestic end of the continuum in their orientation. Large airlines often like to portray themselves as 'global' carriers, but close inspection of their route networks reveals that no carrier serves all parts of the world and even in those countries which are served, it is usually only the largest city that is served.

Similarly, the large international hotel chains have expanded to include many countries, but rarely penetrate local markets beyond the principal cities. By way of contrast, the major soft drinks brands such as Coca Cola are widely available throughout the world and are widely dispersed within individual countries.

Porter's global generic strategies

Porter (1980) argues (see Chapter 8) that competitive advantage rests upon an organization selecting and adopting one of three generic strategies to modify the five competitive forces in its favour so as to earn higher profits than the industry average.

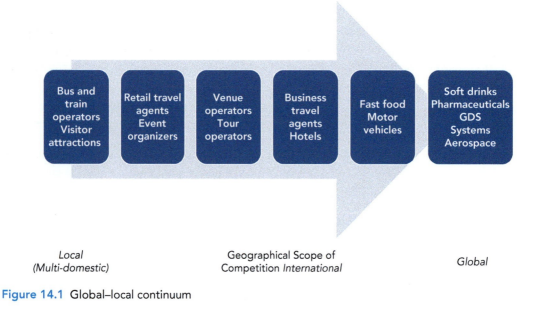

Bus and train operators Visitor attractions | Retail travel agents Event organizers | Venue operators Tour operators | Business travel agents Hotels | Fast food Motor vehicles | Soft drinks Pharmaceuticals GDS Systems Aerospace

Local (Multi-domestic)   Geographical Scope of Competition *International*   *Global*

Figure 14.1 Global–local continuum

The three generic strategies are:

- differentiation;
- cost leadership; or
- focus.

In 1986 Porter extended the generic strategy framework to global business.

The model suggests that a business operating in international markets has five strategy alternatives (as shown in Figure 14.2). The five strategic postures are defined according to their position in respect to two intersecting continua:

- The extent to which the industry is globalized or country-centred (horizontal axis).
- The breadth of the segments (different customer groups) served by the competitors in an industry.

The five strategic positions are described below.

- *Global cost leadership* – the organization seeks to be the lowest-cost producer of a product globally. Globalization provides the opportunity for high-volume sales and greater economies of scale and scope than domestic competitors.
- *Global differentiation* – the organization seeks to differentiate products and services globally, often on the basis of a global brand name.
- *Global segmentation* – this is the global variant of a focus strategy when a single market segment is targeted on a worldwide basis employing either cost leadership or differentiation.
- *Protected markets* – an organization identifies national markets where its particular organization is favoured or protected by the host government.
- *National responsiveness* – the organization adapts its strategy to meet the distinctive needs of local markets (i.e. not a global strategy). Suitable for purely domestic organizations.

The model suffers from similar flaws to those discussed in Chapter 8 relating to the generic strategy framework. As in the case of the conventional understanding of generic strategy, it is possible for a business to pursue a hybrid international strategy.

For example – some of the low-cost airlines, such as easyJet, Air Asia and Ryanair, clearly are concerned with strict adherence to cost control as their label as 'low-cost' suggests. At the same time, however, they are increasingly seeking to differentiate themselves from each other and from the established 'flag-carriers' by having very young aircraft fleets and by adding features such as priority boarding and pre-allocated seating to their business models.

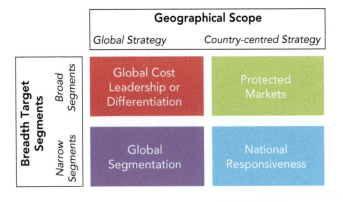

Figure 14.2 Porter's global strategy framework

Porter's global strategy – configuration and co-ordination of internal activities

One of Porter's most important contributions to understanding global strategy is his work on the global value chain (1986b and 1990). Porter makes the case that global competitive advantage depends upon *configuring* and *co-ordinating* the activities of a business in a unique way on a worldwide basis. To put it another way, competitive advantage results from the global scope of an organization's activities and the effectiveness with which it co-ordinates them. Porter (1986b, 1990) argues that global competitive advantage depends upon two sets of decisions:

- *Configuration of value-adding activities* – Managers must decide in which nations they will carry out each of the activities in the value chain of their business. Configuration can be broad (involving many countries) or narrow (involving few countries or one only).

- *Co-ordination of value-adding activities* – Managers must decide the most effective way of co-ordinating value-adding activities, which are carried out in different parts of the world.

Configuration and co-ordination present four broad alternatives illustrated in Figure 14.3.

In the case of configuration, an organization can choose to disperse its activities to a range of locations around the world or it may choose to concentrate key activities in locations which present certain advantages. Many businesses concentrate their operations in countries where costs are low but skill levels are high.

For example – many *THE* (and other) companies have chosen to base call-centre operations and 'back office' functions in countries such as India and the Philippines because they can gain access to high-quality English-speaking employees at relatively low cost.

An organization can decide to co-ordinate its worldwide activities or to manage them locally in each part of the world. The latter approach misses the opportunity for global management economies of scale and scope. For Porter, the 'purest global strategy' is when an organization concentrates key activities in locations giving competitive advantages and co-ordinates activities on a global basis. In the long term, according to Porter, organizations should move towards 'purest global strategy' as far as is practicable.

It is also the case that the degree of globalization of an industry or market may not be uniform. In other words some aspects of an industry or market may be indicative of globalization while others may be indicative of localization.

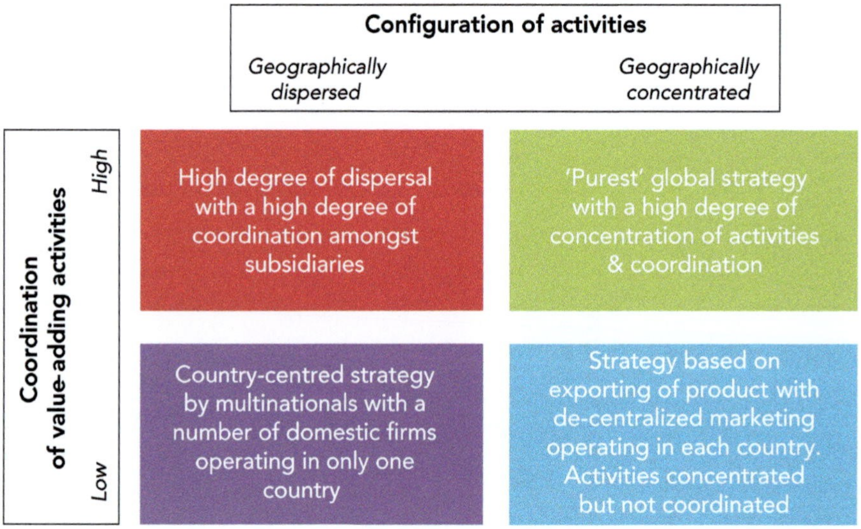

Figure 14.3 Configuration and coordination for international strategy

Configuration of activities

	Geographically dispersed	Geographically concentrated
Coordination of value-adding activities — High	High degree of dispersal with a high degree of coordination amongst subsidiaries	'Purest' global strategy with a high degree of concentration of activities & coordination
Coordination of value-adding activities — Low	Country-centred strategy by multinationals with a number of domestic firms operating in only one country	Strategy based on exporting of product with de-centralized marketing operating in each country. Activities concentrated but not coordinated

The degree of globalization of an industry can be assessed using Yip's globalization driver framework (1992). This widely used framework is generally a more useful framework than Porter's because it makes it possible to evaluate both the overall degree of globalization of an industry and which features of the industry are more or less global in nature.

Yip's framework – globalization drivers

Yip (1992) argues that it is not simply the case that industries are 'global' or 'not global', rather that they can be global in some respects and not in others.

Yip's globalization driver framework shown in Figure 14.4, makes it possible to identify which aspects of an industry are global and which aspects differ locally. Analysis using this framework can play an important role in shaping the global strategy of a business. A global strategy, according to Yip, will be global in many respects but may also include features which are locally oriented.

Yip argues that 'to achieve the benefits of globalization, the managers of a worldwide business need to recognise when industry conditions provide the opportunity to use global strategy levers'.

Yip identifies four drivers (shown in Figure 14.4), which determine the nature and extent of globalization in an industry. These are:

- market drivers;
- cost drivers;
- government drivers; and
- competitive drivers.

The various aspects of each of these drivers are summarized in Table 14.2 and each of these drivers is considered in turn below.

Market globalization drivers

The degree of globalization of a market will depend upon the extent to which there are common customer needs, global customers, global distribution channels, transferable marketing and lead countries. It is not

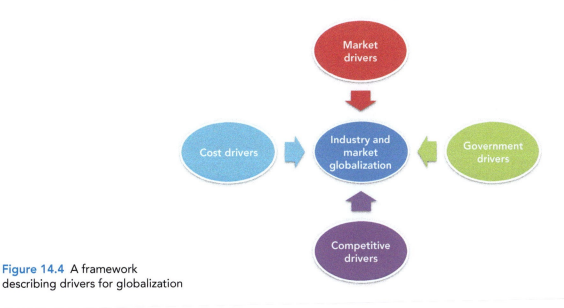

Figure 14.4 A framework describing drivers for globalization

Table 14.2 A summary of the globalization drivers

Market drivers	Cost drivers
Common customer needs	Global scale economies
Global customers	Steep experience curve effect
Global distribution channels	Sourcing efficiencies
Transferable marketing techniques	Differences in country costs (including exchange
Presence in lead countries	rates)
	High product development costs
	Fast changing technology
Government drivers	**Competitive drivers**
Favourable trade policies	High exports and imports
Common marketing regulations	Competitors from different continents
Government owned competitors and customers	Interdependence of countries
Compatible technical standards & common	Competitors globalized
Marketing regulations	
Host government concerns	

simply a case of a market being global or not global. Managers must seek to establish which, if any, aspects of their market are global.

Common customer needs

Probably the single most important market globalization driver is the extent to which customers in different countries share the same need or want for a product. The extent of shared need will depend upon cultural, economic, climatic, legal and other similarities and differences. There are numerous examples of markets where customer needs are becoming more similar. Examples include motor vehicles, soft drinks, fast food. Examples also extend to *THE* where beach and ski resorts, cruise ships, global tours by bands, film and cinema and business travel might be cited.

For example – international business travel is highly fragmented, but a few large internationally diversified companies have emerged (see the BCD illustrative case below) to service the needs of customers around the world. These suppliers include networks of international companies or franchisees such as Uniglobe Travel International, based in Vancouver, Canada; and UK based Travel Solutions International (TSI) and GlobalStar. Some large travel management companies have also developed such as American based Carlson Wagonlit Travel and American Express; UK based Hogg Robinson Group (HRG); and the Dutch based company BCD. In addition many tour operators, leisure based travel agents and hotel companies also operate subsidiaries to service corporate travel management requirements.

Similarly, the various hospitality brands operated by international hotel groups such as Marriott Corporation as well as McDonald's, Burger King and Pizza Hut in fast food, or Coca Cola and Pepsi Cola in soft drinks are all illustrative of converging customer needs in certain markets. Levitt (1983) refers to this similarity of tastes and preference as increasing *market homogenization* – all markets demanding the same products, regardless of their domestic culture and traditional preferences.

SHORT CASE ILLUSTRATION

Market globalization drivers: BCD, international corporate travel management

Corporate Travel Management (CTM) is a diverse field of activity which concerns the strategic management of the travel arrangements for organizations. Many organizations carry out this activity for themselves as an internal function, but many others contract the activity out to other suppliers. The market for supplying organizations is highly fragmented and varies considerably between countries, but a few large internationally diversified suppliers have emerged as multinational corporations have spread their activities.

Services carried out by such companies for their clients differ but include:

- planning and booking travel arrangements for companies at advantageous rates;
- analysing travel market trends and providing consultancy and advice services;
- assessing the risks associated with travel to particular locations;
- documenting travel arrangements and reporting on expenditure; and
- providing visa, passport and foreign currency services.

The large corporate travel management companies (or 'business travel agents' as they are sometimes referred to) are often not well-known consumer brands, but nevertheless constitute sizeable entities.

These companies include BCD; a Dutch privately owned company based in Utrecht, Netherlands. The company which was founded in the 1980s and operates from about 1,500 locations in 97 countries has sales totalling US$21.2 billion. The company operates a wide range of travel management products to meet the demands of internationally based corporate clients. The BCD corporate brochure emphasizes the changing nature of corporate travel:

> The next generation of corporate travel will bear little resemblance to today. The demands of travellers, the promise of technology and the escalating sophistication of corporations will paint a new landscape yet to be envisioned. . . .We see our core business as delivering solutions that serve ever changing business drivers.

The BCD corporate brochure goes on to outline some of the changes taking place which 'are the distinguishing landmarks in the unfolding landscape of corporate travel and meetings management':

- content disaggregation across multiple distribution platforms;
- evolving traveller expectations and services;
- enhanced virtual meeting systems; and
- post-recession business travel behaviour.

Adapted from BCD (2011)

Questions

1. What would you consider to be the principal drivers of globalization in BCD's case?
2. What are the main activities carried out by CTM companies such as BCD and why might the activities be viewed as strategically important for multinational companies?

Global customers and channels

Global customers purchase products or services in a co-ordinated way from the best global sources. Yip identifies two types of global customers:

1. *National global customers* – Customers who seek the best suppliers in the world and then use the product or service in one country.

   For example – a theme park operator might seek the best rides from many countries which are known for providing specialist engineering skills such as Germany, Switzerland, USA and Japan.

2. *Multinational global customers* – they similarly seek the best suppliers in the world but then use the product or service obtained in many countries.

   For example – Cruise lines source their ships from a number of companies in certain countries which are known for building cruise ships such as Finland, France, Germany, Italy and Japan to ensure optimal quality standards delivered at a competitive price. They then use and market the product in many countries.

Alongside global customers there are sometimes global, or more often regional, distribution channels, which serve the global customers. Global customers and channels will contribute towards the development of a global market.

Transferable marketing

Transferable marketing describes the extent to which elements of the marketing mix like brand names and promotions can be used globally without local adaptations.

Clearly, when adaptation is not required it is indicative of a global market. In this way brands like McDonald's, Coca Cola and Nike are used globally, and increasingly travel brands such as Hilton, Thomas Cook and Lufthansa also have global recognition. Yet advertising for such brands can be both global and locally adapted according to the prevailing attitudes in local markets. If marketing is transferable it will favour a global market.

Lead countries

When, as Porter (1990) found, there are certain countries which lead in particular industries, then it becomes critical for global competitors to participate in these lead countries in order to be exposed to the sources of innovation.

Lead countries are those that are ahead in product and/or process innovation in their industry. These lead countries help to produce global standards and hence global industries and markets.

For example – the USA would clearly been seen as the lead country in terms of internet travel distribution systems, airline operations and new hotel and accommodation formats whilst European companies have taken a lead in developing vertically and horizontally diversified leisure travel companies (such as Tui and Thomas Cook). A number of Asian airports such as Singapore, Hong Kong and Kuala Lumpur are consistently ranked among the world's best for the quality of customer experience.

Cost globalization drivers

The potential to reduce costs by global configuration of value-adding activities is an important spur towards the globalization of certain industries. If there are substantial cost advantages to be obtained then an industry will tend to be global.

For example – the international strategic alliances such as Skyteam, OneWorld and Star that have emerged in the airline industry have done so partly due to the need to add value to their customers by being able to offer global connectivity. However their attraction to individual airlines also lies in their ability to save costs (such as business lounges, sales and marketing and procurement) through working cooperatively with other airlines.

Global scale economies

When an organization serves a global market then it is able to gain much greater economies of scale than if it serves only domestic or regional markets. Similarly, serving global markets also gives considerable potential for economies of scope. The differences between scale and scope economies are explained in the Key Concept below.

For example – internationally diversified *THE* companies such as Air France-KLM, Disney, Accor or TUI, which market their activities in many countries, gain large economies of scope in product development, marketing, procurement and financing.

KEY CONCEPT

Economies of scale and scope

Economies of scope and scale are both widely used terms (for a discussion see Ghoshal, 2004), but it is important to understand the differences and be able to apply the terms correctly in various *THE* contexts. The terms are also widely used in the globalization literature.

Economies of scale – describe the benefits that are gained when increasing volume results in lower unit costs.

Although economies of scale can arise in all parts of the value chain, it is probably best understood by illustrating it using purchasing as an example. An individual purchasing one hotel room will pay more *per item* than a large company contracting to purchase hundreds of hotel rooms to provide for their customers for the season. Thus the purchaser who is able to purchase in bulk (because of the size and structure of the buyer) enjoys scale economies over smaller organizations that buy in at lower volumes.

Economies of scope – describe the benefits that can arise in one product or market area as a result of activity in another.

Another way of putting it is that the cost of providing two distinct offers from the same organization is less than providing both separately. Thus if a tour operator expands to market its activities in another country, the costs of the marketing activity can be shared with the activity in the countries in which it already operates through joint advertising, promotion and so on. Website development costs and brochure production costs can be shared between the various markets. Similarly skilled and experienced staff can be transferred from one country to another to share the skills and expertise they have learned in a different market situation.

Steep experience curve effect

When there is a steep learning curve in operations and marketing, businesses serving global markets will tend to obtain the greatest benefits. In many service industries there are steep learning curves yielding the greatest benefits to global businesses.

Experience and good practices from one country can be shared with other countries and regions thereby increasing organizational learning and experience. Those organizations that are able to communicate the lessons from their experience i.e. learning around the organization quickly and effectively are likely to be the most successful in global markets.

For example – for an international hotel group expanding internationally it is crucial that they get their market entry strategy right. However, experience of entering other country markets will help them make the correct decisions when they choose to enter subsequent markets.

KEY CONCEPT

Learning curve

The idea of the learning curve has been used in many areas of life – not just in business. It describes the rate at which an individual or an organization learns to perform a particular task. The gradient of the beginning of the curve is referred to as its 'steepness' and is the most important part. The steeper this first part, the quicker the task is being learned. The general shape of a learning curve is described as *exponential* because the gradient usually decreases along its length as the time taken to perform the task decreases as those performing the task become more accomplished at it.

Sourcing efficiencies

If there are efficiency gains to be made by centralized sourcing carried out globally then this will drive an industry towards globalization. Businesses like those in sports apparel and fashion clothing benefit from global sourcing to obtain lowest prices and highest quality standards.

For example – cruise lines and airlines seeking crew and purchasing ships and aircraft will seek sourcing efficiencies by seeking labour and equipment in the most cost-efficient ways. Many cruise lines select many crew members from Asian countries where good-quality staff members can be recruited at internationally competitive wage rates.

Favourable logistics

If transportation costs comprise a relatively high proportion of sales value, there will be every incentive to concentrate operations. If transport costs are relatively small, such as with consumer electronic goods, production can be located in several locations (thus favouring globalization of activities), which are chosen on the basis of other cost criteria such as land or labour costs.

Differences in country costs

Operational costs (building, labour, etc.) vary from country to country which can stimulate or impede globalization. Thus, countries with lower operational costs will tend to attract businesses to locate activities in the country.

For example – many Asian countries have attracted international hotel chains because of their favourable cost conditions and availability of high-quality labour at reasonable cost (as well as growing demand). Similarly aircraft and ship maintenance and repair is often outsourced to countries with lower labour costs.

Fast changing technology and high product development costs

Product life cycles are shortening as the pace of technological change increases and consumers are becoming more discerning. At the same time research and development (R&D) costs are increasing in many industries. Such product development costs can only be recouped by high sales in global markets. Domestic markets simply do not yield the volumes of sales required to cover high R&D costs, particularly where the domestic market is small.

For example – cruise lines and airlines face very rapidly changing technology and greater degrees of competition, together with high development and equipment purchase costs. These are facets they share with other industries such as pharmaceuticals and automobiles. As a consequence they must operate in global markets so as to ensure they achieve the volumes of sales necessary to recoup these costs.

Government globalization drivers

Since the Second World War many governments have taken individual and collective action to reduce barriers to global trade.

Favourable trade policies

The World Trade Organization and its predecessor, the General Agreement on Tariffs and Trade, have done much to reduce barriers to trade, which have, in the past, hindered globalization of many industries. Although there are still significant barriers to trade in certain areas, the movement towards freedom of trade has been substantial, thus favouring globalization. The growth of customs unions and 'single markets' such as the European Union (EU) and the North American Free Trade Area (NAFTA) have also made an important contribution in this regard.

For example – the airline sector has since its inception been subject to government regulation driven by the need for safety standards and the view that airlines represented important and prestigious national assets. This began to change in the late 1970s when airline deregulation occurred in the USA in 1978 and was followed by Europe in the 1990s and subsequently spread to many other parts of the world. Ownership of airlines by foreign carriers remains as a constraint to full deregulation however.

Compatible technical standards and common marketing regulations

Many of the differences in technical standards between countries, which hindered globalization in the past, have been reduced.

For example – telecommunications standards, which have traditionally differed between countries, are increasingly being superseded by international standards. Similarly standards are converging in the pharmaceutical, airline, and computing industries, which make it easier to produce globally accepted products.

Airlines and shipping have long had common safety standards coordinated through United Nations agencies, as countries have seen it necessary to alleviate consumer safety concerns through having common standards. Shipping, including cruising, is regulated by the International Maritime Organization (IMO). IMO is the London-based, United Nations specialist agency with responsibility for the safety and security of shipping and the prevention of marine pollution by ships.

Similarly, the International Civil Aviation Organization (ICAO) was created in 1944 as another specialist agency of the United Nations to promote the safe and orderly development of international civil aviation throughout the world. Based in Montreal, Canada, the agency sets standards and regulations necessary for aviation safety, security, efficiency and regularity, as well as for aviation environmental protection.

There remain important differences in advertising regulations between countries, but generally, however, these differences are being eroded (albeit slowly) and this serves to favour greater degrees of globalization.

Government-owned competitors and customers

Government-owned competitors, which often enjoy state subsidies and other benefits, can act as a stimulus or a barrier to globalization. They frequently compete with other global competitors, thus being forced to become more efficient and global-market-oriented. On the other hand, government-owned competitors can make it very difficult for other competitors to compete in their home market (since they do not enjoy the same benefits).

There has however been a growing trend towards the privatization of many state-owned businesses in many countries in the world which has reduced this barrier to globalization. Thus government-owned hotel, shipping and airline companies have been sold to the private sector so that governents can concentrate their scarce resources in other areas of activity.

For example – in recent years many governments around the world have chosen to bring private capital and management techniques into the management of state assets such as hotels, airports and other transport infrastructure and airlines. The process of wholly or partly privatizing state assets has been facilitated by factors such as the decline in communism, the need for governments to raise money and reduce their debts, and the recognition that such assets need specialist management skills. The European states of Croatia and Slovenia (amongst others) have privatised state-run hotels in recent years. Assaf and Cvelbar (2010) report that in relation to Slovenian hotels privatization has led to an improved level of performance. Similarly Park *et al.* (2011) evaluate the possible effects of privatization on Incheon International Airport in Seoul, South Korea.

Host government concerns

The attitudes and policies of host government concerns can either hinder or favour globalization.

In certain circumstances, host governments may favour the entry of global businesses into domestic industries and markets and may provide financial or non-financial assistance to do so. Such measures will assist the process of globalization.

For example – in a study of foreign direct investment (FDI) in tourism and related sectors, Endo (2006) states that many countries, including both developed (e.g. Australia, Canada, Switzerland) and developing (e.g. Egypt, India, Jamaica, Kenya), are offering some sort of incentives to tourism-related activities to attract domestic and foreign investors.

The more governments espouse such policies, the greater will be the globalization of an industry. Conversely, in other cases, host governments will seek to protect industries, which they see as strategically important and will attempt to prevent foreign businesses from entry. In these circumstances the legal restrictions placed on competition by governments act as a barrier to the globalization process.

For example – many countries such as the USA limit the ownership of their airlines by foreign companies and restrict access to domestic airline routes for foreign-based competitors.

Competitive globalization drivers

The greater the strength of the competitive drivers the greater will be the tendency for an industry to globalize. Global competition in an industry will become more intense when:

- there is a high level of trade between countries;
- the competitors in the industry are widely spread (they will often be on different continents);
- the economies of the countries involved are interdependent; and
- competitors in the industry are already globalized.

High exports and imports

The higher the level of trade in products and services between countries the greater will be the pressure for globalization of an industry.

Competitors from different continents

The more countries that are represented in an industry and the more widely spread they are, the greater the likelihood of globalization.

Interdependence of countries

If national economies are already relatively interdependent then this will act as a stimulus for increased globalization. Such interdependence may arise through, for example, multiple trading links in other industries, through being a part of a single market or through being in a shared political alliance.

Competitors globalized

If a competitor is already globalized and employing a global strategy then there will be pressure on other businesses in the industry to globalize as well. Globalization in the business travel sector is high because of the pressure on organizations to compete globally.

For example – travel agents which specialize in providing travel arrangements for business customers, so-called corporate travel management companies (such as BCD illustrated previously), are often required to serve the needs of their customers who are themselves global companies. Such companies often wish to deal with an organization, which is able to service its travel needs on a global basis i.e. a company that offers potential *economies of scope*.

Using the globalization driver framework

Yip's globalization driver framework provides a useful tool for analysing the degree of globalization of an industry or market. Equally, it makes possible an understanding of which particular aspects of an industry or market are global and which aspects are localized.

Each of the drivers must be analysed for the industry and market under consideration and the results of the analysis will play an important role in assisting managers to form the global strategy of their organization. It is important that strategy should be fit for purpose in that some aspects of strategy might be standardized across many countries whereas others to be successfully implemented need to be modified for local conditions.

Total global strategy – Yip's stages in total global strategy

Yip (1992) argues that successful global strategy must be based upon a comprehensive globalization analysis of the drivers encountered above.

Managers of a global business must, he contends, evaluate the globalization drivers for their industry and market and must formulate their global strategy on the basis of this analysis. If, for example, they find that customer demand is largely homogeneous for their product then they can produce a largely standardized product for sale throughout the world. If, on the other hand they find that there are few cost advantages of global concentration of operations because of adverse economies of scale or scope, they may choose to disperse their operational activities around the world to be close to their customers in different parts of the world.

The 'total global strategy' of an organization can be a mix of standardization and local adaptation as market and industry conditions dictate.

Thus, the results of the analysis will help to determine:

- Which features of the strategy are globally standardized?
- Which features of the strategy are locally adapted?

Yip goes on to identify three stages in developing a 'total global strategy'.

- *Developing a core strategy* – This will, in effect, involve building core competencies and generic or hybrid strategy which can potentially give global competitive advantage.
- *Internationalising the core strategy* – This will be the stage at which the core competencies and generic strategy are introduced to international markets and when the organization begins to locate its value-adding activities in locations where competitive advantages like low-cost access to resources are available. This will include choice of which markets the business will enter and the means by which it will enter them.
- *Globalizing the international strategy* – This stage is based upon coordinating and integrating the core competencies and strategy on a global basis. It will also include deciding which elements of the strategy are to be standardized and which are to be locally adapted on the basis of the strength of the globalization drivers in the industry and market.

SHORT CASE ILLUSTRATION

Internationalizing events: Rugby Sevens

Top-level sport is by its nature international. If you want to be the best in any sport it has to be proven through international competition. International sport is also highly competitive in a different sense. The various sports vie with each other for international attention, global television audiences and global success.

Football, particularly the large European leagues (Spain's Primera División; Germany's Bundesliga; England's Premier League and Italy's Serie A) and the World Cup held every four years command global attention as do the Olympic Games and American Football. Other sports have to compete for such attention.

One of the ways managers of many sports have competed is by 'internationalizing' sports events by organizing sports events in countries around the world thereby spreading interest and raising commercial revenue. Thus the sports of tennis, golf, motor racing, snooker and badminton for example have successful and growing tours where events are staged in succession in countries around the world. In some cases, such as the annual lucrative Formula 1 Motor Racing tour, cities compete with each other for the rights to stage one of the events. In recent years Singapore was successful in this process and in 2008 staged the world's first F1 Grand Prix at night on its Marina Bay circuit.

Rugby Union is a physical contact sport played with 15 players on each side which originated in late nineteenth-century England at Rugby School – hence the name. It has grown to become a worldwide sport with a loyal following, but success in this physically demanding sport has been concentrated in relatively few countries with New Zealand having the pre-eminent record of achievement in the sport. The Rugby World Cup organized by the sport's governing body (the International Rugby Board) held every four years since 1987 has spread interest in the game.

However, the game has complex rules, is usually played in winter and it is difficult to win without having physically large players; all of which serve somewhat to inhibit its global reach.

As with other sports (such as cricket and football) shorter, faster versions of the game have been developed to help spread its appeal. Thus, rugby sevens (which itself has a long history) has spread in recent years as the game has secured commercial sponsorship and television coverage. With a version of the game involving seven players it has developed rapidly to become a 'global' game with an annual worldwide series of events and Olympic recognition in Rio de Janeiro, 2016.

International competitions have featured for many years with the Hong Kong Sevens competition (dating from 1976) attracting international tourists to Hong Kong from many countries for the annual competition and playing a significant part in raising the tourist profile of the Special Administrative Region. The sevens form of the game is played throughout the year, is less physically demanding but favours athleticism and is far shorter in length, with simpler rules. As a result it lends itself to tournament rather than one-off formats, can be followed more easily by casual spectators rather than rugby aficionados, and represents an attractive package for television.

The profile of sevens rugby has grown considerably with the advent of the HSBC Sevens World Series which is an annual series of international tournaments run by the International Rugby Board featuring national teams and sponsored by HSBC bank. The series, organized for the first time in the 1999–2000 season, was formed to develop an elite-level competition series between rugby nations and develop the sevens game into a viable commercial product for the IRB. The series has developed into an annual competition held between October and April at nine venues around the world in: Australia; Dubai; South Africa; USA; New Zealand; Japan; South Africa; Scotland and England. Since its inception teams from some 36 countries have been involved, and both spectator numbers and television revenues have increased considerably.

Questions

1. How would you categorize the international growth of sevens rugby utilizing the concepts of Yip and Porter covered in this chapter?
2. What are the difficulties and opportunities that might be encountered in internationalizing in this way?

Key strategic decisions

Once a business has developed core competencies and strategies which can potentially be exploited internationally and potentially globally, the decisions must be made as to where and how to employ them. Initial moves into overseas markets will involve *market development* as such markets and segments can be regarded as new to the business. The initial market development may then be followed by product development and, perhaps diversification (see Chapter 10).

When a business enters international and global markets it will be necessary to build new competencies, alongside those which have brought about domestic competitive advantage. These new competencies could well be in the areas of global sourcing and logistics, and global management.

The globalization of a business does not happen overnight. It may well involve entry to key countries with the largest markets first, followed by entry to less important countries later. In the initial stages of globalization the key decisions are usually as follows:

- Which countries are to be entered first?
- In which countries are value-adding activities to be located?
- Which market development strategies are to be employed to gain entry to chosen overseas markets?

THINK POINTS

Using relevant examples from *THE*:

- Explain each of Yip's globalization drivers.
- Explain how Porter develops the generic strategy framework to apply to global strategy.
- Explain the importance of configuration and co-ordination of value-adding activities to global strategy.

Market entry decisions

Decision criteria

The interest in market entry strategy derives from the internationalization and globalization frameworks and can be viewed as one of the most critical strategic decisions for an organization (Root, 1994). There has been extensive research into market entry strategies and several models and theories have emerged to understand and explain this phenomenon. Canabal and White (2008) summarize and evaluate the literature in this field.

Much of the research related to market entry relates to manufacturing as opposed to services and it can be argued (as elsewhere in this book), that there are crucial differences between services, including *THE*, and manufacturing. These differences in relation to foreign market entry are outlined by Brouthers and Brouthers (2003) and Ekeledo and Sivakumar (2004).

Additionally there is also a growing literature which relates specifically to market entry decisions for *THE* organizations, though it is heavily skewed towards the hotel sector (see for example Quer *et al.*, 2007 and Choi and Parsa, 2012).

The decision as to which countries and markets are to be entered first will be based upon a number of important factors.

- *The potential size of the market* – is the market for the product in the country likely to be significant? This will, in turn, be determined by the factors following.
- *Economic factors* – are income levels adequate to ensure that significant numbers of people are likely to be able to afford the product?
- *Cultural and linguistic factors* – is the culture of the country likely to favour acceptance of the product to be offered?
- *Political factors* – what are the factors that may limit entry to markets in the host country?
- *Technological factors* – are levels of technology adequate to support provision of the product in the host market and are technological standards compatible?

To begin with, a business will choose to enter markets in those countries where the above conditions are most favourable.

The case illustration below outlines the balance of risk and opportunity encountered by Tui in entering the Russian and CIS markets and how the company has chosen to deal with the circumstances that it faces.

SHORT CASE ILLUSTRATION

Market entry decisions: Tui enters Russia

Entering a new foreign market is one of the riskiest decisions a business can take and one that must be taken with great care having analysed not only the opportunities of the market itself but also the means of market entry.

The Russian market presents particular challenges and companies such as furniture company Ikea have in the past made costly mistakes. Russia is a vast country with a business culture which is still evolving in the post-communist period; weak legal protection for foreign investors and consumers who are generally inexperienced travellers. Nevertheless Russia and the former soviet states generally referred to as Commonwealth of Independent States (CIS); represent enormous opportunities for foreign tour operators. The harsh winters, over 200 million consumers and few large existing competitors make Russia and CIS attractive markets for outbound travel.

TUI Travel plc is one of the world's leading leisure travel groups, operating in approximately 180 countries worldwide and comprising over 240 brands. Its core source markets, which include UK and Ireland, Germany, France and Scandinavia are mature and growing relatively slowly, hence the need to consider new growth opportunities. Its tour operating strategy is capable of being 'stretched' in that it is similar (with some local adaptation) in all its core source markets. It relies on its:

Content – unique inclusive (packaged) holidays and tailor-made holidays;

Brands and distribution – market-leading brands; trusted brands for safety and security, and high levels of controlled distribution with a focus on online;

Technology – flexible technological platforms to support growth;

Growth and scale – ability to leverage the advantages of scale; and

People – provide the business with knowledge and expertise and drive innovation.

Tui identified the potential for travel growth in Russia and CIS in the early years of this century, but despite its power and size chose not to develop on its own. In 2009 a joint venture company was formed with S-Group Capital Management a Russian group controlled by Russian oligarch Alexei Mordashov, (who also controls a large steel company Severstal). S-Group which also owns 25 per cent of Tui's majority shareholder (Germany's Tui AG) has vital knowledge and experience of the Russian market to match the international travel expertise provided by Tui.

Since forming the joint venture Tui Russia acquired a number of Russian and Ukrainian tour operators and set up a network of travel agencies. Thus Tui Russia and CIS's market entry strategy involved a combination of a joint venture and vertical integration and by 2013 Tui was able to state in its annual report that:

We have established a significant presence in the fast-growing Russian and CIS markets as part of our longer-term growth strategy and these businesses are now starting to reach critical mass. During the year, we consolidated our existing businesses into a single brand (Tui) featuring all destinations, establishing a strong platform for the future. The sector now has close to 600,000 customers, up 15 per cent on prior year.

http://www.tuitravelplc.com *and* www.sgcm.ru

Questions

1. What other market entry methods might Tui have considered?

2. What are the main risks that might Tui might encounter in entering a country like Russia and what steps is the company taking to overcome them?

Location of value-adding activities

Managers must determine within which countries they will locate key value-adding activities of their business. They will seek to gain cost, skill and resource advantages. In other words, they will attempt to locate activities in countries where there are operational advantages to be gained.

Such advantages depend upon:

- *wage levels* – low wage levels will assist in low operational costs;
- *skill levels* – there must be suitably skilled labour available;
- *availability of resources* – suitable resources must be accessible;
- *infrastructure* – transport, communications and ICT must be favourable to the logistics of the business.

The existence of these conditions within a country will, in turn, depend upon:

- *economic factors* – level of economic development, wage levels, exchange rate conditions;
- *social factors* – attitudes to work, levels of education and training;
- *political factors* – legislation favouring investment, etc.; and
- *technological factors* – levels of technology and transport and communications infrastructure of the country.

Market development methods

Once decisions have been made as to which countries' markets are to be entered and where value-adding activities are to be located, the task for management becomes the determination of which method of development to employ to enter another country.

Broadly speaking a business can choose either *internal or external methods for development* of overseas markets (see Chapter 11). Internal methods are usually slower, but tend to entail lower risk. External methods involve the business developing relationships with other businesses. Internal methods of development include direct exporting, overseas operating bases and establishing overseas subsidiaries. External methods include joint ventures and alliances, mergers and acquisitions, franchising and licensing. The choice of method will depend upon a number of factors:

- the size of the investment required or the amount of investment capital available;
- knowledge of the country to be entered and potential risk involved (e.g. of political instability);

- revenue and cash flow forecasts and expectations;
- operating cost considerations; and
- control considerations (some investment options will have implications for the parent to control activity in the host country).

Internal development methods

Internal methods are based upon the organization exploiting its own resources and competencies and involve the organization carrying out some of its activities overseas. This may be exporting its expertise or setting up some form of operations abroad. The advantages of internal methods of development are that they maximize future revenue from sales abroad and they make possible a high degree of control over overseas activities. On the other hand, they can involve significant risk if knowledge of the host country and its markets are limited, and they may require considerable direct investment from the business.

Direct exporting

Direct exporting is the transfer of services across national borders from the home operation. The service may simply be provided from the home country.

For example – a cruise line might advertise its products in a particular country but the line might not have any staff in that country. Instead customers are directed to a sales office in the cruise line's home country. As sales increase, a sales office may be set up in the overseas country.

To avoid some of the pitfalls of direct exporting (like lack of local knowledge and access to distribution channels) many exporting businesses make use of local sales agents to distribute their products (sometimes known as a *piggyback* distribution arrangement). In this way the company avoids direct investment in a foreign country in which it lacks expertise and relies on others with local knowledge to provide key services in a particular market.

Overseas operations

Organizations may choose to offer their products and services themselves directly in foreign countries. There are a number of reasons for such direct investment. The investment allows the company to gain local knowledge, to maintain control over the operations and to tailor the products and marketing to local demands. Relationships can also be forged with local suppliers and government which might be helpful in developing the business.

Internal development may involve establishing a foreign subsidiary of the business. This is the case when it is favourable for the parent company to have total control of its overseas operations, decision-making and profits. Such a subsidiary may carry out the full range of activities of the parent business or it may be only an operational or marketing subsidiary.

External development methods

External methods (or entry 'modes' as they are often termed) of development are the 'vehicle' by which market entry is achieved. These entry modes involve the organization entering into relationships with businesses in a host country. External development methods can take the form of alliances or joint ventures, mergers or acquisitions, or franchises (see Chapter 11 for a discussion of these topics).

Such methods (modes) have certain intrinsic advantages and disadvantages associated with them:

- *Advantages* – Providing local knowledge, potentially reducing risks, and reducing investment costs (except in the case of mergers or acquisitions).
- *Disadvantages* – Providing reduced revenues and reduced control of activities as optimal income is traded off against the advantage of lower financial exposure (again except in the case of mergers and acquisitions).

International alliances and joint ventures

Alliances and joint ventures allow a business to draw upon the skills, local knowledge, resources and competences of a locally based company. They reduce the risks of entry to overseas markets by providing local knowledge and help reduce investment costs.

International mergers and acquisitions

A business may use mergers or acquisitions to enter overseas markets. Such mergers and acquisitions give a business access to the knowledge, resources and competences of a business based in the host country thus reducing some of the risks of market entry.

International franchising and licensing

A franchise is an arrangement under which a franchisor supplies a franchisee with a tried-and-tested brand name, products and expertise in return for the payment of a proportion of profits or sales. The major advantage to the franchisor is that the risk, investment and operating costs of entering overseas markets are reduced considerably. At the same time the franchisee can contribute their local knowledge whilst also benefiting from the lower risks associated with an established business idea.

For example – much activity by *THE* organizations has taken place in foreign markets in this way. The growth of Burger King, Holiday Inn and Choice hotels expanding into overseas markets has come through franchise development.

A conceptualization of market entry

This chapter has discussed a number of facets of market entry. The topic is clearly complex, multi-faceted and has received considerable attention in the academic literature.

It is however useful to have a model or a conceptualization of the main facets of market entry in order to understand the decision-making process that needs to take place. One such conceptualization is provided by Johnson and Tellis (2008) who considered the drivers of success for market entry into China and India in particular, though it is suggested that the generic model could be applicable to other countries.

The conceptualization of Johnson and Tellis is shown as Figure 14.5.

The authors suggest that there are two broad factors which drive firm performance in international market entry and a number of 'constructs' by which the firm and country differentiation can be measured or estimated:

- *Firm differentiation* – This can be achieved through the strategy which is adopted and the way in which resources are accessed and deployed. The key elements of the firm's strategy in this context relate to the mode (method) of entry that is chosen and the timing of the entry. The various modes of entry have been discussed previously but broadly include both external and internal methods. The timing of any strategic move is critical for its success and depends on environmental factors such as the stage in the economic cycle and the positioning of competitors. The authors take firm size as a measure of the resources which a company has available.

● *Country differentiation* – The key variable with regard to country differentiation is the characteristics of the host country, the two most important being identified as the risk associated with investing in a particular country and the openness of the country in terms of regulatory and other barriers to the entry of foreign firms.

In addition to the constructs outlined, firm and country differentiation can be viewed as shaping host-home location. The two measures of this construct which are discussed extensively in the academic literature are economic and cultural distance (see, for example, the work of Hofstedt on cultural distance discussed in Chapter 4).

In order to measure or estimate the firm's performance in relation to the constructs which have been outlined, the model utilizes the historical data as reported by firms in their annual reports and other records.

Though the findings need to be treated cautiously, since they relate to two emerging markets only (albeit very significant markets); the survey carried out was not limited to service companies; and, was based on historical data. Nevertheless the authors present some interesting results. Utilizing their model using historical data the authors draw several conclusions in relation to market entry in China and India:

● success is greater for entry into China than for entry into India:
● success is greater for smaller firms than for larger firms;
● success is greater for entry into emerging markets with less openness and less risk and those that are economically close to the home market;
● success is greater for firms that use a mode of entry with greater control; and
● joint ventures are the most popular mode of entry.

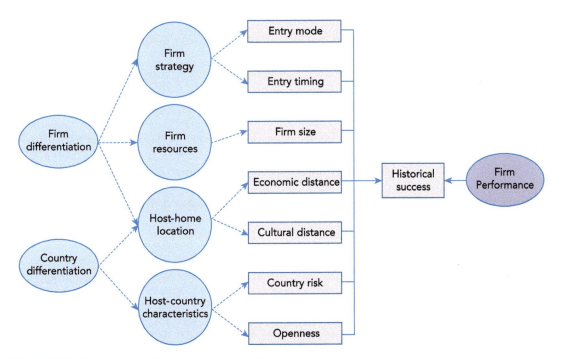

Figure 14.5 A conceptual framework: drivers of entry success

Globalization and market entry strategy – a focus on hospitality

Although we have here considered globalization and market entry strategy separately, they are in reality closely related, since to globalize companies have to carefully consider how they will enter each market in which they plan to operate. Thus here we use the hospitality sector (and international hotel groups in particular) to illustrate the connectedness of these two aspects.

The hospitality sector is at the forefront of globalization, much of the globalization literature focuses on this sector and, it is clear to see that the large branded hotel groups are spreading their interests around the world. International hotels serve to illustrate the opportunities and threats presented by globalization and the variety of market entry strategies that are being implemented in the various markets concerned.

The approach towards globalization varies between hospitality companies, though increasingly companies are utilizing 'asset-light' models which involve managing, leasing or franchising assets rather than owning them. By using such business models companies are seeking to avoid the capital requirements of hotel development and the inherent property risks involved. Market entry strategies also vary considerably both between hotel groups and within each group. In most cases the overall core elements of the strategy used remain in place, regardless of individual market characteristics, but then adaptation takes place for local market conditions.

The short case illustration below outlines the globalization and market entry strategies that have been used by hotel companies using IHG as an example. Though globalization will continue and the larger companies are actively increasing their property portfolios (though they do not necessarily own the properties concerned) it is clear that new competitors are emerging.

It is also the case that notwithstanding the continuing effects of globalization the sector remains highly fragmented. Given the growth in demand and consumer's seeking new product formats there is still room for new and innovative formats to enter the market.

SHORT CASE ILLUSTRATION

Hospitality globalization and market entry strategy: IHG

Over recent decades the hospitality industry has been a significant force in globalization, as evidenced by the proliferation of multinational firms such as Accor, Best Western, Hilton, InterContinental, and Marriott (Cunill, 2006). The internationalization of (primarily Western) brands has been motivated by a variety of factors including: sales expansion; geographic diversification; resource and labour acquisition; and, worldwide brand recognition (Yu, 1999). Most multinationals have deployed either a strategy of concentration or one of scale economies with a brand formula derived from the home country (Gross and Huang, 2011). The typical range of strategic choices for market entry modes consists of strategic alliances, franchising, management contracts, joint venture and acquisition (Athiyaman and Go, 2003).

However, the large multinational groups are being challenged. As Gross and Huang (2011) point out, 'while established mega-chains have attracted the most attention, their corporate domination is being challenged by the growth of smaller domestic hotel chains in countries other than the traditional Western ones that may potentially emerge as hospitality exporters'. Future multinational hotel chains may not come from western sources, but instead, domestic hotel groups (in countries such as China and India) are reaching a stage of development that potentially prepares them for international expansion.

Nevertheless, many of the large 'western' chains and a few selected upscale Asian chains (such as Mandarin Oriental, Shangri-la and Nikko) are firmly established globally both in emerging and developed markets and they continue their growth strategies. In doing so they are targeting not only new countries in which to develop, but also achieving greater geographic penetration in those countries in which they are already operating.

For example – IHG, one of the world's largest hotel grops, has built a strong global presence through a strategy that seeks to build preferred brands with scale positions in the most attractive markets globally.

IHG achieves this through concentrating growth in the largest markets so that IHG and owners can operate more efficiently and benefit from enhanced revenues and reduced costs. The key markets for the hotel brands which constitute IHG include large developed markets such as the US, UK and Germany, as well as emerging markets like China and India.

IHG adapts its strategy and business model by market, choosing partnerships and joint ventures where appropriate.

In China (where it is the largest international hotel company) IHG views the greatest opportunity for growth of any single country in anticipation of increasing demand for hotels, driven by a large, emerging middle-class and growing domestic and international travel. The company's strategy has been to:

● enter the market early;
● develop a relationship with key local third party owners; and
● grow the company's presence rapidly in a country with 659,000 branded hotel rooms.

In Russia and the Commonwealth of Independent States (CIS), IHG views opportunities for new construction and conversions as well as strong demand for branded hotels.

Outside the largest markets, IHG focuses on building presence in key gateway cities where its brands can generate revenue premiums from high business and leisure demand.

Thus IHG, which claims to have the second largest pipeline (hotels being planned and developed) of any hotel group, continues to develop its global reach. In doing so, however, it maintains the principles underlying its strategy, but it carefully selects its targeted development markets and modifies its strategy according to the specific characteristics of that market.

http://www.ihgplc.com/; Cunill (2006); Yu (1999);
Athiyaman and Go (2003); and Gross and Huang (2010).

Questions

1. What are the main elements of IHG's strategy and its adaptation for the Chinese market and consider the threats that IHG might face in its future development in China?

2. Consider the market entry conceptualization provided by Johnson and Tellis and apply it to IHG's entry to the Chinese hospitality market.

THINK POINTS

- Discuss the ways in which a business may develop a 'total global strategy'.
- Discuss the advantages and disadvantages of different market entry methods.
- Distinguish between the approaches adopted by *IHG* and *TUI* in the illustratives cases above.
- Explain the main elements of Johnson and Tellis's conceptualization of market entry above and how it aids understanding to the process.

SMALL BUSINESS FOCUS

It might be thought that internationalization and globalization issues are not directly relevant to most SMEs operating in *THE* sectors because their size precludes them from competing except in the domestic market. Though many *THE* companies are often active internationally because of the inherent international nature of the products, many smaller *THE* companies actually sell their products only in domestic markets.

There are though two reasons why internationalization and globalizations should be of interest to THE managers who are involved with SMEs:

- International competitors may choose to compete in the domestic market thereby challenging the market share of existing SMEs.
- New technology and other advances are increasingly enabling SMEs to internationalize rapidly.

SMEs in all industries (including *THE*) often face difficulties compared to larger competitors. The limited literature on the international activities of SMEs emphasizes constraints to internationalization which inhibit international expansion. These constraints (which are summarized by Freeman *et al.*, 2006), include:

- a lack of economies of scale;
- a lack of financial and knowledge resources;
- an aversion to risk; and
- an inability to manage uncertainty.

However, though SMEs are extremely important in many parts of *THE*, with the accommodation, travel intermediaries and event management sectors remaining highly fragmented, large international groups are developing in each of these sectors and increasing their international market share. As a result managers in smaller *THE* companies have to be aware of the strategic intentions of the larger internationally diversified companies whether they intend to internationalize themselves.

Multi-national companies have the ability to switch substantial resources from one market to another quickly and decisively and can sustain short term losses by cross-subsidizing the business venture from other markets in which they are active. When they do so they can quickly build market share, sometimes at the expense of smaller domestically orientated companies already operating in the market. By contrast, SMEs have smaller resources and cannot afford to sustain losses by cross-subsidy from elsewhere.

For example – the illustrative case of Tui entering the Russian market (discussed earlier in this chapter) presents an example of the strategic market entry by a large, well-established travel company. Tui, with a powerful local partner, was able to enter the fragmented Russian outbound tourism market quickly and decisively. Within a few years it had been able to build a critical mass of activities using its established business model which had been developed in other countries and adapted to Russian market circumstances. Established smaller companies in the fragmented Russian market find it difficult to compete with such competitive pressures.

Conceptualizations of the ongoing globalization of firms are dominated by stage models (Hjalager, 2007:438) which implies that firms normally proceed through a series of stages until they reach a global scale and that in order to trade globally they are likely to have reached a certain size and scale of operations.

However, a new stream of literature emerged in the early 1990s which takes a different view of globalization. It focuses on smaller entrepreneurial firms adopting a global focus from the outset and embarking on rapid and dedicated internationalization (McKinsey & Co., 1993) The evolution of these so-called 'born global' companies has been influenced by an inexorable trend towards globalization and the pervasive impact of new technologies (Knight and Cavusgil, 1996). Their accelerated pace to international markets is driven by a desire to gain 'first mover advantage' and to lock in new customers before competitors can do so. More recently a study (Bell et al., 2001) identifies 'born again' global firms that have internationalized rapidly following a long period during which they have concentrated on the domestic market. Studies of successfully internationalizing born-global SMEs have found that such firms are characterized by an organizational culture that is proactive, risk taking, and innovative (Freeman et al., 2006).

In an inherently international industry such as tourism and associated sectors, which are rarely directly regulated by government, there is an opportunity for born-global firms to develop (Hjalager, 2007; Williams and Shaw, 2011). The approach adopted by the internet intermediary Skyscanner illustrated below provides an example of a born-global approach.

According to Knight and Cavusgil (1996), a number of recent trends have led to the emergence of born global firms. These include:

- The increasing role of niche markets and greater demand for specialized or customized products.
- Advances in communications technology – e-mail, the world wide web and Skype mean that small firms can manage international operations more efficiently and have greater access to information.
- The inherent advantage of small firms in terms of quicker response time, flexibility and adaptability.
- The internationalization of knowledge, tools, technology and facilitating institutions, which provide opportunities for technology transfer and access to funding.
- Trends towards global networks, which are facilitating the development of mutually beneficial relationships with international partners.

SHORT CASE ILLUSTRATION

Born-global companies: Skyscanner travel search engine

The emergence of new technologies, the coalescing needs of consumers and the influence of visionary entrepreneurs has allowed some SMEs to rapidly globalize in a way that was previously not possible for firms of such size.

Skyscanner is an example of such a *born-global* company. Though comparatively recently formed, it has gone through a rapid internationalization process. Skyscanner's three founders including CEO Gareth Williams met at Manchester University and officially launched the company, which is based in Edinburgh, Scotland, in 2003.

Gareth became frustrated with the difficult and tedious process of searching multiple airline and travel agent websites to find the best flight prices and envisioned a solution: a single website that could collect, collate and compare prices for every commercial flight in the world. At a pub brainstorming session between the three friends, from a simple excel spreadsheet, Skyscanner was born.

Skyscanner's comprehensive, proprietary flight search product has grown considerably since that time to become Europe's leading flight search engine and offices have been opened in Singapore, Miami, Beijing and Glasgow. It has demonstrated its appeal to consumers around the world through sister websites in about twenty countries and numerous languages. Its mobile app has been downloaded over 25 million times and its web site attracts over 25 million unique users a month. In late 2013 Sequoia, a leading US-based venture capital firm, announced an investment in the company which valued it at about US$800 million.

Thus in about ten years the travel-based technology company had been able to grow from very small beginnings to substantial global scale.

www.skyscanner.net

Questions

1. What factors enabled Skyscanner to become a born global company?
2. What difficulties might Skyscanner have to overcome to ensure its growth is maintained?

CHAPTER SUMMARY

The focus of global strategy is the attainment of global competitive advantage. Many industries and markets are becoming increasingly global, partly as a result of external factors but also as a result of the strategies of businesses themselves. Global strategy, like domestic strategy is centred on the core competencies of the business itself but it is equally dependent upon an understanding of which aspects of the organization's industry and market are global and which require local adaptation.

Yip's (1992) globalization driver framework provides managers with an essential set of tools for beginning to understand the nature and extent of globalization in their particular industry and markets. Porter provides insight into the importance of global configuration and co-ordination of value-adding activities in achieving and sustaining competitive advantage while Yip (1992) develops the concept of 'total global strategy' to explain how a worldwide approach to strategy can be developed. Finally, the mode of entry by which organizations can develop global strategy by entering foreign markets has been explained.

It is to be remembered that the global business environment is particularly dynamic and that global strategy will have to be constantly adjusted and adapted as circumstances change if competitive advantage is to be sustained and developed.

The use of the frameworks developed in this chapter make it possible for managers to constantly monitor and analyse their global environment and to develop global strategy accordingly.

Developing internationally is one of the riskiest decisions that managers have to consider. In developing internationally managers must carefully consider which markets they will enter and how it will be achieved. This chapter has considered the main modes of market entry strategy, and provided examples of where these are applied in *THE*.

REFERENCES

Al-Kaabi, H., A. Potter and M. Naim (2007) 'An Outsourcing Decision Model for Airlines' MRO Activities', *Journal of Quality in Maintenance Engineering*, 13 (3): 217–27.

Assaf, A. and L. K. Cvelbar (2010) 'The Performance of the Slovenian Hotel Industry: Evaluation Post-Privatisation', *International Journal of Tourism Research*, 12 (5): 462–71.

Athiyaman, A. and F. Go (2003) 'Strategic Choices in the International Hospitality Industry', in B. Brotherton (ed.), *The International Hospitality Industry*, Oxford: Elsevier Butterworth-Heinemann, pp. 142–60.

Bartlett, C. and S. Ghoshal (1987) 'Managing across Borders: New Organizational Responses', *Sloan Management Review*, Fall, 45–53.

—— (1989) *Managing across Borders: The Transnational Solution*, Cambridge, Mass.: Harvard Business School Press.

Bell, J., R. McNaughton and S. Young (2001) '"Born-Again Global" firms: An Extension to the "Born Global" Phenomenon', *Journal of International Management*, 7 (3): 173–89.

Bell, J., R. McNaughton, S. Young and D. Crick (2003) 'Towards an Integrative Model of Small Firm Internationalisation', *Journal of International Entrepreneurship*, 1 (4): 339–62.

Blomstermo, A., D. D. Sharma and J. Sallis (2006) 'Choice of Foreign Market Entry Mode in Service Firms', *International Marketing Review*, 23 (2): 211–29.

Brouthers, K. D. and L. E. Brouthers (2003) 'Why Service and Manufacturing Entry Mode Choices Differ: The Influence of Transaction Cost Factors, Risk and Trust', *Journal of Management Studies*, 40 (5): 1179–204.

Canabal, A. and G. O. White III (2008) 'Entry Mode Research: Past and Future', *International Business Review*, 17 (3): 268–84.

Chen, J. J. and I. Dimou (2005) 'Expansion Strategy of International Hotel Firms', *Journal of Business Research*, 58 (12): 1730–40.

Choi, G. and H. G. Parsa (2012) 'Role of Intangible Assets in Foreign-Market Entry-Mode Decisions: A Longitudinal Study of American Lodging Firms', *International Journal of Hospitality and Tourism Administration*, 13 (4): 281–312.

Creedy, S. (2014) 'Qantas to Send Its Avalon Heavy-Maintenance Work Overseas', *Sydney: The Australian*, 20 January.

Cunill, O. M. (2006) *The Internationalization-Globalization of Hotel Chains, the Growth Strategies of Hotel Chains: Best Business Practices by Leading Companies*, Binghamton, NY: Haworth Hospitality Press, pp. 169–89.

Douglas, S. P. and Y. Wind (1987) 'The Myth of Globalization', *Columbia Journal of World Business*, 22 (4): 19–29.

Ekeledo, I. and K. Sivakumar (2004) 'International Market Entry Mode Strategies of Manufacturing Firms and Service Firms: A Resource-Based Perspective', *International Marketing Review*, 21 (1): 68–101.

Enderwick, P. (1989) *Multinational Service Firms*, London and New York: Routledge.

Endo, K. (2006) 'Foreign Direct Investment in Tourism: Flows and Volumes', *Tourism Management*, 27 (4): 600–14.

Espino-Rodrıguez, T. F. and V. Padro'n-Robaina (2005) 'A Resource-Based View of Outsourcing and Its Implications for Organizational Performance in the Hotel Sector', *Tourism Management*, 26 (5): 707–21.

Evans, N. (2012) 'Tourism: A Strategic Business Perspective', in T. Jamal and M. Robinson (eds.), *The Sage Handbook of Tourism Studies*, Thousand Oaks, Calif.: Sage, pp. 215–34.

Freeman, S., R. Edwards and B. Schroder (2006) 'How Smaller Born-Global Firms Use Networks and Alliances to Overcome Constraints to Rapid Internationalization', *Journal of International Marketing*, 14 (3): 33–63.

Ghoshal, S. (2004) 'Global Strategy: An Organizing Framework' in S. Segal-Horn (ed.), *The Strategy Reader*, 2nd edn, Oxford: Blackwell Publishing, pp. 327–48.

—— (2005) 'Bad Management Theories Are Destroying Good Management Practices', *Academy of Management Learning and Education*, 4 (1): 75–91.

Go, F. and R. Pine (1995) *Globalization Strategy in the Hotel Industry*, London and New York: Routledge.

Gonzalez, R., J. Llopis and J. Gasco (2011) 'What Do We Know about Outsourcing in Hotels?' *The Service Industries Journal*, 31 (10): 1669–82.

Gross, M. J. and S. S. Huang (2011) 'Exploring the Internationalisation Prospects of a Chinese Domestic Hotel Firm', *International Journal of Contemporary Hospitality Management*, 23 (2): 261–74.

Hamel, G. and C. K. Prahalad (1994) *Competing for the Future*, Watertown, Mass.: Harvard Business School Press.

Hamel, G. and C. K. Prahalad (1985) 'Do You Really Have a Global Strategy', *Harvard Business Review*, 63 (4): 139–48.

Hanlon, J. P. (2007) *Global Airlines: Competition in a Transnational Industry*, London and New York: Routledge.

Hjalager, A. M. (2007) 'Stages in the Economic Globalization of Tourism', *Annals of Tourism Research*, 34 (2): 437–57.

Howells, J. (1999) 'Research and Technology Outsourcing', *Technology Analysis and Strategic Management*, 11 (1): 17–29.

Hsu, C. C. and J. J. Liou (2013) 'An Outsourcing Provider Decision Model for the Airline Industry', *Journal of Air Transport Management*, 28 (May): 40–6.

Johnson, G., R. Whittington and K. Scholes (2011) *Exploring Corporate Strategy*, 6th edn, Hemel Hempstead: Prentice Hall.

Johnson, J. and G. J. Tellis (2008) 'Drivers of Success for Market Entry into China and India', *Journal of Marketing*, 72 (May): 1–13.

Knight, G. and S. T. Cavusgil (1996) 'The Born Global Firm: A Challenge to Traditional Internationalization Theory', in S. T. Cavusgil and T. Madsen (eds.) *Advances in International Marketing*, Greenwich, CT: Jai Press, pp. 11–26.

Kobrin, S. J. (1991) 'An Empirical Analysis of the Determinants of Global Integration', *Strategic Management Journal*, 12 (S1): 17–31.

Lamminmaki, D. (2005) 'Why Do Hotels Outsource? An Investigation Using Asset Specificity', *International Journal of Contemporary Hospitality Management*, 17 (6): 516–28.

Levitt, T. (1983) 'The Globalization of Markets', *Harvard Business Review*, May/June: 92–102.

Matheson, C. M., M. Foley and G. McPherson (2006) 'Globalisation and Singaporean Festivals', *International Journal of Event Management Research*, 2 (1): 1–16.

Mathieson, A. and G. Wall (1982) *Tourism: Economic, Physical and Social Impacts*, London: Longman.

McCartney, G. and L. Osti (2007) 'From Cultural Events to Sport Events: A Case Study of Cultural Authenticity in the Dragon Boat Races', *Journal of Sport Tourism*, 12 (1): 25–40.

McKinsey & Co. (1993) *Emerging Exporters: Australia's High Value-Added Manufacturing Exporters*, Melbourne: Australian Manufacturing Council.

Mol, M. (2007) *Outsourcing: Design, Process and Performance*, Cambridge: Cambridge University Press.

Normann, R. (1984) *Service Management Strategy and Leadership in Service Businesses*, Chichester: John Wiley.

Normann, R. (1991) *Service Management: Strategy and Leadership in Service Business*, 2nd edn, Chichester: John Wiley.

Park, J. W., K. W. Kim, H. J. Seo and H. W. Shin (2011) 'The Privatization of Korea's Incheon International Airport', *Journal of Air Transport Management*, 17 (4): 233–6.

Porter, M. E. (1980) *Competitive Strategy: Techniques for Analysing Industries and Competitors*, New York: Free Press.

Porter, M. E. (1986a) *Competition in Global Business*, Cambridge, Mass.: Harvard University Press.

—— (1986b) 'Changing Patterns of International Competition', *California Management Review*, 28 (2): 9–40.

—— (1990) *The Competitive Advantage of Nations*, New York: Free Press.

Quer, D., E. Claver and R. Andreu (2007) 'Foreign Market Entry Mode in the Hotel Industry: The Impact of Country-and-Firm-Specific Factors', *International Business Review*, 16 (3): 362–76.

Quinn, B. (2005) 'Changing Festival Places: Insights from Galway', *Social and Cultural Geography*, 6 (2): 237–52.

Ramón-Rodríguez, A. B., L. Moreno-Izquierdo and J. F. Perles-Ribes (2011) 'Growth and Internationalisation Strategies in the Airline Industry', *Journal of Air Transport Management*, 17 (2): 110–15.

Rieple, A. and C. Helm (2008) 'Outsourcing for Competitive Advantage: An Examination of Seven Legacy Airlines', *Journal of Air Transport Management*, 14 (5): 280–5.

Root, F. R. (1994) *Entry Strategies for International Markets*, New York: Lexington Books.

Segal-Horn, S. (2004) 'The Internationalization of Service Firms', in S. Segal-Horn (ed.), *The Strategy Reader*, Oxford: Blackwell Publishing.

Sharma, D. D. and A. Blomstermo (2003) 'The Internationalization Process of Born Globals: A Network View', *International Business Review*, 12 (6): 739–53.

Stonehouse, G., D. Campbell, J. Hamill and T. Purdie (2007) *Global and Transnational Business: Strategy and Management*, 2nd edn, London: John Wiley & Sons.

Teo, P. (2002) 'Striking a Balance for Sustainable Tourism: Implications of the Discourse on Globalisation', *Journal of Sustainable Tourism*, 10 (6): 459–74.

Tribe, J. (1997) 'The Indiscipline of Tourism', *Annals of Tourism Research*, 24 (3): 638–57.

Tsai, S. P. (2012) 'Place Attachment and Tourism Marketing: Investigating International Tourists in Singapore', *International Journal of Tourism Research*, 14 (2): 139–52.

Wahab, S. and C. Cooper (2001) *Tourism in the Age of Globalization*, London and New York: Routledge.

Whitla, P., P. G. P. Walters, and H. Davies (2007) 'Global Strategies in the International Hotel Industry', *International Journal of Hospitality Management*, 26 (4): 777–92.

Williams, A. M. and G. Shaw (2011) 'Internationalization and Innovation in Tourism', *Annals of Tourism Research*, 38 (1): 27–51.

Yip, G. S. (1992) *Total Global Strategy: Managing for Worldwide Competitive Advantage*, Englewood Cliffs, NJ: Prentice Hall.

Yu, L. (1999) 'The Hospitality Industry as an International Business', in L. Yu, *The International Hospitality Business: Management and Operations*, Binghamton, NY: Haworth Hospitality Press, pp. 3–26.

WEBSITES

www.accenture.com

www. bcdtravel.com

www.ihgplc.com

www.qantas.com.au

www.sgcm.ru/

www.skyscanner.net

www.tuitravelplc.com

FURTHER READING

Reference	Focus
Agndal, H. and J. Elbe (2007) 'The Internationalization Processes of Small and Medium-Sized Swedish Tourism Firms', *Scandinavian Journal of Hospitality and Tourism*, 7 (4): 301–27.	Internationalization Tourism Sweden SMEs
Albers, S., C. Heuermann and B. Koch (2010) 'Internationalization Strategies of EU and Asia-Pacific Low Fare Airlines', *Journal of Air Transport Management*, 16 (5): 244–50.	Internationalization Airlines EU and Asia-/Pacifiic
Aliouche, E. H. and U. Schlentrich (2011) 'A Model of Optimal International Market Expansion: The Case of US Hotel Chains Expansion into China', in M. Tuunanen, J. Windsperger, G. Cliquet and G. Hendrikse (eds.), *New Developments in the Theory of Networks: Franchising Alliances and Cooperatives*, Berlin, Germany: Physica-Verlag, pp. 135–54.	Internationalization Hotels China
Alon, I., L. Ni and Y. Wang (2012) 'Examining the Determinants of Hotel Chain Expansion through International Franchising', *International Journal of Hospitality Management*, 31 (2): 379–86.	Internationalization Hotels Franchising

Baena, V. and J. Cervino (2012) 'International Franchise Expansion of Service Chains: Insights from the Spanish Market', *The Service Industries Journal*, 32 (7): 1121–36.	Internationalization Services Franchising Spain
Barrows, C. W. and E. Giannakopoulos (2006) 'An Exploratory Study of Outsourcing of Foodservice Operations in Canadian Hotels', *Tourism*, 54 (4): 375–83.	Outsourcing Hotels Canada
Bjorkman, I. and S. Kock (1997) 'Inward International Activities in Service Firms: Illustrated by Three Cases from the Tourism Industry', *International Journal of Service Management*, 8 (5): 362–76.	Internationalization Tourism
Blomstermo, A., D. D. Sharma and J. Sallis (2006) 'Choice of Foreign Market Entry Mode in Service Firms', *International Marketing Review*, 23 (2): 211–29.	Internationalization Market entry strategy Services
Bolat, T. and O. Yilmaz (2009) 'The Relationship between Outsourcing and Organizational Performance', *International Journal of Contemporary Hospitality Management*, 21 (1): 7–23.	Outsourcing Performance Hospitality
Brookes, M. and A. Roper (2010) 'The Impact of Entry Modes on the Organizational Design of International Hotel Chains', *The Service Industries Journal*, 30 (9): 1499–512.	Internationalization Market entry strategy Hotels
Bustinza, O. F., D. Arias-Aranda and L. Gutierrez-Gutierrez (2010) 'Outsourcing, Competitive Capabilities and Performance: An Empirical Study in Service Firms', *International Journal of Production Economics*, 126 (2): 276–88.	Outsourcing Performance Services
Campbell, A. J. and A. Verbeke (1994) 'The Globalization of Service Sector Multinationals', *Long Range Planning*, 27 (2): 95–102.	Globalization Services
Chand, M. and A. A. Katou (2012) 'Strategic Determinants for the Selection of Partner Alliances in the Indian Tour Operator Industry: A Cross-National Study', *Journal of World Business*, 47 (2): 167–77.	Internationalization Tour operators India
Chatzoglou, P. D. and L. Sarigiannidis (2009) 'Business Outsourcing and Organizational Performance: The Case of the Greek Hotel Industry', *International Journal of Services Technology and Management*, 11 (2): 105–27.	Outsourcing Performance Greece
Cheung, C., T. Baum and A. Wong (2012) 'Relocating Empowerment as a Management Concept for Asia', *Journal of Business Research*, 65 (1): 36–41.	Internationalization Empowerment Asia
Choi, G. and H. G. Parsa (2012) 'Role of Intangible Assets in Foreign-Market Entry-Mode Decisions: A Longitudinal Study of American Lodging Firms', *International Journal of Hospitality and Tourism Administration*, 13 (4): 281–312.	Internationalization Market entry strategy Hotels
Donada, C. and G. Nogatchewsky (2009) 'Emotions in Outsourcing: An Empirical Study in the Hotel Industry', *International Journal of Hospitality Management*, 28 (3): 367–73.	Outsourcing Hotels
Dunning, J. H. and S. K. Kundu. (1995) 'The Internationalization of the Hotel Industry: Some New Findings from a Field Study', *MIR: Management International Review*, 35 (2): 101–33.	Internationalization Hotels

Espino-Rodriguez, T. F. and V. Padro'n-Robaina (2004) 'Outsourcing and Its Impact on Operational Objectives and Performance: A Study of Hotels in the Canary Islands', *International Journal of Hospitality Management*, 23 (3): 287–306.	Outsourcing Hotels Canary Islands
Espino-Rodriguez, T. F. and V. Padro'n-Robaina (2005) 'The Management Perception of the Strategic Outsourcing of Services: An Empirical Examination in the Hotel Sector', *The Service Industries Journal*, 25 (5): 689–708.	Outsourcing Hotels
Fayed, H. and J. Fletcher (2002) 'Report: Globalization of Economic Activity: Issues for Tourism', *Tourism Economics*, 8 (2): 207–30.	Globalization Tourism
Go, F. (1996) 'A Conceptual Framework for Managing Global Tourism and Hospitality Marketing', *Tourism Recreation Research*, 21 (2): 37–43.	Globalization Tourism Hospitality
Go, F., S. S. Pyo, M. Uysal and B. J. Mihalik (1990) 'Decision Criteria for Transnational Hotel Expansion', *Tourism Management*, 11 (4): 297–304.	Internationalization Hotels Decision criteria
Graf, N. S. (2009) 'Stock Market Reactions to Entry Mode Choices of Multinational Hotel Firms', *International Journal of Hospitality Management*, 28 (2): 236–44.	Internationalization Hotels Finance
Grönroos, C. (1999) 'Internationalization Strategies for Services', *Journal of Services Marketing*, 13 (4/5): 290–7.	Internationalization Services
Guillet, B. D., H. Q. Zhang and B. W. Gao (2011) 'Interpreting the Mind of Multinational Hotel Investors: Future Trends and Implications in China', *International Journal of Hospitality Management*, 30 (2): 222–32.	Internationalization Hotels China
Heung, V. C. S., H. Zhang and C. Jiang (2008) 'International Franchising: Opportunities for China's State-Owned Hotels?' *International Journal of Hospitality Management*, 27 (3): 368–80.	Internationalization Franchising Hotels China
Hoffman, R. and J. Preble (2004) 'Global Franchising: Current Status and Future Challengers', *Journal of Services Marketing*, 18 (2): 101–13.	Globalization Franchising Hotels
Jayawardena, C. (2000) 'International Hotel Manager', *International Journal of Contemporary Hospitality Management*, 12 (1): 67–9.	Internationalization Hotels Management
Johnson, C. and M. Vanetti (2005) 'Locational Strategies of International Hotel Chains', *Annals of Tourism Research*, 32 (4): 1077–99.	Internationalization Hotels Location decisions
Khan, M. A. (2005) 'Internationalization of Services: The Global Impact of US Franchise Restaurants', *Journal of Services Research*, 5 (Special Issue): 187–215.	Internationalization Franchising Restaurants
Knowles, T., D. Diamantis and J. B. El-Mourhabi (2001) *The Globalization of Tourism and Hospitality: A Strategic Perspective*, London: Continuum.	Globalization Tourism Hospitality

Kundu, S. K. and F. J. Contractor (1999) 'Country Location Choices of Service Multinationals: An Empirical Study of the International Hotel Sector', *Journal of International Management*, 5 (4): 299–317.	Globalization Tourism Location decisions
Lam, T. and M. X. J. Han (2005) 'A Study of Outsourcing Strategy: A Case Involving the Hotel Industry in Shanghai, China', *Hospitality Management*, 24 (1): 41–56.	Outsourcing Hotels China
Lee, S. (2008) 'Internationalization of US Multinational Hotel Companies: Expansion to Asia Versus Europe', *International Journal of Hospitality Management*, 27 (4): 657–64.	Internationalization Hotels Market entry strategy
Lee, S. K. and S. C. Jang (2010) 'Internationalization and Exposure to Foreign Currency Risk: An Examination of Lodging Firms', *International Journal of Hospitality Management*, 29 (4): 701–10.	Internationalization Hotels Market entry strategy
Lee, S. K. and S. S. Jang (2013) 'Early Mover or Late Mover Advantage for Hotels?' *Journal of Hospitality and Tourism Research*, published online at http://jht.sagepub.com.	Internationalization Hotels Financial management
León-Darder, F., C. Villar-García and J. Pla-Barber (2011) 'Entry Mode Choice in the Internationalisation of the Hotel Industry: A Holistic Approach', *The Service Industries Journal*, 31 (1): 107–22.	Internationalization Market entry strategy Hotels
Li, L., D. Li and T. Dalgic (2004) 'Internationalization Process of Small and Medium-Sized Enterprises: Toward a Hybrid Model of Experiential Learning and Planning', *MIR: Management International Review*, 44: 93–116.	Internationalization SMEs
Litteljohn, D. (1997) 'Internationalization in Hotels: Current Aspects and Developments', *International Journal of Contemporary Hospitality Management*, 9 (5/6): 187–92.	Internationalization Hotels
Litteljohn, D., A. Roper and L. Altinay (2007) 'Territories Still to Find: The Business of Hotel Internationalisation', *International Journal of Service Industry Management*, 18 (2): 167–83.	Internationalization Hotels Market entry strategy
Lommelen, T. and P. Matthyssens (2005) 'The Internationalization Process of Service Providers: A Literature Review', *Advances in International Marketing*, 15: 95–117.	Internationalization Services
López-Duarte, C. and M. M. Vidal-Suárez (2010) 'External Uncertainty and Entry Mode Choice: Cultural Distance, Political Risk and Language Diversity', *International Business Review*, 19 (6): 575–88.	Internationalization Market entry strategy Cultural distance
Martorell, O., C. Mulet and L. Otero (2012) 'Choice of Market Entry Mode by Balearic Hotel Chains in the Caribbean and Gulf of Mexico', *International Journal of Hospitality Management*, 32: 217–27.	Internationalization Hotels Market entry strategy
Mules, T. (2001) 'Globalization and the Economic Impacts of Tourism', in B. Faulkner, G. Moscardo and E. Laws (eds.), *Tourism in the 21st Century: Lessons from Experience*, London: Continuum , 312–27.	Globalization Tourism Economic impacts
Nurse, K. (2003) 'Trinidad Carnival: Festival Tourism and Cultural Industry', *Event Management*, 8 (4): 223–30.	Internationalization Festivals Trinidad
Ohmae K. (1989) 'Managing in a Borderless World', *Harvard Business Review*, 67 (3): 152–61.	Globalization Management

Paraskevas, A. and D. Buhalis (2002) 'Outsourcing IT for Small Hotels: the Opportunities and Challenges of Using Application Service Providers', *Cornell Hotel and Restaurant Administration Quarterly*, 43 (2): 27–39.	Outsourcing Hotels
Pillmayer, M. and N. Scherle (2013) 'The Tourism Industry and the Process of Internationalization in the Middle East: The Example of Jordan', *International Journal of Tourism Research*, 16 (4): 329–39.	Internationalization Tourism Middle East
Pla-Barber, J., F. León-Darder and C. Villar (2011) 'The Internationalization of Soft-Services: Entry Modes and Main Determinants in the Spanish Hotel Industry', *Service Business*, 5 (2): 139–54.	Internationalization Market entry strategy Hotels Spain
Ramon, A. (2002) 'Determining Factors in Entry Choice for International Expansion: The Case of the Spanish Hotel Industry', *Tourism Management*, 23 (6): 597–607.	Internationalization Market entry strategy Hotels Spain
Rodriquez, A. (2002) 'Determining the Entry Choice for International Expansion: The Case of the Spanish Hotel Industry', *Tourism Management*, 23 (6): 597–60.	Market entry strategy Hotels Spain
Rodtook, P. and L. Altinay (2013) 'Reasons for Internationalization of Domestic Hotel Chains in Thailand', *Journal of Hospitality Marketing and Management*, 22 (1): 92–115.	Internationalization Hotels Thailand
Ruzzier, M., R. D. Hisrich and B. Antoncic (2006) 'SME Internationalization Research: Past, Present and Future', *Journal of Small Business and Enterprise Development*, 13 (4): 476–97.	Internationalization SMEs
Singh, R. K., S. K. Garg and S. G. Deshmukh (2009) 'The Competitiveness of SMEs in a Globalized Economy: Observations from China and India', *Management Research Review*, 33 (1): 54–65.	Globalization SMEs India China
Smeral, E. (1998) 'The Impact of Globalization on Small and Medium Enterprises: New Challenges for Tourism Policies in European Countries', *Tourism Management*, 19 (4): 371–80.	Globalization Tourism SMEs
Sun, K. A. and S. Lee (2013) 'Determinants of Degree of Internationalization for US Restaurant Firms', *International Journal of Hospitality Management*, 33: 465–74.	Internationalization Restaurants USA
Villar, C., J. Pla-Barber and F. León-Darder (2012) 'Service Characteristics as Moderators of the Entry Mode Choice: Empirical Evidence in the Hotel Industry', *The Service Industries Journal*, 32 (7): 1137–48.	Market entry strategy Hotels Service characteristics
Williams, A. M. and G. Shaw (2011) 'Internationalization and Innovation in Tourism', *Annals of Tourism Research*, 38 (1): 27–51.	Internationalization Innovation Tourism
Wood, R. (2000) 'Caribbean Cruise Tourism: Globalization at Sea', *Annals of Tourism Research*, 27 (2): 345–70.	Globalization Tourism Cruising
Xiao, Q., J. W. O'Neill and H. Wang (2008) 'International Hotel Development: A Study of Potential Franchisees in China', *International Journal of Hospitality Management*, 27 (3): 325–36.	Internationalization Hotels Franchising China

Yu, Y., W. H. Byun and T. J. Lee (2013) 'Critical Issues of Globalisation in the International Hotel Industry', *Current Issues in Tourism*, 17 (2): 114–18.	Globalization Hotels
Zhang, H. Q., B. D. Guillet and W. Gao (2012) 'What Determines Multinational Hotel Groups' Locational Investment Choice in China?' *International Journal of Hospitality Management*, 31 (2): 350–9.	Internationalization Hotels China
Zhang, J. and C. Jensen (2007) 'Comparative Advantage: Explaining Tourism Flows', *Annals of Tourism Research*, 34 (1): 223–43.	Internationalization Hotels China

CASE LINKAGES

Case 1	Strategic alliances in the airline industry
Case 2	Tourism Queensland
Case 4	Hyatt Hotels
Case 5	Days Inn
Case 6	Reed Exhibitions
Case 7	Thomas Cook

Chapter **15**

Strategy and tourism, hospitality and event organizations

Theory and practice

Introduction and chapter overview

This is the concluding chapter of the book and brings together a number of themes. Throughout the book we have considered both theoretical concepts relating to strategic management and THE, and stressed the linkages between the two. Practical applications and examples have also been provided. This chapter summarizes some of the theoretical themes covered in the book and provides a practical summary of what factors might be considered in presenting a strategy and what the 'finished product' might look like.

The subject matter of this book is concerned with two quite young and interrelated areas, namely tourism, hospitality and events management and strategic management. It is also concerned with the application of one to the other, i.e. applying strategic management concepts and frameworks to THE. This chapter is concerned with summarizing some of the key theoretical debates within THE and strategic management subject matter and providing practical guidance for producing a strategy.

Tourism, hospitality and events are service sectors with particular characteristics which are highly distinctive, not only when compared with manufacturing but also when compared with many other services. In this chapter we return to some of the themes introduced in Chapters 1 and 2. The distinctiveness of the subject area is discussed and the implications for the study and application of strategic management principles are discussed.

At the heart of strategic management is the desire to explain why certain businesses achieve competitive advantage through superior performance. The view in the 1980s was that competitive advantage was based upon the competitive positioning of the organization in its environment based upon highly systematic planning (Argenti, 1980; Porter, 1980 and 1985).

In the 1990s this view was challenged by strategists who believe that in a turbulent business environment, strategy can be developed incrementally and that competitive advantage depends upon the ability of the business to build core competencies which cannot be easily replicated by competitors (Prahalad and Hamel, 1990; Heene and Sanchez, 1997; Kay, 1993).

This chapter, intended to be a summary of the book, serves the dual purpose of summarizing some of the key theoretical themes in the interaction between *THE* and strategic management before considering in a practical sense how strategy might be presented.

LEARNING OBJECTIVES

After studying this chapter you should be able to:

- understand the nature of the distinctive challenges that managers in *THE* face;
- explain the relevance of strategic management to managers operating in *THE*;
- explain the 'disciplinary' debate which has taken place in both strategic management and *THE* subjects;
- explain and explore the planned/prescriptive approach to strategic management;
- explain and explore the emergent/incremental approach to strategic management;
- explain and explore the competitive positioning school of strategic management;
- explain and explore the resource/core competence school of strategic management; and
- understand how to present strategy in a clear, coherent and convincing way.

Themes in strategic management for tourism, hospitality and events

The growth of *THE* and the managerial challenges presented

The antecedents of 'mass' international tourism and hospitality can be traced back to Thomas Cook in 1850s Britain (Withey, 1998). Events management is a highly diverse field but performances, festivals and events of various descriptions have taken place throughout history. However, as highly structured sectors of many economies *THE* can primarily be viewed as a creation of more recent times. The rise of these sectors has been traced by a number of authors including Gee *et al.* (1997) and Holloway and Humphreys (2009). Since the early 1950s the growth of international tourism (and the associated sectors we are considering) has been phenomenal in its scale, and remarkably resilient to periodic economic and political adversity (Evans, 2012:215).

In product life cycle terms, and taking a global perspective, international tourism might be categorized as having passed through the 'introductory' phase into the 'growth' phase. The number of international arrivals, for example, has shown an evolution from a mere 25 million international arrivals in 1950 to an estimated 1,087 million arrivals in 2013 (UNWTO, 2013). However, since many more countries and new consumers are being drawn into the international tourism net, further growth is to be expected before 'maturity' is reached. Such growth will be uneven, both spatially and with regard to time, and is likely to take place against the backdrop of dramatic changes in the business environment thereby creating both managerial and marketing opportunities and dilemmas for private sector leaders and public sector policy makers.

Given the dominance and drive of the private sector in the development of international tourism, hospitality and events management and the growth in the services which support these, a business management-oriented approach to *THE* studies has evolved over the past 30 years and has become the dominant frame for teaching *THE* in universities and colleges. The study of strategic management (or strategy) is a part of this development as it represents what is sometimes called a 'capstone' module on many *THE* courses. It is referred to in this way because strategic management:

- Takes a holistic approach integrating the study of different business subjects such as human resource management, finance and marketing.
- Is usually studied towards the end of courses so that prior knowledge of relevant underpinning subjects can be integrated appropriately.
- Takes a 'real-world' perspective in that, just as in business itself, there is rarely a 'right' or 'wrong' answer but it is concerned with the analysis of issues, and the formulation and implementation of strategies to address the issues identified.

Tourism, hospitality and events are frequently referred to as 'industries', though we have generally used the terminology 'sectors' to describe the constituent parts of the linked *THE* industry. Whatever terminology is used, managers working within these contexts are driven by the practical needs of organizations seeking commercial success. Those working in *THE* contexts need to understand not only the actual business changes taking place, but also to have an understanding of the underlying characteristics of the industry. Such characteristics (discussed in Chapter 2 and elsewhere in the book), raise a number of managerial issues which, if not necessarily unique, are certainly highly distinctive.

Managers working within *THE*, policy makers, regulators and others concerned with the industry's continuing development, need to not only be knowledgeable about these characteristics and issues, but also to recognize the potential managerial responses that are possible and the impact they might have. These managerial actions responding to identified challenges often fall within one of the recognized functional areas of business: marketing, human resource management, finance and operations but in bringing together the major issues in one place they are considered as part of the emerging academic field we consider here of strategic management.

Strategic management for tourism, hospitality and events – a disciplinary dilemma?

Strategic management is a comparatively young discipline, if indeed it can be called a discipline when it is in fact a multi- and inter-disciplinary field of study (Campbell *et al.*, 2002: 291). Strategists draw heavily upon disciplines as diverse as organization theory and behaviour, human resource management, economics, accounting and finance, and marketing as well as attempting to formulate their own theories and analytical frameworks. The future of strategic management will undoubtedly be longer than its past. For this reason, the theories, tools and techniques employed in strategic management in many cases are far from fully formulated. The subject will continue to evolve and the sophistication of its methods and methodology will develop and improve over time.

Similarly, it is also the case that studies of tourism, hospitality and events are relatively recent in their origins, and there is some doubt as to whether they are indeed disciplines at all.

Since their relatively recent entries into mainstream higher education the linked studies of tourism, hospitality and events have attracted debate regarding their disciplinary status and how they should be studied. The debate has primarily focused on how tourism, hospitality and event management should be conceptualized and the implications it might have for educators and practitioners. In relation to the debate in tourism, hospitality and events, see for example: Faulkner and Ryan (1999); Ottenbacher *et al.* (2009); and Getz (2002); respectively for a consideration of the three sectors.

A flavour of the sort of debates that have emerged is provided in the discussion contained in the Key Concept overleaf.

KEY CONCEPT

Tourism, hospitality and events: A disciplinary dilemma?

Since its entry into mainstream higher education the study of tourism has attracted debate regarding its disciplinary status and the advantages and disadvantages of various approaches to its understanding. By extension the same debate can be extended to the linked fields of hospitality and events.

The articulation of this debate continues to reveal division of opinion (Evans, 2001). On the one hand, authors such as Leiper (1981) have advocated that tourism should be treated as a distinct discipline. Others, on the other hand, maintain that tourism as an area of study fails to meet the necessary criteria in order to be treated as a distinct discipline (Echtner and Jamal, 1997; and Tribe, 1997).

Tribe (1997) maintains that not only is tourism *not* currently a discipline but also that the search for tourism as a discipline should be abandoned. To continue to advocate that tourism should be viewed as a discipline would involve 'casting adrift of important parts of tourism studies in the quest for conceptual coherence and logical consistency' (Tribe, 1997:656).

Instead, Tribe (1997) and others argue that tourism should be treated as a 'field' of study. In this way tourism becomes similar to housing, engineering, or business and strategic management, in that they:

- Concentrate on particular phenomena or practices; and
- Call upon a number of disciplines to investigate and explain their areas of interest.

In contrasting fields and disciplines Henkel (1988:188) noted that disciplines 'are held together by distinctive constellations of theories, concepts and methods' whereas fields 'draw upon all sorts of knowledge that may illuminate them'.

Many of the concepts which have been utilised in tourism, hospitality and events such as life cycle analysis, impact studies, multiplier analysis and yield management are concepts that have been adapted to be used in *THE,* but are not unique to *THE* studies.

Thus while economics, sociology and psychology are all disciplines, since they represent a way of studying, it can be argued that tourism (as with education or leisure) is not, since it represents something to be studied (Tribe, 1997).

Partly adapted from Evans (2012)

If it is accepted that tourism, hospitality and events are fields of study, rather than disciplines, it has a significant consequence: that the study of tourism, hospitality and events (and the associated international travel industry) can be viewed as having much in common with the business and management subject areas. The techniques and applied knowledge in the 'functional' business areas such as marketing, human resource management, finance and operations and the holistic study of organizations through the study of strategic management are 'derivative partly from the disciplines that contribute to them and partly from the world of business practice' (Henkel, 1988:188).

Strategic management in *THE* contexts

This book has argued throughout that *THE* businesses are different, and indeed it provides the underlying rationale for the book itself. *THE* businesses are different in a number of ways from businesses which produce physical products and they are also different in emphasis from other service industries. These differences (discussed in Chapter 2), lead to important consequences the implications of which, managers of *THE* businesses have to consider. The result lies in various distinctive managerial responses to the issues faced which are discussed throughout the book.

In all industries, including the component sectors of *THE*, some organizations prove to be more successful than others. The superior performers conceivably possess something special that competitors do not have access to that allow them to outperform their rivals. The sources of 'competitive advantage' lie in combining:

- the superior application of competencies (skills);
- the deployment of superior resources (assets); and
- in creating value for consumers.

Sustainability is achieved when the advantage resists erosion by competitive behaviour (Porter, 1985).

Thus in order to achieve the goal of competitive advantage managers must have an understanding of how value is added in an organization and a number of approaches have been used in the emergence of a new managerial paradigm – 'strategic management'.

The overall aim of strategy and strategic management is to:

- Develop an effective framework for thinking ahead – for thinking strategically.

Since the 1960s the subject area has been widely considered as a topic of academic interest and a vast literature in the field has been assembled including influential early works from writers such as Chandler (1962) and Ansoff (1987).

> **THINK POINTS**
>
> - Explain why *THE* may or may not be considered a discipline.
> - Consider why *THE* organizations might benefit from taking a strategic approach.

Approaches to the study of strategic management

The developing nature of strategy as a coherent academic study is reflected in two related debates revolving around what constitutes the most appropriate approach to strategic management (see for example Jones, 2004 for an overview on the various perspectives on strategy).

There is some disagreement among strategists on the best way of understanding the determinants of competitive advantage. Some writers advocate an approach to strategic management which is *planned* or *prescriptive* (sometimes called *deliberate*) while others argue that it is better to evolve strategy incrementally (the *emergent* approach to strategy – see the Key Concept in Chapter 1). In this book we have primarily adopted a prescriptive approach whilst acknowledging that strategy in contemporary, fast-moving environments must be flexible and thereby may include some elements that change and may be viewed as emergent.

A parallel debate centres upon whether competitive advantage stems primarily from the competitive position of the business in its industry or from business-specific core competencies.

The debate surrounding the development of strategic management can thus be summarized under two broad headings:

- The planned/prescriptive versus emergent/incremental controversy.
- The competitive positioning versus resource-/core competence-based strategy controversy.

We discussed these debates in various parts of this book.

Here, we summarize the main features of these approaches and briefly explore their advantages and disadvantages (see Table 15.1). The arguments are discussed below.

The prescriptive versus emergent strategy debate

Planned or prescriptive strategy

The planned or prescriptive approach (sometimes also described as 'deliberate') views the formulation and implementation of strategic management as a logical, rational and systematic process.

After analysis of the business and its environment, strategists must set well-defined corporate and business objectives and formulate, select and implement strategies which will allow objectives to be achieved. Such an approach has been criticized on the grounds that there is often a major discrepancy between planned and realized strategies (Mintzberg, 1987). It is also argued that the increasing turbulence and chaos of the business environment makes highly prescriptive planning nonsense. Rigid plans prevent the flexibility which is required in an environment of volatile change. Being over-prescriptive, it is argued, also stifles the creativity which often underpins successful strategy.

On the other hand, it is argued that systematic planning makes it possible to organize complex activities and information, unite business objectives, set targets against which performance can be evaluated and generally increases the degree of control which can be exercised over the operation of the business. The planned or prescriptive approach is often linked to the *competitive positioning* school (see later in this chapter).

Emergent or incremental strategy

The emergent or incremental view of strategy adopts the position that strategy must be evolved incrementally over time. This view is based upon the premise that businesses are complex social organizations operating in rapidly changing environments. Under such circumstances, strategy will tend to evolve as a result of the interaction between stakeholder groups and between the business and its environment. It is argued that an emergent approach has the advantages of increased organizational flexibility. It can form a basis in organizational learning and can provide an internal culture for managers to think and act creatively rather than have to act within the rigid framework of deliberate strategy.

The danger is that an emergent approach may result in a lack of purpose in strategy and it can make it difficult to evaluate performance (because if an organization has no explicit objective, performance against it cannot be measured).

To counter the criticisms of emergent strategy, Quinn (1978) and Quinn and Voyer (1994) see a role for some planning in the context of emergent strategy, advocating 'purposeful incrementalism'. This approach places a strong emphasis on *organizational learning*.

The two approaches towards strategy discussed above are summarized in Table 15.1

Table 15.1 A comparison of prescriptive and emergent approaches to strategy

Prescriptive (deliberate, planned) strategy		
Strategic implications	Advantages	Criticisms
Strategic management is a highly formalized planning process. Business objectives are set and strategies are formulated and implemented to achieve them.	Clear objectives provide focus for the business. Objectives can be translated into targets against which performance can be measured and monitored. Resources can be allocated to specific objectives and efficiency can be judged. The approach is logical and rational.	There are often major discrepancies between planned and realized strategy. Rigid planning in a dynamic and turbulent business environment can be unproductive. Prescriptions can stifle creativity. Rigid adherence to plans may mean missed business opportunities.
Emergent (incremental) strategy		
Strategic implications	Advantages	Criticisms
Strategy emerges and develops incrementally over time in the absence of rigid planning.	Emergent strategy increases flexibility in a turbulent environment allowing the business to respond to threats and exploit opportunities. Changing stakeholder interactions can mean that strategy is often, of necessity, emergent.	There is a danger of 'strategic drift' as objectives lack clarity. It is more difficult to evaluate performance, as targets are less well defined.

The competitive positioning versus resource/core competence debate

Competitive positioning

This school of thought dominated strategic management from the 1980s and though it has been widely criticized in the 1990s, the analytical frameworks devised by Porter in the 1980s (1980 and 1985) are still widely used by both managers and academics. The major strength of the approach lies in the ready applicability of these frameworks to analysis of the business and its environment.

The approach to strategy is essentially 'outside-in' (McKiernan, 1997) to establish a competitive position for the business in its environment which results in it outperforming its rivals.

In terms of procedure, the process of analysing competitive position begins with the *five forces framework*. This is used to analyse the nature of competition in the organization's industry. This is followed by selection of the appropriate *generic strategy* together with *value chain analysis* to ensure that the business configures its value-adding activities in such a way as to support a strategy based on either differentiation or cost leadership.

In the 1990s, this approach was criticized for its over-emphasis of the role of the *industry* in determining profitability and its under-estimation of the importance of the individual business (Rumelt, 1991). Porter's frameworks have also been criticized as being too static although Porter argues that they must be applied repeatedly to take account of the dynamism of the environment. The reality is that without Porter's work, strategic management would be devoid of many of its most practical and applicable analytical tools.

Resource- or core competence-based strategy

The 1990s witnessed the rise of what is known as *resource-* or *core competence-based* strategic management (Prahalad and Hamel, 1990; Heene and Sanchez, 1997; Kay, 1993).

The major difference to the competitive positioning approach is that the importance of the individual business in achieving competitive advantage is emphasised rather than the industry. The approach is therefore 'inside-out'. Although this approach came to prominence in the 1990s, its origins lie in the work of Penrose (1959) who emphasised the importance of the business and its resources in determining its performance. Interest in the approach was revived by Prahalad and Hamel's work 'The Core Competence of the Corporation' (Prahalad and Hamel, 1990). A core competence is some combination of resources, skills, knowledge, and technology which distinguishes an organization from its competitors in the eyes of customers. This distinctiveness results in competitive advantage.

The approach also emphasizes organizational learning, knowledge management and collaborative business networks as sources of competitive advantage (Sanchez and Heene, 1997; Demarest, 1997).

Table 15.2 A comparison of competitive positioning and resource- or competence-based schools of thought

Competitive positioning school		
Strategic implications	Advantages	Criticisms
Competitive advantage results from an organization's position in respect to its industry. The business analyses the strength of the competitive forces in its industry and selects an appropriate generic strategy. The business configures its value adding activities to support this generic strategy. The approach to strategy is 'outside-in'.	Well-developed analytical frameworks like Porter's five forces, value chain and generic strategies. Structured approach helps to simplify the complexity of business and the business environment. Good for identifying opportunities and threats in the environment.	Neglects the importance of business-specific competencies as opposed to industry wide factors. Some of the analytical frameworks (e.g. generic strategies) have been widely criticized.
Resource- or competence-based school		
Strategic implications	Advantages	Criticisms
Organizations must identify and build core competencies or distinctive capabilities which can be leveraged in a number of markets. The school's approach to strategy is 'inside-out'.	The school emphasizes the importance of the individual business in acquiring competitive advantage. Strategic intent, vision and creativity are emphasized.	Analytical frameworks are in their infancy and are currently poorly developed. The importance of the environment in determining competitive advantage is underestimated.

The resource/core competence approach has focused the search for competitive advantage on the individual business. However, its critics argue that it lacks the well-developed analytical frameworks of the competitive positioning school and, perhaps, understates the potential importance of the business environment in determining success or failure.

The two schools of thought towards strategy are summarized in Table 15.2.

Towards an integrated approach to strategy

Similarities and differences between the approaches

The prescriptive approach and competitive positioning school are often seen as related to each other because they both adopt a highly structured view of strategic management.

Similarly, the emergent approach and competence-based school are often linked to each other because of their shared focus on organizational knowledge and learning.

On the other hand, the prescriptive and emergent approaches are often presented as being diametrically opposed, as are the competitive positioning and competence-based approaches. The reality is that the approaches are in many ways complementary as they present different perspectives of the same situation.

Mintzberg *et al.* (1995) argue that the competence-based and competitive positioning approaches ought to be seen as 'complementary, representing two different forms of analysis both of which must be brought to bear for improving the quality of strategic thinking and analysis'. Similarly, Quinn and Voyer (1994) recognize that within logical incrementalism 'formal planning techniques do serve some essential functions'.

Acknowledging the contribution of each approach

The point is that each approach has its merits. By acknowledging the contribution of each approach, managers can arrive at an enriched method of understanding the complex area of strategic management. The contribution of each approach to an integrated understanding is summarized in Table 15.3 below.

Accordingly, it is suggested that strategy must be both inward and outward looking, planned and emergent. By adopting this synthesis, a broader understanding of competitive advantage can be gained.

Table 15.3 The contribution of the different strategic management approaches and schools

Strategic management approaches and schools: contribution	
Approach/school	
Prescriptive (planned, deliberate)	A degree of planning is necessary to provide focus for the strategy of the organization and to assist in the evaluation of performance.
Emergent/incremental	Plans must always be flexible to allow organizations to learn and adapt to changes in the environment.
Competitive positioning	Emphasizes the importance of the environment and provides useful tools for analysing the business in the context of its industry.
Resource-/competence-based	Focuses on the importance of the business and assists in identifying company-specific sources of competitive advantage.

THINK POINTS

- Explain the differences between the planned/prescriptive approach and the emergent/incremental approach to strategic management.
- Discuss the view that the competitive positioning and resource/competence based schools of strategic management are *not* mutually exclusive.

Key strategic management writers

Building on the categorization of strategic management approaches into prescriptive (deliberate) and emergent, Whittington (2001) adds two further opposing variables; the desired outcomes which might be 'profit-maximization' or 'pluralistic'. In some organizations he argues that the key outcome of strategy is profit-maximization whilst others take a pluralist approach in that they pursue several objectives simultaneously.

The variables allow Whittington to identify four categories of approach to strategy:

- *Classical* – Stresses rationality and analysis.
- *Evolutionary* – Stresses the unpredictability of the environment which makes irrelevant much of what is traditionally regarded as strategic analysis. The analogy that can be drawn is 'the survival of the fittest' model from the natural world.
- *Processual* – A pragmatic view of strategy. The world and our knowledge are imperfect so organizations have to take account of this in their strategic processes.
- *Systemic* – Stresses the importance and to an extent, the uniqueness of social systems within which diverse attitudes to and conceptualizations about strategic issues occur. In this view strategy will in part reflect the social system in which it occurs.

Whittington shows diagrammatically his categorization of strategy and illustrates the approaches through the identification of key authors.

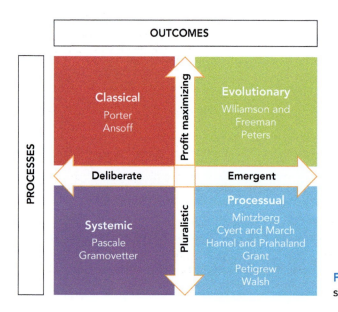

Figure 15.1 Whittington's four generic strategy types

Strategy in practice – how should it be presented

Factors determining how strategy is presented

The chapter has up to this point given an overview of theoretical approaches to strategic management and its application in *THE* contexts.

We now turn our attention (briefly) to a consideration of strategy in practice and specifically: How should the strategy be presented?

Of course there is no absolute answer to this question, since the presentation of the strategy is a subjective matter and styles vary enormously. The presentation of the strategy will vary according to a number of factors including those shown in Table 15.4.

Styles of strategy presentation

As a result of the factors outlined in Table 15.4 there are a wide range of styles adopted for the presentation of strategies. In fact it is true to say that every strategy is unique.

Table 15.5 summarizes some of the ways in which the presentation of strategies differ.

It is difficult to be precise about what constitutes good practice when it comes to presenting a strategy because as outlined above it is largely subjective and is determined by the context in which it is written.

One way of considering and remembering the importance of presentation to producing a 'good' strategy is to remember the 'seven Cs of presentation'.

Table 15.4 Factors determining the way in which organizations present their strategies

Factor	Implication
Who the strategy is aimed at	Is it aimed mainly at the owners or is it aimed at a range of stakeholders? Those aimed predominantly at shareholders and other investors will focus predominantly on financial information and financial prospects for the future.
Private or public companies	Private companies normally do not disclose as much information as public companies because they do not need to do so in order to attract investment and inform shareholders. Many privately held companies are controlled by one person or a small team and the strategy may be closely aligned with these people.
Size and complexity	Some strategies are written for large and complex organizations in dynamic environments and therefore the strategy to be meaningful has to address a wide range of issues. Conversely other strategies may be written for smaller less complex organizations and the range of issues is narrower.
Competitive pressures	Sometimes the strategy (at least its published version) is deliberately vague or ambiguous. This reflects the competitive environment within which the organization is operating. In some cases the organization will not want to divulge too much information which could be useful to competitors.
Strategic approach	This chapter has outlined different approaches or views of strategy. In particular prescriptive vs. emergent views have been highlighted. Where the strategic approach is prescriptive it implies a detailed process has been undertaken and a strategic plan has been prepared. Conversely, if an emergent view is taken, it might be decided that the environment is too turbulent for a strategy to be written or that it should be minimalist in style.

Table 15.5 Differences in the presentation of an organization's strategy

Factor	Implication
Length	Some strategies are long and complex.
	Some strategies are short and simple.
	In some cases the strategy is mainly presented as a short summary with supporting reports and appendices that provide evidence and analysis.
Style	Some strategies are very colourful professionally produced documents, with many elaborate charts and illustrations.
	Others strategies are drab and have few illustrations.
Language	Some strategies use very simple language while others are laden with jargon. The 'language of strategy' is full of different words that are used to denote the same aspect and conversely the same words that are used to denote different aspects.
	The situation is made more complicated by the fact that strategy is a field that has many 'gurus', academics and consultants involved, who make their own uses for words and sometimes create their own terminology.
Strategic terminology	Closely linked to the previous point is the strategic terminology that is used. In many cases organizations will avoid using the strategic terminology we have used in this book (or any other strategic terminology that is commonly used).
	This is because just as a doctor is likely to explain an illness to a patient in non-technical language, so the strategy is explained in non-technical language that has meaning for all the stakeholders involved.
	Thus the strategy may be presented with words such as 'where we want to get to' rather than use the word 'vision'.
Detail	Some strategies are highly detailed and clearly can be applied to all parts of the business.
	Other strategies lack detail and apply only to the organization as a whole.
Measures of success	Some strategies contain measurable objectives, key performance indicators (KPIs) and an indication of critical success factors (CSFs) which will allow for the strategy to be delivered – or not.
	Other strategies contain only vague qualitative statements which cannot be measured and there is little indication of what might constitute success; to use the strategic terminology – 'What does success look like?'

The seven Cs of presentation

The strategy should be:

1. Clear — Written in a style that is easily comprehended.
2. Coherent — There is a logical flow through the document.
3. Consistent — Each aspect is consistent with all other aspects.
4. Concise — Excessive words and documentation are avoided.
5. Convincing — Based clearly on evidence and analysis and presents arguments logically with measurable targets.
6. Context-specific — Takes account of the specific *THE* context for which it is written.
7. Comprehensive — Relates to all parts of the organization.

Source: Author's classification.

Table 15.6 Suggested guidelines for the presentation of strategy

Aspect	Guidelines
Presentation	The strategy should be clear, interesting and 'professional' in its presentational standards.
Length	The strategy may be detailed; have supporting documents; and have adaptations for all parts of the organization. Other strategies might be short but equally effective. In either case the outcome should be the result of a robust process. However, the essence of the strategy should be capable of being captured on a single page for ease of communication and dissemination.
Language	The strategy should be written in such a way that it is clear, concise and appropriate for the stakeholders it is trying to address.
Internal consistency	All parts of the strategy should be consistent with each other, so that it is not ambiguous or contradictory and there is a logical flow to the document. All parts of the organization should be aligned so that objectives (what is tryng to be achieved) at every level and each part of the organization are consistent.
Measurement of success	The strategy should contain measureable and achievable objectives of some sort – unless there are measurable objectives, how does anyone know whether the strategy has been successful and how will staff be motivated to achieve them?

It is suggested that flowing from the seven Cs of Presentation a number of guidelines, considered in Table 15.6, would apply in most cases:

An example of what a strategy might look like is shown in Table 15.7.

In this example the strategy is summarized on a single page and the European airline easyJet is used as an example.

In relation to Table 15.7 the following should be noted:

- *The left-hand column* uses the sort of strategic terminology used in this text and others to describe the 'strategic hierarchy'. Most strategies involve a strategic hierarchy of some sort (though they vary in detail). It provides a logical journey through the strategic process.
- *The middle column* gives a description of what the strategic terms (used in the left-hand column) mean in short easily understood sentences, e.g. 'values' are described as 'what we want to be'.
- *The right-hand column* presents the easyJet strategy, by way of example.

The strategy which is adapted from the company's 2012 annual report (easyJet, 2012) utilizes the same terminology and emphasis that the company used in its document. Note the capitalization of SAFETY FIRST is also taken directly from the easyJet report.

> **THINK POINTS**
>
> - Discuss the factors you might take into account when presenting a strategy for a *THE* organization of your choice.
> - Using relevant examples from *THE*, explain why it is necessary for strategy to be internally consistent.
> - Why do you think strategic management is sometimes considered a 'difficult' subject to study?

Table 15.7 What a strategy document might look like

Our strategy		
MISSION	Why we exist?	*Ambition*: Europe's preferred short-haul airline delivering market leading returns
VALUES	What we want to be?	*Our Values*: Safety, Pioneering, One Team, Passion, Simplicity, Integrity
VISION	What we believe in? or Where we want to get to?	*Cause:* To make travel easy and affordable
STRATEGY KEY THEMES	What is our plan for the future?	*Strategic Intent:* Leverage easyJet's cost advantage, leading market position and brand to deliver point-to-point low fares with operational efficiency and friendly service for our customers
STRATEGY IN ACTION	What we need to do?	*Guiding Principles:* <ul><li>SAFETY FIRST</li><li>Operational Excellence</li><li>Efficient asset utilization</li><li>We are an online business</li><li>Aim to be No.1 or No.2 in the market with significant market share</li><li>Focus on large volume markets</li><li>Aim for at least 30–40% cost advantage</li></ul> *Enablers:* <ul><li>Low cost production model with simple defined processes and organization</li><li>Culture of engagement and going the extra mile</li><li>Strong balance sheet and flexible fleet arrangements</li><li>Driving demand through targeted marketing and excellent customer insight</li><li>Converting demand into effective revenue per seat mile (RSM)</li></ul>
MEASURING SUCCESS	How we know if we have been successful?	*In order to execute against our strategy, easyJet is focused on four key objectives:* <ul><li>Build strong number 1 and 2 network positions</li><li>Maintain cost advantage</li><li>Drive demand, conversion and yields across Europe</li><li>Disciplined use of capital</li></ul>

Source: Adapted from easyJet, 2012

CHAPTER SUMMARY

Strategic management is fundamentally concerned with understanding the nature of competitive advantage and the means by which it is acquired and sustained.

This chapter has argued (as elsewhere in this book) that the contexts presented in *THE* are different from those in other sectors. They are different from manufacturing in particular, but there are also defining characteristics which make *THE* different from other service-based sectors. Consequently managers in *THE* must be aware of these distinctive factors and take them into account when designing appropriate strategies.

This chapter has explored the major approaches adopted by strategists seeking to better understand the factors which underpin competitive advantage, allowing certain organizations to outperform their competitors. The different approaches when applied to *THE* contexts, it is argued, should not be regarded as mutually exclusive, but rather they provide alternative methods for better understanding the means by which strategy is formulated and implemented. A degree of planning of strategy is required, but equally strategy might also emerge incrementally to take account of the dynamic nature of the environment.

The chapter concludes by taking a more practically oriented approach to strategy. In pulling all the disparate threads together what factors underpin the presentation of the strategy and what should the 'finished product' look like? It is difficult to be definitive, since there is room for innovation and creativity and judgement as to what constitutes successful presentation are subjective. However, five guidelines are suggested which would appear to apply in most cases.

REFERENCES

Ansoff, I. (1987) *Corporate Strategy*, Harmondsworth: Penguin.

Argenti, J. (1980) *Practical Corporate Planning*, London: G. Allen & Unwin.

Argyris, C. (1992) *On Organisational Learning*, London: Blackwell.

Campbell, D., G. Stonehouse and B. Houston (2002) *Business Strategy: An Introduction*, 2nd edn, Oxford: Butterworth-Heinemann.

Chandler, A. D. (1962) *Strategy and Structure*, Boston, Mass.: MIT Press.

Demarest, M. (1997) 'Understanding Knowledge Management, ' *Long Range Planning*, 30 (3): 374–84.

easyJet (2012) *Annual Report*, available at www.easyjet.com (accessed March 2014).

Echtner, C. M. and T. J. Jamal (1997) 'The Disciplinary Dilemma of Tourism Studies', *Annals of Tourism Research*, 24 (4): 868–83.

Evans, N. (2001) 'The Development and Positioning of Business Related University Tourism Education: A UK Perspective', *Journal of Teaching in Travel and Tourism*, 1 (1): 17–36.

— (2012) 'Tourism: A Strategic Business Perspective', in T. Jamal and M. Robinson (eds.), *The Sage Handbook of Tourism Studies*, Thousand Oaks, Calif.: Sage, pp. 215–34.

Faulkner, B. and C. Ryan (1999) 'Innovations in Tourism Management Research and Conceptualisation', *Tourism Management*, 20 (1): 3–6.

Gee, C. Y., J. C. Makens and D. J. L. Choy (1997) *The Travel Industry*, 3rd edn, New York: John Wiley.

Getz, D. (2002) 'Event Studies and Event Management: On Becoming an Academic Discipline', *Journal of Hospitality and Tourism Management*, 9 (1): 12–23.

Grant, R. M. (1991) 'The Resource Based Theory of Competitive Advantage: Implications for Strategy Formulation', *California Management Review*, 33 (spring): 114–35.

Hamel, G., Y. Doz and C. K. Prahalad (1989) 'Collaborate with Your Competitors and Win', *Harvard Business Review*, 67 (1): 133–9.

Hamel, G. and C. K. Prahalad (1989) 'Strategic Intent', *Harvard Business Review*, 67 (3): 63–78.

Heene, A. and R. Sanchez (eds.) (1997) *Competence-Based Strategic Management*, London: John Wiley.

Henkel, M. (1988) 'Responsiveness of the Subjects in Our Study: A Theoretical Perspective', in C. Boys, J. Brennan, M. Henkel, J. Kirkland, M. Kogan and P. Youll (eds.) (1988) *Higher Education and Preparation for Work*, Chichester: John Wiley, pp. 134–95.

Holloway, J. C. and C. Humphreys (2009) *The Business of Tourism*, 9th edn, London: Pearson.

Jones, G. (2004) 'Perspectives on Strategy', in S. Segal-Horn (ed.), *The Strategy Reader*, Oxford: Blackwell, pp. 491–508.

Kay, J. (1993) *Foundations of Corporate Success: How Business Strategies Add Value*, Oxford: Oxford University Press.

Leiper, N. (1981) 'Towards a Cohesive Curriculum in Tourism: The Case for a Distinct Discipline', *Annals of Tourism Research*, 8 (1): 69–83.

McKiernan P. (1997) 'Strategy Past; Strategy Futures', *Long Range Planning*, 30 (5): 790–8.

Mintzberg, H. (1987) 'Crafting Strategy', *Harvard Business Review*, July–August: 66-79.

Mintzberg, H., J. B. Quinn and S. Ghoshal (1995) *The Strategy Process: Concepts, Contexts and Cases*, Englewood Cliffs, NJ: Prentice Hall.

Ottenbacher, M., R. Harrington and H. G. Parsa (2009) 'Defining the Hospitality Discipline: A Discussion of Pedagogical and Research Implications', *Journal of Hospitality and Tourism Research*, 33 (3): 263–83.

Penrose, E. (1959) *The Theory of the Growth of the Firm*, Oxford: Oxford University Press.

Porter M. E. (1980) *Competitive Strategy: Techniques for Analysing Industries and Competitors*, New York: The Free Press.

— (1985) *Competitive Advantage*, New York: The Free Press.

Prahalad, C. K. and G. Hamel (1990) 'The Core Competence of the Corporation', *Harvard Business Review*, 68 (3): 79-91.

Quinn, J. B. (1978) 'Strategic Change; Logical Incrementalism', *Sloan Management Review*, 20 (1): 7–19.

Quinn J. B. and J. Voyer (1994) *The Strategy Process*, Englewood Cliffs, NJ: Prentice Hall.

Rumelt, R. (1991) 'How Much Does Industry Matter?' *Strategic Management Journal*, 12 (3): 167–85.

Sanchez, R. and A. Heene (eds.) (1997) *Strategic Learning and Knowledge Management*, New York: Wiley.

Tribe, J. (1997) 'The Indiscipline of Tourism', *Annals of Tourism Research*, 24 (3): 638–57.

UNWTO (2013) *United Nations World Tourism Organization Annual Report*, Madrid: World Tourism Organization, available at www.unwto.org

Whittington, R. (2001) *What Is Strategy – and Does It Matter?* 2nd edn, London: Cengage Learning.

Withey, L. (1998) *Grand Tours and Cook's Tours: A History of Leisure Travel, 1750 to 1915*, London: Aurum Press.

FURTHER READING

Reference	Focus
Argyris, C. (1977) 'Double Loop Learning in Organisations', *Harvard Business Review*, 55 (5): 115–25.	Organizational learning Double-loop learning Emergent strategy
— (1992) *On Organisational Learning*, Oxford: Blackwell.	Organizational learning Emergent strategy
Argyris, C. and D. Schon (1978) *Organisation Learning: A Theory of Action Perspective*, Reading, Mass.: Addison Wesley.	Organizational learning Emergent strategy
Cravens, D. W., G. Greenley, N. F. Piercy and S. Slater (1997) 'Integrating Contemporary Strategic Management Perspectives', *Long Range Planning*, 30 (4): 493–506.	Strategy approaches
— (1997) 'The Knowledge-Based View of the Firm: Implications for Management Practice', *Long Range Planning*, 30 (3): 450–4.	Resource based theory Organizational knowledge
Hamel, G. and C. K. Prahalad (1994) *Competing for the Future*, Cambridge, Mass.: Harvard Business School Press.	Resource based theory Core competencies Corporate futures
Heracleous, L. (1998) 'Strategic Thinking or Strategic Planning', *Long Range Planning*, 30 (3): 481–7.	Strategy approaches Strategic planning

Mintzberg, H., B. Ahlstrand and J. Lampel (2005) *Strategy Safari: A Guided Tour through the Wilds of Strategic Mangament*, New York: Simon & Schuster.	Strategy critique Srategy literature Emergent strategy
Quinn, J. B. (1992) *The Intelligent Enterprise*, New York: Free Press.	Emergent strategy Incrementalism Organizational Learning
Senge, P. M. (1997) 'The Fifth Discipline', *Measuring Business Excellence*, 1 (3): 46–51.	Emergent strategy Leadership Organizational learning
Wang, C. L. and P. K. Ahmed (2003) 'Organizational Learning: A Critical Review', *The Learning Organization*, 10 (1): 8–17.	Organizational learning

CASE LINKAGES

Case 7	Thomas Cook

Part **6**

Case analysis for tourism, hospitality and events

Case analysis

Case study analysis invariably forms a part of most courses in strategic management. Originally developed as a teaching tool in the major American Business Schools, particularly, Harvard, case studies are now widely used by most universities when studying business related courses. Case studies are used so as to enable students to understand the complex nature of strategic decision making and the inter-related nature of such decisions i.e. a decision taken in one part of a business will have a knock on effect upon other parts of the business. The case study approach enables academic points to be illustrated in context rather than in an abstract way enabling learning to be more relevant, interesting and easier to understand.

It has been argued throughout this book that managers in THE have to be aware of the distinctive characteristics of these sectors and the managerial implications of these characteristics. Cases that cover various facets of tourism, hospitality and events management provide an illustration of the specific strategic management challenges that managers face in these contexts.

Case studies are thus a valuable tool in several ways. Case studies:

- Provide experience of organizational problems and issues that it might not be possible or feasible to encounter directly.
- Serve to illustrate the theory and concepts of strategic management applied to relevant examples from *THE*.
- Allow active participation in strategic analysis, choice and implementation and of presenting results persuasively.
- Illustrate the linkages inherent in strategic management in that internal decisions have impacts on other parts of the organization and on external stakeholders.
- Illustrate the holistic nature of strategic management in that decisions often require knowledge of other subject fields such as marketing, finance and human resource management.

Although there is perhaps no substitute for management experience in the real world, case studies represent the next best thing!

What do case studies cover?

The case studies you are asked to analyse indicate the broad range of strategic decisions managers need to take in real world *THE* organizations. The cases may vary in a number of ways which may affect the type of analysis that is carried out and the way in which the results of the analysis are presented.

Cases are diverse and may relate to organizations:

- that are large or small scale;
- that are complex in their structure and management or which are relatively simple to understand;
- with exposure to particular types of risk;
- that are successful or that are in difficulties;
- that are known to you or where their true circumstances are changed in order to illustrate particular points;
- that are totally fictitious and created just for illustrative purposes or in which the company name, the names of managers and so on are altered so as to disguise the real company being considered;
- in the present day or at a date in the past;
- where they are working collectively or on their own.

In all cases considered, however, it is important to realise that what you are normally being asked to do is to:

Place yourself in the position of a manager of an organisation or within an indusry sector at a particular moment in time.

The important point is not what actually happened to the company in reality, but given the available information, how would you have made sense of the information available to you at the time and what actions would you have recommended in the circumstances.

Reading and studying the case

In considering cases you are expected to go beyond merely *describing* the circumstances of the case. The case method requires you to analyse the cases in detail and develop sound reasoned judgements that will lead to recommendations being made.

In so doing it is important to recognize the key or strategic points of the case and to distinguish these points from less substantial or trivial points.

Many cases contain 'red herrings', which are designed to mislead and confuse. In this way the 'real-world' is replicated because in real situations information:

- comes from several directions;
- reaches managers by different means; and
- is often confusing or incomplete.

A manager has to make sense of the information and discern the important or urgent from the less important or less urgent. So in analysing a case it is important to ask:

What are the central issues?

There will be instances when you feel that you do not have all the information you need to make the best decision. The information presented in the case, however, is often incomplete by design and again reflects the situation pertaining in the real world. Managers often have to make decisions based on the information available to them at the time, and although they might wish they had further information it is either unavailable or not available within the necessary time-scale with the resources available. Thus you are required to make the best possible use of the information that you actually have at your disposal.

You are also asked to make your analysis at the time of the case. Managers do not have the benefit of hindsight when managing their companies, (much as they might want it), they have to manage with the information available to them at that time and so it is with case studies.

For example – A case considering a tour operatior set in 2000 would not have known for instance of the terrorist attacks on America in September 2001 and its subsequent effects upon international travel and the companies involved.

One of the difficulties in analysing cases is the lack of a *'right'* answer. Whilst there may be some answers that are clearly *'wrong'*, it is less easy to prove that an answer is right.

For example – If you propose that a small events management company operating in its local market that has demonstrated growth of 10 per cent per annum over the last 5 years should grow to become the largest event management company in the world over the next three years, it would almost certainly be unrealistic and therefore *'wrong'*.

However, there may be several strategic options available and the strength of the answer depends upon the strength of the arguments presented, which in turn depend upon the analysis carried out. The analysis of the case should be based upon:

- the facts of the case;
- sound and logical reasoning; and importantly;
- the application of strategic principles, theories and concepts from the academic literature.

Doing the analysis

A few tips on the analysis of cases are suggested in the table below.

Analysis aspect	Tips
Reading the case	Read the case twice initially. First read the case quickly as if you were reading a newspaper getting a feel for the structure and layout of the case.
	On the second reading of the case, make notes, underline important passages, mark sections for later analysis and identify the central issues. Once you have an adequate grasp of the case and the issues presented you can begin an in-depth analysis.
Organize the case facts	The facts of a case may be presented in a bewildering or misleading way.
	It may be necessary for you to reorganize the information or label the data so that it makes more sense.
	For example – sometimes it might be necessary to re-order the material chronologically or to separate the organization into its constituent parts (SBUs).
Avoid vacuous terms	Terms, which are hollow and lacking in content, make the analysis unsound.
	For example – 'good', 'bad', 'many', 'few' are vacuous without precise meaning as each individual could interpret them in a different manner. Instead use precise language.
Do not contact the company	The case provides the information you need to analyse and the information may have been changed for teaching purposes.
	The case is designed to put you in the position of a company manager at a particular point in time.
	What actually happened is not normallty relevant and companies should not be burdened by numerous enquiries – unless you are specifically instructed to do so.
Appeals to authority	Use of references, application of concepts and empirical evidence to support your case are valid ways of justifying your arguments.
	However, care must be taken. Just because an 'expert' supports a view does not necessarily make it correct and different experts can present different views.
Applying concepts	If you use a concept to organize the information or to support your views make sure that it is applied appropriately.
	For example – Porter's Five Force Model may be an appropriate way of analysing the competitive environment but make sure that it is applied to the facts of the case and not merely presented in its abstract form.
	A common mistake is to use every conceivable strategic concept or framework available. Be selective. Usually some concepts are more appropriate in the circumstances than others.
	The concepts are only useful in that they aid understanding.
	Which concepts are appropriate will depend upon the facts of the case and the material presented to you.

Analysis aspect	Tips
Case linkages	The case may be presented in a confusing manner but look for opportunities to make links between different parts of the case and thereby demonstrate that you have understood the case and its complexities.
	For example – The case may state within the text that a new sales and marketing director was appointed. In another part of the case a table may indicate a falling sales trend and the financial statements may indicate a vastly increased advertising budget. By bringing together the three disparate pieces of information appropriate conclusions might be drawn.
	Similarly, bringing together information from differing parts of the case and presenting it in a different form may be useful to aid understanding. Putting the figures into a graph or table might be useful, for example.
Adding value to the information	Look for opportunities when analysing a case to add value through your analysis. In other words it is of far more value to interpret the information rather than merely to repeat the information contained in the case in your answer.
	For example – A case on an airline might state that the aircraft fleet contains 10 Boeing 737-800 and 6 Boeing 787 aircraft purchased at various stated dates between 2000 and 2014. Rather than repeat this information in your answer it is much more useful to calculate the average age of the fleet. Is the fleet relatively young or relatively old? *Similarly* – A hotel operator may present sales figures for the last ten years. A calculation showing the percentage growth (or decline) of sales from year-to-year would add value. Such a calculation would clearly show whether the rate of growth has risen or declined.

CASE STUDY SUMMARY

Case	Strategy focus	Geographic focus	Sector focus
Strategic Alliances in the Airline Industry	History and development of international airlines Alliances as a strategic method for growth International regulation of airlines External Analysis	Global	International Airlines
Tourism Queensland: Strategic Positioning and Promotion	Strategy for developing Queensland as an international tourism and events destination Sustainability Product and markets Public/private partnerships	Asia/Pacific	Tourist destinations and events
Ryanair: Evolution of Competitive Strategy	Cost leadership competitive strategy Approaches to customer care Leadership styles Change	UK and Europe	International Airlines
Hyatt Hotels: A family firm goes for growth	International growth strategies in the hotel industry Methods of growth e.g. franchising and management contracts Market segmentation and brand development Corporate governance	US and Global	Hotels
Days Inn: Franchising Hospitality Assets in China	Analysing the competitive environment Segmenting targeting and positioning hotels Hotel penetration in the Asian market Characteristics of *THE* products	US and China	Hotels
Thomas Cook: Turnaround for an historic travel brand	Historic tourism development Competitive strategy and strategic direction Products and markets Financial analysis and performance Change and leadership Turnaround strategy	Europe and Global	Tour operators and tourism
Reed Exhibitions: Strategic issues for a leading events management company	Planning events Understanding strategic risks Product and market strategy Product innovation Competitive strategy and strategic methods Internationalization	Global	Events

CHAPTER–CASE CORRELATION

CHAPTER	CASE						
	Strategic Alliances in the Airline Industry	Tourism Queensland: Strategic Positioning and Promotion	Ryanair: Evolution of Competitive Strategy	Hyatt Hotels: A Family Firm Goes for Growth	Days Inn: Franchising Hospitality Assets in China	Thomas Cook: Turnaround for an Historic Travel Brand	Reed Exhibitions: Strategic Issues for a Leading Events Management Company
1. Strategy and strategic objectives		✓					✓
2. Introduction to strategy for tourism, hospitality and events	✓			✓	✓	✓	
3. The operational context – competencies, resources and competitive advantage	✓	✓	✓	✓		✓	✓
4. The Human Context			✓	✓			
5. Financial Analysis and Performance Indicators				✓		✓	✓
6. Products and Markets		✓	✓	✓	✓	✓	✓
7. The external environment – The macro context	✓	✓		✓	✓		
8. The external environment – The micro context	✓	✓		✓	✓		
9. SWOT analysis	✓	✓		✓	✓		
10. Competitive strategy and strategic direction		✓	✓	✓	✓	✓	✓
11. Strategic methods of development	✓			✓	✓	✓	✓
12. Strategic evaluation and selection				✓	✓		
13. Strategic implementation		✓		✓	✓	✓	
14. International and global strategies	✓	✓	✓	✓	✓	✓	✓
15. Strategy: Theory and practice						✓	

Strategic alliances in the airline industry

Introduction

The airline sector has a long history of working in partnership exemplified by the International Air Transport Association's (IATA) annual conferences and bilateral agreements (which split markets equally between pairs of national airlines). Under the auspices of IATA, on a global scale, a tradition of cooperation between airlines was built up and on individual routes co-operation has commonly included revenue-pooling agreements between the carriers operating a route.

Airlines have, in recent years, rushed to form alliances in the fear of being left behind and the stage has now been reached where the international airline sector has coalesced into three large alliance groupings: the *Star Alliance, Oneworld Alliance* and the *SkyTeam Alliance*. Each of the alliances contains one of the large American so-called legacy airlines.

It is not only the number of airline alliance agreements being made that is significant, but the deepening relations between partners in these alliances. The alliances are no longer mere loose arrangements between a couple of carriers to share flight codes and cross-sell tickets. The alliances have developed in a way that is so wide-ranging that they are 'virtual mergers', despite national rules often forbidding foreign ownership.

However some notable gaps in the coverage of the major strategic alliances remain as some airlines have adopted a different competitive stance. In particular the fast-growing and cash-rich Middle East Airlines of Emirates and Etihad, based at the developing hubs of Dubai and Abu Dhabi respectively, have so far avoided joining the alliances and pursue their own individual strategies. Unlike the other fast-growing Middle East airline – Qatar Airways, which joined the Oneworld Alliance during 2014 – Emirates and Etihad have chosen different methods in striving for growth.

These methods involve individual partnership arrangements with other airlines, over which the respective two United Arab Emirates airlines have some degree of control. In the case of Emirates this has involved some individual cooperation agreements with airlines, particularly Qantas, while Etihad has taken several minority stakes in airlines including German carrier Air Berlin. An illustration of this approach was provided by Tim Clark, president of Emirates, when interviewed for the London based Financial Times (Parker, 2013). He said that 'Emirates has no interest in joining one of the global alliances, because it does not want to be "beholden" to some of the most powerful carriers within these groupings'.

Motivations for alliance formation in the airline sector

British Airways attempted to introduce a degree of empiricism to the analysis of the external driving forces underpinning alliance formation. The airline used scenario-planning techniques to develop strategies for the future given uncertainties in the macro environment (Moyer, 1996). Scenarios representing possible futures were developed which sought to identify the key driving forces shaping the world economy and in turn the airline industry as their starting point. Enormous changes have occurred in technology, education and world trade, and with a quickening pace of change. These four forces have combined and manifested themselves in the form of the information revolution, economic restructuring and global competition, representing major environmental shifts making existing strategies vulnerable.

External drivers

Information revolution

In the 1960s and 1970s information technologies mainly played a facilitating role in international tourism, creating mass, standardized and rigidly packaged tourism but merely facilitating its development (Poon, 1993). The US Airline Deregulation Act of 1978 introduced airlines operating in the USA to a new world of competitive threats and opportunities. The key change, whereby price-regulating power was removed from the Civil Aeronautics Board (CAB), enabled airlines to increase the variety of fares offered and the increased frequency by which fares were changed necessitated the extensive development of advanced computer reservations systems (CRS).

The CRS systems allow airlines to monitor, manage and control their capacity through yield management and their clients through frequent flyer programmes. The growth in CRS systems, first in the US, then in Europe and elsewhere created a marketing tool of considerable power, giving travel agents' preferences for booking flights towards the first to appear on their screens. The spread in the coverage of CRS systems and their increasing sophistication with many functions other than reservations has led to them being termed Global Distribution Systems (GDS).

In the past the airlines that owned the GDS undoubtedly favoured their own flights (or those of their code-sharing partners), but to a significant extent such bias has now been eliminated at least in Europe and North America through codes of conduct. The power given to airlines by the GDS system has been replicated by the power given directly to consumers by the internet. A vast amount of information is available to consumers to compare prices and its growth has allowed airlines to communicate directly with consumers cutting out the need for intermediaries to be involved. Many airlines, particularly the low-cost carriers, take the majority of their bookings through this distribution channel.

Economic restructuring

Economic restructuring through the philosophy of 'economic disengagement' by governments in many parts of the world has, over the last few decades, had a major impact on airline industry structure. This philosophy influenced by the widespread adoption of the 'Theory of Contestable Markets' (which advocated the removal of restrictive market entry barriers) from the early 1980s (Baumol, 1982) manifested itself in the forms of deregulation and privatization.

The Chicago Convention of 1944 established the bilateral system of air service agreements between pairs of national governments, which have since governed international air transport. The international market that developed was characterized by national airlines from each country serving routes, airlines charging the same fares, and often sharing markets and revenues. Some bilateral agreements also stipulate conditions governing responsibility for such matters as ground handling. The terms of the bilateral agreements reflected the negotiating power and current aviation policies of the countries involved – the resulting productivity was often low and costs were high (OECD, 1997).

Deregulation of domestic services occurred in the United States in 1978 followed by Canada, the United Kingdom, Australia and New Zealand in the 1980s and the completion of deregulation within the European Union in April 1997. Parallel liberalization in international air services has taken place much more slowly. Notwithstanding the change that has occurred in some markets, even the liberalized structures are restrictive on market entry. Requirements for designated airlines to be owned by nationals of the states involved are common and airport congestion and slot allocation practices often further impede effective market entry (Doganis, 2009). Evidence is mounting, however, that the removal of bilateral agreements and similar intervention barriers can reduce fares.

Another, and linked, aspect of *economic disengagement* is the worldwide movement towards the privatization of state owned airlines. However, despite this gradual process many international airlines remain publicly owned or have major government shareholdings. Controls on foreign ownership remain in most markets, but some foreign ownership of airlines or stakes in airline ownership now exist and with planned privatizations this will increase.

The European Union's third air transport package (implemented from April 1997), for instance, sets no limit on the stake a Union national or a Union airline can hold in an airline registered in another European Union state. With limited exceptions, however, non-European Union investors cannot hold a majority stake in any European Union airline. In the United States, foreign shareholdings of up to 49 per cent of equity under certain circumstances and 25 per cent of voting stock is possible, although the US government also imposes an ad hoc control test to determine whether the foreign shareholder would substantially influence decision making irrespective of equity held.

Liberalisation, privatization, foreign ownership and trans-national mergers will have a major impact upon the future structure of the airline industry but many regulatory and ownership barriers remain in force worldwide. As a result alternative methods of strategic development, namely internally generated growth and mergers and acquisitions are often precluded as viable growth strategies for international airlines and consequently the formation of strategic alliances has been, in many cases, the only available form of market entry.

Global competition

Organizational form has been dramatically influenced by the rise of globalization and it has been argued that success or failure of larger businesses in the future will depend upon their ability to compete effectively globally (Ohmae, 1989a). Certainly many industries in the post-war era have seen a rapid concentration of activity with the emergence of a few dominant companies. Global competition is clearly well advanced in industries such as motor vehicles, pharmaceuticals, soft drinks and more recently financial services, but is a more recent phenomenon in the airline business, having been restricted by regulation, government ownership and consumer preferences.

In an influential article, Levitt (1983) argues that advances in communication and transportation technologies and increased worldwide travel have homogenized world markets with consumers worldwide, increasingly demanding the same products and exhibiting similar preferences. In such an era the strategic imperative is for businesses to achieve the economies of scale and scope that the global market affords and produce standardized products sold through a standardized marketing programme. However, such a standardized approach has been increasingly questioned and the need to recognize the differences between local market conditions has been stressed. Bartlett and Ghoshal (1989), for instance, contend that success depends on whether a business can achieve a 'transnational capability' whereby global efficiency and national flexibility are achieved simultaneously.

Airlines are seeking to maximize their 'global reach', in the belief that those that offer a global service (with a competitively credible presence in each of the major air travel markets) will be in the strongest competitive position. The importance of what Ohmae (1989b) terms the 'triad' markets of Japan, North America and Europe is shown in figure shown in Appendix 6. In a global airline context the triad is modified so as to broaden the Japanese leg of the triad to include the wider Asia-Pacific region and for the crucial markets to include not only the constituent markets of the triad but also the flows between them. Thus, globalization, and particularly developments in the key markets is an important external driver for alliance formation. The growth in international air travel will continue to outstrip the growth in economic activity as measured by GDP, but it will not be uniform across the world with some regions significantly outpacing others.

The external driving forces serve as the backdrop to an organization's decision to form strategic alliances, but firms will only enter into such agreements when their internal circumstances make this the correct strategic move. The major internal drivers identified in the literature are discussed below.

Internal drivers

Risk sharing

Strategic alliances are seen as an attractive mechanism for hedging risk because neither partner bears the full risk and cost of the alliance activity (Porter and Fuller, 1986). The need to spread the costs and risks of innovation has increased as capital requirements for development projects have risen. Developing new or existing routes, for instance, becomes far less risky if the partners operating the routes have firmly entrenched marketing strengths in the two markets at either end of the routes.

Economies of scale, scope and learning

A prime driver for alliance formation is for airlines to achieve cost economies, which can be categorized as economies of scale, scope and experience (OECD, 1997). Economies of scale exist where the average cost per unit of output declines as the level of output increases (Hanlon, 2007). Empirical evidence reveals little evidence of economies of scale however (OECD, 1997), except for the smallest operators and specific areas such as marketing. Indeed one study of United States domestic aviation suggests possible diseconomies at the largest airlines (Spraggins, 1989). Furthermore, the evidence also suggests that airlines' unit costs do not fall greatly as they expand their networks. Cost savings appear to stem largely from attracting more traffic to a given network rather than expanding it to cover more destinations.

The airline industry may lack substantial scale economies, but other economies related to the size and nature of operations exist (OECD, 1997) which help to explain the growing market concentration and the move towards alliances. Economies of scope occur when the cost of producing two (or more) products jointly is less than the cost of producing each one alone. Such economies can be achieved if alliance partners link up their existing networks so that they can provide connecting services for new markets, and where marketing costs can be shared between alliance partners (Hanlon, 2007) who may have strong entrenched positions in certain markets.

For example, the alliance between KLM and Northwest formed in 1989 had a substantial impact on passenger numbers, market share and both airlines' financial performance (Hannegan and Mulvey, 1995). Through the long standing alliance which lasted for many years, KLM gained access to Northwest's extensive North American route network based on its Minneapolis, Detroit and Boston hubs, whilst Northwest could promote a sizeable international network based on KLM's services from its Amsterdam hub.

A number of authors, such as Hamel (1991) and Inkpen (1998) have suggested that an important motivator to form alliances is the benefit to be derived from economies of learning (such as experience). Incumbent suppliers have more information on the market being served and can tailor their services to specific customer needs, whereas new entrants would have to sink resources to acquire such information in order to win market share; alliances allow the information to be gained from existing suppliers.

Access to assets, resources and competencies

Specific resource, skill or competence inadequacy or imbalance can be addressed by collaborating with partners which have a different set of such attributes and can therefore compensate for internal deficiencies. The regulatory framework of 'bilaterals' (see Appendix 3) and landing rights and congestion at certain airports means that airlines possessing licenses to operate on a route and slots at congested airports have important and marketable assets that are attractive to alliance partners. Alliances can thus offer relatively easy access to a route (Bennett, 1997) through allowing access to a partner's assets which may have been established over prolonged periods and which may have been protected by government intervention.

Shape competition

Strategic alliances can influence the companies that a firm competes with and the basis for competition (Porter and Fuller, 1986) since they can hinder the abilities of competing firms to retaliate by binding them as allies. Furthermore, current strategic positions may be successfully defended against forces that are too strong for one firm to withstand alone (Glaister and Buckley, 1996).

Strategic alliances may, therefore, be used as a defensive ploy to reduce competition since an obvious benefit of strategic alliances is converting a competitor into a partner (Jennings 1996). Smaller, relatively weak airlines may view alliances as the only viable way in which to compete with larger, more sophisticated rivals. The purchase of a 40 per cent share of Sri Lankan Airlines in 1998 by Emirates Airlines, for instance, can be viewed as part of a defensive alliance strategy aimed at retaining international competitiveness through allying with a commercially stronger rival.

Alternatively, alliance formation may form part of an offensive strategy, by linking with a rival, for example, in order to put pressure on the profits and market share of a common competitor (Contractor. and Lorange, 1988). The long standing operating alliance between British Airways and American on transatlantic routes, as part of the wider Oneworld alliance is an example of such an offensive positioning. As such it has attracted criticism in that the two airlines have large market shares on these routes and dominant positions at their respective hubs.

Alliance structure and scope

Considerable time and effort may be expended in developing the structure and scope of an alliance. The unique nature and operating environment of the airline sector dictates that alliances must be structured around diverse requirements (Mockler, 1999). Determining the structure and scope of an alliance requires detailed consideration of issues across a broad spectrum. Mockler *et al.* (1997) group the decisions into five categories relating to: marketing; products and services; computer systems technologies; equipment; and equipment servicing and logistics.

Evaluation of alliance performance

Evaluating the performance of alliances is complex given the multifaceted objectives of many alliances and the difficulties involved in ascribing financial measures. The situation is often further complicated by the asymmetric performance: one firm achieves its objectives while others fail to do so. For instance several studies have reported cases of alliances in which one partner had raced to learn the other's skills while the other partners had no such intentions (Khanna et al., 1988; Hamel et al., 1989). Despite these evident measurement obstacles, several writers have attempted empirical studies of alliance performance primarily through examining the factors leading to the termination of alliance arrangements. These studies, which have not focused directly on the airline industry, have cited various contributory factors in the termination of alliances including: partner asymmetry, the competitive overlap between partners, the presence of other concurrent ties, and the characteristics of the alliance itself such as autonomy of operations and flexibility (Kogut, 1989). Such an approach to the study of alliance performance is limited by two factors. First, not all alliance terminations can be viewed as failures since in some cases they may have been intended as interim transitional arrangements. Second, not all on-going alliances can necessarily be viewed as being successful, since inertia or high exit costs may provide an explanation for their continuation.

Taking a more pragmatic approach to the evaluation of alliance success, Mockler (1999) suggests that four basic criteria should be fulfilled. First, that the alliance must add value to a participant. That is, it must be worth more to the company to enter into an alliance than to undertake a venture on its own. Second, that the participant must be able to learn something from collaborating with partners. Third, a participant must be able to protect its own competencies even while interacting with the alliance over a continuing period of time, and fourth, the firm must retain flexibility, and not be over-reliant on any one partner.

Airline alliance success and failure (examples)

The long list of failed airline alliances, supposedly bolstered by equity stakes, includes Air Canada/ Continental Airlines, Scandinavian Airlines System/Continental Airlines and Sabena/Air France highlights the lack of stability in airline strategic alliances. Airlines forming alliances now have higher expectations from their alliances, than was previously the case, and are becoming more willing to cancel agreements and switch partners if agreements do not perform.

Political sensitivities lay behind the failure of another proposed airline alliance between the Dutch airline KLM and Belgian airline Sabena in the early 1990s (Shaughnessy, 1995). Both airlines had held talks with British Airways before talking to each other about a possible alliance or merger. Both airlines were loss-making and feared absorption by larger competitors, but the failure to cement an alliance highlights the uniquely political nature of the airline sector. Political considerations are transparent when both companies involved are 'national flag carriers' (Shaughnessy, 1995) carrying the prestige of the home country around the world. For Sabena (which later went bankrupt in 2001) to ally with KLM would have created a predominantly Dutch-speaking company which would have proved politically unacceptable in bilingual Belgium. Sabena had to bow to political pressure from Belgium's French-speaking community and pull out of negotiations.

The airline alliance between KLM and the American airline Northwest dating from 1989 could claim some success, at least in part, since it demonstrated uncharacteristic sustainability, and appears to have been revenue enhancing for the two partners (Hannegan and Mulvey, 1995). The alliance was borne out of necessity when KLM, in return for a 20 per cent equity stake, contributed $400 million to the $700 million that was required when senior Northwest executives put together a leveraged buyout of the airline. Notwithstanding the financial success of this strategic alliance, cultural differences and personal incompatibilities between the two parties repeatedly threatened to force them apart. Jennings (1996) highlighted these differences in stating that 'the alliance has been a saga of personal spats, fights over "creeping control" and threats of separation that were hidden behind a marriage that works well on a daily basis'. The Dutch partners, it is said, are inclined to be quiet, stay out of the limelight and focus on strong operational expertise whereas the US partners are more inclined to Hollywood lifestyles and a financial engineering approach to management (Medcof, 1997).

Conclusion

Clearly the growth of airline strategic alliances is one of the most fundamental developments in the airline industry over the last 20 years. Airlines have rushed to form alliances in the fear of being left behind and many have later changed their partners as they have become more sophisticated at identifying the potential 'strategic fit' between them. The alliances have developed from individual relationships between pairs of airlines (which were subject to many changes and modifications) to a situation where there are now three major strategic alliance groupings that have added member airlines over the years.

To some degree alliance formation can be viewed as an inevitable result of the regulatory framework within which the international airline industry operates. Regulatory and legal restrictions often prevent the full ownership of airlines by foreign companies and consequently alliances have been perceived as the only viable market entry mechanism at least in the short-to-medium term. However, some observers view strategic alliances as inherently unstable and transitory forms of organization, a 'second best' solution that is disturbingly likely to break up under commercial pressure. Porter (1990), for instance, has suggested that alliances rarely result in a sustainable competitive advantage being established, whereas Hamel (1991) views them as a race to learn, in which the winner will eventually establish dominance in the partnership thereby leading to instability. It can be argued that the benefits of alliances can probably be achieved more completely and effectively through mergers and thus alliances are only really a stopping-off point on the way towards full mergers if the lifting of regulatory and legal restrictions were to make them possible.

The role and characteristics of the strategic alliances have continued to evolve. French (1997) summarizes the recent evolution of the alliances. In the late 1980s strategic alliances were seen as a rather crude way in which to grow quickly through the avoidance of bilateral restrictions and some airlines rushed to form alliances in the fear of being left behind. The cyclical slump and heavy losses of the early 1990s turned attention to the efficiency improvements made possible by alliances and consequently airlines focused more clearly on the strategic logic of the particular partners that had been chosen. The importance of 'strategic fit' thus came to be stressed, i.e. that the proposed partners should have a culture, management style and geographical coverage that were compatible.

The commercial logic for airlines to form alliances seems to have been established as a range of external and internal drivers exert pressure. This logic, if extended, has led to the larger, multi-airline, globally encompassing alliance structures which developed from the late 1990s and which are still evident in today's industry. A growing body of research points to the role of alliance structure and scope in promoting stable relationships and improved organizational performance. Less attention has been paid to the implications of airline alliances for consumers (both internationally and in local markets) and how alliance success can be determined (Wang, 2014).

Consumers receive several benefits from those alliances that are successful in producing integrated products. Consumers are provided with an enhanced choice of destinations through the marketing of alliance partners' route networks. Schedule co-ordination between partners often produces shorter transfer times between connections and co-ordination of flight timings can avoid bunching of flight schedules. Additionally consumers benefit from: one-stop check-in for passengers (although they are taking an onward connecting flight provided by the partner airline); the pooling of frequent flyer programmes; shared airport lounge facilities; ground-handling arrangements; and the improvement in technical standards brought about through the sharing of expertise.

However, a critical unknown remains: whether consumers are paying higher or lower fares because of the strategic alliances. If carriers collaborate on many of their activities, what incentive is there for competing on price? Some independent evidence has suggested that fares in non-stop markets offered by European alliance partners have increased somewhat faster than fares in non-alliance non-stop markets. Analysis of pricing is difficult, however. The UK Consumers' Association (1997) pointed to the difficulties involved with analysis being 'hampered by the extremely complex web of factors regulations and processes that involve the industry. The airline industry is characterised by tight regulation in some areas and dominance of policy by airlines and their industry bodies in others'. By their very nature alliances often limit supply and thereby would be expected to force up prices. Alliance arrangements often allow one carrier to fly aircraft in a market where two may have been doing so otherwise, possibly leading to higher fares. Thus, the fares outlook for consumers in the rush to form alliances is far from clear.

A number of trends relating to strategic airline alliances are discernible:

- The number of airlines involved in alliances has continued to grow. Three key alliances have emerged each headed by one of the major American airlines. The focus in the coming years will be on these alliances adding further airlines so as to fill gaps in their global coverage. Equally second-level feeder airlines will be added to the existing alliances.

- Substantial new alliances may be difficult to form since the major international players from the 'triad' countries are all now involved in alliances and new ones would therefore lack the substantial marketing presence that appears to be necessary to ensure success. The existing alliances are also likely to have significant gaps in their global coverage as some notable world airlines choose different growth strategies.

- Airlines from outside the 'triad' countries will increasingly become involved with the established alliances. To date, airlines from Africa, South America and parts of Asia have largely been excluded from the major alliances. Although many such airlines are currently operating in highly protected domestic markets, the degree of protection will progressively decrease and these airlines will increasingly want to secure their commercial future through involvement with the major alliance groupings.

- Increasing consumer pressure is likely to be evident. Whilst the case for alliances has robustly been made by the airlines, less attention has been focused on consumers. Increasingly, international regulators will be attempting to ensure that the supposed cost savings (that the airlines argue result from alliance activity) are passed on to consumers and that the dominant positions at hub airports are scaled down so as to allow more 'contestability' of markets.

- Competition between the alliance groupings as entities (as opposed to the individual airlines comprising them) is increasing. The alliances promote themselves as 'umbrella' brands with the individual airlines being sub-brands, offering similar service standards and an increasing level of integration between the constituent airlines will be evident.

Appendix 1: The major airline strategic alliance groupings

	Star alliance	SkyTeam alliance	Oneworld alliance
Alliance founded	1997	2000	1999
Constituent airlines	28	19	14
Destinations	1,328	1,024	883
Countries	195	178	151
Annual passengers (Million)	727	569	354
Headquarters	Frankfurt, Germany	Amsterdam, Netherlands	New York City, USA
Daily departures	21,900	15,189	10,117
Constituent airline employees (thousands)	460	452	357
Constituent airlines include:	Air Canada Air China Air New Zealand All Nippon Airways Avianca EgyptAir Ethiopian Airlines Eva Air Lot Polish Airlines Lufthansa Scandinavian Airlines Shenzhen Airlines Singapore Airlines South African Airways TAM Airlines TAP Portugal Thai Airways Turkish Airlines United Airlines	Aeroflot Aoerolineas Argentinas Air France China Airlines China Eastern China Southern; Kenya Airways KLM MEA Qatar Airways Saudia Tarom Vietnam Airlines XiamenAir	Air Berlin American Airlines British Airways Iberia Cathay Pacific Finnair Japan Airlines Lan Malaysia Airlines Qantas Qatar Royal Jordanian AirlinesS7 US Airways

Appendix 2: External driving forces underpinning strategic alliance formation in the airline industry

Appendix 3: Freedoms of the sky and bilateral agreements

Freedoms of the sky

In 1944, delegates from 52 nations met in Chicago to develop a multilateral treaty securing each nation's rights over its airspace. These 'freedoms of the sky' have been the fundamental building blocks of air transportation regulation and each subject to specific conditions, such as establishing the frequency of flights or airport usage.

There are five basic freedoms that are recognized by virtually all countries:

- First freedom – The right to fly over another nation's territory without landing (overflight).
- Second freedom – The right to land in a foreign country for non-traffic reasons, such as maintenance or refuelling, without picking up or setting down revenue traffic.
- Third freedom – The right to carry traffic (people or cargo) from own State A to treaty partner State B.
- Fourth freedom – The right to carry traffic (people or cargo) from treaty partner State B to own State A.
- Fifth freedom – The right to carry traffic between two foreign countries with services starting or ending in own State A.

Bilateral air service agreements

International air transport services are regulated by bilateral air services agreements (ASAs) between States. When negotiating ASAs, States generally wish to secure that the rights exchanged with their partners will benefit the air carriers of both parties but not air carriers of other states who are not parties to the agreement and thus not providing reciprocal rights.

The simplest way to reserve rights for air carriers of the parties is for each party to restrict designation to air carriers majority owned and effectively controlled by that party. At the same time, restrictions are also reflected in national laws of the parties. Indeed, an obvious reason for national restrictions has been the logic of ASAs with respect to securing the benefits as described above.

(ICAO 2013)

Appendix 4: Ownership of airline equity stakes (examples)

Investor	Stake	Company	Comments
Delta	49%	Virgin Atlantic	$360 million purchase in 2012
Air France/KLM	100%	Air France	Air France-KLM is the Paris-based holding company formed in 2004
		KLM	
	26%	Kenya Airways	
	25%	Alitalia	
	20%	Air Cote d'Ivoire	
	12%	Air Corsica	
	7%	Air Tahiti	
	3%	Air Mauritius	
	3%	Royal Air Maroc	

Investor	Stake	Company	Comments
Etihad	10%	Virgin Australia	
	25%	Air Berlin	
	40%	Air Seychelles	
	3%	Aer Lingus	
IAG	100%	British Airways	IAG is the holding company based in the UK
		Iberia	
	2.3%	Air Mauritius	
	0.95%	Royal Air Maroc	
LAN/TAM	100%	Tam Airlines	LATAM is the holding company based in Chile
		Lan Airlines	
Lufthansa	100%	Austrian Airlines	2008 acquisition
	100%	Germanwings	2008 acquisition
	100%	Lufthansa Regional	
	100%	Swiss International	2005 acquisition
	50%	Sun Express	
	45%	Brussels Airlines	
	14.44%	Luxair	
	15.85%	Jet Blue	2005 acquisition for $300 million

Source: Company reports (various)

Appendix 5: Reasons for foreign ownership restrictions

- National air carriers were predominantly government owned and controlled.
- National air carriers were considered as key strategic assets.
- National security concerns about the foreign control of strategic assets.
- The intention to make aircraft readily available when needed for the purposes of national defence, emergency needs or providing air services for public interest, for example, to/from remote areas of the country.
- Market access rights, especially cabotage, were reserved to national air carriers.
- Labour issues such as the concern that foreign investors may not maintain the same labour standards.

(ICAO 2013)

Appendix 6: Airline traffic growth by airline domicile

Region	2012 % share of world RPKs	20 year average annual growth 2012–2032	2032 % share of world RPKs
Asia-Pacific	29%	5.5%	34%
Europe	26%	3.8%	22%
N America	25%	3.0%	18%
Middle East	8%	7.1%	12%
Latin America	5%	6.0%	7%
CIS (Russia & former USSR states)	4%	5.0%	4%
Africa	3%	5.1%	3%

Note: RPK – Revenue passenger kilometres
Source: Airbus Global Market Forecast 2012–2032 available at www.airbus.com

REFERENCES

Bartlett, C. A. and S. Ghoshal (1989) *Managing Across Borders: The Transnational Solution*, Cambridge, Mass.: Harvard Business Press.

Baumol, W. J. (1982) 'Contestable Markets: An Uprising in the Theory of Industry Structure', *American Economic Review*, 72 (1): 1–15.

Bennett, M. M. (1997) 'Strategic Alliances in the World Airline Industry', *Progress in Tourism and Hospitality Research*, 3 (3): 212–23.

Consumers' Association (1997) *Airline Competition: A Long Haul for the Consumer*, London: Consumers Association Policy Report.

Contractor, F. and Lorange, P. (1988) 'Why Should Firms Cooperate? The Strategy and Economic Basis for Cooperative Ventures', in F. Contractor and P. Lorange (eds.) *Cooperative Strategies in International Business*, Lexington, Mass.: Lexington Books, pp. 3–30.

Doganis, R. (2009) *Flying Off Course: Airline Economics and Marketing*, 4th edn, London and New York: Routledge.

French, T. (1997) 'Global Trends in Airline Alliances', *Tourism Analyst*, 4: 81–101.

Glaister, K. W. and P. J. Buckley (1996) 'Strategic Motives for International Alliance Formation', *Journal of Management Studies*, 33 (3): 301–32.

Hamel, G. (1991) 'Competition for Competence and Inter-Partner Learning within International Strategic Alliances', *Strategic Management Journal*, 12 (Special Summer Issue): 83–104.

Hamel, G., Y. L. Doz and C. K. Prahalad (1989) 'Collaborate with Your Competitors – and Win', *Harvard Business Review*, 67 (1), 133–9.

Hanlon, P. (2007) *Global Airlines: Competition in a Transnational Industry*, 3rd edn, Oxford: Butterworth-Heinemann.

Hannegan, T. F. and F. P. Mulvey (1995) 'International Airline Alliances: An Analysis of Code-Sharing's Impact on Airlines and Consumers', *Journal of Air Transport Management*, 2 (2): 131–7.

Inkpen, A. (1998) 'Learning, Knowledge Acquisition and Strategic Alliances', *European Management Journal*, 16 (2): 223–9.

International Civil Aviation Organization (2013) National Restrictions on Air Carrier Ownership and Control, Working Paper, Montreal, Canada: International Civil Aviation Organization.

Jennings, M. (1996) 'Immune Deficiency Syndromes', *Airline Business*, June, 52–5.

Khanna, T., R. Gulati and N. Nohria (1998) 'The Dynamics of Learning Alliances: Competition, Co-operation and Relative Scope', *Strategic Management Journal*, 19 (3): 193–210.

Kogut, B. (1989) 'The Stability of Joint Ventures: Reciprocity and Competitive Rivalry', *Journal of Industrial Economics*, 38: 183–98.

Levitt, T. (1983) 'The Globalization of Markets', *Harvard Business Review*, November/December, 92–102.

Medcof, J. W. (1997) 'Why Too Many Alliances End in Divorce', *Long Range Planning*, 30 (5): 718–32.

Mockler, R. J., D. G. Dologite and N. Carnevali (1997) 'Type and Structure of Multinational Strategic Alliances: The Airline Industry', *Journal of Strategic Change*, 6 (5): 249–60.

Mockler, R. J. (1999) *Multinational Strategic Alliances*, London: John Wiley.

Moyer, K. (1996) 'Scenario Planning at British Airways: A Case Study', *Long Range Planning*, 29 (2): 172–81.

Ohmae, K. (1989a) 'The Global Logic of Strategic Alliances', *Harvard Business Review*, 67 (2): 143–54.

—— (1989b) 'Managing in a Borderless World', *Harvard Business Review*, 67 (3): 152–61.

Organisation for Economic Co-operation and Development (1997) *The Future of International Air Transport Policy: Responding to Global Change*, Paris: OECD.

Parker, A. (2013) 'Gulf Carriers Destabilise Alliances', *The Financial Times*, 14 November.

Poon, A. (1993) *Tourism, Technology and Competitive Strategies*, Wallingford: CAB International.

Porter, M. E. (1990) *The Competitive Advantage of Nations*, London: Macmillan.

Porter, M. E. and M. B. Fuller (1986) 'Coalitions and Global Strategy', in M. E. Porter (ed.), *Competition in Global Industries*, Cambridge, Mass.: Harvard Business School Press.

Shaughnessy, H. (1995) 'International Joint Ventures: Managing Successful Collaborations', *Long Range Planning*, 28 (3): 10–17.

Spraggins, H. B. (1989) 'The Impact of Airline Size upon Efficiency and Profitability', *Journal of Transportation Management*, 23: 73–104.

Wang, S. W. (2014) 'Do Global Airline Alliances Influence the Passenger's Purchase Decision?' *Journal of Air Transport Management*, 37: 53–9.

Case **2**

Tourism Queensland

Strategic positioning and promotion

Background

Queensland is Australia's second largest and third most populous state with a population of over 5 million and many natural attractions for tourists. These include the Great Barrier Reef, a long and spectacular coastline, areas of rainforest and the 'outback'.

Tourism is one of Queensland's key sectors, generating $48 million per day – or $17.7 billion per year in overnight visitor expenditure. Tourism also directly accounts for 124,000 or 5.4 per cent of Queensland jobs and directly contributes $8.4 billion or 3.1 per cent to Queensland's gross state product.

Tourism and Events Queensland (TEQ) is the Queensland Government's lead marketing, experience development and major events agency, representing the state's tourism and events industries. TEQ operates on a national and international level, looking at new and innovative ways to make the most out of emerging opportunities which benefit the Queensland tourism industry and economy.

As the second largest export earner (behind coal), tourism generates $5 billion in overseas export earnings for Queensland. The industry supports 55,700 businesses, representing 12.9 per cent of all registered businesses in the state. TEQ works closely with the state's 13 membership-based regional tourist organizations (RTOs) which together represent around 4,400 Queensland tourism operators. The RTO network is widely regarded as one of the most influential in Australia and has played a major role in Queensland's tourism success.

TEQ provides strategic industry leadership and coordinates stakeholders in the planning, industry development, marketing and application of resources to grow tourism in each Queensland destination. Strategies and activities are developed in close consultation with the RTOs. TEQ maintains a network of 13 international offices, working closely with Tourism Australia to target established and emerging international markets.

Queensland's tourism industry has developed greatly since 1929, when the then Queensland Government Tourist Bureau was transferred to the Railway Department and the first attempt was made to correlate publicity with a travel booking organization. Tourism and Events Queensland began as the Queensland Tourist and Travel Corporation (QTTC). The QTTC was established by Act of Parliament in August 1979, taking over from the Department of Tourism.

As a statutory authority, under the jurisdiction of the then Minister for Maritime Services and Tourism, the corporation operated as a marketing and development organization, with the sales arm trading under the name, Queensland Government Tourist Bureau.

The functions of the Corporation as defined in the act were to:

- promote and market tourism and travel;
- make tourism and travel arrangements;
- provide tourism and travel information services;
- encourage the development of the tourist and travel industry;
- advise the Minister on matters relating to tourism and travel.

The primary responsibility of the corporation was described in the act as one of promoting, marketing and arranging travel and tourism to and within Queensland.

As the tourism industry grew and developed, so did the QTTC and in 1982, a wholesale division Sunlover Holidays was created to give Queensland tourism operators better access to the domestic market. In the 1990s, the QTTC pioneered the destination marketing approach in Australia, highlighting the many unique visitor experiences on offer in Queensland and working alongside a network of RTOs to support destination marketing and development.

In February 1999, the *Where Else But Queensland* marketing campaign was launched, positioning the state as the undisputed premier holiday destination in Australia. In keeping with the new *Where Else* branding, the QTTC became Tourism Queensland, adopting the stylised 'Q' into all communications and making it synonymous with Queensland. In June 2005, Tourism Queensland signed a licence agreement with SL Holidays Pty Ltd, a wholly owned subsidiary set up by the AOT Group, to operate its commercial enterprises, Sunlover Holidays, and the Queensland Travel Centres.

Early in 2006, a new brand was launched which flowed through to new websites being developed. The Queensland Holidays site (www.queenslandholidays.co.au) offers visitors a refreshed experience and aims to present Queensland as a vibrant, fun, warm, friendly, colourful and relaxing place to visit and provides booking options for users. The consumer site provides a comprehensive tool for retrieving up-to-date news, information, research, policies, plans and strategies relating to Queensland's 12 destinations, special interests and the international sector.

In 2008, Tourism Queensland continued to lead the development of the tourism industry in Australia as it commenced the implementation of the $4.16 million Global Brand Strategy. This strategy aimed to deliver a sustainable, compelling and effective brand for Queensland, strengthening the State's position as the number one Australian holiday experience. Tourism Queensland launched the phenomenally successful *Best Job in the World* campaign in 2009. Undoubtedly Tourism Queensland's most successful campaign ever, *Best Job* received a long list of prestigious international awards and set off a number of copycat campaigns around the world. As at June 2010 the campaign had generated an estimated $410 million worth of media exposure for Queensland domestically and internationally.

In November 2012 the *Tourism and Events Queensland Bill 2012* was passed, successfully merging Tourism Queensland and Events Queensland into Tourism and Events Queensland.

Tourism and events Queensland

Tourism and Events Queensland's purpose is to achieve economic and social benefits for the State through the marketing and promotion of tourism, tourism experience and destination development, and securing major events to be held in Queensland.

Thus, in Queensland the interaction and connectivity between tourism and events is explicitly recognized in the title and purposes of the statutory body established to promote and develop activity. Hospitality activities are not explicitly mentioned but are subsumed within the all-embracing umbrella of tourism. Combining the resources and expertise of the former Tourism Queensland and Events Queensland formally into one entity enabled a continued focus on driving growth in Queensland's tourism and event industries in close partnership with Government and industry.

The functions of the Tourism and Events Queensland include to:

1. Attract international and domestic travellers to travel to and within Queensland through the promotion and marketing of Queensland, and tourism experience and destination development.
2. Identify, attract, develop and promote major events for the state that contribute to the Queensland economy.
3. Attract visitors to Queensland.
4. Enhance the profile of Queensland.
5. Foster community pride in Queensland.
6. Work collaboratively with the Tourism, Major Events, Small Business and the Commonwealth Games department and other public sector units and Queensland tourism industry participants to identify opportunities to increase tourism and travel to and within Queensland.
7. Conduct research into, and analysis of, tourism in Queensland.

Recognizing that tourism and events are intrinsically linked, the creation of Tourism and Events Queensland ensured the most coordinated and strategic approach to maximize domestic and international visitor markets and support the Government's goal of growing annual overnight visitor expenditure to $30 billion by 2020.

Operating in a competitive national and international environment in an industry where global economic conditions and other external shocks such as natural disasters may influence visitor numbers and expenditure, Tourism and Events Queensland identifies new and innovative ways to maximize emerging opportunities for the benefit of industry and the Queensland economy as a whole. Events play an important role in the tourism industry by creating exposure, promoting community pride and driving visitation and expenditure to the host region.

Organization structure

Tourism and Events Queensland's vision and operational focus is an efficient and collaborative tourism and events business system that engages and provides a sense of ownership for all stakeholders, working towards the goal of $30 billion in overnight visitor expenditure by 2020. To support the collaborative business system, Tourism and Events Queensland has developed a holistic business structure that supports the critical interrelationships between the Minister, Tourism and Events Queensland, the Department of Tourism, Major Events, Small Business and the Commonwealth Games, Queensland destinations, other Government partners and industry.

Branding

In September 2010, after 18 months of extensive research and industry consultation, Tourism Queensland (now Tourism and Events Queensland) launched its first truly global tourism brand. *Queensland, Where Australia Shines* introduced a new vision for Queensland as a tourism destination.

Though the new branding represents an umbrella brand to promote the whole of Queensland, the state has a unique position in Australia of having a number of strong destination brands, each having distinctive attributes, target markets and a sufficiently developed tourist industry to warrant a portfolio approach to their management as destinations. The approach reflects the diversity and scale of Queensland (and its tourism industry) and translate into different destination images, target markets, positional and promotional programmes for each destination.

The main tourism destination areas and their positioning have previously been summarized in an academic study, as shown in the Table below:

Destinations	Positioning elements	Brand personality	% Domestic visitors
Tropical North Queensland (TNQ)	Great Barrier Reef and tropical rainforest	Relaxed, friendly, natural, adventurous, active	57
Brisbane	Stimulating subtropical capital city experience	Plenty to see and do, relaxed fresh outdoors	75
Gold Coast	Beach and excitement, nightlife and entertainment	Exciting, fast-paced, fun	70
Sunshine Coast	Beach and relaxation	Relaxed, simple, the way things used to be	90
Whitsunday Islands	Aquatic playground	Relaxed, fresh, friendly, vibrant, natural	75

Sources: Adapted from Scott et al. (2000).

Appendix 1: Tourism and events Queensland: Brand strategy

To build a sustainable, compelling and effective global brand platform for Queensland, and to position Tourism Queensland as the brand leader in that process.

- Grow global awareness and Queensland's market share of tourism expenditure and visitation.
- Develop a sustainable, compelling and effective global brand platform for Queensland, then continue this to develop sustainable, compelling and effective brands for the five major destinations that link strongly to brand Queensland.
- Position Queensland as the brand leader – Australia's number one holiday experience.
- Build brand advantage over competitors through a brand that emotionally connects with our target markets.
- Strengthen awareness of Queensland and its destinations.

Objective

The key objective of the creative journey was to evolve Queensland as a holiday destination rather than reinvent it. Queensland has always been a popular holiday destination for Australians and travellers from across the globe, and Tourism Queensland undertook the process of refreshing Queensland's image to inspire travellers to come for the first time, or to come back.

Laying the foundations

Determining the right positioning for Queensland and five regional marketing brands involved an extensive research, consultation and creative process. Tourism Queensland sought input from over 6,000 consumers and the industry – input from the consumer in terms of understanding what was important to them, and input from the industry to make sure the industry's vision was understood.

The consumer input resulted in domestic segmentation based on consumer psychographics (wants and needs) as opposed to more traditional demographic segmentation based on age and income. Traditional methods of research assume everyone in the same age group or with the same income acts in a similar way. However, it is more productive to understand our visitors' needs and wants, thus maximizing the impact. By understanding the genuine holiday needs and motivations of visitors, communications can be customized by offering tailored experiences.

Creative strategy

The new strategic proposition was derived from the understanding that people are drawn to Queensland for a holiday not just because of beautiful places and experiences, but more so because of the way our visitors feel as a result of their holiday. The strategic proposition *Queensland, Where Australia Feels Most Alive* was the inspiration for the brand line *Queensland, Where Australia Shines*.

The evolution of the Queensland brand represents a move away from just talking about the great places and experiences on offer in Queensland. It adds to the mix the amazing feelings the places, experiences and people of Queensland generate – an emotional territory for Queensland as a whole and its five regional marketing brands. Queensland's tourism industry will also use the creative elements to support their marketing campaigns.

Brand launch

From September 2010, Tourism Queensland's new brand campaign hit the market to drive the new brand message to potential visitors and showcase new imagery through social media, TV, radio, print, online and outdoor activity. Domestically, this includes online holiday deals through Tourism Queensland's website (queenslandholidays.com.au) and special airline fares from anywhere in Australia to Queensland through the campaign's airline partner, Virgin Blue.

Internationally the brand rolled out via marketing campaigns, trade and consumer shows in key target markets. An integral part of the brand launch involved enhancements to Tourism Queensland's websites, which included: increased exposure for holiday deal offers; new navigation tools which invite site visitors to find their own holiday in three easy steps; greater opportunities to generate leads for tourism operators through increased exposure direct to operators; and improved search and filter functionality and integration of social media across the sites.

Brand summary

Brand summary		
Who we target	Category Definition:	Tourism
	Customer Target:	Domestic holiday makers: Social Fun Seekers, Connectors, Active Explorers, International holiday makers: Global Experience Seekers
	Customer Insight:	For the main segments (Social Fun Seekers and Connectors), the people aspect of a holiday is key, whether it's reconnecting with friends and family, or sharing good times with friends new and old. For Active Explorers, its more about achievement and personal development through connecting with a place.
What we do	Attributes:	'DO' There is huge variety and different attributes will feature depending on the communication, but some of the key ones are Beach, Natural attractions, Tropical islands, Great Barrier Reef, Rainforest, Theme parks, Natural encounters, Dining and Shopping
	Customer Benefits:	'FEEL' Connected, with loved ones, friends, locals, the place, even with a deeper part of themselves. Relaxed, Happy, Energised, Rejuvenated. A Queensland holiday lets you be 'The person I want to be', even if it's only for the duration of the holiday.
Who we are	Brand Values:	Pride in Queensland Hospitality Authenticity Creating holiday experiences that delight visitors The Holiday State
	Brand Personality:	'SEEN AS' Warm, Friendly, Welcoming, Outgoing, Positive, Carefree, Cheeky, Accepting, Non-judgmental, Unpretentious, Down-to-earth
What we promise		WHERE AUSTRALIA FEELS MOST ALIVE

Appendix 2: TEQ – Organization values and executive responsibilities

Values

Tourism and Events Queensland created a set of values for the organization.

- We lead together – Guided by the Minister and the Board, we are clear on our purpose, direction and priorities and our team is empowered to implement.

- We are one team – We work in partnership with our teammates and always act for the good of the whole.

- We are agile and responsive – We embrace emerging trends and opportunities. To thrive in a competitive industry environment we are proactive, flexible and adaptable.

- We go beyond – We are creative, innovative and solutions driven. We strive for continuous improvement and make a difference where it really counts for Queensland.

Board

TEQ's Board of directors is responsible for the overall performance of the organization; its composition includes private sector tourism interests and academic representatives as well as public sector representatives.

TEQ senior executive team

TEQ's senior executive team comprises of six Group Executives, led by the Chief Executive. The key areas of focus for each Group Executive are outlined below.

Executive team responsibilities	
Destination partnerships	Partners in collaboration with key destination stakeholders to deliver strategies and actions within the destination tourism plan.
	Ensures cross-organization leadership and coordination of destination focused strategies and activity.
	Leads partnerships with other key stakeholders such as the Department of Tourism, Major Events, Small Business and the Commonwealth Games and the Queensland Tourism Industry Council.
Acquisition	Builds a portfolio of major, business and regional events, supporting the destination tourism plans.
	Develops strategic partnerships with airlines and airports in order to attract the required flight capacity to Queensland.
Development	Develops events in destinations to stimulate visitation in shoulder and low seasons, consistent with *DestinationQ* objectives, and tourism experiences that align with the destination tourism framework.
	Manages the allocation of funding to the Queensland Convention Bureaux and the International 'Bid Fund'.
	Enables tourism operators to build their domestic and international marketing skills;
	Develops tourism experiences within each destination.
	Undertakes research and development, and implements identified strategic projects associated with nature based tourism and ecotourism, drive tourism, experience development, product development and renewal, Indigenous tourism, cruise tourism and investment facilitation to increase economic benefits.
Marketing services	Partners with regional stakeholders to develop consumer-driven destination experience marketing, targeted at priority markets, in line with the destination tourism plans.
	Implements the 2020 Strategic Marketing Plan for Tourism and Events in Queensland.
	Partners with event rights holders to market major events in the Tourism and Events Queensland portfolio.
Business services	Supports Tourism and Events Queensland's senior management and Board in the delivery of the organization's operation, strategic, research and financial activities.
	Provides leadership across all areas of the business to maximize efficiencies.
Corporate affairs	Coordinates the media and communications activities across all areas of Tourism and Events Queensland.
	Provides effective and timely liaison between tourism and events key stakeholders.
	Manages effective relationships with key stakeholders.

Appendix 3: *DestinationQ*

Context

DestinationQ is a partnership agreement between the Queensland Government and the state's tourism industry (represented by Queensland Tourism Industry Council) which recognizes tourism as one of the four pillars of the economy. The 20-year plan for Queensland tourism – *Destination Success* – was launched in February 2014 as a long-term shared vision between the government and the Queensland tourism industry. The vision for tourism has state-wide commitment with themes and a clear vision that was formalized with delegates at the 2013 *DestinationQ* forum.

The key elements of *DestinationQ* are:

- *Ambition* – Setting a growth target for the industry to double overnight visitor expenditure to $30 billion by 2020.
- *Leadership* – Focusing whole-of-government support for tourism and events as one of the four pillars of the Queensland economy.
- *Partnership* – Developing a strong partnership with industry, driving enhanced and collaborative marketing and development efforts, and a focus on events for Queensland.
- *Investment* – Attracting new investment in tourism product and new aviation routes to Queensland, and reducing the red-tape burden on tourism operators.
- *Accountability* – Assigning roles and responsibilities, tracking progress and reporting on outcomes at an annual forum of industry stakeholders.

Destination success

What will success look like?	
Goal	Queensland is Australia's leading tourism destination.
Target	Increase visitor expenditure to $30 billion (overnight visitor expenditure) by 2020.
Vision	Our diverse iconic experiences will be the foundation of our destinations, and our destinations will be the foundation of our tourism success.
	Our destinations will showcase the best of Queensland – our people and lifestyle, our culture and heritage, our natural wonders and climate, and our communities.
	The tourism industry will be strong and prosperous, fully engaged with governments and the community, and universally recognized as fundamental to Queensland's economic, environmental and social future.
Strategic directions	*Build strong partnerships* • Industry and governments will work in partnership at all levels, unified in their approach to support the growth of tourism. • The tourism industry will have strong leadership that works collaboratively across other industries, with communities and towards a common long-term vision. • The community will be ambassadors for tourism, welcoming visitors and recognizing the benefits that the industry brings to Queenslanders. *Preserve our nature and culture* • Natural assets will continue to be the heart of the Queensland experience – able to be enjoyed by visitors and locals alike, and preserved for future generations. • Our unique, authentic character and cultural heritage will be preserved and enhanced, and will always be at the heart of the Queensland experience.

Deliver quality, great service and innovation
- We will deliver authentic, quality experiences with a local feel and high standard of service, showcasing the best of the Queensland spirit – friendly, welcoming and down to earth.
- Our industry will be led by career-oriented professionals who are passionate about tourism and their communities.
- Our operators will be technologically smart, connected and efficient, doing business better and reaching consumers in new and innovative ways.

Target a balanced portfolio of markets
- Visitors from Australia and around the world will aspire to visit our destinations many times, exploring the diversity of our state.
- We will target a balanced portfolio of markets that match our competitive strengths and deliver the best results for our destinations.
- We will always look to the future, understanding and acting on consumer trends to appeal to traditional markets and grow new markets.

Offer iconic experiences
- We will focus on the consumer, and the experiences we offer will create lifelong memories.
- Our destinations will build on and leverage their strengths and heroes – iconic people, places and events – giving visitors many reasons to stay, explore and return.
- Our hero experiences and icons are our points of difference, and this is what we will showcase.

Grow investment and access
- Well-planned, timely public and private infrastructure will enable tourism growth and visitor access.
- The ability of the industry to invest and innovate will be encouraged through the continued reduction of unnecessary red tape.

Megatrends

Megatrends that will shape the future of tourism and events in Queensland. There is evidence of some of the big shifts, or 'megatrends', that are likely to shape the industry over the coming decades and we can use these to set the context for long-term planning. Research commissioned by the Queensland Government identified seven megatrends.

Megatrend	Description
The orient express	The world economy will significantly change over coming decades. Rapid income growth within emerging economies will create new markets and new sources of competition. There are major growth opportunities through attracting new tourists from the developing Asia region and ensuring Queensland is a differentiated and aspirational destination for domestic and international travellers.
A natural advantage	Global biodiversity is decreasing. Natural habitats are disappearing at alarming rates, and remaining areas of pristine natural habitats are increasing in value. As the world's population grows and becomes more urbanized, tourists will be drawn to nature-based experiences. Queensland's natural assets will become an increasingly important drawcard for locals and visitors alike.
Great expectations	As incomes grow, people shift their discretionary expenditure towards experiences rather than products. Future tourists will seek experiences that are personalized, 'authentic' to the destination and its people, involve social interaction and create emotional connection.

Megatrend	Description
Bolts from the blue	Sudden and unexpected events such as extreme weather and infectious disease outbreaks are more likely in a world with a changed climate, antimicrobial drug resistance and increased human mobility. When combined with the growing importance of safety perceptions, these events will have both positive and negative impacts on Queensland tourism expenditure, depending on where they occur in the world and the perceptions potential travellers have regarding their impacts.
Digital whispers	In the digital age, models of human communication and decision-making are changing. Information flows much more rapidly and via more widely distributed channels than it did in even the recent past. The perceived credibility of information sources is also changing. The online world has created new risks and opportunities for the tourism sector.
On the move	People are becoming increasingly mobile. While leisure remains a strong motivator for travel, people are travelling further and more frequently for many reasons including trade, business, events, conferences, education and healthcare. Technological advances in the transport sector, particularly aviation, will enable the continued rise in mobility as people are able to move greater distances faster.
The lucky country	Queensland and Australia have weathered the financial turbulence of the last decade exceptionally well compared to many other countries. However, for some travellers, they are expensive destinations. Local tourism operators face higher costs than many overseas competitors.

Appendix 4: Tourism and Events Queensland: Events strategy (summary)

Events showcase Queensland's destinations in key domestic and international markets, attracting visitors and generating expenditure for the state.

TEQ recognizes that tourism and events are intrinsically linked, and its events strategy focuses on:

- Developing Queensland events to maximize tourism outcomes before, during and after the event.
- Marketing events to maximize visitor numbers and promote the destination.
- Fostering a partnership approach with RTOs, including the incorporation of an event strategy within each region's Destination Tourism Plan.

In 2012–13 Tourism and Events Queensland secured a calendar of major events to contribute to Queensland's economy and promote the State to interstate and overseas markets. New major events included a number of international sporting and cultural events such as the Sunshine Coast Ironman triathlon event.

Appendix 5: Tourism and Events Queensland – Summary of recent performance

Overnight visitor expenditure

In 2013 22 per cent of all overnight visitor expenditure was made by international visitors with the balance of 78 per cent being made by Australians. Queenslanders travelling within the state contributed 32 per cent of all overnight visitor expenditure.

Total overnight visitor expenditure for Australia and the States of Queensland, New South Wales and Victoria is shown below.

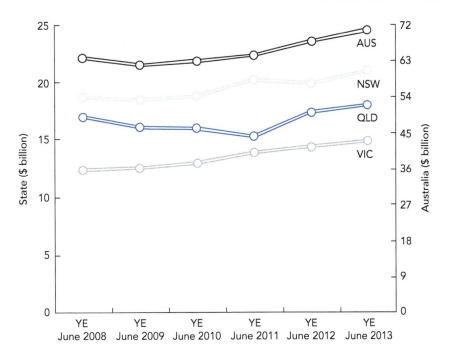

Total

Over a third of all international visitors to Australia visit Queensland during their trip. International visitors tend to spend more on their visits than domestic visitors and often visit more than one state. During 2013 there were a range of impacts on international visitation to Australia which were felt in varying degrees by Queensland and the other states, which included the effect of domestic economic conditions in European markets and youth unemployment in many countries. Positive impacts on visitation included the growth of the Chinese market and a range of world-class sporting and entertainment events also attracted a broad cross-section of international visitors.

Percentage of international visitors visiting particular Australian states						
State	Year ending Jun 08	Year ending Jun 09	Year ending Jun 10	Year ending Jun 11	Year ending Jun 12	Year ending Jun 13
Queensland	41.3%	40.0%	37.9%	37.0%	35.6%	35.9%
New South Wales	54.2%	53.4%	52.9%	51.9%	51.0%	51.5%
Victoria	28.9%	29.2%	29.6%	31.7%	32.4%	32.7%
Rest of Australia	26.3%	26.4%	25.9%	26.2%	25.5%	25.8%

Percentage of domestic visitors visiting particular Australian states						
State	Year ending Jun 08	Year ending Jun 09	Year ending Jun 10	Year ending Jun 11	Year ending Jun 12	Year ending Jun 13
Queensland	24.0%	24.0%	23.6%	23.6%	24.5%	23.9%
New South Wales	33.2%	33.4%	34.2%	34.8%	33.1%	33.2%
Victoria	24.0%	23.8%	24.2%	24.1%	24.4%	23.8%
Rest of Australia	22.3%	22.1%	21.5%	20.8%	21.5%	22.3%

Note: Visitors frequently visit more than one state

International visitors to Queensland (Year ending June 2013 in A$)		
Origin	Visitor numbers	% Change from previous year
TOTAL NEW ZEALAND	396,000	(–4%)
Japan	169,000	1%
Hong Kong	44,000	5%
Singapore	76,000	41%
Malaysia	42,000	5%
Indonesia	25,000	32%
Taiwan	45,000	15%
Thailand	15,000	15%
Korea	58,000	(–6%)
China	294,000	24%
India	36,000	20%
Other Asia	28,000	8%
TOTAL ASIA	832,000	13%
USA	163,000	10%
Canada	46,000	(–6%)
TOTAL N. AMERICA	209,000	7%
UK	205,000	7%
Germany	74,000	9%
Scandinavia	35,000	(–5%)
France	41,000	8%
Italy	24,000	26%
Netherlands	17,000	(–11%)
Switzerland	19,000	27%
Other Europe	65,000	3%
TOTAL EUROPE	479,000	6%
OTHER	149,000	(–4%)
TOTAL	2,065,000	6%

Appendix 6: Queensland Tourism and Industry Council (QTIC)

Background

QTIC is the industry-led body for tourism in Queensland. A private sector, membership-based organisation, QTIC represents the interests of the tourism and hospitality industry across the state. All of Queensland's 14 Regional Tourism Organisations (RTOs) are members of QTIC, as are 20 industry sector associations and in excess of 3,000 regional members, operating in all sectors of the tourism industry. QTIC works in partnership with government agencies and industry bodies at a local, state and national level, to strengthen the voice of tourism in all relevant policy forums. QTIC has been actively involved in the development a number of state and national strategic documents for the tourism industry,

QTIC's analysis of Queensland tourism

In November 2011, QTIC published a document which considered Queensland's Tourism industry. It reached a number of conclusions including:

- Australia's international tourism receipts are growing but at a lower rate than worldwide tourism receipts over the last decade and Australia is losing market share.
- Queensland is losing relatively more market share in the total Australian international market.
- Queensland is losing market share in terms of domestic visitor expenditure.
- Queensland is also facing a declining consumer 'travel preference' rating, compared to other states.

Contrasting these trends for both Australia and Queensland, the growth rates proposed in the Tourism Potential 2020 appear ambitious. This would suggest that significant change must occur for current trends to approach the growth targets. The disparity between actual and aspirational trends cannot be explained by recent, 'one off', external shocks. Such shocks occur in some form on a regular basis and have to be assumed in any prediction or forecast.

Global tourism in terms of visitor numbers and visitor expenditure has exhibited high growth rates over the last decade, despite a brief decline during the Global Financial Crises (GFC). While Australia has not felt the GFC in the same way, the trend growth rate has lagged the worldwide rate. Queensland's share of international visitor expenditure in Australia was 20 per cent in the year ended June 2011 (down 2.2 per cent) whilst NSW 36 per cent and VIC 23 per cent, both increased marginally.

Domestic visitor expenditure growth for Australia has been very modest at best over the last decade. Considering population growth impacts and increased general consumer spending, the evidence suggests that domestic tourism is losing 'share of wallet'. The aggregate domestic visitor expenditure decline over the last four years appears to be mainly reflecting the decline over the same period in Queensland. This state is particularly exposed to price competition from international destinations (the outbound market) and as a consequence, Queensland has lost share in the domestic market.

Appendix 7: Tourism Australia – China and India 2020 strategy plans

Why China?

China is Australia's most valuable inbound tourism market. In 2010 the China inbound market contributed $3.26 billion to the Australian economy. By 2020, this market has the potential to contribute $7 to $9 billion annually. Australia has experienced faster arrivals growth from China than any other market. In 2010, China was Australia's fourth largest source of visitor arrivals with 454,000 Chinese visitor arrivals to Australia, 24 per cent higher than 2009.

Tourism Australia (formerly the Australian Tourist Commission) opened an office in Shanghai in 1999 after Australia received 'Approved Destination' Status.

Why India?

India is one of the world's fastest growing outbound travel markets, with the United Nations World Tourism Organisation predicting 50 million outbound travellers by 2020. Now Australia's 10th most valuable inbound tourism market, India contributed A$867 million to the Australian economy in 2011.

Starting from a low base of 41,000 in 2000, Indian arrivals have grown at a compound annual growth rate of 12.3 per cent to reach 148,200 visitors in 2011. In the Tourism 2020 projections, India has the second fastest rate of growth, behind China, from a much smaller base.

Currently the number of Indian visitors for holidays is small compared to other countries (only 19 per cent of visitors compared to the average of 44 per cent of visitors). In fact the number of short-term arrivals for education and employment is about the same size as holiday arrivals. Education and employment drive a relatively large visiting friends and relatives (VFR) market (33 per cent of visitors), supported by a strong business market (20 per cent of visitors). The profile of visitation from India is unique and emphasizes the opportunity of advocacy to build the holiday market. Advocacy is also very important to help rebuild the safety image of Australia following a safety incident involving an Indian student that occurred in 2009.

Not surprisingly other National Tourism Offices (NTOs) are also targeting the growth and potential of the Indian market. It is estimated there are over 70 NTOs active in India. Australia needs to further invest to grow its competitive advantage over other destinations. Australia ranks eighth amongst all out-of-region outbound destinations for Indian travellers. Tourism Australia opened an office in Mumbai in 2008, recognizing the potential of the market.

Tourism Australia's China and India 2020 strategic plans

To ensure Australian tourism remains competitive in the fast-growing markets for outbound travel from China and India, Tourism Australia's China and India 2020 Strategic Plans were launched in 2011. The plans were developed by Tourism Australia in collaboration with industry and government stakeholders. They are key deliverables of the 'Grow Demand from Asia' plank of the Australian Government's Tourism 2020 Strategy. Under the Tourism 2020 Strategy, China is projected to be worth between A$7.4 billion and A$9 billion by the end of the decade and India has the potential to contribute between A$1.9 and A$2.3 billion annually. (A$1.00 = US$0.90, £0.55 or €0.66)

The plans identified pivotal themes in achieving China and India's 2020 tourism potential and winning market share as indicated by the table below. The China and India plans have five and four themes respectively.

Strategic themes	China	India
Knowing the customer	Who they are? Two principal target groups: Leisure Customers Business Events Target Customers (See profiles below)	
Geographic strategy	The geographic strategy identifies the focus for Tourism Australia's resources to maximise the Chinese market growth opportunities and achieve the 2020 goal. Tourism Australia is currently active in 13 cities, with distribution development in all 13 and	Research indicates that wealth is highly concentrated in India, and will remain so. In the short term the focus will be on Delhi and Mumbai, ensuring marketing and distribution are optimised. Four additional cities have been identified for possible targeted marketing and strengthening of distribution. By focusing resources more tightly, better marketing cut through is expected to have greater impact in the two major centres.

consumer marketing in five. Over time Tourism Australia will develop and implement a competitive expansion strategy informed by an analysis of over 600 Chinese cities.

Delivering quality Australian tourism experiences	While Chinese consumers generally rate Australia as a highly desirable destination, there are instances where visitor expectations have not been met – particularly relating to group travel and shopping experiences. Other issues impacting visitor satisfaction include the availability of Mandarin speaking guides and relevant products for Chinese visitors.	Research indicates that Indians are motivated to travel to Australia by the experiences of nature and journeys. Indians find Australia an easy place to visit particularly since most affluent travellers speak English. Although there is a high awareness of Australia amongst Indian travellers, they have relatively low levels of knowledge about places outside of the major east coast cities. The development of new products that meet the needs of the target customer, along with in-market promotions that showcase new destinations and reasons to visit will be prioritized as part of the Quality Experiences Strategy. Indian travellers enjoy a culture in their home country where shopping and dining are available into the late hours, and this can be a challenge for Australia to provide. A key part of the strategy will be to deliver a distribution strategy that leverages the strong current support of travel sellers through the Aussie Specialist and Preferred Agency Scheme programs. The focus will be on the identified target cities in order to reach the largest pool of affluent consumers.
A healthy aviation development environment	A healthy aviation environment will be critical to the success of the China 2020 goal. More planes, with more connections to more destinations in Australia, aligned to the geographic strategy will be essential to bring the increase in economic value to Australia.	Aviation capacity is critical to Australia achieving the India 2020 potential. While there are currently no direct nonstop services between India and Australia, Qantas, Virgin Australia and Jet Airways serve the route through code share arrangements. Supporting a sustainable and competitive aviation market will be the focus of the Aviation Development Strategy. It is estimated that an extra 345,000 seats will be required by 2020 to meet the expected demand from India. As per the Geographic Strategy, aviation development priorities will focus on Delhi and Mumbai. Air services arrangements are in place, and there is sufficient capacity available for airlines of both sides to commence services should they choose to.
Strong partnerships	Tourism Australia's success in the Chinese market has been achieved through effective partnerships with Government and industry including Qantas, China Southern Airlines and other carriers along with States and Territories. Expanding and strengthening partnerships will be integral as Tourism	

Strategic themes	China	India
	Australia expands to new cities in China. Tourism Australia will continue to work with partners by leading: the China Industry Advisory Group (based in China), and the China Market Advisory Panel (based in Australia).	

Knowing the customer – Target profiles

Following the publication of its China and India 2020 Strategic Plans, research was carried out to profile the two principal target segments: leisure customers and business events

Leisure customers: China

Who they are:

- *Affluent couples* – Men and women aged 30–49 years who are amongst the wealthiest of China's population.
- *Live in* – The primary cities of Beijing, Shanghai and Guangzhou and secondary cities including Chongqing, Chengdu, Hangzhou, Nanjing, Shenyang, Shenzhen, Tianjin, Wuhan and Xiamen.
- *Experienced travellers* – With an independent travel mind-set who want to explore and experience local culture.

Australia is viewed by its target leisure customers as a 'must visit' holiday destination:

- *Offers what the target customer wants* – Nature and laid back lifestyle with the comforts of a developed country. This appeals to target customers in both primary and secondary cities.
- *Group travel* – Preferred when visiting a destination for the first time, but as Chinese travellers become more experienced they like some flexible travel options.
- *Traditional travel advertising and travel media* – Key influencers, with social media becoming increasingly important.
- *The internet is used to research and plan* – But target customers rely on travel agents to book their travel.
- *Chinese travellers* – Welcome 'China friendly' products and services, e.g. Chinese food, signage, Mandarin-speaking guides.
- *Australia's visa processing system* – Viewed as comparable with or better than most other countries.

Leisure customers: India

Who they are:

- *Affluent, mid-life travellers* – Self-employed or entrepreneurs; highly qualified professionals or senior executives at multinational companies.
- *They will travel as couples* – Including honeymoon, often with their children; increasingly as free independent travellers (FIT); usually first time visitors to Australia.
- *Living in or near the target cities.*

Australia is a relatively expensive holiday choice when compared to competitor destinations such as Europe and the USA. Most Indians travel to Australia after first travelling short-haul within Asia (an inexpensive holiday) and then after a first long-haul trip, usually to Europe or the USA. Australia's target customer is therefore older and better able to afford the cost of a long-haul holiday. Highlighting the expected growth in wealth over the coming decade, research has also shown that the more affluent households in India will grow faster than other segments.

Business events target customers: China

With the appetite for business events increasing in China, Business Events Australia and the Association of Australian Convention Bureaux commissioned research on Australia's business events opportunities in China to provide insights into how to capitalize on these opportunities.

Who they are:

- *Corporate business events decision-makers* – From selected industry sectors, including direct selling, insurance, pharmaceutical, automotive, IT and electronics.
- *Business event planners* – Work in primary cities of Shanghai, Beijing and Guangzhou.

Australia is viewed as:

- *A highly aspirational business event destination* – With one in five survey respondents choosing Australia as their preferred destination.
- *Innovative team-building activities in Australia's natural landscapes* – Should be included in communications as they provide a real point of difference for the Chinese business events customer.
- *Value for money and safety* – Important factors when choosing the destination for an incentive trip. Australia needs to promote its vast range of options for incentive itineraries as well as its safety and security.
- *Customized event experiences* – Encourage recommendation and repeat visitation, whether this be involvement by Australian Government officials or services provided in Mandarin.
- *Building relationships* – With travel and event agencies as well as corporate clients it is vital to winning business.

Business events target customers: India

The business events profiling continues to be researched, but the target sectors have been identified as consumer goods, automobile, pharmaceuticals, information technology and life insurance.

CASE SOURCES

Australia Tourism 2020 Strategic Plan, Sydney Australia: Tourism Australia.

China 2020 Strategic Plan, Sydney Australia: Tourism Australia.

India 2020 Strategic Plan, Sydney Australia: Tourism Australia.

Scott, N., Parfitt, N., Laws, E., Faulkner, B., and Moscardo, G. (2000), Destination management: co-operative marketing, a case study of the Port Douglas brand in Eds. B. Faulkner, G. Moscardo and E. Laws, *Tourism in the twenty-first century: Lessons from experience*, London: Continuum, 198-221.

Queensland Tourism Industry Council (2011), *Game Changing Priorities for the Future of Tourism in Queensland: A Path towards Regaining Queensland's Status as the Leading Tourism State*, Brisbane, Australia: QTIC.

Tourism and Events Queensland Annual Report, 2012–13.

WEBSITES

www.tourism.australia.com
www.qtic.com.au
www.queensland-australia.eu
www.queenslandholidays.com.au

Ryanair

Evolution of competitive strategy

The launch and early development

Ryanair, now firmly established as Europe's largest low-fare airline, began operations back in 1985 with the launch of a daily flight on a 15-seater turbo prop aircraft between Waterford Airport in the South East of Ireland and London Gatwick. The company had a commitment to low-fare air travel and making air travel affordable for people in Ireland and the UK, but in the early years problems were encountered in delivering this commitment. In the company's first year, its 57 employees carried just over 5,000 passengers on its one route.

In 1986, Ryanair broke the high-fare cartel, which was then operated by the two state airlines Aer Lingus and British Airways on the Dublin–London route. The Dublin–London route had stagnated at about 1 million passengers per annum between 1975 and 1985 and was then characterized by some of the highest air fares in Europe. Prior to Ryanair, the normal air fare between Dublin and London in 1985 was £209 return. Ryanair began services on the 23 May 1986, with two turbo prop BA 748 aircraft and an introductory launch fare of £94.99 return. Ryanair was the first European airline specifically set up to offer low fares on short-haul intra-European routes.

Over the next three years (1987 to 1989) Ryanair expanded, rapidly opening many new routes between Ireland and the UK, increasing the fleet by adding jets, and additional turbo prop aircraft. Whilst customers continued to flock to Ryanair for the low air fares, costs were not controlled and the company continued to rack up losses. By 1989, the company employed 350 people, operated 14 aircraft (four different types), was carrying 600,000 passengers a year, but had managed to lose £20m in just four years.

New management team

Under a new management team, a major overhaul of the airline was undertaken in 1990/91, with Ryanair re-launched as the first of a new breed of *'low fares/no frills'* airlines. In re-launching the airline in this way, the management was adapting the formula so successfully pioneered by Southwest Airlines in the U.S. in the period following deregulation of the American domestic aviation market which took place in 1978. Non-profitable routes were eliminated, the network was cut back from 19 to just five routes, the turbo prop aircraft were disposed of and air fares across the remaining network were substantially reduced with 70 per cent of all seats offered at the two lowest fares. On the Dublin–London route, for example, a new promotional fare of just £69 return was launched which stimulated a whole new era of growth for Ryanair. By 1991, Ryanair was operating an all jet fleet of six aircraft, employing 350 people, carrying 700,000 passengers on just five routes, and it had recorded its first ever profit, despite the damage done to the airline industry by the Gulf War in 1991.

Over the next few years, schedules on the key Dublin–London route were increased, average air fares were lowered, new routes were launched from Dublin to Birmingham, Glasgow, Manchester, and Gatwick, while traffic continued to grow strongly. By 1994, Ryanair was employing over 500 people, carrying over 1.5 million passengers per annum, offering lower than ever air fares of just £49 return on the Dublin–London route, and had recorded its fourth continuous year of profitability. 1994 also saw the acquisition of Ryanair's first Boeing 737 aircraft with an order for six 737-200 series aircraft (130 seats) being purchased direct from Boeing. Over the subsequent three years a further 15 737-200 aircraft were purchased bringing the fleet to 21.

To coincide with this expansion of the fleet, many more new routes were opened by Ryanair between Ireland and the UK, increased frequencies were offered on all routes and air fares were lowered yet further. As a result in 1995, the airline's tenth anniversary, Ryanair had become the biggest passenger carrier on the Dublin–London route, with total passengers of 2.25 million per annum and the work force exceeded 600 people.

1997 – A milestone year

1997 represented a milestone year for Ryanair. Thanks to the full deregulation of European Union air transport, the airline was free for the first time to open up new routes to Continental Europe. Services were launched from London's smaller Stansted Airport to Stockholm and Oslo, as well as from Dublin to Paris and Brussels. Again Ryanair entering these markets offered air fares which were more than 50 per cent lower than the cheapest fares then provided by the *flag carrier* airlines.

Passengers responded enthusiastically and in great numbers to the arrival of low fares for the first time in these European markets. Ryanair was the first low fares airline to offer scheduled services from the UK to Continental Europe and vice versa. 1997 also saw Ryanair Holdings plc float on the Dublin and New York (Nasdaq) Stock Exchanges enabling all of its then 700 employees to become shareholders in the airline. At the time the airline was capitalized at a market value of about US$400 million, and was carrying over 3 million passengers per annum on its network of 18 routes. Ryanair was competing head to head with many of Europe's biggest airlines including British Airways, SAS, Alitalia, Lufthansa, Air France and Aer Lingus.

Continuing growth

In 1999, Ryanair announced its next major investment programme with a huge US$2 billion order for up to 45 new Boeing 737-800 series aircraft. These were the latest and most modern aircraft manufactured by Boeing. The first five aircraft were delivered to Ryanair in 1999 and five more were scheduled for delivery each year thereafter. In 1999 Ryanair announced another set of record results, operating 35 routes to 11 countries and carrying almost 6 million passengers. The company was then employing over 1,200 people, and also had its shares listed on the London Stock Exchange in addition to the Dublin and New York (Nasdaq). In 1999 Ryanair was awarded 'Airline of the Year' by the Irish Air Transport Users Committee, and was voted one of the Best Managed Airlines in the world by the International Aviation Week magazine.

The following year the airline launched its website at www.ryanair.com, which within three months of its launch was taking over 50,000 bookings per week by offering low airfares starting from as little as £9 return plus taxes on the Dublin–London routes.

From the very beginning Ryanair had an aggressive direct sales approach. By 2007, the airline was reporting over 90 per cent of its direct sales via the Internet. The airline has continued to grow rapidly in the new century despite other airlines copying aspects of its low fares, no frills business model. It has become the largest airline in Europe through the aggressive and relentless addition of extra routes and new operating bases. It has spread its activities far beyond its Irish routes and operates throughout Europe. In 2012 the airline carried over 79 million passengers and had over 7,000 staff, but remains committed to offering low fares since its average fare in that year was €43.

The growth of the airline's passenger numbers has not, however, been mirrored by a growing reputation for customer service as lower fares has generally led to a lack of focus on service standards. The Times reported in 2002 for instance that they receive more customer complaints about Ryanair than any other airline (Chesshyre, 2002) and the Advertising Standards Authority which monitors the accuracy of advertising claims in the UK had upheld several claims against the airline. Complaints included: the inability to change ticket details once they have been booked, charging for every conceivable additional extra, flying to secondary airports sometimes remote from the city they claim to serve; and, the lack of clarity in the advertising messages Ryanair used.

Despite these difficulties with customers, it did not seem to deter them from booking cheap travel with Ryanair. In 2002 Ryanair CEO Michael O'Leary bluntly challenged existing assumptions about customer service and made it clear what 'the deal' was with customer service at his airline when he defended his 'well defined' service. 'We guarantee to give you the lowest airfare. You get a safe flight. You get a normally on-time flight. That's the package. We don't and won't give you anything more on top of that' (Chesshyre, 2002).

Ryanair in 2013/14

The formula certainly seems to have worked. The International Air Transport Association (IATA, 2013) statistics confirms that Ryanair carried more international passengers than any other airline. In 2013 Ryanair carried 81.3 million international passengers, almost 29 million more than second placed Easyjet (52.7 million) and 30 million more than third placed Lufthansa (50.7 million).

Passenger numbers at Ryanair had continued to grow, but increasingly the airline was being challenged as new competitors came into the market, existing low-cost competitors (such as easyJet) offered additional features; and, traditional carriers adjusted their business models to compete more effectively. At the same time consumers had become more sophisticated. Comparative shopping for the best deals on the internet had become the norm. Though there was a continuing appetite for the lowest possible fairs, adverse publicity and a complicated website had led to perceptions that the lowest fares were not necessarily those of Ryanair once the cost of 'extras' (of which there were many) had been included.

The Sunday Times reported that 'Michael O'Leary, the fast-talking, outspoken boss of Ryanair, has had his wings clipped — he says he is finally listening to his customers' (Barber, 2014). In September 2013 Ryanair had issued a profit warning and the following month the airline announced that it would be rolling out what it called a series of 'customer service improvements'. Michael O'Leary himself criticized the website for its lack of clarity and several other aspects of the airline's operations and carried out a series of media interviews in which he claimed that the airline must become more responsive to customer needs and learn from its mistakes, through:

- an easier to use Ryanair.com website (17 to 5 clicks to book);
- twenty-four hour grace periods (for minor booking errors);

- a free small 2nd carry-on bag;
- 'My Ryanair' customer registration service;
- accepting group and corporate bookings;
- allocated seats on all flights.

The airline operates over 500,000 flights a year. Punctuality statistics over the previous 12 months to March 2014 are shown below.

Airline	Punctuality
Ryanair	93%
EasyJet	87%
Lufthansa	83%
BA	85%
Air France	83%
Aer Lingus	82%

Sources: www.ryanair.com

Appendix 1: Ryanair – Passenger numbers

Year	Passengers carried (000s)	Year	Passengers carried (000s)	Year	Passengers carried (000s)
1985	5	1995	2,260	2005	34,769
1986	82	1996	2,950	2006	42,509
1987	322	1997	3,730	2007	50,932
1988	592	1998	4,629	2008	58,566
1989	644	1999	5,358	2009	66,504
1990	745	2000	7,002	2010	72,063
1991	651	2001	9,355	2011	75,816
1992	945	2002	15,737	2012	79,325
1993	1,120	2003	23,133	2013	81,300
1994	1,666	2004	27,593		

REFERENCES

Barber, L. (2014) 'Cabin Pressure: Interview with Michael O'Leary', *The Sunday Times*, 14 January.
Chesshyre, T. (2002) 'Interview with Michael O'Leary', *The Times*, 5 January.
International Air Transport Association (2013) *World Air Transport Statistics*, 58th edn, Montreal: International Air Transport Association.

WEBSITE

www.ryanair.com

Case **4**

Hyatt Hotels

A family firm goes for growth

The hospitality context

Hospitality is an interesting industry sector in many respects. It is growing rapidly around the world, and, though there are many individually owned properties or small chains, consolidation is taking place so that a small number of large internationally diversified groups have become established.

Many of the first groups to establish themselves internationally have been from the USA or Europe, but in more recent times chains from Asia and elsewhere have established substantial international operations. Hospitality is also a sector which represents the principal physical manifestation of business and leisure travel, since the buildings the hotels occupy are often prominent features of cities, resorts, roadside locations and scenic areas.

The industry has many of the characteristics often associated with service sectors such as the inseparability of production and consumption, the perishability of its product offerings and, at least in part, product intangibility. Managers operating in the business also have to deal with international currency risks. Revenues and expenditures will often be denominated in different currencies and assets and debts may well be denominated in currencies other than the company's accounting currency.

Furthermore the patterns of business activity often give rise to further need for managerial attention. Volatile levels of business and cash flow are common due to both cyclicality and seasonality. Hospitality generally follows, on a lagged basis, the overall economy. There is a history of increases and decreases in demand for hotel rooms, in occupancy levels and in rates realized by owners of hotels through economic cycles. Variability of results through some of the cycles in the past has been more severe due to changes in the supply of hotel rooms in given markets or in given categories of hotels.

The combination of changes in economic conditions and in the supply of hotel rooms can result in significant volatility in results for owners, managers and franchisors (and franchisees) of hotel properties. The costs of running a hotel tend to be more fixed than variable. Because of this, in an environment of declining revenues the rate of decline in earnings will be higher than the rate of decline in revenues. Conversely, in an environment of increasing demand and room rates, the rate of increase in earnings is typically higher than the rate of increase in revenues.

The effects of seasonality are geographically specific. In a diversified portfolio of properties its effects will vary from property to property and from country to country driven by a number of factors such as: climate, school holidays, cultural and religious festivals, sporting events and changing tastes and fashions. Beach resort hotels generally fill during summer months for example, as city business hotels find activity levels are lower.

In the highly competitive hospitality industry in which hotel groups operate, trademarks, trade names and logos are very important in the successful sales and marketing of accommodation and vacation ownership properties and services. The major international chains work assiduously to establish their brands and their market positioning and many sub-brands have been formed so as to target perceived new segments and their needs. The companies concerned devote sizeable revenues to promoting and positioning their brands effectively and in protecting their brands from intellectual property infringement.

But everything is not always as it appears in the hospitality industry. The branding can mean different things in different circumstances. The branding or the 'sign above the door' can denote that the hotel building and the hotel operations are owned and managed by the owner of the brand. However, in many cases the position is far more complicated with the ownership of the building, the management of the hotel and the provision of the brand and its values and attributes, all being carried out by different companies.

Thus, there is frequently a three-way arrangement that separates the physical asset, its management and the brand-holder. First of all, the hotel property may be owned by a commercial landlord or a real estate investment trust (REIT). Secondly, there are several large hotel management companies (and many smaller ones) which manage hotels and often do so under the 'umbrella' of several brands. These companies (which might also act as the property owner), include companies such as White Lodging, Highgate Holdings and Interstate Hotels and Resorts. In the B2B market in which they operate, these companies are well known and are sizeable and powerful companies with which the brand owners have to negotiate, but they are largely unrecognized by consumers.

Interstate Hotels and Resorts, for example, is a leading US-based global hotel management company which is itself a joint venture between the US Thayer Lodging Group and China's Jin Jiang Hotels. The company manages 380 hotels with more than 73,000 rooms located throughout the United States and around the world, including only six which are wholly owned. The hotels are operated under the brands of some of the world's most widely recognized hospitality names including: Hilton, Marriott, Sheraton, Westin, Holiday Inn and Hyatt.

The third party in this arrangement is the brand holder – the franchisors, who put their name on the front of the hotel and back it up with global reservations, marketing, advertising, training, branded items and other services. Many chains continue to own and manage properties, particularly in the upscale part of the market, but the trend is towards separation of these activities in what the internationally recognized branded hotel groups refer to as an 'asset-light model'. The US-based Wyndham group, for example (which owns brands such as Wyndham, Ramada, Days Inn and Howard Johnson), has almost 7,500 hotels in its portfolio, but owns or manages very few of them and sometimes only for short periods while negotiations take place.

As a result of this separation, brand changes are a regular feature of the industry. The changes are sometimes simply due to the expiration of the contract or the change of ownership of the building. The changes may also be due to the failure to agree after contract negotiations as all parties jostle for the most favourable terms. The franchise arrangements permit the branded hotel companies to roll out their brands more quickly with far less capital commitment, but at the price of losing some degree of control over the brand.

The franchisee takes most of the financial risk, but is able to gain access to a respected branded product and the services provided by the brand owner.

There is intense competition in all areas of the hospitality industry. Competition exists for hotel guests, management agreements and franchise agreements and sales of vacation ownership properties. The number of branded lodging operators with a global reach and depth of product and offerings is, however, limited. Those companies that have a strong customer base, prominent brand recognition, strategic property locations and global development capabilities are likely to be most successful.

The global hotel industry appears to provide good continuing investment opportunities. US lodging demand, as measured by number of booked hotel rooms, has improved with the economic recovery in recent years, experiencing growth of 4.9 per cent over the last three years, significantly exceeding the 25-year average of 1.8 per cent. In contrast, over the last three years US lodging industry capacity has grown at a rate of 0.9 per cent, well below the 25-year average of 2.0 per cent. This positive imbalance between demand and supply growth has contributed to a RevPAR growth in the US of 6.8 per cent over the last three years and projections indicate that this real rate of growth will continue for the next few years.

The broader global macroeconomic climate also appears positive which will continue to drive longer-term growth in the lodging sector, but periodic regional economic and political difficulties will make the growth spatially uneven. In particular a growing middle class, which the Organization for Economic Co-operation and Development (OECD), expects will grow from approximately two to five billion people by 2030 will exhibit the desire and have the resources to travel both within their home regions and elsewhere, which will support growth in global tourism. The United Nations World Tourism Organization (UNWTO) projects global tourism will grow on average between 3 per cent and 4 per cent annually through to 2030.

Hyatt Hotels Corporation: profile

Chicago's Pritzker Family are one of America's richest families with most of the wealth derived from the Hyatt Hotels Corporation, which was developed by family members.

Hyatt was founded by Jay Pritzker in 1957 when he purchased the Hyatt House motel adjacent to Los Angeles International Airport. In 2004 the hospitality assets owned by Pritzker family business interests, including Hyatt Corporation and Hyatt International Corporation, were consolidated under a single entity whose name was subsequently changed to Global Hyatt Corporation. In June 2009, Global Hyatt Corporation changed its name to Hyatt Hotels Corporation. and a public offering of its shares (for the first time) was made in November 2009.

Hyatt Hotels Corporation is a hospitality company with broad international operations, widely recognized, brands and a tradition of innovation developed during a history spanning over 55 years. Hyatt manage, franchise, own and develop the Hyatt portfolio of hotels, resorts and residential and vacation ownership properties around the world. The full service hotels and resorts operate under five established brands: Park Hyatt, Andaz, Hyatt, Grand Hyatt and Hyatt Regency and are supported by two 'select service' brands Hyatt Place and Hyatt House, an extended stay brand. The company introduced the Hyatt Ziva and Hyatt Zilara brands in 2013, which marked the company's entry into the all-inclusive resort segment. Hyatt also develops, sells or manages vacation ownership properties in select locations as part of the Hyatt Residence Club. Hyatt provide services or license trademarks with respect to residential ownership units that are often adjacent to a full service hotel that is a member of the Hyatt portfolio of hotels.

Hyatt has over 500 hotels, a significantly lower number than some of its rivals, but Mark Hoplamazian, Hyatt's CEO, told the Financial Times that 'having a smaller "footprint" does not impact our ability to perform. We just have to be thoughtful, deliberate and have a presence in key markets'. Hoplamazian, a 20-year veteran of Hyatt, has been in control since 2006, but the board is chaired by a member of the

Pritzker family who retain a 60 per cent shareholding and 75 per cent of the voting rights. He is credited with navigating the fractious family politics and fusing the hotel business's multiple strands (Raval, 2014).

Like other US-based hotel companies, Hyatt has been pursuing an aggressive overseas expansion, utilizing a strong balance sheet and strong brand recognition in large growing markets such as China, India and Brazil. The growth emphasis has hitherto been on the luxury segment and with Asia being a particular focus. Future international growth is likely to target India, China and neighbouring countries, but it is likely to be achieved in the lower-price brackets as Hyatt targets the growing number of middle-class travellers in these rapidly emerging markets.

The company has more than 95,000 associates, as they are usually termed, who work for companies promoting and operating Hyatt-branded products. Of these approximately 45,000 are employees at Hyatt's corporate offices, regional offices, owned and managed hotels and residential and vacation ownership properties. The rest of the associates are employed by certain third-party owners and franchisees of the hotels.

Most hotel general managers are trained professionals in the hospitality industry with extensive hospitality experience (averaging 22 years) in their local markets and host countries. The general managers of the managed properties are empowered to operate their properties on an independent basis using their market knowledge, management experience and understanding of the Hyatt brands. The associates and hotel general managers are supported by the regional management teams located in cities around the world and the executive management team, headquartered in downtown Chicago. Costs are managed by setting performance goals for hotel management teams and granting general managers operational autonomy. Cost management efforts are reinforced with tools and analytics provided by Hyatt offices and by compensating hotel management teams based on property performance.

Revenues are primarily derived from hotel operations, management and franchise fees, with other revenues from managed properties and sales of vacation ownership properties. For the year ended December 31 2013 revenues totalled $4.2 billion and net income attributable to shareholders totalled $207 million. 78.2 per cent of revenue was derived from US operations and 74.4 per cent of long-term assets were located there. Total debt was $1.5 billion, there were cash and cash equivalents available of $454 million and the company had a borrowing capacity of $1.4 billion under bank credit facilities. These sources provide Hyatt with significant liquidity and resources to fund future growth.

Hyatt's 'Gold Passport' guest loyalty program is designed to attract new guests and to demonstrate loyalty to the company's best customers. In the year ending December 2013, new membership enrolment in the program increased by 13.6 per cent, bringing total enrolment to over 16 million members. Stays by Hyatt Gold Passport members represented 34.3 per cent of total room nights during 2013. In 2013, Hyatt Gold Passport won four Freddie Awards, including best elite travel programme. The Hyatt Card, a co-branded Visa credit card launched in 2010 by Hyatt and Chase Card Services, has shown strong growth in both card member acquisitions and existing member spend.

Hyatt Hotels Corporation: corporate realignment

In October 2012 Hyatt carried out a realignment of corporate and regional operations to enhance organizational effectiveness and adaptability. The changes were designed to facilitate innovation and further advance the company towards its goal of becoming the preferred hospitality brand for the company's associates, guests and owners. The organizational evolution was designed to position Hyatt to adapt quickly and effectively to guest and hotel owner needs during the expansion and growth anticipated across all brands in multiple markets over the next few years.

As part of the realignment, three operating segments – Americas management and franchising; Southeast Asia, as well as China, Australia, South Korea and Japan ('ASPAC') management and franchising; and

Europe, Africa, the Middle East and Southwest Asia ('EAME/SW Asia') management – together with the owned and leased hotels, form the four reportable segments of the business. The results of the vacation ownership business, Hyatt co-branded credit card and unallocated corporate overhead continue to be reported within 'corporate and other'.

Additionally, as part of the realignment, two new functions, the Real Estate and Capital Strategy Group and the Global Operations Center, were established. The Real Estate and Capital Strategy Group, whose costs are included as part of 'corporate', is responsible for implementing Hyatt's overall capital strategy, managing its hotel asset base and providing support to Hyatt's development professionals around the world. The Global Operations Center whose costs are allocated to the management and franchising businesses is charged with ensuring that Hyatt's operating segments function according to company-wide principles and standards and enabling ongoing transformation and collaboration to ensure that structures and resources are optimized.

Hyatt Hotels Corporation: business model

Hyatt operates a business model that involves both ownership of properties and management and franchising of third-party owned properties. This allows the company to pursue diversified revenue streams that balance both the advantages and risks associated with these lines of business. Expertise and experience in each of these areas gives flexibility to evaluate growth opportunities across these lines of business.

Growth in the number of management and franchise agreements and earnings from these, typically results in higher overall returns on invested capital because the capital investment under a typical management or franchise agreement is not significant. This is because the capital required to build and maintain the hotels that Hyatt manages or franchises for third-party owners is typically provided by the owner of the respective property. Minimal capital is required from Hyatt as the manager or franchisor.

However, during periods of increasing demand Hyatt does not share fully in the incremental profits of hotel operations (for hotels that are managed for third-party owners). This is because the fee arrangements generally include a base amount calculated using the revenue from the hotel and an incentive fee that is typically a percentage of hotel profits that is usually less than 20 per cent, with the actual level depending on the structure and terms of the management agreement.

Hyatt also does not share in the benefits of increases in profits from franchised properties because franchisees pay an initial application fee and ongoing royalty fees that are calculated as a percentage of gross room revenues with no added fees based on profits.

Owning hotel properties allows Hyatt to capture the full benefit of increases in operating profits during periods of increasing demand and room rates. The cost structure of a typical hotel is more fixed than variable, so as demand and room rates increase over time, the pace of increase in operating profits typically is higher than the pace of increase of revenues. Hotel ownership is, however, more capital intensive than managing hotels for third-party owners, as Hyatt is responsible for the costs and all capital expenditures for its owned hotels. Hence the profits realized in Hyatt's owned and leased hotel segment are generally more significantly affected by economic downturns and declines in revenues than the results of management and franchising segments.

There is intense competition in all areas of the hospitality industry. Competition exists in B2C markets for hotel guests, and in B2B markets for management and franchise agreements; vacation ownership properties; and branded residential properties. Hyatt's principal competitors are other operators including other major hospitality chains with well-established and recognized brands as well as smaller chains and independent and local owners and operators. The number of branded lodging operators with a global reach and depth of product and offerings similar to Hyatt is, however, limited.

Appendix 1: Hyatt Hotels Corporation – history

Year	Activity
1957	Jay Pritzker purchases the very first Hyatt House hotel from business partners, Mr. Hyatt von Dehn and Mr. Jack Dyer Crouch. The small motor hotel is adjacent to the Los Angeles International Airport in California.
1962	Hyatt goes public, changing its name to Hyatt Corporation.
1963	Advertised as 'The World's First Fly-In Hotels', Hyatt has three divisions: Hyatt House hotels, Hyatt Chalet motels and Hyatt Lodges. Properties are primarily in the western United States, but in 1963 Hyatt expands east with a property in Lincolnwood, Illinois near the Pritzkers home. An innovative program directed towards executive secretaries responsible for travel arrangements called HERS (Hyatt Executive Reservation Secretaries) is established.
1964	Three new regional sales offices are established, serving Northern and Southern California and greater Chicago and the Midwest. A toll-free, direct reservation line to Hyatt House Hotels is set up for approximately three-dozen major US cities.
1967	The first Hyatt Regency is introduced in Atlanta, Georgia. Its first major John Portman designed hotel, Hyatt Regency Atlanta features original, groundbreaking design with a dramatic, 21-story atrium lobby. The revolutionary architecture spawns scores of atrium lobbies around the world, effectively changing the course of the lodging industry and reshaping the Hyatt brand as an innovative and significant global hospitality leader.
1968	Hyatt International is formed and subsequently becomes a separate public company.
1969	Hyatt Regency Hong Kong welcomes its first guests as the first international Hyatt hotel.
1972	The Company opens a central reservations office with an 800 number in Omaha, Nebraska.
1973	Hyatt Regency San Francisco opens its doors.
1976	The Company manages a total of more than 50 hotels.
1977	Hyatt headquarters moves to Chicago, first to an airport location and later downtown.
1979	Hyatt Corporation is taken private by the Pritzker family business interests.
1980	The Grand Hyatt brand is introduced with the Grand Hyatt New York. Additionally, the Company adds the Park Hyatt brand to its portfolio and also solidifies its entry into the luxury resort market with the opening of *Hyatt Regency Maui Resort and Spa* in Hawaii. Hyatt Regency Chicago opens its west tower, making the hotel the largest in Chicago with more than 2,000 guestrooms.
1982	Hyatt International, which had operated separately from Hyatt Corporation, is taken private by the Pritzker family business interests.
1987	Hyatt Gold Passport makes its debut.
1990s	The Company emphasizes the *Hyatt touch*, placing the tag line 'Feel the Hyatt Touch' on Hyatt's advertising, featuring the new Hyatt crescent logo. The crescent shape is meant to symbolize Hyatt's 'sunrise-to-sunset service'. Hyatt.com is launched and Hyatt Residence Club is born.
1998	Grand Hyatt Shanghai becomes the world's highest hotel, occupying floors 53–87 of an 88-story tower.
2004	Almost all hospitality assets are consolidated under a single identity, Global Hyatt Corporation. In December, Hyatt announces it will acquire AmeriSuites, an upscale chain of all suite business class hotels. The properties are rebranded as Hyatt Place in 2006.
2005	Hyatt's corporate office moves into the newly opened Hyatt Center building in downtown Chicago.
2006	The Hyatt Place brand debuts in Lombard, Illinois. Hyatt acquires a second select service brand, Summerfield Suites, and rebrands the properties to Hyatt Summerfield Suites.

2007   Hyatt introduces its Andaz brand and opens its first hotel without the Hyatt name, the Andaz Liverpool Street in London.

2008   Park Hyatt Shanghai takes the title of world's highest hotel occupying floors 79–93 of the 101-story Shanghai World Financial Center. The hotel does not retain this title, but it continues to be in the rankings as one of the world's highest.

2009   Global Hyatt Corporation changes its name to Hyatt Hotels Corporation. Hyatt launches Hyatt Concierge, making it the first hospitality company in the world to deploy a designated concierge site on Twitter. In November, Hyatt completes an 'initial public offering' of stock (shares) which begins trading publicly on the New York Stock Exchange.

2010   The Hyatt Card is introduced, partnered with Visa. Hyatt increases social media presence with its blog 'Keyed Into Hyatt' (blog.hyatt.com).

2011   Hyatt announces its select service brands are expanding internationally.
Hyatt announces that one of its wholly owned subsidiaries acquired a portfolio of assets from LodgeWorks. The transaction includes the purchase of twenty hotels and the management or franchise rights to an additional four hotels. Key members of the LodgeWorks management and development team join Hyatt as part of the transaction.
Park Hyatt Paris-Vendôme is awarded a five-star classification of the highest distinction – it is named by the government as one of eight official palace hotels in France. The Company introduces Hyatt Thrive (thrive.hyatt.com), Hyatt's global corporate responsibility platform.

2012   Hyatt evolves its extended-stay brand into a distinctive new hotel concept – Hyatt House. As a part of the rebranding, all Hyatt Summerfield Suites and 15 Hotel Sierra properties undergo official name and signage changes. Hyatt completes an approximately $190 million acquisition of its first hotel in Mexico City. The 755-room hotel is rebranded as Hyatt Regency Mexico. Mexico City is the premier political, business and commercial hub in Mexico and the gateway to Latin America. Hyatt 'select service' makes its international debut with the opening of Hyatt Place San Jose in Costa Rica. In October Hyatt realigns its corporate and regional operations.

2013   Hyatt acquires the historic landmark hotel, The Driskill, in Austin, Texas, for approximately $85 million and The Peabody Orlando hotel for approximately $717 million and the 1,641-room hotel is rebranded as Hyatt Regency Orlando. Hyatt Ziva and Hyatt Zilara debut in Mexico as the Company's first all-inclusive resort brands, marking Hyatt's entry into the fast growing, all inclusive segment.

Appendix 2: Hyatt Hotels Corporation – mission, goal and values

Our Mission

- Our mission is to provide authentic hospitality by making a difference in the lives of the people we touch every day, including our associates, guests and owners.

Our Goal

- Our goal is to be the most preferred brand in each customer segment that we serve for our associates, guests and owners.

Our Values

- We aim to foster a common purpose and culture within the Hyatt family through shared core values of mutual respect, intellectual honesty and integrity, humility, fun, creativity and innovation.

Our mission, goal and values are interdependent, and we refer to this interdependence as the Hyatt value chain. The Hyatt value chain begins with our associates. We believe that our efforts to engage our associates in planning for how we can better serve our fellow associates, guests and owners contributes to their commitment to genuine service, which is the first step to achieving high levels of guest satisfaction.

In our view, motivating our associates to become personally involved in serving and demonstrating loyalty to our guests is central to fulfilling our mission. We rely upon the management teams at each of our managed properties to lead by example and we provide them with the appropriate autonomy to make operational decisions in the best interest of the hotel and brand. We believe the managers of our franchised properties are experienced operators with high standards and have demonstrated commitment to our values and our approach to guest service that is designed to enhance guest satisfaction.

High levels of guest satisfaction lead to increased guest preference for our brands, which we believe results in a strengthened revenue base over the long term. We also believe that engaged associates will enhance efficient operation of our properties, resulting in improved financial results for our property owners.

Sustained adherence to these principles is a basis for our brand reputation and is one of the principal factors behind the decisions by our diverse group of hotel owners and developers to invest in properties in the Hyatt portfolio of hotels around the world. We work with existing and prospective hotel owners and developers to increase our presence around the world, which we expect will lead to guest satisfaction, brand preference, and new channels for professional growth for our associates.

(Source: Hyatt Corporation 2013 Annual Report)

Appendix 3: Hyatt Hotels Corporation – Summary of hotel portfolio and selected competitors

Brand	% of total portfolio	Americas region	ASPAC region	EAME/SW Asia region	Primary selected competitors	Key locations
Park Hyatt	4%	1,630	2,416	2,489	Four Seasons, Ritz-Carlton, Peninsula, St. Regis, Mandarin Oriental	Buenos Aires, Dubai, Paris, Shanghai, Sydney, Washington D.C.
Andaz	2%	1,577	303	389	Mondrian, The Standard	Amsterdam, London, Los Angeles, New York, Shanghai
Hyatt	6%	7,213	—	1,396	Marriott, Hilton, InterContinental, Westin, independent and boutique hotels	Abu Dhabi, New York, San Francisco, Seattle, Key West
Grand Hyatt	15%	8,989	9,789	3,484	Mandarin Oriental, Shangri-La, InterContinental, Fairmont	Beijing, Berlin, Dubai, Hong Kong, New York, Tokyo
Hyatt Regency	48%	52,102	9,909	8,984	Marriott, Sheraton, Hilton, Renaissance, Westin	Boston, Delhi, London, Los Angeles, Mexico City, Orlando, San Francisco

Hyatt Place	17%	25,365	—	210	Courtyard by Marriott, Hilton	Atlanta, Dallas, Houston, Miami, Phoenix
Hyatt House	6%	8,154	—	—	Residence Inn by Marriott, Homewood Suites	Austin, Boston, Dallas, Miami, San Francisco
Hyatt Ziva	<1%	619	—	—	Club Med, Sandals, Beaches	San Jose del Cabo, Mexico
Hyatt Zilara	<1%	306	—	—	Club Med, Sandals, Beaches	Cancun, Mexico
Hyatt Residence Club	1%	963	128	973	Hilton Vacation, Club, Marriott, Vacation Club, Starwood Vacation Ownership	Aspen, Beaver Creek, Carmel, Dubai, Fukuoka, Key West, Mumbai

Notes:

Rooms/units as at December 31 2013.

Room/unit counts include owned, leased, managed, franchised, vacation ownership, branded residential and joint ventures.

Appendix 4: Hyatt Hotels Corporation – Summary of brands

Brand	Segment	Description and positioning
Park Hyatt	Full service/ luxury	Provide discerning, affluent individual business and leisure guests with elegant and luxurious accommodation. Guests receive gracious service and rare and intimate experiences in a thoughtfully designed contemporary environment. Located in many of the world's premier destinations, each hotel is custom designed to combine sophistication with distinctive regional character. Hotels feature well-appointed guestrooms, meeting and special event spaces for smaller groups, critically acclaimed art programmes and signature restaurants featuring award-winning chefs.
Andaz	Full service/ upper upscale	Boutique-inspired hotels where guests experience a vibrant yet uncomplicated atmosphere geared towards today's individual business and leisure travellers. The hotels are designed to reflect local culture and feature a unique and innovative service model. Signature elements include lounges, which are open, communal settings replacing the traditional lobby, and studios, which are creative and inspiring spaces for small meetings; hosts, who assist guests with everything.
Hyatt	Full Service/ Upper Upscale	Smaller-sized properties conveniently located in diverse business and leisure areas. Associates at Hyatt hotels are knowledgeable about their community and focus on offering guests the opportunity to experience the neighborhood like a local. Hotels accommodate individual business and leisure travellers, as well as smaller scale business meetings and social gatherings.
Grand Hyatt	Full service/ upper upscale	Feature distinctive hotels in major gateway cities and resort destinations. With presence around the world and critical mass in Asia, these hotels provide sophisticated global business and leisure travellers with elegant accommodation, extraordinary restaurants, bars, spas and fitness centres, as well as comprehensive business and meeting facilities. Signature elements include dramatic architecture, state of the art technology, and facilities for an array of business or social gatherings of all sizes.

Brand	Segment	Description and positioning
Hyatt Regency	Full service/ upper upscale	Designed to offer a full range of services and facilities tailored to serve the needs of meeting planners, business travellers and leisure guests. These convention hotels feature spacious meeting and conference facilities designed to provide a productive environment allowing guests to convene and connect. The hotels in resort locations cater to couples seeking a getaway, families enjoying a vacation together and corporate groups seeking a functional and relaxed atmosphere in which to conduct business and meetings.
Hyatt Place	Select service/ upscale garden inn	Creates a modern, comfortable and seamless experience, combining style and innovation to create a casual simple hotel experience for today's multi-tasking traveller. Modern spacious guestrooms feature a sofa sleeper, the Hyatt Grand Bed and 42" HDTV with plug and play capability. Guests stay connected with free Wi-Fi and enjoy the a complimentary hot breakfast. Hyatt Place hotels also feature the new Gallery Menu, Fresh 24/7, specialty coffees, premium beer, wine and spirits. Properties typically have 125 to 200 rooms and are located in urban, airport and suburban areas. Hyatt Place caters to business travellers as well as leisure guests and families. Hyatt Place properties are also well suited to serve small meetings and events.
Hyatt House	Select service/ extended stay	Designed to create contemporary experiences in casual home comfort, providing a residential atmosphere with spaces and services to keep routines rolling while guests are away from home. Residentially inspired studio, one and two bedroom suites feature contemporary full kitchens and separate living and sleeping areas with flat panel HDTVs. Guests stay connected with free Wi-Fi and enjoy the complimentary hot breakfast and evening social hour. The all-suite hotels are located in urban, airport and suburban areas. Caters for extended stay business and leisure travellers as well as families. Properties are also well suited to serve small meetings and events.
Hyatt Ziva	All inclusive	All-inclusive resorts cater to vacationing guests of all ages and offer a wide variety of activities that allow them to explore unique destinations where the properties are located. Properties will be larger resorts catering to families and accommodating groups with varied and well-appointed meeting facilities
Hyatt Zilara	All inclusive	Adult-only all inclusive resorts will be located in sought after, unique resort destinations. They will offer a wide array of food and beverage services and social activities as well as a variety of meeting spaces. Properties will be medium sized where couples or small groups can enjoy sophisticated surroundings.
Hyatt Residence Club	Vacation ownership/ branded residential	Provides members with vacation ownership opportunities in regionally inspired and designed residential-style properties with the quality of the Hyatt brand. Members pre-purchase time at a property and have the flexibility of usage, exchange and rental. Members can choose to occupy their vacation home, to exchange time among 15 Club locations, to trade their time for Hyatt Gold Passport points or to travel within the Hyatt system. Alternatively, members can exchange their time for time at properties participating within Interval International's program, a third-party company with over 2,800 resorts in its exchange network worldwide.

Appendix 5: Selected Hotel Groups – Portfolio of hotels

Hotel group	Owned and leased	Managed	Franchised	Total
IHG (UK)	10	658	3,954	4,622
Wyndham (USA)	2	45	7,290	7,337
Accor (France)	1,324	986	770	3,080
Marriott (USA)	43	1,015	2,645	3,703
Starwood (USA)	48	559	548	1,155
Hilton (USA)	156	530	3,394	4,080
Hyatt (USA)	97	366	182	648
Total	1,686	4,114	18,755	24,555

Appendix 6: Hyatt Hotels Corporation – Hotel portfolio changes

Category	Dec 2013	Dec 2012	Dec 2011	Dec 2010
Americas management and franchising				
Full service managed	117	119	122	121
Full service franchised	33	24	20	16
Select service managed	98	97	95	81
Select service franchised	150	128	120	114
ASPAC management and franchising				
Managed	57	51	51	49
Franchised	2	2	2	2
EAME/SW Asia management				
Full service managed	62	53	50	46
Select service managed	2	1	–	–
Properties				
All-inclusive properties	2	–	–	–
Vacation ownership properties	15	15	15	15
Residences	10	10	8	9
Owned and leased hotels				
Full service hotels USA	27	31	31	29
Full service Other Americas	4	4	3	3
Full service ASPAC	1	1	1	1
Full service EAME/SW Asia	11	11	9	9
Select service USA	54	56	64	54

Appendix 7: Hyatt consolidated statement of income (US$ million except share data)

	2013	2012	2011	2010
Owned and leased hotel revenues	2,142	2,021	1,879	1,859
Management and franchise fee revenues	342	307	288	255
Other revenues	78	78	66	45
Other revenues from managed properties	1,622	1,543	1,465	1,368
Total revenues	4,184	3,949	3,698	3,527
Direct and selling, general, and administrative expenses	3,951	3,790	3,545	3,419
Income (loss) from continuing operations	205	87	111	52
Net loss attributable to non-controlling interests	2	1	2	11
Net income (loss) attributable to Hyatt Hotels Corporation	207	88	113	67
Income (loss) from continuing operations per common share	$1.29	$0.53	$0.66	$0.30

Appendix 8: Hyatt consolidated balance sheet (US$ million)

	2013	2012	2011	2010
Cash and cash equivalents	454	413	534	1,110
Total current assets	1,163	1,758	1,591	2,165
Property and equipment, net	4,671	4,139	4,043	3,453
Intangibles, net	591	388	359	280
Total assets	8,177	7,630	7,497	7,233
Total current liabilities	871	618	568	596
Long-term debt	1,289	1,229	1,221	714
Other long-term liabilities	1,240	962	890	802
Total liabilities	3,400	2,809	2,679	2,112
Total stockholders' equity	4,769	4,811	4,808	5,108
Total liabilities and equity	8,177	7,630	7,497	7,145

Appendix 9: Hyatt and Hilton performance measures

HYATT	RevPAR		Occupancy		ADR	
	2013	2012	2013	2012	2013	2012
Owned and Leased						
Full Service	$161	$152	74.7%	73.7%	$215	$206
Select Service Hotels	$88	$83	77.8%	77.6%	$113	$105
Total Owned and Leased Hotels	$139	$131	75.7%	74.9%	$183	$175
Managed and Franchised						
Americas Full Service	$133	$126	74.1%	72.9%	$179	$172
Americas Select Service Hotels	$82	$78	76.2%	75.1%	$108	$104
Managed and Franchised						
ASPAC Full Service	$155	$159	68.0%	66.9%	$227	$237
Managed and Franchised						
EAME/SW Asia Full Service	$149	$144	63.6%	60.4%	$235	$238
HILTON SYSTEMWIDE	$100	$93	73.5%	71.1%	$136	$131

RevPAR

- RevPAR is the product of the average daily rate and the average daily occupancy percentage. RevPAR does not include non-room revenues, which consist of ancillary revenues generated by a hotel property, such as food and beverage, parking, telephone and other guest service revenues. Managers use RevPAR to identify trend information with respect to room revenues from comparable properties and to evaluate hotel performance.

- RevPAR changes that are driven predominantly by changes in occupancy have different implications for overall revenue levels and incremental profitability than do changes that are driven predominately by changes in average room rates. For example, increases in occupancy at a hotel would lead to increases in room revenues and additional variable operating costs (including housekeeping services, utilities and room amenity costs), and could also result in increased ancillary revenues (including food and beverage). In contrast, changes in average room rates typically have a greater impact on margins and profitability as there is no substantial effect on variable costs.

Occupancy

- Occupancy represents the total number of rooms sold divided by the total number of rooms available at a hotel or group of hotels. Occupancy measures the utilization of hotels' available capacity. Managers use occupancy to gauge demand at a specific hotel or group of hotels in a given period. Occupancy levels also help determine achievable ADR levels as demand for hotel rooms increases or decreases.

Average Daily Rate (ADR)

- ADR represents hotel room revenues divided by total number of rooms sold in a given period. ADR measures average room price attained by a hotel and ADR trends provide useful information concerning the pricing environment and the nature of the customer base of a hotel or group of hotels. ADR can be used to assess the pricing levels that can be generated by customer group, as changes in rates have a different effect on overall revenues and incremental profitability than changes in occupancy, as described above.

Appendix 10: Hyatt Hotels Corporation – Performance measures by brand

Hotel brand	Performance measure	2013	2012
Park Hyatt	ADR	$343	$348
	Occupancy	66%	61%
	RevPAR	$227	$215
Andaz	ADR	$281	$280
	Occupancy	77%	75%
	RevPAR	$216	$211
Hyatt	ADR	$169	$162
	Occupancy	74%	74%
	RevPAR	$125	$119
Grand Hyatt	ADR	$240	$240
	Occupancy	74%	73%
	RevPAR	$177	$175
Hyatt Regency	ADR	$165	$165
	Occupancy	71%	69%
	RevPAR	$119	$114
Hyatt Place	ADR	$102	$99
	Occupancy	75%	74%
	RevPAR	$77	$73
Hyatt House	ADR	$124	$119
	Occupancy	80%	78%
	RevPAR	$99	$93

Appendix 11: Hyatt Hotels Corporation: bases for competition

Category of Hyatt business	Main bases for Hyatt's competitive offering
Hotel guests	Brand name
	Recognition and reputation
	Location
	Customer satisfaction
	Room rates
	Quality of service
	Amenities and quality of accommodation
	The ability to earn and redeem loyalty program points.
Management and franchise agreements	Value and quality of management services
	Brand name recognition and reputation
	Ability and willingness to invest capital in third-party owned hospitality venture projects

Level of management fees

Economic advantages to the property owner of retaining Hyatt management services and using Hyatt's brand name

The room rate that can be realized and total revenues Hyatt can deliver to the properties

Marketing support and reservation and e-commerce system capacity and efficiency

Links to institutional investors

Sales of vacation ownership properties

Location

Quality of accommodation

Price and financing terms

Quality of service

Flexibility of usage

Opportunity to exchange into other vacation properties and

Brand name recognition and reputation

Appendix 12: Hyatt Hotels Corporation: Capital deployment model 2009–2013

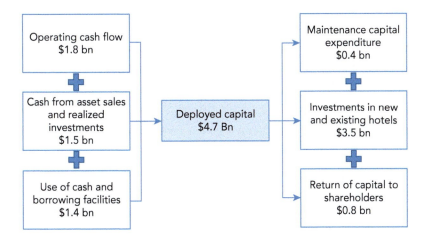

Appendix 13: Hyatt Hotels Corporation: Asset recycling example 2011

Appendix 14: Hilton Worldwide Inc – Hotel brands

Brand	Segment	Countries	Hotels	Rooms
Waldorf Astoria	Luxury brand in selected gateway cities	10	24	10,335
Conrad	Global luxury brand	17	23	7,877
Hilton Hotels and Resorts	Upper upscale, global flagship brand which ranks no. 1 for global brand awareness in hospitality	79	554	196,225
Doubletree by Hilton	Upscale, full service designed to provide true comfort to business and leisure travellers	51	361	90,409
Embassy Suites	Upper upscale, all-suite hotels	5	214	51,217
Hilton Garden Inn	Upscale brand that aims to provide busy travellers with what they need to be productive on the road	19	575	79,135
Hampton Inn hotels	Moderately priced upper midscale hotels with limited food and beverage	15	1,929	189,681
Homewood Suites by Hilton	Upscale extended-stay hotels that feature residential style accommodation	3	329	36,237
Home2 Suites by Hilton	Hilton's newest brand, Upper midscale hotels providing a modern and savvy option to budget conscious extended-stay travellers	1	22	2,423
Hilton Grand Vacations	Timeshare brand	3	41	6,404

Appendix 15: Hilton value proposition

- Hilton's value proposition starts with our award-winning brands and industry-leading commercial services platform
- This leads to satisfied customers, including nearly 39 million HHonors loyalty members
- As a result, we are able to drive premium performance to the hotels in our system
- These hotel operating premiums drive strong financial returns, which benefit our hotel owners
- Satisfied existing and new owners continue to invest in growing our brands, making us a global leader in hotel supply and pipeline
- We believe the reinforcing nature of these activities will allow us to outperform the competition

SOURCES

Hyatt Corporation 2013 Annual Report.
Hilton Worldwide IPO Filing, NASDAQ Exchange, 2013.
Hotel Group Annual Reports: Various.
Raval, A. (2014), 'Hyatt Opens up and Bets on Expansion', London: The Financial Times, March 18th.

Case **5**

Days Inn

Franchising hospitality assets in China

Historical development and ownership of the Days Inn brand

The Days Inn brand was created by Cecil B. Day in 1970 when the US hospitality industry consisted of just a dozen national lodging brands rather than the proliferation of brands encountered by today's consumers. The Atlanta-based company, Days Inns of America Inc., began franchising hotels in 1972 and within eight years had created a system of more than 300 hotels in the United States, Mexico and Canada.

Cendant Corporation, Wyndham Worldwide's predecessor, acquired the Days Inn brand in 1992. Wyndham Worldwide Corporation is the holding company for Wyndham Hotels & Resorts, Group and timeshare exchange group RCI and other lodging brands such as Ramada and Howard Johnson. Wyndham Worldwide, which has its headquarters in New Jersey, USA, was formed when it was de-merged from Cendant Corporation in July 2006.

The Days Inn product characteristics

Days Inns and Days Hotels are economy hotels located throughout the world that offer guests single, double and sometimes suite accommodation. All properties in North America, and most properties in other regions, feature high-speed Internet access, expanded cable television, in-room coffee-maker and continental breakfast. In addition Days Hotels typically offer meeting and business facilities, fitness centre, swimming pool and restaurant. Days Suites properties are economy hotels located throughout the United States that offer guests one- and two-bedroom suite accommodation.

In China the brand is somewhat different. Known as Days Inn Hotel & Suites in China, properties are mid-to-upscale hotels that, in addition to the amenities found at their global counterparts, offer multiple bars and restaurants, 24-hour room service and expanded meeting and banquet facilities.

Service-based products

The service sector has grown rapidly in both developed and developing countries during the past three decades. The hotel industry is characterized by high capital intensity, contrary to most other industries in the service sector, and its logistics and supply chain can be as complex as those in manufacturing operations (Chen and Dimou, 2005). When internationalizing, service firms may enter foreign markets using a variety of entry modes, such as, exports, licensing, joint ventures, or establishing a subsidiary abroad.

The choice of foreign market entry mode can however be viewed as critical and is related to control. Control is crucial in that it ensures achievement of the ultimate purpose of the organization. Control is also the single most significant factor that determines risks and returns, the amount of relational friction between buyers and sellers, and ultimately the performance of the investment abroad (Blomstermo *et al.*, 2006).

Services can be defined as:

> *An activity or series of activities of a more or less intangible nature that normally, but not necessarily, take place in interactions between the customer and service employees and/or physical resources or goods and/or systems of the service provider, which are provided as solutions to customer problems.*

> *Gronroos (1990: 27)*

An analysis of this definition shows that services are characterized by intangibility, and inseparability of production and consumption, which, in turn, are related to perishability and heterogeneity. These four characteristics are central to the analysis of the international operations of service firms (Bouquet *et al.*, 2004; Palmer, 2001).

Intangibility entails that there is no physical product to act as a catalyst to bind international business units and business partners together. This gives rise to a greater need for internal marketing and a stable partner relationship. Intangibility also affects perceptions of service quality.

A number of writers have attempted to meaningfully reduce the large diversity of the service sector on the basis of the inseparability of production and consumption. This is done particularly in the context of internationalization so that useful insights about international entry modes for individual service industries can be gained (Ekeledo and Sivakumar, 1998). In doing so they frequently distinguish between 'hard' and 'soft' services. For some internationally marketed services a decoupling of production and consumption is feasible. Hard services are those where production and consumption can be decoupled. For example, software services and architectural services can be transferred in a document, email attachment, or some other tangible medium. They can often be standardized, making mass production feasible.

However, with regard to soft services, where production and consumption occur simultaneously, decoupling is not viable. The soft-service provider must be present abroad from their first day of foreign operations (Blomstermo *et al.*, 2006). Thus both the supplier and customer must be present during performance of the service, and since the service is being 'performed' implying that there is a large degree of personal involvement with product delivery standardization becomes much more difficult. Whilst hotel services generally fall into this category, hotel companies go to great lengths in attempting to standardize some product features (so as to ensure consistent quality is achieved). They also attempt to provide distinctive products partly through the quality of their staffing.

There are important implications of simultaneous production and consumption. Customers may demand specific adaptations and information exchange to suit local requirements in foreign markets. Services with a high degree of intangibility and buyer–seller interaction frequency and simultaneous production and consumption are location-bound and must be available in full from the day of foreign market entry (Anand and Delios, 1997).

Because services are to a large degree experience-based and dependent on individual perceptions in time and space, they are difficult to evaluate before and even after consumption, thus it is difficult to perform quality control in traditional ways. With customer as co-producer, service outcomes are highly variable, making provision of service guarantees. Finally, because many services cannot be stored, buffering demand fluctuations through holding inventory is impossible (Blomstermo *et al.*, 2006).

One of the central questions in considering international expansion and mode of market entry is the extent to which customer needs are homogeneous worldwide and whether their needs can be met through a standardized strategic approach or whether adaptation will be necessary. The answer to this question is vital because as Takeuchi and Porter (1986) state, standardization across national markets has an impact on value-chain activities. For example, homogeneous customer needs may allow economies of scale and a common marketing approach. Heterogeneous needs, by contrast, may require an organization to adopt different product designs, brand names and product features for each national market (Altinay, 2007).

Market entry decisions

The mode of entry is a fundamental decision a firm makes when it enters a new market because the choice of entry automatically constrains the firm's marketing and operational strategy. The mode of entry also affects how a firm faces the challenges of entering a new country and deploying new skills to market its product successfully (Gillespie *et al.*, 2007).

A firm entering a foreign market faces an array of choices to serve the market. Johnson and Tellis (2008) categorize the choices open to companies into five main classes, listed in order of increasing control:

1. Export – a firm's sales of goods/services produced in the home market and sold in the host country through an entity in the host country.

2. Licence and franchise – a formal permission or right offered to a firm or agent located in a host country to use a home firm's proprietary technology or other knowledge resources in return for payment.

3. Alliance – agreement and collaboration between a firm in the home market and a firm located in a host country to share activities in the host country.

4. Joint venture – shared ownership of an entity located in a host country by two partners, one located in the home country and the other located in the host country.

5. Wholly owned subsidiary – complete ownership of an entity located in a host country by a firm located in the home country to manufacture or perform value addition or sell goods/services in the host country.

A firm can choose any of these entry modes or use them in combination, though clearly exporting is not an option for soft service-based products. The distinguishing attribute regarding the different modes of entry is the degree to which they give another firm control over its marketing resources. At one end of the spectrum is the export of goods, which has the lowest degree of control. Licences, franchises, and various forms of joint venture provide a progressively increasing degree of control for the firm; at the other end of the spectrum, ownership-based entries, such as wholly owned subsidiaries, afford the highest control.

In making the decision about the appropriate market entry mode for a particular country a firm needs to consider a complex set of factors which include factors such as the timing of the entry; the extent to which the company has knowledge of the relevant economic and cultural circumstances in the particular country; the size and expertise of the company; and, the assessment of the risks that could be encountered in a particular country (Johnson and Tellis, 2008).

Franchising and management contracts

Hotel chains have generally preferred to use non-equity forms of organization for international expansion and operations mainly due to cost-efficiency concerns. Non-equity-based agreements such as franchising and management contracts are the most common forms of organizational structure for market entry among hotel chains, partly because of the high initial capital requirements involved in setting up a hotel (Contractor and Kundu, 1998).

On the face of it, both franchising and management contracts seem to provide a company with similar advantages and disadvantages, but there are important differences between them regarding the degree of control (Chen and Dimou, 2005). In the case of a hotel franchise, a company operates a hotel under one of the brands owned by one of the large international chains and the company benefits from the services and expertise of the international chain. In return a franchise fee is paid (by the franchisee) to the international hotel group (the franchisor). The fee is based on revenues received. Operational decision making and day-to-day management control lies with the franchisee.

Alon (2012) found that hotels are different from other service franchisors such as retail and business services franchises' internationalization. Franchising related costs are highest in terms of the required capital investment for hotels. Total investment required by Choice Hotels International ranges from $2.3 to 14.6 million, InterContinental Hotels Group (IHG) $2–20 million, Motel 6, $1.9–2.3 million, and Hilton 53.4–90.1 million, to give a few examples (Alon et al., 2012). In contrast, most other service franchising industries require less than $1 million for start-up costs.

Notwithstanding the high initial capital outlays required of franchisees, franchising systems in the hotel industry are among the most mature of the franchised services, and therefore they are further along the product life cycle. They also face stiffer domestic and global competition and declining profit margins, which together contribute to a greater awareness of the need to think of the world in global terms (Alon et al., 2012).

Burton and Cross (1995:36) define international franchising as:

> *a foreign market entry mode that involves a relationship between the entrant (the franchisor) and a host country entity, in which the former transfers, under contract, a business package (or format), which it developed and owns, to the latter.*

By way of contrast, with a management contract the hotel property is operated by the international branded hotel company for the property owner. Operational decision making and day-to-day management control lies with the hotel company which has been contracted to manage the hotel. Management fees are paid to the hotel group which are based on revenue and operating profits.

Franchising provides scope for rapid international expansion for hotel companies and has the potential to overcome many of the cultural, linguistic, technical, legal, and employment problems commonly associated with internationalization.

The hotel industry is capital-intensive, requiring a big financial up-front outlay to establish facilities. Franchising provides an opportunity for hotels to lower the risks and the level of investment to expand. Franchising also allows hotel and motel franchisors to share the costs of expansion with the franchisees, who typically pay the start-up costs, initial fees, and ongoing royalties. In return, the franchisees obtain brand-name recognition, economies of scale, and managerial expertise from the franchisors. A franchise is a way to transfer tangible and intangible expertise with limited capital risks.

However, internationalization through franchising can be a complex process affected by many forces, particularly organizational factors and market conditions (Alon et al., 2012). The use of franchising potentially causes two main problems for an international hotel company: the risk of proprietary knowledge leakage and the possible 'free-riding' behaviour of the franchisee, in which the franchisee is able to reap most of the benefits from a partnership. However, the franchising model provides powerful incentives since the franchisee's compensation is mainly linked to the unit performance. The use of high-powered incentives can reduce the need for monitoring the franchisee because the behaviour is self-correcting.

The Wyndham business model

Wyndham Worldwide, which is headquartered in the suburban New Jersey town of Parsippany, is one of the world's largest hospitality companies, employing approximately 26,000 people. Wyndham offers individual consumers and business-to-business customers a broad suite of hospitality products and services across various accommodation alternatives and price ranges through its portfolio of brands. Wyndham is the world's largest franchisor of hotel-branded products.

The company also has other substantial business interests in its two other divisions:

- Wyndham Exchange and Rentals offers leisure travellers, including its 3.8 million members, access to approximately 97,000 vacation properties located in approximately 100 countries.
- Wyndham Vacation Ownership develops, markets and sells vacation ownership interests and provides consumer financing to owners through its network of over 160 vacation ownership resorts serving nearly 815,000 owners throughout North America, the Caribbean and the South Pacific.

Wyndham is one of the world's largest hotel companies with almost 7,500 properties and approximately 650,000 rooms. However, very few of the properties operating under the Wyndham Worldwide owned brands are managed by the company and only two are actually owned directly. The rapid international rise of Wyndham Worldwide has largely resulted from it adopting the franchised model to facilitate growth. Such an 'asset-light' model, pioneered by Holiday Inn and fast food chains in 1950s America, has been widely copied and adapted by hospitality groups to facilitate rapid growth, leverage finite resources and to devolve risk.

In North America, Wyndham generally employs a direct franchise model for its brands, whereby the company contracts with and provides various services and reservations assistance directly to independent owner-operators of hotels. Under the direct franchise model, Wyndham's lodging brands are principally marketed to hotel developers, owners of independent hotels and hotel owners who have the right to terminate their existing franchise affiliations with other lodging brands. Existing franchisees are also targeted because many own, or may own in the future, other hotels that can be converted to one of Wyndham's brands.

The standard franchise agreement grants a franchisee the right to non-exclusive use of the applicable franchise system in the operation of a single hotel at a specified location, typically for a period of 15 to 20 years. It also gives the franchisor and franchisee certain rights to terminate the franchise agreement before its conclusion under certain circumstances, such as upon the lapse of a certain number of years after commencement of the agreement. Early termination options in franchise agreements give flexibility to terminate franchised hotels if business circumstances warrant. Under such agreements Wyndham also have the right to terminate a franchise agreement for failure by a franchisee to bring its property into compliance with contractual or quality standards within specified periods of time, pay required franchise fees or comply with other requirements of the franchise agreement.

Although a direct franchise model is generally employed in North America, Wyndham's currently has two company-owned hotels. The Bonnet Creek hotel, which opened in late 2011, is situated in the Bonnet Creek vacation ownership resort near the Walt Disney World resort in Florida. This property enables synergies to be leveraged between the company's hotel and vacation ownership elements. In late 2012, the Rio Mar hotel in Rio Grande, Puerto Rico was acquired. This is a luxury vacation destination. The oceanfront property includes premier restaurants, a spa, casino, golf course, and comprehensive business centre. These two hotels represent mixed-use opportunities whereby cross product brand loyalty can be generated by exposing repeat hotel guests to the vacation ownership product. Additionally, under the mixed-use business model, hotel guests and vacation property owners can benefit from accessing higher quality amenities.

In other parts of the world Wyndham employ both a direct franchise and master franchise model. The master franchise model is generally used in regions where the company is not yet ready to support the required infrastructure for a specific region. While Wyndham's employs a direct franchising model in China for its Wyndham and Ramada brands, the master franchise model is used for the company's Super 8, Days Inn and Howard Johnson brands. Similarly, within Canada, a direct franchising model is generally applied for the company's brands with the exception of the Days Inn, Howard Johnson, Travelodge and Knights Inn brands, for which the master licence model is used.

Franchise agreements in regions outside of North America may carry a lower fee structure based upon the breadth of services Wyndham is prepared to provide in that particular region. Under the master franchise model, the lodging brands are principally marketed to third parties that assume the principal role of franchisor, which entails selling individual franchise agreements and providing quality assurance and marketing and reservations support to franchisees.

Since only limited services are provided to master franchisors, the fees received in connection with the master franchise agreements are typically lower than the fees received under a direct franchising model. Master franchise agreements, which are individually negotiated and vary among the different brands, typically contain provisions that permit Wyndham to terminate the agreement if the other party to the agreement fails to meet specified development schedules.

Franchise and management fees are generally higher in the second and third quarters than in the first or fourth quarters of any calendar year. This is the result of increased leisure travel and the related ability to charge higher room rates during the northern hemisphere spring and summer months.

The ability of an individual franchisee to compete may be affected by the location and quality of its property, the number of competing properties in the vicinity, community reputation and other factors. A franchisee's success may also be affected by general, regional and local economic conditions. For Wyndham the potential negative effect of these conditions on results of operations is substantially reduced by virtue of the diverse geographical locations of franchised hotels and by the scale of the franchisee base. The franchise system is dispersed among approximately 5,500 franchisees, which reduces the Wyndham exposure from any one franchisee. No one franchisee accounts for more than 6 per cent of the franchised hotels or total segment revenues.

Chinese market

Nowhere is the growth of tourism more prominent than China, in terms of inbound tourism, outbound tourism and domestic tourism by its 1.3 billion people. Given the sheer scale of the Chinese population, even though the percentage of the Chinese population travelling overseas is likely to remain relatively small for many years, the impact, both on the companies which have invested in China, and on the destination areas for the tourists, will be profound.

Chinese tourism and hospitality industries have experienced phenomenal development since economic reform was initiated in 1978. At the commencement of this period of development, China's hotels were few in number, with travel having been primarily restricted to that associated with political needs (Zhang et al., 2005).

As part of a strategy to modernize China, the country started with a new economic reform (the so-called 'Open Door Policy'), under the leadership, of Deng Xiaoping. After 1978, the Open Door Policy and further economic reforms helped to contribute to change the old socialist economic system of the former China into a new environment in which foreign investment and expertise were encouraged. The Chinese government officially explicitly recognized the importance of tourism as a driver of economic development in 1986 insofar as the tourism industry was mentioned for the first time in the national plan for social and economic development (Zhang *et al.*, 2000).

Notwithstanding the need for caution in interpreting tourism statistics in China (as elsewhere in the world), Chinese tourism has undoubtedly grown significantly. Tourism, is normally sub-divided into three categories: inbound tourism by overseas tourists; domestic tourism by Chinese travellers; and, outbound tourism by Chinese tourists visiting foreign countries. Unsurprisingly, in a developing country and where economic migration (from rural communities to cities and from the interior to coastal provinces) domestic tourism is the dominant sector, but both inbound and outbound have shown significant growth.

Days Inn in China

There are more than 1,900 Days Inn hotels worldwide, catering largely for the economy segment of the market in which Wyndham, the world's largest hotel franchisor is the clear market leader. Tera Capital Limited is a private investment management firm that invests in both private equities and public sector investment. The firm is the investment holding company for three Singaporean brothers, David Tan, Harry Tan and Ted Fang who in 2003 successfully acquired the Days Inn master franchise for Greater China from Wyndham Worldwide Corporation.

The hotels are operated and managed through the Frontier Group of companies which are based in Beijing and controlled by the Singaporean brothers. Since commencing operations in 2004, the principals have made Days Inn China one of China's fastest growing mid-market hotel chains, with a portfolio across 22 provinces. Tera Capital continues its role as the sponsor of Days Inn China, in steering its strategic direction and arranging real estate deals.

The brothers had spotted an opportunity in that they felt that there was at the time a lack of mid-tier or economy hotels in China, and that some of the nations' secondary markets had been overlooked by most hotel developers. Most of the hotels that had been developed were either luxury or budget hotels and yet growing affluence in China's had led to the emergence of a large middle class. In explaining their market positioning the Singapore newspaper, *The Straits Times*, quotes Harry Tan: 'Our niche market is good because when times are good, the two-star travellers want to upgrade and give themselves a treat to a three-star hotel. When times are bad, the five-star travellers want to save some money and move down to a four-star hotel' (Teo, 2013).

Since its inception in 2004, Days Inn China has become one of the fastest-growing mid-tier hotel chains in China, with a total of 140 projects and more than 20,000 rooms spanning 80 cities and 22 provinces across China by the end of 2013. Many of the hotels are situated in provincial cities such as Chongqing, Suzhou and Xiamen with the majority of properties in the mid-market three- and four-star categories. A typical property would be the Days Hotel in Siping. The town with a population of about 600,000 is at the centre of an agricultural region of about 3 million people and is the third largest in the Jilin province of north east China. The four star Days Hotel in central Siping, which features a restaurant, spa and meeting rooms in the 15-floor property, is the only hotel in Siping featured on the Expedia search engine.

Traditionally an economy brand, Days Inn China has upgraded the brand image and market positioning in China with a range of hotel Days Inn brands:

- Days Hotel & Suites – 5-star luxury hotels and holiday resorts;
- Days Hotel – Superior 4-star hotels;

- Days Inn Business Place – Full-service business hotels;
- Days Inn – 3-star city hotels;
- Days Suites – superior hotel style, service apartments.

Appendix 1: China – Number of hotels and hotel rooms

Year	No. of hotels	Hotel star rating				
		5 star	4 star	3 star	2 star	1 star
1991	853	21	21	235	393	156
1995	1,913	38	38	591	930	248
2000	6,029	117	352	1,899	3,061	600
2005	11,828	281	1,146	4,291	5,497	613
2010	13,991	595	2,219	6,268	4,612	297

Year	No. of rooms	Hotel star rating				
		5 star	4 star	3 star	2 star	1 star
1991	167,195	14,993	21,375	58,985	56,229	15,613
1995	308,587	21,924	40,975	116,047	110,227	19,414
2000	594,678	45,208	84,890	231,244	205,110	28,226
2005	1,332,100	106,532	240,448	542,207	410,982	31,914
2010	1,709,966	218,064	449,207	714,850	313,871	13,974

Source: Gu et al. (2012), based on Annual Tourism Statistics of China National Tourism Administration (1992–2010), Beijing, China Travel & Tourism Press, 2011.

Appendix 2: China – Major hotel groups in 2011

International hotel group	Hotels (Worldwide)	Rooms (Worldwide)	Hotels (China)	Rooms (China)
IHG (InterContinental Hotels Group)	4,432	643,787	227	50,440
Wyndham Hotel Group	7,112	597,674	326	48,821
Hilton Hotels Corp.	3,526	587,813	24	8,695
Marriott International	3,329	580,876	58	21,970
Accor	4,111	492,675	107	28,002
Choice Hotels International	6,021	487,410	3	455
Best Western International	4,048	308,477	34	6396
Starwood Hotels and Resorts Worldwide	979	291,638	72	26,704

International hotel group	Hotels (Worldwide)	Rooms (Worldwide)	Hotels (China)	Rooms (China)
Carlson Hotels Worldwide/Rezidor	1,059	159,756	9	3,817
Hyatt Group	399	120,031	17	NA
Shangri-La	72	30,000	36	NA
Ascott	NA	NA	40	7,000

Source: Adapted from Gu et al. (2012)

Domestic hotel group	Hotels (China)	Rooms (China)
Jinjiang Hotel International	703	105,149
New Century Hotels & Resorts	83	24,610
CTS HK Metro Park Hotels	74	23,964
Jinling Hotels & Resorts	92	23,057
BTG – Jianguo Hotels & Resorts	67	20,283

Source: Adapted from Gu et al. (2012)

Appendix 3: China – Number of tourists (millions)

	2001	2002	2003	2004	2005	2006	2007	2008
Inbound	89.0	97.9	91.7	109.0	120.3	125.0	131.9	130.0
Outbound	12.1	16.6	20.2	28.9	31.0	34.5	41.0	45.8
Domestic	780.0	880.0	870.0	1,100.0	1,212.0	1,394.0	1,610.0	1,712.0

Source: CNTA Annual Reports

Appendix 4: Days Inn – Franchise support

Days Inn franchisees are supported in a number of ways including:

Positioning

Under the 'Best Value Under the Sun' market positioning Days Inn hotels offer value-conscious consumers consistent standards in over 1,900 hotels and free high-speed Internet service in most properties.

Global sales team

Focus is on building the relationships that help deliver business. Acting as an extension of franchisees' sales teams, the Global Sales Department consists of hospitality professionals around the world and provides revenue-building support in key segments:

- group – meetings, incentive, conferences and exhibition (MICE);
- corporate, associations and group sales;

- specialty market – transportation, sports, government, member benefits, and tour and travel;
- travel – travel management companies (TMC), consortia, tour operators and wholesalers;
- corporate transient – business travel and relocations.

Procurement

Strategic sourcing is committed to lowering costs while providing higher-quality products for an enhanced guest experience. This is done by leveraging the combined purchasing power of Wyndham Worldwide. Through WynSource, an online purchasing tool, operating supplies and equipment can be purchased and spending can effectively be tracked.

Training

Wyndham Hotel Group's School of Hospitality Operations (SoHO) is focused on helping Wyndham Hotel Group's family of franchised and managed hotels enhance customer experiences. From general manager orientations to self-paced online courses, the goal is to help employees attain relevant skills and knowledge.

Brand marketing

Marketing Services including powerful promotions, advertising and public relations help drive consumers, travel agents and corporate meeting planners to properties. Support is provided by trained call-centre staff available at all times. Consultation regarding rates and inventory management are provided to stay competitive in the marketplace.

REFERENCES AND ACKNOWLEDGEMENTS

Martina Müller at Teesside University aided the author with some of the material for this case.

Alon, I., L. Ni and Y. Wang (2012) 'Examining the Determinants of Hotel Chain Expansion through International Franchising', *International Journal of Hospitality Management*, 31 (2): 379–86.

Altinay, L. (2007) 'The Internationalization of Hospitality Firms: Factors Influencing a Franchise Decision-Making Process', *Journal of Services Marketing*, 21 (6): 398–409.

Anand, J. and A. Delios (1997) 'Location Specificity and the Transferability of Downstream Assets to Foreign Subsidiaries', *Journal of International Business Studies*, 28 (3): 579–603.

Blomstermo, A., D. D. Sharma and J. Sallis (2006) 'Choice of Foreign Market Entry Mode in Service Firms', *International Marketing Review*, 23 (2): 211–29.

Bouquet, C., L. Hebert and A. Delios (2004) 'Foreign Expansion in Service Industries: Separability and Human Capital Intensity', *Journal of Business Research*, 57 (1): 35–46.

Burton, F. N. and A. R. Cross (1995) 'Franchising and Foreign Market Entry', in S. J. Paliwoda and J. K. Ryans (eds.), *International Marketing Reader*, London and New York: Routledge, pp. 35–48.

Chen, J. J. and I. Dimou (2005) 'Expansion Strategy of International Hotel Firms', *Journal of Business Research*, 58 (12): 1730–40.

Contractor, F. and S. Kundu (1998) 'Modal Choice in a World of Alliances: Analysing Organisational Forms in the International Hotel Sector', *Journal of International Business Studies*, 29 (2): 325–57.

Ekeledo, I. and K. Sivakumar (1998) 'Foreign Market Entry Mode Choice of Service Firms: A Contingency Perspective', *Journal of the Academy of Marketing Science*, 26 (4): 274–92.

Gillespie, Kate, Jean-Pierre Jeannet and H. David Hennessy (2007) *Global Marketing*, 2nd edn, Boston: Houghton Mifflin.

Gronroos, C. (1990) *Service Management and Marketing: Managing the Moments of Truth in Service Competition*, Lexington, Mass.: Lexington Books.

Gu, H., C. Ryan and L. Yu (2012) 'The Changing Structure of the Chinese Hotel Industry: 1980–2012', *Tourism Management Perspectives*, 4: 56–63.

Johnson, J. and G. J. Tellis (2008) 'Drivers of Success for Market Entry into China and India', *Journal of Marketing*, 72 (3): 1–13.

Palmer, A. (2001) *Principles of Services Marketing*, 3rd edn, London: McGraw-Hill.

Takeuchi, H. and M. Porter (1986) 'Three Roles of International Marketing in Global Strategy', in M. Porter (ed.), *Competition in Global Industries*, Boston, Mass.: Harvard Business School, pp. 111–46.

Teo, E. (2013) 'Brothers Hit Jackpot in China Hotel Sector: A Travel Boom Has Helped Them Take the Days Inn Brand to Greater Heights', *The Straits Times* (Singapore), 6 May.

Zhang, G., R. Pine and H. Q. Zhang (2000) 'China's International Tourism Development: Present and Future', *International Journal of Contemporary Hospitality Management*, 12 (5): 282–90.

Zhang, H. Q., R. Pine and T. Lam (2005) *Tourism and Hotel Development: from Political to Economic Success*, Binghampton, NY: Haworth Hospitality Press.

Case **6**

Reed Exhibitions

The world's leading events organizer

Background

'Events management' is an all-embracing term which covers a multitude of activities and sub-divisions ranging from wedding planning to international festivals. The events that are organized differ in a number of ways.

The scale of events ranges from small local events through to globally important events such as the Olympics and the World Cup. Events also differ in their target audiences in that some are clearly targeted by businesses at consumers (B2C) while others are targeted at other businesses (B2B). In most cases while the event itself may have a very high profile, those organizations that organize the events are generally in the background and have a much lower public profile. Some events are organized in a regular cycle in that they occur perhaps every year, or in the case of the Olympic Games or the World Cup given their enormous scale every four years. Other events are one-offs such as a concert by a particular artist at a particular venue.

There is a continuum of events in relation to their finances. Some are financed by local or national government and are viewed as a service which can be subsidized, while others are run as not-for-profit ventures, often by public–private partnerships, but do not receive a public subsidy. Other events are organized in a purely commercial way, with the company that manages the process expecting to do so in a way that is profitable for its shareholders.

Given the number and diversity of events and festivals being organized and managed and the sheer scale of the activities involved, it is not surprising that the industry that has grown up to provide these services remains highly fragmented. It is also the case that the overall events and festivals sector is often broken down into various segments and that companies are often highly specialized in the type of events they manage or the customers that they target.

One such segment is the meetings, incentive travel, conventions, and exhibitions segment, often referred to by the acronym 'MICE'. The MICE set of events has been recognized as a significant hospitality market segment over the past few decades. The segment is multi-faceted in that it brings together hospitality services, including lodging, food and beverage, catering, convention service, convention facility supply, transportation, tourism, retail and entertainment and consequently often represents an economic driver of great importance for the local economy of a destination. Many destinations have developed large-scale facilities to cater for this segment with convention centres, large-scale exhibition spaces and meeting resources having been developed in many cities around the world.

MICE activity is essentially urban in its focus because it requires ease of access, a nucleus of facilities and ancillary attractions and hospitality capacity. Some destinations such as London, Dubai, Singapore and Hong Kong derive enormous revenues from attracting MICE tourism activity with delegates drawn by their status as major world cities. Others such as Las Vegas and Macau have built their MICE activity as an adjunct to gambling and utilizing the extensive hospitality resources developed in these cities. Other cities such as Frankfurt and Geneva as ancient well positioned trading cities, have ancient trade fairs that long pre-date the use of the MICE terminology. Resorts such as Davos in Switzerland, Australia's Gold Coast and the Indonesian island of Bali, have also targeted MICE activities since they represent highly attractive destinations for visitors who provide a means of filling their large hospitality facilities during 'off-peak' and 'shoulder' seasons.

Companies have emerged to organize and manage much MICE activity. The industry is highly fragmented with many local and regional companies operating and many have particular specialisms such as meetings or exhibitions; or a concentration on particular industry sectors such as healthcare or automotive. Notwithstanding the industry fragmentation that exists, there is very keen competition for organizing MICE events. Several large diversified companies have emerged and the major international hotel groups often commit large resources to developing these activities centred on their hotel properties and associated banqueting and convention spaces.

The scale of MICE activity is vast and growing quickly. Yang and Gu (2012), cite studies that illustrate the scale of the industry in the USA and Singapore for example. According to a study by consultants PricewaterhouseCoopers US (2011), the MICE industry contributes $263 billion in annual spending to the US economy, provides $25.6 billion in tax revenue, and creates 1.7 million jobs for the American workforce across the United States. For Singapore, which relies on MICE heavily for its tourism industry, the MICE business contributes even more to the nation's economy. According to International Enterprise Singapore (2001), every dollar generated by the MICE industry adds another $12 to the national gross domestic product (GDP).

This is a multifaceted business in which convention and exhibition centres, specialized facilities, tourism, trading partners and distribution operate systematically in generating revenue. MICE activities are generally recognized as high-value-adding business opportunities worldwide and many countries and cities are committed to strengthening and enhancing the infrastructure to accommodate internationally renowned events.

Exhibitions

Exhibitions are a large constituent part of MICE events, though many of them go relatively unnoticed by the general public since many are B2B events. The exhibitions vary considerably in their scale and focus, with many concentrating on very specialized industry sectors and sub-sectors. It is also the case that it is sometimes difficult to disaggregate exhibitions from other MICE activity since many other activities such as meetings, conventions and conferences cluster around the exhibitions and delegates often benefit from incentive travel opportunities provided by their organizations.

A number of specialized companies have formed to organize and manage exhibitions around the world and while there are many 'one-off' events the companies have also with their partners tried to create recognized exhibition brands in their chosen specialisms the formats of which get repeated in subsequent years and 'cloned' and adapted to serve different geographical markets. Some of the companies which specialize in these events have long histories while others are of much more recent origin. The trade fairs (messe) were established in large Continental European cities, particularly in Germany (such as Frankfurt, Munich and Hannover) in medieval times.

The global exhibitions market saw robust growth in 2012, after several years affected by the world economic downturn, expanding by 5 per cent to reach $27bn. Global growth slowed slightly in 2013 in most countries, but 2014 is expected to return to 5 per cent growth with this level of trend growth continuing thereafter (AMR, 2013). A particularly important constituent of this growth is likely to come from the so-called BRIC countries (Brazil, Russia, India and China) with the rapid emergence of the Gulf Region also continuing to drive global growth. In addition to these countries, 'tier two' emerging markets such as Indonesia and Malaysia are seeing heightened M&A and launch activity. The large international organizers are expanding into these countries as they continue to rebalance their portfolios to emerging markets. Substantial growth in mature markets is more difficult to achieve; but a compelling offering including digital can drive exhibition value and provide additional revenue opportunities for organizers (AMR, 2013).

Apart from its solid growth prospects, the exhibitions sector remains highly attractive for many other reasons: events can be highly profitable; they have excellent cash flow characteristics, with stand space deposits often paid a year in advance; there is also a high degree of revenue integrity with exhibitor renewal rates typically in the 65 per cent to 85 per cent range (AMR, 2013). Furthermore, the exhibitions market remains fragmented and still offers considerable opportunities for consolidation. The $950m acquisition of a large American events management company, illustrates the attractiveness of the exhibitions sector for investors. Nielsen Expositions, which had grown from a US publishing business Miller Freeman was acquired by Onex, a Canadian private equity investor in 2013 and subsequently changed its name to Emerald Expositions. The subsequent acquisition of another US exhibition organizer (GLM) propelled Emerald to the position of the leading trade exposition organizer in the USA.

There are, however, significant differences between the world's most attractive exhibition markets and between the requirements of the industry sectors on which the events focus. Thus though organizers are trying to create branded concepts which can be replicated in various parts of the world, they nevertheless have to try to understand the local market dynamics and make relevant adaptations to their products accordingly. Local knowledge, expertise and contacts are hard to acquire and though the industry is not heavily regulated, it is common for local partners to become involved. These partnerships may take the form of a joint venture but may also involve looser arrangements such as contractual agreements with local organizations such as venue owners, travel, hospitality and marketing companies and trade associations. In doing so event organizers are able to reduce risks by acquiring local expertise and knowledge, sharing marketing activities and having specialized support at the particular location.

Furthermore an increasingly important part of the exhibition market is the digital interface that occurs between exhibitors, buyers and intermediaries prior to the event, during the event and after the event. These 'digital platforms' allow: connections to be made; partnerships and alliances to be formed; a deeper understanding of products to be gained; and price and product comparisons to be made. Generally these digital platforms are an adjunct to the exhibition and related events, but in a small (but rapidly growing) number of cases 'virtual exhibitions' have been held, thereby avoiding the costs and logistical effort of organizing a physical exhibition involving all parties meeting in one place at a specified time. This is likely to be a growing trend in the industry, though those with vested interests such as: hotel operators; destination organizations; venue owners; travel companies; and exhibition organizers are all involved in stressing the advantages of face-to-face meetings which they claim are more effective in generating results.

Increasingly event organizers are deploying extensive resources in developing and maintaining their digital platforms and making it part of their positioning relative to competitor offerings. The organizers which have developed digital platforms stress the quality, networking opportunities and the business facilitation offered by their particular digital platforms and point to the inability of smaller organizers to provide similar coverage.

Reed Elsevier

Reed Elsevier is a major international business publisher and business services provider based in the UK and the Netherlands with offices and operations worldwide.

Reed Elsevier came into being in Autumn 1992 as the result of a merger between Reed International, a British trade book and magazine publisher, and the Dutch science publisher Elsevier. The respective businesses were merged to form two jointly owned companies, Reed Elsevier Group plc, a UK-registered company which owns the publishing and information businesses, and Elsevier Reed Finance BV, a Dutch-registered company which owns the financing activities. Reed Elsevier PLC and Reed Elsevier NV have retained their separate legal and national identities and are publicly held companies. Reed Elsevier PLC's securities are listed in London and New York, and Reed Elsevier NV's securities are listed in Amsterdam and New York.

Reed Exhibitions – Origins and growth

Reed Exhibitions is a division of Reed Elsevier plc which prominently claims to be the 'world's largest events organizer', though in a diverse, segmented industry this claim is difficult to verify. Undeniably, it certainly is a very large events organizer and the market leader in its primary segment. The origins of Reed Exhibitions can be traced back to 1966 when a British publishing company, IPC, purchased a stake in the US company Cahners Publishing which also had a portfolio of exhibitions which it organized. IPC was acquired by Reed International in 1970 and over the next 15 years, Reed and Cahners continued to grow their exhibition business in the US, Asia and Europe through acquisitions and mergers, becoming Reed Exhibition Companies in 1986.

With the purchase of Miller Freeman Europe (a US publisher with a European exhibition business) in 2000, Reed Exhibitions became the world's largest exhibition organizer. In the decade since, there has been a strategic shift in emphasis towards the growth markets of China, Latin America, Russia and the Middle East, fuelled by joint venture partnerships and the leveraging of market-leading Reed brands.

Reed's first major presence in China (Reed Huayin) was established in 2003, followed by Reed Sinopharm in 2005 and Reed Huabo in 2007. In 2007 Reed also acquired Alcantara Machado in Brazil, making it the number one events organizer in Latin America. Reed is seeking to increase the proportion of the portfolio in Asia and emerging markets from 24 per cent to 35 per cent.

Reed Exhibitions is the global market leader in a fragmented industry, holding less than a 10 per cent global market share. Other international exhibition organizers include UK-based UBM and Informa (which also includes the Taylor and Francis publishing business including the Routledge imprint), US-based Emerald and some of the larger German and Swiss Messe, including: Frankfurt, Düsseldorf, Hannover, Munich and Basel. Competition also comes from industry trade associations and convention centre and exhibition hall owners.

Reed Exhibitions also has to compete in other ways. As a division of a large diversified corporation it has to compete with other parts of the business for investment and in the allocation of resources. It also has to consider the efficiency of its internal processes to ensure that it delivers in a value-for-money way carrying out those tasks where it is important to have direct control but outsourcing and partnering where it is sensible and cost effective to do so. The relevant balance will be different in each case and according to environmental circumstances and is likely to change over time as more experience is gained and learning is acquired by other parties. Reed Exhibitions operates in many countries and in many sectors but the company must continually monitor the relative performance of both sectors and countries so as to focus its activities appropriately.

Reed Exhibitions – Business model, competition and strategy

Reed Exhibitions' stated strategic goal is 'to understand and respond to its customers' evolving needs and objectives better than its competition through deep knowledge of its customers and the markets they serve'. The primary focus of Reed Exhibitions' activities is on business-to-business (B2B) events, although it also runs a small number of consumer events, and consequently the organization is not widely recognized by consumers. However, that is not to say brands are unimportant, for it has acquired, developed and grown a number of strong market leading brands in its chosen B2B segments. During 2013 Reed organized about 500 events in over 30 countries bringing together over 6 million event participants from around the world.

The industry has significant 'multiplier' effects in that it helps generate billions of dollars of business activity (for exhibitors), facilitates entry into new markets and boosts the local economies where the events are hosted. Reed Exhibitions which has about 3,400 employees had revenues for the year ended 31 December 2013 of £862m. It is a global business headquartered in suburban south-west London and with principal offices in Paris, Vienna, Norwalk (Connecticut), São Paulo, Abu Dhabi, Beijing, Moscow, Tokyo and Sydney.

The substantial majority of Reed Exhibitions' revenues are from sales of exhibition space with the balance being derived from other sources which include conference fees, online and offline advertising, sponsorship fees and, for some shows, admission charges. Exhibition space is sold directly or through local agents where applicable. Reed Exhibitions often works in collaboration with trade associations, which use the events to promote access for members to domestic and export markets and with governments for whom events can provide important support to stimulate foreign investment and promote regional and national enterprise.

Increasingly, part of the business proposition is to offer visitors and exhibitors the opportunity to interact before and after the event through the use of online tools such as directories and matchmaking. In 2013, approximately 16 per cent of Exhibitions' revenue came from North America, 43 per cent from Europe and the remaining 41 per cent from the rest of the world on an event location basis. While growth (during 2013) in Europe was modest, the US, Japan, Brazil and other markets all grew well. In the other parts of the Reed Elsevier group, there has been transformational and rapid shift to electronic revenue generation. This has been far less pronounced in the Exhibitions division with 97 per cent of revenues being derived from 'face-to-face' activities and only 2 per cent and 1 per cent coming from electronic and print media respectively. It is likely there will be some shift towards electronic revenue generation in future years and its central role in supporting face-to-face activity will become more important; new and enhanced tools are likely to be developed.

Growth in the exhibitions market is influenced by both B2B marketing spend and business investment. Historically, these have been driven by levels of corporate profitability, which in its turn has followed overall growth in GDP. Emerging markets and higher growth sectors provide additional opportunities for Reed Exhibitions. As some events are held other than annually, growth in any one year is affected by the cycle of non-annual exhibitions.

Like most companies in its field Reed specializes in particular industry sectors where it can leverage its market knowledge, experience, marketing expertise, established networks and financial strength. In Reed's case its main specialisms are: aerospace and aviation, automobiles, beauty and cosmetics, broadcasting, building and construction, electronics, energy, oil and gas, engineering and manufacturing, food service and hospitality, gifts, healthcare, interior design, IT and telecoms, jewellery, life science and pharmaceuticals, machinery, marketing, business services and training, medical education, printing and graphics, security and safety, sports and recreation and travel.

At an operational level Reed clearly has proven, geographically dispersed expertise in envisaging, designing, planning and delivering large scale exhibition events. The strategic priorities of Reed though reflect broader concerns. A business such as Reed exhibitions has to respond to investors' demands relating to growth and delivering attractive rates of return. In doing this the company must be concerned with the 'one-off' nature of the underlying business, and differential growth rates in various sectors and geographical localities.

Many events are one-off events, which are successfully delivered and then the organizing company moves on the next event. The company though has to develop consistent returns. To counteract the one-off nature of this industry, the company has built up some strong B2B exhibition brands in certain sectors which have become well established and generally run annually or biannually. Consequently in considering its strategy Reed Exhibitions needs to focus on a number of aspects. These include: how the company can build and develop successful exhibition propositions, responding to customer needs and market conditions; which methods of development should be utilized; and which markets should be targeted. At the same time the company has to be driven by deploying its resources effectively and in a highly competitive, fragmented and cost sensitive sector ensuring that cost-effective operational delivery can be achieved with appropriate quality assurance.

In delivering its strategic priorities Reed Exhibitions tries to deliver a platform for industry communities to conduct business, to network and to learn through a range of market-leading events in growth sectors, especially in higher growth geographies, enabling exhibitors to target and reach new customers quickly and cost effectively. The company believes that organic growth is an important part of its development since its existing and potential product portfolio is strong, capable of further penetration in its existing markets and can be adapted to access new market opportunities. As some events are held other than annually, growth in any one year is affected by the cycle of non-annual exhibitions.

Growth in this industry is difficult to achieve. The industry is highly susceptible to changes in the local economy and in a fragmented industry with relatively low entry barriers many companies are jostling for competitive advantage. Furthermore as with most service sectors there is a focus on the quality of the customer experience which is delivered by a workforce that is dispersed, under pressure to deliver results to tight schedules and which contains many part-time employees and employees working for independent suppliers.

For a company such as Reed Exhibitions to compete effectively it must leverage the advantages it derives from being large, well-established and having a record of product innovation. Thus a number of aspects of the way in which the company operates are likely to be crucial to future strategic growth prospects. These aspects might include: continuing to generate greater customer value through the intelligent application of customer knowledge; developing a pipeline of new or 'cloned' events; and building and maintaining the technology platforms to ensure the rapid deployment of innovation and best practice. In addition Reed Exhibitions is also shaping its portfolio through a combination of strategic partnerships and acquisitions in high-growth sectors and geographies. At the same time strategic withdrawal will be considered by the company in markets and industry sectors with lower long-term growth prospects.

In 2013 Reed Exhibitions launched 37 new events. These included events which extended the geographical footprint of the luxury travel brand, ILTM, to Africa and the art brand, Paris Photo, to Los Angeles. Reed Exhibitions Japan responded again to customer demand by replicating its Tokyo-based World Smart Energy Week in Osaka. The UK-based event, Oceanology International, was successfully launched in China through a collaborative effort between the Chinese and UK teams. Regional strategies remain a key element of building business in China and Brazil, taking more events to China's second tier cities and cloning events from São Paulo to Recife in Brazil's fast developing north east. Reed Exhibitions now organizes nearly 200 events in emerging markets.

A number of targeted acquisitions were completed during 2013. These included the Capsule portfolio of contemporary fashion events, located mainly in North America; Travelweek São Paolo, a high-end travel event servicing premium buyers across Latin America; and Expo Ferretera, the leading hardware event in Mexico. Elsewhere, acquisitions were made to expand Reed Exhibitions' footprint in China and its global position in the advanced materials sector. Reed Exhibitions also entered into a partnership with Thebe Exhibitions, one of the leading events companies in South Africa, to form Thebe Reed Exhibitions, which will run a number of events, primarily in the travel and interior design sectors.

Reed Exhibitions – Travel events

One sector in which Reed has developed particular expertise is the international travel industry, and the sector accounts for about 7 per cent of the exhibition division's revenues. Though the travel industry is clearly of massive proportions and has grown enormously (and will continue to do so) it is somewhat difficult to identify, define and communicate with. However, the expos that Reed have developed enable diverse suppliers, buyers and those with an interest in the industry to be brought together in one place and at one time and for business negotiations and transactions to be carried out. The development of relevant and targeted electronic platforms supplements the face-to-face acuity with resources deployed in developing, maintaining and updating a series of dedicated websites, industry blogs, Twitter feeds and Facebook pages.

In the travel sector Reed has developed a number of leading brands which increasingly it is 'cloning' and replicating the formats albeit in locally adapted ways for different geographical regions. The World Travel Market for example is a well-established global event held annually in London since 1980 which has achieved strong brand recognition. The global brand strength has been utilized to produce regionally focused events in strong emerging regional markets. Similarly EIBTM (the global meetings and events expo) and ILTM (International Luxury Travel Market) were acquired by Reed in 1998 and 2005 respectively. EIBTM and ILTM are long-established leading global expos in their fields with annual events in Barcelona, Spain and Cannes on the French Riviera. Subsequently both events have been progressively cloned to encompass new geographies though this has happened systematically so that Reed does not over stretch its resources, can learn from its experiences elsewhere and so that it ensures that existing successful events are not 'cannibalized'.

Though there has been much discussion and some development of electronic meetings, virtual exhibitions and other electronic communications face-to-face expos remain highly relevant and popular in the global travel industry. Perhaps this is partly driven by the nature of the underlying product 'travel' and the propensity of industry professionals to gather together in one place, but the importance of such gatherings seems to be replicated in other sectors. The travel events are often viewed by leading professionals as 'must attend' events allowing exhibitors and visitors to achieve a number of objectives such as enhancing brand awareness, directly meeting relevant trade colleagues, education, media exposure, networking and competitor monitoring. In addition crucially the expos allow for commercial transactions to be initiated, discussed and in some cases concluded whilst at the event allowing delegates to be able to demonstrate a return on investment for their involvement.

There is, however, an increasing focus on customer value and in travel, as in others sectors, Reed has to work hard on constant product evaluation and enhancements to its offerings. The ways in which the product might be enhanced include enhancing the face-to-face format, adding value through technology and extending community reach.

Innovation at large exhibitions include clearly brokered relationships offering a customized experience and the arrangement of pre-scheduled meetings of exhibitors and buyers whereby both parties identify who they want to meet. Formats have evolved further over the past few years with the development of so-called 'table-top' summits for focused markets in which exhibitors purchase a table, and receive a diary of pre-scheduled meetings with buyers. The benefits of table-top summits for exhibitors are that they are able to test new markets at lower cost (no stand build) and that they have guaranteed time with buyers and for Reed Exhibitions' expansion it represents a way of quickly becoming involved with new market opportunities.

Technology now permeates all Reed Exhibitions (and those of many of its competitors) and it acts to enhance the face-to-face experience in that it provides a year round community beyond the show-floor and provides content for users. In doing so Reed's position as a broker is strengthened and it can charge for some of the content display. The technology can also extend to software which identifies preferences for matching buyers and suppliers and creating customized schedules of meetings at mutually agreeable times. In 2013 Reed Travel Exhibitions pre-scheduled some 210,000 meetings. Smartphone apps and online tools allow for each visitor to events to build up their own personalized schedules and to interact with exhibitors, event organizers, and the media while receiving reminders and updates about activities within the event.

Increasingly active steps are taken to extend the 'footprint' of events using social media, digital channels, TV and print media. At larger events activities include roving social media reporters, dedicated, onsite video teams for instant online content and conference sessions broadcast online. Such exposure increases brand awareness, beyond the exhibition, for the event itself but also for the products being promoted by exhibitors. At the same time it spreads the perception of Reed Exhibitions, that it is more than an exhibition organizer and that in an increasingly competitive industry (such as exhibitions) that on the face of it appears quite straight forward, innovation, technology and customer service are as important as in any other service-based sector.

Appendix 1: Importance of 'face-to-face' business activities

A global research report found that companies could increase revenue by investing in more face-to-face events. InterContinental Hotels Group (IHG) released its first-ever Business Meetings in a Modern World global research report (2013), revealing that businesses around the world could be missing out on nearly a quarter (24 per cent) of additional revenue because they are not investing enough time in face-to-face contact.

The report surveyed more than 2,000 businessmen and -women across five major markets – the UK, US, United Arab Emirates (UAE), China and India – to better understand how business professionals are using both virtual and face-to-face meetings and the possible economic impact.

The survey found that:

- Nearly half (47 per cent) of businessmen and -woman surveyed believe they had lost a contract or client simply because they didn't have enough face-to-face meetings, which resulted in the estimated yearly revenue loss of 24 per cent – a significant loss for any business.
- In fact, 81 per cent of businessmen and -women state that face-to-face meetings are *better* for building long-term trust and ensuring strong client relationships.
- However, nearly two thirds (63 per cent) reported that the number of virtual meetings they attended has increased in the past five to ten years further demonstrating that the value of face-to-face meetings is being overlooked in favour of cost- and time-saving technologies, such as video conferencing.
- Starting a new business relationship (57 per cent), finalizing a deal (54 per cent) and contract negotiation (53 per cent) are the top subjects respondents prefer to discuss face to face.
- 53 per cent of respondents believe that connecting with a business associate on social media can help them develop a stronger and more trusted relationship. Facebook came out more popular than the business networking website LinkedIn, with 48 per cent saying they had used Facebook and 42 per cent had looked at an associate's LinkedIn page.
- Small talk is recognized as a good business meeting tool, with the average meeting starting with about seven and a half minutes of light-hearted conversation.

- The UK and the US spend the first few minutes of a meeting discussing the weather, as opposed to news and current affairs, which is the main topic of conversation in China (64 per cent), India (59 per cent) and the UAE (49 per cent).

(www.ihg.com/, accessed March, 2014)

Appendix 2: World exhibition space

Country	Exhibition space 2011 (in m²)	% of world capacity	Increase since 2006
USA	6,712,342	21%	+ 5%
China	4,755,102	15%	+ 48%
Germany	3,377,821	10%	+ 2%
Italy	2,227,304	7%	+ 3%
France	2,094,554	6%	+ 3%
Spain	1 548 057	5%	+ 13%
Netherlands	960,530	3%	+ 15%
Brazil	701,882	2%	+ 6%
United Kingdom	701,857	2%	+ 13%
Canada	684,175	2%	+ 6%
Russia	566,777	2%	+ 17%
Switzerland	500 570	2%	+ 1%
Belgium	448,265	1%	+ 1%
Turkey	433,904	1%	+ 25%
Mexico	431,761	1%	+15%

Approximately 31,000 exhibitions per year corresponding to 124 million m² of total net exhibition space rented and where 4.4 million exhibiting companies welcomed 260 million visitors.

Note: The 15 countries with the largest capacities account for 80 per cent of the total increase of indoor exhibition space between 2006 and 2011.

The total net exhibition space rented by organizers (in m²)			
Region	2008	2010	2012
Europe	53.0	47.7	46.4
North America	52.3	45.6	47.8
Asia Pacific	19.8	20.6	21.6
Central and South America	4.0	4.4	5.1
Middle East	2.4	2.5	2.6
Africa	1.0	1.0	1.0

Source: UFI (2014)

Global exhibition market projections

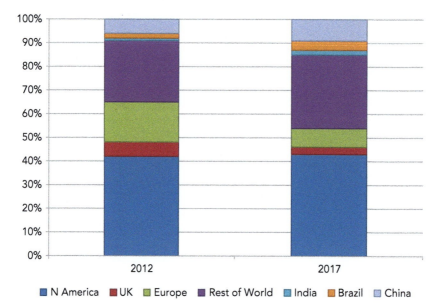

Appendix 3: Exhibition organizers – Key competitor revenues and market shares

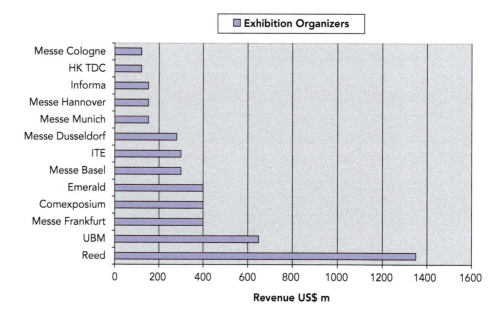

Company	Head office	Market share
Reed	London, UK	5%
UBM	London, UK	3%
Messe Frankfurt	Frankfurt, Germany	2%
Comexposium	Paris, France	2%
Emerald	California, USA	2%
Messe Basel	Basel, Switzerland	1%
ITE	Paris, France	1%
Messe Dusseldorf	Dusseldorf, Germany	1%
Messe Munich	Munich, Germany	<1%
Messe Hannover	Hannover, Germany	<1%
Informa	Zug Switzerland and London, UK	<1%
HK Trade Development Council	Hong Kong, China	<1%
Messe Cologne	Cologne, Germany	<1%
Others	–	80%

Source: AMR, 2013

Appendix 4: Reed Elsevier – Market segments, revenues and profits

Market segments	Reed Elsevier business focus	Segment position	Key brands
Scientific, technical and medical	Provide information and tools to help customers improve scientific and healthcare outcomes. Its products and services include electronic and print journals, textbooks, reference works, and workflow solutions for researchers and practitioners.	Global No. 1	Elsevier
Risk solutions and business information	Provide data, analytics and insight that enable customers to evaluate and manage risks, and develop market intelligence, supporting more confident decisions, improved economic outcomes, and enhanced operational efficiency.	Global No. 1	LexisNexis, Risk Solutions, Reed Business Information
Legal	A world leading provider of legal, regulatory and news and business information and analysis to legal, corporate, government and academic customers.	US No. 2 Outside US No. 1 or No. 2	LexisNexis, Legal and Professional
Exhibitions	The 'world's leading events business', with 500 events in over 30 countries.	Global No. 1	Reed Exhibitions

Revenue by geographic market (2013)			
Market segments	Europe	North America	Rest of the World
Scientific, technical and medical	30%	38%	32%
Risk solutions and business information	59%	28%	13%
Legal	21%	68%	11%
Exhibitions	43%	16%	41%

	Revenue				Operating profits			
	2013	2012	2011	2010	2013	2012	2011	2010
Scientific, technical and medical	2,126	2,063	2,058	2,026	826	780	768	724
Risk solutions	933	926	908	927	414	392	–	–
Business information	547	663	695	718	119	107	110	89
Legal	1,567	1,610	1,634	1,691	238	234	229	238
Exhibitions	862	854	707	693	213	210	167	158

Appendix 5: Reed Exhibitions: Vision and values

Our Global Vision: to deliver contacts, content and communities with the power to transform your business.

Delivering:

- *Contacts* – the essence of what we do; bringing people together for mutual business, professional and personal benefit.
- *Content* – customers achieve more at Reed events; more information, more innovation, more education.
- *Communities* – we draw industries and markets together under a common banner, fostering relationships.

With the power to transform – our vision is to offer each and every customer the potential for dramatic change.

Your business – we are committed to helping our customers grow their business and to maximize their return on investment. This is measured through improved performance in sales, education, brand building, sourcing, solutions and networking.

Our Values:

- At Reed Exhibitions we have a clear set of values for delivering our vision.

These are:

- Customer focus: Everything we do is driven by our customers' needs. We want to be their indispensable partner and have a passion for understanding and exceeding our customers' expectations. We are committed to providing demonstrably superior products and services with the highest level of quality and excellence. Plus, we strive to be professional in all our customer dealings and are highly valued and respected by our customers.

- Valuing our people: We put the highest priority on recruiting, developing and retaining outstanding people. Our managers are directly responsible for the development of their people and we recognize and reward achievement. What's more, we enjoy what we do and celebrate success. Our people are empowered to maximize their potential and contribution. Above all, we respect our people, encourage open and honest communication and behave in an ethical and principled manner.

- Passion for winning: We are determined to outperform and beat the competition i.e. we want to be the best. We are a high energy, fast moving, decisive organization that has a strong propensity for action. We always execute well and deliver on our intentions. We set aggressive goals and strive to beat them, and we hold ourselves and each other accountable for outstanding results.

- Innovation: We welcome and push change; we challenge the status quo. We encourage our people to be entrepreneurial, take some risks and learn from mistakes. We are ready to make bold moves and decisions. We constantly look for new ideas, and value 'out-of-the-box' thinking. We keep things simple and minimize bureaucracy.

- 'Boundarylessness': We welcome the global nature of our business and encourage people to work collaboratively across business units, hierarchy and functions. We constantly strive to break down barriers between organizations and we seek partnerships with customers and suppliers.

Appendix 6: Reed Travel Exhibitions – Bringing together key travel industry professionals

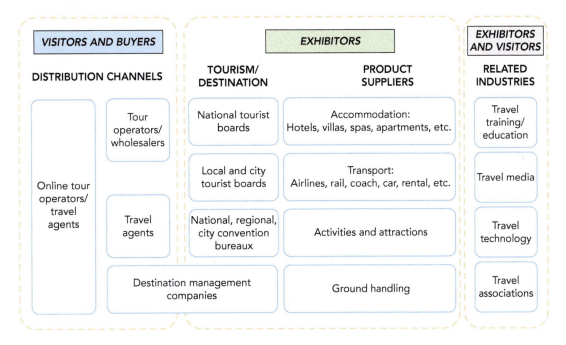

Reed Exhibitions travel industry events			
Leisure travel	IBTM global events	Luxury travel	Sports travel
World travel market, London, November	EIBTM: Global meetings and events expo, Barcelona, November	International Luxury Travel Market, Cannes France, November	International Golf Travel Market, November

Reed Exhibitions travel industry events			
World travel market, Latin America, April/May	CIBTM: Incentives, Business travel and meetings expo, China, August	International Luxury Travel Market. Asia, April	International Ski Travel Market, March
World travel market, Africa, April	AIBTM: Incentives, Business travel and meetings expo, America, June	International Luxury Travel Market, Americas, September	
Arabian travel market, Dubai, May	GIBTM: Incentives, Business travel and meetings expo, Gulf, February/March	International Luxury Travel Market, Africa, April	
IFTM, Paris, September	IBTM: Incentives, Business travel and meetings expo, India, September	International Luxury Travel Market, Japan, March	
	IBTM: Incentives, Business travel and meetings expo, Africa, April	International Luxury Travel Market, Spa, August	
	AIME: Asia Pacific Incentives and Meetings Expo, Melbourne Australia, February		

Source: www.reedexpo.com, investors presentation Reed Exhibitions, 2013.

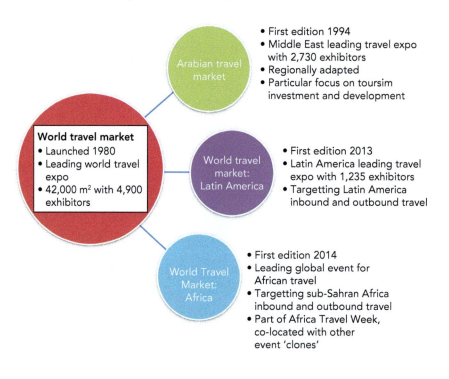

Arabian travel market
- First edition 1994
- Middle East leading travel expo with 2,730 exhibitors
- Regionally adapted
- Particular focus on toursim investment and development

World travel market
- Launched 1980
- Leading world travel expo
- 42,000 m² with 4,900 exhibitors

World travel market: Latin America
- First edition 2013
- Latin America leading travel expo with 1,235 exhibitors
- Targetting Latin America inbound and outbound travel

World Travel Market: Africa
- First edition 2014
- Leading global event for African travel
- Targetting sub-Sahran Africa inbound and outbound travel
- Part of Africa Travel Week, co-located with other event 'clones'

Appendix 7: AMR International – Winning exhibitions strategies in 2015 and beyond

A leading events industry consultant AMR International produced a report in 2012 entitled *Winning Exhibitions Strategies In 2015 And Beyond* which found that exhibitions organizers will increasingly need a dual strategy. While emerging markets will continue to offer strong growth opportunities, in mature markets organizers will need to compete more vigorously to maximize their share of visitors' time and, by extension, exhibitor marketing budgets. Key points include:

- In mature markets, two factors combine to mount a structural challenge to exhibitor value: the decline of total visitor time at events and the steady march of prices per square metre.

- Organizers need to compete more effectively for share of visitor time, both during and outside the show. This means adopting measures to maximize visitors' Return on Time (RoT) at show, while increasing contact with visitors through tools and resources that are available on demand throughout the year.

- As well as delivering value, trade shows are under increasing pressure to measurably demonstrate value to exhibitors. This will require smarter use of digital tools, to understand and track exhibitor value and support exhibitors with their broader marketing needs.

- From their solid base of community engagement, organizers are well positioned to develop resources that address their audiences outside the traditional show format. These in turn should provide revenue generating opportunities, be it through advertising, sponsorship or user fees.

- As emerging markets continue to offer strong underlying growth, organizers will look for a variety of ways to increase their portfolio exposure to these markets, such as cloning shows and brands and acquiring or partnering with local players. Organizers will furthermore increasingly look to second and third tier growth markets as competition in the top-tier intensifies.

www.amrinternational.com

REFERENCES

AMR (2013) *Global Exhibition Market Report*, London: AMR International Strategy Consultants.
International Enterprise Singapore (2001) 'The Shows Will Go On: Findings Confirm the Economic Benefits One Trade Exhibition Can Bring to Singapore', press release.
PricewaterhouseCoopers US (2011) 'The Economic Significance of the Meeting and Events Industry to the US Economy', available online at http://www.conventionindustry.org/Libraries/ESS/CIC_Final_Report_Executive_Summary.sflb.ashx (accessed February 2013).
Rankine, D. (2012) *Winning Exhibitions Strategies in 2015 and Beyond*, London: AMR International, available at www.amrinternational.com (accessed March 2013).
Reed Elsevier (2013) Annual Report and Accounts, available at www.reedelsevier.co.uk.
UFI (2014) Global Exhibition Industry Statistics, Paris: UFI, the Global Association of the Exhibition Industry, March.
Yang, L. T. G. and Z. Gu (2012) 'Capacity Optimization Analysis for the MICE Industry in Las Vegas', *International Journal of Contemporary Hospitality Management*, 24 (2): 335–49.

WEBSITES

www.amrinternational.com
www.ihg.com
www.reedexpo.com
www.ubm.com

Thomas Cook

Turnaround for a historic travel brand

Background

Thomas Cook is one of the world's best-known brands in travel and it has sometimes been referred to as the world's oldest travel company. Thomas Cook began his international travel company in 1841, with a successful one-day rail excursion he organized between the English cities of Leicester and Loughborough. From these humble beginnings Thomas Cook began to develop first with domestic excursions and then from the 1850s the development of tours in Continental Europe.

From these modest beginnings, Thomas Cook Group plc has developed into one of the world's leading leisure travel groups with sales of over £9 billion and more than 20 million customers in the year ending 30 September 2013. About 27,000 employees are employed by the group which operates from offices in 17 countries. It is number one or two in all its core markets. The company's shares are listed on the London Stock Exchange. However, in recent years the company has experienced some difficulties and radical steps had to be taken to alleviate the situation.

Although the antecedents of what might be termed 'mass' international tourism can be traced back to the roots of Thomas Cook in 1850s Britain, as a highly structured and vigorous sector of many economies it can primarily be viewed as a creation of more recent times. Since the early 1950s in particular the growth of international tourism has been phenomenal in its scale and remarkably resilient to periodic economic and political adversity.

In product life cycle terms, and taking a global perspective, international tourism might be categorized as having passed through the 'introductory' phase into the 'growth' phase. The number of international arrivals, for example, has shown an evolution from a mere 25 million international arrivals in 1950 to an estimated 806 million in 2005, and a figure of almost 1.1 billion in 2013 corresponding to an average annual growth rate of 3.8 per cent between 2005 and 2013. The overall growth disguises many differences in performance across the world's regions and a marked slowdown during the years of economic slowdown within this period.

However, many more countries and new consumers are being drawn into the international tourism net. On a global scale, further growth is to be expected before 'maturity' is reached. Such growth will be uneven, both spatially and with regard to time, and is likely to take place against the backdrop of dramatic changes in the business environment thereby creating both managerial and marketing opportunities and dilemmas for private-sector leaders and public-sector policy makers. The growth in the number of tourist arrivals, particularly international arrivals, has been mirrored by the growth of a vast complex travel industry which supports the activity.

The 'package' concept

In Europe in particular, the world's largest international tourist destination, the leisure travel industry grew particularly as a result of putting the various elements of travel and holidays together as part of a 'package'. Tourists travelling abroad can purchase each separate component of a holiday – accommodation, transportation, activities, ground handling, etc. – as individual items. During the 1960s, however, the foreign inclusive tour or 'package' holiday became established in Western Europe (and later elsewhere) and brought with it a substantial expansion in the numbers of tourists venturing abroad.

A 'package' can be defined (European Commission, 1990) as a pre-arranged combination, sold or offered for sale at an inclusive price, of not less than two of the following three elements: transport; accommodation; and, other tourist services not ancillary to transport or accommodation and accounting for a significant part of the package.

The role of tour operators has been the key element in the expansion, which has continued progressively since the 1950s. This role goes beyond that of the wholesaler, in that they not only purchase or reserve the separate components in bulk but, in combining these components into an 'inclusive tour', also become producers, since a new product, the inclusive tour or package holiday, is created. A tour operator typically combines tour and travel components to create a holiday. The most common example of a tour operator's product would be a flight on a 'charter' airline plus a transfer from the airport to a hotel and the services of a local representative, all for one price.

The traditional appeal of the tour operators' product has been to offer a complete holiday package at the lowest price to a population often lacking the linguistic knowledge or the knowledge and confidence to organize independent travel. As a result tour operation has become the dominant feature of the holiday market in most tourist-generating countries, though the companies involved vary in their structures. In North America, for instance, the activities are often carried out by vacation subsidiaries of the major scheduled airlines and hotel groups, whereas in Europe several large tour-operating companies have come to dominate the industry.

Benefits of the package concept

Many predictions have been made that the package holiday product is set to decline and die. The growth of low-cost airlines, the ability of consumers to put their own packages together through the use of the internet and the growth of more experienced travellers are all factors which have been cited as contributing to this demise. However, such predictions have generally proved unfounded since the companies concerned continue to allow consumers to benefit from the advantages of packaged products. These benefits include the convenience of purchasing all the elements of a holiday in one purpose-designed 'bundle'; delivery of product quality assurance, reliability and protection; and, perceived good-value prices.

Although the future of the 'package' seems assured, changes in consumer preferences and changes in the environment in which tour-operating products are provided are changing the characteristics of these packages. This will in turn have an effect on the future structure of this industrial sector. The tour-operating sector as a whole, and the smaller independent operators in particular, are facing a number of pressures which have led to marked differences in recent performance. Changes that have taken place in recent years include the growth of all-inclusive holidays (in which almost all holiday costs at the destination are pre-paid); the growth of long-haul travel destinations and cruising; and the emergence of significant outbound travel markets in the rapidly emerging economies of countries such as those of the BRIC group (Brazil, Russia, India and China).

The growth of UK outbound tour operations

Anyone who knows the climate of northern Europe will be aware that summers are unpredictable and unseasonably cold or wet weather is common. Consequently, it is not surprising that warmer more dependable climates within easy reach should be sought when circumstances allowed. When the necessary circumstances did indeed come together during the 1950s – rising incomes, paid holiday entitlements, aircraft technology and entrepreneurial vision – a new industrial sector was born. The 'air inclusive tour' (AIT) industrial sector developed across Europe separately and took different forms in various countries.

Nowhere was its development more vigorous than in the UK where travel habits were to change fundamentally and irreversibly in a generation. As an island nation (at that time lacking the Channel Tunnel), air travel represented the only real, feasible option for quickly reaching the warmer weather of Mediterranean resorts. This was not the case for many continental countries where car, coach and rail travel presented feasible alternatives. The UK's geography presented a spur to the industry's development and continues to play an important part in underpinning demand for such a product offering.

Vladimar Raitz, a Russian émigré, is widely credited with operating the first air inclusive tour (AIT) charter to Corsica in 1950 at an inclusive price of £32.10. Part of his original company, Horizon, continued until the 1990s as a trading name of Thomson, a well-known current UK brand which is owned by Tui plc. Others who pioneered AITs during the 1950s in the UK were Captain Ted Langton, who set up Universal Skytours which was also later to become part of Thomson; Joe and Syril Shuman, founders of Global Holidays; Christopher and Stephen Lord whose Lord Brothers firm was later absorbed by the now defunct Laker Airways; and George Jackman and Wilf Jones, who built up the Cosmos brand which still operates as a subsidiary of the Swiss privately owned company Globus.

Other companies missed out on the early market opportunities. Thomas Cook failed at this time to achieve the market leadership in air holidays that it had in rail holidays, while British European Airways (BEA), a forerunner of British Airways, was slow to react to the threat posed by the 'charter' airlines, which were created to operate services for the fledgling businesses. In the 1950s foreign travel remained a luxury commodity within the reach of only a privileged few who had both plenty of free time and considerable purchasing power. The market changed during the 1960s, from that of a privileged 'niche' market to a 'mass' tourism market as a result of innovations in aircraft technology, changes in labour legislation (which provided for paid holidays) and changes to the structure of the tour-operating industry itself.

New entrants and consolidation

The strategic entry into the marketplace of the Canadian-based International Thomson Organisation (ITO) in 1965 proved to be a major turning point for the industry. It represented the initiation of a period of consolidation within the UK industry, which continued until the late 1990s, and the entry to UK tour operations of a large, sophisticated and diversified international group of companies. During the summer of 1965 Thomson had around 100,000 holidays on offer.

The reasons for this rapid growth of the UK outbound AIT market and that of the operators that service it are inextricably linked, but perhaps two major factors stand out. First, many UK residents travel abroad for their holidays in order to obtain reliable sunshine and warmth. The UK's island location has necessitated the development of well-organised, packaged transportation to service this need. Second, UK residents accord holidays and travel a high priority in terms of their discretionary expenditure even in times of economic hardship. Again, a highly sophisticated holiday travel industry has developed to service this need.

Relatively low barriers to entry and continual striving among operators for increased market share led to price wars, (particularly in the early 1970s and the mid 1980s), which resulted in a highly volatile record of profitability over the period. The price wars, low margins and the vulnerability of the travel industry to external economic and political factors inevitably took their toll on operators and a number of large operators failed. The International Leisure Group (ILG), which, when it failed in March 1991 was Britain's second largest tour operator, provides an example of a failed tour operator which could not withstand a business setback. The downturn in business at the time of the Gulf War, exposed ILG's strategy of using strong tour operating cash flows to diversify into scheduled air services through its airline Air Europe.

During the 1970s to the 1990s the large tour operators came to increasingly dominate the AIT market, as mass market operators were determined to increase their market share and to reap the anticipated rewards of market dominance. Thomson (now part of Tui plc), the market leader had since its inception faced major challenges to its market leadership position, but had hitherto always successfully defended its position.

Major competitors had disappeared from the scene but Thomson's major challengers during the 1990s were of more recent prominence: Owners Abroad (re-named First Choice) was founded in 1972 and, as its name suggests, specialized in serving the needs of expatriate overseas property owners; and north-west England-based Airtours, started in 1978. The demise of ILG removed from the industry a privately held company that had targeted Thomson through aggressive pricing in a bid for an ever-greater share of the market. Both Airtours (from 1989) and First Choice are Public Limited Companies (PLCs). Their status as PLCs necessitated the targeting of profitability rather than market share as the primary objective of the two companies to satisfy their shareholders and as a result competition from 1991 focused on matching supply much more closely to demand, and thereby avoiding damaging price wars. The latter part of the 1990s saw a flurry of activity in the UK tour-operating sector with Airtours, Thomson and First Choice consolidating their leading positions with the takeover of smaller groups, adding aircraft to their airline subsidiaries and acquiring further high-street travel agents to boost their distribution outlets.

Clearly, given the scale and complexity of their operations and the vertically and horizontally integrated structure of their businesses, the largest operators in the UK came to dominate the sector. However, a marked polarization has occurred in the UK industry dividing it into a relatively small number of 'mass' tour operators and a much larger number of 'independent' operators largely serving specialized niche markets.

One of the key features of the independent tour operators is that they are not vertically integrated, in that they do not own their own travel agencies or other distribution channels nor do they own their own airline and thus rely on the supply in the market place for individual components of the package. In the UK the term 'independent tour operator' also has a more precise meaning, in that it can refer to those companies that are members of The Association of Independent Tour Operators (AITO). AITO, formed in 1976, has grown to represent about 120 members that collectively carry almost a million customers per annum.

Tour operating risks

Increasingly however, given the size and international complexity of the companies concerned, it became apparent in the in the late 1990s that a pan-European view of competition issues in the tour-operating sector was necessary. Scale matters in a business where the better performers still only make thin profit margins of perhaps 4 per cent. Consequently, if an operator can negotiate cost efficiencies of 1 per cent to 2 per cent through better buying of, say, hotel rooms and aircraft fuel, that has a very material impact on profitability. These are the sort of factors that have driven consolidation over the last 20 years or so.

Tour operating has always been viewed as an inherently risky business in which seasonal and cyclical effects are prominent and where the underlying product is relatively expensive and viewed as a luxury rather than a necessity. Most profits are generally made during a short summer period, and the sector experiences 'good' and 'bad' years as economic, climatic and other external pressures exert their influences on consumers who can be fickle in their buying habits.

The principal risks usually perceived by external observers of the travel industry for a tour operating group are those of under-utilized aircraft and excess hotel and other accommodation, for which payment has already been made. The reality is that in many cases the major tour operators have considerable flexibility in contracting of both of these services. Aviation contracts with third-party suppliers usually have a variety of cancellation options, which can be exercised once booking patterns have been established. With regard to accommodation requirements a great deal of the stock required by tour operators is not negotiated on an irrevocable basis, meaning that adjustments to capacity can be made, though such changes can prove costly.

Perhaps more critical to the business, and common to other businesses dealing with international conditions, are changes in exchange and interest rates; and aviation fuel. Most companies develop policies of 'hedging' against all major risks on the financial and commodity markets prior to each holiday cycle. This usually involves the practice of negotiating a range of forward contracts and options. In this way the costs of hedging these risks can be built into the overall selling prices that customers are asked to pay.

The holiday business is well known for generating substantial cash flows as customers traditionally pay in advance and the holiday companies pay most of their suppliers in arrears. There is a degree of seasonality to this cash flow with large cash surpluses commonly built up during the spring period (as sales are made), which are eroded as payments to suppliers are made during the summer period. Autumn and winter are the seasons of greatest risk as business costs are still incurred but relatively few customer payments are received. Thus effective 'cash management' of these balances and potential seasonal deficits has become a very important part of managing the business for many tour operators.

European expansion

The tour operators responded to the perceived risks in several ways in both the two leading European markets (Germany and the UK). In the 1990s the sector increasingly became vertically integrated and horizontal expansion followed first at the national level and then internationally when domestic opportunities became more limited.

The new century, however was characterized not by the largest players in Germany and the UK purchasing smaller, weaker rivals, but by consolidation among the largest players themselves which eventually resulted in the emergence of two dominant groups: Tui and Thomas Cook. The European industry was largely shaped at corporate headquarters in Toronto, Canada, and Hanover, Germany, by the changing strategies of two large industrial companies. Thomson, a large Canadian Media group, withdrew from the travel sector by floating its Thomson Holiday group subsidiary in the UK during 1998. Preussag AG, a German industrial and logistics group, decided to withdraw from these sectors in order to concentrate its activities on the travel industry. In 1999 Preussag purchased Germany's largest travel group (Tui) and followed up this purchase a year later with the acquisition of Thomson Travel. Further consolidation and ownership changes considerably strengthened Tui's position in the European market in 2007.

Tui Travel plc, a British leisure travel group listed on the London Stock Exchange, was formed in September 2007 with the merger of a leading UK-based tour operator, First Choice Holidays plc, and the Tourism Division of the German company Tui AG (which had changed its name from Preussag). Tui AG continues to own 56.4 per cent of the company. First Choice had emerged in the mid-2000s reinvigorated having modified its strategic positioning. First Choice's emphasis had been to shift away from high volume/low margin businesses towards a portfolio of individually branded more specialist products with an emphasis on 'all-in-clusive' arrangements offering potentially higher returns. All-inclusive products involving the provision of most destination services, including food and beverage within the package price, have proved increasingly popular. Such arrangements allow the tour operator to provide more rigorous quality standards through the control of a greater part of the supply chain and gain additional revenues from the services provided. Cost efficiency was maintained through the utilization of centralized systems and corporate buying power.

Thomas Cook had become a subsidiary of the UK's Midland Bank Group during the 1980s and was later sold to Westdeutsche Landesbank, Germany's third largest bank, and LTU Group, Germany's leading charter airline. Thomas Cook became a wholly owned subsidiary of WestLB in 1995 and a period of rapid expansion followed with the acquisition of a number of well-known tour operator brands culminating in the company's merger with Carlson Leisure Group's UK travel interests which included a large number of high street travel agents.

In 2001 Thomas Cook was acquired by C&N Touristic AG, one of Germany's largest travel groups. Within a matter of months, recognizing inherent brand strength, C&N Touristic AG had changed its name to Thomas Cook AG and launched a new logo and brand identity.

The summer of 2007 was pivotal in creating the two major European-based tour operating groups, which still dominate the industry sector. Tui, in its present form, was created at that time and so was the current configuration of the Thomas Cook group. In June 2007, Thomas Cook AG and MyTravel Group plc (which was a major listed UK travel group which had changed its name from Airtours) merged to form Thomas Cook Group plc.

Under the terms of the merger, German Department Store Group Arcandor, the owners of Thomas Cook (and owner of C&N Touristic), owned 52 per cent of the new group. The shareholders of MyTravel Group owned the remaining 48 per cent of the shares with the shares being listed on the London Stock Exchange. Arcandor subsequently went bankrupt in 2009 and its shares in Thomas Cook plc were sold by its creditors to market investors.

Another merger followed in October 2011, when Thomas Cook amalgamated its UK high street travel and foreign exchange businesses with those of the Co-operative Group and the Midlands Co-operative Society to create the UK's largest retail travel network of over 1,200 shops. In October 2013 Thomas Cook officially unveiled its new 'unified' brand to the world. The 'Sunny Heart' and 'Let's go!' taglines will form an important part of Thomas Cook's future plans.

European tour operators – Current challenges

The vertically integrated model whereby a single group became the full owner (or had equity in) airline operations, tour operations and travel retailing and sometimes accommodation is now firmly established. A few large integrated Europe-based groups have emerged of which Tui and Thomas Cook are the largest and which have access to stock market capital. Other large European groups such as Kuoni and Globus based in Switzerland and France's Club Med have also emerged. The industry does, however retain a large number of smaller operators competing for customers in certain niches. Increasing polarization has occurred as companies have to make the strategic choice to become complex vertically, horizontally or in some cases diagonally integrated organizations or to specialize as niche players targeted at discrete market segments.

One of the reasons often cited for ever-greater concentration by a few large suppliers for an industry is that larger companies enjoy the advantages derived from economies of scale and scope. These economies clearly exist in tour operating, in terms of marketing, operational and purchasing economies for instance, but savings have been hard to achieve in the recent adverse economic circumstances particularly in Europe. The markets that the companies serve are increasingly 'mature' and there has been a trend away from standard 'summer sun' packages towards a more diverse range of package options. Tour operators are increasingly being forced to respond to a much more complex holiday market than has hitherto existed, through diversification, narrower market segmentation and responding to independently minded and increasingly experienced customers.

The larger Europe-based companies have also looked to spread their geographical coverage away from their focus on the mature markets of Western Europe. New markets have been sought with expansion taking place into Eastern and Central Europe, Russia, India and China in particular. Large emerging middle classes with high propensities to spend on international travel make these markets attractive to travel company investors. However, each international marketplace is different with their own complexities and are at varying stages of development. In such cases companies have to carefully consider their mode of market entry and the business model to be adopted in each individual case.

Companies have also had to consider the balance of their activities so as not to over stretch their resources and capabilities. Even for the larger, well-established companies competitive and resource pressures and entry to new markets necessitate consideration of newer ways of working. These include the increasing emphasis on collaborative strategy through the formation of strategic alliances and franchising; the separation of ownership of tourist assets from their management; and outsourcing some activities previously handled 'in-house'.

Furthermore tour operators have had to respond to two further challenges, which place far more power in the hands of consumers.

Many new technology entrants to the travel industry and consumers were quick to recognize the power of the internet. It enables consumers to search online for information, to access reliable, accurate and up-to-date information and to quickly compare comparative product offerings. Furthermore the availability of such information enables consumers to make reservations in a fraction of the time necessary for some other methods and with a minimum of inconvenience. The internet is driven by both the increasing volume and diversity of tourism demand and by the power it gives consumers to buy personalized 'bundles' of tourism products. In some cases this leads to the avoidance of the traditional tourism 'packages' leading instead to consumers assembling their own packages (so-called 'dynamic packaging') from individual component parts on offer.

Though such distribution does not totally undermine the advantages that tour operators enjoy or the need for specialist advice that can be offered by retail travel agents, it clearly has a significant impact. In particular the tour operators have had to adjust their own distribution activities investing in enhanced interactive websites supported by call centres and reassessing the scale of their networks of retail shops. Furthermore, the internet allows (at reasonable cost) suppliers an unprecedented opportunity to communicate globally with their target markets and to establish direct relationships with consumers. Some smaller companies have successfully developed a niche in the market, usually by targeting particular customer types or by focusing on specific destinations, and often by using the internet as a cost-effective tool.

The rapid rise of low-cost airlines such as easyJet, Ryanair, Norwegian and Air Berlin in Europe over the last 20 years has provided further challenges for managers at the tour-operating companies. The airlines by definition cut their costs wherever possible and by operating modern aircraft fleets are able to ensure high rates of utilization for their planes. However, the charter airlines such as Thomsonfly, Thomas Cook and Monarch owned by the tour-operating groups have provided stiff competition through careful exploitation of the inherent advantages of charter flights.

The low-cost airlines have to operate to a pre-arranged schedule regardless of sales levels achieved. Managers of charter carriers, as in all airlines, watch load factors very carefully and are fully conscious of the load factor at which breakeven is achieved. Beyond the breakeven point as in all travel operations, profitability quickly accumulates with each additional passenger. Usually the charter carriers are able to achieve very high load factors by matching seats available to demand and if necessary changing the aircraft type, consolidating flights and even changing departures (or arrivals) to a different airport.

A broader challenge to the tour operators is also provided by the low-cost carriers in that, as with the internet, they allow consumers to easily and at reasonable cost put their own packages together. A low-cost flight can easily be combined with accommodation and ancillary services such as ground transportation can quickly be added. The multitude of search engines available can facilitate making these arrangements and price comparisons can easily take place. Tour operators have had to respond to these challenges by offering more flexible products. Mass tourism is increasingly being replaced by mass customization in an industry that has to cater for ever-more discerning and experienced consumers.

Thomas Cook Group in 2011

2011 was not a 'good' year for Thomas Cook; in fact it was a year the company would wish to forget, for it was the year in which a respected and historic name in travel came perilously close to failure.

The travel group had been hit by tough trading brought on by the global economic downturn, high fuel costs and social unrest in popular destinations for the company such as Egypt, Tunisia and Greece. The cumulative effect had forced the company to negotiate and renegotiate banking lifelines, make disposals to raise cash and reduce debt and led to senior managerial changes.

The situation reached crisis point in late November 2011 as the following statement was released by the company:

> *Thomas Cook Group plc announces that as a result of deterioration of trading in some areas of the business in the current quarter, and of its cash and liquidity position since its year end, the Company is in discussions with its principal lending banks with regard to its facilities during the seasonal low period of cash in the business.*
>
> *While the Company currently remains in compliance with its financing covenants, it also intends to seek agreement from its lending banks to adjustments that will improve its resilience if trading conditions remain difficult.*
>
> *As a result, the Company will delay its announcement of its full year results until these discussions are concluded. The Company expects to report a headline operating profit for the year ended 30 September 2011 broadly in line with previous guidance.*

Manny Fontenla-Novoa, the group's long serving chief executive who had worked for the company from the age of 18, resigned in the summer of 2011 as a result of the adverse reactions to profit warnings and the sliding share price. His departure had been widely anticipated, following rumours of discontent among shareholders as the group's debt burden rose to more than £900m.

Although the company's position had deteriorated, with three profit warnings having been made during the year, the statement nevertheless came as a bombshell and the shares subsequently lost 70 per cent of their value later that week. Shares that had traded at 300 pence at their spring 2009 peak tumbled. The shares in Europe's second-biggest tour operator closed 75 per cent down at just over 10 pence, giving it a market capitalization of just £89 million.

Sam Weihagen, the interim chief executive who had previously been Fontenla-Novoa's deputy, said trading since the group's end of year in September had been worse than expected, piling further pressure on Thomas Cook's cash flow during the slow winter booking season: 'We have seen some deterioration in our trading post the year-end, and that has put pressure on our cash and liquidity position'. He blamed the group's lack of bookings on the Eurozone crisis and a sluggish recovery in tourism to the Middle East and North Africa (Wembridge and Blitz, 2011). It was also acknowledged that costs had risen for holidays in Turkey, where the company is market leader, as a result of the effects of the Arab Spring and that its fuel-buying policy was only 80 per cent hedged against fuel increases compared to rival's Tui Travel at more than 90 per cent. Weak performance in the UK had prompted the company to undergo a wide-ranging review of its British operations; a key component of the business and a step seen by some analysts as admission that the business model was flawed.

Whereas rival Tui had weighted its offerings towards higher-margin 'differentiated' package holidays, the UK's second-biggest tour group by revenues was still heavily exposed to more basic trips, which people book later or reject completely in favor of planning their own flights and hotels (Wembridge and Jacobs, 2011). While Thomas Cook was suffering, its bigger rival, Tui, while not soaring, was certainly doing better. Customer numbers in its big British, German and French markets were either flat or only marginally ahead in 2010/11, full-year revenues increased by 9 per cent and pre-tax profits were £144m compared with a £73m loss in the previous year. Tui appeared to try to make the most of its rival's misfortunes. It ran adverts on its website in late 2011 containing lines such as 'Unlike a certain holiday company we could mention, you don't need to worry about the way we run our business'. The adverts elicited complaints from Thomas Cook and were quickly removed.

The underlying problem faced by both Thomas Cook and Tui was that the recession across its major European markets had taken its toll, while some important core destinations had become unattractive due to political instability. Thomas Cook's cash flow is seasonal because fewer holidays are booked and paid for in the winter, prompting speculation that the group could breach its obligations around Christmas time. However, an old adage in banking is that 'if you owe the bank a million pounds you have a problem; if it's a billion pounds then the bank has a problem'. Consequently whereas a smaller company might have been forced into failure as banks failed to agree extended credit terms, Thomas Cook's lenders agreed that the group's net debt could now be up to 4.5 times earnings, before interest, tax, depreciation, amortization and restructuring costs at the end of December. That was an increase from 3.75 times ebitdar that was agreed in May 2010. This gave the company some leeway and it survived 2011, having had a close call.

Thomas Cook Group in 2013

Wind the clock forward two years and the position of the company is very different. In July 2012 a new CEO, Harriet Green, who had previously led an electronics distribution business, was appointed. Although the company had survived the previous winter in a subsequent interview with the UK trade paper Travel Weekly she said (with understatement) that when she joined the company was 'not very well' (Taylor, 2013). In the same interview she said that there were three things that struck her on joining the company:

- First, that the travel business was insular and that there were relatively few outsiders (such as her) for a business of such scale and complexity.
- Second, that the workforce was shattered as the brand had been publicly beleaguered.
- Third, that the Thomas Cook business appeared to operate as a number of unconnected 'siloes'. There had been lots of acquisitions, but there appeared to be little evidence of integration as it seems the synergies had stayed in the boardroom. For example, the online travel agent was a completely separate business competing with the company's own high street shops.

The new CEO works from a modest office and is clearly not afraid to speak her mind: 'I don't really give a damn whether people like what I have to say and I am not trying to win any popularity contests' (Saunders, 2014). While clearly having a strategic vision for the company she is also not afraid to deal with operational detail and communicate freely. She has 3,000 followers on her Twitter account and deals with all her own emails encouraging staff to contact her and providing answers within 24 hours; 'When people realized that it sent the most symbolic ripple through the organization and it allowed me to say that we've got to do these things at pace' (Saunders, 2014).

By mid-2013, Thomas Cook's share price had recovered to the level of about 145 pence, valuing the group at about £1.3 billion. The company took advantage of the surge in the share price to make a £400 million rights issue of shares to help cut the holiday company's £1.3 billion debt burden.

A series of asset sales (including its North American division) had been made and a cost-cutting regime had been implemented to restore the tour operator to financial health. In March 2013, 2,500 jobs had been cut in its British business and around 200 high street travel agents had been closed.

Appendix 1: International tourist arrivals – 2013

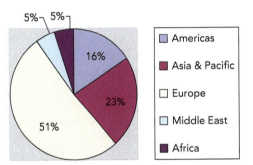

Source: United Nations (2013)

Appendix 2: International tourist arrivals – percentage change

	2013	Average 2005–2013	Forecast 2014
Europe	5.4%	2.9%	3 to 4%
Asia and Pacific	6.0%	6.2%	5 to 6%
Americas	3.6%	3.0%	3 to 4%
Africa	5.6%	6.2%	4 to 6%
Middle East	0.3%	4.6%	0 to 5%
World	5.0%	3.8%	4 to 4.5%

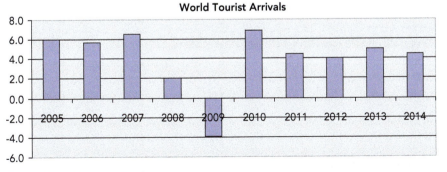

Source: United Nations (2013)

Appendix 3: Changing tourism consumers

Mass tourism can be seen as a phenomenon of large-scale packaging of standardized leisure services at fixed prices for sale to a mass clientele. Such tourism remains central to the outbound tourism product of European countries and emerging markets, but underlying trends towards a new type of more independent and experienced traveller can be discerned. These 'new tourists' are 'consumers who are flexible, independent and experienced travellers, whose values and lifestyles are different from those of mass tourists' (Poon, 1993). Six key attributes are characteristic of these 'new tourists' are shown below.

Characteristic	Comments
New consumers are more experienced	In many countries in Europe a foreign holiday has become routine and has come to be expected. Thus many people have become experienced tourists. More experienced travellers are more knowledgeable and consequently more quality and value conscious, demand greater choice and flexibility and are more certain of what they want and what they find unacceptable.
New consumers have changed values	Values of conservation, health and nature are being reflected in the tour operators' products and there are some signs that the fashion for the sun is beginning to fade.
New consumers have changed lifestyles	Krippendorf (1986) argues that society has moved through three key phases between the industrial era and today. First, from the industrial era in which people live to work to the post-industrial era in which they worked to live, to the third phase where a new unity exists between work and leisure, and travel and leisure become integral aspects of daily life.
	These changes in the role of travel and leisure in society have implications for the travel industry. People who live to work have simple holiday and travel motivations while people who work to live view leisure as the counterpoint to everyday life. Those seeking unity of everyday life want to reduce the polarity between work and leisure and are looking for fulfilment throughout all sectors of life, during working time, through humanized working conditions, and at home through more habitable cities and a more colourful everyday life.
New consumers are the products of changing population demographics	Population demographics in the tourism-generating countries are changing. In particular the population is ageing. These demographic changes will have profound effects upon buyer behaviour in tourist-generating countries. In Europe this includes the growth in the proportion of people aged over 65, and in the middle-age categories and a relative decline in the 18–35 age category. This reflects a significant European demographic trend: the rise of the 'baby boomers', that is those born between the Second World War and the mid-1960s. This category is inheriting wealth on a large scale leading to the higher net worth of middle-age households and higher expectations of the products than previous generations. Improvements in health care also means that these consumers will continue to be active until later in life than was hitherto the case.
New consumers are more flexible	Consumers are becoming 'hybrid' in nature in that they may consume in an unpredictable way making the traditional stereotypical categories of rich, poor or middle-income people no longer sufficient to segment holiday markets. Some consumers may for instance take the cheapest charter flight available but stay in the most luxurious accommodation available at the destination. Other consumers may stay in relatively modest accommodation but partake in the most expensive sporting activities such as heli-skiing or hot air ballooning. Another aspect of the flexible consumer is the spread of impulse buying to the travel industry. There are shorter lead times before booking and paying for holidays, a changing consumer preference which partially explains the growing number of shorter and more frequent breaks.

New consumers are more independent	Increasingly consumers are asserting their individuality and independence and seeking more flexible and custom-made travel and leisure options and resisting the standardised and sanitized product options. This trend towards independence, individuality and more experimentation in travel and leisure is clearly underpinned by the value, lifestyle and demographic changes. Such changes are likely to manifest themselves in the continuing demand by consumers for the core advantages provided by packaged travel products relating to pricing, convenience, reliability and easy access. However, consumers are increasingly rejecting some of the traditional drawbacks of packaged travel products relating to the inflexibility of products and resistance to travelling in organized groups.

Appendix 4: Harriet Green – Interview extracts

'My style is to understand very quickly who is on the bus, who is likely to get on the bus and who is not going to be on the bus. The first 32 weeks have been about the turnaround, about how to make the business better and ignite interest in it. We have achieved over 70 major changes. For the next 32 weeks we are into the transformation. We have a number of brands that are competing [with one another] or duplicating or not adding value and we will consolidate and make things simpler and clear. We had this period of buying lots of businesses that did the same thing with different names'.

She insisted: 'There is no intention of shrinking, but of being simpler. We have a credible, profitable-growth story. [Now] the company has to prove it can execute it'. She describes some of what has been achieved thus far: 'We have consolidated the senior team – one third I inherited, one third we promoted and one third we have hired from outside. Travel is fact free: people tend to say "I know this". So we carried out a survey of 18,000 consumers across Europe, looking at their travel behaviour and demographics and at the differences with our own data. We developed customer focus groups and this will be a big piece of what we do going forward.

'We will invest in improving the quality of sun, beach and package-holiday vacations across a wide range of income brackets. We will continue to invest in dynamic packaging. We will expand our [exclusive] "concept" hotels and quality, low-budget hotels. We will expand our winter sun – to Gran Canaria, Cape Verde, the Dominican Republic. Customers have said they would like to stay connected with Cook when not on vacation so we are developing an array of networks to stay connected.

'We have an option whether we continue to have our own airline. In the past, airline capacity has dominated the economic footprint of the business. Cook had capacity and had to fill it. We have said let's have less capacity at the start of a programme.'

Asked if she has achieved the goals she set herself, Green said: 'I'm the sort of woman who has stretch targets on the fridge. I have the feeling I'm always behind on my targets.'

The important thing is: 'We have made extraordinary progress. We have the loyalty and trust of 23 million customers and we would like it to be 24 million or 25 million or 28 million. To do that, we have to be better. One final thing Green has learned, she said, is: "The business is not that complex. It is not the nuclear industry. It's travel. How difficult can it be to give people a good holiday?"

Adapted from: Taylor (2013)

Appendix 5: Thomas Cook Group – New strategy from March 2013

The new Thomas Cook Group plc profitable growth strategy is focused on simplification, web innovation and flexible new products and services, and enabled by rigorous execution and an integrated IT platform. It builds on a trusted brand with a 171-year heritage. The new strategy aspires to delight customers by delivering personalized holiday experiences through a high-tech, high-touch approach.

Strategic highlights

- A strategy of simplification, focused on delivering trusted, personalized holiday experiences delivered through a high-tech, high-touch approach.

- The new strategy has been based upon extensive research and analysis including a comprehensive, in-depth survey measuring the attitudes and changing needs of almost 18,000 travellers, validated against the experiences of many of Thomas Cook's own customers.

- Clear metrics developed to measure and report on progress, with the following measures established. 2015 Targets include:

  - New product revenue > £500m
  - Increase Group web penetration to > 50 per cent
  - Cost Out/profit improvement of £350m Sales increasing at > 3.5 per cent
  - Underlying Gross margin improvement >1.5 per cent.

- The strategy will deliver on-going product and service innovation through four major initiatives:

  - Expand our successful, proven international hotel concepts across our markets.
  - Creating a new portfolio of flexible, trusted, products and services.
  - Creating a single, consistent, channel gateway for customers to access personal recommendations from our extensive range of products and services.
  - All underpinned by the powerful Thomas Cook brand and an integrated IT platform.

The implementation of this strategy will be carefully phased over the next five years to balance the desire for rapid improvements, where possible, against the necessary lead times for major infrastructure projects (for example in relation to concept hotels) and the Group's investment requirements.

Over the next two years Thomas Cook expects to expand on our concept hotels, and introduce the first wave of new products, including the scale-up of dynamic packaging capabilities. Web penetration is expected to climb as the single gateway and ancillary propositions develop. Thereafter, the concept expansion will continue, the quality- assured inventory will grow and the single gateway will reach maturity.

www.thomascookgroup.com, accessed February 2014

Appendix 6: Thomas Cook Group financial statements

Thomas Cook Group: Balance sheet (£m)

	2013	2012	2011
Non-current assets	4,281.8	4,382.6	5,043.9
Current assets	2,003.0	1,524.2	1,645.9
of which cash and cash equivalents	1,088.8	460.3	359.3
Total assets	6,284.8	5,906.8	6,689.8
Current liabilities of which borrowings	(3,704.6)	(3,540.1)	(3,883.8)
	(176.5)	(37.8)	(179.5)
Non-current liabilities of which borrowings	(2,032.1)	(1,908.8)	(1,722.8)
	(1,113.8)	(977.6)	(967.8)
Total liabilities	(5,736.7)	(5,448.9)	(5,506.6)
Net assets	548.1	457.9	1,183.2
Total equity	548.1	457.9	1,183.2

Thomas Cook Group: Income statement (£m)

	2013	2012	2011
Revenue	9,314.5	9,195.0	9,808.9
Cost of providing tourism services	(7,294.2)	(7,163.6)	(7,711.2)
Gross profit	2,020.3	2,031.4	2,097.7
Personnel expenses	(1,075.9)	(1,107.1)	(1,123.3)
Depreciation and amortization	(171.7)	(167.9)	(167.1)
Net operating expenses	(720.7)	(727.0)	(756.3)
Other	(39.0)	(199.5)	(317.6)
Profit/(loss) from operations	13.0	(170.1)	(266.6)
Finance income	47.6	48.1	47.9
Finance costs	(219.4)	(216.4)	(182.7)
Other	0.7	1.6	3.2
Profit/(loss) before tax	(158.1)	(336.8)	(398.2)
Tax	(49.5)	(104.1)	(119.8)
Loss from continuing operations	(207.6)	(440.9)	(518.0)
Profit/(loss from discontinued operations	(0.3)	(149.2)	–
Loss for the year	(207.3)	(590.1)	(518.0)

Thomas Cook Group: Principal revenue streams (£m)

	2013		2012	
	Revenue	Earnings before interest and tax	Revenue	Earnings before interest and tax
UK and Ireland	2,977	66	3,110	2
Continental Europe	4,195	77	4,085	52
Airlines Germany	1,312	48	1,165	36
Northern Europe	1,239	109	1,174	101

REFERENCES

European Commission (1990) *Council Directive 90/314/EEC of 13 June 1990 on Package Travel, Package Holidays and Package Tours*, Brussels: European Commission, available at www://eur-lex.europa.eu/legal-content

Krippendorf, J. (1986) 'Tourism in the System of Industrial Society', *Annals of Tourism Research*, 13 (4): 517–32.

Poon, A. (1993) *Tourism Technology and Competitive Strategies*, Wallingford: CAB International.

Saunders, A. (2014) 'The MT Interview: Harriet Green', *Management Today*, February.

Taylor, I. (2013) 'Big Interview: Harriet Green on the Transformation of Thomas Cook', *Travel Weekly*, 15 March.

United Nations World Tourism Organization (2013) *World Tourism Barometer*, January.

Wembridge, M. and R. Jacobs (2011) 'Thomas Cook Chief Stands Down', *The Financial Times*, 3 August.

Wembridge, M. and R. Blitz (2011) 'Thomas Cook Plunges on Debt Concerns', *The Financial Times*, 22 November.

Glossary

Acquisition   The purchase of a controlling interest of one business's shares by another. The acquired business becomes a subsidiary of the acquirer but may be subsequently absorbed fully into the parent's structure.

Added value   The difference between the full cost of a product and its financial value to the market. High added value is one of the objectives of strategy. It tends to be measured in terms of profit.

Annual report and accounts   Audited annual communication between a limited company and its shareholders. In the UK, it has five compulsory statements by law (the chairman's statement, the auditors' statement, the profit and loss statement, the balance sheet and the cash flow statement).

Asset stripping   The process of breaking a company up and selling them off for a sum greater than that paid for the whole.

Augmented benefits   Benefits added to core (or basic) benefits that are intended to differentiate a product.

Backward vertical development   The acquisition of one or more parts of the backward direction in the supply chain. This is typically done by acquisition of or merger with a supplier.

Barriers to entry   Obstacles preventing entrant firms from being established in a particular market.

BCG matrix (Boston Consulting Group matrix)   Framework used to rationalize and understand a business's product portfolio. It divides products according their market share and the rate of market growth. Four categories are identified, stars (high market share in high growth market), cash cows (high market share in low growth market), question marks (low market share in high growth market) and dogs (low market share in low growth market).

Benchmarking   A collection of techniques used to compare certain aspects of business practice and the transfer of good practice procedures from benchmark companies to 'followers'.

Break-even point   The point at which costs or expenses and revenue are equal, i.e. there is no net loss or gain.

Business ethics   An area of research in which the nature of the relationship between business organizations and their role as moral agents is explored. It also describes research into the interface between business organizations and their social constituencies.

Capacity   In *THE*, capacity refers to the number of people that can be accommodated in a hotel, aircraft, bus, resort, venue, etc. The important figure is how much of the capacity is actually used at any time. This can be measured in various ways but is usually expressed as the occupancy rate for accommodation and venues or the load factor for transportation.

Capital   The finance used to invest in a business with a view of making a return from it in future years. It is used to purchase the other resource inputs that enable an organization to carry out business activity.

Carrying capacity   The ability of a site, resort, region or country to absorb tourists without deteriorating. The notion of carrying capacity is central to the concept of sustainability.

Change agent   One of the models of change management wherein the change process is overseen and managed by a single individual (the change agent). Offers the advantages of specialist management of a change process and the personification of the need for change.

Clusters   In many industries companies group together. Clusters are geographic concentrations of inter-connected companies and institutions in a particular industrial field. They encompass an array of linked industries and other entities, which are important to competition.

Collaboration   Businesses are said to collaborate when, instead of (or perhaps as well as) competing, they choose to work together in pursuit of both parties' strategic objectives.

Commercially sensitive   Confidential business information the disclosure of which may harm the business.

Competencies   The abilities that an organization possesses that enable it to compete and survive in an industry. It includes an element that is tangible (its physical resource base) and another which is intangible (know-how, networks, etc.).

Competitive advantage   The ability of an organization to out-perform its competitors. It can be measured in terms of superior profitability, increase in market share or other similar performance measures.

Competitive positioning (school of thought)   The approach to business strategy that argues that an organization's success in strategy rests upon how it positions itself in respect to its environment. This is in contrast to the resource-based approach.

Consortia/consortium   Various types of collaborative arrangements in which more than two organizations join together to undertake a cerain tasks (such as marketing and promotion) or for the duration of a certain project.

Contestable market   A contestable market is characterized by insignificant entry and exit barriers, so there are negligible entry and exit costs.

Core competencies   Competencies are core when they become the cause of the business's competitive advantage. Also called distinctive capabilities.

Corporate reports   *see* Annual report and accounts.

Cost benefit analysis   One of the non-financial tools sometimes used in evaluating strategic options. It involves weighing up the benefits that will arise from a course of action against its costs.

Cost leadership (in generic strategy framework)   The approach to business that seeks to achieve higher than industry-average performance by keeping unit costs lower than those of competitors. It is characterized by an emphasis upon the high volume production of standard products.

Critical success factors (CSFs)   Those elements that are vital for a strategy to be successful.

Culture   The character or personality of an organization. A culture can be understood by examining its manifestations under the categories of the cultural web.

Deliberate strategy   Strategy that is planned in advance and which follows a rational process through each stage from analysis through to implementation.

De-layering   Cutting costs through reducing the numbers of people employed particularly at middle levels of the organization.

Demerger   The disposal of a business (usually a subsidiary) by making it into a stand alone business and selling it off, usually via a flotation.

Diagonal integration   A process whereby firms use information technologies to logically combine services for best productivity.

Differentiation (in generic strategy framework)   The approach to business that seeks to achieve higher than industry-average performance by being distinctive rather than cheap (more distinctive than competitors). It presupposes that markets will pay more for extra product features.

Disintermediation   The removal of intermediaries in the supply chain, or 'cutting out the middleman' as it is often refered to. Customers can often deal directly with the supplier offering a service rather than through an intermediary such as a travel agent. This has been greatly facilitatated through the growth of the Internet.

Distinctive capability   *See* Core competencies.

Diversification   Business growth that involves developing new products for new markets.

Dynamic packaging   A method used in the travel industry to enable consumers to build their own package of flights, accommodation, and ancillary services such as car rental instead of purchasing a pre-defined package.

Earnings   Profit after interest and tax. Attributable to the company's shareholders who may elect to not withdraw the total earnings as dividends in order to leave some retained profit for future investment.

Economies of scale   The benefits gained in unit costs (cost per item) of increases in size, and hence, the dilution of fixed costs.

Economies of scope   The benefits gained in unit costs (cost per item) of increases in scope or number of services provided and hence, the dilution of fixed costs.

Efficiency   A comparison of a systems output to its inputs with a view to testing how well the input has been turned into output.

Emergent strategy   Strategy that is not planned in advance and that arises from a consistent pattern of behaviour.

Empowerment   Giving employees the authority to take decisions in order to resolve issues as they occur

Entry barriers   The obstacles that a new entrant to an industry needs to negotiate in order to gain market entry. Examples include the cost of capital, the legal and regulatory obstacles, access to supply and distribution channels, the costs of competing (especially lack of scale economies), etc.

Environmental analysis   Essentially the same as strategic analysis – an analysis of an organization's internal environment and its external macro-environment and micro-environment.

Experience effect   Unit costs are reduced as companies learn from their expriences.

External analysis   The analysis of the external environments in which an organization exists (micro and macro) with a view to identifying opportunities and threats.

External growth   Growth of a business by merger or acquisition (in contrast to organic or internal growth).

Factors of production   Inputs into an organizational process that make normal operation possible (otherwise called resources).

First mover advantage   Occurs when the first product becomes the established provider and establishes a barrier to entry for subsequent entries to the market.

Fiscal policy   Regulation of a national economy by the use of government revenues and expenditure.

Five forces analysis   A conceptual framework for understanding an industry's or organization's position in respect to the forces in its micro-environment. Can be used to explain the structure of the industry and the performance of competitors within it.

Focus strategy (in generic strategy framework)   Competitive advantage gained through serving one (or few) market segments.

Foreign exchange risk   Arises out of uncertainty about the future exchange rate between two currencies. The risk can be categorized as transaction, translation or economic (or political) exposure to risk.

Forward vertical development   The acquisition of one or more parts of the forward direction in the supply chain. This is typically done by acquisition of or merger with a buyer.

Frame conditions   Those conditions operating in the organization's commercial environment that frame (or influence) strategic decision making for a particular organization.

Franchising   An arrangement for business growth where the idea or format is rented out (from a franchisor to a franchisee) rather than directly developed by the originator of the idea.

Generic strategy   A distinctive posture that an organization adopts with regard to its strategy. It is suggested that superior performance arises from adopting a cost leadership or differentiation strategy with either a narrow or broad product and market scope.

Globalization   The most extensive stage of business development in which an organization's interests are spread throughout the world and are configured so as to compete and respond to differing customer requirements in many different national and local cultures.

Heterogeneity of services   Services, unlike mass-produced manufactured goods, are never identical. The human element and other factors in delivering services, ensures that services will be heterogeneous, i.e. varied.

Hierarchical congruence   Objectives set at various levels must be aligned with each other in such a way that each level of organizational decision making contributes to the organizations overall strategic objectives.

Horizontal development   Merger with or acquisition of a competitor or a business at the same stage of the supply chain. Increase in market share.

Hostile takeover   An acquisition attempt that is not supported by the board of the target company.

Human resource   One of four resource inputs that can be deployed to help create competitive advantage. Comprises the employees and any other people's skills that are used by the organization (such as consultancy skills that it has access to).

Human resource audit   An investigation into the size, skills, structure and all other issues surrounding those currently employed by the organization.

Hybrid strategy   An approach to generic strategy that adopts elements of both cost leadership and differentiation.

Implementation   The part of the strategic process that involves carrying out the selected strategy. It involves making the requisite internal changes and reconfiguring the organization's resource base to make it possible.

Incremental change   Organizational change that is carried out in many small steps rather than fewer large steps.

Industry   A group of producers of close substitute products. The players in an industry compete against each other for resource inputs and in product markets.

Industry analysis   Part of strategic analysis. The analysis of an industry, usually using the five forces framework, with a view to gaining a greater understanding of the micro-environment.

Inseparability of services   The production and consumption of service products are inseparable. The implication of this inseparability is that the consumers have direct experience of the production of the service in contrast to the production of a physical product.

Insolvency   The inability to pay bills as they become due.

Intangible resources   Sometimes called intellectual resources – resource inputs that are not physical but which can be amongst the most important at causing competitive advantage. Examples include patents, legal permissions, licences, registered logos, designs, brand names, etc.

Intangibility of services   Services cannot normally be seen, touched, smelt, tasted, tried on for size or stored on a shelf prior to purchase. Their intangibility makes them harder to buy but easier to distribute.

Integration   The collective name given to mergers and acquisitions.

Intellectual resources   *See* Intangible resources.

Intermediaries   The individuals and companies that act as 'middlemen' by purchasing and packaging products and services from their owners (the principals) and selling them on to customers. Travel agents and tour operators are examples of intermediaries.

Internal analysis   Part of strategic analysis (along with external analysis) wherein the internal parts are examined for strengths and weaknesses. The value chain framework is often used to assist the process.

Internal growth   Growth in the size of a business without the use of mergers and acquisition. It involves the reinvestment of previous years' retained profits in the same business venture.

Internationalization   Business growth involving development across national borders. Can be achieved by using market entry strategies such as exporting, direct investment, international joint ventures, alliances or franchising.

Job enrichment   Employees are given a greater deal of discretion or *empowerment* to make decisions.

Job rotation   Employees rotate jobs between them so that teamwork is encouraged and knowledge and skills are gained.

Job sharing   Employees' jobs are shared between two or more employees thereby sharing burdens and responsibilities.

Joint ventures   A collaborative arrangement between two or more companies. JVs tend to be for limited time periods, usually for a project or similar. Can also take the form of multi-partner consortia.

Just in time   An operational philosophy which aims to carry out (usually) production without any waste. Sometimes called stockless production.

Key issues   The issues that 'fall out of' the SWOT analysis which is, in turn, the summary of the strategic analysis. In practice, key issues are those issues that are the most pressing, the most important and the most critical.

Key Performance Indicators (KPIs)   Represent a measurement tool. They are measures that quantify management objectives, and enable the measurement of strategic performance.

Licensing   The renting-out of a piece of intellectual property so that the licensee enjoys the benefits of the licensor's innovation upon the agreement of a royalty payment. Most commonly applied to recipes, formulations, brands (such as lager brands), etc. Not to be confused with franchising.

Limited liability   A type of liability that is limited to the amount that has been invested.

Macro-environment   The outer 'layer' of environmental influence – that which can influence the micro-environment. It comprises five categories of influence – sociodemographic, political, economic, natural and technological influences.

Management buy-out   Occurs when a company is sold to its current management.

Management contracts   A popular form of joint development method whereby the ownership of the physical asset (such as a hotel or other accommodation) is separated from its management.

Market   The group of customers that a business or industry can sell its outputs to. Can also mean the specific part of a total market that an individual business sells to. In economics, market is taken to mean the 'place' or arena in which buyers and sellers come together.

Market segmentation   The practice of subdividing a total market up into smaller units, each of which shares a commonality of preference with regard to a buying motivation. Markets are segmented by applying segmentation bases – ways of dividing customers in a market from each other.

Market share   The proportion (usually expressed as a percentage) of the market for a product type held by a supplier to the market. Can be defined in terms of value of volume.

Mass tourism   Large-scale packaging of standardized leisure services at fixed prices for sale to a mass clientele.

Mergers   A form of external growth involving the 'marriage' of two partners of (usually) approximately equal size. The identities of both former companies are submerged into the new company.

Micro-environment   The near or immediate business environment that contains factors that affect the business often and over which, individual businesses may have some influence. Usually comprises competitors, suppliers and customers.

Mission statements   A formalized statement of the overall strategic purpose of an organization.

Moment of truth   *See* Service encounter.

Near environment   *See* Micro-environment.

Objectives   The state of being to which an organization aims or purposes. It is the end to which strategy aims.

Oligopoly   A commercial environment in which a particular market is controlled by a small group of firms.

Operational objectives   To be distinguished from strategic objectives. The level of objectives which tend to be short to medium-term in timescale and which have the sole purpose of helping to achieve the higher level strategic objective.

Opportunity cost   The cost of an alternative that must be forgone in order to pursue a certain action.

Organic growth   *See* Internal growth.

Outsourcing   The practice of a company entrusting to an external entity the performance of activities previously performed within the company.

Overtrading   Overtrading often occurs when companies expand their own operations too quickly and risk failure due to lack of financial resources.

Package holiday   A package holiday is a pre-arranged combination, sold or offered for sale at an inclusive price, including at least two of transport, accommodation and other tourist services ancillary to transport or accommodation.

Paradigm   The worldview or way of looking at the world held by an individual or organization. It is a very powerful determinant of the culture and behaviour (and hence performance) of a business.

Perishability of services   Since production and consumption are simultaneous, services are instantly perishable if they have not been sold at the time of production.

Planned strategies   *See* Deliberate strategy.

Portfolio   Can refer to either the spread of interests in respect to products and markets. The principle behind any portfolio is to spread opportunity and risk with a view to making the organization less vulnerable to trauma in any one product or market segment and to enable it to be in the position to quickly exploit any opportunities.

Power distance   A measure of how far removed subordinates feel from their superiors in an organization.

Prescriptive strategy   *See* Deliberate strategy.

Price elasticity of demand   The relationship between the price of a product and the quantity of the product sold. Price elastic products are those whose quantity sold is relatively price responsive. Price inelastic products are those where a change in price would be expected to bring about a proportionately lower change in quantity sold.

Product   The output of an organization intended for consumption by its markets. The result of the adding value process.

Product life cycle   The concept is based on the analogy with living things, in that all products would be expected to have a finite life, whether it is long or short and that products move from introduction through growth towards maturity and eventually decline.

Profit   The surplus of sales against total costs; tends to be measured either before or after tax.

Profit and loss account   One of the three compulsory financial statements in a company annual report. The P&L statement reports on the total sales, the costs incurred in creating those sales and hence (by subtraction), the profit made over a reporting period.

Profit Impact of Market Strategy (PIMS) study   On examining thousands of companies in many industries this study found that one of the primary determinants of profitability is market share.

Public–private partnerships   Various forms of collaborative activity bringing public and private sector involvement together to develop assets and resources.

Quality   Usually defined as 'fitness for the purpose'. It is not to be defined in terms of luxury or premium.

Ratio analysis   A comparison (by quotient) of two items from the same set of accounts.

Related diversification   External growth by developing new products for new markets. Related diversification suggests that the new products or markets have something in common with existing products or markets such that the risk of the diversification is lessened. Related diversification is in contrast to unrelated diversification.

Resource-based approach   A way of understanding the source of competitive advantage as arising from the way in which an organization obtains and deploys its resources to build and develop core competences.

Resource immobility   Many resources that are used cannot be moved either in terms of place or time.

Resource substitution   The substitution of one resource category with those of another.

Resources   The key inputs into an organization that enable normal functioning to take place. There are four categories of resource – physical (e.g. stock, land, buildings, etc.), financial, human and intangible (or intellectual).

Resource markets   The markets in which a business competes with other businesses for resource inputs. Examples include labour markets, real estate and property markets, finance markets (for capital), etc.

Retained profit A balance sheet measure of the profit that is attributable to the shareholders once all other allocations are accounted for, i.e. profit after interest, tax and extraordinary items.

Reverse segmentation Process by which customers select suppliers that meet particular specified criteria.

Satisficing Behaviour linked to the behavioural theory of the firm. In this view of the firm (which often applies to smaller companies) a critical level of profit is achieved by firms; thereafter, priority is attached to the attainment of other goals as the owners are satisfied with the levels of profit that have been achieved.

Service encounter The time and place where the customer interacts with the organization.

SERVQUAL A framework developed to consider service quality.

Selection of strategy The second stage in the overall strategic process which takes the information gained in the strategic analysis and uses it to evaluate options and to decide upon the most appropriate option.

Service dominant logic A strand of academic thought that developed in the early years of the current century which attempts to distinguish between marketing and strategy in services and manufacturing contexts

Service Profit Chain Assesses the sources of profitability and growth in labour dominated service firms.

Situational leadership Adjusting the leadership style adopted according to the circumstances encountered.

Stakeholders 'Any group or individual who can affect or [be] affected by the achievement of an organisation's objectives' (Freeman, R. E. and D. L. Reed (1983) 'Stockholders and Stakeholders: A New Perspective in Corporate Governance', *California Management Review*, 25: 88–106).

STEEP analysis The key stage in macro-environmental analysis. It involves auditing the macroenvironment for sociodemographic, political, economic, environmental, and technological influences.

Stakeholder theory The belief that the objectives of an organization are determined by the relative strengths of the various stakeholders.

Step change Change that occurs rapidly as an organization moves from its current level to a new level.

Stockholder approach The belief that business objectives should be determined predominantly for the financial benefit of the owners (shareholders). In practice, this position is taken to mean that the objectives of a business should be to maximize its profits.

Strategic alliances A collaborative arrangement between (usually) two businesses where part of all of the two companies' value chains are shared for mutually-beneficial strategic purpose.

Strategic analysis The first part of the strategic purpose. Its purpose is to gather information about a business's internal and external environments so that sufficient information is available to make possible the informed evaluation of options.

Strategic business units (SBUs) The primary constituent parts of an organization. This is the level at which most business level strategy decisions are made.

Strategic congruence The integration of multiple objectives either within an organization (at various levels) or between multiple groups so that they are aligned with each other.

Strategic drift Occurs when an organization fails to change at a rate that is equal to or faster than the rate of change in the external environment in which it operates.

Strategic fit The weaknesses of one partner are complemented by the strengths of another and vice-versa.

Strategic groups The subgroups within an industry that compete head on with each other for the same types of customers or for similar resource inputs. The members of a strategic group will normally consider an ongoing monitoring of each others' activities to be an essential part of their strategic analysis.

Strategic implementation *See* Implementation.

Strategic objectives In contrast to operational objectives, strategic objectives are those pursued at the highest level of an organization. They concern the whole organization, are concerned with the overall product and market scope, and tend to concern longer time scales than operational objectives.

Strategic options Generated as part of the second stage of the strategic process (evaluation and selection). The options that are considered as possible courses of action for the future.

Strategic process One way of looking at strategy is to conceptualize it as an iterative process. According to this view, the process has three distinct stages – strategic analysis, strategic evaluation and selection and then finally, strategic implementation. In practice, all stages are carried out continually.

Strategic selection   *See* Selection.

Strategy   There are a number of definitions of strategy, perhaps best understood in terms of Mintzberg's five Ps – plan, ploy, pattern, perspective and position. A strategy is usually taken to mean the process that is performed in order to close the gap between where an organization is now and where it aims to be in the future.

Strengths   Those internal features of an organization that can be considered to add to its ability to compete in its strategic group (or industry) and to increase its competitive advantage. Strengths are positive attributes that an organization owns.

Structure   The term used to describe the shape of an organization. In strategy, a consideration of structure usually refers to its height, width, complexity and the extent to which it is decentralized.

Stuck in the middle   A phrase used to describe the position of an organization that, in respect to the generic strategy framework, is neither purely cost leadership nor differentiation. It has been argued that to be stuck in the middle is to expose an organization to the probability or returning below-average profits because the organization experiences competition from those pursuing all other competitive strategies (narrow and broad, cost and differentiation). This view has been challenged.

Substitute products   Products that provide identical or comparable benefits to those of the organization's products.

Supply chain   Not to be confused with the value chain. Usually refers to the entire path that a product and its component parts takes from the primary industry stage to when it is sold to the final consumer on the chain.

SWOT Analysis   Standing for Strengths, Weaknesses, Opportunities and Threats is the key technique for presenting the results of strategic analysis, and provides a platform for going on to formulate the strategy for the future. Strengths and Weaknesses should be based upon the internal analysis of the organization whilst the Opportunities and Threats should be based upon an analysis of the organization's external environment.

Synergy   The effect that is observed after two or more parties (e.g. businesses in a merger) come together and the whole becomes greater than the sum of the parts. Sometimes expressed as $2+2=5$.

Targeting   When the possible range of segments has been identified and the characteristics of each of the segments has been analysed, an organization then has to decide which market segments to target.

Time value of money   A sum of money received now is preferable to the same sum of money received some time in the future.

Tour Operator   Tour operators purchase or reserve the separate components of a package holiday in bulk and in combine these components into an 'inclusive tour' or package.

Tourist Area Life Cycle (TALC)   Destinations go through a similar evolution to that of products, but visitor numbers are substituted for product sales. Destinations move from evolution through involvement, development, consolidation before reaching stagnation. Decline will follow unless actions are taken which result in rejuvenation.

Turnaround   A process dedicated to corporate renewal using analysis and strategy to turn troubled companies around and return them to solvency.

Unrelated diversification   External growth by developing new products for new markets. Unrelated diversification suggests that the new products or markets have little or nothing in common with existing products or markets such that the risk of the diversification is increased, but that portfolio benefits are maximized. Unrelated diversification is in contrast to related diversification.

Value adding   *See* Added value.

Value chain analysis   A conceptualization of the internal activities of an organization. The framework divides the internal activities of an organization into two categories – those that directly add value (primary activities) and those that support the primary activities (support or secondary activities). The analysis of an organization's value chain is intended to show up the strategic importance of any key linkages or any blockages – points where value is added less efficiently than it might be.

Values   Set out how managers and employees should conduct themselves, how they should do business and what sort of business they should build in order to help the organization achieve its mission.

Vertical development   The acquisition of forward or backward competencies such as through merger with, or acquisition of a supplier (backward vertical development) or a customer (forward vertical development).

Vision   Sets out some desired future state. It articulates often iin bold terms what the organization wants to achieve.

Waste   Anything that does not add value in an organizational process (such as machine inefficiencies, tooling up and tooling down, bad quality, stock, etc.).

Weaknesses   Those internal features of an organization that can be considered to detract from its ability to compete in its strategic group (or industry) and to reduce its competitive advantage. Weaknesses are negative attributes that an organization owns.

Weighted average cost of capital   The rate that a company is expected to pay on average to finance its assets weighted in accordance with proportion of finance provided.

Subject index

Index of names